EBLA TO DAMASCUS

ART AND ARCHAEOLOGY OF ANCIENT SYRIA

AN EXHIBITION FROM
THE DIRECTORATE-GENERAL OF ANTIQUITIES
AND MUSEUMS
SYRIAN ARAB REPUBLIC

EDITED BY HARVEY WEISS

SMITHSONIAN INSTITUTION TRAVELING EXHIBITION SERVICE
WASHINGTON, D.C.   1985

PUBLISHED WITH THE ASSISTANCE OF THE J. PAUL GETTY TRUST

Library of Congress Cataloging in Publication Data
Main entry under title:

Ebla to Damascus.

Exhibition held at Walters Art Gallery, Baltimore,
Md. and others, Sept. 1985–Sept. 1987.
1. Art, Ancient—Syria—Exhibitions. 2. Art—Syria—
Exhibitions. 3. Syria—Antiquities—Exhibitions.
I. Weiss, Harvey, 1945– . II. Syria. Mudīrīyat
al-Āthār wa-al-Matāḥif. III. Smithsonian Institution.
Traveling Exhibition Service. IV. Walters Art Gallery.
N5460.E35 1985   709′.39′4074013   85-14333

ISBN 0-86528-029-0
ISBN 0-295-96576-2 (cloth)

Published on the occasion of an
exhibition organized by the
Smithsonian Institution Traveling
Exhibition Service and the Directorate-
General of Antiquities and Museums of
the Syrian Arab Republic and shown
from September 1985 to September
1987 at the following museums:

Walters Art Gallery
Baltimore, Maryland

Museum of Natural History
Denver, Colorado

**Los Angeles County Museum of Natural
History**
California

Virginia Museum of Fine Arts
Richmond

Cincinnati Art Museum
Ohio

Detroit Institute of Arts
Michigan

National Museum of Natural History
Smithsonian Institution
Washington, D.C.

Cover illustration: Cat. No. 55;
frontispieces: Cat. No. 109 (p.1); Cat.
No. 61 (p.2)

CONTENTS

Cat. No. 11   Cat. No. 12

Cat. No. 13   Cat. No. 14

Cat. No. 29

Cat. No. 35

Cat. No. 54

Cat. No. 57

Cat. No. 36, top left

Cat. No. 37, top right

Cat. No. 38, bottom right

Cat. No. 39, bottom left

13

FOREWORD

AFIF BAHNASSI
Director-General of Antiquities and Museums
Syrian Arab Republic

THE HISTORY OF CULTURAL DEVELOPMENT IN THE LAND OF SYRIA extends millennia into the past and provides one of the world's unique perspectives on the cultural heritage shared by all peoples. Beginning with the earliest periods of tool use in the Lower Paleolithic, at such sites as el-Kowm and Latamné, the documentation extends through the first advances toward food production and agriculture at places like Mureybit and Abu Hureyra. These early settlements along the Syrian Euphrates are now a part of the prehistoric archaeological record through the accomplishments of the international archaeological campaign to save the antiquities threatened by the Euphrates dam. As such, these efforts surely rank among the most successful examples of international cooperation in the salvage of mankind's ancient heritage.

In an earlier period of archaeological activity, accident alone was able to bring to the world's attention the early accomplishments of ancient Syrian peoples. In 1933 a nomad, searching for stones with which to erect a funerary monument, uncovered a headless statue which soon came to the attention of the colonial authorities. The statue eventually was reported to the archaeologists of the Louvre, who charged a young curator, André Parrot, with responsibility for pursuing additional research at the site of the statue's recovery. Parrot's excavations at Tell Hariri on the Euphrates River eventually indicated that the site was none other than the ancient capital of Mari.

Archaeological excavations at Mari have continued ever since: street upon street, palace upon palace, temple upon temple have yielded themselves to the archeologists' tools and patient labors. The unique representations of Mari's successive civilizations have become well known to the world at large. Long ago these works of art provided André Parrot with the opportunity to remark, "They have confirmed the ancient expression *'Ex oriente lux.'* "

Cat. No. 55

15

The two major periods of Mari's history are the third millennium and the early second millennium B.C. More than 30,000 clay tablets bearing cuneiform inscriptions have been recovered from the excavations, as well as many artistically significant stone statues. The latter include the major sculpture of the singer Ur-Nanshe (Cat No. 66) in the Ninni-zaza Temple, and the statue of Lamgi-Mari, king of Mari (Cat No. 62). Among the statuary known from the second-millennium city and the great palace of Zimri-Lim, the "goddess with flowing vase" (Cat. No. 90), the statue of Ishtup-ilum, and the headless statue of Idi-ilum are counted among the most famous examples of ancient artistic accomplishment.

More recently the recovery of the ancient city of Ebla ranks as a rival archaeological accomplishment to that of Mari. The Italian archaeological mission had been pursuing its scientific work at Tell Mardikh for eleven years when in 1975 a discovery of singular importance for the history of civilization was made. Within the reception hall of the Royal Palace, dated to the second half of the third millennium B.C., the archives of the city were recovered within two rooms preserving thousands of cuneiform documents. These must now be considered the most extensive and the most ancient archives known. No less important for the history of civilization is the recovery of the world's oldest bilingual dictionary within the archive rooms.

The historical significance of the Ebla archives extends beyond the bounds of the ancient site, for the new documents show that the city was one of the most important in southwest Asia, with political, economic, and cultural influence extending as far as southern Mesopotamia. A new chapter in the history of the origins of civilization is thus opened, with northwestern Syria now understood to be a primary locus for early city and state development.

While Mari played a major role in the history of the Orient in the early second millennium B.C., Syria continued to serve as the theater for the important cultural developments of the second half of the second millennium as well. Ancient Ugarit, the major port city of the Orient, was discovered at the site of Ras Shamra, just north of the modern port of Lattakiah in 1929. A French-sponsored archaeological mission under the direction of Prof. Claude Schaeffer initiated the excavations at Ras Shamra, and these continue to the present. Ugarit had been an important settlement since Neolithic times, but in the history of the ancient Near East the city assumed singular importance in the second millennium as a port center for Canaanite civilization and its expanding commercial involvements with Egypt, the Aegean, and Anatolia.

The precisely arranged Royal Palace at Ugarit, as well as the temples of Baal and Dagan are among the most significant monuments of ancient Canaanite culture. Ugaritic, like Eblaite which preceded it, remains one of the most important literary vehicles of the ancient world. Apart from the historical, religious, and mythological contents of the Ugaritic tablets, which illuminate the otherwise closed world of the Bible, Ugaritic preserves for us the first steps toward the development of a truly alphabetic writing system. Replacing the unwieldy syllabic scripts of cuneiform which preceded it, the alphabetic Ugaritic script was the source for later scripts, including that which served as the model for the Greek and eventually Latin alphabets.

The great deserted cities of ancient Syria, presenting mounded sites (in Arabic, called *tell*) preserving the cultural accomplishments of antiquity, are not the only sources of the Syrian past. Sites still occupied and presenting unique contrasts between the old and the new also preserve the past for us. Two among these are the famous cities of Aleppo and Damascus.

Aleppo is sometimes said to be the oldest city in the world. Certainly this epithet contains more than a grain of historical truth, for Aleppo is mentioned as early as the third millennium B.C. and was the capital of the kingdom of Yamkhad, under the name Halab, in the second millennium B.C. During this period the city was allied with Hammurabi and concluded treaties with Mari, Ebla, and Babylon. The later historical monuments of Aleppo, such as the famous Citadel, the Great Mosque, the maristans, and the bazaars, make the city one of the most historic and interesting for the modern tourist.

Damascus, a name which possibly signified "land that is irrigated" in ancient Aramaic, has flourished as a city for more than forty centuries. Initially the capital city of the Aramaeans, Damascus later served as a Roman and Christian metropolis before becoming the capital of the most powerful Islamic kingdom, the Umayyad state. Monuments from Aramaean as well as Roman times can be seen throughout Damascus. The great columned gateways to the city, the towers, and the remains of the Temple of Jupiter still stand. Among the ancient Christian monuments the church of St. John and the church of Hananiah, as well as "St. Paul's Gate," are perhaps the most famous. As for Islamic-period monuments, there is the city itself: its mosques, the madrassas, the maristans, the khans, and the takiyas (monasteries), which are maintained and preserved by the Directorate-General of Antiquities and Museums.

With the victory of Alexander the Great over Darius, king of the

Persians, at the Battle of Issus, Greek domination over Syria, and then Roman domination, ensued. During this period Palmyra became a focus of particularly Roman concern. Within the ruins of this great caravan city we can still see the peculiar mix of indigenous Aramaic and Arab with Roman culture. The importance of the city, its wealth, and its military significance can still be understood not only in light of its oasis cultivation and strategic trade location, but as well from the standing monuments which make it one of the most impressive ancient sites in the Orient. The Temple of Bel, the great avenues lined with workshops and emporia, the forum and the theater, the hypogeum, and the columned avenues, all bear witness to the city's ancient activities.

Bosra, less well known than Palmyra to some, is nevertheless in many regards a more important city. An Arab and Nabataean center initially, from A.D. 106 Bosra became an important Roman city, receiving the name Mother of Cities under Alexander Severus. The Roman amphitheater at Bosra is the best preserved example of such architecture in the ancient world. Apamea, the second capital of the Seleucids, became a Roman city in 50 B.C. Archaeological research here has, in recent years, begun the restoration of important fora and theaters.

The Islamic period has left Syria with a bounty of magnificient monuments, of which the Umayyad Mosque in Damascus is perhaps the best known. Constructed by the caliph al-Walid ibn Abd al-Malik, the mosque is situated upon an earlier church, where from the time of the conquest of Damascus Moslems had prayed side by side with Christians. The plan of the mosque has served as the prototype for subsequent structures. The famous multi-color mosaic which decorates the interior facades of the mosque's courtyard represents the paradise promised to all Moslems.

Among the Umayyad palaces, perhaps the most famous is that of Qasr al-Hayr al-Gharbi, which was constructed by the caliph Hisham ibn [Abd al-Malik] (A.D. 724–743) on the plain south of Palmyra. Other palaces built by this ruler include those at Qasr al-Hayr al-Sharqi and two at Rusafa. In the later Islamic period, under the Ayyubid monarchs, the citadel of Aleppo was restored and renovated. Similarly, the citadel in Damascus remains a powerful monument to the needs of the medieval state with its pigeon towers for communications, workshops, armories, prisons, baths, bazaars, and mosques.

Our mention of these monuments and periods of cultural development comprise but slight glosses upon a span which mirrors the unfolding of Western culture as a whole. Each in turn would therefore require a separate monograph to justly express its significance and the forces which brought it into existence. The present exhibition can hope only to introduce the American public to the history of Syrian culture and to encourage further study of its details.

Much of the historical materials, artifacts, and works of art presented here are the products of the enquiring spirit and determination which stimulate archaeological research. At this time there are more than forty archaeological expeditions working in Syria. Some are Syrian, others are foreign projects sponsored by internationally recognized universities and research institutions from France, Belgium, the Netherlands, Great Britain, Japan, Poland, Australia, and the United States. The bounty of archaeological materials retrieved through these scientific activities has required a terrific expansion of facilities for storage, study, and display. In the past ten years the number of museums in Syria has quadrupled, with much emphasis placed upon the construction and expansion of facilities, not just in Damascus and Aleppo, but in the regional centers, the provinces (*Mohafazat*), where such facilities can be enjoyed by the local populace.

The great number of ancient sites and monuments in Syria presents unique problems for a country dedicated to the preservation of its past and the development of its future. Restoration and preservation projects are a constant need in this situation, as the government's responsibilities extend in both directions. More than 120 such preservation and restoration projects are now in progress throughout Syria, each equipped with technicians, materiel, and support staffs dedicated to the protection of Syria's past. Additional projects are included within the next Five Year Plan for Bosra, Der'a, Palmyra, and other ancient sites.

We hope that this exhibition, and the volume which serves as its guide, will assist the viewer and reader to appreciate the historical record which so many have labored to retrieve, record, preserve, and display for future generations.

PREFACE

HARVEY WEISS
Yale University

EBLA TO DAMASCUS PRESENTS THE VAST EXPANSE OF SYRIAN CUL-
tural history and as a part of that history the still larger context within
which Syrian culture has evolved over the past ten thousand years.
The exhibition therefore illustrates the origins and development of
Old World civilization in the Near East—where Syrian developments
were crucial and determinative—and the trajectory followed by Syrian and Near Eastern cultures through the classical and medieval
periods. It is a world very different from our own, yet one from which
ours has slowly evolved and directly borrowed.

The historical stages and cultural epochs which define the past ten
thousand years of Syrian history are clearly marked within the archaeological and historical record that frames this exhibition. Often
the Syrian record is so well defined and exemplary that it provides us
with a key or model for unravelling prehistoric or ancient developments in adjacent regions or even other periods. In this regard *Ebla to
Damascus* expresses what is known and what is still not known about
the long-term course of Near Eastern history and hence has an
importance far beyond that which 281 objects intrinsically possess.

These objects have never before travelled to the New World, and
therefore they provide a unique opportunity for Americans to exam-
ine directly the major material remains of the prehistoric, ancient,
and medieval cultures of Syria. The objects were initially selected by
the staff of the Directorate-General of Antiquities and by Dr. Eva
Strommenger and Dr. Kay Kohlmeyer of the Museum für Vor- und
Frühgeschichte, Berlin, Prof. Dr. Christine Strube, Universität Heidelberg, and Dr. Michael Meinecke, German Archaeological Institute, Damascus. They and their colleagues presented the exhibition
Land des Baal in Germany in 1982–1983 and later in Austria.

Under the direction of Pierre Amiet, chief curator of the Departe-
ment des Antiquités Orientales of the Louvre, the German exhibition

was considerably expanded by material from the Louvre for an exhibition held in Paris in 1983–1984: *Au pays de Baal et d'Astarté*. In Rome in 1985 the original *Land des Baal* was supplemented by objects from third- and second-millennium Ebla which the Directorate-General of Antiquities had graciously made available to Prof. Paolo Matthiae. The objects from Ebla which were added to the Roman exhibition have been incorporated into the American one as well.

The individual catalogue entries for the objects illustrated are for the most part translations of the entries first published in *Land des Baal*, prepared by German archaeologists and art historians, and carefully edited by Dr. Eva Strommenger and Dr. Kay Kohlmeyer. The catalogue entries for the twelve supplementary objects from Ebla have been written by Prof. Paolo Matthiae and his colleagues. In all cases the author's initials follow each entry. In some cases slight emendations have been made to suit the American audience or the American academic community, and the most recent bibliographic references have been appended. Several of the more important emendations of the German text have been written by Ulla Kasten, editor and manager of the Yale Babylonian Collection, who also translated the German and Italian catalogue entries and has been unfailingly helpful throughout the project. The final editing of the entries was my responsibility.

In addition to the descriptions of the individual objects, forty-five essays are included which attempt to explain the historical and cultural significance of the archaeological sites from which the objects are derived. Eighteen of these essays, the product of German and Syrian scholars under whose names they appear, have been translated by me from their original publication in *Land des Baal*. Twenty-seven new essays have been prepared especially for *Ebla to Damascus* by American and Italian scholars.

As editor of *Ebla to Damascus*, and on behalf of those who have worked with me to prepare this book, I wish to thank the Directorate-General of Antiquities and Museums, Damascus, for making this exhibition possible. Primary initiative and responsibility rest with Dr. Afif Bahnassi, Director-General, and it is to his far-sighted vision that we are all extremely indebted.

The efforts of those who worked with Dr. Bahnassi in the organization of the exhibition, especially Adnan Joundi, Director of Museums, and Wahid Khayata, Director of the National Museum, Aleppo, are also gratefully acknowledged. The collaboration and encouragement of Dr. Adnan Bounni, whose advice and judgment sustain field research in Syria, are apparent throughout this volume and this exhibition. I also wish to express my gratitude to Mohammed Muslim for his contributions to field research and to Antoine Suleiman, curator of the Ebla collections at the National Museum, Aleppo, for his assistance.

Ebla to Damascus reflects its complex subject, but it is hoped that it also clarifies much that would otherwise remain obscure. Its multiple authors and multiple original languages have required perduring patience from Diana Menkes, whose editorial and managerial skills have sustained this project with determination, rigor, and charm. I assume responsibility for this volume's faults, and acknowledge her responsibility for its merits.

CONTRIBUTORS TO EBLA TO DAMASCUS

ALI ABU ASSAF
University of Damascus
Syrian Arab Republic

ALFONSO ARCHI
Università di Roma
Italy

JERE L. BACHARACH
University of Washington
Seattle

JANINE BALTY
Mission Archéologique à Apamea
Brussels, Belgium

MARIA GIOVANNA BIGA
Università di Roma
Italy

ADNAN BOUNNI
Directorate-General of Antiquities
and Museums, Damascus
Syrian Arab Republic

GIORGIO BUCCELLATI
University of California
Los Angeles

JEANNY VORYS CANBY
Columbia University
New York

FRANK MOORE CROSS
Harvard University
Cambridge, Massachusetts

MARIANNE EATON-KRAUSS
Freie Universität
Berlin, Federal Republic of
Germany

BENJAMIN R. FOSTER
Yale University
New Haven, Connecticut

OLEG GRABAR
Harvard University
Cambridge, Massachusetts

ULLA KASTEN
Yale University
New Haven, Connecticut

MARILYN KELLY-BUCCELLATI
California State University
Los Angeles

DAVID A. KING
New York University, New York
and
Johann Wolfgang Goethe
Universität
Frankfurt-am-Main, Federal
Republic of Germany

KAY KOHLMEYER
Museum für Vor- und
Frühgeschichte
Berlin, Federal Republic of
Germany

SUSAN MATHESON
Yale University
New Haven, Connecticut

PAOLO MATTHIAE
Università di Roma, Italy

GABRIELLA SCANDONE MATTHIAE
Consiglio Nazionale delle Ricerche
Rome, Italy

MICHAEL MEINECKE
Deutsches Archäologische Institut,
Abteilung Damaskus
Syrian Arab Republic

VIKTORIA MEINECKE-BERG
Deutsches Archäologische Institut,
Abeteilung Damaskus
Syrian Arab Republic

ANDREW M. T. MOORE
Yale University
New Haven, Connecticut

JAMES D. MUHLY
University of Pennsylvania
Philadelphia

JOSEPH NASRALLAH
Paris, France

DENNIS PARDEE
The Oriental Institute
Chicago, Illinois

KLAUS PARLASCA
Universität Erlangen
Federal Republic of Germany

FRANK E. PETERS
New York University
New York

EDITH PORADA
Columbia University
New York

WOLFGANG RÖLLIG
Universität Tübingen
Federal Republic of Germany

JACK M. SASSON
University of North Carolina
Chapel Hill

GLENN M. SCHWARTZ
Yale University
New Haven, Connecticut

DANIEL C. SNELL
University of Oklahoma
Norman

EVA STROMMENGER
Museum für Vor- und
Frühgeschichte
Berlin, Federal Republic of
Germany

CHRISTINE STRUBE
Universität Heidelberg
Federal Republic of Germany

KASSEM TUWEIR
Directorate-General of Antiquities
and Museums, Damascus
Syrian Arab Republic

HARVEY WEISS
Yale University
New Haven, Connecticut

IRENE J. WINTER
University of Pennsylvania
Philadelphia

ACKNOWLEDGEMENTS

PEGGY A. LOAR
Director
Smithsonian Institution Traveling Exhibition Service

EBLA TO DAMASCUS PRESENTS THE CULTURAL SIGNIFICANCE OF ancient Syria, and its role in the development of Western civilization, primarily through the archaeological discoveries of the past fifty years. The exhibition spans cultural developments from 8000 B.C. to A.D. 1600, from the origins of agriculture through the genesis of cities, the revolutionary discoveries from third-millennium Ebla, the famous civilizations of Mari and Ugarit in the second millennium, and the urban complexities of Hellenistic, Roman, Byzantine, and Islamic Syria.

The 281 objects in the exhibition appear in the United States through the generosity and consideration of the Syrian Arab Republic, and in particular the Ministry of Culture and Education and the Directorate-General of Antiquities and Museums. These objects have been selected from the extensive holdings of the National Museum of the Syrian Arab Republic, with its various branches in Damascus, Aleppo, Palmyra, Homs, Deir-ez-Zor, and Hasseke. The National Museum's collections represent the cumulative archaeological and curatorial efforts, spanning the twentieth century, of dedicated scholars, Syrian as well as foreign. These collections include objects usually on display to the public in the National Museum, Damascus, the National Museum, Aleppo, and the provincial museums, as well as the study and storage collections preserved and catalogued for the professional and scientific world of archaeologists, historians, and epigraphers. The metaphor of the iceberg, of course, applies to all museums; the National Museum of the Syrian Arab Republic however is more than one museum; its rich holdings extend across the country and across cultural periods to which most museums are exclusively dedicated. The objects presented in this exhibition are therefore only a small selection from the range of cultural treasures preserved by the Directorate-General of Antiquities and Museums.

The extent of those treasures can be imagined when viewing the array we present.

The generous loans of the Directorate-General of Antiquities and Museums have made possible this magnificent presentation of the archeological treasures of Syria. In particular, I would like to thank Dr. Afif Bahnassi, Director-General, for his unfailing cooperation. Dr. Nadjah al-Attar, Minister for Culture and National Guidance, has been instrumental in the overall organization of the exhibition.

Special thanks are due to His Excellency Rafic Jouejati, Ambassador of the Syrian Arab Republic, in Washington, D.C. Abbas Hakeem, Cultural Affairs Attaché, and others at the Syrian Embassy have assisted in numerous ways.

While a good number of museum professionals at the Smithsonian Institution Traveling Exhibition Service (SITES) have devoted themselves to realizing this project, I would like to note one in particular. It is largely due to the efforts of Anne R. Gossett, SITES Assistant Director for Exhibition Development and project director for *Ebla to Damascus*, that this exhibition and its accompanying publication have come to fruition. Her interest in and devotion to the subject and her substantial previous experience in coordinating major SITES exhibitions are in equal part responsible for our ability to present this exhibition to the American public.

ACKNOWLEDGEMENTS

ANNE R. GOSSETT
Project Director
Smithsonian Institution Traveling Exhibition Service

THE ORGANIZATION OF EBLA TO DAMASCUS HAS BEEN AN EXCITING undertaking. Its successful realization is the result of the collaboration of many individuals in the United States and abroad, whose involvement is gratefully acknowledged.

Dr. Harvey Weiss, Associate Professor of Near Eastern Archaeology, Yale University, and director of the Tell Leilan Project in Syria since 1978, was curatorial consultant for the exhibition and general editor of the accompanying catalogue. His thorough knowledge of the ancient Near East and his selection of outstanding scholars, whose essays are herein published, have guided the publication of a volume which will make a long-standing contribution to our knowledge of ancient Syria. Diana Menkes has brought to this complex project her considerable editorial skills.

Other scholars who have assisted in the important area of preparation of the exhibition interpretative materials and texts are Suzanne Heim, Carol Bier, Gary Vikan, and Ellen Reeder Williams. Their dedication is greatly appreciated and their accomplishments will enlighten all visitors to the exhibition.

I would like to add my personal thanks to Dr. Afif Bahnassi, Director-General of Antiquities and Museums of the Syrian Arab Republic. His associates, Adnan Joundi, Director of Museums for the Directorate-General; Wahid Khayata, Director of the Aleppo Museum; Khaled Assad, Director of the Palmyra Museum; and Assad Mahmud, Director of the Deir ez-Zor Museum, have facilitated the presentation of important artifacts from their respective museums, for which we are all grateful.

Many of the objects included in this exhibition were originally presented in *Land des Baal,* an exhibition organized by the Museum für Vor- und Frühgeschichte, Berlin. The Smithsonian Institution wishes to thank Dr. Eva Strommenger and Dr. Kay Kohlmeyer for their cooperation and permission to draw on research and information disseminated in that exhibition and its accompanying publication.

A major grant for the exhibition was provided by an anonymous sponsor. Additional financial support came from the Arabian American Oil Company (Aramco), Shell Companies Foundation, Inc., Mobil Oil Corporation, and Mrs. H. C. Stevens. Without their help the exhibition would not have been possible. The exhibition is supported by an indemnification from the Federal Council on the Arts and the Humanities. This book is published with the assistance of the J. Paul Getty Trust.

Throughout the period of planning for the exhibition I have had the benefit of the interest and advice of members of the diplomatic community who have served in Syria and the Near East. I would particularly like to thank Louis Hoffacker, Mr. and Mrs. Talcott Seelye, Mr. and Mrs. Alfred E. Atherton, and Mr. and Mrs. Richard W. Murphy.

The staff of the American Embassy in Damascus has been enormously helpful in facilitating arrangements for the exhibition. Ambassador and Mrs. William Eagleton have taken a keen interest in the project. Albert W. J. Dalgliesh, Public Affairs Officer, has assisted in countless ways, as did his predecessor, Richard Undeland. James Callahan, desk officer for Syria at the United States Information Agency, has cheerfully provided advice and support throughout the organizational period.

Many departments of the Smithsonian Institution have provided support and technical expertise to the realization of the exhibition. Under the direction of James Mahoney and his assistant Karen Fort, the Office of Exhibits Central has undertaken the critical responsibility for the design and production of the exhibition. Mary Dillon has created an elegant design for the traveling exhibition, and Rosemary Regan has prepared an excellent exhibit script in consultation with the curatorial committee. John Widener, Walter Sorrell, James Speight, Ken Clevinger, and the combined staffs of the Model Shop, Graphics Shop, and Cabinet Shop have given their special attention to the presentation and preparation of works of art in the exhibit. The staff of the Conservation Analytical Laboratory has been most helpful in consultation about and treatment of the objects.

At the Smithsonian Institution Traveling Exhibition Service various members of the staff have been deeply involved in the development of the exhibition. During the lengthy planning period the following persons have made special efforts: Antonio Diez and Marie-Claire Jean in financial administration: Julia Shepherd, Emily Stern, and Cherie Faini in educational programming; Ronald Geatz and his assistant Ann Singer in promoting public information; Andrea Stevens in managing the production of all publications accompanying the exhibition; and Linda Schmoldt, who acted as exhibition assistant, looking after the many and varied organizational details. Mary Jane Clark, SITES Head Registrar, and her capable assistants Gwen Hill, Janet Freund, and Fredric Williams, deserve thanks for their diligent efforts.

INTRODUCTION

HARVEY WEISS

MODERN SYRIA, WHICH ONLY GAINED ITS INDEPENDENCE FROM France in 1946, was the homeland of a multitude of ancient and medieval cultures, each of which vies for the attention of the exhibition viewer while none can be represented adequately in a single exhibition. Nevertheless, *Ebla to Damascus* does attempt to reveal the historical role which Syrian cultures have played in prehistoric, early historic, and medieval times. It is our hope therefore that this exhibition will deepen American awareness of Syrian cultural history, a history which extends beyond the borders of one nation or state.

The title *Ebla to Damascus* refers to the great urban centers of Syria from the third millennium B.C. through the second millennium A.D. and thereby stresses the role which cities have played within the grand epochs of Syrian, Near Eastern, and Old World history. The genesis of cities was the genesis of civilization, and the transformation of these cities through time precisely reflects the transformation of social and economic relations which has characterized the landscapes of Syria and the Old World for the past five thousand years.

The nine chapters which frame this exhibition are convenient divisors of a broad range of archaelogical material, but the historical and cultural particularities which they illustrate can be grouped into still larger units amounting to five essential stages:

1. The origins of sedentary village life
   Prehistoric Background, ca. 8000–5000 B.C.
2. The origins of civilization and ancient cities
   Protohistoric Period, ca. 3500–3000 B.C.
   Third Millennium Cities, ca. 3000–2100 B.C.
3. The historical trajectory and interactions of these ancient societies
   Old Syrian Period, ca. 2100–1600 B.C.
   Middle Syrian Period, ca. 1600–1200 B.C.

New Syrian Period, ca. 1200–330 B.C.

4. The intrusion and then integration of Hellenistic and Roman culture and its Byzantine succession
   Hellenistic and Roman Periods, ca. 330 B.C.–A.D. 400
   Byzantine Period, ca. 400–600
5. The Arab conquest of the Near East, the transformation of Byzantium, and the creation of Islamic civilization
   Islamic Period, ca. 600–1600

The archaeological and epigraphic record of these developments is extensive and detailed. Modern students of Syrian history must choose narrow paths or otherwise lose their way in a diachronic maze of languages, disciplines, dialects, and data. Much of the record is archaeological, and *Ebla to Damascus* therefore confronts the American audience with that which this science has only recently been able to salvage from both the mute prehistoric periods and the complex historic periods.

Throughout most of this exhibition it will be obvious to the viewer that material objects are not the isolated products of individuals but the products of cultures, each one moving across stretches of time and space, interacting, transforming, and being transformed. While the process is as old as time, the actors and the stage in this exhibition are uniquely Syrian.

Syria: The geographical background

The Syrian coastline along the Mediterranean has always served as a major outlet to the west for the peoples and cultures of the Asian interior. In the medieval period the transit trade which united western Europe with eastern Asia flowed through the port cities of Syria, as did the long-distance trade of antiquity and prehistory. At the same time the Syrian interior served as a central arena for the crucial prehistoric, ancient, and medieval developments within the Fertile Crescent—the lands which extended from Mesopotamia to Palestine and Egypt.

Slightly inland from the Mediterranean coast are parallel mountain ranges, the Jebel Ansariyah, which run northward from Lebanon to form the first barrier to traffic from the coast. Along the eastern slopes of the Jebel Ansariyah passes the Orontes River (flowing from south to north), whose basin constitutes one of the fertile regions of western Syria. Here were situated, within an essentially Mediterranean climate, the ancient cities of Homs, Hama, and Antioch. Much as their modern counterparts do now, they thrived on the plain's soils, rainfall, and resulting fertility.

Farther eastward is the barren, low-rainfall steppe, deeply etched with the annual meanders of seasonal streams. The little vegetation here is exploited by the pastoralists' herds of sheep and goat. But beyond the western steppe the valley and floodplain of the Euphrates intervene and impose upon the otherwise harsh landscape the fertility which absence of rainfall has otherwise denied it.

The waters of the Euphrates provide two essential resources to the Syrian landscape: water for irrigation agriculture and water for long-distance transport of harvests, bulk trade goods, and other supplies. Water-borne transport remains today the least expensive means for moving bulk goods; in antiquity its benefits were even greater. Upstream and downstream, barges loaded with timber, cereal harvests, metals, asphalt, and luxury goods made low-cost exchange and regional integration possible.

Between the Orontes and the Euphrates are the extensive *terra rosa* plains which surround the city of Aleppo. The tablelands here are watered by the Qoueiq River as well as by sufficient annual rainfall to ensure agricultural yields equal to those of the plains of Homs and Hama. Additionally, the plains of Aleppo provide the essential linkage between the traffic along the Euphrates and the Mediterranean coast.

A fourth agricultural region is the Habur Plains in the northeastern corner of Syria. Here the mean annual rainfall ranges from 300 to 500 millimeters across gently rolling plains with fertile brown soils. This region today is the granary of Syria, producing more than 25 percent of its cereal harvest. In antiquity it was always densely occupied and served as the base for successive independent polities, occasionally powerful enough to control regions to the east and west.

A last extensive agricultural region is the oasis around Damascus, fed by the Barada River, and the basalt areas of the southern Hauran region. Clear transit links to the northeast across the wastelands of the desert toward the Euphrates have traditionally tied this region with the oasis at Palmyra. The surrounding territory near the Jebel Bishri and extending north to the union of the Balikh River with the Euphrates provides seasonal grazing for the flocks of sheep and goat which pastoral nomads have herded for millennia in this region.

Figure 1 outlines the essential climatic conditions within Syria in terms of mean annual rainfall. Here it is possible to note the region which receives at least 200 millimeters of rain, the lower limit for an annual cereal crop on cultivable soils. Immediately apparent are the advantages of the coastal plains, of those stretching between Homs, Hama, and Aleppo, and the Habur Plains of the northeast.

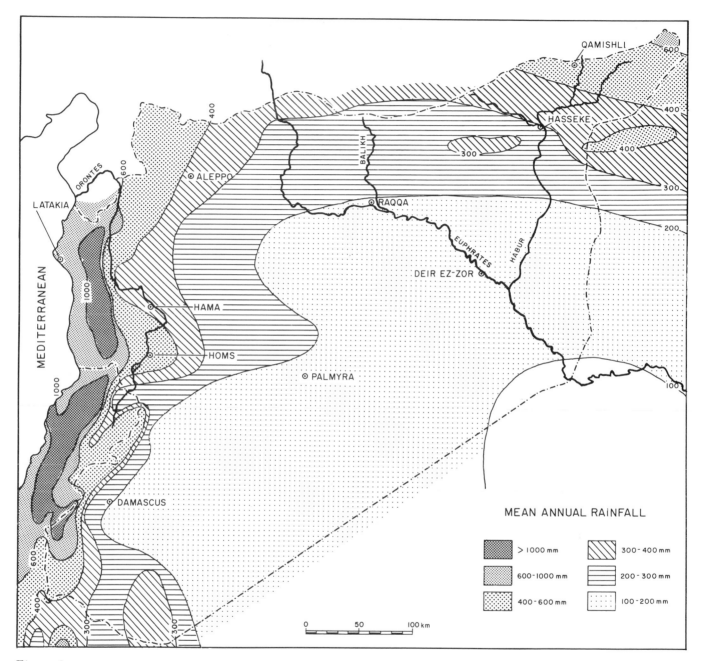

Figure 1
Climatic regions of Syria.

Within the map:

QAMISHLI

HASSEKE

ALEPPO

LATAKIA

ORONTES

BALIKH

RAQQA

MEDITERRANEAN

EUPHRATES

HABUR

DEIR EZ-ZOR

HAMA

HOMS

PALMYRA

DAMASCUS

MEAN ANNUAL RAINFALL

▓	> 1000 mm	⧄	300 - 400 mm
▒	600-1000 mm	☰	200-300 mm
░	400-600 mm	⋮	100-200 mm

0   50   100 km

The map in Fig. 2 combines the essential 200-millimeter isohyet with the fundamental ground conditions for agriculture. These are represented as three regions:

The areas where non-saline ground water is readily accessible from wells and springs

The areas where soil types and topographic relief are most favorable for dry-farming agriculture

The areas adjacent to the four major rivers (Orontes, Euphrates, Balikh, and Habur), where simple irrigation agriculture is possible

The area encompassed within these three regions is startlingly small. Modern settlement in Syria, in fact, extends to probably twice this area, but this is a function of the availability of gasoline-powered pumps and drills which are able to tap underground water resources inaccessible until the twentieth century. Hence the cultivable areas indicated in Fig. 2 are probably an accurate depiction of the areas which were occupied in antiquity by sedentary agricultural societies.

Languages and peoples of ancient Syria

In modern Syria Arabic is the official language, and indeed it has been the language spoken by most peoples of Syria since the Arab conquest in the seventh century. But what is Arabic? What languages were spoken in Syria before Arabic? What is the relationship of these languages to each other? This broad set of questions falls into the realm of linguistics, which is important to separate from the related but quite different category encompassing that durable expression of language—writing.

To illustrate the difficulties associated with just the asking of these questions, it may be useful to recall that without writing there is no certain evidence for language. That is, we do know that early *Homo erectus* populations were capable of speech and were probably communicating with each other through language by 400,000 B.C. But writing was only developed as another means of expression a mere 5,000 years ago (at approximately 3500–3000 B.C.). Hence it is almost impossible to discuss the cultures which existed before writing in terms of languages which they might have shared. Archaeologists who treat the preliterate, prehistoric cultures refer to them by the modern names of the sites or regions which they occupied and designate them by area, level of technology and tool use, and artifact types.

Semitic languages

The people of ancient Syria who can be identified by their written

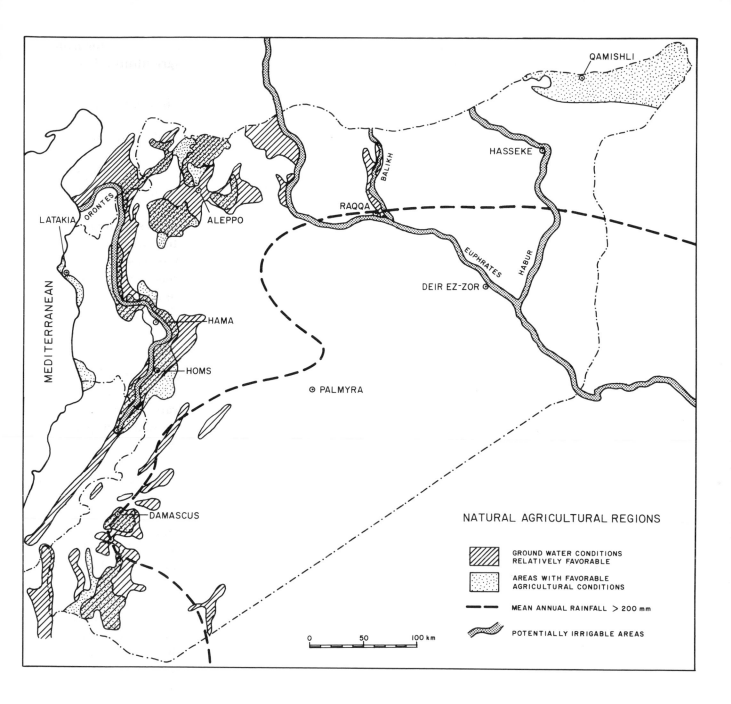

Figure 2
Regional agricultural utility.

Within the map:

MEDITERRANEAN

LATAKIA

ORONTES

ALEPPO

HAMA

HOMS

DAMASCUS

PALMYRA

RAQQA

BALIKH

HASSEKE

QAMISHLI

EUPHRATES

HABUR

DEIR EZ-ZOR

NATURAL AGRICULTURAL REGIONS

GROUND WATER CONDITIONS RELATIVELY FAVORABLE

AREAS WITH FAVORABLE AGRICULTURAL CONDITIONS

MEAN ANNUAL RAINFALL > 200 mm

POTENTIALLY IRRIGABLE AREAS

0   50   100 km

remains spoke for the most part languages which are classified as Semitic. It is worth examining just what this term means, because it is often misused.

Genetic relationships among languages allow for their classification into families. In the Old World alone at least twelve families are recognized, while in the New World far more are distinguished. The Old World language families include many which are quite familiar to Americans: Chinese, Niger-Congo, and Indo-European, for instance.

Semitic is another Old World language family, but the affinity between the Semitic languages is similar to that between the Romance or Germanic divisions of Indo-European. The Semitic languages are sometimes linked with the Hamitic to form a larger Hamito-Semitic grouping. The terms for these two families were derived 200 years ago from the names of the sons of Noah—Shem and Ham—listed in the genealogical table of Genesis 10.[1] The Hamitic languages include those of northern Africa, such as ancient Egyptian, the Cushitic languages of Somalia and Ethiopia, and Berber spoken across northern Africa and southward to the Sahara. The Semitic family includes about seventy different languages, all spoken, some to this day, in what we call the Near East and northern Africa. The people who spoke Semitic languages are of great historical interest, for so much of the Near Eastern, European, and eventually American cultural traditions are derived from their literature and history. *Ebla to Damascus* captures much of that history from the primary documents themselves. In fact, the exhibition presents some artifacts—clay tablets inscribed with a heretofore-unknown Semitic language—which now challenge the previously "well-established" history of the Semitic languages and peoples.

The chart of Semitic languages on page 38 presents a classification commonly accepted, at least for discussion purposes, among modern scholars. The horizontal axis represents similarity and divergence among the major language groupings within the Semitic family, while the vertical axis represents time (neither axis has anything but a rough and nonuniform "scale"). The similarities and divergences of vocabulary, verb morphology, and syntax result in a generally accepted classification of the Semitic languages which reflects their geographical distribution: Northwest Semitic, Southwest Semitic, Southeast Semitic, and East Semitic. With the exception of the Southeast languages, many of these have been or still are spoken in Syria. *Ebla to Damascus* presents the cultural history of people who spoke Eblaite, Akkadian, Amorite, Ugartic, Aramaic, and Arabic.

[1] A. L. Schlozer *Repertoire für Biblische unde Morgendlandlische Literatur* 8 (1781) 161.

Outside the Semitic family, two other languages appear in ancient Syria. Hurrian, a language isolate, was spoken by people occupying the Habur Plains during the late third millennium B.C., when the region was known as Subir; during the early second millennium B.C., when it was known as Subartu; and also in the mid-second millennium B.C., when it was known as Mittani or Hanigalbat. The influence of these Hurrian-speakers across Syria is an unresolved archaeological and historical matter. To be sure, however, Hurrian documents have been retrieved on the Habur Plains, at Mari, and at Ugarit.

The second non-Semitic language in ancient Syria may have been only written, not spoken. This is Luwian, an Indo-European language written with a hieroglyphic script initially developed in Late Bronze Age Anatolia. Its continued use on stone monuments of the twelfth to ninth centuries B.C. in northwest Syria may only indicate that the language was no longer spoken (see the essay "End of the Bronze Age").

Akkadian

The first steps toward writing—clay tablets impressed with seals and small numerical notations—occur at a wide range of sites across the Near East. This notation system developed first at Susa and Warka at the beginning of the Late Uruk period (ca. 3500 B.C.) and then was used by scribes at "colony"-type settlements such as Jebel Aruda and Habuba Kabira/Tell Qannas (see the chapter "Protohistoric Period").

It is not possible to determine the language in which these numerical notations were read. Shortly thereafter, however, the first ideograms appear alongside the notations, and these in turn soon appear with phonetic indicators which allow us to read the signs in particular languages. The earliest certain indicators tell us that the writing in southern Mesopotamian was expressing Sumerian, a language isolate. Only a few hundred years later, by 2750 B.C., some of these cuneiform signs suggest that they are to be read in the East Semitic language known as Akkadian, while some scribe names appended to the bottom of tablets are also Akkadian.[2] The appearance of these traces of early Akkadian in southern Mesopotamia has been traditionally understood as an "immigration" or "conquest" of the Sumerian south by Akkadians. More likely, Akkadians were present in southern Mesopotamia from the earliest historical moments.[3] The gradual replacement of one language-defined population by another in the Near East is one of the region's most repetitive historical

[2]R. D. Biggs Review of W. von Soden and W. Röllig *Das akkadische Syllabar* in *JNES* 29 (1970) 138 / "Semitic Names in the Fara Period" *Orientalia* 36 (1967) 55 / *Inscriptions from Tell Abu Salabikh* (Oriental Institute Publications 99) (Chicago 1974).

[3]J. Cooper "Sumerian and Akkadian in Sumer and Akkad" *Orientalia* 42 (1973) 239.

THE SEMITIC LANGUAGES IN THE NEAR EAST CA. 3000 B.C.–A.D. 1600

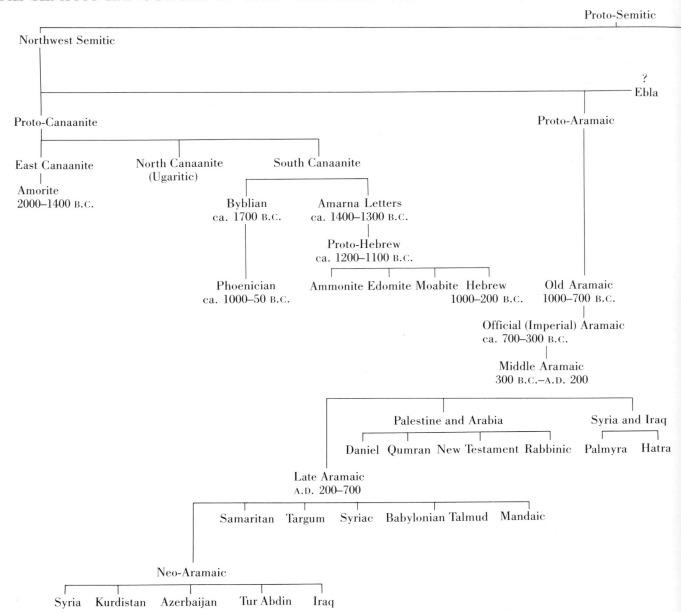

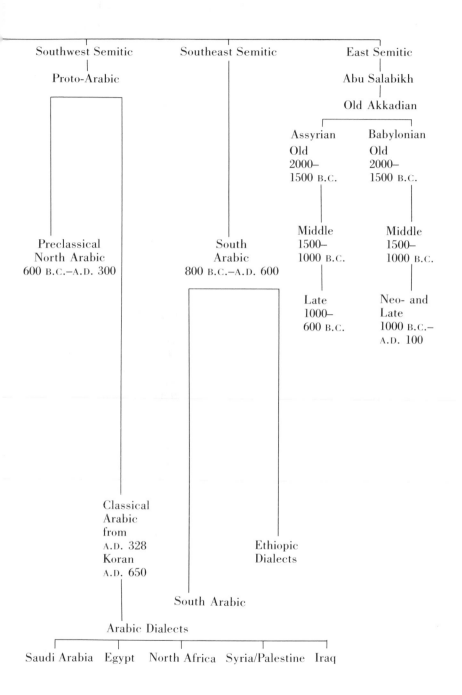

Southwest Semitic   Southeast Semitic   East Semitic

Proto-Arabic

Abu Salabikh

Old Akkadian

Assyrian
Old
2000–
1500 B.C.

Babylonian
Old
2000–
1500 B.C.

Preclassical
North Arabic
600 B.C.–A.D. 300

South
Arabic
800 B.C.–A.D. 600

Middle
1500–
1000 B.C.

Middle
1500–
1000 B.C.

Late
1000–
600 B.C.

Neo- and
Late
1000 B.C.–
A.D. 100

Classical
Arabic
from
A.D. 328
Koran
A.D. 650

Ethiopic
Dialects

South Arabic

Arabic Dialects

Saudi Arabia Egypt   North Africa Syria/Palestine Iraq

The construction of this chart is
based essentially on discussions in
Sabatino Moscati (ed.) *An Introduction
to the Comparative Grammar of the
Semitic Languages* (Wiesbaden 1969).

themes. In many cases the "conquest" was simply the gradual movement and integration of successive ethnic groups, often from pastoral communities, into the arenas of urban power and state officialdom.[4]

The Assyrian and Babylonian dialects of Akkadian, which are derived from and resemble Old Akkadian of the third millennium, were spoken and written in Syria and Mesopotamia during the second millennium B.C. and were only gradually replaced by Aramaic, a Northwest Semitic language, and its alphabetic script, during the first millennium B.C. The last cuneiform scribes, writing their astronomical observations in Late Babylonian and still copying older Sumerian literature, have left us dated documents from the first century A.D.[5] The cuneiform writing of Akkadian in Mesopotamia is therefore the lengthiest written record known, spanning almost three thousand years. The tens of thousands of inscribed clay tablets written during this period at a multitude of Syrian and Mesopotamian cities and towns provide our detailed historical record. *Ebla to Damascus* presents Akkadian texts from the archives of the palace at Mari, the great Old Syrian city on the Euphrates, as well as texts from the Middle Syrian city of Emar farther north near the great bend of the Euphrates.

Eblaite, Amorite, Ugaritic, and Aramaic

The stability and conservatism represented by the Akkadian or East Semitic languages is countered by the innovation and divergence within the Northwest Semitic languages. This probably reflects the relative dispersion of settled populations in the western portion of the Near East, as opposed to the lineal, riverside ties of settled communities in the Mesopotamian world. It is probably also a function of the movement between the "desert and the sown," the areas of sedentary agriculture and the seasonal grazing lands serving the needs of pastoral nomads situated between the agricultural regions. The historical variation in Semitic languages within these Syrian regions is still providing the academic world with surprises.

The recovery of third-millennium Ebla through Paolo Matthiae's excavations at Tell Mardikh has radically altered the history of the Near East and of the Semitic languages. The early documentation for Akkadian, perhaps as early as 2750 B.C., is limited to a few phonetic notations and scribal names. Literature in this language does not really appear until the Akkadian dynasty after the twenty-fifth century B.C. The palace archives from Ebla dating to the twenty-fifth century, with their literary texts, letters, and juridical documents are therefore "uniquely early documents in a Semitic language," as

[4]M. Rowton "Autonomy and Nomadism in Western Asia" *Orientalia* 42 (1973) 247 / "Dimorphic Structure and the Tribal Elite" *Studi Instituti Anthropos* 28 (1976) 219.

[5]W. W. Hallo "Toward a History of Sumerian Literature" in S. J. Lieberman (ed.) *Sumerological Studies in Honor of Thorkild Jacobsen* (Assyriological Studies 20) (Chicago, 1976) 181 // Timothy Doty "Cuneiform Archives from Hellenistic Uruk" Ph.D. dissertation (Yale University 1977).

INTRODUCTION

Alfonso Archi writes in his essay on the Ebla archives. The classification of Eblaite within the branches of Semitic remains uncertain. As Professor Archi notes, Eblaite's grammatical ties are with Old Akkadian, while its lexical ties are closest to the Northwest Semitic languages.

In the early second millennium, Amorite, clearly distinguished from Akkadian, is documented in the proper names and linguistic peculiarities of contemporary Akkadian documents in the Mari archives. Texts written in the Amorite language do not exist. Amorites, as individuals and as groups of people, are identified in Akkadian texts, however. In the fourteenth and thirteenth centuries the language of the letters and the literary and administrative texts from Ugarit illustrates yet another Northwest Semitic innovation and the beginnings of alphabetic writing as well.

The emergence of the Aramaeans, the foundation of the Aramaean city states at Damascus, Hama, Arpad (Tell Rifa'at near Aleppo), and Sam'al (Zinjirli), the adoption of Aramaic as the *lingua franca* of the Achaemenid empire, and the continued use of Aramaic within the communities of southern Mesopotamia, Syria, and Palestine through the Hellenistic, Roman, and Byzantine periods is a record almost one thousand years long. Varieties of Neo-Aramaic are still spoken in communities near Damascus and in towns and villages along the upper Habur River and across the Habur Plains. The origins of the Aramaeans, their initial settlement on the Habur Plains, and the early history of their amalgamation into city-states remain to be explored. The recent recovery and publication of a life-size statue with a bilingual Akkadian and Aramaic inscription from Tell Fekheriye (near Tell Halaf) has created another stir in the world of Semitic studies. The Aramaic portion is the oldest text of its kind and the only monumental text from the Habur Plains.[6]

Included among the Aramaic languages is Nabataean, spoken and written in the state organized at Petra between the first century B.C. and the third century A.D. The Arabic script evolved from the Nabataean, but classical Arabic texts only occur relatively late. The new evidence, therefore, for the oldest inscription (A.D. 328) in classical Arabic is as dramatic as the Syrian evidence for Eblaite, Amorite, Ugaritic, and Aramaic. The Namarah tomb inscription, first found some 100 kilometers southeast of Damascus in 1901 and recently restudied, was written in the Nabataean alphabet "well on its way to becoming Arabic," and adds 150 years to the history of classical Arabic.[7]

[6]A. Abou-Assaf, P. Bordreuil, and A. Millard *La statue de Tell Fekheriyeh et son inscription bilingue assyro-araméene* (Paris 1982) // D. Pardee and R. Biggs *JNES* 43 (1984) 253.

[7]James A. Bellamy "A New Reading of the Namarah Inscription" *JAOS* 105 (1985) 31.

New perspectives

The wealth of new data and new perspectives which Syrian archaeology has generated during the past ten years will require still longer to integrate into our working knowledge of the ancient Near East. In the spirit of *Ebla to Damascus*, two examples may illustrate this point.

The origins of cities and civilization in the Near East has been understood as a function of the high yield of irrigation agriculture in southern Mesopotamia. *Ebla to Damascus* redefines the problem of urban origins to include dry-farming Syria within the early urban terrain. As the number of known third-millennium cities in Syria grows, the challenge to present historiographic and anthropological paradigms becomes clearer. Attention will soon focus not just upon the difference between irrigation agriculture and dry farming in antiquity but upon the variabilities inherent in each system with regard to transport, production, exchange, settlement, and subsistence.

As a second example of the use of recent archaeological data, our understanding of the origins of classical Islamic civilization has also experienced very substantial revision through Syrian research. A long-held view among historians and archaeologists saw the Islamic conquest as a disruption of the urban forms which passed from Rome to Syria and other parts of the Near East. Classical cities with their broad arcades and large public buildings were transformed into mazes of crowded and winding alleys, the agora market and assembly areas disappeared, and the large public buildings were replaced by mosques and bath houses. In short, in this view the Arab conquest only brought the desert to the city. New perspectives, however, drawing together the evidence from archaeology and epigraphy, challenge this idea. The changes in urban design and function seem, in fact, to have already appeared before the Arab conquest. Planned Islamic towns, such as Qasr al-Hayr al-Sharqi, were constructed in Syria and display the open central square surrounded by arcades which characterize earlier cities. Such changes as did occur after the conquest seem to have been useful accommodations to economic changes, changes in short- and long-distance transport, and changes in urban administration.[8] These perspectives typify a substantial shift within recent archaeological concerns. They suggest that Syrian archaeology may carry us to deeper understandings of ancient civilizations in general.

[8]Richard Bulliet *The Camel and the Wheel* (Cambridge, Mass. 1975) // Hugh Kennedy "From Polis to Madina: Urban Change in Late Antique and Early Islamic Syria" *Past and Present* 106 (1985) 3.

A note on chronology

The absolute—that is, calendar year—dates used in this volume for the pre-Hellenistic period are of three different qualities.

First, there are the dates until the middle of the fourteenth century B.C. which are documented through regnal years of the kings of Mesopotamia, Syria, and Egypt, have many synchronisms, and therefore can be considered secure.

Second, there are the dates from the fourteenth back to the twenty-seventh century B.C. A "dark age," providing few chronological linkages, separates the fourteenth-century kings of northern and southern Mesopotamia from their predecessors, the partial contemporaries Shamshi-Adad of Assyria and Hammurabi of Babylon. The dates of the latter and still earlier rulers are therefore dependent upon the span of time assigned to the "dark age." Three different absolute chronologies have been proposed for this period. The reign of Hammurabi is assigned 1848–1806 by the "high chronology," 1791–1750 by the "middle chronology," and 1728–1686 by the "low chronology." In the English-speaking world the middle chronology advocated by Sidney Smith and Michael Rowton has acquired general acceptance.[9] This is the chronology used for this period in this book, although a recent probabilistic analysis now suggests that the "high chronology" may be correct.[10]

Third, there are the dates preceding the twenty-seventh century. Dependent upon stratigraphic sequences, relative chronologies, and radio-carbon dating, these are only approximate. An older, more general, periodization for the third through first millennia B.C. discussed in this volume is the Bronze–Iron Age terminology occasionally referred to. That terminology can be summarized approximately as follows:

Iron Age	1200–535 B.C.	New Syrian period
Late Bronze Age	1550–1200 B.C.	Middle Syrian period
Middle Bronze Age	2000–1550 B.C.	Old Syrian period
Early Bronze Age	3000–2000 B.C.	Third Millennium

[9]J. A. Brinkman "Mesopotamian Chronology of the Historical Period" in A. L. Oppenheim *Ancient Mesopotamia* (Chicago 1977) 335.

[10]P. J. Huber et al. "Astronomical Dating of Babylon I and Ur III" *Occasional Papers on the Near East* 1/4 (Malibu 1982).

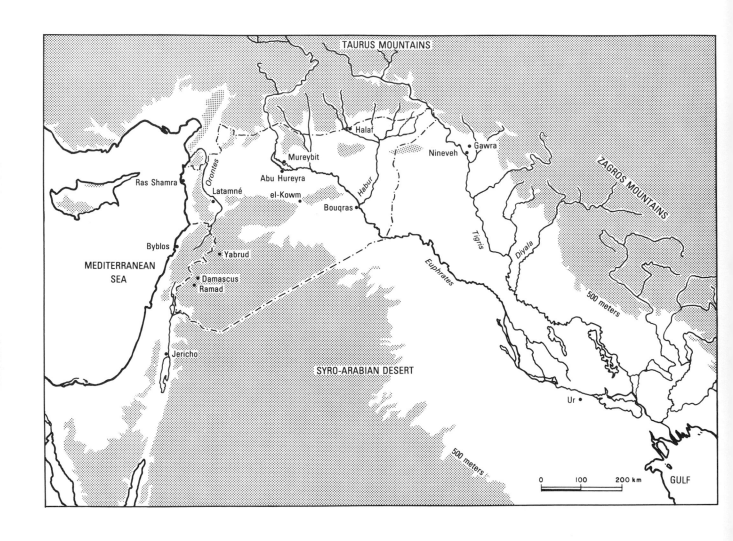

TAURUS MOUNTAINS

ZAGROS MOUNTAINS

MEDITERRANEAN
SEA

Ras Shamra

Byblos

Latamné

Abu Hureyra

Mureybit

el-Kowm

Bouqras

Halaf

Nineveh

Gawra

Yabrud

Damascus
Ramad

Jericho

SYRO-ARABIAN DESERT

Orontes

Habur

Euphrates

Tigris

Diyala

500 meters

500 meters

Ur

GULF

0   100   200 km

PREHISTORIC BACKGROUND
CA. 8000–5000 B.C.

PREHISTORIC ORIGINS

HARVEY WEISS

BY DEFINITION PREHISTORY ENCOMPASSES THAT VERY LONG PERIOD of life on earth prior to the use of writing, which was invented first in the Near East a mere 5,000 years ago. As the archaeological record of the cultural activity of humans or humanlike species, prehistory extends as far back as 1.6 million years, when the earliest archaeologically recognizable activities associated with hominids can be detected at several locations in East Africa. Geologically that time period represents the end of the Pliocene epoch and the beginning of the Pleistocene.

The Pleistocene epoch was marked by very severe but gradual alterations in climate. Some parts of the world, such as western Europe, were repeatedly covered by glaciers, advancing and retreating from northern climes as temperature conditions varied. The last of these cold periods, and the last glacial retreat, ended only about 10,000 years ago. Many geologists believe that present conditions on earth are but one of the interglacial periods characteristic of the Pleistocene.

The species of humans which lived on earth during the Early and Middle Pleistocene are designated *Homo erectus*. They appeared first in Africa, and within the course of a million years became the first widely distributed species of early humans. By about 100,000 years ago the *Homo erectus* population had altered to the point that it is possible to speak of *Homo sapiens*. This was a gradual change which resulted in a population very much like our own.

The archaeological record for cultural activity during almost the entire span of the Pleistocene indicates that human groups were essentially small bands of hunters of wild animals and gatherers of plants, adapting by degree over the course of tens of thousands of years to gradually changing environmental conditions. Much of the evidence for the culture of this period consists of the durable artifacts manufactured by these populations as a means of subsisting and successfully reproducing themselves. That durable record is mostly chipped stone tools; they provide archaeologists with their most important guide to the changes within human societies during the long span of the Pleistocene.

The stone tools manufactured in prehistory are usually categorized by their method of manufacture, which gradually varied to meet changing methods of hunting, gathering, collecting, and preparing food, as well as making shelters. The earliest types of tools were made by chipping flakes off stone cores; hence they are labelled core or flake tools. Such tools, characterizing the toolmaking traditions of the Old World during most of the Pleistocene, are called Paleolithic, or Old Stone Age, tools, and the societies which produced them are also labelled Paleolithic. During the Lower Paleolithic most tools have the shape of hand axes chipped on both sides (bifacially) and were probably used to butcher large game, such as varieties of elephant and rhinoceros now extinct. Important evidence for the activities of Lower Paleolithic bands in the Near East is derived from the Syrian sites of Latamné and el-Kowm, while surface and occasional finds of Lower Paleolithic tools have been recovered along the terraces of the Nahr el-Kebir River and the Euphrates, where early geological strata have been exposed by natural erosion processes.

About 90–100,000 years ago in the Near East and Europe a very different tradition of manufacturing stone tools appeared which archaeologists label Middle Paleolithic. Instead of chipping large flakes off a stone core and then manipulating the residue core as a tool, the new technique prepared the cores in such a way that flakes of predetermined size and shape could be formed. This technique, called Levalloisian after the French site of Levallois where such tools were first identified, is also associated in Europe, the Near East, and other parts of Asia with a *Homo erectus* population slightly different from earlier ones. This population, the Neanderthals, received its name from the Neanderthal Valley in Germany where such individuals were first identified in nineteenth-century excavations. The Neanderthals were quite different from us physically but hardly merit the qualities with which their name is associated among the public. They were much stronger and heavier than modern *Homo sapiens*, their teeth were larger, their faces probably broader, and their cranial capacities probably larger as well. The elaboration of culture among the *Homo sapiens neanderthalensis* has suggested to some that "language" had certainly evolved by this time; its evidence, however, will always be uncertain.

The origins and then disappearance of the Neanderthal population remain poorly understood archaeological phenomena. The last evolutionary stage in the history of our species was irreversibly reached by about 45,000 years ago, and at approximately the same time the tool tradition which archaeologists can distinguish also changes from Middle to Upper Paleolithic. The Levalloiso-Mousterian technique of core and flake preparation gives way to a tool tradition in which long, slim blade tools begin to predominate.

There is much debate as to the causal relationships between the biological and cultural changes of this period; in fact, the nature of cultural change in general throughout the long Paleolithic period is a matter of great controversy among archaeologists. Similarly, the transition from Paleolithic to Neolithic (New Stone) cultures in Syria, the Near East, and elsewhere is poorly understood and thus the subject of much research.

One of the intriguing questions which remain to be answered about the Paleolithic period and the Pleistocene epoch is the apparent stability of the hunting-and-gathering groups whose remains we can observe in the archaeological record. For instance, the long span of time during which Lower Paleolithic cultures persisted, with an essentially unchanged tool kit, raises the question why changes eventually appeared at all. Is the stage which we label Middle Paleolithic the result of different physical qualities and needs of the Neanderthals? Why does the pace of tool-assemblage change quicken so rapidly thereafter as well? Perhaps most important, if hunting and gathering, to judge from its persistence as a way of life for millions of years, was such a successful means of subsistence for hominid and human populations, why did Upper Paleolithic societies abandon it for an agricultural way of life?

One promising source of information for the eventual resolution of such questions is the study of modern hunters and gatherers, the few remnant Paleolithic cultures which are available for documentation. The study of one such population suggests that the hunter-gatherer way of life required relatively little in the way of labor expenditures compared with the requirements of early agriculture. Although the accuracy of the parallels between modern and prehistoric cultures is very difficult to establish, inquiries such as this have prompted some archaeologists to suggest that Paleolithic stability was due to a relative abundance of resources, while the way of life, essentially a nonsedentary seasonal round, placed upper limits on population growth.

Why then did hunting and gathering give way to agriculture and sedentary village life? The gradual amelioration of climatic conditions at the end of the Pleistocene and beginning of the recent epoch, the Holocene, coincides with the early evidence for agricultural societies in Syria and the Near East. Most archaeologists believe that this alteration of climate helped to promote the new means of subsistence. The actual mechanism, however, still remains uncertain. After all, we might ask, why did the transition to an agricultural way of life not take place during one of the earlier interglacial periods of the Pleistocene epoch?

Recommended Reading

J. Cauvin (ed.). *Cahiers de l'Euphrate* 1— (Paris: C.N.R.S., 1978—).

Richard B. Lee and Irven DeVore (eds.). *Man the Hunter* (Chicago: Aldine, 1968).

David R. Pilbeam. "The Descent of Hominoids and Hominids." *Scientific American* 250/3 (1984) 84–96.

Eric Trinkhaus and William W. Howells. "The Neanderthals." *Scientific American* 241/6 (1979) 118–134.

SYRIA AND THE ORIGINS OF AGRICULTURE

ANDREW M. T. MOORE

FOR TWO MILLION YEARS EARLY HUMANS PURSUED A HUNTING-AND-gathering way of life, moving in small groups among several camp-sites in the course of the year. Then about 11,000 years ago people began to cultivate their own crops and to raise livestock, providing an increased and more accessible supply of food. The development of agriculture and settled life was one of the most important transformations in human history, and there is reason to believe that it occurred earlier in the Near East than anywhere else in the world.

This economic revolution had far-reaching consequences. Since an agricultural way of life could best be carried out in the vicinity of a settlement, people were encouraged to live in permanent villages for the first time. An immediate result was that their numbers grew dramatically, partly because of the increased supply of food but also because the birth rate was no longer slowed by the physiological demands of a mobile way of life. The village inhabitants now required new forms of social organization to regulate their affairs, arrange access to land, and resolve disputes.

There were other consequences, too. The agricultural year in simple societies consists of periods of intense work at planting and harvest time, separated by spells of relative leisure. Some members of these early societies took advantage of their times of ease to engage in crafts. Thus we find evidence for the manufacture of a wide range of new artifacts—a flowering of craft production—soon after the initial development of agriculture. In time, an increasingly productive agricultural economy made possible the rise of civilization. This, too, occurred in the Near East earlier than elsewhere. Archaeological research in the last twenty years has demonstrated that Syria was one of the main areas of agricultural development and may be taken as a model for similar changes in the Near East.

Epipaleolithic (ca. 18,000–8500 B.C.)

During the Epipaleolithic age Syria was inhabited by small groups of people who were widely scattered across the landscape. Their camp-sites have been found at Yabrud, near Palmyra, and around el-Kowm. They hunted a variety of game and collected wild plant foods. The climate was cool and dry, and much of the country was semiarid plains, or steppe. About 13,000 B.C. both temperature and rainfall increased; the forest zone in the coastal mountains expanded eastward while the steppe became better watered. Under these more favorable conditions population increased and groups began to settle in more permanent camps and to construct dwellings. These first villages have been found at Abu Hureyra on the Euphrates and at Jayrud near Nebek. The Epipaleolithic settlement at Abu Hureyra, inhabited about 9000 B.C., consisted of pit dwellings sunk into the ground and roofed with branches and reeds on a timber framework.

The inhabitants of these first villages required a regular supply of food in the immediate vicinity of their settlements. But to intensify their traditional hunting and gathering was by itself not enough. They went further and began to exert a degree of control over certain animals such as gazelle, caprines, and onagers and to deliberately cultivate cereals and pulses.

Taming wild animals and cultivating wild plants are the necessary first steps in the process of domestication. At first the plants and animals maintain the normal characteristics of wild species, but later, under selection pressures imposed by man, their morphology changes and they are visibly different from their wild ancestors. In the case of cereals like wheat and barley the changes in the form of the ear are of crucial importance for the reproduction of the plant. Each cereal grain is attached to a segment of the stem called the rachis. In wild plants the rachis is brittle, so that at maturity the ear shatters easily and the seeds fall to the ground and readily enter the soil, to sprout again the following year. Once cereals were cultivated, man encouraged the growth of plants with a tough rachis so that the seeds would remain in the ear until they were harvested. This was convenient, since it allowed more time to reap the plant, but it seriously reduced the ability of the seeds to reproduce themselves. They became dependent on man for this. The morphology of lentils, peas, and other pulses changed less dramatically. The most notice-able initial trend was an increase in seed size, so that cultivated varieties would yield more than their wild counterparts.

Domesticated animals are also different in size from their fore-bears. Early domesticated cattle, in particular, were much smaller than their wild ancestors. Domesticated sheep and goats exhibited other morphological changes as well: the horns of both species became shorter, disappearing altogether in female sheep, while the shape of the horns altered. In the case of pigs, the most distinctive change was a shortening of the snout.

Such differences enable the archaeobotanist and archaeozoologist to distinguish generally between wild and domestic plants and animals. It is difficult on the basis of these criteria, however, to discern when domestication was just beginning, for at that stage the morphological changes resulting from man-imposed selection are not yet manifest. When changes do become apparent, we must assume that deliberate cultivation and herding had been under way for some time.

Other kinds of archaeological evidence are also helpful in determining where and when agriculture began. Once human groups began to interest themselves in the possibilities of farming, they sought to locate their sites near fertile, moist land. They also developed the necessary artifacts to process the fruits of their farming, in particular grinding tools to crush the seeds of cereals. It is precisely these changes that we see taking place at Abu Hureyra and other sites in Syria about 11,000 years ago, earlier than anywhere else in the world.

Abu Hureyra was surrounded by easily cultivable land, watered by a tributary of the Euphrates. It seems that the inhabitants of the site were beginning to grow cereals and perhaps pulses as early as 9000 B.C. These plants were still wild in form but would later acquire all the characteristics of domesticated species as man adjusted his methods of harvesting them. In the pit dwellings at Abu Hureyra were flat querns for grinding grain (see Fig. 3).

Neolithic (ca. 8500–5000 B.C.)
Agriculture was already well established in Syria by the early Neolithic period. At Tell Aswad, near Damascus, a site inhabited soon after 8000 B.C., domesticated emmer wheat, lentils, and peas were all being cultivated. Abu Hureyra was reoccupied about 7500 B.C. by people who grew both domesticated emmer and einkorn wheat, barley, and a wide range of pulses. The diet was still supplemented by plants and animals taken from the wild, but as more productive varieties of crops were developed, agriculture provided an increasing proportion of food.

It seems that in Syria early in the Neolithic only light control was exercised over the available animals such as gazelle, onager, and cattle. Then quite suddenly about 7000 B.C. sheep and goats were

Figure 3
Abu Hureyra, Epipaleolithic, ca.
9000 B.C. Two querns found in
position within a pit dwelling,
which suggests that the inhabitants
of this early village were already
processing grain for food. (Scale:
0.2 meter.)

introduced, probably from Mesopotamia and the Zagros Mountains, where it is thought they were first domesticated. From this time on flocks of sheep and goats became a mainstay of the economy. The two other important species, cattle and pigs, were fully domesticated by 6000 B.C.

During the Neolithic the normal form of settlement was a village of mud-brick houses. These were inhabited over many centuries, indicating how stable the new sedentary, agricultural way of life was. Neolithic villages were more numerous and substantially larger than Epipaleolithic settlements. Abu Hureyra, the largest of them all, covered 11.5 hectares and was big enough to have served as a regional center. It is clear that by the seventh millennium the population of Syria had increased dramatically as a consequence of the development of agriculture.

Early in the Neolithic the houses of these villages were circular in shape, best seen at Mureybit, another village on the Euphrates. These were simply mud-brick examples of the huts built during the Epipaleolithic. Then, during the eighth millennium, people started to build rectangular mud-brick houses, relatively large, with several rooms. Each house was free-standing and probably lodged a single family. These dwellings often had plaster floors inside with hearths, ovens, and sleeping platforms for additional comfort. The walls and floors of some rooms might be decorated with painted designs, as were those found at Abu Hureyra and Bouqras. These large Neolithic villages were densely packed settlements. The houses tended to be aligned in a single direction with narrow lanes and courts between them (see Fig. 4). Food preparation and other activities of daily life were carried on as much outdoors as inside.

Figure 4
Abu Hureyra, Neolithic, ca. 6500 B.C. The walls of a rectangular mud-brick house with five rooms. The corner of another house is visible in the lower part of the photograph. These two houses were separated by a narrow lane and surrounded by open spaces. (Scale: 2 and 0.5 meters.)

PREHISTORIC BACKGROUND

It was the custom during the early Neolithic to bury many of the dead within these settlements, under the floors of houses or in the yards outside. The graves contained only the simplest of goods, and there were no significant differences between one burial and another. This, coupled with the fact that houses were similar in size, suggests that there were no marked status differences in these societies.

The inhabitants of the villages manufactured a variety of new artifacts, both utilitarian and ornamental. They chipped great quantities of fine flint tools: sickle blades for reaping, arrowheads for hunting, and scrapers for preparing leather, as shown in Cat. No. 19. Bone was used to make everything from awls to pins, needles, fishhooks, and fasteners for clothing. There is some evidence that yarn and textiles were manufactured, while mats and baskets were regularly woven. Early in the Neolithic dishes and bowls were carved from limestone (Cat. No. 3), gypsum, and steatite. During the seventh millennium heavy containers were fashioned out of white plaster, perhaps for storing foodstuffs. Pottery began to be made about 6000 B.C., and soon after a wide variety of vessels for cooking and storage were being produced (see Cat. No. 18). The development of the craft of potting probably created a minor revolution in food preparation, since a cook could now make a variety of stews, soups, and porridge in addition to the simple baked dishes and roasts that had been the only possibilities before.

Weaving, potting, and other crafts first developed during the Neolithic may be seen as an immediate consequence of sedentary village life based on agriculture. Nor were the inhabitants of these settlements interested simply in making practical articles; they also fashioned jewelry in the form of beads and pendants out of bone, shell, and colored stones. Some of the stones were imported from distant regions: the Taurus Mountains (serpentine and agate), Sinai (turquoise), and even the Zagros Mountains (steatite). Simple clay models of animals and humans were also made, together with occasional objects that aspired to art such as the delightful tiny carving in granite of a gazelle's head found at Abu Hureyra (Fig. 5; cf. Cat. No. 7).

Trade in attractive stones for ornamental artifacts was sporadic, but obsidian was regularly acquired by the inhabitants of all Syrian Neolithic villages. Obsidian, which was prized for the sharp knife blades that could be made from it, was exchanged in the form of partly prepared cores (see Cat. No. 4). Trade in this material began about 8000 B.C., soon after the founding of the first villages, and continued throughout the Neolithic.

Figure 5
Abu Hureyra, Neolithic, ca. 6500
B.C. The head of a gazelle carved
from granite. This miniature work
of art is a superb example of
Neolithic craftsmanship. (Scale:
0.05 meter.)

About 6000 B.C. the environment began to deteriorate as the climate grew warmer and drier and the forest zone began to shrink. The increased population was also having a deleterious effect on the surroundings of many sites in the steppe. A fresh adjustment in the location of sites and subsistence economy became necessary, and there followed a major shift of settlement out of the steppe westward toward the coast and northward to the present frontier with Turkey. New villages were founded on heavier soils in the forest zone, which had a higher rainfall and so offered a more reliable climate for farming.

Hitherto the economy had been based on cultivation and herding supplemented by wild plants and game. From now on agriculture and domesticated animals provided almost all the food. This agricultural system was quite similar to that practiced until very recently in Syria, based as it was on the cultivation of wheat, barley, and pulses and the raising of sheep and goats with some cattle. It was a system of food production that could be intensified to produce greater yields which in turn would support higher levels of population. There is archaeological evidence that by 5000 B.C. the population of Syria had indeed increased further as a result of the adoption of a fully agricultural economy.

Syria was ready for another major cultural change that would transform the simple Neolithic farming villages with their egalitarian social system into a more stratified society with an emergent political organization. The first indications of these changes were evident about 5000 B.C. A new culture known as Halaf, named after a site in north Syria, developed out of the later Neolithic. It too had a firm agricultural base, but trade and craft specialization played more important roles than they had before. The most notable example was the production and exchange of beautifully painted pottery, the hallmark of the Halaf culture. Halaf sites were especially numerous in the Jezireh on the Habur Plains and westward across north Syria from the Euphrates to the Mediterranean. These sites were often set close together on the most fertile land. This suggests that some intercommunity agreement would have been necessary to regulate affairs, and we may see in this the beginning of a more complex pattern of political organization. Civilization was not to arise in Syria until late in the fourth millennium, but already the first steps had been taken beyond the Neolithic village way of life that was the immediate consequence of the development of agriculture.

Recommended Reading
B. Bender. *Farming in Prehistory* (London: Baker, 1975).

J. Mellaart. *The Neolithic of the Near East* (New York: Scribner's, 1976).

A.M.T. Moore. "A Pre-Neolithic Farmers' Village on the Euphrates." *Scientific American* 241/2 (1979) 62–70.

MUREYBIT

Location: Left bank of the middle Euphrates
Dates: Phase I, 8500–8200 B.C.; Phase II, 8200–8000 B.C.; Phase III, 8000–7600 B.C.; Phase IV, 7600–6800 B.C.
Excavations: 1964 and 1965 (University of Chicago); 1971–1974 (Centre de Recherches d'Ecologie Humaine et Prehistoire, France)
Publications: J. Cauvin *AAAS* 22 (1972) 105 / *AAAS* 24 (1974) 47 / *Les premiers villages* // M.C. Cauvin and D. Stordeur "Les outillages lithiques et osseux de Mureybet, Syrie (Fouilles Van Loon 1965)" *Cahiers de l'Euphrate* 1 (Paris 1978) // J. Cl. Margueron (ed.) *Le Moyen Euphrate* 21

According to the available evidence, humans began living in permanent, sedentary communities about 11,000 years ago in the Near East. Mureybit is one of the earliest known examples of these primary villages. Occupation began at the site in the middle of the ninth millennium B.C. and continued for almost 2,000 years, providing us with a document of long-term changes experienced by early village society.

The inhabitants of the oldest occupation level, Mureybit I, acquired their food through hunting and gathering. They practiced a "broad-spectrum" food procurement strategy, in which the available resources from a wide range of ecological niches were exploited. The wild gazelle, onager, and cattle of the steppe were hunted, fish and mussels were caught in the river, and plants were collected from wild stands. The plants included such cereals as einkorn wheat and barley, which were later subject to intentional cultivation, a process which may well have begun even in this early stage.

Only limited architectural remains were recovered from Mureybit I. The earliest contexts yielded floor surfaces and three fire pits filled with pebbles, probably used to roast grain in order to remove the tough husks characteristic of primitive forms. Upper levels included remnants of a round house 6 meters in diameter, a dwelling common in later levels as well. The flint tools employed by the inhabitants of Mureybit I included many geometric-shaped microliths, tiny blades set in wood or bone hafts to form composite tools. These tools are comparable to those used in sites in Palestine of the same period (Natufian). The similarities in the tool kits and the architecture of these Palestinian sites and Mureybit I have led archaeologists to consider them part of a single cultural zone encompassing the entire Levant.

The succeeding settlement, Mureybit II, occupied an area of 2 to 3 hectares, at least double the size of Mureybit I. Village size was increasing in this period, although the number of villages diminished. At Mureybit a settlement of many round houses existed. Sometimes semi-subterranean and sometimes built on level ground, the houses measured 3 to 4 meters in diameter and were constructed of packed mud or red clay, with wooden posts acting as roof supports. The broad-spectrum hunting-and-gathering strategies of the earlier settlement were continued. Many stone implements used for the processing of plant food were found, including querns, mortars, pestles, and stone bowls. By this point, the manufacture of microliths had declined and arrowheads took their place.

Evidence of ideological innovation is apparent in Mureybit II. The "cult of the bull," common in later Neolithic settlements all over the Near East, is attested by the discovery of a bull cranium imbedded in a clay bench in one of the houses. Clay nude female "goddess" figurines, prevalent in the Near East for thousands of years thereafter, were also found first in this settlement (see Cat. No. 1, from Phase III).

By the time of Mureybit III there is a discernible change in food procurement, including a decline in hunting and fishing. Evidence of plant cultivation is now available: analysis of the pollen from this

Figure 6
Round houses at Mureybit.

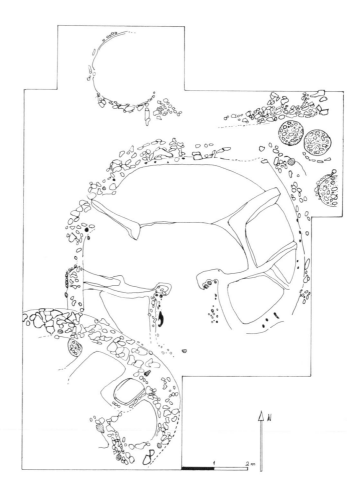

phase revealed a quantity of cereal pollens which would be unexpected in the absence of agriculture. There is architectural change as well. While the round houses persist, in some cases their interiors are divided by partition walls creating rectangular rooms (Fig. 6). Completely rectangular buildings also make their first appearance here.

One of the round houses in Mureybit III contains the earliest example of wall painting within a manmade structure, a mural with a geometric design. Another surprising find is a group of five lightly fired clay vessels. There is no other pottery from the site, and pottery does not appear elsewhere in the Levant for another 1,500 years.

The excavated area from the latest settlement at the site, Mureybit IV, is relatively small, but the evidence indicates that rectilinear architecture continued in use. Another ideological innovation appears at this point: the "cult of the skulls." Human skeletons were found buried under the floor of a building, but the skulls were discovered in the room above the floor, resting on red-clay supports against the walls. Similar treatment of skulls of the dead is found at sites to the south, such as Jericho and Ramad (see Cat. No. 16). It has been suggested that the cult of the skulls represents a form of ancestor worship which developed with the advent of sedentary society: when people began to live in permanent dwellings and possess hereditary territory, the veneration of deceased family members became important to the inheritors of property.

Mureybit was at last abandoned in the early seventh millennium after almost 2,000 years of occupation. The history of the site demonstrates the shift from round to rectangular domestic architecture in early Neolithic times. It has been observed that circular dwellings are associated in the ethnographic literature with nomadic or semi-nomadic hunting-and-gathering societies, while rectangular dwellings are connected with sedentary agricultural societies. In a circular hut settlement each structure is occupied by one or two adults, and storage is shared. In a rectangular house community the nuclear family is the basic organizational unit, with each family having its own storage area. New elements can be easily added to rectangular structures as new members of the family are born or enter the family through marriage. At Mureybit we also have evidence for the gradual adoption of agriculture by the earliest villagers, who began by simply collecting wild plants but eventually assumed an active control over the planting and growing process themselves.

GLENN M. SCHWARTZ

BOUQRAS

Location: 35 km southeast of Deir-ez-Zor on the right bank of the Euphrates, opposite the mouth of the Habur River
Dates: Four phases, ca. 6400–5900 B.C.
Excavations: 1965 (French); 1976–1978 (University of Amsterdam and University of Groningen)
Publications: H. de Contenson and W. J. van Liere *AAAS* 16,2 (1966) 188 // P. A. Akkermans et al. *AfO* 26 (1978–1979) 152 // P. A. Akkermans et al. in *Prehistoire du Levant* 485 // P. A. Akkermans et al. *Proceedings of the Prehistoric Society* 49 (1983) 335

In the period following the abandonment of Mureybit, large villages with rectilinear, multi-room houses became common in the Levant. A notable example of such a village is Bouqras, a 3-hectare site some 250 kilometers downriver from Mureybit. Much of the architecture of the ancient village was visible from the surface of the site and could be mapped; as a result, we have an extensive plan of the architecture of the site (Fig. 7). In addition, a sizable sample of houses

Figure 7
Settlement at Bouqras.

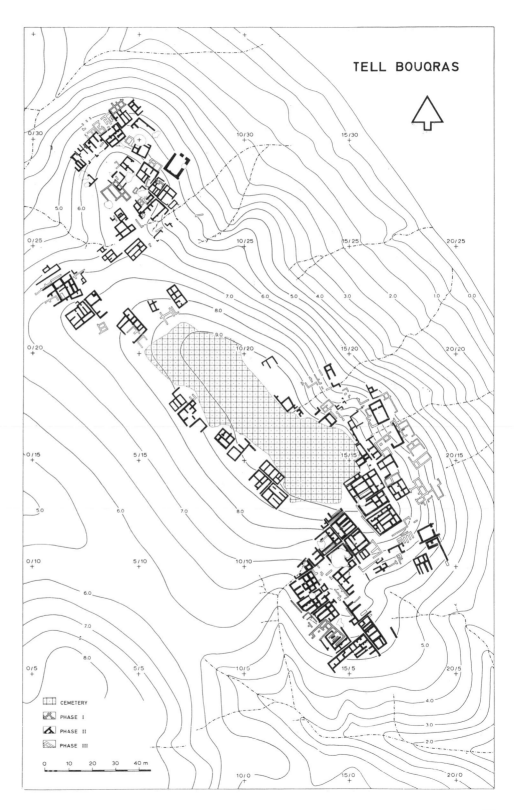

TELL BOUQRAS

CEMETERY
PHASE I
PHASE II
PHASE III

0 10 20 30 40 m

was excavated and provides much valuable information on a large village of this period.

The buildings were constructed with rectangular sun-dried mud bricks of a uniform size. In one excavation area at the apex of the mound, the typical house plan consisted of a courtyard with a horseshoe-shaped oven, flanked on one side by a large rectangular room and on the other by three small squarish rooms with small ovens and floor bins (possibly storage or kitchen space). House walls are often plastered with gypsum, available in abundance from the nearby steppe. In the southwest part of the site, the typical house plan consists of a series of three narrow rectangular rooms with three small squarish rooms added on one side. Sometimes an extra series of small rooms appears as well. The majority of the excavated buildings were clearly intended for domestic purposes, since they yielded features like ovens, hearths, and bins. Two houses contained wall paintings of red ochre, one of which depicts a row of birds (cranes?) on gypsum plaster (Fig. 8).

The flint tool industry included many arrowheads and spearheads comparable to types known from elsewhere in the Levant in the Pre-Pottery Neolithic B period. A large quantity of obsidian tools were also manufactured. Since we know that the obsidian was obtained from the Lake Van region in eastern Anatolia, we have evidence of the existence of long-distance exchange in this period. Anatolian contacts are also attested by similarities in material culture: a baked clay seated female figure from Bouqras (Cat. No. 5) resembles examples from Çatal Hüyük in south-central Ana-

tolia, as do the stone vessels with small feet shown in Cat. Nos. 13 and 14. Shared material culture characteristics can also be seen at early sites to the east in Mesopotamia, especially Tell es-Sawwan on the middle Tigris and Umm Dabaghiyah south of the Jebel Sinjar.

The manufacture of pottery was under way in the Levant in this period, and thousands of sherds are associated with the later levels at Bouqras. Another type of vessel characteristic of the period was "white ware," made of gypsum or lime and salty gray ashes built up in coils around a basket which was then dried and fired. Although white ware is sometimes thought to have been a step toward the manufacture of pottery, it appears no earlier than pottery at Bouqras. In use alongside white ware and pottery were stone vessels (Cat. Nos. 11–14), including small cups, four-footed vessels, plates, and dishes. Three gypsum vessels in the shape of a hedgehog (Cat. No. 9), a hare (Cat. No. 8), and a bull were among the many objects found in a burned house.

By this point, there is clear-cut evidence for agriculture in the Levant, but the people of Bouqras seem to have partaken very little of plant food. Domesticated emmer, breadwheat, hulled and naked barley are attested at the site, but the number of recovered seeds was quite small. Evidence of wild food plants was equally rare. This lack of emphasis on plant exploitation is understandable in light of the environment of the site: Bouqras is located in a steppe zone with an average annual rainfall of some 125 millimeters, only half of the required minimum for rainfall agri-

Figure 8
Wall paintings at Bouqras.

culture. What agriculture the people of the site did practice was probably conducted in the moist bottoms of nearby wadis, where low-yield farming without the benefit of irrigation is still practiced today.

It was animals that the inhabitants of Bouqras primarily depended upon for their food. Herding was the major subsistence activity of the site, and a huge number of animal bones were retrieved from the excavations. The bones of domestic sheep, goats, and cattle were identified, among others. Hunting was practiced too, with such quarry as gazelle and wild goat from the steppe.

The excavators estimate that the village of Bouqras contained some 180 houses and a population of 700–1,000 people. A community of this size must have required a more complex form of social organization than the small villages of earlier Neolithic times. Likewise, the regular layout, standardized plans, and uniform mode of construction of the houses at Bouqras imply the existence of specialized craftsmen and some form of community organization. However, there is no evidence for individuals of high status; the houses are all of a similar size, with similar collections of artifacts.

GLENN M. SCHWARTZ

RAMAD

Location: Near Qattana, 15 km southwest of Damascus at the foot of Mount Hermon
Dates: Level I, 6250–6000 B.C.; Level II, 6000–5800 B.C.; Level III, 5800–5500 B.C.
Excavations: 1963–1973 (Directorate-General of Antiquities and Museums, Damascus, and Commission des Recherches Archéologiques à l'Etranger de Paris, Centre National de la Recherche Scientifique)
Publications: See especially W. J. van Liere and H. de Contenson *AAAS* 13 (1963) 179 / *AAAS* 14 (1964) 109 / *AAAS* 16,2 (1966) 167 // H. de Contenson *AAAS* 17 (1970) 77 / *AAAS* 24 (1974) 17 / *Archaeology* 24 (1971) 278

Approximately contemporary with Bouqras and about the same size is the site of Ramad, located at the foot of Mount Hermon, southwest of Damascus. The environmental situation of the two sites differs dramatically, however; while Bouqras is located on a dry steppe, Ramad is situated in an area with abundant rainfall for dry farming. Consequently, there is ample evidence for plant domestication and a reliance on rainfall agriculture at Ramad. Domestic emmer, barley, lentils, and flax were grown. Wild plants were still collected, and gazelle, equids, and deer were hunted.

The transition from round huts to rectilinear houses observed at Mureybit is also in evidence at Ramad. In Ramad I, the earliest occupation, the inhabitants lived in semi-subterranean oval dwellings some 3 to 4 meters in diameter, built of packed mud with lime-plastered floors. The treatment of human skulls observed in Mureybit IV also appears here; the skulls were plastered and painted, with shells set into the empty eye sockets. Small clay figurines of women and animals were also found in Ramad I. Flint and obsidian tools were worked at the site, the obsidian coming mainly from central Anatolia. Long-distance exchange with Anatolia is also attested by a bead of native copper, probably derived from the Ergani Maden copper mines of eastern Anatolia.

In Ramad II, round houses are displaced by rectilinear mud-brick houses with plastered floors, sometimes with stone foundations. Vessels of white ware appear for the first time. More modeled skulls were discovered in this settlement, found resting on headless seated clay female figurines coated with plaster and red paint (see Cat. No. 16 and Fig. 9).

Pottery was introduced by the time of Ramad III, a variety known as dark-faced burnished ware (Cat. No. 18). Burnished ceramic heads of figurines produced in this period are comparable to examples from Byblos and Yarim Tepe. The appearance of domesticated animals (goats, sheep, pigs, cattle, dogs) points to a new emphasis on herding in addition to the already entrenched practice of plant cultivation. No substantial architecture is associated with Ramad III.

Ramad is an example of a late-sixth-millennium Near Eastern site which made the transition from a settlement of circular houses to a village with standardized rectilinear house plans and streets. Agriculture was practiced on an increasingly intensive scale, and religious innovations associated with the beginnings of sedentary society are apparent here as they were in Bouqras and Mureybit.
GLENN M. SCHWARTZ

1

1
Standing female figurine

Site: Mureybit
Date: Phase III, 8000–7600 B.C.
Material: White limestone
Height: 9.5 cm
Museum No.: Aleppo 64/1
Literature: J. Cauvin *AAAS* 24 (1974) 48, Fig. 3

At Mureybit figurines representing humans were
either modelled of clay or carved in soft limestone.
In form they range from being extremely simplified
to quite naturalistic. The oldest examples are female,
and since we hesitate to assume that the populations
of the hunter-gatherer villages were depicting themselves, we tend to classify such works as divine images relating to fertility cults. There are examples of
such fertility goddesses at Mureybit which predate the
introduction of agriculture. It was not until a thousand
years later, ca. 7000 B.C., that the female deity was
joined by a male, who remained less important, however.
E.S.

2
Idol

Site: Mureybit
Date: Phase III, 8000–7600 B.C.
Material: White limestone
Height: 12 cm; *depth:* 3.3 cm
Museum: Aleppo
Literature: J. Cauvin *AAAS* 22 (1972) 110, Fig. 6

This object belongs to a group of very schematic
human representations. The upper part of a face is
carved on an oval stone with a flint tool. At the level of
the nose the sculpture is divided by a horizontal indentation; two vertical grooves form the lower parts.
We are not sure which part of the human head or body
these horizontal and vertical lines represent. The simplified carving of the upper part of the face is reminiscent of a stone stele from Upper Mesopotamia,[1] which
was meant to represent an entire human figure. Since
we would like to assume the same about this small
sculpture from Mureybit, we label it an idol.
E.S.

[1]H. Th. Bossert *Altsyrien* (Tübingen 1951) No. 419.

2

3

3
Bowl

Site: Mureybit
Date: 8000–7000 B.C.
Material: White limestone
Height: 3.4 cm; *diameter:* 8.8 cm
Museum No.: Aleppo MB 74.2979

In the early Near Eastern settlements of hunter-
gatherers, as well as in early agricultural villages,
containers were either made of reeds or carved in
stone. This slightly rounded small bowl was carved
of soft limestone, then polished.
E.S.

4
Stone tools

Site: Mureybit
Date: 8000–7000 B.C.
Material: (a,b) flint; (c) obsidian
Length: (a) 13.2 cm; (b) 7.1 cm; (c) 9.6 cm
Museum Nos.: Aleppo (a) MB 71.598; (b) MB 73.1215; (c) MB
    72.4025
Literature: M. C. Cauvin and D. Stordeur "Les outillages
    lithique et osseux de Mureybet, Syrie (Fouilles Van Loon
    1965)" *Cahiers de l'Euphrate* 1 (Paris 1978) 29, Figs. 13–23

An axe, a scraper, and a drill are typical of the many
stone tools found at Mureybit. The axe (a)—a particularly important tool—has been found in all levels at
this site. In this example the blade is flat on one side,
rounded on the other, and "retouched" on the striking
edge and the flat side (i.e., it has closely connected
chip marks to give greater sharpness). The oldest axes
from the Near East were rounded with the back ta-
pered to fit the handle. Scrapers (b) have also been
found in all levels at this site. Their edges were
"retouched" on one side to make them sharper. The
drill (c) was made from a small flake split off from a
larger core of obsidian. The pointed end has been
"retouched" on both sides.
E.S.

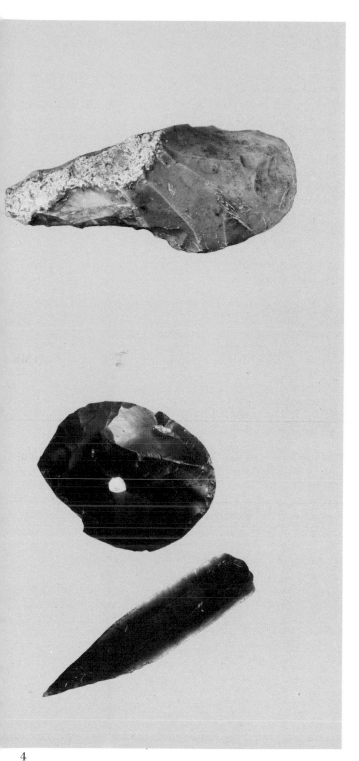

5
Torso of a female figure

Site: Bouqras
Date: 6400–5900 B.C.
Material: Limestone
Height: 4.4 cm; *width:* 5.4 cm; *depth:* 4.5 cm
Museum No.: Deir ez-Zor BJ 145/2162
Literature: Cf. Mellaart *Çatal Hüyük* Fig. 51.53

The woman is sitting with her legs folded under her.
The head, right arm, and right knee are broken off. In
spite of the fragmented condition of this figure, the
high quality of carving is recognizable in the distinctive details. The individual parts of the body are
more carefully rendered, especially the buttocks,
breasts, and arms, than they were in Cat. No. 1. The
underside (not visible because of the stand) is modelled like the rest. Similar female figurines are known
from the almost contemporary site of Çatal Hüyük in
Southern Anatolia.
E.S.

5

6
Head of a small human figure

Site: Bouqras
Date: 6400–5900 B.C.
Material: Dark burned terracotta
Height: 2.9 cm; *width:* 2 cm; *depth:* 2.4 cm
Museum No.: Deir ez-Zor BJ 132/2161

This small, carefully executed head belonged to a figurine whose body was not preserved. It is broken off at the neck, and the skullcap, the left cheek, and ear are damaged. The rendering of the face is considerably more detailed than the older examples from Mureybit (Cat. Nos. 1 and 2). Since the eye sockets are drilled, one may assume that they originally had inlays, which would have lent a strong radiance to the face. Comparable naturalistic representations of the human head are not known elsewhere in prehistoric ancient Near East.
E.S.

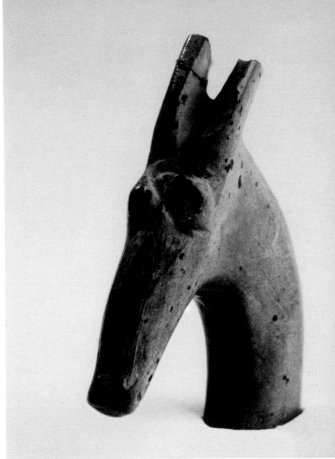

7
Head of a gazelle

Site: Bouqras
Date: 6400–5900 B.C.
Material: Bone
Height: 4.6 cm; *greatest width:* 0.8 cm; *depth:* 3.1 cm
Museum No.: Deir ez-Zor BJ 121/2159

This head may have formed part of a tool handle. The neck and the horns are partly broken off. The eyes and the nostrils are carefully rendered, the surface smoothly polished.
E.S.

8
Vessel shaped as a hare
See color plate p. 9

Site: Bouqras
Date: 6400–5900 B.C.
Material: Burned alabaster
Height: 9 cm; *length:* 17.5 cm; *width:* 9.4 cm
Museum No.: Deir ez-Zor BJ 100/2136

Apparently this animal-shaped vessel was burned in a fire in antiquity; as a result it is blackened, cracked, and partially deformed. Although only the essential details are rendered, the hare is quite naturalistic. The sculptor paid as much attention to the bottom of the vessel as he did to the visible sides. The spherical eyes are drilled.

Vessels such as this and the following one were not meant for everyday domestic use; rather, they may have been offerings to a deity, and as such the symbolic quality of the hare in its proverbial fertility may have been established. Similar animal-shaped vessels, but made of terracotta, are known from Çatal Hüyük in Southern Anatolia.
E.S.

9
Vessel shaped as a hedgehog
See color plate p. 9

Site: Bouqras
Date: 6400–5900 B.C.
Material: White alabaster
Height: 6.6 cm; *length:* 14.2 cm; *width:* 7.6 cm
Museum No.: Deir ez-Zor BJ 119/2138
Literature: Cf. H. G. Buchholz *BJV* 5 (1965) 66

Parts of the back of this hedgehog were broken in antiquity, and unfortunately not all the fragments were retrieved in the excavation. The details of the body are even more carefully rendered than the hare of Cat. No. 8. Crosshatching indicates the quills, and the vessel has small stubby legs.

The hedgehog was ascribed power to ward off evil in antiquity, probably because of its ability to capture snakes and its immunity to reptilian poison.
E.S.

10
Pestle decorated with relief

Site: Bouqras
Date: 6400–5900 B.C.
Material: Limestone
Height: 3 cm; *greatest length;* 14.2 cm; *width:* 7.1 cm
Museum No.: Deir ez-Zor BJ 131/2168
Literature: Cf. Mellaart *Çatal Hüyük* Plate VI, Fig. 31

The rounded side of this elongated oval pestle is decorated with a relief of a quadruped which is so schematically rendered that it is impossible to identify. The only clue—the drill holes—possibly indicate the spotted hide of a panther. Several other pestles, also decorated with reliefs, were found at Bouqras, but only this example has a figurative decoration. Again we find certain parallels at Çatal Hüyük, where similar animals with spotted hides were painted on the mud walls.
E.S.

11
Bowl
See color plate p. 10

Site: Bouqras
Date: 6400–5900 B.C.
Material: Striated marblelike stone
Height: 4.5 cm; *diameter:* 7.1 cm
Museum No.: Deir ez-Zor BJ 62/2120

12
Tall bowl
See color plate p. 10

Site: Bouqras
Date: 6400–5900 B.C.
Material: Striated marblelike stone
Height: 10.9 cm; *diameter:* 11.2 cm
Museum No.: Deir ez-Zor BJ 91/2100

Both these finely polished bowls have been carefully carved so that the striated grain of the stone forms horizontal rings. The smooth and harmonic play of colors is especially accentuated by the simple shape of the bowl shown in Cat. No. 12.
E.S.

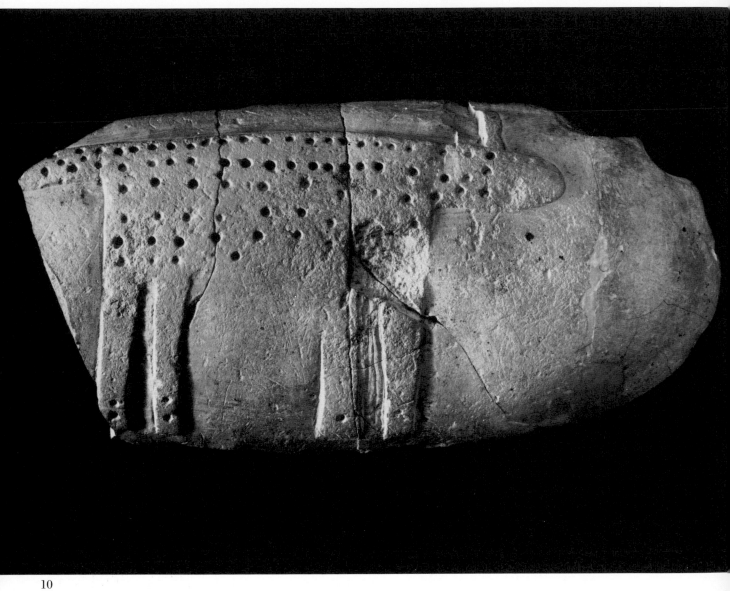

10

13
Cup with feet
See color plate p. 10

Site: Bouqras
Date: 6400–5900 B.C.
Material: Speckled marblelike stone
Height: 4–4.3 cm; *diameter:* 5.3 cm
Museum No.: Deir ez-Zor BJ 102/2146

14
Tall cup with feet
See color plate p. 10

Site: Bouqras
Date: 6400–5900 B.C.
Material: Gray-veined marble
Height: 6.6 cm; *diameter:* 3.3–3.4 cm
Museum No.: Deir ez-Zor BJ 111/2140
Literature: Cf. el-Wailly and Abu es-Soof *Sumer* 21 (1965)
    Plates XXVIII–XXVIV // Mellaart *Çatal Hüyük* Plate 111

Cups were made of various kinds of stone deemed especially attractive because of color and grain. Both of these examples have a thick rim and stubby feet. We know of very similar stone cups from Tell es-Sawwan on the Tigris and of related vessels, carved in wood, from Çatal Hüyük in Southern Anatolia. The occurrence of a special shape in several places may indicate cultural relations or far-reaching trade connections. In any case it raises the question whether such pieces were made locally or imported. The answer can only be determined under particularly lucky circumstances, such as the discovery in one place of the finished product together with unfinished vessels, raw materials, and tools. Further excavations may resolve this question.
E.S.

15
Polished stone axe

Site: Bouqras
Date: Surface find, 6000 B.C.
Material: Greenish-gray stone (diorite?)
Length: 12 cm; *height:* 6 cm; *width:* 3.3 cm
Museum No.: Damascus B.65.2.91

Polished stone pendants intended for jewelry were produced as early as the ninth millennium B.C., and stone vessels were also smoothly polished (see Cat. Nos. 11–14); but such meticulous work was then reserved for so-called luxury items. Only later do we find polished tools such as this axe, which is superior to the older one from Mureybit shown in Cat. No. 4a but similar to the polished axes at Mureybit dating to the end of Phase III, ca. 7700 B.C.
E.S.

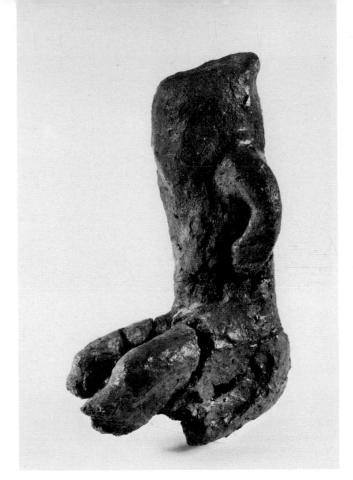

16
Seated human figure

Site: Ramad
Date: Level I, 6250–6000 B.C.
Material: Clay, lightly fired
Height: 25 cm; *width:* 8.5 cm; *depth:* 16 cm
Museum No.: Damascus R.67.4.94
Literature: H. de Contenson *AAS* 17 (1967) 20, Plate III

Settlement Levels I and II at Ramad featured pits with deposits of human skulls which were covered with a lime paste modelled to look like complete human heads. White chalk set off the eyes; red paint may have indicated the hair. While a deposit of about a dozen such skulls was being cleaned in the workrooms of the National Museum in Damascus, two fragmentary figures of undetermined sex were found. They were modelled in clay and covered with a thin whitish slip which had remnants of red paint. The better-preserved figure is shown here. The legs are stretched out (see the reconstruction in Fig. 9) but broken off at the knees and the right side is missing. The break is smooth and flattened, which leads one to believe that the figure may have been attached to something, perhaps a wall. The left arm is set on the body like a handle, with the hand at the waist of the figure. The head is merely a cylindrical shape, levelled off at the top. It has been suggested that such figures may have served as stands for the ancestral skulls which they were found with (cf. the find from Mureybit, discussed on p. 60) and, later on, stands with their skulls were put in a common repository.
E.S.

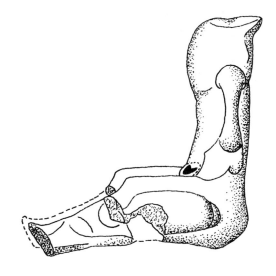

Figure 9
Reconstruction of clay figurine
from Ramad (see Cat. No. 16).

17
Stone bowl

Site: Ramad
Date: Level I, 6250–6000 B.C.
Material: Reddish-beige marbled stone
Height: 4.9 cm; *diameter:* 9.8 cm
Museum No.: Damascus R.67.37.85
Literature: Cf. H. de Contenson *Archaeology* 24 (1971) 280

This stone vessel, of exactly the same shape as Cat. No. 11, connects Ramad with Bouqras. As we have already seen, such carefully produced bowls made of choice materials were popular everywhere.
E.S.

18

17

18
Ceramic bowl

Site: Ramad
Date: Level III, 5800–5500 B.C.
Material: Fired clay
Height: 9.8 cm; *diameter* 15.5–16 cm
Museum No.: Damascus R.63.288.78
Literature: H. de Contenson *Archaeology* 24 (1971) 284

In the two oldest levels at Ramad there were no vessels made of fired clay; only in Level III does pottery appear, in the form of dark-colored hand-modelled bowls, simply shaped, with a finely smoothed surface. This type of pottery—called "dark-faced burnished ware"—was widespread from Palestine to Anatolia.
E.S.

19
Stone tools

Site: Ramad
Date: Level I, 6250-6000 B.C.
Material: Flint
Height: (a) 14.3 cm; (b) 7 cm; (c) 10.5 cm
Museum Nos.: Damascus (a) R.68.1; (b) R.63.188; (c) R.69.49
Literature: Cf. H. de Contenson *Archaeology* 24 (1971) 278

These three flint tools—an axe (a), an arrowhead (b), and a sickle blade (c)—belonged to the household of a Ramad inhabitant. The point of the arrowhead is finely "retouched" (see Cat. No. 4), as is the sickle blade, creating serrated edges. Along the edge of the blade is "sickle gloss," which shows that this tool was used in harvesting grasses or grains.
E.S.

PROTOHISTORIC PERIOD
CA. 3500–3000 B.C.

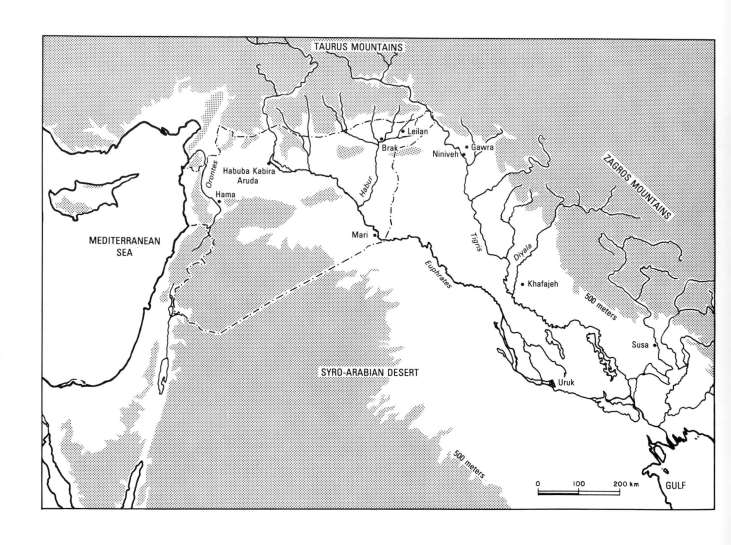

TAURUS MOUNTAINS

ZAGROS MOUNTAINS

MEDITERRANEAN
SEA

Leilan
Brak
Niniveh Gawra

Habuba Kabira
Aruda

Orontes

Hama

Habur

Mari

Tigris

Diyala

Khafajeh

500 meters

Susa

Euphrates

SYRO-ARABIAN DESERT

500 meters

Uruk

0   100   200 km

GULF

PROTOHISTORIC SYRIA AND THE ORIGINS OF CITIES AND CIVILIZATION

HARVEY WEISS

ALONG THE SOUTHERNMOST REACHES OF THE TIGRIS AND EUPHRA-
tes rivers, in southern Mesopotamia just north of the Persian Gulf,
the landscape dotted with small village farming settlements underwent a profound and irreversible transformation in the late fourth
millennium B.C. For the previous 2,000 years the banks of the Euphrates had been sparsely lined with these small villages of farmers
and herders who seasonally drew the water for their fields from small
canals branching off the slow-moving waters of the Euphrates. These
small villages, usually less than 10 hectares in size, occasionally
included small temples, but were more often simply composed of
fairly uniform houses of mud brick and reeds sheltering family units
which had relatively equal access to fields, water, and the annual
wheat and barley harvest.

The profound transformation of this landscape during the period
4000–3000 B.C. saw the emergence of large cities, royal dynasties,
temples and palaces, bureaucrats and administrators, huge teams of
laborers, and writing. The appearance of this new form of society is
considered by archaeologists to mark the dawn of civilization. That it
took place first in southern Mesopotamia along the Euphrates, and
(possibly contemporaneously) in lower Egypt along the Nile, is beyond doubt. Why this transformation first occurred in these regions
remains uncertain despite decades of archaeological research.

Consensus does exist among archaeologists, however, with regard
to the incentives for growth, change, and disequilibrium within the
agricultural system of these early southern Mesopotamian settlements. Understanding the natural environment of the areas will
perhaps allow us to comprehend why southern Mesopotamia underwent this urban tranformation, the important role which we now
understand the Syrian landscape to have played within it, and the

impressive but still unexplained Syrian urbanization of the third millennium B.C.

The southernmost portion of Mesopotamia receives less than 250 millimeters of rainfall per annum, not enough to generate an annual crop of wheat or barley. Southern Mesopotamian farmers throughout the ages have thus been forced to expend large amounts of labor irrigating their fields with water drawn from small canals leading from the Euphrates. Although costly in terms of labor input, the rewards have been substantial: irrigation agriculture in antiquity probably produced between one and a half and two times the amount generated by rainfed agriculture, or dry farming, as it is sometimes called. These considerable yields, it is argued, would have been sufficient to sustain those not directly involved in food production: rulers, technicians, artisans, priests, scribes. Small-scale societies, freed from the need to expend all their time in the fields, could have branched off on a road to civilization paved with the surplus production of irrigation agriculture.

In many respects this theory of civilization's origins is in accord with the Garden of Eden status assigned to southern Mesopotamia in Genesis. This theory, however, actually fails to account for the means whereby the surpluses of irrigation agriculture were actually deployed or expended upon the non-food producers whose very existences, positions, and efforts were to take these small societies along new paths. Indeed, the very generation of agricultural surplus requires the prior existence of some authority or agency which could define this "social" surplus and assign it for specific uses or personnel. After all, rather than generating a surplus, small-scale village farmers could easily have chosen instead to produce less by working less.

Hence most archaeologists have come to understand that some very substantial alterations of social organization were actually behind the changes in economic organization which enabled the urban revolution to proceed. How these changes came about is still uncertain but probably was affected by the prevailing inequalities of land availability, natural variation in the kind and quality of land and water accessible for farming, and the slight but persistent perturbations which accompany village farming communities in environmentally fragile settings. The results, however, were dramatic: communities which had been essentially egalitarian were now highly stratified; landscapes once dotted with small villages were now dominated by large cities 50 or even 100 hectares in size; fields once cultivated by small family or clan units counted in the dozens were now cultivated by large teams of laborers working estates of land controlled by palaces, temples, or "nobles"; villages and towns composed mainly of small domestic residences were now dwarfed by cities with central areas devoted to huge temples and palaces busy with the administration of land and laborers. Civilization had evolved.

Economic life of early cities

Geographers have long understood that cities do not just emerge; countrysides set them up to accomplish what must be performed in central places. The earliest cities neither originated nor sustained themselves in isolation: they were in fact centers for small regions adjacent to the bed of the Euphrates or its effluents. The economic life of these cities reflected their regional situation with regard to smaller villages and towns on the surrounding countryside. These economies comprised in great part the exchange of goods and services.

Dense agglomerations of individuals residing in a city required large areas of grain-producing land around them, an agricultural hinterland. Workers employed in cereal production were apparently paid rations—uniform measures of food—for their services. Grain produced on such lands, often "owned" by large temples or private estates, was redistributed from the local level of its production into the organizational orbit of the land-owning temple, and then back down to the individuals working in the service of the temple, palace, or estate. Also moving among the various levels of ownership, production, and distribution were countless other items, such as finished or almost finished manufactured goods, raw materials destined for workshops or exchange such as stone for toolmaking or artistic decoration, various kinds of foods such as fish from the rivers and canals, and of course labor, being moved, transported, deployed, relieved, and shifted across the landscape as needs arose. In the context of such exchanges, writing developed.

Writing

One of the fascinating qualities of the archaeological record is that it can inform us of the origins of such everyday tools as writing, refine our understanding of the why and how of such inventions, and provide us with a firmer knowledge of the genesis of long-lasting technological changes in general. Writing first developed in the ancient Near East during precisely the period we are discussing as one of the tools used for the administration, control, and extension of the new society and economy—civilization.

The archaeological documentation for the development of writing takes us to these first cities on the lower Mesopotamian plains, cities such as Warka in southern Iraq and Susa in southwestern Iran. Our best documentation at the moment, retrieved and analyzed from the site of Susa, indicates that four kinds of recording devices were introduced into the administrative tool kit during this period: cylinder seals, bullae, calculi, and clay tablets.

Cylinder seals with engraved designs were first introduced for the purpose of marking containers, storerooms, and documents, and thereby either protecting them or insuring their integrity. Hollow clay balls, or bullae, contained small clay tokens, calculi, which apparently expressed the quantities of commodities being exchanged or otherwise deployed (and in some cases were used to impress specific shapes upon the bullae). Marking the quantity of calculi on the outside of the bulla allowed the cylinder-sealed bulla to be read without breaking it open (and destroying its utility as a document). These three devices were employed at the beginning of the late Uruk period at Susa and Warka.

Archaeological evidence indicates that synchronously a fourth innovation was employed—the clay tablet. Small tablets, shaped like fluffed pillows, were sealed with cylinder seals, then impressed with a reed stylus in such a way as to imitate the impressions made by the small clay calculi. These numerical notation tablets mark a literary revolution. Shortly thereafter small ideograms expressing the kind of commodity being enumerated were added to the tablet's surface, and these soon acquired phonemic values. Writing—the durable expression of language—had begun. The manipulation and exchange of raw materials, finished products, labor, land, tools, seed and harvests could now be controlled in ever more complex but efficient ways.

Syrian cities

An intriguing question is why cities and states did not emerge first from the late prehistoric villages along the banks of the Syrian Euphrates. Indeed, phrasing the question of urban origins in this manner has the advantage of forcing us to define the range of specific circumstances which did generate the first steps toward cities and civilization. Part of the answer to this question may reside in the fact that Syria and the landscape upstream along the Euphrates present a different set of environmental and agricultural conditions from that of southern Mesopotamia. The area along the Euphrates banks as the river passes through the core of Syria en route from the mountains of Turkey to the marshes of southern Iraq falls within the rainfall zone where dry farming is impossible and irrigation a necessity. However, unlike the peaceful, slowly meandering channel that the Euphrates is in the low-lying areas of southern Mesopotamia, in Syria the Euphrates is a very strong river, with a steep gradient moving the currents swiftly toward the lower elevations. The Euphrates and its valley may not have offered the same opportunities for small-scale, easily controlled irrigation agriculture that were present in the southern marshlands of Mesopotamia. Hence settlement along the Syrian Euphrates in this period was rather sparse and consisted of small villages continuing the still older village agriculture traditions of the sixth and fifth millennia B.C.

Colonies from southern Mesopotamia

Fifteen years ago it would not have been possible to say more about this period other than that protohistoric and protourban developments and influences seem to have been concentrated in southern Mesopotamia. An almost synchronous series of archaeological events, however, has now radically altered this picture. In the 1960s the Directorate-General of Antiquities of Syria coordinated an intensive international program of archaeological projects aimed at recovering as much data as possible from the ancient sites soon to be flooded by the waters of the Euphrates dam under construction at Tabqa.

Several sites in the archaeological salvage area proved to be extensive settlements of the middle-late Uruk period in southern Mesopotamia. Two of these in particular, Habuba Kabira South/Tell Qannas and Jebel Aruda, provide new evidence for the early city economy of the ancient Near East and the use of early writing. These settlements were undoubtedly "colonies" of the larger urban centers in southern Mesopotamia. This is clear from the lack of any precedent in the region for the sudden appearance of southern Mesopotamian artifacts which are indistinguishable from those actually manufactured in the south. These artifacts include ceramics, cylinder seals, architectural forms, and even the tools and devices of writing. Distant from such colonies, indigenous native settlements continued to thrive within the traditions of agricultural and craft production long maintained by them. From Habuba there is some evidence that local populations supplied the colonists with certain foodstuffs. Why, however, were the colonists there, and what were they doing?

The distribution of these sites suggests very strongly that they represent part of a lengthy chain of towns following the Euphrates trade route to the north and onto the Anatolian plateau where sites such as Arslantepe near Malatya, excavated by Alba Palmieri, provide additional evidence for the distribution. To the east, in the high intermontane valleys of the western Zagros Mountains, similar settlements, with artifact and architectural assemblages precisely like those of Susa, are well documented from excavations such as those at Godin Tepe and from surface surveys through the valleys between the east-west Khorasan Road, which passes through the Zagros, and the lower-elevation valleys to the south toward Susa. In all of these cases the towns display the same characteristics with startling uniformity: no previous direct contact with southern Mesopotamian centers and then the sudden appearance of the entire assemblage of southern Mesopotamian artifacts including architecture, ceramics, cylinder seals, seal impressions, and even the tools, devices, and remnants of southern Mesopotamian writing.

As a function of southern Mesopotamian culture, these colonies seem to attest to Warkan and Susian needs for materials, finished or unfinished, not present in the south and only available at great distances within the surrounding highlands. These materials may have been mineral resources such as copper ores for smelting and tool manufacture or lapis lazuli and other semi-precious minerals for decorative and symbolic uses. The objectives of these trade colonies may even have been exotic biological resources such as skins, leathers, or animals. The nature of the exchanges remains obscure, however, in spite of the presence of the earliest writing for the purpose of documenting the transactions. The calculi, bullae, seal impressions, numerical notations, and tablets only rarely provide us with an ideogram such as a jar or container. The presence of these writing and accounting devices, however, assures us that the transactions were considered important enough for the colonies and their southern overseers to maintain durable, sophisticated records.

These colonies on the Euphrates, like their counterparts in the Iranian Zagros, were relatively short-lived. None were maintained in the immediately succeeding archaeological period. Their short life and nonreplacement may indicate that other sources for materials were now available, or that the needs for these materials were no longer felt in the south, or that other forms of exchange which did not require colonies had come into existence. Shortly thereafter, however, a new type of settlement appeared in the dry-farming regions of Syria and a new relationship with southern Mesopotamia developed.

Recommended Reading

Robert McC. Adams. *The Evolution of Urban Society* (Chicago: Aldine, 1966).

Dietrich Sürenhagen. "Late Uruk Period Developments in Syria." In Harvey Weiss (ed.) *The Origins of Cities in Dry-Farming Syria and Mesopotamia in the Third Millennium B.C.* (Winona Lake, Ind.: ASOR, 1985).

HABUBA KABIRA SOUTH/TELL QANNAS AND JEBEL ARUDA

Location: Right bank of the middle Euphrates
Date: 3500–3300 B.C.
Excavations: Habuba Kabira South 1969–1975 (Deutsche Orient Gesellschaft); Tell Qannas 1967–1973 (Comité Belge de Recherche Historiques); Jebel Aruda 1975–1979 (Dutch expedition)
Publications: Habuba Kabira South: *MDOG* 102 (1970) 27 / 103 (1971) 5 / 105 (1973) 5 / 108 (1976) 5 // E. Strommenger *AASOR* 44 (1979) 63 / *Habuba Kabira* (Mainz 1980) / *AJA* 84 (1980) 479 // D. Sürenhagen *APA* 5/6 (1974–1975) 43. Tell Qannas: A. Finet *Syria* 52 (1975) 157 / *AASOR* 44 (1979) 79 / *Lorsque la royauté descendit du ciel . . .* (Musée royale de Mariemont 1982). Jebel Aruda: G. van Driel *Phoenix* 23, 42 / *Akkadica* 12 (1979) 2 / "Tablets from Jebel Aruda" in G. Van Driel et al. (eds.) *Zikir Šumim* (Leiden 1982) 12 / *Akkadica* 33 (1983) 34–62 // G. van Driel and C. van Driel-Murray *Akkadica* 33 (1983) 1 // J. H. Tenison *Akkadica* 33 (1983) 27

Habuba Kabira South/Tell Qannas and Jebel Aruda are among the most important discoveries of the last decade of research in the Near East. In close connection with the oldest literate cultures of Sumer and Elam in southern Iraq and southwestern Iran, these Syrian settlements of the middle Euphrates document the economic and cultural blossoming of the area around 3500 B.C.

The center of the north Syrian Euphrates lay on the mountain plateau of Jebel Aruda, a dominant position high above the river valley. Two temples and several large houses excavated at Jebel Aruda indicate that the site was the seat of important rulers and their divinities. The majority of the local population, however, lived in settlements near the river, a much easier locus for food and water than the 60-meter-high cliffs of Jebel Aruda. Long-distance trade by water and land probably occupied many of these communities, to judge from the extensive excavations at Habuba Kabira South/Tell Qannas.

Protected by a strong fortified wall, Habuba Kabira was a densely settled town with living quarters and workshops stretching along the bank of the Euphrates (see Fig. 10). A central district contained buildings for cult and administrative activities; irrigated gardens were situated to the south. The city wall was a massive construction some 3 meters wide, protected by bastions or towers, although only the bot-

Figure 10
Reconstruction of settlement at
Habuba Kabira South.

PROTOHISTORIC PERIOD

tommost of the sun-dried bricks remain. Another, smaller wall stood in front of the city wall. Two gates provided entrance into the city. Toward the south the last traces of the wall have fallen victim to wind and rain erosion; hence the southern extension of the city cannot be traced. A reasonable estimate for the maximum extent of the town, however, is approximately 18 hectares.

The few main streets of the city plan are clearly recognizable. They bordered a court around which various buildings are grouped (Fig. 11): a "middle hall" house for dwelling, wide rooms for receiving guests, and various rooms for conducting business. The middle hall house—the favorite domestic architectural form of the period—was a tripartite structure with a large middle room and a series of equally wide side rooms on each long side. A strikingly symmetrical form was regulated by groupings of towers and niches. In the religious and administrative center of the site, designated Tell Qannas, were other middle hall houses, some of which may have served as temples. They differ from ordinary dwellings only in their size.

Figure 11
House with adjacent construction at Habuba Kabira South.

The city wall fortifications of Habuba, the city plan with its center and main streets, and the mechanisms for water drainage by means of clay pipes as well as open and closed canals all attest to extensive planning and considerable technical ability. A few houses were destroyed by fire and the collapsed roofs have preserved the room contents. Hence from Habuba we can learn both the kind and quantity of household tools and devices, insofar as they were manufactured of nonperishable materials. Cylinder sealings, numerical notation tablets, and clay bullae bear witness to the active economic life of the Habuba community and its concern to protect property from foreign hands.

The economic floruit of the Euphrates Valley around Jebel Aruda was relatively brief, perhaps no more than 100 or 150 years. The city wall hints at a threat which eventually forced the inhabitants to abandon their houses. Only centuries later did settlements appear here again.

EVA STROMMENGER

TELL BRAK

Location: Southern portion of the Habur triangle, 1 km west of the Jagjagh River, one of the effluents of the Habur River, approximately 40 km north of Hasseke

Date: Ca. 5500–1500 B.C.

Excavations: 1937 and 1938 (British School of Archaeology in Iraq); since 1976 (Institute of Archaeology, University of London)

Publications: M. E. L. Mallowan *Iraq* 9 (1947) 1 / *Mallowan's Memoirs* (London 1977) 125 // D. Oates *Iraq* 39 (1977) 233 / *Iraq* 44 (1982) 187 / "Tell Brak" in J. Curtis (ed.) *Fifty Years of Mesopotamian Discovery* (London 1982) 62 // J. Oates *Iraq* 44 (1982) 205 // K. J. Fielden "The Chronology of Settlement in Northeast Syria . . . in the Light of Ceramic Evidence from Tell Brak" (Ph.D. diss. Oxford 1981)

Two important social and economic phenomena of the late fourth millennium have already been examined: (1) the emergence of cities and states, and (2) the creation and extension of their "colonies" along the Euphrates to the west up into Anatolia and to the east within the western Zagros mountain valleys. As examples of the early city-states we have mentioned Warka and Susa. Well-documented examples of the colonies along the Euphrates are the famous Syrian sites of Habuba Kabira South/Tell Qannas and Jebel Aruda. In the Zagros mountain valleys of western Iran an example is Godin Tepe. With these settlements we have then discussed the southern, western, and eastern portions of the ancient Near East during the late fourth millennium, but we have not yet treated developments in the north. The northern portion of the lowlands of Syria and Mesopotamia extends across the Habur Plains, the northeasternmost corner or the "duck's bill" of modern Syria. Contemporary communities in this region may have been quite different from the colonies of the late Uruk period characteristic of the Euphrates in the west and the Zagros valleys of the east. The gently rolling topography of the Habur Plains is segmented by the deep-cut streams passing out of the Taurus Mountains of Turkey to the north. Across most of the plains the prevailing rainfall patterns present a situation as unique as, but quite different from, the situation in southern Mesopotamia. Here the quantity and reliability of the rainfall is as plentiful and persistent as that in the most fertile areas of the surrounding highlands and mountain valleys of the Taurus and the Zagros. Indeed the winter-spring rainfall in this area marks the region as the most favorably situated in southwest Asia for dry farming: the combination of extensive, cultivable soils and plentiful, reliable rainfall produces exceptional cereal yields. The region is known as the granary, for today the northeastern province produces one-quarter of Syria's cereal crop, with the area immediately around Qamishli enjoying the highest per-hectare yields at the lowest production costs. Under circumstances such as these, therefore, it is hardly surprising to encounter large, structurally complex, late prehistoric settlements, such as Tell Brak.

A glance at the peculiar geographical configuration of the Habur Plains allows us to understand, as well, the special relationship of Tell Brak to southern Mesopotamia and to the larger realm of the plains. Tell Brak is situated at the southern corner of the Habur triangle, that confluence of streams, wadis, and other seasonal channels which flow out of the

Taurus Mountains and join together south of Brak, near modern Hasseke, to form the Habur River. Flowing almost due south into the Euphrates, which it joins near Meyadin, the Habur constitutes a primary communications route between the Euphrates and the Habur Plains. Indeed, passing north from the Euphrates, only the valley of the Habur River makes settlement and traffic possible through the semi-arid wastelands of the Jezireh, "the island," as this tract of land between the Euphrates and the Tigris is known. The Habur then passes between two short mountain ranges, the Jebel abd al-Azziz on the west and the Jebel Sinjar on the east, above which its feed streams unite. At just this juncture sits Tell Brak: a gateway into the Habur Plains.

The sequence of protohistoric, late Uruk temples excavated by Sir Max Mallowan at Tell Brak is represented in this exhibition by several artifacts which vividly illustrate the unique nature of this settlement: the gold sheathing (Cat. No. 35) which enveloped the altar or podium within the Eye Temple (Fig. 12) and the "eye idols" themselves (Cat. Nos. 41–43), apparently votive objects placed within the temple precincts. The walls of this temple were also decorated with stone-inlaid clay cones (see Fig. 13), a distinctive variation upon the typically simple clay cones of southern Mesopotamian wall decor.

Some archaeologists have been able to conclude, now that contemporary colonies have been uncovered along the Euphrates and elsewhere, that Tell Brak and its temple series represent a similar phenomenon: a southern Mesopotamian intrusion into the Habur

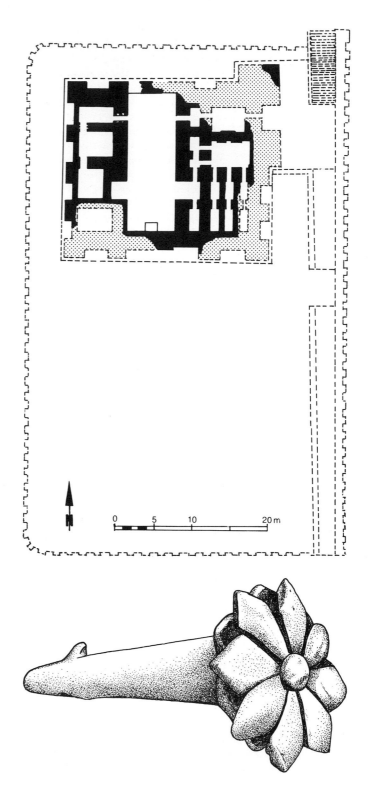

Figure 12
Eye Temple and Terrace, Tell Brak.

0   5   10   20 m

Figure 13
Ceramic cone wall decoration from
the Eye Temple, Tell Brak.

PROTOHISTORIC PERIOD

Plains. To be sure, the material culture of Tell Brak during this period does show considerable influence from the south in its ceramic inventory, cylinder seal impressions, and even the early appearance of numerical notation tablets. Southern influence on Tell Brak, however, was not a new feature of the late fourth millennium, but rather extends back at least a millennium on the Habur Plains. In that respect it seems doubtful that this was the same kind of southern intrusion as is apparent at Habuba Kabira or Jebel Aruda along the Euphrates, up into the highland valleys of Anatolia, or the Iranian plateau.

Fourth-millennium developments on the Habur Plains may have been to some degree endogenous, a function of local social and economic conditions and forces. Considering the uniquely high agricultural productivity of the region, this possibility seems reasonable. Indeed, a further suggestion may be available in the archaeological record: the Eye Temple, unlike the temples retrieved at the colonies along the Euphrates, does not resemble the plan of Sumerian temples in southern Mesopotamia. Its plan falls within a native northern tradition, perhaps visible also at Tepe Gawra across the border in northern Iraq.

Recent survey efforts by Kate Fielden in the region immediately surrounding Tell Brak have adduced another archaeological phenomenon which also suggests the endogenous nature of Tell Brak, in contrast to Habuba Kabira South and Jebel Aruda. Within one mile of Tell Brak a ring of smaller late Uruk settlements surrounds the site. We cannot be certain of the contemporaneity of these settlements, but they do suggest that Tell Brak in the late Uruk period may have grown to its 43-hectare size through the coalescence of smaller sites clustered around it.

Along the Jagjagh River, one of the effluents which form the triangle of streams joining together at Hasseke, and along the several other large feed streams of the Habur, a range of late Uruk, protohistoric sites are situated. Several are located farther north than Tell Brak and hence receive still more annual rainfall. One such site, Tell Hamoukar, may have been as large as or even larger than Tell Brak during this period. Future archaeological research at Tell Brak will probably illuminate the site's gateway status between the interior regions of the Habur Plains and the exterior, irrigation-agriculture regions to the south.

HARVEY WEISS

SYRIAN SEALS FROM THE LATE FOURTH TO THE LATE SECOND MILLENNIUM

EDITH PORADA

LESS THAN TWENTY YEARS AGO A GREAT SURPRISE WAS SPRUNG ON the archaeological world: it was discovered that northern Syria had participated in the precociously early urban development of about 3400 B.C. of Uruk in southern Mesopotamia (Iraq) and Susa in Iranian Khuzistan. German, Belgian, and Dutch salvage excavations necessitated by the Middle Euphrates Tabqa dam project revealed an Uruk- or Susa-related town at the modern site of Habuba Kabira and similarly related sanctuary sites at Tell Qannas and Jebel Aruda. These early, highly developed settlements made use of clay tablets inscribed with numerals and impressed with engraved cylinder seals (Cat. Nos. 22, 23). Such cylinder seals were also used to make impressions on balls of clay enclosing counting devices (Cat. No. 24). The cylinder seals, usually made of stone, were engraved in intaglio with various designs which left relief impressions when the seals were rolled over damp, soft clay. The hardened clay retained the seal designs over thousands of years.

Cylinders were chiefly used in Mesopotamia and Iran and in the regions that were politically and economically related to these countries. Early cylinders appeared at the northern Syrian sites in the period called Protohistoric, corresponding to the Late Uruk period in Mesopotamia, and remained in general use in Syria until the thirteenth century B.C., after which they were replaced by stamp seals. Mesopotamia and Iran, however, retained cylinder seals until the Persian period.

Aside from providing a means of authentication for tablets, which doubtless served to record the movement of commodities, the impressions of cylinders on lumps of clay served to secure goods in jars, boxes, and baskets and in storage rooms behind bolted doors. Most important was probably the fact that cylinder seals had some amuletic value like the stamp seals that preceded them in Syria, northern Mesopotamia, and Iran. Some of the Syrian stamp seals were contemporary with the cylinder seals, and they are often in the form of animals in folded poses, occasionally with lovely naturalistic forms (Cat. Nos. 36–39).

In the earliest phases the Syrian seals and sealings are clearly dependent on Mesopotamian glyptic traditions but sometimes contain certain local features. Most of the cylinders of the early period from Habuba Kabira show flocks of goats or sheep in slightly varying postures, often with different types of horns, which give a lively appearance to the scenes (Figs. 29 and 31 on pp. 108 and 109). Or the animals stand on their hind legs in various formal, symmetrical schemes, as in Fig. 30 (on p. 108). A distinctive Syrian Protohistoric feature in the seal impression in Fig. 30 is the entwined tails of what may be bovine animals (since no other domestic horned animals have long tails). Such entwined tails are also seen on a cylinder from Godin Tepe in northwestern Iran and on seal impressions from Susa.

In the same impression shown in Fig. 30 a special feature of Syrian seals is displayed in the bodies of the lions: their hind parts are turned in the opposite direction from the foreparts. Such torsion of the body is not a single accidental occurrence but a feature that is paralleled in the impression of a stamp seal from Tepe Gawra, near Mosul in northern Iraq, and in later cylinder seal designs from the ancient harbor town of Byblos, near Beirut. The appearance of related distinctive features in different places provides pointers toward the existence of relations between these sites. Another characteristic of the Protohistoric cylinders of Syria is the frequent association of seated pigtailed figures with animals (Cat. No. 20). A special motif is presented by the cylinder with juxtaposed scorpions (Cat. No. 21), which may have been meant to ward off these noxious creatures as well as other evil forces. In general, scorpions are remarkably frequent in Syrian cylinders.

The settlements of this period in northern Syria—whose cylinders show strong relations to those of distant sites like Susa and Uruk—were probably established for purposes of trade and were of rather short duration, perhaps lasting no more than a century. Although cylinder seals remained in use in Syria in the early third millennium, shape and design changed. Some looked like beads with geometric decorative designs in which a rosette was favored. These were called Nineveh 5 cylinders after Level 5 of the site near Mosul where they were first discovered. Very fine examples have now been found in Syria, particularly at Tell Leilan, Period III.

In the second third of the third millennium B.C. cylinders of northern Syrian sites like Mari and Tell Chuera resembled those of the Early Dynastic period of Mesopotamia in subject matter and style, showing interlocking friezes of animals and composite creatures standing on their hind legs, battling superhuman heroes (Cat. Nos. 51–53). The Syrian versions of the cylinders, however, have some distinctive features; they show, for example, the greater use of the bow drill, a mechanical tool that made holes in the seal, which appear as smaller or larger spheres in the impression. This is especially obvious in a cylinder seal from Mari (Cat. No. 53). The upper register of the cylinder also depicts a festive meal, another favored motif of Early Dynastic cylinders, but here the principal figures sit on either side of a large table holding big jars instead of drinking through tubes from a vessel between them or raising cups to drink as in cylinders from Ur. Nevertheless, such cylinders from Mari show the close relation between the artistic standards of important Syrian and Mesopotamian sites. Some Syrian cylinders of the same period, however, are extremely crude and merely indicate the desire by members of the population of provincial districts to participate in the conventions of the period without having well-trained artisans to equal the work produced in the major sites.

The most original of the early Syrian seal designs are those of Ebla (Fig. 14) which, if compared to Mesopotamian seal styles, appear to be transitional between Early Dynastic and Akkadian period styles. Characteristic of the Ebla style are the delicacy of execution, the frequent frontality of the figures and their vertical postures, as well as the alignment of dissociated heads of animals and superhuman beings, often seen above or below a principal design. Also distinctive is the rendering of fleeced garments so that tufts of wool are so big as

Figure 14
Seal impression from Royal Palace G at Ebla.

PROTOHISTORIC PERIOD

to suggest leaves. This leaflike impression has already appeared in Syrian cylinders of unknown provenance (purchased on the antiquities market) belonging unquestionably to the Early Dynastic style. A certain naturalism in the appearance of the figures suggests that they were carved close in time to the Akkadian style when naturalistic renderings prevailed. However, so far none of the distinctive Akkadian cylinders have been found at Ebla, a fact which confirms the abandonment of the site at the height of the Akkadian Dynasty.

Mari, however, has yielded at least one of the characteristic cylinders of the period which presents divine figures with such extensive detail that their function can be recognized although their names are unknown (Cat. No. 85). This last remark even includes the god enthroned on a mountain with two stars placed before him. The stars have been interpreted as the name of the supreme sky god Anu, although they do not look at all like cuneiform signs. Even if the scene represents a cosmic event, which is entirely possible, there is no evidence linking the god on the mountain with the sky. From the bottom of the mountain emerge two serpentlike creatures that eject streams of water which rise to form the bodies of two goddesses of vegetation. A male deity seems to thrust his spear into the waters of one of the goddesses. This god has been tentatively associated by Pierre Amiet with the later Syrian storm god. The concepts underlying this representation have not been fully determined.

After the fall of the Akkadian Dynasty and the assumption of power in Mesopotamia by the Third Dynasty of Ur (ca. 2112–2004 B.C.) Mari was ruled by governors or viceroys possibly under the suzerainty of southern Mesopotamian kings. The close relation with Ur is manifested in the court style of a cylinder seal belonging to a priest who was an official of the governor Idi-ilum (Cat. No. 86). The audience standing before an enthroned goddess is beautifully carved, but the facts that the deity holds the saw which is the exclusive emblem of the sun god in Mesopotamia and that one of the worshipers approaches the throne holding a staff are features unthinkable in a cylinder carved within the sphere of metropolitan Mesopotamian conventions.

Somewhat later than the court style of Ur III there emerged a genuinely independent style in northern Syria, here called Old Syrian I (Fig. 15). Its most frequent motif is that of a seated god, characterized as such by his wearing the traditional Mesopotamian multiple-tiered, flounced robe, drinking through a tube from a vessel under the bent curve of which usually appears an enigmatic object, a staff with a ball attached to its side. Usually a small vessel accom-

Figure 15
Impression of a cylinder seal of Old Syrian I style.

Figure 16
Seal impression of Old Syrian II style on an Old Assyrian tablet from Kültepe.

panies the staff. These two objects also occur on Old Babylonian and Old Assyrian cylinders, but their meaning has not been convincingly determined. The style of the Old Syrian I cylinders is deeply cut, and most of the details are produced by linear hatching. Some cylinders in this style with other motifs show the principal personage wearing headgear with a feather or horn rising from the front. From the discovery of the first cult basin at Ebla (Cat. No. 116) in which a figure with a similar headgear carved in a similar style is portrayed in a ceremony opposite a female partner, it became obvious that the figure is a ruler and that the Old Syrian I style is a reflection of the sculptural style of northern Syria.

A group of cylinders from Ebla showing processions of identical figures, crudely carved in a style derived from the Old Syrian I cylinders (Fig. 15), was related by Stefania Mazzoni to cylinders found at Kültepe, the ancient Assyrian trading center of Kanesh on the Anatolian plateau in modern Turkey. These seals were found in Level Ib of Kültepe, dated in the late nineteenth and the earlier eighteenth centuries B.C. These dates indicate the time at which the Old Syrian I style had disintegrated into monotonous, coarsely executed seals.

Probably contemporary with the Old Syrian I style are seal impressions (Fig. 16) on tablets found at Kültepe Level II, roughly dated 1920–1840 B.C. On several of these impressions appears a personage that wears the same royal headgear seen on the cult basin from Ebla. Other details, such as garments, seats, and tables, correspond to the inventory of the cult basins of Ebla, indicating the extension of the northern Syrian artistic province in the twentieth and nineteenth centuries B.C.

A limited number of extant cylinder seals seems to belong to the same style as the Old Syrian seal impressions on Old Assyrian tablets. For these cylinders the classification of Old Syrian II is suggested (Figs. 17 and 18). They show a distinctly Syrian repertory with a figure wearing the royal headgear just discussed and with the appearance of a post topped by a female head over a male head (Fig. 18). The female has the long hair of the ladies portrayed in the cylinders of this group, whereas the male head is very summarily executed. Characteristic of the group (but not illustrated in the cylinders here reproduced) are composite creatures such as bird-headed winged demons, male and female sphinxes, and lions whose hindquarters are formed by scorpions. This group must have furnished the Syrian elements used by the accomplished seal engravers of Mari, who created what may be called the first classic style of Syrian cylinder seals.

Several seal impressions on tablets from the reign of King Zimri-Lim of Mari (ca. 1781–1758 B.C.) indicate the inception of the finest Syrian style at that site. Fortunately, one of the beautiful cylinders of Zimri-Lim's court has surfaced in our time, though the delicately cut original inscription of the king's official was erased and replaced by a larger and more crudely carved Old Babylonian inscription of a

Figure 17
Impression of a cylinder seal of Old Syrian II style.

Figure 18
Impression of a cylinder seal of Old Syrian II style.

second seal owner. Still, the engraving of the scene is in its original condition (Fig. 19), showing as the most important figure the goddess, drawing back her heavily bordered military mantle to reveal her alluring nude body. Jewelry and a tambourine stress the goddess's female nature, while military boots with upturned toes add to her warlike aspect. At Mari this goddess was doubtless Ishtar, who also aided the king in his military exploits, as seen in an unillustrated set of seal impressions from Mari.

Characteristic of these seals is the delicate execution, the slenderness of the figures, especially of their hands, as noted by Hisham El-Safadi, and the restraint in the depiction of the modeling and motions of the bodies. The garment of the king is the Babylonian cap with upturned brim and the bordered mantle, but in the Syrian cylinders the brim turns up slightly at the ends, indicating the rounding of the headgear. A similar tendency toward curved lines transforms the angular edge of the Old Babylonian royal mantle into the Syrian one which has a rounded outline.

Contemporary with the cylinders of the First Classic Syrian style and perhaps even slightly earlier, belonging to the end of the nineteenth century B.C., was a group distinguished by the appearance of male figures who wear a short pleated kilt or a thin garment of which only the belt is visible. These male figures are usually seen controlling lions, griffins, or serpents—that is, life-threatening creatures. The most elaborate cylinder of the group was found at Chagar Bazar on the Habur Plains of northeast Syria (Fig. 20), but a considerable number of closely related examples were discovered at Ugarit (Ras Shamra) on the Syrian coast, some of them found in graves together with pottery of the late nineteenth or early eighteenth century B.C. Another group of cylinders also belonging to the same period has the

Figure 20
Impression of a cylinder seal of the early eighteenth century B.C. *found at Chagar Bazar.*

Figure 21
Impression of a cylinder seal of the early eighteenth century B.C.
(Bibliothèque Nationale).

Figure 22
Seal impression of King Abban of Yamkhad belonging to the Aleppo Group.

[1]Dominique Collon "The Aleppo Workshop" *Ugarit-Forschungen* 13 (1981) 34.

field divided into vertical frames each containing repetitions of one type of animal or object (Fig. 21). Ruth Mayer-Opificius has suggested that the textile industry of Syria might have inspired such designs.

The next stylistic phase in Syria, here called Second Classic style, is dated in the second half of the eighteenth century and was centered in Aleppo, according to Dominique Collon on the basis of the seal impressions from Alalakh, Level VII. The royal cylinders are likely to have been carved at Aleppo, called Halab in antiquity, when it was the center of the country of Yamkhad. A feature of the style is the "well balanced composition . . . generally divided into two parts either vertically or horizontally, with every possible permutation including scenes at 90 degrees to the axis of the seal."[1] Further traits are the strong modeling of the figures; the heavy, rolled, strongly curved borders on mantles of kings and goddesses, which bring to mind baroque forms; and the appearance of the long-robed goddess with a polos-like cap on a pair of horns (Fig. 22).

Perhaps the transition to this group is represented by the 7-centi-meter-high "super cylinder" twice as tall as the normal Syrian cylin-der, which was rolled over the shoulder of a vessel at Ebla (Cat. No. 102). The excavator dated the seal impression at about 1750 B.C., and its style seems indeed to fit between the restrained First Classic style and the increased modeling of the Second Classic group. The scene includes the figure of the storm god Adad, who was the most impor-tant iconographical figure of Syrian glyptic art next to Ishtar, the goddess of war and love. He usually stands in a smiting posture, brandishing a mace or an ax. Here he is thought also to hold the rein of the bull, his emblematic animal. Occasionally he uses a tree as a weapon to kill a snake, as Elizabeth Williams Forte has pointed out.[2] According to the conventions of ancient Near Eastern art, in which one element of a scene frequently represents the entire dramatic event, the god often holds only one or the other symbol, tree or serpent. A god of water, generally enthroned as a major deity, a nude bearded hero with streams, probably identifiable with the constella-tion Aquarius, and a bird-headed demon are frequent elements in Syrian cylinders of the late eighteenth to early seventeenth centuries. In addition to these divine or demonic beings, the figure of the king appears often with his attire varying according to the time and place of the cylinder's manufacture. As mentioned before, the royal gar-ment of Babylonian origin—the cap with upturned brim and a mantle with linear borders—is somewhat earlier than the tall oval cap and the mantle with heavy rolled borders, though there also seems to be a geographical difference. The mantle with rolled borders seems to be more common in the western areas, the Babylonian type of garment in the eastern parts of Syria. Within these two major categories, however, there are many variations that probably correspond to the local royal costume.

Some cylinders included in the Aleppo group have compositional features which associate them with the style of later Aegean wall paintings. An example, Fig. 23 shows leaping acrobats with a bull portrayed in the "flying gallop." Such cylinders may have originated in a region which had very close contacts with Aegean style. Whether this was Ugarit (Ras Shamra) or some other site remains to be discovered.

Toward the end of the period associated with Level VII at Alalakh there seems to have been a "tendency which leads away from the solid shapes and figures toward thinner, more spidery ones" (Fig. 24), according to Dominique Collon. Instead of the "baroque curves" that characterize seals of the Aleppo group, there appear "the narrow,

[2]L. Gorelick and E. W. Forte
Ancient Seals and Bible (Malibu 1983)
24 ff.

PROTOHISTORIC PERIOD

Figure 23
Seal impression of a cylinder with Aegean elements (Erlenmeyer Collection).

Figure 24
Seal impression of King Niqmepa of Yamkhad, grandson of Abban, showing thinner figures.

Figure 25
Early Mitannian cylinder of sintered quartz from Alalakh.

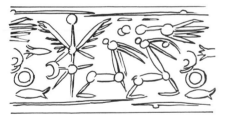

Figure 26
Syro-Mitannian cylinder of hematite from Ugarit.

[3]Dominique Collon "The Seal Impressions of Tell Atchana/Alalakh" *AOAT* 27/3 (1975) 140.

linear bodies of the later seals."[3] Alalakh Level VII came to an end between 1650 and 1615 B.C. From the levels Alalakh VI and V, dated in the latter part of the seventeenth and the sixteenth centuries, a few cylinder seals found by C. L. Woolley and carefully republished by Dominique Collon present the only evidence of the stylistic trends which resulted in the fully developed Mittanian style of the fifteenth and fourteenth centuries.

Characteristic of the early Mittanian style is the use of sintered quartz (identified earlier as faience), and the appearance of abstract geometric forms for the bodies of humans and animals (Figs. 25 and 26). It is not known how the designs on cylinders of sintered quartz were produced, whether with tools agitated only by hand or by mechanical drills, which were certainly employed on cylinders made of hard stones. In both types of seals the Syrian composition prevailed: one major scene accompanied by secondary motifs usually in two registers. Both hard stone seals and seals of sintered quartz were widely distributed, especially the latter. A large number of seal impressions were found at the north Mesopotamian site of Nuzi, near Kirkuk, which, like Alalakh, was part of the Mitannian empire. Cylinders like the one from Ugarit, reproduced in Cat. No. 119, which shows a palmette and sphinxes characteristic of Syrian style (though ultimately derived from Egypt), are refered to as Syro-Mitannian. One of the most common seals is small, made of hard stone, most often hematite but sometimes colored marble or chalcedony, and shows as the design apparently unconnected forms of horned animals, birds or bird-demons, fish, and a human hand, as exemplified by a seal from Ugarit (Fig. 26), dated by C. F. A. Schaeffer ca. 1450–1350 B.C.

One of the finest cylinders of the Syro-Mitannian style was the dynastic seal of the northern Syrian country of Amurru, which was impressed on the tablets recording the dowry of a princess of Amurru who was married to the king of Ugarit. The dynastic cylinder of Ugarit was a much older type (Cat. No. 159), probably even earlier than the Old Babylonian cylinder from Mari in the present exhibition (Cat. No. 87). These Old Babylonian cylinders manifest the close ties which existed between Syrian and Babylonian courts and their workshops from the nineteenth to the seventeenth century.

In the International Age of the fifteenth and fourteenth centuries the relationships had shifted northward on the one hand and included Egypt and the Aegean on the other. Of the several hundred cylinder seals found at Ugarit (Ras Shamra) a few have been selected for the exhibition to show the foreign influences that came together in that town and palace in the International Age. One cylinder (Cat. No. 123) shows figures of Egyptian type in unusual compartments. One might think that it was recut, but it was made of blue sintered quartz, which belongs in this period. An Egyptian chain of lotus blossoms and buds in another cylinder (Cat. No. 120) serves as the base for graceful griffins and a goat, which Joan Aruz has recognized to be of a Cretan type. Another cylinder (Cat No. 124) has the heroic figure with a Syrian pointed cap standing on a lion in a manner seen several centuries later on a Phoenician stele. Whether the figure holds two spears or two serpents is difficult to decide. In either case it was surely meant to protect its wearer against all evil. Another cylinder (Cat. No. 121) shows in its irregular cutting that there were poor engravers or perhaps homemade seals for people who could not afford the expense of well-carved cylinders. An especially interesting cylinder (Cat. No. 122) foreshadows Hittite influence in the posture of the divine or heroic figure shouldering an axe in the Hittite manner while spearing a lion that pursues a bull.

The tablets from Ugarit provide much more definite evidence of Hittite influence in the impressions of the cylinders of the king of Carchemish, a Hittite dependency on the Euphrates at the modern border between Syria and Turkey. The term Syro-Hittite was suggested by Dominique Beyer for the style of these seal impressions. In one of the sealings (Cat. No. 160) there are such characteristic Hittite elements as the small mountain gods who support a major deity; there is also a storm god who can be recognized as a Hittite deity by his tall pointed headgear, also worn by a facing god who is supported by a bird-headed demon. Especially distinctive of cylinders from Carchemish is a bull who stands almost upright on a support, resting his forelegs on the top of a second support (here a cuneiform sign), and turns his head back in a curiously artificial posture which makes one think of a circus act performed by a trained animal. The framing angular twist above and below the scene suggests that the cylinder was engraved in metal, probably silver, of which several Hittite seals were made.

Another cylinder belonging to the same king, of which two almost identical versions are known, was found on seal impressions on tablets from Ugarit and also from the site of Emar (Cat. No. 164). It shows a god holding an axe and a mace; the cuneiform inscription identifies him as the god Sharumma. At Emar, which was under Hittite rule, many persons used not cylinder but stamp seals, the common seal form in the Hittite capital of Hattusha (modern Boghazköy in Turkey). Thus the seal of King Tudhaliya IV (ca. 1250–1220 B.C.) was a round stamp showing the royal winged disk and the protective deities of the king (Cat. No. 161). Sharumma, who is mentioned in the texts as the protector of Tudhaliya IV, puts his arm around his protégé in a very expressive gesture. The seal was impressed on a tablet which bore the text in which the Hittite king ordered the king of Ugarit to divorce his wife, the princess of Amurru, whose dowry had been enumerated on the tablet bearing the imprint of the dynastic cylinder of Amurru.

Hittite influence may be responsible for the replacement in Syria of cylinder seals by stamps and seal rings. In a grave of the middle or late thirteenth century at Ugarit, belonging to the owner of the largest of several houses, probably a man called Rap'anu, was found a silver ring (Cat. No. 125) engraved with a goat and a palmette in what looks like one of the Cypriot styles. Although Rap'anu's tablets found in his archive bear impressions of Cypriot cylinder seals, his personal seal seems to have been the easier-to-wear, more modern seal ring.

**Chronology of the Styles of Syrian Cylinder Seals
ca. 3400–1200 B.C.**

Syrian Protohistoric (ca. 3400–2900 B.C.) Syrian Early Dynastic (ca. 2900–2350 B.C.)	Dependence on Mesopotamian styles
Early Syrian (ca. 2400–2200 B.C.)	New stylistic elements at Ebla (Fig. 14), Mari, Tell Chuera
Old Syrian I (ca. 2000–1800 B.C.)	Glyptic style related to the sculptures of Ebla (Fig. 15)
Old Syrian II (ca. 1920–1840 B.C.)	Impressions of Syrian style on Old Assyrian tablets (Fig. 16) Corresponding to Syrian seal impressions on tablets of Kültepe, Level II (Figs. 17, 18)
First Classic Syrian Style (ca. 1800–1730 B.C.)	Finest Old Babylonian style transformed into a Syrian style at Mari (Fig. 19) Contemporary styles: heroic male figures, usually kneeling on one knee (Fig. 20); vertical rows of identical animals or other designs (Fig. 21)
Second Classic Syrian Style (before 1720 to ca. 1650 B.C.)	Corresponding to Level VII at Alalakh (Fig. 22) Aegean elements (Fig. 23)
Attenuated style toward the latter part of Level VII at Alalakh	(Fig. 24)
Syro-Mitannian cylinders (fifteenth and fourteenth centuries B.C.)	Geometric stylization in two styles and two different materials: sintered quartz and hard stone, chiefly hematite
Cylinders of the court of Carchemish (thirteenth century B.C.)	

Recommended Reading

Every collection of ancient Near Eastern seals contains some Syrian cylinders of one or more of the stylistic and chronological phases surveyed here. Therefore only works which have contributed insights into the classification of Syrian seals or into the explanation of their iconography are listed here.

Pierre Amiet. "Notes sur le répertoire iconographique de Mari à l'époque du Palais." *Syria* 37 (1959) 215–232 / "La glyptique de Mari . . . note additionelle." *Syria* 38 (1961) 1–6 / "La glyptique syrienne archaïque." *Syria* 40 (1963) 57–83 / "Cylindres syriens présargoniques." *Syria* 41 (1964) 189–193 / "Le sceau de Sumirapa roi de Tuba." *RA* 56 (1962) 169–174.

Dominique Beyer. "Notes préliminaires sur les empreintes de sceaux de Meskené." *Le Moyen Euphrate.* J. Margueron (ed.) 265–283 / "Le sceau cylindre de Shahurunuwa, roi de Karkemish." *La Syrie au Bronze Récent* (Paris 1982) 67–77 / "Stratigraphie de Mari. . . ." *Mari, Annales de recherche . . .* 2 (Paris 1983) 37–60.

Dominique Collon. "The Seal Impressions from Tell Atchana/Alalakh." *AOAT* 27 (1975) / "The Alalakh Cylinder Seals." *BAR* int. ser. 132 (1982) / "The Aleppo Workshop." *Ugarit-Forschungen* 13 (1981) 33–43.

Hartmut Kühne. *Das Rollsiegel in Syrien* (Tübingen 1980).

Ruth Mayer-Opificius. "Betrachtungen zur Darstellungs und Kompositionsform einiger syrischer Rollsiegel." *Ugarit-Forschungen* 11 (1979) 597–600.

Stefania Mazzoni. "Tell Mardikh et una classe glittica Siro-Anatolica del periodo di Larsa." *Annali* 35/N.S. 25 (1975) 21–43.

Anton Moortgat and Ursula Moortgat Correns. "Archäologische Bemerkungen zu einem Schatzfund im vorsargonischen Palast in Mari." *Iraq* 36 (1974) 155–167.

Edith Porada. "Syrian Seal Impressions on Tablets Dated in the Time of Hammurabi and Samsu-iluna." *JNES* 16 (1957) 192–197 / "Les cylindres de la jarre Montet." *Syria* 43 (1966) 243–258 / "On the Complexity of Style . . . of Cylinder Seals from Cyprus. . . ." Acts Int. Arch. Symposium: *The Mycenaeans in the Eastern Mediterranean* (Nicosia 1973) 268–272 / "The Cylinder Seal from Tomb 66 at Ruweise." *Berytus* 24 (1976–1977) 27–33 / "A Cylinder Seal with a Camel in the Walters Art Gallery." *Journal of the Walters Art Gallery* (1977) 1–6 / "Cylinder Seal from Jericho." *Jericho* 2 (1983) 774–776 / "Syrian Seal from East Karnak." *Journal of the Society for Studies of Egyptian Archaeology* 13 (1983) 237–240.

Hisham El-Safadi. "Die Entstehung der syrischen Glyptik und ihre Entwicklung in der Zeit von Zimrilim bis Ammitaqumma." *Ugarit-Forschungen* 7 (1975) 433–476.

C. F. A. Schaeffer. "Recueil des sceaux et cylindres hittites imprimés sur les tablettes des archives sud du palais de Ras Shamra." *Ugartica* III (1956) 1–163 / "Le cylindre A 357 de Chagar Bazar." *Iraq* 36 (1974) 223–228 / *Corpus I des cylindres-sceaux de Ras Shamra-Ugarit et d'Enkomi-Alasia* (Paris 1983).

Henri Seyrig. "Les dieux de Hierapolis." *Syria* 37 (1960) 233–252 / "Antiquités syriennes." *Syria* 32 (1955) 31–58 / "Quelques cylindres syriens." *Syria* 40 (1963) 255–260 / "Cylindre représentant une tauromachie." *Syria* 33 (1956) 169–174.

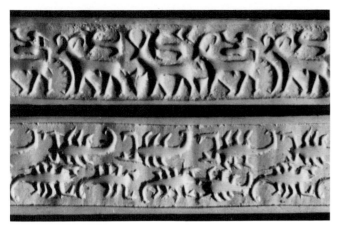

20/21

The cylinder seals from Habuba Kabira South are some of the oldest known. The design of Cat. No. 20 leads us into the world of herding, an important aspect of ancient economic life. Here goatlike animals with three different types of horns stride to the left; above them are two lizards with their heads turned back and a squatting human figure. The spaces between the goats are filled in with a triangle, a plant, and a pot. This seal is carefully carved, and the edges are smoothly honed.

The cylinder shown in Cat. No. 21 is rather crudely cut yet creates a spectacular frieze of scorpions when rolled. Because of its poisonous sting the scorpion was considered able to ward off evil. Later, the goddess Ishkara was symbolized by the image of a scorpion.
E.S.

20
Cylinder seal with animal design

Site: Habuba Kabira South
Date: 3500–3300 B.C.
Material: Black stone
Height: 2.4 cm; *diameter:* 2.5 cm
Museum No.: Aleppo BB X: 7
Literature: E. Strommenger *Journal für Geschichte* 2/4
(1980) illus. bottom p. 42

21
Cylinder seal with scorpion design

Site: Habuba Kabira South
Date: 3500–3300 B.C.
Material: Reddish limestone
Height: 2.5 cm; *diameter:* 2.5 cm
Museum No.: Aleppo M II: 123
Literature: E. Strommenger *Habuba Kabira* Fig. 43 bottom

Toward the middle of the fourth millennium cylinder seals came into use, replacing the stamp seals used earlier. A seal impression on a vessel or a cuneiform tablet identified the owner just as a signature does today. In Mesopotamia and its neighboring states cylinder seals were in use for more than 3,000 years. Since every citizen who was involved in any kind of business transaction needed a personal seal, unique in design, an immense number of seals were produced. The vast quantity of seals that remain from all periods in the ancient Near East constitute a valuable source for historians of ancient art.

22
Sealed tablet

Site: Habuba Kabira South
Date: 3500–3300 B.C.
Material: Unfired clay
Height: 5.5 cm; *length:* 5.2 cm; *depth:* 1.2 cm
Museum No.: Aleppo M II: 127
Literature: E. Töpperwein *MDOG* 105 (1973) 25, Fig. 4

One side of this tablet is flat and smooth, while the other and all four edges are covered with seal impressions. However, the seal was only incompletely rolled onto the wet clay; Fig. 27 shows a reconstruction combining the several partial rollings. There are two intertwined snakes rising from a small vessel, a lion, flying birds, and a human figure squatting in front of a vessel with grain hanging over its sides.

After the small clay tablet had been sealed it was inscribed with numbers forming groups of four—that is, one vertical and three horizontal signs. The numbers were inscribed with a stylus made of either reed or wood. The tablet thus signified a certain number of goods (of unknown type) belonging to a person who could be identified by his seal impression. The tablets of Habuba Kabira South exemplify Mesopotamian writing in its earliest stage, when it consisted entirely of numbers, the value of which depended on the number of signs, their shape, and their size. Only later were objects more precisely indicated by the use of pictograms.
E.S.

22

Figure 27
Reconstructed cylinder seal impression of Cat. No. 22.

Like Cat. No. 22 this tablet was first sealed, then inscribed. Both sides and all four edges are completely covered with seal impressions. The design shows a row of cattle and horned goats with depictions of pots and grain in the spaces above and between the animals.

The scribe used styli of three different sizes to indicate the various numbers. The largest and the smallest styli were impressed vertically, while the medium-sized one was held at an angle. The system of number writing employed here was widespread and standardized, since it had to serve trading partners over long distances and very likely across different language barriers.

E.S.

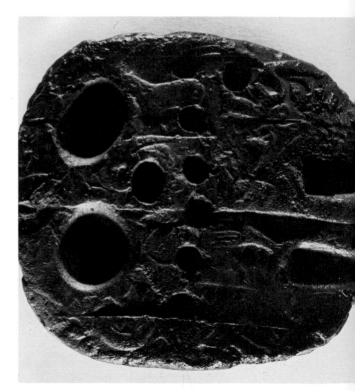

23

23
Sealed tablet

Site: Jebel Aruda
Date: 3500–3300 B.C.
Material: Burned clay, blackened in certain places
Height: 8 cm; *length:* 9.2 cm; *depth:* 2.8 cm
Museum No.: Aleppo JA'DD 370.3(24)
Literature: Antiquités de l'Euphrate 82, top right

24
Sealed bulla

Site: Habuba Kabira South
Date: 3500–3300 B.C.
Material: Unfired clay
Diameter: 6.3 cm
Museum No.: Aleppo M II: 33
Literature: E. Töpperwein *MDOG* 105 (1973) 26, Fig. 5

This hollow clay ball (or bulla) with small clay tokens
(calculi) inside served as an inventory which accompanied a delivery of goods. The shape of the tokens
would indicate the type of goods—oil is very likely
represented here—and the number of tokens would
correspond to the number of oil vessels. To prevent
the messenger from tampering with the contents of
the shipment, the tokens were covered with a ball of
clay which was impressed with the seal of the sender
and then inscribed with the number of tokens inside.
When the shipment was delivered, the receiver could
check the number and type of goods sent, as well as
the identity of the sender. If there was any doubt
about the honesty of the messenger, who might have
changed the numbers on the outside of the clay bulla,
it could be opened and the tokens inside counted.
Both the numbering system on clay tablets and the
meaning of tokens was well known on wide-ranging
trades routes.

Since it was not easy to roll a cylinder seal over a
curved clay surface, we often find incomplete impressions, as in the case here (see Fig. 28 for a reconstruction). In the design we can recognize a jar with grain
hanging over its sides, like that on the tablet of Cat.
No. 22, and a goat standing on his hind legs.
E.S.

24

Figure 28
Reconstructed cylinder seal impression of Cat. No. 24.

25
Sealed bulla

Site: Habuba Kabira South
Date: 3500–3300 B.C.
Material: Unfired clay
Length: 7.5 cm
Museum No.: Aleppo M II: 140
Literature: E. Strommenger *Habuba Kabira* Fig. 57

Certain goods were safeguarded from tampering by
the use of string knots covered with a lump of wet clay
which then was sealed by the sender and sometimes
also inscribed with the number of items being
shipped. If an unauthorized person opened the knots,
he would not be able to reseal the shipment without
the sender's personal seal. At Habuba Kabira there
were many such bullae which had been broken upon re-
ceipt, then thrown away This one is broken length-
wise exactly in the middle so that the string marks are
clearly visible. The almost completely reconstructed
seal design (see Fig. 29) shows two animals lying inside a round enclosure, while the rest of the herd is
grazing in the field. A human figure sits in front of a
vessel, perhaps processing dairy products.
E.S.

25

26

Figure 29
Reconstructed cylinder seal impression of Cat. No. 25.

Figure 30
Reconstructed cylinder seal impression of Cat. No. 26.

structed in Fig. 30. Two goats stand upright, back to back with tails intertwined over a vessel. Next to this group are two resting lions with a predatory bird between them. Beautifully carved seals occasionally included such symmetrical compositions and a pleasing, well-balanced distribution of decorative elements. Unlike the other bullae from Habuba Kabira this one was also impressed with the uncarved end of the cylinder seal, which produced a circular smooth indentation.
E.S.

26
Sealed bulla

Site: Habuba Kabira South
Date: 3500–3300 B.C.
Material: Unfired clay
Length: 8.1 cm
Museum No.: Aleppo M II: 139
Literature: E. Töpperwein *MDOG* 105 (1973) 30, Fig. 8

This almost completely preserved bulla bears the impression of an elaborate and well-carved seal recon-

27
Sealed bulla

Site: Habuba Kabira South
Date: 3500–3300 B.C.
Material: Unfired clay
Length: 6.5 cm
Museum No.: Aleppo M II: 138
Literature: E. Töpperwein *MDOG* 105 (1973) 27, Fig. 7

27

The only complete and undamaged bulla from Habuba
Kabira South is covered with impressions of a beautifully cut seal (see Fig. 31). Unlike the heraldic composition of the previous seal, this design shows a free-
flowing naturalistic rendering of the herd. It depicts
male and female sheep and goats with their young, a
few of them placed in rectangular pens inside an enclosure. The seal was rolled several times, but incompletely. Only the legs of the shepherd and a small
dog remain of the upper part of the design.
E.S.

Figure 31
Reconstructed cylinder seal impression of Cat. No. 27.

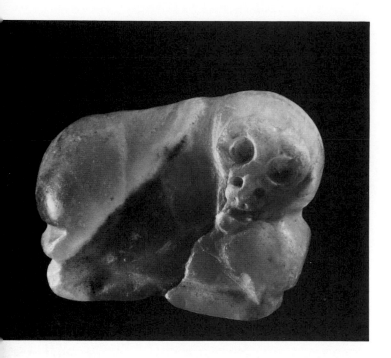

29
Small four-lugged vessel
See color plate p. 11

Site: Habuba Kabira South
Date: 3500–3300 B.C.
Material: Blue-green stone
Height: 3.1 cm; *greatest diameter:* 3.1 cm
Museum No.: Aleppo BB XII: 4
Literature: E. Strommenger *AAAS* 25 (1975) 158, Fig. 11

In Near Eastern excavations it is uncommon to find objects that have been perfectly preserved and look as if they were made yesterday, since most have suffered from their burial in saline soil. This pretty miniature bowl is one of the rare exceptions. It was carved very carefully from an unusual type of stone and finely polished. The inside shows horizontal and slanting traces of the grinding and cutting tools. The rounded shape with four lugs is common in contemporary pottery. What purpose was served by this miniature version, made of precious material, is not known. It may have contained small amounts of valuable cosmetics or foods.
E.S.

28
Amulet in the shape of a lion

Site: Habuba Kabira South
Date: 3500–3300 B.C.
Material: Greenish alabaster
Height: 3.7 cm; *length:* 4.8 cm
Museum No.: Aleppo FF XII: 18
Literature: E. Strommenger *MDOG* 108 (1976) 21, Fig. 11

The body of this predatory cat has been quite schematically rendered. The legs and the shanks are carved underneath; the head is turned toward the observer. Eyes, nostrils, and teeth are indicated by drill holes of different sizes. The back is flat. This miniature sculpture has a vertical bore for suspension, which indicates that it may have been used as an amulet.

Amulets in the shape of different animals had symbolic power. This was also the case with various parts of the human body, such as hands or feet, or demonic masks. Even the material used for the amulets had protective value, especially the highly prized blue lapis lazuli. The strong and wild lion was believed to frighten away enemies and ward off evil, and lion amulets were highly prized in the ancient Near East.
E.S.

30
Four-lugged jug with handle

Site: Tell Qannas
Date: 3500–3300 B.C.
Material: Alabaster
Height: 22 cm; *greatest diameter:* 30 cm
Museum No.: Aleppo TK 74/1272
Literature: A. Finet *AASOR* 44 (1979) 94, Fig. 23

The precious alabaster jug was found broken into several pieces in a large room in the religious and administrative center of Habuba Kabira South/Tell Qannas. The otherwise shiny white alabaster surface shows some traces of the effect of a fire which burned the large buildings in the center of the city. The incised decorative band and the shape of the jug with its sharply bent shoulder, four double-roped lugs, ribbon-shaped handle, and heavy spout copies exactly contemporary popular pottery. Considering the high value of such a vessel, it is certainly no accident that it was found in the cultural center of the city.
E.S.

30

31
Small bottle

Site: Tell Qannas
Date: 3500–3300 B.C.
Material: Alabaster
Height: 13.4 cm; *greatest diameter:* 6 cm
Museum No.: Aleppo TK 74/1269

This small bottle is made of the same kind of translucent alabaster as the vessel in Cat. No. 30. The outer surface is smoothly polished, while the inside retains elongated traces of the cutting tool. There are a few pieces missing from the sides, and the foot is broken off. This shape was also quite common in contemporary pottery production.
E.S.

32
Eight-lugged jar with stamped decoration

Site: Habuba Kabira South
Date: 3500–3300 B.C.
Material: Pottery
Height: 34 cm
Museum No.: Aleppo M V: 6.10

This jar, which unfortunately is not completely preserved, is one of the outstanding examples of pottery produced in Habuba Kabira. Pairs of rounded bands lead from the foot to the shoulder of the jar. They are groved to represent cords, each of which ends in a lug at the top. It looks as if they might depict a carrying apparatus made of strings or cords that could be tied together around the neck of the jar. The wider spaces between the cords were decorated with diamond-shaped stamps in a regular pattern before the pot was fired. Both stamps with and without design were used; a row of incised triangles on the shoulder of the jar connects the lugs.
E.S.

33
Loop-shaped libation jug

Site: Tell Qannas
Date: 3500–3300 B.C.
Material: Pottery
Height: 44 cm; *greatest diameter:* 33 cm
Museum No.: Aleppo TK 74/1207

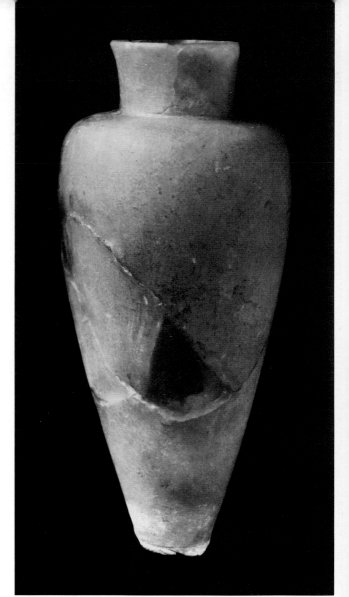

31

In this period pottery was mainly mass-produced, so that various types would be abundantly available. Occasionally, however, a particular workshop or even an individual artisan would make special or unique shapes. Catalogue Nos. 32–34 belong to this category. This unusual jug in Cat. No. 33 was definitely not meant for ordinary household use; rather it was used

32, right

33

Libation vessel in the shape of a hedgehog

Site: Jebel Aruda
Date: 3500–3300 B.C.
Material: Pottery
Height: 24 cm; *length:* 28 cm
Museum No.: Aleppo JA'DD 300 (34)
Literature: Antiquités de l'Euphrate 83, bottom fig.

This vessel was used only on special occasions, probably in connection with religious ceremonies. Its shape, as well as its presumed symbolic power to ward off evil, is similar to the much older vessel from Bouqras (Cat. No. 9). The egg-shaped body of the hedgehog was thrown on a potter's wheel, which gave the surface its slanting, striated look. The opening at the snout was closed, and eyes, ears, the protuberance on the neck for the quills, and the short legs were attached. Holes were punched into the back and the two spouts, one for filling the vessel and the other for pouring, were put on. Both spouts were prefabricated, standard parts.

In antiquity this vessel lost a leg and the top of the spout. The broken places were dipped in bitumen and the pieces were reattached with this adhesive. This ancient restoration measure attests to the original value of the vessel.
E.S.

34

Frieze from an altar
See color plate p. 11

Site: Tell Brak, in the last Eye Temple
Date: 3500–3300 B.C.
Material: Gold, silver, copper, bituminous limestone, white marble, green slate
Height: 12.3 cm; *length:* 1.25 m
Museum No.: Aleppo G. 564
Literature: M. E. L. Mallowan *Iraq* 9 (1947) 93, Plates III, IV, L

This frieze assembled from different materials is an example of early interior decoration. Originally it decorated the upper part of an altar in a temple. The individual pieces were once mounted on a wooden backing, of which nothing remained when it was excavated. The edges at the top and bottom formed a molding which was covered with gold foil nailed into place with gold-headed silver nails. The different-colored stone

for pouring libations at religious ceremonies. This assumption is corroborated by the fact that the vessel was found in the city's religious and administrative center.

To construct the jug the potter first shaped a wide clay band, which he formed into a tube; then he bent the tube to form a loop. The seams were filled in, on the bottom he attached a tall foot, and on the top he pressed out two holes in the loop to accommodate the two spouts, one for filling and one for pouring. Finally the entire surface was carefully smoothed with a spatula-like instrument.
E.S.

34

bands were put together from rectangular strips that had perforations at the back so that a thin copper wire could be threaded through them and attached to the wooden backing.

The frieze was not only a decorative ornament; it depicted a type of facade common on temples and public buildings at the time. Placed directly below the roof, such facades often had a row of mosaic made from clay strips interspersed with black-painted heads. Under the mosaic the wall had receding niches. The green slate in our example only partly succeeds in creating the illusion of niches. The use of different-colored materials for an object was popular in the ancient Near East, especially in ancient Sumer and Elam (southern Iraq and southwestern Iran). E.S.

36
Stamp amulet in the shape of a predatory bird
See color plate p. 12

Site: Tell Brak, level of the Grey Temple
Date: 3500–3300 B.C.
Material: Black serpentine
Height: 3.1 cm; *length:* 5.8 cm
Museum No.: Aleppo F. 692
Literature: M. E. L. Mallowan *Iraq* 9 (1947) 98, Plates VIII
   1, XLV 5

The earliest seals in the ancient Near East were
stamps, but after the invention of cylinder seals,
stamp seals gradually went out of use for a long time.
We do not exactly know the reason for this. Stamp
seals shaped like animals (Cat. Nos. 36–39) were often
contemporary with the earliest cylinder seals; their
function was not restricted to identifying ownership,
for they also served as amulets. The shape would symbolize the power attributed to the animal depicted.

   The unusually large seal in No. 36 is rather crudely
worked. The wings and the tail of the resting bird are
indicated by deeply cut grooves, the feathers by shallow ones. Originally the eye was inlaid with colored
stone, which has been lost. The top of the beak is
broken off. On the stamp surface are three resting
goats with curved horns and a snake-like design above
them (see Fig. 32). In quality and beauty this seal almost matches Cat. No. 39, but the composition suffers
from lack of space. The first goat is only imperfectly

fitted into the narrow space of the head of the amulet.
This object has a vertical bore for suspension and
could be worn as an amulet.
E.S.

37
Bear-shaped stamp amulet
See color plate p. 12

Site: Tell Brak, level of the Grey Temple
Date: 3500–3300 B.C.
Material: Reddish-brown stone
Height: 3 cm; *width:* 2 cm
Museum No.: Aleppo G. 41
Literature: M. E. L. Mallowan *Iraq* 9 (1947) 103, Plates XI
   2, XLV 2

This amulet is also of high quality, although the workmanship does not match that of Cat. No. 39. The
stamp surface has a few irregularly cut grooves.
E.S.

38
Eagle-shaped stamp amulet
See color plate p. 12

Site: Tell Brak
Date: 3500–3300 B.C.
Material: White stone
Height: 2.5 cm; *length:* 4.3 cm
Museum No.: Aleppo G. 47
Literature: M. E. L. Mallowan *Iraq* 9 (1947) 98, Plate VIII 4

A bird of prey, very differently executed than Cat. No.
36; here the characteristic features of the eagle are
more convincingly rendered. The beak is broken off,
and the inlay for the eye is lost, but the shiny, smoothly polished surface has hardly suffered through the
millennia. Certainly the strong and courageous eagle
had symbolic powers to ward off evil. The seal design,
shown in Fig. 32, consists of groups of simply drilled
round indentations. This seal has a vertical bore for
suspension.
E.S.

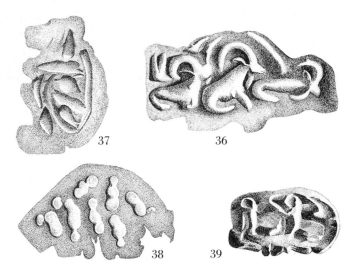

Figure 32
Amulet impressions from Tell Brak of Cat. Nos. 36–39.

39
Gazelle-shaped stamp amulet
See color plate p. 12

Site: Tell Brak, below the Grey Temple
Date: 3500–3300 B.C.
Material: Bone
Height: 1.8 cm; *length:* 3.4 cm
Museum No.: Aleppo G.1
Literature: M. E. L. Mallowan *Iraq* 9 (1947) 103, Plates XI
   3, XLIV 4

This is one of the most beautiful examples among the
wealth of early animal-shaped stamp amulets. The
characteristic shape of the gazelle at rest is so convincingly rendered that it does not lose its charm,
even when considerably enlarged in the photograph on
p. 12. The seal surface has carvings of similar animals, but they are quite crudely cut and without detail
(see Fig. 32). The cutting of the seal was not done by
the same artist who carved the body. Only after the
customer had purchased the piece was the desired
motif cut on the flat side by a less-skilled artisan.
However, the seal design had somehow to correspond
to the shape of the amulet, since its impression would
serve as identification of the owner, like a signature
today. This seal also has a vertical bore for suspension.
E.S.

40
Masklike human head

Site: Tell Brak, level of the Grey Temple
Date: 3500–3300 B.C.
Material: White alabaster
Height: 9.2 cm; *width:* 3.7 cm; *depth:* 3.4 cm
Museum No.: Aleppo G. 445
Literature: M. E. L. Mallowan *Iraq* 9 (1947) 92, Plate II 3

This schematically rendered human face with large
eyes, which was found together with a few similar
pieces, may have belonged to the unexcavated Grey
Temple. The function of the head has not been clearly
established, but it might have been a votive object
dedicated to a deity. These masks all have a deep vertical groove on the back so that they could be fitted to
a wooden staff or standard. Two holes at the neck and
on top of the head served to secure the mask to the
wood by means of either wire or nails. We might suggest that such masks were indeed used as cult decora-

40

tions on standards. Similar cult objects are depicted in
pairs on Syrian cylinder seals from the second millennium.
E.S.

117

41–43
Three "eye idols"

Site: Tell Brak, level of the Grey Temple
Date: 3500–3300 B.C.
Material: White alabaster
Height: (No. 41) 4.5 cm; (No. 42) 4.8 cm; (No. 43) 8.1 cm;
   depth: 0.5–0.6 cm
Museum Nos.: (No. 41) Aleppo 2103; (No. 42) 2122; (No. 43)
   2121
Literature: M. E. L. Mallowan *Iraq* 9 (1947) 150, Plates
   XXV, XXVI, LI

More than 300 of these peculiar schematically rendered figurines were found embedded in the Eye Temple platform, together with thousands of fragments.
Most of them were carved of alabaster. In these representations of humans only the shoulders, the neck,
and the eyes are indicated. The figurines are in the
form of individuals, pairs, and mother-with-child
groups, as shown in Cat. Nos. 41–43.

This extraordinary find has been widely discussed
by scholars. Some have connected the figurines with
the belief in the evil eye and assumed they were
amulets against it, because of emphasis given to the
eyes. The excavator, Sir Max Mallowan, thought they
were symbols for a specific god. Since such eye idols
have been found only at Tell Brak, they may have been

closely associated with a deity worshipped there. Considering the large number of idols, one may assume they were votive gifts.

E.S.

44
Figure of a bear

Site: Tell Brak
Date: 3500–3300 B.C.
Material: White alabaster
Height: 4.8 cm; *width:* 2.2 cm
Museum No.: Aleppo G. 409
Literature: M. E. L. Mallowan *Iraq* 9 (1947) 212, Plate
   LII 23

Figurines representing seated bears were found in large numbers in the vicinity of the Eye Temple at Tell Brak. The excavator, Sir Max Mallowan, suggested that the proximity of the site to the natural habitat of bears may have inspired the artists. One does in fact get the impression that the living model was not unknown to the sculptor. Even the very stylized renditions have the proportions and lines characteristic of this animal. The bear figurine exhibited here is one of the best examples from Brak. The surface was originally smoothly polished, but has suffered some deterioration.

E.S.

45
Figure of a lion

Site: Tell Brak, level of the Grey Temple
Date: 3500–3300 B.C.
Material: White alabaster
Height: 5.7 cm; *length:* 9 cm
Museum No.: Aleppo G. 433
Literature: M. E. L. Mallowan *Iraq* 9 (1947) 101, Plates IX
   6, LII 18

Very lifelike sculptures of lions are typical quite early in antiquity, and this form was often depicted at Tell Brak. There were lions in Mesopotamia until this century, so the ancient inhabitants would have been familiar with this animal, considered "king of beasts" both in Mesopotamia and Egypt.

E.S.

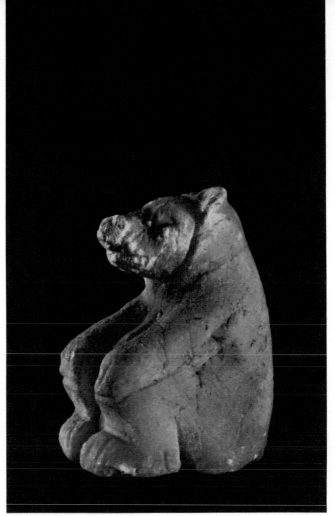

44

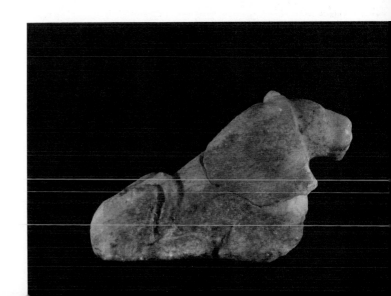

ca. 3500–3000 B.C.

46
Frog-shaped amulet

Site: Tell Brak, level of the Grey Temple
Date: 3500–3300 B.C.
Material: White alabaster
Height: 2.3 cm; *length:* 4.6 cm; *width:* 4 cm
Museum No.: Aleppo F. 683
Literature: M. E. L. Mallowan *Iraq* 9 (1947) 100, Plate IX 3

Figurines in the shape of frogs were even more common at Tell Brak than those representing bears. This example is bored through the lower part of the back so that it could be worn as an amulet. Similar votive objects are known from other temples in the ancient Near East. The frog was considered a symbol of fertility, and may have been donated to the temple by worshipers. Here the shape of the animal is very accurately rendered. The left eye has remnants of paint and part of the pupil.
E.S.

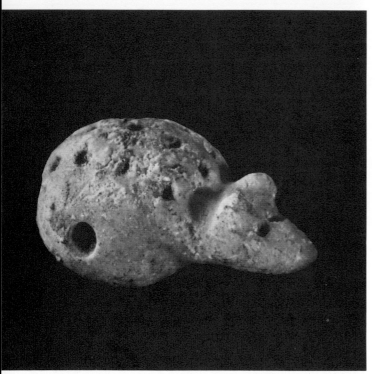

47
Hedgehog-shaped amulet

Site: Tell Brak, level of the Grey Temple
Date: 3500–3300 B.C.
Material: White alabaster
Height: 1.2 cm; *length:* 3.2 cm
Museum No.: Aleppo F. 658
Literature: M. E. L. Mallowan *Iraq* 9 (1947) 101, Plate X 2

The many hedgehog idols found at Tell Brak were all quite small. Our example has drill holes on the back, probably meant to indicate quills. They may have had colored inlays originally. See Cat. Nos. 9 and 34, where the symbolic powers of hedgehogs are discussed.
E.S.

THIRD MILLENNIUM CITIES
CA. 3000–2100 B.C.

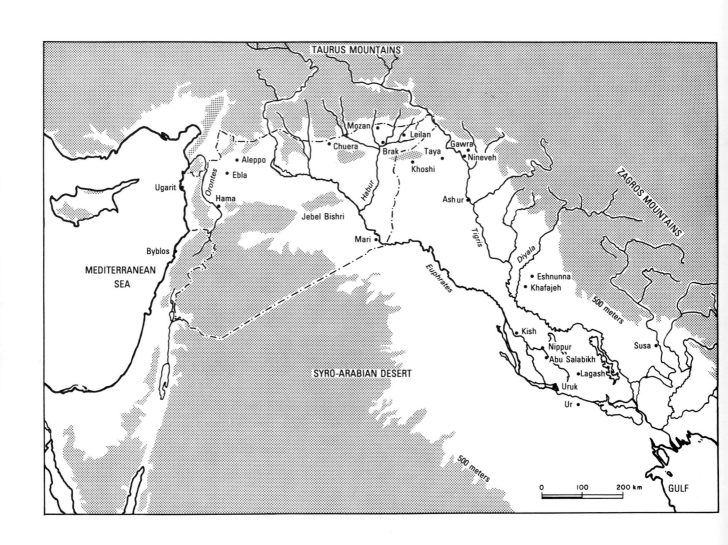

TAURUS MOUNTAINS

ZAGROS MOUNTAINS

Mozan

Leilan

Chuera

Brak

Taya

Gawra

Khoshi

Nineveh

Aleppo

Ebla

Ugarit

Hama

Orontes

Habur

Ashur

Tigris

Jebel Bishri

Byblos

Mari

Diyala

MEDITERRANEAN
SEA

Euphrates

Eshnunna

Khafajeh

500 meters

Kish

Susa

Nippur

Abu Salabikh

Lagash

SYRO-ARABIAN DESERT

Uruk

Ur

500 meters

0   100   200 km

GULF

THIRD MILLENNIUM SETTLEMENT AND SUBSISTENCE

HARVEY WEISS

THE CITIES OF SOUTHERN MESOPOTAMIA WHICH EMERGED IN THE late fourth millennium B.C., with their Syrian trade colonies as far-ranging and massive as Habuba Kabira, came to dominate the landscape and the people of the south in the third millennium. According to the estimates available from Robert Adams' surface survey of the lower Mesopotamian plain, as much as 80 percent of the population of southern Mesopotamia resided in large cities of more than 40 hectares by ca. 2500 B.C. Over the next thousand years the percentage living in cities steadily fell, until by the middle of the first millennium barely 15 percent of the population was urban. The third millennium was then the pinnacle of Mesopotamian urbanism in the south, and from this period we derive many of our paradigmatic notions of Mesopotamian civilization.

Early Dynastic period

Cities in southern Mesopotamia were ruled by dynasties of kings, probably only a newly emergent feature of the urban landscape. The span from the end of the Uruk period until the ascension of the Akkadian Dynasty is therefore labelled the Early Dynastic period in southern Mesopotamia. During this time the first large public buildings which can be identified as palaces, as opposed to temples, were constructed. For the archaeologist these serve as important indicators of the wealth which could be accumulated by royal dynasties ruling over a large labor force working a rich land with terrific organizational efficiency. Indeed, the wealth of these dynasties with their absolute rule is, along with the cities themselves, the hallmark of this period.

At a city such as Ur in southern Mesopotamia dynastic rule and wealth were such that enormous masses of precious metals and other materials, including gold, silver, electrum, and lapis lazuli, worked by skilled craftsmen and artists, could be expended toward the vainglory of deceased rulers, their families, and servants in truly immense royal cemeteries. The veneration of royalty in such ostentatious fashion surely reflected the pervasive ideology of the period in the south, an ideology adequately enough reflected in the cosmological literature of the Sumerians as well.

By the middle of this period, what archaeologists term the Early Dynastic II period, the centrally located city of Kish had probably already begun to assume a prime position in the affairs of the Sumerian heartland. Indeed, the location of Kish, only a few kilometers east of Babylon (then but a village), suggests that the region for reasons of efficient transport, communications, and military concerns was always the capital district of southern Mesopotamia. The paramount position of the city of Kish during the later Early Dynastic period is reflected in such varied sources as the famous Sumerian King List (known from southern Mesopotamian texts), the "chariot burials" retrieved there by an early archaeological expedition, and by the title "king of Kish" which during this period was the equivalent of "king of the entire world." Although much of ancient Kish remains to be excavated, we know that its position within the third-millennium world of Sumerian-speaking southern Mesopotamia was essentially unchallenged, or if challenged, integrated and adopted into the successful challenger's realm.

By the last part of the Early Dynastic period, scribes with names which can only be understood as Semitic, not Sumerian, were already appending their names to the colophons (last lines) of cuneiform documents written in Sumerian. Most scholars now understand such documents as evidence for the gradual emergence of the Semitic-speaking element within Sumerian society into positions of urban power and control. By about the twenty-fifth century B.C. persons who undoubtedly were speaking Akkadian already appear as royal officials within the Sumerian courts.

Akkadian period

In the middle of the twenty-fourth century, to use the standard but by no means assured "middle chronology," the dominant position of the city of Kish within the Sumerian south was rudely, and probably forcefully, displaced by a new ruler, a new dynasty, a new capital city. Little is known of the historical circumstances within which this process occurred. What larger forces were shaping the social and economic relations of the period are similarly still poorly understood and do not at the moment allow us to comprehend why these events occurred. It is certain, however, that by the middle of the century Kish was overthrown by a ruler with the grandiose name—probably taken only upon his accession to power—Sargon, "true king" in Akkadian.

At some point, probably early in his reign, Sargon abandoned the ancient capital at Kish and created a new capital for his realm at a place called Akkade or Agade (meaning unknown). It is from the name of this capital city that we derive the name for the language spoken by these dynasts, Akkadian, our name for the dynasty itself, and the general name for the region, Akkad. The location of the capital Agade remains unknown. It is one of the last great cities of antiquity which still elude archaeologists. The large mound of Ishan Mizyad, only a few kilometers from Kish, if not some otherwise unknown major city, is likely to be the missing Agade.

According to his own inscriptions, later copies, and the varied traditions which he inspired, Sargon undertook far-reaching military campaigns, even to the Mediterranean, and managed to "conquer" much of the "entire world," claiming domination of all of southern Mesopotamia and the conquest of most of the rest. His sons were no less ambitious, nor less vain. Documentation for Sargon and his sons' activities is not difficult to find, as they left their inscriptions in most places they conquered or tried to conquer. The legendary Sargon, however, was even outdone by his grandson Naram-Sin ("beloved of the [moon-god] Sin"). For the first time in Mesopotamian history we find a king actually deifying himself (Naram-Sin's scribes begin to use the "god-sign" not just in front of the Sin part of his name, but in front of Naram as well). Naram-Sin's royal inscriptions, like his grandfather's, include extensive paeans to his might, the might of the gods protecting him and his armies, and the terrible defeats which he inflicted upon distant cities.

This picture of southern Mesopotamian dynastic power, economic development, broad-scale urbanization, and far-ranging conquest is essentially self-generated. The southern Mesopotamian city-states presented their activities in this light and historians have pretty much followed in their path. The conquests, given the state of archaeological research, always seemed well substantiated, and certainly the uniformity of the boasting and the consensus among the scribal reporters left little doubt that southern Mesopotamia was the center of a larger Mesopotamian world whose peripheral regions began at the borders of Akkad.

Historiographically, and even archaeologically, little research devoted to southern Mesopotamia has been able to account for the "sudden" expansionary activities of Sargon and his dynastic successors. The available documentation suggests, however, that the persistent and very efficient deployment of ration-paid labor across a landscape lined with canals continued to generate huge returns in the annual barley harvest. Some mid-third-millennium accounts indicate 76-fold seed-to-harvest yields, while late-third-millennium texts suggest still-impressive 20-fold yields. These high cereal yields were certainly the product of irrigation agriculture exploiting fertile soil horizons not yet burdened with the residue salts which irrigation would inexorably bring to the surface. The extensive cultivation of irrigated tracts, however, would have been difficult if not impossible were it not for the efficiency of water-borne transport presented by the canal system of southern Mesopotamia.

New data and new perspectives: Ebla

Sargon was by no means the first southern ruler to attempt far-ranging conquest, although his reign is simplistically often labelled the beginnings of the transition to empire from the period of exclusively city-state rule. Similarly, indications that this picture of southern Mesopotamian domination was too simplistic have been accumulating for many years. In the 1960s the late Anton Moortgat undertook a series of excavations at the very large (>100 hectare) site of Tell Chuera in northeastern Syria, on the western fringe of the Habur Plains. Although Tell Chuera is relatively isolated, and in that sense remains enigmatic, Moortgat's excavations indicated that remote from the southern centers, and very likely remote from the kind of irrigation agriculture which characterizes southern production, very large urban configurations were emerging in the north during the Early Dynastic period.

Further to the east, just across the Syrian border, the British archaeologist Julian Reade had by the early 1970s concluded the topographic mapping of an exceptionally large walled site called Tell Taya, near Tell Afar in northwestern Iraq. Like Tell Chuera, Taya is approximately 100 hectares or more in size, and like Tell Chuera appears to have emerged as a major urban center in the north as early as the twenty-fifth century B.C.

Without doubt the excavations of Professor Paolo Matthiae at Tell Mardikh have now definitively shown that in the late Early Dynastic and early Akkadian periods urban life on a social and economic scale as complex, productive, extractive, efficiently organized, and socially conscious as any recorded in southern Mesopotamia was functioning in northwestern Syria. The entire record of late Early Dynastic and Sargonic historical inscriptions must now be re-examined. Toponyms previously considered to be distant, weak towns useful only as a base for Sargonic boasting, must now be re-evaluated as the probable sites of early urban cultures stratified, specialized, militarized, and expansive enough to have merited Sargonic attack for the threats which they posed to southern Mesopotamian interests.

The cultural details of Ebla's civilization, its literature, writing system, language, religion, art, and political arrangements are described in some detail in the essays which follow, along with the all-important outline of the city's archaeological monuments and periodization. Here it may be useful to consider another of the problems raised by the existence of Ebla: its origins.

Two regions of Syria are particularly noteworthy for their agricultural production: the plains of Aleppo, Hama, Homs, and Idlib in northwestern Syria and the Habur Plains of northeastern Syria. Both areas offer a similar combination of soils, rainfall, and topography: gently rolling plains of fertile Mediterranean red and brown soils enjoying more than 350 millimeters of rainfall per annum. These conditions permit the extensive cultivation of wheat and barley without irrigation, that is, by dry farming, and the extensive raising of sheep and goat herds. The circumstances of these plains, therefore, make for extremely large harvests in the aggregate, as contrasted with the cereal harvests of southern Mesopotamia, where irrigation agriculture provides high per-hectare yields, but solely with the relatively limited stretches of land which can be brought under irrigation.

This contrast between the irrigation agriculture of southern Mesopotamia and the dry farming of northern Syria (and parts of northern Iraq) is one framework within which much of the late prehistoric and early historic cultural history of the ancient Near East can be understood. Cereal agriculture as a mode of production with its own organizational and distributional requirements conditioned in many respects the development of other organizational forms, such as those of human settlement across agricultural regions.

The Sumerian colonies of Syria, some of them extremely large like Habuba Kabira, left no visible successors upon the landscape they briefly dominated, except for their abandoned settlements. Life apparently returned to normal after the departure of the colonists. Why they departed and how they came to dominate the landscape in the first place remain largely unanswered archaeological questions.

The period which follows this late Uruk (Protohistoric) expansion from southern Mesopotamia into Syria is still not well known. In northwestern Syria it is termed the Proto-Syrian period, or Tell Mardikh IIA. It is likely to be the next frontier in Syrian archaeology. In the succeeding period, Mardikh IIB1, Palace G and its archives present us with a fully developed, highly articulated regional economy centered on Ebla. The analysis of the archives, especially the administrative texts, indicates the source of Ebla's wealth: extensive dry farming of cereals and, most important, of flax, as well as wool products derived from sheepherding.

In northeastern Syria and northern Iraq this period, falling between the south's late Uruk and Akkadian periods, is known as Ninevite V after Nineveh, the site in Iraq where it occupies the fifth level of an early excavation. Most recently the long-debated chronological position of Ninevite V ceramics has been refined to define the nature of settlement and subsistence during the third millennium on the Habur Plains where Tell Leilan is located.

Tell Leilan

Settlement in the Leilan region during the Ninevite V/Leilan III period was not very dense: only fourteen sites were situated within 15 kilometers of Tell Leilan, and their average size was only 5.5 hectares. Leilan may have been the largest of these sites but could not have been larger than 15 hectares. To judge from the floral samples retrieved from house floors of this period excavated at Leilan, the Leilan III people were prosperous farmers, harvesting barley and emmer wheat. Throughout the region larger settlements are not known.

This apparently quiet period of well-established village farming came to a sudden end with the beginning of Leilan Period II. At some point after the abandonment of the stratum-16 house in Leilan operation 1, and probably well after a few additional house strata had been occupied and abandoned, some rather considerable new forces appeared upon the scene, forces which have yet to be adequately defined or understood but which apparently changed the face of the Habur Plains and much of northwestern Syria and northern Iraq for the next several hundred years. At Tell Leilan the archaeological indicators of these changes are quite clear.

First, the last of the wall stubs of the domestic structure sequence in operation 1 were leveled, probably with some kind of a shovel, and upon this prepared surface an enormous wall of mud brick, at least 15 meters wide, was constructed. At the same time, settlements at Leilan expanded beyond the acropolis area and began to fill the lower town defined by the site's walls. Then the city wall itself was built: an enormous effort of mud brick, at least 10 meters wide and 15 meters tall, extending around the settlement's circumference for almost 3.5 kilometers.

The simultaneous construction of the city wall and settlement of the lower town were not isolated events. The ceramics which characterize the early lower town and strata upon which the city wall was contructed can now be identified at other large walled settlements on the Habur Plains and across the border in northern Iraq. Additionally, a series of radiocarbon measurements taken during the Leilan excavations provides an absolute date for these developments: ca. 2500 B.C. Inscriptions from a slightly later date suggest that these cities were ruled by Hurrian-speaking dynasties.

These observations at Tell Leilan supplement and help configure a variety of other archaeological data from the Habur Plains, as well as the plains of northwestern Syria. Taken together these data indicate that a radical reorganization of settlement in the dry-farming plains of Syria was visible by about 2500 B.C. This is precisely the same period as that when Tell Mardikh, another massive city in a dry-farming situation, was beginning to dominate the regional landscape, and it is the precise period when southern Mesopotamian dynasts were beginning—just before the ascension of the Akkadian dynasts—to claim conquests of distant cities.

Mari

An important third-millennium example or variant of city life dependent upon irrigation agriculture is represented in *Ebla to Damascus* by Mari, on the left bank of the Euphrates. Through the long-term efforts of André Parrot, and now the excavations of Jean-Claude Margueron, more third-millennium structures have been excavated at Mari than at any other Syro-Mesopotamian city. These excavations are just beginning to provide the kinds of archival materials already available from Ebla and the south. These documents represent one aspect of another research frontier looming on the horizon—the comparative developmental histories of southern Mesopotamia, Mari, Ebla, and the Habur Plains.

The Mari excavations have already documented the religious and political centers of the city's third-millennium wealth: the richly decorated statue-filled temples of Ishtar, Ninni-zaza, Ishtarat, Ninhursag, and Dagan and the successively rebuilt Early Dynastic palace (P-3, P-2, P-1) with its centrally located temple. The wealth and power of Mari extended beyond its walls and brought military involvements with the south and Ebla, and probably the Habur Plains as well. The Sumerian King List records Mari as the "tenth dynasty after the Flood" to control southern Mesopotamia, while the powerful southern King Eannatum of Lagash (late Early Dynastic) records his conquest of Mari in a royal inscription.

The relationships between Mari and Ebla are now being explored within the third-millennium documents recently retrieved from excavations at both sites. It is already certain that an economic and military rivalry based upon conflicting regional interests resulted in huge payments ("gifts") of silver and gold from one city to the other. The famous Treasure of Ur, recovered within the Early Dynastic palace temple, probably represents only the smallest part of the wealth which moved between the cities of the third millennium.

It is still far too early to define with any certainty the precise nature of settlement and political organization across the plains of Syria and Mesopotamia. But archaeological research in Syria during the past fifteen years has radically altered some of the most fundamental conceptions which historians, archaeologists, and anthropologists have shared for decades concerning the origins and early development of civilization. The high-yield productivity of southern Mesopotamian agriculture was certainly matched by the extensive dry-farming agriculture—cereal and flax cultivation as well as sheep-herding—on the plains of northwestern and northeastern Syria.

Recommended Reading

Robert McC. Adams. *Heartland of Cities* (Chicago: University of Chicago Press, 1981).

I. J. Gelb. "Ebla and Lagash: Ecological and Developmental Contrasts." In Harvey Weiss (ed.). *The Origins of Cities in Dry-Farming Syria and Mesopotamia in the Third Millennium B.C.* (Winona Lake, Ind.: ASOR, 1985).

Harvey Weiss. "Excavations at Tell Leilan and the Origins of North Mesopotamian Cities in the Third Millennium B.C." *Paléorient* 9/2 (1983) 39–52.

MARI (TELL HARIRI)

Location: 10 km northwest of Abu Kemal, on the right bank of the Euphrates
Dates: Ca. 4000 B.C.–ca. 312 B.C.
Excavations: From 1933 (Musée du Louvre and Centre National de la Recherche Scientifique)
Publications:
  Preliminary reports: A. Parrot *Syria* 16 (1935) 1, 117 / 17 (1936) 1 / 18

(1937) 54, 325 / 19 (1938) 1 / 20 (1939) 1 / 21 (1940) 1 / 29 (1952) 183 / 30 (1953) 196 / 31 (1954) 151 / 32 (1955) 185 / 39 (1962) 151 / 41 (1964) 1 / 42 (1965) 1, 197 / 44 (1967) 1 / 46 (1969) 191 / 47 (1970) 225 / 48 (1971) 253 / 49 (1972) 281 / *AAAS* 1 (1951) 193 / 2 (1952) 137 / 3 (1953) 71 / 4 (1954) 29 / 11 (1961) 173 / 14 (1964) 15 / 15 (1965) 25 / 16 (1966) 5 / 17 (1967) 1 / 19 (1969) 15 / 20 (1970) 1 / 22 (1972) 9 / 23 (1973) 9 / 25 (1975) 9 // M. Birot *Syria* 50 (1973) 1 // J.-Cl. Margueron (ed.) *Mari: annales de recherches interdisciplinaires* 1— (1981—)

Final reports: A. Parrot *Mission archéologique de Mari I. Série archéologique:* I. *Le temple d'Ishtar* (1956); II. *Le palais:* 1. *Architecture* (1958); 2. *Peintures murales* (1958); 3. *Documents et monuments* (1959); III. *Les temples d'Ishtarat et de Ninni-zaza* (1967); IV. *Le trésor d'Ur* (1968)

Publication of cuneiform documents: A. Parrot and G. Dossin (eds.) *Mission archéologique de Mari* II. *Série épigraphique, historique et littéraire: Archives royales de Mari* I— (1950—) and numerous articles (see J.-G. Heintz *Index documentaire des textes de Mari. Fascicule 1: Liste/Codage de textes. Index des ouvrages de reference* (= *ARMT* 17/1, Paris, 1975)

General introduction: A. Parrot *Mari: capitale fabuleuse* (Paris 1974) with extensive bibliography pp. 194–206

In August 1933, a Bedouin preparing a burial tomb at the mound known as Tell Hariri accidentally came upon a large fragment from a stone statue. This chance discovery was brought to the attention of the French colonial authorities, and thus began archaeological research at Mari. By December of the same year, in the course of the very first season of excavations, it was possible to identify Tell Hariri with the city of Mari already known from southern Mesopotamian docu-

Figure 33
Plan of the Temple of Ishtarat and Ninni-zaza at Mari.

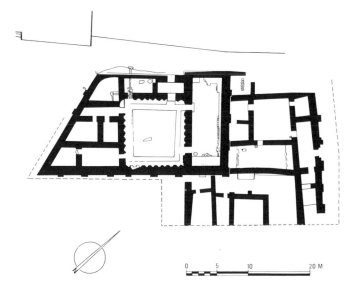

0   5   10   20 M

ments. A completely preserved statue, discovered with several others, bore on its shoulder a votive inscription which names the statue's patron, Lamgi-Mari, king of the city of Mari (Cat. No. 62). From 1933 to the present, systematic excavations at Tell Hariri have exposed large portions of the 60-hectare city.

A massive western city wall was constructed in the Early Dynastic period. Adjacent to this wall excavation has revealed three construction phases of a temple dedicated to the goddess Ishtar and sheltering her priestly attendants. Phase A, the latest of the three, was heavily destroyed in antiquity but is the most completely exposed. Two cellas (sacred rooms) were situated adjacent to each other, separated by a doorless wall. Benches and a pedestal were built-in features. The walls of the structure, constructed from sun-dried mud brick, were set on limestone foundations. Within the wall foundations of these cellas a total of thirteen "foundation deposits" were buried: seven deposits from level c of the Ishtar temple and six similar deposits from level a. Each of these deposits consists of a D-shaped copper ring-bolt, a pointed copper peg, and stone tablets (see Cat. No. 60).

An asphalted court north of the two cellas was part of the cultic area: a basin for liquid sacrifices, an offering table, and an altar are evidence of the activities once performed here. Adjacent rooms to the east were presumably used by the priests. Objects found within the court, the cult rooms, and another court south of these include jewelry, weapons, inlaid figurines of the type appearing in the friezes of

Cat. Nos. 49 and 50, a steatite vessel (Cat. No. 71), and more than a hundred statuettes and fragments of statuettes. In addition to the figure of Lamgi-Mari, two others are illustrated: a female (Cat. No. 63) and a seated couple (Cat. No. 65). The famous statue of Ebih-Il, perhaps the most beautiful of this group, is now in the Louvre.

A number of other shrines were erected within the city, but they have not been excavated as extensively as the Temple of Ishtar. One of these temples, that of the god Dagan, is set within a brick mass, the "*massif rouge*," part of a terrace which may be the forerunner of the famous Mesopotamian ziggurat (stepped tower) tradition.

The temple dedicated to the goddess Ishtarat is arranged like the multi-room domestic structures in the western and center portion of the city: a central courtyard provides entry to the other rooms (see Fig. 33). Cult rooms with pedestals (for statues) at both ends were entered through the courtyard. The Temple of Ishtarat was constructed against the niched outer wall of the Temple of Ninni-zaza, a far more richly embellished structure. The central court of the temple features a conical basalt stele 1.5 meters long. This type of stele is otherwise associated with religious architecture and practice in Palestine and hence is sometimes identified as Canaanite. Similar stelae also occur at Tell Mardikh. A long cult room with two doors opens onto the courtyard. Here too evidence of severe destruction, resulting in the abandonment of precious objects, has been found. From the Temple of Ishtarat the exhibition features the large votive statue from the time of King Ikun-Shamagan (Cat.

No. 61) and a seated female figure (Cat. No. 64). A figure of the cult-singer Ur-nanshe (Cat. No. 66) and a particularly finely worked head (Cat. No. 67) were retrieved from the contemporanous Temple of Ninni-zaza, a deity who appears to be unique to Mari.

A third group of third-millennium objects from Mari was also derived from religious buildings. In the course of exploring the structures which preceded the enormous palace of the late third and early second millennia, two or perhaps even three overlapping architectural complexes were discovered. Within the largest of these palaces an architecturally independent temple unit was constructed (Fig. 34). The famous Treasure of Ur, buried within a clay vessel, is derived from the last period of this palace temple's use.

André Parrot explained the treasure as a royal gift from the southern Mesopotamian city of Ur, but the majority of the objects may be the products of mid-Euphrates-region workshops. The treasure consists of fourteen pristine cylinder seals, three statuettes, a pair of stick pins, arm and neck rings, and an inscribed lapis lazuli bead, all perhaps the remains of a temple inventory associated with priests or a cult statue. The selection from the Treasure of Ur in this exhibition includes two cylinder seals made of shell (Cat. Nos. 52 and 53), a necklace (Cat. No. 54), a stick pin (Cat. No. 59), a lion-headed eagle (Cat. No. 55), an inscribed lapis lazuli bead (Cat. No. 56), and a small copper, lapis, and electrum figurine of a goddess (Cat. No. 57).
KAY KOHLMEYER

Figure 34
Plan of the temple in the palace at Mari.

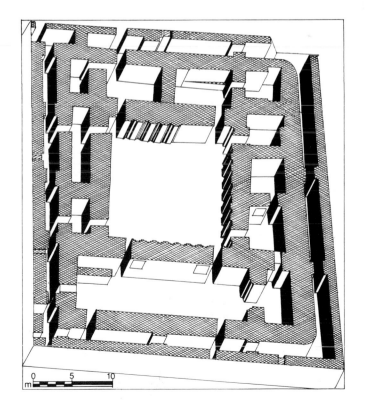

EBLA RECOVERED

PAOLO MATTHIAE

EBLA (TELL MARDIKH)

Location: 55 km south of Aleppo
Dates: Period I, 3500–3000 B.C., through Period VI, 560–530 B.C.
Excavations: 1964 to present, annually (University of Rome)
Publications:

Preliminary reports: P. Matthiae et al. *MAIS* 1964 (1965) / *MAIS* 1965 (1966) / *SEb* 1 (1979)— // P. Matthiae *AAAS* 15 (1965) 83 / *AAAS* 17 (1967) 25 / *AAAS* 18 (1968) 5 / *AAAS* 20 (1970) 55 / *Akkadica* 2 (1977) 2 / *Akkadica* 17 (1980) 1 / *MonANE* 1/6

General: P. Matthiae *Ebla: An Empire Rediscovered* (Garden City 1981) / *I Tesori di Ebla* (Rome 1984) // G. Pettinato *The Archives of Ebla: An Empire Inscribed on Clay* (New York 1981)

Royal Palace G: P. Matthiae *BiblArch* 39 (1976) 94 / *Archaeology* 30 (1977) 244 / *AJA* 82 (1978) 540 / *SMS* (1978) 13 / *CRAI* 25 Berlin 1978 (1982) 125

Palace Archives: S.G. Beld et al. *The Tablets of Ebla: Concordance and Bibliography* (Winona Lake, Ind. 1984) (See also bibliography at end of following essay, "The Royal Archives of Ebla")

Figure 35
Topographic plan of Tell Mardikh, with areas excavated through 1978.

Tell Mardikh, located 55 kilometers south of Aleppo, is one of the largest ancient sites in inner Syria, almost 60 hectares in area. The archaeological expedition of the University of Rome has been excavating the site since 1964 (see Figs. 35 and 36). The first decade of research at Tell Mardikh resulted in three major accomplishments:

1. Identification of the period ca. 2400–1600 B.C. as the time when the city flourished.

2. Retrieval of detailed information about the Old Syrian period of the early second millennium B.C.

3. Identification of Tell Mardikh with ancient Ebla, already known from Sumerian, Akkadian, Egyptian, Hurrian, and Syrian sources, and previously hypothesized to be located in southern Turkey.

In 1974 we began the excavation of the administrative quarter of the Royal Palace, Area G, of the early Proto-Syrian period, ca. 2500–2250 B.C. One year later, the largest portion of the cuneiform documents of the royal archives was discovered in Palace G. The archival inventory of more than 17,000 items includes more than 2,000 complete tablets.

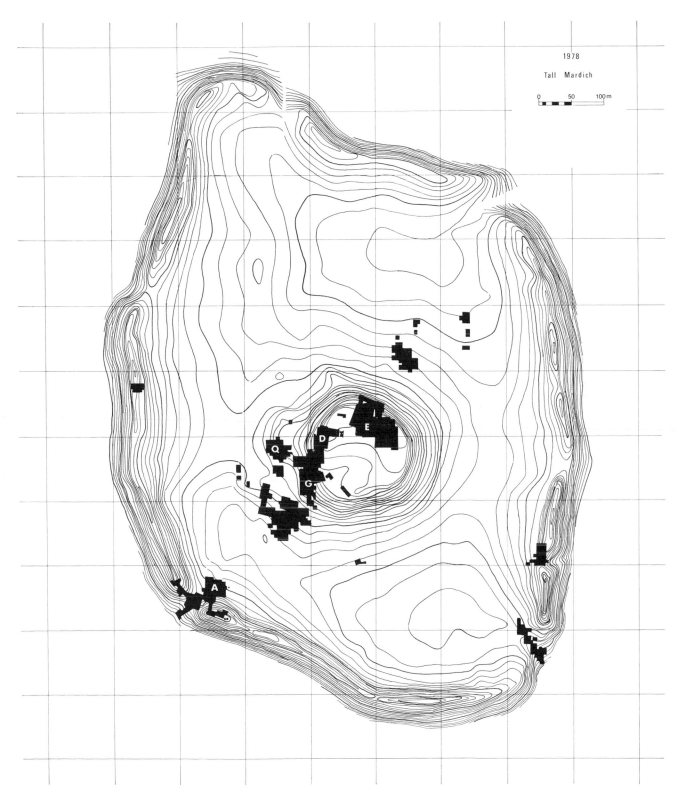

ca. 3000–2100 B.C.

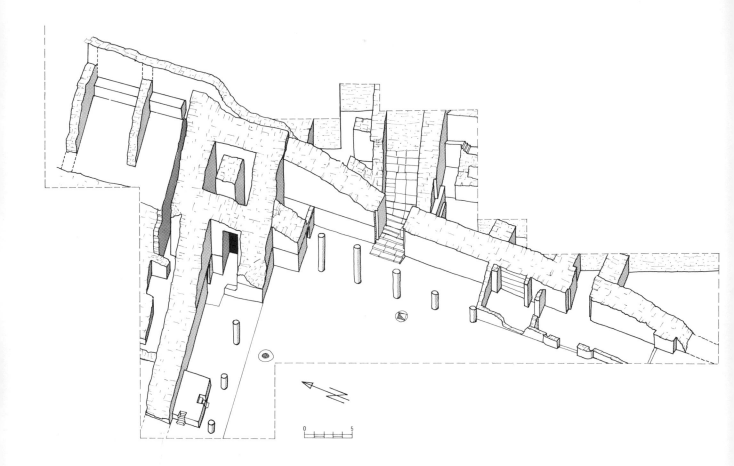

Figure 36
Axiometric plan of Royal Palace G,
Ebla (Tell Mardikh).

Since 1978 we have been uncovering the very large Western
Palace, Area Q, built around 1900
B.C. and stretching for more than
three-quarters of a hectare. We
have also been retrieving the royal
necropolis of the Amorite dynasties
who reigned in the Western Palace.
Three of these tombs, including
that of the "Lord of the Goats,"
were explored in 1978 and 1979. In
1983 our attention turned again to
Royal Palace G, where we uncovered an additional 2.4 hectares
and also exposed portions of a
building dating to shortly after 2500
B.C.

Our excavations have resulted in
the following dating of the history
of settlement at Tell Mardikh:

Mardikh I:
ca. 3500–2900 B.C.
Mardikh IIA:
ca. 2900–2350 B.C.
The oldest urban settlement at
Ebla should date to the last centuries of the fourth millennium
B.C., and some materials from Tell
Mardikh, although retrieved out of
their archaeological context, can
be dated to Mardikh I, ca. 3500–
2900 B.C. During the succeeding
period, Mardikh IIA, ca. 2900–

2350 B.C., the settlement became increasingly more significant. Building levels of this period have been found in the southern region of the Mardikh acropolis. The accelerated urbanism may have been a function of control exerted over the trade routes in the region involving the exchange of timber, copper, and silver from northern Lebanon, the Amanus mountains, and the Taurus mountains.

Mardikh IIB1: ca. 2400–2250 B.C.

During Mardikh IIB1 Ebla reached its economic, political, and cultural apogee. The city probably expanded to nearly 50 hectares, and a large palace complex was constructed over much of the acropolis, including its southern and western slopes. Three wings of this structure have been identified: (1) the central complex in the south part of the acropolis, (2) the administrative quarter to the west, (3) the southern quarter.

Only the administrative quarter, with its large audience court, has been completely excavated. Here we have retrieved the thousands of cuneiform tablets—economic, administrative, juridical, lexical, and literary—of the royal archives. We have also uncovered other important artifacts which illuminate the international relations of the city, including more than 20 kilograms of raw lapis lazuli from Afghanistan and fragments of diorite and alabaster bowls of pharaonic Egyptian provenance. The large audience court was apparently a center of administrative and commercial activity. Here officials organized the trading caravans which distributed Ebla's textile products, collected gold and silver tribute, delivered food rations to officials and messengers, maintained the royal accounts, and received messengers from foreign powers.

During this period Ebla probably controlled all of northwestern Syria from Hama to the south up to the Euphrates and Balikh rivers. The city had close relations with other urban centers, such as Mari along the middle Euphrates, and with cities along the Tigris in northern Mesopotamia. Ebla's political power, however, was undermined by the military expeditions of Sargon and Naram-Sin of Akkad in southern Mesopotamia. Royal Palace G and the remainder of the city were destroyed by either of these two kings in the reign of Ibbi-Zikir, the last Ebla king mentioned in the archives, around 2300 or 2250 B.C.

Mardikh IIB2: ca. 2250–1900 B.C.

During this period a much poorer and smaller settlement was rebuilt. At the same time, political power in the region shifted to the city of Urshu, probably not far from Ebla and well known even to Gudea, the ruler of the southern Mesopotamian city of Lagash.

Mardikh IIIA: ca. 1900–1800 B.C.

Mardikh was rebuilt during this period with heavy fortified ramparts, some of which still stand more than 22 meters high along the eastern perimeter of the site. These ramparts, four city gates, the large, ring-shaped lower city, and the central hillock of the acropolis created the urban topography of Ebla during this period. The large Western Palace of the lower city (in area Q), and Ebla's major temples were also constructed during this period.

The latter included Temple D, dedicated to the goddess Ishtar; Temple B1 for the cult of Resheph, the lord of war and the netherworld; and Temple N, seemingly related to the sun god Shamash. During this period Ebla was probably the most powerful city between Hama and Aleppo and had close ties with Anatolia and Palestine. Royal patronage exerted its influence upon the arts of the city at this time, as can be seen by carved ritual basins, such as the one discussed in Cat. No. 116.

Mardikh IIIB: ca. 1800–1600 B.C.

At the beginning of this period, political supremacy over the region extending from Homs to the Euphrates shifted to the kingdom of Yamkhad (modern Aleppo), ruled by Yarim-Lim I. Ebla became a vassal of Aleppo at this time but did not suffer destruction or attack. To this period belong the following excavated structures: private houses in the lower city (Area B); City Gate A; Sanctuary B2, probably related to the cult of royal ancestors; Royal Palace E in the north portion of the acropolis; Fortress M, built on the eastern ramparts.

The tombs of the royal necropolis belong to the period 1800–1650 B.C. and are topographically as well as ideologically related to the Western Palace, Temple B1, and Sanctuary B2. The Tomb of the Princess is not older than ca. 1825 B.C. The Tomb of the Lord of the Goats, the most important of the graves, dates to ca. 1700 B.C. It is likely that its owner was one Immeya, for his titleless name was inscribed on a silver bowl in the tomb. His royal lineage is indicated

by the presence in the vault of a ceremonial mace of ivory, silver, gold, and limestone of the Thirteenth Dynasty Egyptian Pharaoh Hetepribre Hornedjheryotef (ca. 1770 B.C.), as well as other rich furnishings (see Cat. Nos. 109–114).

At the end of Mardikh IIIB, 1650–1600 B.C., Ebla was conquered and destroyed again. This destruction can be associated with the end of the settlement at Alalakh (near Antioch), Level VII, and is historically tied to the conquests in this region by Hattushili I and Mursili I, kings of the Hittite empire in Turkish Anatolia. Hattushili I conquered Alalakh, Urshu, and Aleppo. Thereafter, Mursili I conquered Aleppo and then embarked on a lightning raid of Babylon in 1595 B.C.

Ebla is not mentioned in the Mari archives, which overlap chronologically with part of Mardikh IIIB. Perhaps the city's region or "state" was mentioned instead with a different name, such as Elahut. Ebla's king, apparently a vassal of Aleppo, does appear, however, in the archives of Alalakh Level VII.

Mardikh IV: ca. 1600–1200 B.C.

Ebla was definitely abandoned after the destruction of Mardikh IIIB. During Mardikh IV all of the lower city was deserted, although some very small settlements were built on the acropolis. Temple D underwent one last building phase in the area of its cella (inner holy chamber). Shortly before 1450 B.C. the Egyptian army of Thutmosis III passed near Ebla, and upon the pharaoh's return to Egypt, the city's name was included among the more than three hundred cities of Palestine and Syria recorded on the monumental pylon at Karnak.

Mardikh VB: ca. 900–720 B.C.
Mardikh VC: ca. 720–535 B.C.

Scattered private houses and perhaps a very poor fortification were still present on the north and west areas of the acropolis during these periods, which correspond to those designated Iron Age II and III, or the Aramaean period, and to the decades of Neo-Assyrian and Neo-Babylonian rule.

Mardikh VIA-B: ca. 535–60 B.C.
Mardikh VII: ca. A.D. 300–500

During the Persian and Hellenistic periods there was a revival of rural settlements in Syria. The northern part of the acropolis was occupied by a small country manor house (Area E), and smaller dwellings were built on the slopes of the acropolis. The site was probably completely abandoned during the second century B.C. In the late Roman and Byzantine periods, a very poor monastic settlement was built at the western foot of the acropolis.

The significance of Ebla

The excavations of Ebla are important primarily for their revelation of the unanticipated qualities of Proto-Syrian culture and secondarily for their demonstration of the continuity of historical development within inner Syria. The urban culture of Proto-Syrian Ebla is the only one known in southwest Asia outside of southern Mesopotamia for the third millennium B.C. It is immediately contemporary with the city-based societies of Sumer and Akkad. The sophisticated administrative organization of Proto-Syrian Ebla at approximately 2300 B.C. has no parallel outside of Sumer, while the linguistic, religious, ethnic, and other cultural characteristics of the city remain indigenously Syrian. The brief temporal and cultural gap between Proto-Syrian Ebla (ca. 2300 B.C.) and Old Syrian Ebla (ca. 1900 B.C.) notwithstanding, the excavations at Tell Mardikh have made it possible to distinguish elements of continuity within the ideology, religion, economy, art, and architecture previously neglected in our reconstructions of the historical development of pre-Hellenistic Syria.

THE ROYAL ARCHIVES OF EBLA

ALFONSO ARCHI

THE CUNEIFORM ARCHIVES OF ROYAL PALACE G AT EBLA PROVIDE unique documentation for the third millennium B.C.: almost 2,000 complete clay tablets, approximately 6,000 large tablet fragments, and thousands of smaller tablet fragments. Within this corpus 80 percent of the documents are administrative texts recording expenditures and exchanges involving the palace and its personnel, while the remainder is comprised of literary texts and lexical lists. These documents now permit us to write the history of northwestern Syria during the second half of the third millennium B.C. and help us to better understand the early history and classification of the Semitic languages.

The archives rather systematically cover a period corresponding to three dynastic generations totalling approximately forty years: Ar-Ennum, Ibrium, and Ibbi-Zikir. A few documents are associated with two previous kings, Igrish-Halam and Irkab-Damu. The entire archives can be dated to approximately the middle of the twenty-fourth century, that is, the late pre-Sargonic age and the early part of the reign of Sargon of Akkad (2340–2284 B.C.). This date for the archives is founded upon the following observations:

1. The latter part of the reign of Iblul-il of Mari cannot extend beyond the first years of Ar-Ennum.

2. The city of Akkad is never mentioned in the Ebla texts, whereas Kish is mentioned frequently.

3. Pepi I, third pharaoh of the Sixth Dynasty, whose cartouche was found on an alabaster jar lid with the tablets of Palace G, probably ruled during the middle of the twenty-fourth century.

The royal archives document the activities of the various administrative sectors of the Eblaite state, including those concerned with the provision of food for the court, agricultural harvests, and animal husbandry. A central portion of the archives, located in a room under the eastern portico of the audience hall where the king performed many of his duties, contained the monthly and annual accounts of each economic activity controlled by the palace. This archive, which spans a period of several decades, contains just over fifty letters, decrees, and political treaties, all probably a selection from a larger number of documents. In contrast, an archive retrieved from a small adjacent room contained twenty-eight letters and royal decrees all dating from the period immediately preceding the city's destruction. Comparative study of the separate archives suggests that tablets with individual administrative entries were cancelled and destroyed once the data had been entered into the appropriate accounts.

Within the central archives, some tablets were originally stacked upon wooden shelves along the walls. The destruction of the shelves during the intense fire which destroyed the palace caused the tablets on the upper shelves to slide toward the center of the room. Within large groups, however, the original placement of the shelved tablets is reconstructable. Most tablets were stored on the floor, including the larger tablets and those of lenticular shape. The latter, stacked one upon the other, were probably kept in baskets which were completely consumed by the fire. On the shelves along the north wall, the mythological texts were placed along with the magical incantations, the lexical lists, and the juridical documents. Along the same wall, but on the lower shelves, were kept the tablets concerned with the administration of agricultural land and livestock breeding. Documents recording the palace revenues—textile production and tributes in precious metals—were stacked in the east corner of the same room. (See Figs. 37 and 38.) In contrast the entire western wall held the texts documenting palace economy output, especially textiles destined for palace dependents or for export.

There are approximately twenty literary texts, some written in Sumerian, others in Eblaite. Among the latter are equal numbers of original compositions and translations from Sumerian, as indicated by the appearance of Sumerian deities like Enlil alongside indigenous Syrian gods like the deified Balikh River. These texts, together with the Eblaite letters and juridical documents, comprise some of the oldest texts in a Semitic language. Certainly scribes with Semitic names are documented as the authors of tablets within southern Mesopotamian archives of the twenty-fifth century B.C. But within these archives the tablets themselves are written in Sumerian. Similarly, southern Mesopotamian economic documents of this period use formulaic Sumerian bureaucratic expressions, although some, to be

Figure 37
Cuneiform tablets in situ *along east wall of the archives room, Palace G, Ebla.*

sure, may have been read as Semitic. These Ebla documents, therefore, are uniquely early documents in a Semitic language.

Lexical texts

One series of Ebla texts are lexical lists grouping words according to their graphemes (the cuneiform signs used to express them) and conceptual resemblances. Lists of graphemes, objects and animals, geographical names and names of professions and occupations, already generated by Sumerian scribes in southern Mesopotamia, were

imported into the scribal traditions of Ebla. The Ebla scribal schools then rearranged all of this foreign material by their own principles.

The Sumerian words were rearranged in a canonical list, and the Semitic Eblaite translation was added to the majority of the entries. These lists therefore are the oldest dictionaries. Additionally, all known words were grouped under their first syllabic cuneiform sign, for example, NIG-, KA-, SAG-. In this manner three large dictionaries of approximately 1,500 words were compiled, each duplicating the other, while another fifteen or so smaller tablets presented abstracts of the larger documents' contents.

Our understanding of Eblaite grammar is founded upon an analysis of the letters and decrees, the data provided by the lexical lists, and even the administrative accounts. The last, although brief, stereotypical, and often using formulaic Sumerian expressions, do provide us with several thousand Eblaite personal names for palace functionaries and consignees. These names, like those expressed in other ancient Semitic languages, are often "sentence names"; for example, Mi-ga-il = "Who is like [the god] Il?" The sentence names therefore provide additional data for Eblaite vocabulary, grammar, and even religion.

Classification

Taxonomies are usually hierarchical; that is, they assign priorities, or weigh some categories of attributes over others. In language classification, grammatical similarities, for instance, are usually considered more important than lexical (vocabulary) similarities. By commonly accepted criteria, therefore, the classification of Eblaite within the family of Semitic languages is not very surprising, especially when we consider the age of the Ebla tablets. Grammatically, Eblaite is closest to Old Akkadian, the Semitic language utilized by the Akkadian Dynasty in southern Mesopotamia which is documented just slightly later than Eblaite. Some grammatical forms, however, seem closer to Arabic and South Arabian. On the other hand, from the lexical point of view, an entire series of isoglosses links Eblaite to the western Semitic languages: Ugaritic, Hebrew, Aramaic. Eblaite words, for example, with west Semitic cognates include: *'arzatum* (cedar), *badalum* (merchant), *kinnarum* (lyre), and *urpum* (window).

Outside of Ebla, where was Eblaite spoken? An answer to this question rests within a study of the personal names for which the Ebla texts provide places of origin. These names cover a large portion of the ancient Near East, from the Mediterranean to the Persian Gulf. Specifically Eblaite names appear only in north-central Syria, around Hama, the plain of Antioch, Carchemish and Harran to the north, Emar on the Euphrates, and Kakmium, possibly in northeast Syria. "Mesopotamian"-type names appear at Mari, just above the present Syro-Iraqi border.

Religion and deities

Two sets of deities, overlapping only in part, comprised the Ebla pantheon. One set, the deities of the official cult, are listed in documents which record the sacrifices performed at the court. Another group, those of the popular cults, are known from the Eblaite personal names composed with the name of a god. Among these appear familiar west Semitic deities such as Baal, Damu, Lim, Malik ("king"), Rasap, Zikir ("remembrance"), and gods well known from the Mesopotamian culture area such as Ada, Ishtar, and Ishar ("the just one"). Il or El, common to all the ancient Semitic cultures, also appears, either as a proper divine name ("[the god] El") or as an appellative ("god").

Within the official cult the three principal deities were Kura (apparently not a Semitic name, it also appears in some personal names), the weather god Adad and the sun god Shamash. Baal does not appear in the official offering lists. The situation here then is quite different from that at second-millennium Ugarit where Baal, an epithet of Ada(d), is quite common. A fourth deity, mentioned almost as frequently as Kura, and probably also not Semitic, is Idakul. There are also many other Mesopotamian deities such as Ishtar, Ishara, and Dagan, and many other west Semitic deities such as Rasap (Ugaritic Rashap), Kasalu (Ugaritic Koshar), and Kamish (the first-millennium Moabite deity). Local deities included the deified Balikh River, and Adamma and Ashtappi, non-Semitic gods who also appear, a millennium later, within the Hurrian pantheon at Ugarit.

Kingdom of Ebla

City states dominated the cultivable plains of northwestern Syria, just as in southern Mesopotamia, during the third millennium B.C. It is not possible, however, to envisage an Eblaite "empire," for there were local rulers already at Hama, only 90 kilometers to the south, while to the west Eblaite territory stopped at the mountains which delimit the Syrian coastal region. The kingdom of Ebla certainly included the plain of Antioch to the north, but its northern border was probably marked by the foothills which today define the border between Syria and Turkey. Carchemish, on the Euphrates, apparently was Eblaite territory, but the Euphrates was certainly the kingdom's easternmost border in places, with some cities like Emar (modern Meskene) on the river's right bank and settlements in the Jabbul Plain maintaining their independence. The economic resources of the Eblaite kingdom, however, apparently allowed for the extension of its influence and interests through northern Syria as far as the Tigris River and southeast as far as the territory of Mari.

Ebla was ruled by a king, *malikum*, but the monarchy was not ordinarily hereditary; only with the last of the five kings known to us, Ibbi-Zikir, was the reign passed from father to son. A council of elders, representing major family groupings, assisted the sovereign and in some manner was integrated into the palace organization. This king-elders grouping was also recognized in international relations, as is shown by shipments of textiles sent from Ebla to other cities and addressed to both the king and elders.

Approximately fourteen higher-ranking functionaries bore the Sumerian title *lugal*, corresponding to the Semitic *šarrum*, and understood in Eblaite—in accordance with west Semitic usage—as "lord." Two of these functionaries served as judges (Sumerian $d\ i\ =\ k\ u_5$, perhaps Eblaite *dayyanum*). Two others apparently controlled important sectors of the palace organization, such as livestock raising.

Ebla's economic foundations were above all in extensive agriculture. Linen (from flax) was an important agricultural product, although the well-watered areas which flax requires were rather limited. Barley was the most prevalent cereal, with olive trees (for oil) and vineyards (for grapes, raisins, and wine) also cultivated. Sheep constituted a very important source of wealth. Flocks belonging to the king numbered more than 80,000, in addition to those belonging to outlying villages, a portion of which were presented to the palace. Apart from the wool derived from their annual shearing, an extremely large supply of meat was derived from the 12,000 sheep butchered every year at Ebla.

The majority of the Ebla tablets are the records of the textile industry. Warehouse inventories were kept on small tablets listing items of clothing in stock. One, for example, reads:

2,510 garments,
220 girdles of first quality
and 1,970 girdles of second quality
present in the wool warehouse.
110 cloaks: supplementary count.

Hundreds of larger, quadrangular tablets with approximately eleven columns per side list the items of clothing issued, unit by unit.

Apart from the state's highly productive sheep raising and textile manufacturing, Ebla's superior economic position was probably a function of its control of the supply routes bringing metals from the Anatolian plateau to the lowland plains of Syria. One result of this was the common presence at Ebla of full-tin bronzes, alloyed with the requisite 10 or 12 percent tin. Other, perhaps more dramatic, indications of the ancient city's wealth are the documents which record the total amounts of precious metals received each year. During the reign of the last king, Ibbi-Zikir, for instance, the quantities received averaged 1,000 pounds of silver and from 10 to 12 pounds of gold per annum. It is interesting that these metals were kept in the same "wool warehouse" which stored the city's textile products. A typical "cash account," for instance, reads, "Total: 580 pounds of silver issued; 430 pounds remain in the 'wool warehouse.' " Silver apparently was exchanged regularly for gold, which was then smelted into bars, as another example indicates: "25 pounds of silver in exchange for 7 pounds of gold, to make 26 bars of 16 shekels each." Gold and silver, however, were not only used as standard values but also as a means of exchange. The evidence for this is derived at present solely from the royal archives, but it leaves no doubt that the trade carried out with silver and gold "money" was not restricted to exchanges between palaces.

Bibliography

An international committee of cuneiform scholars assembled by Professor Paolo Matthiae, Rome, and the Directorate-General of Antiquities, Damascus, is supervising the publication of the Ebla texts by the Università di Roma in the series Archivi Reali di Ebla, Testi. The following volumes which present photographs, hand copies, transliterations, translations, and commentaries have already been published, or will soon be available:

I. Alfonso Archi. *Testi amministrativi: assegnazioni di tessuti (Archivio L. 2769)* (1984).

II. D. O. Edzard. *Verwaltungstexte verschiedenen Inhalts (aus dem Archiv L. 2769)* (1981).

III. A. Archi and M. G. Biga. *Testi amministrativi di vario contenuto (Archivio L. 2769 TM75.G.3000–4101)* (1982).

IV. M. G. Biga and L. Milano. *Testi amministrativi: assegnazioni di tessuti (Archivio L. 2769)* (1984).

V. D. O. Edzard. *Hymnen, Beschworungen und verwandtes (aus dem Archiv L. 2769)* (1984).

VI. A. Archi and P. Fronzaroli. *Bilingual, Sumerian/Eblaite Lexical Texts* (in preparation).

VII. A. Archi. *Administrative Texts: The Registration of Metals and Textiles* (in preparation).

VIII. E. Sollberger. *Administrative Texts Concerning Textiles* (in preparation).

In addition to these volumes, the series Studi Eblaiti (Università di Roma), edited by Paolo Matthiae and published in several annual issues, presents archaeological, philological, and historical analyses of materials from the excavations at Tell Mardikh.

Among the wealth of articles and books which have been published on the archives, the following ones in English may be singled out for their usefulness:

Alfonso Archi. "The Epigraphic Evidence from Ebla and the Old Testament." *Biblica* 60 (1979) 556–566 / "Further Concerning Ebla and the Bible." *BiblArch* 44 (1981) 145–154.

Robert D. Biggs. "Ebla and Abu Salabikh: The Linguistic and Literary Aspects." In L. Cagni (ed.). *La Lingua di Ebla* (Naples: Istituto Universitario Orientale 1981), pp. 121–133.

P. Fronzaroli. *The Ebla Language and Semitic Linguistics* (Florence: Istituto di Linguistica, 1984).

I. J. Gelb. "Ebla and the Kish Civilization." In L. Cagni (ed.). *La Lingua di Ebla* (Naples: Istituto Universitario Orientale, 1981), pp. 9–73.

Lorenzo Vigano. "The Ebla Tablets: Literary Sources for the History of Palestine and Syria." *BiblArch* 47/1 (1984) 6–16.

48, right

frieze and arranged the pieces using the Standard of Ur (mentioned in Cat. No. 49) as a model. The pieces were found in one of the rooms in the Temple of Dagan, god of agriculture. The three registers of the frieze depict religious scenes. In the top register we see a procession of priests approaching a libation vessel on a tall stand. Some of them carry small vessels, cups, bowls, and a libation jug. Pottery of this sort is known from contemporary archaeological assemblages. The other priests have their hands crossed over their chests in a traditional gesture of worship.

In the middle register (not illustrated) are women who, judging from their outstretched arms, probably originally carried similar vessels. One of them holds a libation vessel like the one in the upper register. The central scene is fragmentary and uncertain: at the back there is a bench with animal feet over which two women are draping a throw with tassels, possibly made of fur. In front of the bench, partly obscured by the feet of the women are three stands for libation vessels, or possibly three standards.

The right side of the lower register (not illustrated) also depicts a religious scene. A female worshiper is bringing votive gifts, and various objects are being carried in procession. In the left corner, however, there is a group of (originally) two pairs of women, one standing and one sitting on a stool engaged in a domestic activity, namely spinning wool.

The males in this mosaic inlay wear long fringed robes which are held together with a tie at the waist. The women wear fringed ankle-length garments and shawls. We find similar costumes and headdresses in sculpture from Mari.

K.K

51
Cylinder seal

Site: Mari (Tell Hariri), Temple of Ishtar, level c
Date: Early Dynastic period, ca. 2500 B.C.
Material: White stone
Height: 4.3 cm; *diameter:* 3.4 cm
Museum No.: Aleppo 6297 (M. 1080)
Literature: A. Parrot *MAM* I (1956) 190, Plate LXV

The three examples of cylinder seals from the Early Dynastic period shown in Cat. Nos. 51–53 all have bands of animal figures, wild or domestic, always standing upright either on their hindlegs or forelegs,

51

along with naked heroes and bull-men. The figures are either closely grouped together or crossed to form a harmoniously designed band. On the seal in Cat. No. 51 there are two such bands divided by a horizontal line. Groups of naked heroes and bull-men grasp the heads, tails, or legs of goats, lions, or bulls. In the upper register they are all connected by the crossed animal bodies, while in the lower register they hold onto each other. The individual figures are quite crudely rendered. Next to a salamander are three cuneiform signs in a frame. The Sumerian inscription reads: *šita dumu-nun,* " 'Incantation' of a child-deity Dumu-Nun" (after M. Lambert).

K.K.

52
Cylinder seal

Site: Mari (Tell Hariri), Treasure of Ur
Date: Late Early Dynastic period, ca. 2500 B.C.
Material: Sea-snail shell
Height: 4.3 cm; *diameter:* 2.7 cm
Museum No.: Damascus S 2410 (M.4441)
Literature: A. Parrot *MAM* IV (1968) 35, Fig. 22, Plate XVIII // A. Moortgat and U. Moortgat-Correns *Iraq* 36 (1974) 155 // H. Kühne *Das Rollsiegel in Syrien* (1980) 47

Like Cat. Nos. 51 and 53 this seal shows very clear traces of the tools used in carving the design. The tails of the animals end in a row of crudely drilled indentations; the feet and ankles are similarly rendered. The bodies were also pre-drilled but were carved carefully afterward, as were the fine lines.

The scene shows a lioness, a lion, a goat, and a human-headed bull (cf. Cat. No. 76 on p. 177) in contest. A naked hero attacks the group from one side, a bull-man from the other.

This seal and the following one are made from the core of the shell of a large sea snail such as a whelk or a triton. To drill a bore through such a shell would likely have damaged it, but in any case the shell's natural central hollow is wide enough for a string to be threaded through so that the seal could be worn around the neck.

K.K.

53
Cylinder seal

Site: Mari (Tell Hariri), Treasure of Ur
Date: Late Early Dynastic period, ca. 2500 B.C.
Material: Sea-snail shell
Height: 5.1 cm; *diameter:* 3.0 cm
Museum No.: Damascus S 2411 (M. 4440)
Literature: A. Parrot *MAM* IV (1968) 33, Fig. 21, Plate
    XVIII // A. Moortgat and U. Moortgat-Correns *Iraq* 36
    (1974) 155 // H. Kühne *Das Rollsiegel in Syrien* (1980) 48

This seal has two registers, the lower one showing a row of figures similar to Cat. No. 51. In the center of a symmetrical composition stands a naked hero grasping two antelopes being attacked by lions, which are in turn being attacked by bull-men who wield long daggers. There is also a group of three figures: a naked hero and a deer being attacked by a lion. Finally we see a male figure dressed in a knee-length robe who is carrying a sacrifical animal, either a sheep or a goat.

The upper register shows a banquet scene, a motif

52/53

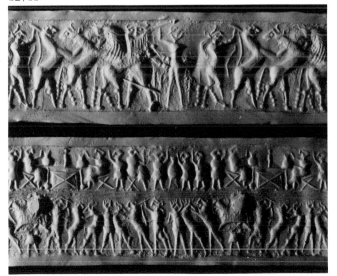

which was very popular in Early Dynastic times. Two seated figures holding fat-bellied drinking jugs face each other across a table with a staff. This motif, which may be presumed to have religious significance, is here elaborated by a servant standing behind with one arm raised. Behind the servant is a seated figure watching three figures in short robes raising one hand toward a large jar.

K.K.

54
Necklace
See color plate p. 13

Site: Mari (Tell Hariri), Treasure of Ur
Date: Late Early Dynastic period, ca. 2500 B.C.
Material: Lapis lazuli, carnelian
Length of longest bead: 9.2 cm
Museum No.: Damascus S 2407 (M. 4430/4432/4434)
Literature: A. Parrot *MAM* IV (1968) 31 Plate XVII 2 //
    A. Moortgat and U. Moortgat-Correns *Iraq* 36 (1974) 162

This necklace of round, grooved lapis lazuli beads and elongated, double-conical beads of carnelian has been restrung in modern times. Similar beads were found at the sites of Kish, Tell Asmar, and Ur in southern Mesopotamia. Neither lapis lazuli nor carnelian, both highly prized in the ancient Near East, occurs in Syria or Mesopotamia. Both stones had to be imported from far away, mainly from Badakshan in northern Afghanistan, where there are large deposits of high-quality lapis lazuli in the Sar-i-Sang and Koksha valleys. Lapis lazuli from the Koksha mines has the same property as that found in Sistan (east Iran) at the site of Shahr-i-Sokhta, a settlement which flourished and grew wealthy by processing and trading lapis lazuli, carnelian, and turquoise. In the Shahr-i-Sokhta workshops the imported blocks of lapis lazuli were purified of their calcite and pyrite content, a process which reduced the weight by as much as 60 percent. The refined lapis lazuli was then ready for further shipment. Archaeological evidence shows that some of the purified stone was made into beads at this site: remains from bead production were found, such as flint drills, half-finished beads, with and without bores, partly polished and finished beads.

In addition to this southern trade route through Iran to Mesopotamia, bead workshops at Tepe Hissar in northern Iran indicate that a northern route existed as well. In Afghanistan carnelian also occurs in large de-

posits. It was transported along the same trade routes as lapis lazuli but apparently not fashioned into beads until it reached Mesopotamia proper, where workshops have been found at the Early Dynastic site of Diqdiqqa near Ur and at Uruk. It is not known whether trade existed between Syria and the areas around the Red Sea where carnelian deposits also occur.
K.K.

55
Lion-headed eagle
See color plate p. 14

Site: Mari (Tell Hariri), Treasure of Ur
Date: Late Early Dynastic period, ca. 2500 B.C.
Material: Lapis lazuli, gold, bitumen, copper
Height: 12.8 cm; *width:* 11.8 cm
Museum No: Damascus S 2399 (M. 4405)
Literature: A. Parrot *MAM* IV (1968) 22, frontispiece, Fig. 16, Plates IX, X // A. Moortgat and U. Moortgat-Correns *Iraq* 36 (1974) 158 // J. Boese in *Propyläen Kunstgeschichte* 14, 211, Fig. 122a // Tokyo Exhibition No. 55

This small sculpture of an eagle with the head of a lion is one of the most valuable items from the Treasure of Ur, found in a temple in the late Early Dynastic palace at Mari. The exact mythical powers of this animal have yet to be understood. In Sumerian it was called Anzu and was the symbol of the god Ningirsu, whose main temple was in the city of Lagash in southern Mesopotamia.

We are not exactly sure what function our small figure had; the excavator, André Parrot, thought it might have been a pendant. Three drilled holes in the wings and the body and a fourth at the back of the neck may have served for attachment. The outline of the body and the wings are incised in flat lapis lazuli; the body itself is decorated in a schematic yet ornamental herringbone and fish-scale pattern. The head and the tail feathers, attached to the body with copper wire, are fashioned in bitumen covered with gold leaf. Such details as the whiskers and the feathers are very carefully rendered. The eye sockets are filled with bitumen but may once have had inlays of semi-precious stone. The best comparison is an Anzu pendant (now in Baghdad) found in an Early Dynastic context at Tell Asmar on the Diyala River. Its body is also carved in lapis lazuli, while the head, tail, and wing tips are made of silver foil.
K.K.

56
Inscribed bead
See color plate p. 14

Site: Mari (Tell Hariri), Treasure of Ur
Date: Late Early Dynastic period, ca. 2500 B.C.
Material: Lapis lazuli
Length: 11.8 cm
Museum No.: Damascus S 2409 (M.4439)
Literature: A. Parrot *MAM* IV (1968) 44 Fig. 35, 37, Plates XXI, XXII // G. Dossin *ibid.* 53 // W. von Soden *OLZ* 66 (1971) 141 // J. Boese *ZA* 68 (1978) 6

This faceted oblong bead has an engraved inscription mentioning Mesannepada, king of the First Dynasty of Ur. Unfortunately, it is very worn and therefore invites a number of reconstructions and interpretations. The first two epigraphers working on the text came to opposite conclusions as to the origin of the entire Treasure of Ur. One agreed with the excavator that it was a gift from Mesannepada to his fellow ruler at Mari. The other thought that it was a gift intended for Ur from the ruler at Mari. A third scholar later suggested that it might have been a wedding gift or dowry for a princess who came to Mari from Ur. Most of the contents of the treasure were produced in northern or central Mesopotamia, very likely at Mari.

According to a new interpretation, the traces of cuneiform signs read: "to the god An, King [of the land?] Mesannepada, King of Ur, son of Meskalamdu(g), King of [Kish?], has dedicated (this object)." An was the highest deity in the Sumerian pantheon, father of both Enlil and Inanna. If the new reading is correct, an important chronological link can be established between the earliest known king of the First Dynasty of Ur and a ruler, buried at the Royal Cemetery at Ur, whose name is mentioned on a cylinder seal.
K.K

57
Standing figure of a goddess
See color plate p. 13

Site: Mari (Tell Hariri), Treasure of Ur
Date: Late Early Dynastic period, ca. 2500 B.C.
Material: Copper, lapis lazuli, electrum
Height: 11.3 cm; *width:* 3.2 cm; *depth:* 3.0 cm
Museum No.: Damascus S 2366 (M. 4403)
Literature: A. Parrot *MAM* IV (1968) 16, Figs. 7, 8, Plates IV–VI // A. Moortgat and U. Moortgat-Correns *Iraq* 36 (1974) 155 // D.P. Hansen *Propyläen Kunstgeschichte* 14,

170, Fig. 396 // Spycket *La Statuaire* 80 // Tokyo
Exhibition No. 56

Aside from two female statuettes carved in ivory, the
Treasure of Ur contained this small figurine of a naked
female made of solid copper. The two small bull horns
decorating her head indicate that she was a goddess.
Throughout this exhibit and catalogue we will see examples of such horns indicating divinity (e.g., Cat.
No. 90, the water goddess from Mari; Cat. No. 170,
the god from Arslantash). The feet of this highly stylized goddess were originally attached to a stand or
base. Her face is dominated by large wide-open eyes;
the angular shoulders and wide hips contrast with the
narrow waist and slender legs. She stretches her bent
arms forward; the remains of wire in the closed hands
indicate that she held objects, perhaps snakes, which
are now lost. On her hair are traces of electrum, glued
on with bitumen; the headband is also electrum. Her
pierced ears had earrings, now lost. The eyes are inlaid with a white material and lapis lazuli.

Covering less precious material with a thin layer of
precious metal is a technique often used on Middle
Syrian statuettes (see Cat. No. 133), but we also find
the technique employed on Early Dynastic votive reliefs at Mari (Cat. No. 70). There is no convincing
comparison piece. Probably this statuette originated in
a northern Syrian workshop.

K.K.

Figure 39
Shell inlay figure of a woman
wearing a stick pin, from
Mari (see Cat. No. 58).

Many similar pins were found in the Early Dynastic
Royal Cemetry at Ur. We also find it depicted in contemporary shell inlays from Mari (see Fig. 39), where
it is shown holding a shawl together. From the eye of
the pin hang threaded beads and possibly a cylinder
seal.

K.K.

58
Stick pin

Site: Mari, Zimri-Lim Palace, room 65
Date: Early Dynastic period, 2900–2500 B.C.
Material: Gold or electrum
Length: 9.6 cm; *weight:* 17 g
Museum No.: Aleppo 1657 (M. 790)
Literature: A. Parrot *MAM* II, 3 (1959) 94, Fig. 69, Plate
  XXXIII 790

This garment stick pin was found in the throne room
of the Zimri-Lim Palace. The excavator assumed
rightly that it originated in a much earlier period—the
Early Dynastic—and that it was used much later, like
antique jewelry is today. The pin has a mushroom-
shaped head. It was cast in a mold, then hammered
and pierced, and finally the upper part of the pin was
bent at a right angle.

59
Stick pin

Site: Mari (Tell Hariri), Treasure of Ur
Date: Late Early Dynastic period, ca. 2500 B.C.
Material: Gold, silver
Length: 12.5 cm
Museum No.: Damascus S 2395 (M. 4428)
Literature: A. Parrot *MAM* IV (1968) 27, Fig. 20, Plate XIII

Since the gold coating covers the silver core in a thick
seamless layer, we may assume that this is an example
of double casting. In this process the upper part of a
cast or hammered silver pin was first covered with a
heavy layer of wax, in which the details and the head
of the pin were modelled. Then the wax-coated part of
the pin was covered with a clay mold with small drain
channels, so that the wax could be melted out and the
gold poured in. The gold surface was cleaned of im-

perfections and polished, the traces of the drain channels were removed, and the pin pierced. Inlay figures from Mari show women with such stick pins, either worn in crossed pairs or fastened individually (see Cat. No. 50).

K.K.

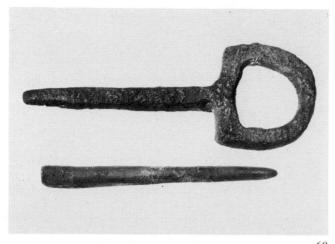

60
Foundation deposit: clevis (D-shaped ring bolt) with peg

Site: Mari (Tell Hariri), Temple of Ishtar, level a, southeast corner of cella 17
Date: Late Early Dynastic period, ca. 2600–2350 B.C.
Material: Leaded bronze
Length of clevis: 42.3 cm; *length of peg:* 33.5 cm
Museum Nos.: Aleppo 6846 (M. 1381), 6849
Literature: A. Parrot *MAM* I (1956) 51, Plate XXIV / *Mari* 52 // R. S. Ellis *Foundation Deposits in Ancient Mesopotamia* (New Haven 1968) 47

Foundation deposits included all kinds of objects buried in the bases of public buildings, usually temples. The objects were often placed in corners, doorways, or tower gates during foundation ceremonies. The range of objects is quite extensive: figures of humans or animals with a spike-shaped lower end, clevises with matching pegs (as in this example), inscribed or uninscribed bricks and tablets, as well as beads, shells, and small stone and metal objects. Often there

would be remains of animal bones from a sacrifice near such deposits.

The deposit here was found in level a of the Temple of Ishtar together with two tablets, one of lapis lazuli, the other of gypsum. The clevis, which was hammered into the corner of the building with its round pointed peg thrust down vertically through the fitting, illustrates the builders' belief in the magical fortification of the structure. Both metal parts were sloppily cast with many air bubbles. They are not made of pure copper but of an alloy of lead and copper, so-called leaded bronze. Similar foundation deposits were found in the temples of Dagan, Ninhursag, Shamash, and in the *"massif rouge"* at Mari.

K.K.

61
Votive statue
See color plate p. 2

Site: Mari (Tell Hariri), Temple of Ishtarat
Date: Late Early Dynastic period, ca. 2600–2350 B.C.
Material: Gypsum, steatite
Height: 114 cm; *width of base:* 36 cm
Museum No.: Damascus S 2061 (M. 2300/2323)
Literature: A. Parrot *Syria* 30 (1953) 208, Plates XXI, XXII / *MAM* III (1967) 37, Figs. 31–36, Plates XII, XIII // Strommenger and Hirmer *Mesopotamien* 70 Figs. 90, 91 // Braun-Holzinger *Beterstatuetten* 51 (Stiltufe II) // Spycket *La Statuaire* 86

"Iku(n)-Shamagan, king of Mari, Shibum, the surveyor of land, dedicated this statue to Ninni-zaza." The donor appears facing his god, bald with large inlaid eyes, a long wavy beard, arms folded over his naked chest. Several scholars have suggested that this statue is a representation of King Iku(n)-Shamagan himself, mainly because of the unusual size of the sculpture. But the inscription on the right shoulder is ambiguous, and the statue more likely depicts a certain "land surveyor" by the name of Shibum. From a later text we know that this title might belong to the second highest office within the state hierarchy.

We call such sculptures votive statues because they are often found in temples, with a dedicatory inscription, praying for long life for the donor as well as his ruler. They might have been positioned in rows on the benches found in many temples at Mari. Such statues were found in large numbers in the Diyala region of Iraq. Examples are also known from Susa and Ashur in Mesopotamia as well as Tell Chuera in northern Syria. The great weight of the statue may explain the rather clumsy rendering of the body. At first glance, this figure seems rather impersonal; yet it does present some individual traits, such as folds of fat at the back of the neck.

The so-called *kaunakes* garment which this figure is wearing is typical of late Early Dynastic statuary (see also Cat. Nos. 62–66). It seems to have been styled from a woven material which was tufted and/or tasseled to resemble a sheep's fleece.

K.K.

62
Votive statue of Lamgi-Mari

Site: Mari (Tell Hariri), Temple of Ishtar, level a, courtyard 20
Period: Late Early Dynastic period, ca. 2600–2350 B.C.
Material: White stone
Weight: 27.7 cm; *base:* 10.3 × 8.6 cm
Museum No.: Aleppo 1486 (M. 174)
Literature: A. Parrot *MAM* I (1956) 68, Fig. 46, Plates XXV, XXVI // Strommenger and Hirmer *Mesopotamien* 70, Fig. 100 // D.P. Hansen *Propyläen Kunstgeschichte* 14, 167, Fig. 30 // Braun-Holzinger *Beterstatuetten* 57 // Spycket *La Statuaire* 88 // Tokyo Exhibition No. 51

This small statue bears an inscription on the upper arm, shoulder, and part of the back: "Lamgi-Mari, king of Mari, chief *ensi* of Enlil, his statue, to Inanna-uš, has dedicated." Lamgi-Mari was chief *ensi* (high priest) for Enlil, the highest Sumerian god, whose main temple was at Nippur.

Lamgi-Mari's gesture of worship is slightly different from the previous statue of Shibum in Cat. No. 61; here the worshiper holds his right wrist with his left hand. He is wearing a wrap-around garment which covers the left shoulder and encloses the arm on the chest, thereby restricting movement considerably. This type of garment was worn only on ceremonial occasions. Both Shibum and Lamgi-Mari wear garments of tufted material. Around the crown of the head he wears a braided headband, tied at the back with a complicated knot. The hair style is similar to that of the golden headdress found at the Royal Cemetery at Ur. The left side of the statue was repaired in antiquity.

K.K.

ca. 3000–2100 B.C.

63
Female statuette

Site: Mari (Tell Hariri), Temple of Ishtar, level a
Date: Late Early Dynastic period, 2600–2350 B.C.
Material: Alabaster
Height: 22.5 cm; *width:* 6.5 cm
Museum No.: Aleppo 1496 (M. 172)
Literature: A. Parrot *Syria* 16 (1935) 27, Plate X1 / *MAM* I
　　(1956) 84, Plate XXXVI // Strommenger and Hirmer
　　Mesopotamien 71, Fig. 109 // Braun-Holzinger
　　Beterstatuetten 60 // Spycket *La Statuaire* 111

This small statue wears the female polos headdress
common at Mari and a capelike robe draped over the
shoulder. The polos may have been a stiff construction
covered with material, or possibly a hat made of such
a material as heavy felt. It has a rolled-up brim. The
hair is covered with a scarf from which a few escaping
strands frame the face; the strands may have had inlays of colored stone. The eye sockets are inlaid with
shell which held the now-lost pupils. The eyes and the
eyebrows may have had inlays of steatite or lapis
lazuli. The ears are pierced for earrings, probably of
precious metal. The robe, which leaves the right arm
and shoulder uncovered, was worn by females at religious ceremonies.
K.K.

64
Seated female

Site: Mari (Tell Hariri), Temple of Ishtar
Date: Late Early Dynastic period, 2600–2350 B.C.
Material: Gypsum
Total height: 34.4 cm; *throne:* 14.0 × 10.2 × 13.5 cm
Museum No.: Damascus S 2072 (M. 2308/ 2368/ 2383)
Literature: A. Parrot *MAM* III (1967) 96, Figs. 134, 135,
　　Plates XLVIII–L // Strommenger and Hirmer
　　Mesopotamien 70, Fig. 95 left // Braun-Holzinger
　　Beterstatuetten 60 (Stilstufe III) // Spycket *La Statuaire*
　　111

Seated on a throne, this woman has a large shawl
draped over her polos and shoulders. Both the shawl
and her robe are made of tufted material described in
Cat. No. 61. The nose and right cheek are slightly
damaged, but details missing in Cat. No. 63—the lapis
lazuli inlaid strands of hair framing the face—are preserved. The upper body and part of the robe as well as
the cube-shaped throne are heavily damaged. The

sides of the throne are carved in relief showing a woodwork design. The feet are rendered naturalistically.

K.K.

65
Seated couple

Site: Mari (Tell Hariri), Temple of Ishtar, level a, cella 17
Date: Late Early Dynastic period, 2600–2350 B.C.
Material: Gypsum
Height: 12.8 cm; *width:* 10.8 cm; *depth:* 8.9 cm
Museum No.: Aleppo 1502 (M. 303)
Literature: A. Parrot *MAM* I (1956) 102, Fig. 65, Plate XLII // Strommenger and Hirmer *Mesopotamien* 70, Fig. 94 // Spycket *La Statuaire* 119

Sitting close together on a bench, this couple embraces lovingly. With his left hand the male figure holds the right wrist of his companion in his lap. Unfortunately, both heads are broken off and the upper bodies are worn by cleaning. Both figures wear clothing made of tufted material: the male wears a wrap-around garment tied at the waist, the female a robe draped over her shoulder. Four holes drilled under the bottom of the sculpture indicate that it originally was mounted, possibly with feet, on a base. Statues of couples are rare. There are a few Early Dynastic examples from the Diyala region and from Nippur.

K.K.

66
Seated figure of the singer Ur-Nanshe
See color plate p. 176

Site: Mari (Tell Hariri), Temple of Ninni-zaza, room 13
Date: Late Early Dynastic period, 2600–2350 B.C.
Material: Gypsum
Height: 26 cm; *diameter of cushion:* 11.6 cm
Museum No.: Damascus S 2071 (M. 2416/2365)
Literature: A. Parrot *Syria* 30 (1953) 209, Plate XXIII / *MAM* III (1967) 88, Figs. 127–31, Plates XLV–XLVI, frontispiece // Strommenger and Hirmer *Mesopotamien* 70, Figs. 92–93, Plate XXI // D.P. Hansen *Propyläen Kunstgeschichte* 14, 165, Fig. 24 // Braun-Holzinger *Beterstatuetten* 59 // Spycket *La Statuaire* 92 // Tokyo Exhibition No. 47

This sculpture of a seated musician is one of the most splendid works of art created by the Mari sculptors. "Iblul-il, king of Mari: Ur-Nanshe, the chief singer,

65, left

dedicated this statue to N[inni-zaz]a" is the inscription on the shoulder. The divine name is damaged, and the meaning of the inscription is open to discussion.

The musicians of Mari were famous. Contemporary tablets from Ebla often mention "great" or "lesser" singers from Mari who served at Ebla. They are also mentioned in the Old Syrian period when the Assyrian ruler Shamsi-Adad asked his son to send singers from Mari to the king of Carchemish. From this period and from the time of the Third Dynasty of Ur we have texts describing the duties of a singer, who had to be able to play various stringed instruments as well as drums. First and foremost he served the palace and the temple, praising in song the gods and the king.

Ur-Nanshe is seated cross-legged on a low round cushion, with his tufted robe pulled over his knees. The arms and a support at the chest are lost. A fragment of the upper body of a similar statue holding a stringed instrument was found in the same room; the arms were held up by supports from the lower part of the body. The eye inlays of shell and lapis lazuli are preserved, while the inlays for the eyebrows have been lost. The long hair is dyed black, parted in the middle, and pushed back behind the ears. The wavy hair hangs down the back in long strands ending in curls.

The ruler Iblul-il, who is known from other dedicatory inscriptions at Mari, was the unlucky opponent of Enna-Dagan, a general from Ebla. Iblul-il also ruled the town of Abarsal, which is mentioned on the tablet shown in Cat. No. 80 as engaging in trade with Ebla.

K.K.

67
Head of male figure

Site: Mari (Tell Hariri), Temple of Ninni-zaza, room 19
Date: Late Early Dynastic period, 2600–2350 B.C.
Material: Pink breccia
Height: 8.5 cm; *width:* 6.2 cm; *depth:* 7.3 cm
Museum No.: Damascus S 2051 (M. 3046)
Literature: A. Parrot *MAM* III (1967) 99, Fig. 138, Plate LIII // Braun-Holzinger *Beterstatuetten* 60

The face of this small head is very lifelike with softly modelled transitions between the individual features. The hair is parted in the middle and pulled forward around the ears. The wide eyelids, the rounded eyeballs, and the broad, bent nose lend distinction to the features.

K.K.

67

69

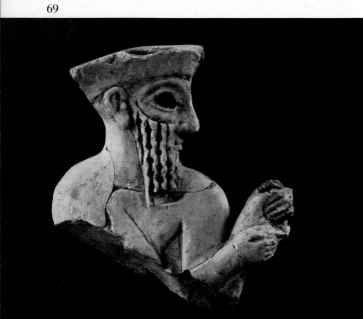

68
Face of a composite figure

Site: Mari (Tell Hariri), *"massif rouge"* temple, northwest side
Date: Late Early Dynastic period, 2600–2350 B.C.
Material: White marble, mother-of-pearl, lapis lazuli
Height: 3.5 cm
Museum No.: Damascus S 2366 (M. 2010)
Literature: A. Parrot *Syria* 29 (1952) 196, Plate XX 2–3 / *Mari* 73, Fig. XI

Figurines assembled from different colored materials were quite popular in the late Uruk and the Early Dynastic periods. Famous examples from southern Mesopotamia of such composite figures are a female head found at Uruk together with various animal figurines, and an Early Dynastic female statuette with a gold foil face found at Nippur (both now in Baghdad).

In this case only the face is preserved. The eyes are inlaid with shell and lapis lazuli, the eyebrows with lapis lazuli; the right eyebrow and the left pupil are lost. A serrated edge ends the upper part of the face, where the hair might have been attached.
K.K.

69
Inlay figure

Site: Mari (Tell Hariri), Presargonic Palace
Date: Early Dynastic (I–II) period, 2900–2600 B.C.
Material: Gypsum
Height: 7.7 cm; *thickness:* 3 cm
Museum No.: Damascus S 2501 (M. 4694)
Literature: A. Parrot *Syria* 44 (1967) 21, Plate IV 2 / *Mari* 58, Fig. 29

Only a triangular piece of the upper body, the bearded face, and the flat conical cap remain of this inlay figure. We can date this piece to the beginning of the Early Dynastic period because of the conical cap and the beard, which is separated into strands rather than rendered in wavy lines as was the fashion at the time of Iku(n)-Shamagan (cf. Cat. No. 61).

The figure has outstretched hands with a vertical bore indicating that originally he held a staff or a standard like the figurines we have seen depicted in shell inlays from Mari. Only the front surface of the figurine is carefully worked; toward the back it narrows and the traces of cutting and carving tools remain, since this area would have been covered by other materials.

68, right

Remnants of black paint in the beard are preserved, the inlay of the eyes lost. A technically similar inlaid frieze from Kish, in southern Mesopotamia,[1] has limestone figurines set off by slate.

K.K.

[1]S. Langdon *Excavations at Kish I, 1923–24* (1924) 59 // D.P. Hansen *Propyläen Kunstgeschichte* 14, 190, Fig. 92b

70
Fragment of relief

Site: Mari (Tell Hariri), Presargonic Palace
Date: Late Early Dynastic period, 2600–2350 B.C.
Material: Gypsum
Height: 11.6 cm; *width:* 6.3 cm; *maximum thickness:* 1.7 cm
Museum No.: Damascus S 2380 (M. 4393/M. 4454)
Literature: A. Parrot *Syria* 42 (1965) 215, Plate IV 2 / *Mari* 57, Fig. 28a // J. Boese "Altmesopotamische Weihplatten" *UAVA* 6 (1971) 90, Plates XXVI–XXVII

This relief was divided into small squares framed by ridges, each square worked into a carefully balanced symmetrical scene. The upper square shows a naked hero with a long beard and side curls, a figure often depicted in ancient Near Eastern art in animal contest scenes. Here he grasps two human-headed bulls standing on their hind legs (cf. the color plate of Cat. No. 76 on p. 177). We have already seen this popular motif on an Early Dynastic cylinder seal (Cat. No. 52). In the lower register a lion-headed eagle, called Anzu (see Cat. No. 55 on p. 14) sinks his claws into two reclining ibexes.

Our piece, put together from four adjacent fragments, was probably originally the lower left corner of a larger relief with nine squares. A few other fragments found nearby corroborate this suggestion, since these fragments have similar motifs (Anzu, animal contests). If this assumption is correct, the complete relief (see reconstruction, Fig. 40) may be compared to the temple-dedicated votive reliefs of Early Dynastic southern Mesopotamia. Like the statues of worshipers (Cat. Nos. 61–66) such reliefs were meant to protect the donor's welfare. The middle register was left blank, so that the relief could be fastened to the temple wall. Faint traces indicate that the relief was covered with silver.

K.K.

Figure 40
Reconstruction of gypsum relief plaque, Cat. No. 70.

foreign origin, since pottery of the same shape was produced both at Mari and in Mesopotamia at the time, the fragments of a vessel shown in Cat. No. 72 make it perfectly clear that these were not locally produced.

A few years ago in excavations in southern Iran, 225 kilometers south of Kirman, workshops were found near natural deposits of steatite. Like the case of the lapis lazuli workshops discussed in Cat. No. 54, pieces from various stages of production were found there. The export market must have been vast: besides Iran it included all of Mesopotamia as well as regions on the Persian Gulf.

K.K.

71

71
Vessel with carved relief

Site: Mari (Tell Hariri), Temple of Ishtar, level a, courtyard 20
Date: Early Dynastic period, 2900–2500 B.C.
Material: Steatite
Greatest height after restoration: 26.2 cm
Museum No.: Aleppo 1509 (M. 185)
Literature: A. Parrot *MAM* I (1956) 116, Plate XLVIII //
Tokyo Exhibition No. 60

This jar was found in the Temple of Ishtar near one of the most important Early Dynastic sculptures from Mari, the statue of Ebih-Il (now in the Louvre). Only the bottom of the jar has been restored.

The jar from the shoulder to the center is decorated with two wavy, interwoven bands of carved relief. We see these parallel bands as purely decorative snake bodies winding their endless way around the vessel. In antiquity the indentations were decorated with inlays of shell, red or green stone, or paste. Such vessels did not originate in Syria or Mesopotamia. Even though it would be difficult to immediately recognize this jar's

72a

plant. His shaved bald head is distinguished by a large protruding nose, characteristic for this type of decorated vessel. A palm trunk separates him from a scene depicting three goats with curved horns, one above the other. On the other fragment (72b) we recognize a similar horned goat, probably standing on its hind legs eating leaves off a tree.

K.K.

73
Wig for a composite figure

Site: Ebla (Tell Mardikh), Royal Palace G
Date: Late Early Dynastic to early Akkadian period, 2400–2300 B.C.
Material: Dark gray-green stone
Height: 30.3 cm; *width:* 14.5 cm
Museum Nos.: Aleppo TM. 76. G. 433 a–c/TM. 77. G. 116 + 155 + 175 + 184 a–c/TM. 78 G. 178 + 221
Literature: P. Matthiae *Akkadica* 17 (1980) 43, Fig. 5 / *JNES* 39 (1980) 249, Figs. 3–5, 13–15

72b

72
Fragments of a vessel with carved relief

Site: Mari (Tell Hariri), Temple of Shamash
Date: Early Dynastic period, 2900–2500 B.C.
Material: Steatite
Dimensions: (a) 20 × 20 × 2.0–3.4 cm; (b) 19.7 × 11.5 × 1.0–1.6 cm
Museum Nos.: Damascus S 2058 (a) M. 2226; (b) M. 2151/M. 2182
Literature: A. Parrot *Syria* 30 (1975) 204, Fig. 4 / *Mari* 39, Fig. 11 // Strommenger and Hirmer *Mesopotamien* 59, Fig. 39 bottom // Tokyo Exhibition No. 62

The two fragments of the sides of a vessel enable us to reconstruct the shape of the jar, that of a truncated cone. The outer surface was decorated with two friezes carved in relief. The larger fragment, No. 72a, has bands of wavy lines on either side of a wide guilloche. Above this is a kneeling male figure, dressed in a horizontally striped garment, tending a

This wig of stone, assembled from ten parts, was intended for a statue or a head that was almost life-size. Drilled holes on the inside once had metal nails or wooden pegs with which it was fastened to a head, presumably of wood. The ends of the separately worked strands of hair were attached to the back of the statue in a similar fashion. The pieces of the wig (only a few pieces are missing) were glued together with bitumen. The face was framed by a semi-circle of the waved and incised strands of hair. Fragments of two additional heads were found in Palace G but no body fragments, leading the excavator to suggest that such wigs may have belonged to heads or possibly busts rather than to complete statues.

K.K.

74
Headdress for a composite figure

Site: Ebla (Tell Mardikh), Royal Palace G, L. 2764
Date: Late Early Dynastic to early Akkadian period, ca.
　2400–2300 B.C.
Material: Beige limestone
Height: 1.7 cm; *width:* 3.2 cm; *greatest diameter:* 3.5 cm
Museum No.: Aleppo TM. 76. G. 830
Literature: Matthiae *Ebla* 78, Fig. 36 / *SEb* I/2 (1979) 20, Fig.
　4 a–d

75
Miniature head

Site: Ebla (Tell Mardikh), Royal Palace G, L. 2913
Date: Late Early Dynastic to early Akkadian period,
　2400–2300 B.C.
Material: Beige limestone
Height: 3.0 cm; *width:* 2.3 cm; *depth:* 1.8 cm
Museum No.: Aleppo TM. 77. G. 220
Literature: P. Matthiae *Académie des inscriptions et belles-
　lettres, Comptes rendues* (1978) 227, Fig. 18 / *JNES* 39
　(1980) 264, Fig. 16

Both of these pieces formed parts of composite figures. The small beardless head is flattened on the back. Details on the forehead and in front of the ears, where a wig and the separate strands of hair were once attached, still show traces of bitumen. The deeply carved eye-sockets and eyebrows were once inlaid.

The headdress of Cat. No. 74 may be a representation of a cap made of fur, as the design seems to indicate. A thick braided brim goes all around the cap,

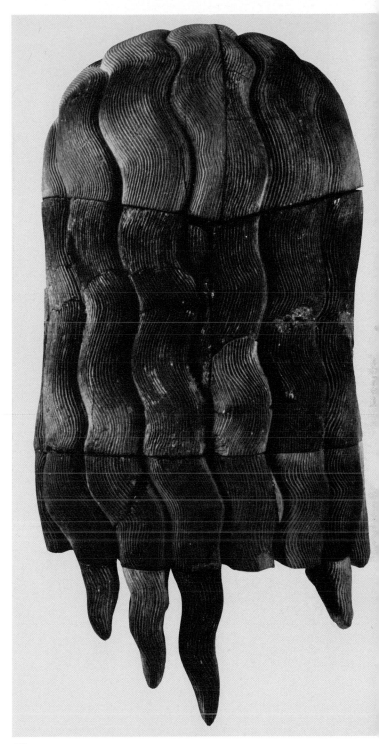

73

74

76
Figure of a human-headed bull
See color plate p. 177

Site: Ebla (Tell Mardikh), Royal Palace G, L. 2764
Date: Late Early Dynastic to early Akkadian period, ca.
2400–2300 B.C.
Height: 4.2 cm; *length:* 5 cm; *depth:* 1.8 cm
Museum No.: Alleppo TM. 76. G. 850
Literature: Matthiae *Ebla* 76, Fig. 28

A wooden core covered with gold foil forms the body
of this small human-headed bull. The head is turned
at a right angle to the body, looking straight at the observer. The hair is inlaid steatite, carefully worked in
wavy strands ending in two rows of curls. The eyes
were originally inlaid. In Early Dynastic glyptic art the
human-headed bull is often depicted being attacked
by lions or by naked heroes.
K.K.

75

ending in a short tassel with wavy strands. Inside the
cap are traces of bitumen.
K.K.

77

77
Statuette of a bull

Site: Ebla (Tell Mardikh), Royal Palace G, L. 2913
Date: Late Early Dynastic to early Akaddian period, ca.
  2400–2300 B.C.
Material: Limestone
Height: 3.3 cm; *width:* 1.9 cm; *length:* 2.3 cm
Museum No.: Aleppo TM. 78.6.320
Literature: P. Matthiae *SEb3* (1980) 99–120, Figs. 201–203 / *I*
  Tesori di Ebla (Rome 1984) 13–14, 45, Plates 39 a–b

This fragment of a resting bull formed part of the furnishings from the internal courtyard of the administrative quarters of Royal Palace G, which functioned as
the entrance to the audience chamber. Like similar
statuettes which are better preserved but of inferior
quality, this bull could be fastened to a base with pegs
inserted into two circular holes on the bottom. The
base was probably made of perishable material and is
now lost. It is possible that this statuette once was fastened on top of a ritual standard, or it may have been
part of the furniture decoration in the royal palace.

Although the technique used for producing these
animal figurines generally was inspired by the Protohistoric animal figurines from Uruk in southern Mesopotamia, this small Eblaite sculpture has only one true
iconographic and stylistic parallel, namely a calf found
at the slightly earlier Royal Cemetery at Ur. It is possible that the figurine at Ur originally came from the
palace at Ebla.
P.M.

78
Pieces of unworked lapis lazuli

Site: Ebla (Tell Mardikh), Royal Palace G, L. 2913
Date: Late Early Dynastic to early Akkadian period, ca.
  2400–2300 B.C.
Material: Lapis lazuli
Dimensions: (a) *length:* 11.2 cm, *width:* 4.5 cm, *thickness:*
  2.6 cm; (b) *length:* 8.3 cm, *width:* 8.2 cm, *thickness:* 2 cm;
  (c) *length:* 9.8 cm, *width:* 6.7 cm, *thickness:* 2.5 cm; (d)
  length: 11.8 cm, *width:* 5.4 cm, *thickness:* 4.8 cm
Museum Nos.: Aleppo TM.76.G824, TM.78.G.352klv
Literature: F. Pinnock *Bull. Society for Mesopotamia Studies*
  1 (1983) 19–36 // P. Matthiae *I Tesori di Ebla* (Rome 1984)
  47–48, Plate 36d

Unworked blocks of lapis lazuli were found in large
quantities in the inner courtyard of the administrative
center of Palace G; they may have been stored on the
top floor of the small portico in bags which were destroyed when the building burned. Although the
weight of the blocks varies, there is no doubt that in
most cases they were broken into standard pieces for
further distribution. More than a third of the raw lapis
lazuli retrieved from Palace G was in blocks of about
500 grams, which is approximately the same weight
used for distribution of the precious material from the
mines in Afghanistan.

The lapis lazuli trade was almost certainly a royal
monopoly. Whether the precious material traveled
through Mesopotamia via the northern route and the
region called Khamazi or the southern route through
the city of Adab (both are mentioned in Eblaite economic texts), it had to pass through Mari and Ebla on
its way to the Mediterranean or to Egypt. Only a small
fraction of the enormous quantities of lapis lazuli
found at Ebla—more than 22 kilograms—was worked
there into personal jewelry, especially necklaces, or
small ornamental pieces, difficult to reconstruct, and
inlays for composite reliefs.
P.M.

78

tion, much used by the Egyptians. The preserved hieroglyphs mention a Sixth Dynasty pharaoh: they begin with the name of Pepi I and continue "King of Upper and Lower Egypt, son of Hathor, the ruler of Dendra, Pep(i)." As attested in a number of other inscriptions, Pepi I worshiped especially the goddess Hathor of Dendra. Dendra was an important religious center of Upper Egypt, and Hathor, goddess of love, sometimes also called the ruler of Dendra, was the main deity there. She was worshiped as far as Byblos, the Levantine harbor, where several fine Egyptian objects similarly inscribed were found. Economic texts from Ebla show trade relations between Ebla and Byblos, so we may assume that this lid was made in the reign of Pepi I and meant for export to Byblos, from where it later made its way to Ebla.

M.E.-K.

79
Fragment of Egyptian jar lid

Site: Ebla (Tell Mardikh), Royal Palace G
Date: 2300–2270 B.C.
Material: Calcite
Diameter: Ca. 16.7 cm
Museum No.: Aleppo TM. 77. G. 600
Literature: G. Scandone-Matthiae "Vasi iscritti di Chefren e
  Pepi I dal Palazzo Reale G di Ebla" *SEb* I/3–4 (1979) 33–44
  / "Inscriptions royales egyptiennes de l'Ancien Empire a
  Ebla" *CRAI* XXV Berlin 1978 (1982) // cf. H. G. Fischer
  *Dendera in the Third Millennium B.C. down to the Theban
  Domination of Upper Egypt* (Locust Valley, N.Y., 1968) 37
  // C. Vandersleyen (ed.) "Das alte Ägypten," *Propyläen
  Kunstgeschichte* 15 (Berlin 1975) Plates 353 a–c

In the 1977 season of excavations at Tell Mardikh several fragments of Egyptian stone vessels were found on the floors of Palace G. This fragment of a lid, which shows traces of having been in a fire, once covered a typical Egyptian jar meant for salve or body lo-

79   *80, right*

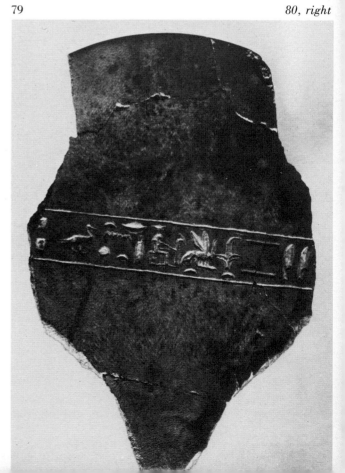

81

THIRD MILLENNIUM CITIES

80
Contract tablet

Site: Ebla (Tell Mardikh), Royal Palace G
Date: Late Early Dynastic to early Akkadian period,
　　2350–2300 B.C.
Material: Fired clay
Height: 22.1 cm; *width:* 23.9 cm; *depth:* 6 cm
Museum No.: Aleppo TM. 75. G. 2420
Literature: E. Sollberger *SEb* III (1980) 129–155

This tablet is inscribed with a contract between the
ruler of Ebla and a prince, who unfortunately is not
mentioned by name, from the city of Abarsal, a site
not yet located. The text is not altogether understood,
and we can therefore only present a partial translation.

After a census of the twenty surrounding towns under the jurisdiction of Ebla a treaty follows: Abarsal is
obligated to take care of provisions for messengers
from Ebla. In the case of theft of sheep from the Ebla
region, the neighbors are threatened with annihilation.
In case of revolt in Abarsal, Ebla reserves the right to
intervene. In case of negligence regarding deliveries of
seed as well as the provision for messengers, the
prince of Abarsal is threatened with deposition. Abarsal must also guarantee Ebla's unlimited use of their
waterways. The ruler of Ebla seems to have less direct
power over individual citizens and property at Abarsal: in case of breach of contract the people of Abarsal
are threatened by severe punishment inflicted on them
by the sun god, the weather god, and a third unspec-
ified god. A curse formula closes the document:

　All (of those who. . .) assemble for evil (purposes)
　Shamash (and) Adad shall cause its (that assembly's)
　words to perish in (its) bile. To (its) couriers who go
　in (their) travels no one shall bring drinking water
　nor (give) shelter. And you (Abarsal) (if) you go on an
　evil expedition you shall be cast out.

W.R.

81
Administrative text

Site: Ebla (Tell Mardikh), Royal Palace G, L. 2769
Date: Late Early Dynastic to early Akkadian period,
　　2350–2300 B.C.
Material: Clay, burned in a fire
Height: 19.7 cm.; *width:* 21.0 cm; *depth:* 3.6 cm
Museum No.: Aleppo TM. 75. G. 1274
Literature: Pettinato *Catalogo* 42, No. 713; *Testi ammini-
　　strativi della biblioteca L. 2769.* Parte I: *Materiali
　　epigrafici di Ebla* (1980) 59, No. 7

This tablet, written in Eblaite, lists amounts of dyed
and fine cloth, clothes, and valuable jewelry distributed by the royal family, the king and queen (*mal-
iktum*). Part of column 2, lines 12 ff. reads:

　1 piece of *Edaum* material for 2 (maybe the mea-
　　surement or length)
　1 piece of *Aktum* material
　1 excellent and colorful garment
　1 silver bracelet weighing 32 shekels given to Ish-
　　putu, by his guardian, the lord
　2 pieces of *Edaum* material for 2
　2 pieces of *Aktum* material
　2 excellent and colorful garments via Darzimu and
　　Sarmilu
　1 piece of *Edaum* material for 2
　1 piece of *Aktum* material
　1 excellent and colorful garment to Ishputu, his
　　guardian, the queen, has given.

At the end the scribe adds up the individual materials
and garments, calculates the final sum, and dates the
text.

K.K.

82

83

82
Administrative text

Site: Ebla (Tell Mardikh), Royal Palace G, L. 2769
Date: Late Early Dynastic to early Akkadian period,
  2350–2300 B.C.
Material: Clay, burned in a fire
Size: 4.2 × 4.2 cm; *maximum thickness:* 1.9 cm
Museum No.: Aleppo TM. 76. G. 790

Shorter administrative texts were usually inscribed on
round curved tablets. This Eblaite account of a business transaction is written in two columns on the obverse and the reverse of the tablet. The text mentions
metals, including gold, and a smith.
K.K.

84

83
Cuneiform legal text

Site: Ebla (Tell Mardikh), Royal Palace G, L. 2769
Date: Late Early Dynastic to early Akkadian period,
    2350–2300 B.C.
Material: Fired clay
Height: 14.7 cm; *width:* 13.4 cm; *thickness:* 3.7 cm
Museum No.: Aleppo TM.76.G.1444
Literature: D.O. Edzard *Verwaltungstexte verschiedenen*
    Inhalts. Archivi Reali di Ebla, II (Rome 1981) 35–39

This tablet belongs to a group of texts, often royal decrees, from the royal archives of Ebla which are characterized by the typical introduction formula of direct
speech, also used in the beginning of letters: *enma*
personal-name *sin* personal-name = "Thus (says) one
person to another person."

    This tablet is difficult to understand and to trans-
late. It has several instances of direct speech from
Ibrium to the king of Ebla, who is not mentioned by
name. The text begins by mentioning three people,
Gir-Damu, Ir-Damu, and Napkha-Il, to whom the king
assigns various pieces of land in different cities, all
carefully listed. Then other persons, both male and
female, are mentioned; a certain Tiludu and his sons
together with the sons of Ibrium are assigned property
by the king. The tablet ends with an oath formula,
guaranteeing these properties in the names of deities,
specifically Kura, Adad, and Shamash.
M.G.B.

84
Cuneiform lexical text

Site: Ebla (Tell Mardikh), Royal Palace G, L. 2769
Date: Late Early Dynastic to early Akkadian period,
    2350–2300 B.C.
Material: Fired clay
Length: 9.3 cm; *width:* 9.6 cm; *thickness:* 2.8 cm
Museum No.: Aleppo TM.75.G.1404
Literature: G. Pettinato *Testi lessicali bilingui della*
    biblioteca L. 2769 (Naples 1982) 93–95

This tablet is a Sumerian-Eblaite vocabulary consisting of 58 Sumerian words translated into Eblaite. It is
one of the lexical texts, found in the royal archives of
Ebla, which formed the basis for deciphering the
Eblaite language; both monolingual texts in Sumerian
and bilingual texts in Sumerian-Eblaite were found.
From a number of other tablets it was possible to reconstruct a large Sumero-Eblaite vocabulary which
has several duplicates but still remains incomplete.
This text did not form part of the larger vocabulary; it
belonged to another dictionary. Here, there is a
cuneiform sign after the Eblaite word indicating that it
is translated; in the case of other words, the Sumerian
pronunciation is indicated.
M.G.B.

Cat. No. 66

Cat. No. 76

Cat. No. 100

Cat. No. 103

Cat. No. 85

178

Cat. No. 99

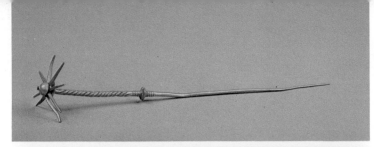

Cat. No. 104

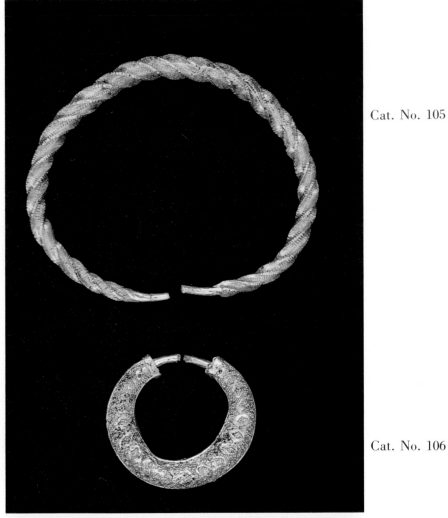

Cat. No. 105

Cat. No. 106

Cat. No. 107

Cat. No. 108

Cat. No. 115

Cat. No. 111

Cat. No. 118

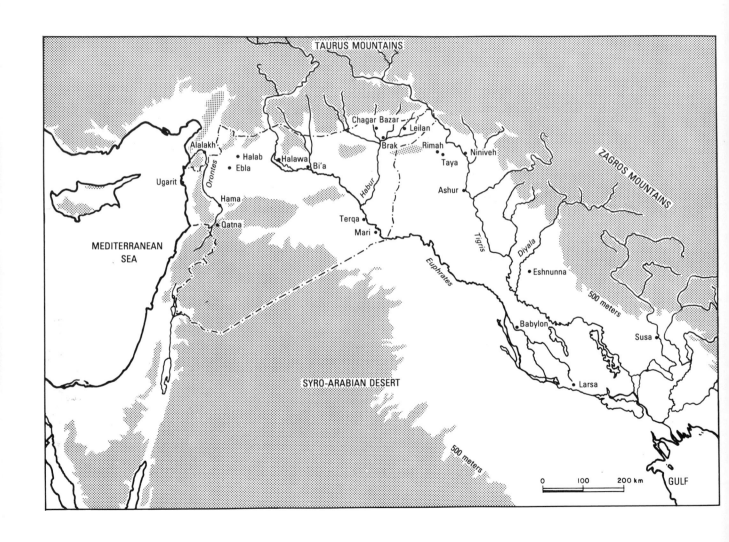

TAURUS MOUNTAINS

Chagar Bazar
Leilan
Brak
Rimah
Niniveh
Taya
Halab
Alalakh
Halawa
Bi'a
Ebla
Ugarit
Orontes
Habur
Ashur
ZAGROS MOUNTAINS
Hama
Terqa
Mari
Tigris
MEDITERRANEAN
SEA
Qatna
Diyala
Eshnunna
500 meters
Euphrates
Babylon
Susa
SYRO-ARABIAN DESERT
Larsa
500 meters
GULF

0   100   200 km

OLD SYRIAN PERIOD
CA. 2100–1600 B.C.

CONFLICT AND CONQUEST AMONG THE AMORITE KINGDOMS

HARVEY WEISS

THE OLD SYRIAN PERIOD, THE FIRST HALF OF THE SECOND MILLEN-
nium B.C., encapsulates the time from the destruction of Ebla to the
destruction of Halab, the "Great Kingdom of Aleppo." In other
words, it may be perceived as the period when the second great west
Syrian kingdom, Yamkhad, with its center at Halab (modern Aleppo),
arises upon the ruins of the former great west Syrian power, Ebla.
This, however, is not the usual perception of this period, for the
centers of Syro-Mesopotamian power were only slowly shifting across
time and space, and along this spiralling path the persistent conflicts
between regions, modes of subsistence, and ethnic power bases
continued to mark highly visible, increasingly shorter intervals, each
revealed through sources which vary considerably.

In the traditional historiography of this period the centers of power
and cultural development in Western Asia are often considered to
have been Babylon and perhaps Mari. New data and new perspectives now suggest that this period witnessed the shift from southern
Mesopotamian to west Syrian power, a shift presaged by the role
played by Ebla in the third millennium and fulfilled by the kingdom of
Yamkhad in the second.

Ethnically, or from the perspective of peoples speaking different
languages, this period is certainly denoted by the expansion and
political ascension of the Amorites. As noted in our Introduction, the
term Amorite remains linguistically somewhat indefinite; Amorite
documents do not exist, and the language was probably never recorded. The sole evidence for the language consists of personal names
and names of deities. These names, however, allow us to identify a
language whose phonology and verbal structures can be distinguished from other Semitic languages and can be classified as West
Semitic. Whether these personal names present us with enough
information to be sure that there was one language or several is

uncertain; it is likely that with more evidence, several "Amorite" languages could be discriminated.

The collapse of Akkad and Amorite origins

The destruction of Ebla, whether by Sargon or his grandson Naram-Sin, was the result of one of the many long-distance raids staged by the Sargonic kings. These reached their greatest frequency during the reign of Naram-Sin, a period that also marks the collapse of Akkadian expansion and was even recognized in antiquity as the end of an era.

The centralization of wealth and political power within the heartland of Akkade, and the period of long-distance raiding which accompanied it, was surprisingly short-lived, perhaps no more than 150 years. Within a century of Ebla's destruction, the imperial aspirations of this dynasty began to crumble under the weight of intrusive forays by surrounding peoples. Later traditions ascribe to the still-unlocalized Gutians the most important role in the dismemberment of the Akkadian empire, but possibly neighboring Elamites to the east and Hurrians to the north played energetic roles as well. The succeeding Gutian period was literally an interregnum of about fifty years, till ca. 2100 B.C., characterized by the phrase "who was king, who was not king" according to the Sumerian King List. But the downfall of the Akkadian "empire" was probably due as well to the activities of the Amorites.

Regnal years were assigned names rather than numbers during this period; these names are therefore a primary source of historical information. A year-name of Shar-kali-sharri, Naram-Sin's successor, proclaims that he "defeated the Amorite at Basar," the first reference to the people who will dominate the Syrian and Mesopotamian stage during the early second millennium. Basar is the Akkadian name for the modern Jebel Bishri, the range of foothills and mountains in the Syrian desert south of Raqqa and due west of Deir ez-Zor. Today this region is heavily utilized by nomads in winter and spring as a foraging ground for their extensive flocks of sheep and goat. It seems possible that this pastoral activity, predetermined by seasonal and geographical conditions, has a very long history.

By the middle of the twenty-second century, with Akkadian power in eclipse, the southern city of Girsu was briefly able to exert some control over its neighbors and embark upon long-distance expeditions for raw materials. Under the rule of Gudea, perhaps the most powerful of these Girsu kings, we hear again of the Amorites near "the mountains of the Amorites (Amurru)," named "Basalla" (or Basar) and "Didanum, the mountain of the Amorites."

Syria and the Third Dynasty of Ur

The successors to the Akkadian state in the south were based in the city of Ur, where the famous Third Dynasty rulers had established themselves by about 2100 B.C. Many of these kings ventured forth upon the same long-distance campaigns as their predecessors, and sors, and from these it is possible to learn much about the state of affairs in Syria proper. This period probably saw the flowering of Mari on the Euphrates under its *shakkanakku* ("governors"). Elsewhere to the west, southern documents make clear the importance of Syrian cities such as Urshu, possibly Tell Touqan near Ebla, Hahhum, possibly further north, and Tuttul, probably Tell Bi'a at the juncture of the Balikh and the Euphrates rivers. Some of these settlements are now just beginning to come under excavation; no doubt the next few years of research in Syria will radically change our understanding of the importance of sedentary urban life outside the confines of southern Mesopotamia during the early centuries of the second millennium.

It was once assumed that the rulers of the Third Dynasty of Ur controlled most of lowland Mesopotamia and Syria. Much new data now suggest a considerable re-evaluation of this period and the nature of the Ur III kingdom's control over the Near East. Indeed, this period, much as the preceding Sargonic period, seems destined for historiographic revision. The Habur Plains, for instance, were once considered to have been colonized and directly controlled by Ur-Nammu, because an inscription bearing his name was retrieved within the ruins of the Naram-Sin fortress at Tell Brak. We now know that the inscription does not bear his name at all, and the rebuilding of the Naram-Sin fortress may have been a result of local forces, now resurgent with the demise of the short-lived Akkadian emplacement. This period also presents us with the considerable evidence for local Hurrian dynasties being well established upon the Habur Plains.

Amorites of the Ur III period

The Ur III kingdom in southern Mesopotamia was apparently quite powerful but nevertheless short-lived. The sources of its wealth, like those of its predecessors, remained the production of grain in staggering quantities, utilizing ration-paid laborers organized in efficient teams for tilling, sowing, harvesting, and storing barley and wheat and for the perennial tasks of canal maintenance. A new feature of the southern economy, which may have contributed to its perduring strength, was the expansion of highly efficient water-borne transport of cereal harvests between cities, perhaps reflecting the specialization of city economies within the region as a whole.

The wealth of southern documents from this period allows us to perceive the continued intrusion into and eventual domination of the kingdom by the Amorite-speakers first encountered in the reign of Shar-kali-sharri. Many persons identified as Amorites in the texts from southern cities already bear Sumerian and Akkadian personal names, perhaps indicating the gradual assimilation of this population into the amalgam of southern ethnic groups. Elsewhere, however, the Amorite population is carefully distinguished in the south from the "native" population, not only by their names, but even in literary descriptions which set them apart as "the one who does not know city life," "who eats uncooked meat," "who does not know grain," "who digs truffles in the piedmont." These native descriptions are supplemented by royal inscriptions, year names, and other accounts which show that at least some Amorites, probably tribally organized, were a hostile, fearful force from whom the Ur III rulers had to protect their territory, wealth, and power.

Ur-Nammu's successor was the first of the Ur III rulers to construct an enormous earthern wall, perhaps 280 kilometers long, intended to control or prevent the entry of Amorites into the heartland of the south. The third Ur III ruler Shu-Sin explicity labeled the wall the *muriq Tidnum*, "that which keeps the Tidnum at a distance." Tidnum is the ancient name of the Amorite peoples, the first encountered in Akkadian times by Shar-kali-sharri and Gudea at Jebel Bishri. Shu-Sin's successor, Ibbi-Sin, was not able to hold back these forces; and the Amorites apparently broke through the wall and with the assistance of the Elamites, who attacked the city of Ur from the east, helped bring down the Third Dynasty. Control of the south then passed to the city of Isin and then Larsa, where the emergent dynasty had already adopted Amorite ancestry, and quickly thereafter to the city of Babylon and Mari.

Amorite rule of Babylon and Mari

The first two rulers of the First Dynasty of Babylon bore Amorite names, were followed by three with Akkadian names, and then six rulers, beginning with Hammurabi, with Amorite names. Through the first 100 years of this dynasty and its first five rulers, little more than an area of perhaps 50 kilometers around the city was actually under the city's control, and in this respect Babylon differed little from its successors or predecessors. With the dynasty's sixth ruler, however, the city was propelled onto the complex stage of Mesopotamian history as contending dynasties along the Euphrates and its effluents battled with each other for control of land, booty, revenue, and prestige.

Since the contending forces were mostly Amorite-led, this might be called the Amorite age. In fact it is frequently called the age of Mari, for the excavations at this Syrian city have revealed more about the political and economic and social life of the period than any other source. Amorite rulers dominated Mari during the twentieth and nineteenth centuries, beginning with the famous Lim dynasty and its founder Yaggid-Lim. During this period one very large palace at Mari, initially constructed in the twentieth century, underwent considerable reconstruction and expansion. The son and successor of Yaggid-Lim, Yakhdun-Lim, boasted in typical terms of his exploits and the extent of his control over neighboring territories. The foundation tablet which he set within the Shamash Temple at Mari is displayed in our exhibition (Cat. No. 94). In stereotypical royal Mesopotamian fashion, Yakhdun-Lim includes the following boasts in his dedicatory inscription:

> . . . no other king residing in Mari had ever—since, in ancient days the god built the city of Mari—reached the (Mediterranean) Sea, nor reached and felled timber in the great mountains, the Cedar Mountain and the Boxwood Mountain, he, Yakhdun-Lim, son of Yaggid-Lim, the powerful king, the wild bull among kings, did march to the shore of the sea, an unrivalled feat, and offered sacrifices to the Ocean as (befitting) his royal rank while his troops washed themselves in the Ocean. . . . (translation A.L. Oppenheim).

Yakhdun-Lim's son Zimri-Lim was deposed from the throne of Mari by Shamshi-Adad, another Amorite, probably of tribal origins, whose enigmatic reign united all of northern Mesopotamia from the Euphrates on the west to the Zagros Mountains on the east. Aspects of Shamshi-Adad's rule are discussed in the essays "Letters from Mari" and "Tell Leilan and Shubat Enlil." Here we may caution that the brilliance and intrigue of the political and military affairs of the period, and the detail with which much of these are known, should not obscure from view the larger pattern of regional domination. The deposed Zimri-Lim found sanctuary in the court of Yamkhad, with its capital at Aleppo, an important indication of the power which still remained upon the terra-rosa plains of western Syria. With the death of Shamshi-Adad, his son Yasmakh-Adad was unable to hold the throne of Mari, and Zimri-Lim returned and quickly set about restoring his order upon adjacent territories, including the Habur Plains formerly controlled by Shamshi-Adad.

Hammurabi of Babylon, however, was eventually able to emerge as the dominant figure in the southern Mesopotamian arena and even briefly extend his control to northern Mesopotamia. In his thirty-third regnal year Hammurabi destroyed the Mari of his former ally Zimri-Lim and then moved to conquer and presumably destroy the city centers of the Habur region. Hammurabi did not extend his domination farther to the west, nor was his control of the south more than temporary. The centers of Near Eastern power seem to have shifted radically during this very period.

The kingdom of Yamkhad

In about the year 1775 B.C. one Itur-Asdu, an emissary of King Zimri-Lim, advised a meeting of tribal leaders on the Euphrates:

> There is no king who is mighty by himself. Ten or fifteen kings follow Hammurabi, the man of Babylon, a like number Rim-Sin of Larsa, a like number Ibal-piel of Eshnunna, a like number Amut-pi-el of Qatna, and twenty follow Yarim-Lim of Yamkhad.

This oft-cited portion of a letter from Mari describes the alignment of political forces in lowland Syria and Mesopotamia in terms which must have approximated the truth, for they were designed to convince rather than dissuade. As such, these words more than others allow us to understand how it was that Hammurabi, unlike his predecessors, never travelled to the Mediterranean nor boasted of having conquered territories farther west than Mari. Hammurabi's kingdom made no lasting impression upon his contemporaries, and with his death the kingdom dissipated more rapidly than it was assembled. To judge from the testimony of Itur-Asdu, the most powerful city of the period probably remains to be excavated. The kingdom of Yamkhad led the largest alliance of rulers in the region and played a decisive role in the political and military affairs of the period. Yamkhad's capital, called Halab in the ancient sources, is now probably covered by the successive occupations which climax in the burgeoning modern city of Aleppo.

The dependent vassal states of Yamkhad included Alalakh, the city which controlled the plain of Antioch to the northwest, and Emar, which controlled the transit trade from the Euphrates to the east. Slightly more distant, but nevertheless subject to the king of Aleppo, were the cities of Hashshum, Urshu, Carchemish, Tunip, and the port city Ugarit. When the ruler of Ugarit sought an invitation to visit the palace of Zimri-Lim at Mari, he did not address himself directly to the Mari ruler but to Hammurabi of Yamkhad, who in turn wrote to Zimri-Lim: "The 'man' of Ugarit wrote to me as follows: 'Show me the house of Zimri-Lim, I want to see it.' Now then, I am sending his servant to you."

The royal tombs of Ebla, which during this period was a dependency of Yamkhad, make clear the continued importance of that city. Amorite rulers at Ebla, as well as at Yamkhad and Qatna, probably account for the transmission of royal Amorite ideology into the second half of the second millennium and its documentation at centers such as Ugarit on the Syrian coast. The cult of the *Rephaim* at Ugarit, for instance, has now convincingly been explained as the cult of long-departed kings, explicitly associated with the ancestors of the Amorites, the "council of the *Ditanu/Tidanum*," the Amorite homeland or tribal name first encountered in the time of Gudea.

Shamshi-Adad seems to have once dared to engage the king of Yamkhad in battle, carefully protecting himself with added support from a coalition of other rulers. But thereafter, Shamshi-Adad avoids all mention of Yamkhad and Halab, while allying himself with Qatna, Yamkhad's powerful southern neighbor, through the marriage of his son Yasmakh-Adad to the daughter of the king of Qatna. The value which Shamshi-Adad assigned to his relationship with Qatna is revealed in another of the famous Mari letters where Shamshi-Adad rebukes his son, the philandering governor of Mari, in the following terms:

> Did not the former kings set their wives in the palace? (But) Yakhdun-Lim honored his concubines, set his wife aside, and moved her into the desert. Perhaps you are planning to set the daughter of Ishi-Adad [king of Qatna] in the desert. Her father will be deeply troubled by this. It is not good. There are many rooms in the "Palm-Tree" palace. Let them choose a room for her there, let her stay in that room. Don't set her in the desert!

The center of power, then, had clearly shifted in Syria and Mesopotamia from the southernmost portion of the Tigris-Euphrates alluvium to the dry-farming plains of the Habur region in the reign of Shamshi-Adad, and then to the westernmost plains of Syria around Yamkhad and Qatna in the period following the death of Hammurabi. It seems quite possible that this alteration in the centers of power reflects the inexorable decline in the yields of southern Mesopotamian agriculture as irrigated land became salinized and waterlogged. The consequences of this can be seen in the secular decline in urbanization, noticeable already in the second millennium. Early-second-millennium southern cities were not locally producing enough to sustain the densely packed populations which had characterized the third-millennium cities. The dry-farming plains of northern Mesopotamia and western Syria, however, did not suffer this decline in agricultural yields. Although temporarily cut off by the circumstances of Shamshi-Adad's death and Hammurabi's last grasp for power, the Habur Plains and northern Mesopotamia later served as the base for imperial expansion under the kingdom of Mitanni and the Assyrian empire.

Yamkhad with its center at Aleppo was clearly the successor state to third-millennium Ebla. The same fertile, rain-fed terra-rosa soils characterize the region around Aleppo as are found at nearby Ebla. Hence it is easy to comprehend the ability of the second-millennium center to generate wealth in cereals, flax, and sheep herding, even though we still have yet to retrieve direct archaeological evidence from the city. More than third-millennium Ebla, however, the situation of Aleppo provided for, and still provides, direct control of the most important trade route across the Near East linking the Euphrates and north Mesopotamian routes with the Mediterranean. Since it was the dominant power in the Near East in the early second millennium, the eventual excavation of Aleppo will be the great archaeological project of future generations.

The Orontes River waters the great interior western valley of Syria with the modern cities of Homs, Hama, and Idlib. Qatna, situated in the fertile plain near modern Homs, benefited from the productivity of its dry-farming agriculture and its strategic trade location linking via Palmyra the Euphrates trade route with the Mediterranean. Qatna's role in the history of the Near East, like Aleppo's, has yet to be fully appreciated. A few seasons of limited archaeological excavation were undertaken at Qatna between 1924 and 1929. These confirmed the identification and significance of the site but were not expanded. The site itself is one of the largest walled mounds of the Near East: its city walls rise more than 25 meters above plain level and enclose an area of more than 100 hectares. The Syrian government, through the Directorate-General of Antiquities, has purchased the land and houses of the families which over the generations settled within the ancient walls of Qatna and has provided these families with equivalent plots and houses on nearby land. Qatna, one of the great ancient cities of Syria, will shortly reveal its history.

Recommended Reading

Giorgio Buccellati. *Amorites of the Ur III Period* (Rome, 1966).

J.-R. Kupper. *La civilisation de Mari* (Liege, 1966) / "Northern Mesopotamia and Syria." *Cambridge Ancient History.* Vol. II, Part 1 (3rd ed. Cambridge, 1973).

MARI (TELL HARIRI)

Location: 10 km northwest of Abu Kemal, on the right bank of the Euphrates
Dates: Ca. 4000–ca. 312 B.C.
Excavations: From 1933 (Musée du Louvre and Centre National de Recherche Scientifique)
Publications: See earlier description of Mari, p. 130

The approximately 25,000 cuneiform-inscribed clay tablets from the palace archive of the late third and early second millennium B.C. give us—from the perspective of the palace—insight into the life of the city and its relations within Syria. Besides the palace, only a few shrines and no dwellings have been excavated; hence private archives do not yet supplement this picture.

The economic basis for city life at Mari was irrigation agriculture, making use of the banks of the Euphrates where intensive garden and date palm planting was possible. Under Zimri-Lim, the territory controlled by Mari reached to the Balikh and the Habur rivers and, to the southeast, far into what is now Iraq. Many documents from the archives treat issues raised by agriculture, irrigation, and the difficult relationship between the city authorities and cattle thieves and nomadic tribesmen seasonally crossing the river valleys with their herds.

Among the important tribal groups named in the Mari documents, the Jaminites and the Hanaeans are prominent. The relationship of the Mari population to these tribesmen was rarely hostile: sedentary agriculturalists and pastoral nomads relied on each other and profited from the exchange of goods. Cheese, leather, livestock, wool, and woven fabrics, and the products of steppe-land foraging such as herbs and truffles were offered on the urban markets by nomads for exchange with agricultural and handiwork products from the urban economy.

As guides, the nomads were matchless in their knowledge of the steppe and desert with their springs and oases. Tribesmen such as the Jaminites under the Assyrian king Shamshi-Adad also served in the armies of the urban forces. Nevertheless, the seasonal movement of pastoral nomads, coordinated with the changing availability of fodder for sheep flocks, posed a threat to urban rulers fearful of uncontrolled alliances among the tribesmen or with enemy cities seeking their military assistance or simple caravan raiding.

Much of Mari's extraordinary riches may have been a function of long-distance trade, as commercial traffic between southern Mesopotamia, Anatolia, and western Syria passed along its Euphrates shores. Even the route to southern Syria departed from Mari, with donkey caravans following a chain of groundwater oases to Tadmor (Roman Palmyra) and the fertile agricultural plains around ancient Qatna (modern Mishrifé). According to the supply lists from Mari, such a trip would have taken about ten days.

The palace not only extracted tolls from long-distance traders, but also engaged itself in trading enterprises. Its horizons reached from Hazor in Palestine, to Crete and Cyprus, over to Hattusas in Anatolia and Dilmun on the Persian Gulf. Among the foreign embassies whose arrivals and departures were registered, even Elamites from southwestern Iran appear. The most important goods involved in this exchange were for the production of bronze: tin and copper. Large quantities of tin were, as we know from the Mari tablets, protected in palace magazines. Tin came mostly from northwestern Iran; sources in the western Mediterranean or western Europe were too distant to be involved in this trade. Copper was obtained from Cyprus. Other goods exchanged were wood, oils, wine, and semi-precious stones.

In the center of the city of Mari, among other shrines, stood the Dagan Temple. In the customary style it consisted of an oblong room with two sides chambers abutting a ziggurat. Stone monuments and columns stood in the courtyard. Not far from the Dagan Temple was the palace, so famous in its own day that the king of Ugarit, on the Mediterranean coast, longed to see it. More than 300 rooms, corridors, and courts covered an area of about 2.5 hectares. Constructed in several stages, the palace underwent many additions and functional changes in the course of successive reigns. The oldest section, on the east, with a construction tradition extending back to the Early Dynastic period, was probably also used by the *shakkanakku*, or governors. It is likely that the western section was added during the reign of Shamshi-Adad and his son the governor of Mari, Yasmakh-Adad. At this time and under the reign of the last Mari ruler, Zimri-Lim, the palace was richly decorated.

Through a gate, a vestibule, a court (A), and another wide room whose doors interlock, one arrived at the central eastern court (see Fig. 41). The central kitchen for the outer palace realm (B) was adjacent to the entrance courts. On the east side of the large palace court lay a row of rooms in which arriving goods were registered prior to further distribution; pots and clay jar sealings from sealed goods were retrieved here (C). The southwest area of the palace featured a shrine (D). The fragmentary statue Cat. No. 89 was found in this shrine. An audience hall (E) opened onto the semi-circular stair to the court. The wall paintings depicting the royal sacrifices may hark back to the period of the Third Dynasty of Ur. In the back of the palace were workshops where smiths, described in the archives,

	palace kitchen		store room		bath
	administration		private residence		guest room
	temple		treasury or school		archive

Figure 41
Plan of the Zimri-Lim Palace at Mari.

probably labored. One inaccessible room in this area (F) was also decorated with mural paintings.

Through a corridor passing an archive room, one entered the west palace court. This was decorated with large wall paintings, of which one fragment (Cat. No. 99) is included in the exhibition. On its south side lay a wide room with a pedestal (G); court entrance, door, and pedestal are all arranged in one axis. Whoever wished to see the enthroned king had to cross a

stretch of 45 meters through the large court. Two paths led to an oblong room (H) behind the court with a cella connected to it by a staircase. The plan of this room suggests that it was a sacred place, associated with cultic activity represented in a mural (Fig. 42) to the right of the entrance to the pedestal room (G) showing the "investiture" of the king (see the discussion of Cat. No. 90).

The southern side of the palace was occupied by a bazaar-like room (I). Wares from the eastern palace court had to be transported through a long corridor. A crafts area (J)—the molds, Cat. Nos. 95–98, are from this area—with surrounding sleeping quarters (K), and an additional throne room were adjacent. Next to these lay a group of rooms which the excavator interpreted to be the palace school with tablets and benches, but which is now considered to have been the royal treasury (L).

Large portions of the palace are assumed to have been two-storied. Baked bricks were employed in only a few places. The walls of sun-dried mud brick are only today, some forty-five years after their excavation and restoration, beginning to collapse.

KAY KOHLMEYER

LETTERS AT MARI

JACK M. SASSON

OVER 2,000 LETTERS WERE RECOVERED FROM THE VAST PALACE AT Mari, with the largest harvest coming from the small room called number 115, although stray examples have been found in dozens of spots. Recent discoveries outside the palace indicate that letters, even "official" ones, could be placed in the private homes of the top administrators. The letters are written on clay by scribes who used styli to make the wedges (cuneiforms). The size of individual letters varies, but normally they measure around 8 x 5 cm. Because Mari was sacked by Babylonian troops on two occasions over a three-year period, many letters have not survived in good condition. Thus there are breaks and areas showing pulverized cuneiform, invariably at the most crucial points in the text.

It will be useful to remember that at the time these letters were written literacy was limited to a very small percentage of the population. This was so, not simply because the cuneiform system of writing was remarkably complex, but mainly because in most societies until relatively recent times literacy was not regarded as an advantage for any but the professional scribe and occasionally the priestly figure. The scribes in Mari were female as well as male. (One roster gives the names of nine women who were scribes, but no text has yet been located which can definitely be assigned to a female scribe.) In addition to learning the cumbersome cuneiform system, Mari scribes had to learn a new language in which to display their skills; for their native language, which was most certainly Amorite, was not that used for state and private transactions, which was Akkadian. The distinction between the two is like that between Spanish and French or German and Dutch, enough to make it impossible for a hearer to understand anything but occasional words. Therefore, whenever scribes were recording statements, they had to translate into Akkadian before they wrote.

Letters are easy to distinguish from other texts because of the convention that was followed by scribes during the second millennium B.C. The opening is addressed to the scribe, who is asked to report to the real addressee the content of the letter. This is followed by a line stating the name of the sender and, most commonly, establishing a relationship between the correspondents. Thus, if Queen Shiptu wrote to her husband, King Zimri-Lim, her letter would open as follows: "Tell Zimri-Lim, thus (says) Shiptu, your handmaid." ("Handmaid" was a conventional term by which a wife politely addressed her husband.) The letter then enters into the main message, which can be very simple or rather developed, shifting from topic to topic by means of the word *shanitam*, "another matter." The end of the letter may or may not include a parting remark. The more elaborate letters can hold as many as 80 or so lines, allocated to two sides. It is not uncommon to find the scribe running out of space and entering tightly drawn cuneiform on the sides of the tablet. Letters are rarely "signed"; if they bear the impression of seals, it will be found on the clay envelope in which the letter is secured. The letters do not have such marks as the pressing of thumbnails or fringes of clothing that are found in juridical or administrative documents.

It might be expected that the letters found at Mari would be only those that were sent to that city, and this is certainly the case of a large portion of them. But since an appreciable number of documents were sent to the king when he was on campaigns or visiting provincial palaces to fulfill administrative or cultic functions, this correspondence was brought back to the palace at the end of the journey and then added to the archives. The same can be said for a smaller number of examples that were exchanged between the king and his ambassadors and mercantile representatives (often the same post). One can also find a number of letters which could have reached their final destination only if copied from the original before their dispatch or, as is the case of official correspondence between two powers, intercepted by larcenous methods. Additionally, a very few letters could have been penned by scribes for purely aesthetic reasons and might be labelled literary. One such example, which purports to contain a declaration of war between the powerful king of Aleppo and his erstwhile vassal, is translated below.

The letters found at Mari spanned approximately a forty-year period. Only a handful are assignable to King Yakhdun-Lim of Mari, those found as strays in room 153, which came to be a guard post and may also have served as a bath. Characterized by one cuneiform sign written in an archaic style, these letters from a vassal contain heart-rending appeals not to be abandoned to the machinations of a merciless (and ultimately successful) king of Assyria, Shamshi-Adad.

Who corresponded? Rulers and their allies, their vassals, their enemies. We actually have letters found at distant Tell al-Rimah from King Zimri-Lim of Mari that were dispatched to a foreign ruler and were kept there. Mari kings wrote to their officials to give instructions, to their wives, daughters, sons, in-laws, even their gods, and we have responses from practically every one of those but the latter. Since it is not always possible to match a letter with a suitable response, the context for a letter is often unknown, and it is a stroke of good fortune when continuity and sequence can be established for a specific correspondence.

The mounds (*tell*) of other city-states in Mesopotamia have yielded letters to the spade. The Mari letters, however, are unique to the ancient world in the number of recovered examples, in the variety of correspondents, in the breadth of topics, and especially in the light they shed on diverse aspects of Mesopotamian culture. May the French, excavating under Syrian sponsorship, continue to enrich us by their discoveries.

Sampling from letters found at Mari are given below. Some are but extracts, others are complete. The conventional opening of each letter is not given, but the source for each is appended, with Roman numerals referring to the Archives Royales de Mari *series. This series also includes matching companion volumes wherein are found transliterations of the Akkadian into Latin alphabets and translations of the originals into French.*

1. *Abi-samar writes his overlord, Yakhdun-Lim (I:2)*

Do not be offended by what I am about to say. To whom should I have expressed it if not to my "father"? Even if you hate Abi-samar, do you also hate your cities? In the matter which I am about to mention, I cannot do anything myself . . .

Perhaps you may think as follows: "Abi-samar is not my 'son' and my house is not related to his!" But my house is your house, and Abi-samar is indeed your "son."

2. *Shamshi-Adad of Assyria writes to his son, Yasmakh-Adad of Mari (I:5)* [This letter contains a proverb that must surely be the oldest continuously cited example in recorded history, having parallels in Sumerian, Greek, Latin, and Arabic as well as in contemporary European languages.]

All of you are constantly trying tricks and maneuvering endlessly to destroy an enemy. The enemy likewise constantly tries tricks and endlessly maneuvers against you, just as wrestlers try to trick one another all the time. I hope that—following the old proverb that says "By her squinting the bitch dropped a litter of blind puppies"—you will now avoid doing the same. I hope that the enemy will not maneuver you into ambush. . . .

3. *Yasmakh-Adad to his father, Shamshi-Adad (I:108)*

I have heard Papa's letter to me with the following message: "You there, how long must we care for you? Are you a child and not a man? Are there no whiskers on your chin? How much longer will you be unable to govern your house? Can you not see your brother guiding huge armies? You must run your own palace and household!" This is what Papa wrote me.

Now then, am I supposed to be still young and unable to govern? But Papa himself reared me, and he fixed my destiny by his very own order. And I am now not supposed to control either slave or my household. . . . How come? Ever since childhood, I grew up in Papa's presence. But now they begin, the slaves, this one or the other, to separate me from Papa's affection. . . . I have decided: "I shall go before Papa and shall share with Papa my distress. . . ."

4. *King Ishme-Dagan of Ekallatum to his brother Yasmakh-Adad of Mari (IV:65)*

The drug which your doctor fixed as poultice on me is excellent. As soon as a new wound breaks out, this drug heals it! Now I am dispatching to you Samsi-Adad-tukulti, the doctor; have him promptly inspect the drug and send him back.

5. *King Zimri-Lim of Mari to his wife Shiptu (X:129)*

I have heard: "Nanna has an infection, and since she is often at the palace, it will infect the many women who are with her."

Now give strict orders: No one is to drink from the cup she uses; no one is to sit on the seat she takes, and no one is to lie on the bed she uses, lest it infect the many women who are with her. This is a very contagious disease!

6. *King Zimri-Lim to Queen Shiptu (X:126)*

I am now directing to you female weavers, among which there are priestesses. Select the priestesses and assign (the rest) to weaving establishments. Choose from among these and previous weavers thirty—or as many as are worth selection—handsome ones, who have no blemishes from toe to head hair, and assign them to Warad-ilishu. Have Warad-ilishu teach them Subarean dances; but their figures(?) are not to be changed. Be careful with their ration so that their looks won't change.

Let Warad-ilishu be there when you make selections, but Mukan-nishum ought not alter the appearance of the weavers of choice whom you assign to him.

7. *Princess Shimatum to her father, King Zimri-Lim (X:26)*
I have given birth to twins: a boy and a girl! Be happy, my lord.

8. *A provincial governor to King Zimri-Lim (XIV:8)*
The mayors of the district took hold of me regarding the gods that are held in the cities of Saggaratum and Dur-Yakhdulim and said about the matter: "It is time for sacrifices! Release the gods so that they can offer them sacrifices in their own temple."

But since I had not asked my lord, I am not releasing the gods. May my lord write me whether the gods are to be conveyed to the villages or not, one way or another, so that I could follow my lord's order.

9. *A provincial governor to King Zimri-Lim (XIV:10)*
I had asked my lord regarding my trip to Qattunan, and he answered me: "I shall go myself; come along with me."

Now I reached Saggaratum, but two female servants had died in the household. I investigated the matter to find out that it was because of the sacrifice to the god Amu-Tikhran. If it is agreeable to my lord, let me go and satisfy this god. My round trip ought to take five days; but ought I not tarry there a while to allow me to pray for my lord during this sacrifice?

10. *A provincial governor to King Zimri-Lim (XIV:35)*
Ever since I reached Saggaratum five days ago, I have continually sent truffles to my lord. But my lord wrote me: "You have dispatched truffles that are not good." But my lord ought not condemn(?) with regard to truffles. I have sent to my lord what they have brought me. . . .

11. *An old woman, Addu-duri, writes King Zimri-Lim (X:50)* [The letter was sent when the king was at the height of his power]
Since the restoration/destruction [the word has double and opposite meanings] of your father's house, I have never had a dream such as this. Previous portents of mine were like this pair.

In my dream, I entered the chapel of the goddess Belet-ekallim; but Belet-ekallim was not in residence! Moreover, the statues before her were not there either. Upon seeing this, I broke into uncontrollable weeping. —This dream of mine occurred during the evening watch—

I turned around, and Dada, priest of the goddess Ishtar-pishra, was standing at the door of Belet-ekallim's chapel; but a hostile voice kept uttering: "Return, o god Dagan; return, o god Dagan." This is what it kept on uttering.

More! A female ecstatic arose in the temple of the goddess Annunitum to say: "Zimri-Lim, don't go on a journey; stay in Mari and it is I who will remain responsible."

So my lord should not neglect to protect himself. Now I have sealed locks of my hair and fringes from my garment and have sent them to my lord.

12. *King Zimri-Lim to the river god Naru* (Syria *19[1938] 126*)

I am herewith dispatching a gold vessel to my Lord. Previously when I sent my request to my Lord, my Lord revealed for me a sign; may my Lord fulfill the sign which he revealed; may he not neglect to protect me; may my Lord not turn his attention elsewhere; may my Lord not favor anyone else but me.

13. *King Yarim-Lim, of Aleppo, writes his vassal, Yashub-Yakhad, king of Der, some 300 miles away* (Syria *33[1956] 66–67*) [The letter is actually a rare example of a declaration of war; however, it may well be a literary creation by the Mari scribe]

The god Shamash ought to investigate and decide on your conduct and mine. I have acted as a father and brother toward you; toward me you have acted as a villain and enemy.

What good was it that by means of the weapons of the god Adad and of Yarim-Lim, I saved the city of Babylon and gave life to your land and to you? Were it not for the god Addad and for Yarim-Lim, 15 years ago the city of Der could have been windblown (matter?); as if it were chaff, one would never have found it.

Would you then have been able to treat me like this?

Certainly Sin-gamil, king of Diniktum, very much like you would repeatedly respond to me by means of lies and provocations. Having docked 500 boats in Diniktum's quay, I "sank" (?) his land as well as him for 12 years.

I swear to you by Adad, my city's god, and by Sin, my own god (may I be cursed) should I ever go away before annihilating your land and you. Now therefore, I shall come in springtime and shall encamp at your city's gate. I shall have you witness the galling weapons of the god Adad and Yarim-Lim.

Recommended Reading

A. Leo Oppenheim. *Letters from Mesopotamia* (Chicago: University of Chicago Press, 1967).

Archives Royales de Mari (Paris): I–III (1950), IV (1951), V (1952), VI (1954), X (1967; 1978), XIII (1964), XIV (1974; 1976), XVIII (1976; 1977).

TELL LEILAN AND SHUBAT ENLIL

HARVEY WEISS

The city of Shubat Enlil is a fortress, founded in the heart of the land. . . . (Archives Royales de Mari XIV: 101)

Speak to Hatnu-rapi: thus Bunu-Ishtar your brother. "Since you are bringing out Zimri-Lim's share from the spoil that you are bringing out of Shubat Enlil, why are you still keeping his share? Will he just look on? Now, when you have read this letter. . . ." (S. Dalley et al. The Old Babylonian Tablets from Tell al-Rimah *[London 1976] No. 5)*

SHORTLY AFTER THE DISCOVERY OF MARI AND THE RETRIEVAL OF ITS early-second-millennium palace archives in the 1930s, a new historical arena—the Habur Plains of northeastern Syria—was opened to archaeologists concerned with the ancient Near East. To be sure, earlier archaeological excavations on the Habur Plains had already pointed to the terrific fertility of the region, the density of ancient mounded sites, and the probable interaction between this region and southern Mesopotamia in antiquity. It was the Mari archives, however, which brought historical inquiry to the Habur.

From at least the sixth millennium B.C. the Habur Plains were dotted with small villages and larger towns containing populations enjoying the easy-to-produce, rain-fed harvests of wheat and barley for which the region is famous. Walled cities first appeared on the Habur Plains, apparently rather suddenly, in the twenty-fifth century B.C., probably in association with the emergence of dynastic rule among the Hurrian-speaking towns and villages which had previously dominated the rolling fertile plains. For approximately six hundred years thereafter the history of the Habur Plains is virtually unknown, except for occasional south Mesopotamian references to the land or princes of "Subir" and the periodic mention of "Subarian" slaves, individuals captured from this region and then installed as workers in southern Mesopotamian plantations and workshops.

Suddenly, however, in a still-unexplained flash of historical stardom, there emerged upon the Habur Plains the singular Shamshi-Adad, who in the space of some thirty-five years of rule consolidated all of the small local towns and cities of the northeastern plains and extended his decidedly imperial control across all of northern Mesopotamia, from the big bend of the Euphrates in northwestern Syria to the foothills of the Zagros Mountains in northeastern Iraq. By the end of the nineteenth century B.C. there were none who could rival the power of Shamshi-Adad. Even the border states of southern Mesopotamia sought alliance with him. It was only his partial contemporary Hammurabi of Babylon who eventually was able to check, counter, and prevail against the alliances and confederations which comprised Shamshi-Adad's northern realm.

Shamshi-Adad's origins are exceptionally obscure: perhaps his kin were the tribally organized Amorite-speakers along the Euphrates near Terqa, north of Mari; perhaps his roots were already established within the communities of the Habur Plains. The available documentation is only historiographically reliable for the period after his ascension to power.

The Mari letters record much of the diplomatic intrigue, military maneuverings, and economic administration which allowed for this imperial domain to survive the thirty-five years of Shamshi-Adac's reign (see the preceding essay "Letters from Mari"). Within the archives we can trace the fortunes of the Amorite-named Lim dynasty, its founder Yaggid-Lim, his son and successor Yakhdun-Lim (whose foundation inscription is a key historical document), and the intrusive appearance of Yasmakh-Adad, son of Shamshi-Adad. The documentation is the most extensive available for the early second millennium. Nothing of the sort can be utilized for the history of Babylon, where the early-second-millennium Old Babylonian levels are too far below the present water table to permit excavation. The intrusive reign of Yasmakh-Adad at Mari is sometimes referred to by historians as the "Assyrian interregnum," in an allusion to the reign of Shamshi-Adad over the Assyrian capital at Ashur. But Shamshi-Adad himself, of course, was an interloper, and hence the label "Assyrian interregnum" provides an inaccurate impression of north Mesopotamian political rule during this period.

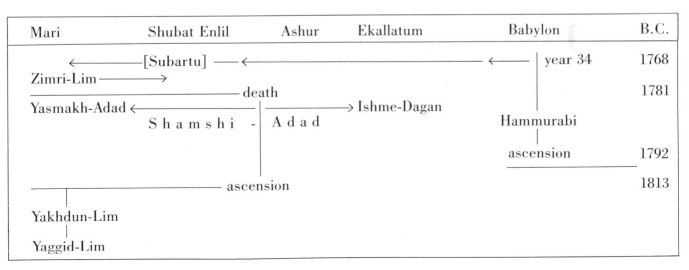

Mari	Shubat Enlil	Ashur	Ekallatum	Babylon	B.C.
←———[Subartu]———←——————————————————————←———				year 34	1768
Zimri-Lim———→					
——————————————— death					1781
Yasmakh-Adad ←——————— | ——→ Ishme-Dagan					
S h a m s h i - A d a d				Hammurabi	
				ascension	1792
——————————————— ascension					1813
Yakhdun-Lim					
Yaggid-Lim					

According to the Assyrian King List, which clearly at this juncture in its narrative has been edited quite heavily by later hands, Shamshi-Adad went down to Babylon, then returned to the north of Mesopotamia and quickly seized the key towns of Ekallatum and Ashur. We know that he then created a new capital city for himself at a site which he called Shubat Enlil (there are no earlier references to such a city), and then installed his two sons in defensive positions, guarding and controlling his realm: one, Yasmakh-Adad, at Mari; the other, Ishme-Dagan, at Ekallatum. Shamshi-Adad himself apparently moved back and forth between Shubat Enlil and Ashur.

The city economy of Mari, founded upon irrigation agriculture and the transient trade along the Euphrates, was also part of a larger Syrian regional economy which integrated the irrigation agriculture of the Euphrates banks with the dry farming of the Habur Plains. Effecting that integration were the pastoral nomadic tribes whose numbers, wealth, strength, and territoriality posed a considerable threat to city-based powers also seeking to exploit the region. The peculiar relationship here—seasonal, spatial, transient, and sedentary—is a very old one, its theater and actors predetermined by the physical landscape, climate, and the fundamental dependence of the Near Eastern economy upon wheat and barley, sheep and goat.

Pastoral nomads, apparently Amorite-speaking, controlled the land between cities, along the Euphrates, and between the Euphrates and the Habur. This territory was seasonally exploited by these pastoralists as they steered their herds, "capital on the hoof," to the grazing lands made available by sedentary agriculturalists after the cereal harvest. The difference in agricultural seasons between the Euphrates and Mari and the Habur Plains with its dry-farming communities made for the efficient exploitation of both territories as a seasonal round: the Euphrates banks in the spring, the Habur Plains in the late summer. This same round is followed to this day by the pastoral nomads who inhabit the "desert" regions of Syria.

Within such circumstances we can see the manipulative activities of the Mari rulers, Yasmakh-Adad reporting back to Shamshi-Adad on the movement of various tribesmen and their flocks, Shamshi-Adad employing these as troops within his armies and as guardsmen upon the walls of his city, Shubat Enlil. The allegiance which these pastoralists felt toward Shamshi-Adad remains enigmatic; we still do not understand how this individual was able to claim the support of armies large enough to organize, defend, and protect his realm and encourage neighboring rulers to enter into vassal treaties.

For more than forty years, from the early days of exploration at

Mari, when the existence of Shamshi-Adad and Shubat Enlil became known in greater detail, the city has remained an archaeological lure, tantalizing those who would seek to penetrate the surface of the Mari archives and emerge with some greater understanding of the historical dynamics of this period. One site has always seemed the most likely candidate for Shubat Enlil: Tell Leilan. With the assistance of the Directorate-General of Antiquities in Damascus, Yale University and the Metropolitan Museum of Art have now conducted three seasons of excavation at Tell Leilan. The results are still inconclusive with regard to the historical identification of the site. Other, equally important issues, however, are now posed by these excavations. Work on the acropolis has uncovered more than 1,300 square meters of massive temple architecture within three building levels. The terminal occupation of the acropolis and the lower town is definitely within the Habur-ware ceramic period, which coincides with the reign of Shamshi-Adad and his immediate political successors.

Building Level I, immediately below the present surface of the acropolis, is clearly a scruffy rebuilding—perhaps it was a platform to fill in or create occupiable areas—within the ruins of a still larger structure. That structure, Building Level II, was a massive temple, itself apparently but a rebuilding of a still larger temple, Building Level III, with an adjoining courtyard. These two temples are indisputably tied to the reign of Shamshi-Adad, for numerous cylinder seal impressions inscribed with the names of "servants" (i.e., royal officials) of Shamshi-Adad littered their floors. Most intriguing for the purposes of historical reconstruction within the Habur Plains is the stratigraphic sequence which records the deposition of some of these cylinder seal impressions relative to those bearing the names of other rulers' servants, also retrieved upon the floors of the last temple construction, Building Level II.

Building Level II, insofar as it has been extensively excavated through the 1982 season, presents us with a unique temple plan (Figs. 43 and 44). The long central room 12 was apparently the cella of the temple, surrounded on each of its long sides by an almost parallel arrangement of side rooms. This long cella is preceded by a wide-room antecella, rooms 10–11, which then appears to lead out of the building through an entrance or gateway which might be situated directly in line with the doorway of the anteroom 10. The entire building in this phase seems to have been constructed up against the side of a mud-brick platform on the west, which certainly antedates the construction of Building Level II.

At this juncture only a small portion, some 9 meters (square

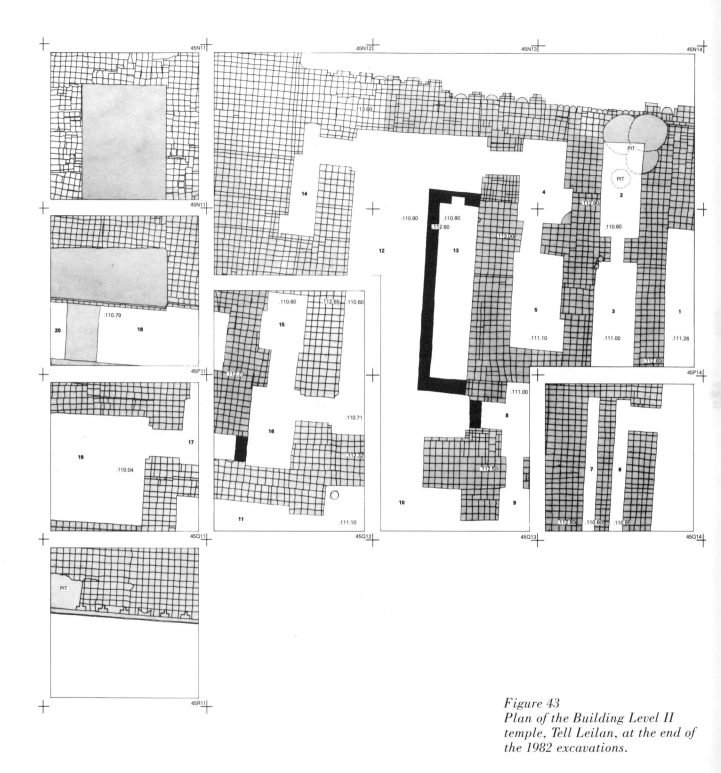

Figure 43
Plan of the Building Level II
temple, Tell Leilan, at the end of
the 1982 excavations.

OLD SYRIAN PERIOD

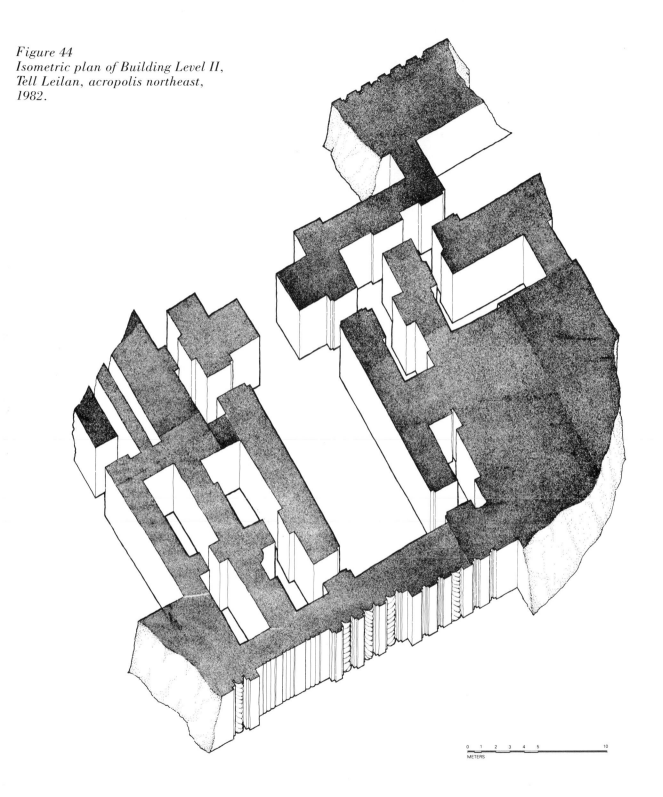

Figure 44
Isometric plan of Building Level II,
Tell Leilan, acropolis northeast,
1982.

0 1 2 3 4 5   10
METERS

45R11), of the southern facade of this building level has been retrieved, so it is not certain that such a doorway actually exists. An argument for its existence, however, is the secondary blockage-walls (hatched areas in Fig. 43) built shortly after the building level's construction by less skilled masons who clearly had other purposes in mind than those conceived by the building's architect. The long central cella was obstructed by the creation of room 13; it clearly no longer was to be used as a sacred room. Access to the central cella, or even its new room 13, was now obstructed by the small walls blocking rooms 16–17 and 8–12. With these secondary walls in place, the only entrance into this building seems to have been through the area which remains to be excavated, the continuation of the southern facade.

If these projections of internal traffic prove correct, then the plan of Building Level II is probably the earliest documented example of the classic Assyrian *langraum* ("long-room") temple, which comes to dominate the architectural conventions of Assyria during the fifteenth through ninth centuries B.C. The temple may have been an innovation of the Shamshi-Adad period, copied by his Assyrian successors much as they copied his name, his literary style, and of course his imperial ambitions. But these temples, and still earlier ones below, may also provide a link to the late prehistoric *langraum* temples at Tepe Gawra (Levels IX–VIIIC) in northern Iraq.

Alternatively, the reveals which decorate the corner walls of the long cella may lead us out of that room into rooms 16, 17, and 19 to some other doorway to the west. The plan of this building then becomes a *knichachse* ("bent axis"), harking back to the famous bent-axis temples of the Diyala region of the third millennium B.C. Perhaps Shamshi-Adad or his architect adopted older traditions of the Habur, which resulted in their perpetuation and sanctification in middle and Neo-Assyrian times.

The sequence of floors which can be associated with these secondary blockages does, however, provide us with an historical and stratigraphic framework for the sequence of occupants within the temple. The cylinder-seal impressions from the early pre-secondary wall construction are tied exclusively to Shamshi-Adad. Those which are associated with the secondary floors and their walls are tied as well to the names of small kings of the Habur region whom the Mari texts portray as participants in the twenty years of bloody drama at Shubat Enlil which followed upon the death of Shamshi-Adad. The city was subjected to repeated pillage and plunder, not only of the storehouses of grain but even of exotic riches. Armies moved in and then out of the city gates as the deposed former ruler of Mari, Zimri-Lim, regained his throne from the ineffective son of Shamshi-Adad and then marched to the north to re-establish Mari's control over the Habur's cereal riches. Armies from the east and the southeast also involved themselves in these follies. Eventually Hammurabi of Babylon, probably feeling threatened by the military chaos and seeing a chance for easy success, advanced first against Mari and destroyed the city, practically forever. He next moved against Subartu in the Habur Plains and probably removed any pretender's hopes for reconstructing a north Mesopotamian coalition or even empire that might seriously challenge the wealth of the south.

The facades of the temples at Tell Leilan display architectural decorations now known from a number of contemporary sites. Among the typical architectural features are niches, panels, and engaged columns, usually decorated with thick mud plaster and then sculpted to resemble the trunk of the palm tree. The northern facade of Building Level II, that which looks over the Habur Plains some 20 meters below and faces the mountains of the Anatolian Plateau only 20 kilometers distant, presented a very imposing array of columns crafted from pre-fashioned curved mud bricks to form spirals turning in opposite directions (see Fig. 45).

Such spiral columns also appear in the contemporary temple of Tell al-Rimah, near Tell Afar in Iraq, and at the É.BABBAR temple of Larsa on the Euphrates in southern Iraq. It is possible that they were a feature associated with Shamshi-Adad at Ashur, where the temple founded by him may not only have been *langraum* but may also have had engaged spiral columns as well. Why were spiral columns manufactured? They probably represent a long tradition in temple architecture of columns fashioned from palm trunks, a custom which can be traced at least as far back as the Uruk period in southern Mesopotamia. On the facade of a massive mud-brick temple such as Building Level II at Tell Leilan, spiral columns are a type of skeuomorph: a decoration resembling some feature which once served a practical, nondecorative function. Palm timbers were still, however, being used in the north by Shamshi-Adad, even at Shubat Enlil. As Shamshi-Adad wrote to Yasmakh-Adad:

> The palms, cypresses, and myrtles that have been brought from the town of Qatanum lie at present in the town of Subrum. Send Mashiya and a few officials with him to Subrum, where they shall divide the palms, cypresses, and myrtles into three lots. Send one third of the palms, cypresses, and myrtles to Ekallatum, one third

Figure 45
Engaged spiral columns along the
north facade of the Building Level
II temple, Tell Leilan, 1982.

to Nineveh, and one third to Shubat Enlil. . . . That which you send to Shubat Enlil is to be transported by ship to the town of Saggaratum, then from Saggaratum to Qattunan. From Qattunan let the men of Qattunan take it in wagons, and let them bring it to Shubat Enlil. (*Archives Royales de Mari* I:7: 4–31.)

Recommended Reading

Harvey Weiss. "Tell Leilan on the Habur Plains of Syria." *BiblArch* 48/1 (1985) 5–35 / "Tell Leilan and Shubat Enlil." *M.A.R.I.* 4 (1985) 1–19.

OLD SYRIAN PERIOD

EBLA (TELL MARDIKH)

Location: 55 km south of Aleppo
Dates: Period I, 3500–3000 B.C., through Period VI, 560–530 B.C.
Excavations: 1964 to present, annually (University of Rome)
Publications of the Western Palace and royal tombs: P. Matthiae et al.
   SEb I/9 (1979) 138 // P. Matthiae *Ugarit-Forschungen* 11 (1979) 563–569
   / *CRAIBL* (1980) 94 / *CRAIBL* (1982) 299 / *Akkadica* 17 (1980) 1 /
   Archaeology 33/2 (1980) 9 / *AfO* 19 (1982) 121 / *Antike Welt* 13/1 (1982)
   3, 129 / *BiblArch* 47/1 (1984) 18 (For other publications, see the earlier
   description of Ebla, p. 134.)

Although references to Ebla continue to appear in the southern Mesopotamian literature of the late third and early second millennium B.C., archaeological research at the site has yet to uncover significant occupational traces for the span from the Akkadian destruction until the Old Syrian period. This situation is particularly intriguing because southern Mesopotamian sources, including the inscriptions of Gudea, the powerful ruler of Lagash, a major city in the south during this period, frequently mention Ebla.

The Old Syrian period at Tell Mardikh is the equivalent of the Middle Bronze I and II periods of Palestinian archaeologists and coincides with the Old Babylonian and Old Assyrian periods of the Mesopotamian archaeologists. At Tell Mardikh itself the period is designated Mardikh IIIA and IIIB. Ebla at this time was probably inhabited by persons who spoke Amorite or were of Amorite descent. As described in the Introduction, Amorite is one of the West Semitic (or Northwest Semitic) languages for which the sole documentation consists of personal names. At this period, persons with Amorite names (as opposed to, for instance, Akkadian ones) controlled the political structures of Mari, Babylon, and the myriad other cities along the Euphrates. As in the case of the tablets found in the Mari archives, however, all cuneiform communication was carried on in Akkadian, although the cuneiform documentation from Ebla is still not extensive.

From this period at Ebla comes a basalt statue fragment with a twenty-six-line Akkadian cuneiform dedicatory inscription of King Ibbit-Lim (Aleppo TM.68.G.61) found in 1968. It was this statue which first made possible the localization of Ebla in this region and possibly at Tell Mardikh. Previously all of the, admittedly slippery, historical and geographical estimates of Assyriologists and archaeologists had placed the city farther to the north.

An enormous earthen wall surrounded Ebla during this period. Massive dressed stone blocks secured its foundations, while its heights were ornamentally faced with clay and plaster. Towers and other fortified emplacements strengthened the wall at strategic locations. One of the city gates in the wall has been fully excavated (Fig. 46). On the inner side of the gate a two-chambered building with double doors guarded the entrance. Enormous rectangular

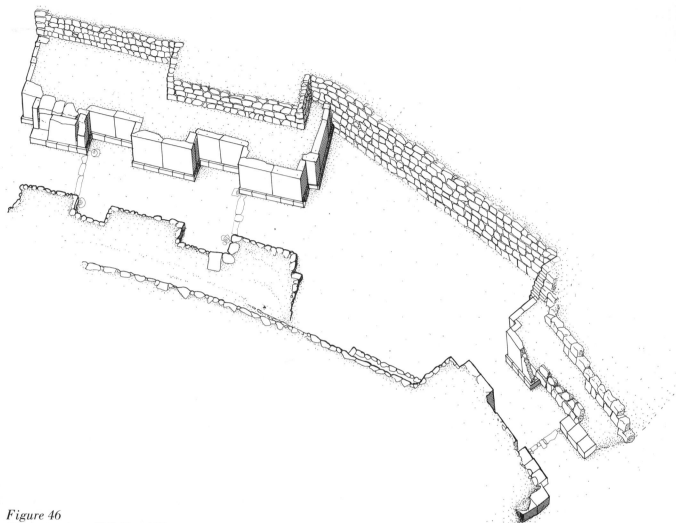

Figure 46
City gate A, at Tell Mardikh.

stone blocks faced the lower parts of the chambers' walls. Moving toward the outside one passed through a large court and then a single-chambered gateway before reaching the city wall's exterior. A large tower protected the city at just this point.

At two loci within the lower city of Tell Mardikh, Professor Paolo Matthiae and his colleagues have uncovered residential structures and religious buildings. The largest of the temples uncovered, called Temple D (Fig. 47), lies on the west side of the acropolis and was probably the city's main shrine during this period. This temple features a long cella with a cultic niche (probably for a statue), preceded by a wide anteroom, guarded by two lion figures, and a similarly oriented wide-form vestibule. This temple plan and room arrange-

OLD SYRIAN PERIOD

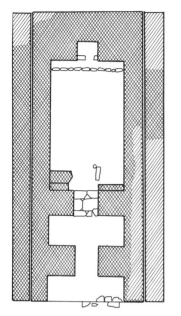

Figure 47
Temple D, Tell Mardikh.

ment—long cella with wide ante-cella—is characteristic of Syrian temple architecture for this period. A large stone ritual basin, part of the temple cult inventory, was retrieved from the corner of the cella (see Fig. 48 and Cat. No. 116).

In the northern part of the acropolis lay the royal residence, a building with many courts constructed like terraces. Similar in some respects to the royal residence is the building initially designated Q and now known as the Western Palace. The signs of destruction and burning which have been detected within the Western Palace associate the structure with other contemporaneous palaces in northwest Syrian cities which were probably destroyed in the expan-

sionary raids of the Old Hittite kings.

The ancients did not consider the future needs of archaeologists at all, which often presents considerable stratigraphic complexities. The Western Palace, for instance, is situated west of the third-millennium Palace G, but its eastern boundary wall was set on the foundations of the west facade of the third-millennium palace's audience court. The Western Palace provides evidence of two phases of use through two, partially overlapping floors.

Subterranean tombs (hypogea) under the floors of the palace reveal the practices and perhaps ideas associated with death and the cosmos during this period in west-

Figure 48
In the center foreground, the ritual basin (Cat. No. 116) in situ in Temple D, Tell Mardikh.

ern Syria. These tombs were cut into the limestone immediately under the surface at Tell Mardikh. Initially they were approached through two entry ways, and additional approaches were later set with large basalt blocks. These tombs were obviously those of royalty, as evidenced by the very unusual wealth and fine workmanship of the burial objects. At least six tombs have been identified, three (designated the Tomb of the Princess, the Tomb of the Lord of the Goats, and the Tomb of the Cistern) have provided the bronze, ceramic, and gold ornaments— many indicating far-ranging trade contacts and artistic influences— which are illustrated in the exhibition (see Cat. Nos. 104–115, 117).

Professor Matthiae has recently explained the subterranean royal burials through an analysis of the afterlife ideology described in Ugarit texts from a period only slightly later. The central location of this royal necropolis, and its relationship to the situation of contemporary temples within the city, and even to the Western Palace, suggest that the city's public loci, whether palace, temple, or necropolis, were all conceived as a unit expressing the cult worship of royal ancestors. In southern Mesopotamia, as well as northwestern Syria, a royal ancestor cult may very well have been a feature of the Amorite societies now characterizing the urban centers of the region. Tell Mardikh provides an impressive range of evidence for this aspect of Old Syrian social and religious life.

The Old Hittite kingdom of the seventeenth century B.C., like many of its successor kingdoms, repeatedly sought control of the fertile lands of northwestern Syria. Under Hattushili I and then Mursili I, the Hittites repeatedly attacked the region, destroying the centers of Alalakh (near ancient and modern Antioch), the large and famous city of Urshu (which Professor Matthiae identifies with Tell Touqan), and probably Ebla as well. The kingdom of Yamkhad, centered on modern Aleppo and certainly the major western power of the period, was also destroyed by the Hittites, who then turned their attention to the south and in a lightning raid in 1595 B.C. managed to sack Babylon before beating a hasty retreat.

HARVEY WEISS // KAY KOHLMEYER

TERQA AND THE KINGDOM OF KHANA

GIORGIO BUCCELLATI AND MARILYN KELLY-BUCCELLATI

THE DISCOVERIES OF MARI, UGARIT, AND EBLA HAVE DONE FOR OUR century what the discoveries of Nineveh, Nimrud, and Khorsabad did for the last: they have riveted the attention of scholars and laymen alike on monumental buildings, on impressive works of art, and—perhaps most important—on vast epigraphic archives. Now that the limelight has shifted to Syria, and the special character of its early urban tradition is emerging in full splendor, we may wonder why such a realization has been so long in coming. It was late in the last century when the first cuneiform tablets of demonstrable Syrian provenance were found at Amarna in Egypt. Where, we may ask, were the first tablets found on Syrian soil? The site was Terqa, about 60 kilometers north of Mari near the juncture of the Habur and Euphrates rivers.

Still in the last century, shortly after the discovery at Amarna, F. Thureau-Dangin published the text of a contract which had been bought on the market but could be shown, on internal evidence, to have come from Terqa. Shortly after the beginning of the century a German archaeologist, who had stopped by accident at the site of Terqa, picked up on the surface a cuneiform document of greater significance: the foundation deposit of the temple of Dagan. Epigraphic finds from Terqa continued to trickle in over the years and came to constitute the group of Khana texts, so-called from the name of the kingdom of which Terqa was the capital. Until the discovery of Mari, the Khana texts, although few in number, represented the major single body of texts from Syria, and as such they were given their due attention by Assyriologists. With the recent excavations at Terqa, the total epigraphic collection reaches about a hundred items, a slender amount numerically but significant in other respects. Not only is the Terqa epigraphic inventory the third oldest in Syria, it is also quite diversified in its provenance (private houses, streets, a temple, and a large administrative building) and in its typology (royal inscriptions, contracts, legal documents, letters, school texts, administrative texts, and a religious/literary text).

Excavations at Terqa are entering their ninth season—the longest American participation in an archaeological project in Syria. What is emerging is the picture of a city which was the successor of Mari on the mid-Euphrates. This much was anticipated on the basis of the Khana texts. Unexpected, on the other hand, was the discovery of massive third-millennium strata, including a large city wall. Also surprising was the extremely scarce evidence of Aramaic presence. Briefly the history of Terqa and its kingdom may be outlined as follows:

(1) It started out as a full-blown city around 3000 B.C., without any evidence of earlier strata at the site itself (there are important fourth-millennium strata at a nearby site, Qraya). The formidable defensive ring was established *ex novo*, indicating perhaps that the city was planned as such rather than having evolved organically and gradually from earlier settlements.

(2) While the defensive system remained in use for some 1,500 years, there is little evidence that Terqa enjoyed major political power in the second half of the third millennium. We may project back to this period the situation of the time (immediately following) when Terqa functioned as a provincial capital in the reign of Mari. Some indirect evidence points, however, to a possible role of Terqa as a religious center of unique significance *vis-à-vis* the capital, Mari. It may also be that the royal family of Mari was in fact originally from Terqa.

(3) Whatever the situation was, Terqa became the capital of the kingdom once controlled by Mari—the Habur and Middle Euphrates basin. (The evidence for Terqa's political position as a capital is circumstantial but compelling.) The territory bordered on Babylon to the south and the Habur triangle to the north, which placed the kingdom of Khana territorially on a par with the other major kingdoms of the Syro-Mesopotamian area, after the short-lived expansionist policies of Hammurabi were replaced by the more traditional patterns of regional distribution of power. We know of thirteen kings ruling the new Khana kingdom from Terqa, and five of them are associated with specific buildings that have been found in the excavations.

(4) The Aramaeans were present at Terqa from 1500 B.C. on, but they left behind very little, perhaps because the site was essentially uninhabited and served the tribe of Laqe only as a ceremonial center. If so, the presumed ancient distinction of Terqa as the center of

Dagan's cult survived after Terqa itself was abandoned as a regularly functioning urban center.

The most important architectural find at Terqa is the city wall. A solid mud-brick structure some 20 meters thick and 1.6 kilometers long, it was built in three stages beginning shortly after 3000 B.C. The impetus for its construction was perhaps danger from the rising Euphrates as much as from military incursions.

Going from the cyclopic dimensions of the city wall to a smaller scale, another discovery at Terqa which deserves special mention is an office-like area in which a scribe sat to conduct his business. Located in a room of a sprawling building, perhaps administrative in nature, this ancient office included all the elements of its modern counterpart. A platform of baked bricks set in a dirt floor corresponds to what we would call a desk. Instead of drawers, there were two jars within reach of the scribe as he squatted on the platform: one contained plain clay, ready for writing, and the other held six tablets. On one side a narrow bin set in a wall served most likely as a filing cabinet where the scribe probably kept his reference works. But as these were precious, he seems to have taken them with him as he left one day, leaving only a small tablet of little consequence. Seven more tablets were scattered on the floor, and just outside the door was a basket, well preserved but empty; if it had been used as a briefcase, then the scribe had filed all its contents away.

The single most important group of artifacts from Terqa are the cuneiform documents, some dating from the period of Mari but most from the Khana period. About 100 in number, they are diversified in content. A well-known document is an official royal inscription which records the dedication of an "ice house." The contracts are very characteristic, showing great concern for the preservation of certain obligations. For example, large numbers of witnesses were present at each transaction, and their names, filiation, and profession are inscribed on the documents. Several witnesses affixed their seals on the documents in lieu of signatures (only scribes could write in cuneiform). The tablets were encased in clay envelopes, which repeated the text of the tablet almost like a carbon copy. In case of a controversy about the authenticity of the contract, the envelope would be opened in front of a judge and only the text inside was considered to be juridically binding. In one rare case well documented at Terqa, not one but two envelopes were placed around the contract.

The punishments for breach of contract were imaginative. For breach of sale, hot asphalt was to be poured on the head of the transgressor. In the case of a will made by a husband with his wife as beneficiary, the punishment envisaged in case the husband were to file for divorce calls for him to leave the house "empty handed" and to go tend the palace oxen. Should the wife file for divorce, she too would have to leave the house "in her nakedness" and be exposed from the roof terrace of the palace. As a guarantor of the juridical order, the palace (i.e., the royal administration) would receive for every case of breach of contract a substantial monetary fine.

While serving the purposes of a legal transaction, the seals are also the embodiment of an important artistic tradition. The corpus of Terqa seals and seal impressions is significant for several reasons. Artistic monuments, especially well-dated ones, are scarce from this period in Syro-Mesopotamia, and Terqa thus provides well-stratified documentation to fill in the gap. This enables us to securely determine the stylistic developments during the approximately 200 years that Terqa was a major power in the region. The Khana style, named after the kingdom, is characterized by a blending of Mesopotamian and Syrian elements, syncretized into a uniquely harmonious whole. The seal carvers chose to depict their figures in such a way that the initial drillings used in the cutting of the stone are still quite obvious. They often placed the principal deity on the left side of the seal, as opposed to the prevailing right-hand orientation of Mesopotamian and Syrian seals. Taking full advantage of the whole area of the seal to display the principal figures, Khana seal carvers did not clutter up the background with a number of smaller figures, which is so often the case in seals carved in the surrounding areas. (See Fig. 49.)

Since many of the seal owners are named in the tablets, we are also able to reconstruct up to three generations of the families living in the city as well as their activities. This is especially the case during the reign of one of the Khana kings, Yadikh-Abu (ca. 1720 B.C.). In one instance we can even determine the economic status of an individual, Puzurum, along with that of his family.

A rich find was made in a corner of the altar room of the temple dedicated to Ninkarrak, the goddess of healing. A total of 6,637 beads were found clustered tightly together in what must have been a bag which had disintegrated (see Fig. 50). The beads were mostly of semi-precious stone, from lapis and carnelian to agate and chalcedony. From religious texts we know that these were the kinds of precious amulets which were given to patients who sought relief from bad omens. Thus it is plausible that a pouch once contained these stones which were to be given to patient-worshipers by a priest.

What at first seemed like a more modest find turned out to be of

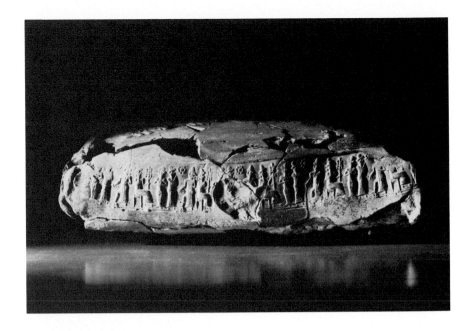

Figure 49
Seal impression on the side of a
clay envelope from Terqa, dating to
ca. 1720 B.C.

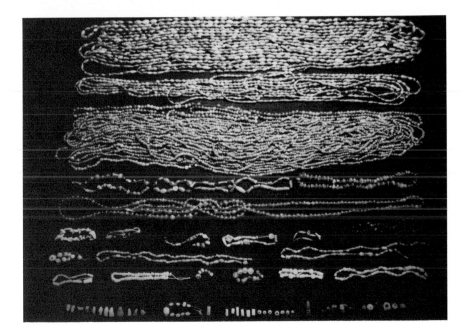

Figure 50
Hoard of beads found in the
Ninkarrak Temple at Terqa.

great historical significance. A few carbonized cloves were found in a jar in a pantry room of a middle-class house. What is remarkable about these cloves is that they originated in the Far East and in fact were not previously known to have been in use in the West before Roman times. Our find extends back in time by almost 2,000 years and out in geographical area by some 6,500 kilometers the range of cultural connections between Terqa and the Mesopotamian area on the one hand and the Eastern trade routes on the other.

Recommended Reading

G. Buccellati et al. "Terqa Preliminary Reports, 1–12." *Syro-Mesopotamian Studies* 1 (1977)–3 (1983).

O. Rouault. *L'archive de Puzurum*. Bibliotheca Mesopotamica 16 (Malibu: Undena, 1984).

86

85
Cylinder seal
See color plate p. 178

Site: Mari (Tell Hariri), Temples Anonymes
Date: Late Akkadian period, ca. 2250 B.C.
Material: Shell with copper caps
Height: 4.0 cm; *with caps:* 6.1 cm; *diameter:* 2.8 cm
Museum No: Damascus S 2184 (M. 2734)
Literature: A. Parrot *Syria* 31 (1954) 153, Plate XV 1 / *Mari* 90, Fig. 47 / *Iraq* 36 (1974) 189 // R.M. Boehmer *Die Entwicklung der Glyptik während der Akkad-Zeit* (Berlin 1965) Fig. 552 // *Propyläen Kunstgeschichte* 14, 236, Fig. 136h // H. Kühne *Das Rollsiegel in Syrien* (Tübingen 1980) 58

The design of this seal features a bearded god wearing a long flounced robe and a horned crown sitting on a stylized mountain holding a staff in his right hand. Long-necked birds' heads appear on either side of the mountain, spewing streams of water. Behind the seated god stands a female deity, apparently with branches growing from her body and head. She wears a horned crown and her hair, gathered in a pigtail, hangs down her back. In her hands she holds a vessel. A bearded god with a long spear, also wearing a horned crown with vegetation on top, stands with one leg forward behind another female deity who presents a branch or standard to the god seated on the mountain. These two figures are both standing in streams of water. Two stars fill the space in front of the seated god. Various interpretations regarding this seal have been offered; for example, that the seated deity may represent Anu, or even the Syrian god El, but the seal definitely belongs to the southern Mesopotamian Akkadian tradition.
U.K.

86
Cylinder seal of Idi-ilum

Site: Mari (Tell Hariri), eastern perimeter of the palace
Date: Late Shakkanakku period, ca. 2000 B.C.
Material: Hematite
Height: 2.75 cm; diameter: 1.4 cm
Museum No.: Aleppo 6296 (M. 1400)
Literature: A. Parrot *MAM* II 3 (1959) 146, Fig. 99, Plate XXXIX

This seal impression depicts a so-called presentation scene. A suppliant goddess and a worshiper stand in front of a seated god. Both deities wear flounced robes and horned crowns, while the worshiper wears a plain fringed robe and skullcap covering his hair. Above the scene is a sun disk in a crescent, the symbol of the sun god Shamash.

This motif was introduced in Akkadian times, but became very popular during the Third Dynasty of Ur. The inscription reads: "Idi-ilum, *shakkanakku* (governor) of Mari: Iddin-Dagan, *shabra* (priest)."
U.K.

87
Cylinder seal

Site: Mari (Tell Hariri), Palace, "appartements privés"
Date: Early Old Syrian period, ca. 1900–1750 B.C.
Material: Hematite
Height: 2.6 cm; *diameter:* 1.4 cm
Museum No.: Aleppo 6307 (M. 828)
Literature: A. Parrot *MAM* II, 3 (1959) 150, Plate XXXIX
   828

Two figures have been added to the presentation scene
on this seal: the goddess standing behind the throne
and "the divine king as warrior." In the central scene
we find the seated god and the suppliant goddess presenting a worshiper who carries a sacrifice. The
bearded god sits on his throne with his feet on a
footstool. Like the two goddesses he is wearing a
horned crown and a flounced robe; he holds a staff or
scepter in his right hand. The worshiper standing before him wears a long robe and a broad-rimmed cap
and carries the sacrificial animal under his left arm.
The suppliant goddess behind him, dressed in a
flounced robe, wears a heavy necklace with a counterweight down her back. Behind her stands the bearded
"divine king as warrior"; he wears a cap with a brim
and a knee-length garment; his pose is victorious. The
filler motifs between the figures are a human head, a
bird, a lion with open jaws, and a horned goat. Behind
the seated god is the symbol of Shamash, a sun disk in
a crescent.
U.K.

88
Statue of a worshiper

Site: Mari (Tell Hariri), Temples Anonymes
Date: Akkadian period, ca. 2350–2250
Material: Gypsum
Height: 23 cm; *width:* 16 cm
Museum No.: Aleppo 1525
Literature: A. Parrot *Mélanges syriens offerts à Monsieur
   René Dussaud* (Paris 1939) 171 / *Syria* 20 (1939) Plate VII /
   Sumer: The Dawn of Art (New York 1961) Fig. 341 / *Mari*
   93, Plate VII 2 // E. Strommenger *BaM* 1 (1960) 54 //
   Spycket *La Statuaire* 161

Among the few Mari art works that date from the
Akkadian period are the cylinder seal shown in Cat.
No. 85 and this statue found east of the Dagan Tem-
ple. It shows the worshiper carrying a sacrificial ani-

mal with one leg hanging over his left arm, reminiscent of Early Dynastic representations. He is dressed in a tufted robe gathered under a thick collar. His hair is covered by a cap with a rolled-up brim tied at the right ear; from somewhat later texts we know that *en*-priests wore such headgear. His upperlip is shaved (cf. the statue of Lamgi-Mari in Cat. No. 62), while his beard is carefully worked in wavy rows ending in curls. The worshiper's features, especially the ears, are naturalistically rendered.

The excavator dated this statue to the beginning of the second millennium. This piece, however, can be compared to a fragment of a statue and a stele from Susa, dating to the even earlier Akkadian period.
K.K.

89
Fragment of a statue

Site: Mari (Tell Hariri), Zimri-Lim Palace, foundation deposit in room 149
Date: Late Shakkanakku period, ca. 2000 B.C.
Material: Red-brown slatelike stone
Height: 19 cm; *width:* 9.5 cm; *depth:* 7 cm
Museum No.: Aleppo 2164 (M. 1389)
Literature: A. Parrot *Syria* 19 (1938) 16, Plate VII 2 / *MAM* II, 3 (1959) 14, Plate XII // G. Dossin *RA* 34 (1937) 176 // E. Strommenger *BaM* 1 (1960) 76 // Spycket *La Statuaire* 242

The inscription on the seam of the garment of this statue reads: "Lashgan, son of Asmatien . . . has dedicated his statue to Anunitum." Anunitum is the equivalent of the militant Ishtar of the Akkadian period. The open wrap-around robe and the beard of this worshiper remind us of the two statues which were dedicated by Puzur-ishtar to the *shakkanakku* of Mari, which once formed an exhibit in the Neo-Babylonian palace "museum" at Babylon. A functionary named Lashgan is mentioned in contemporary texts; this statue may represent the same person.

It is a pity that this beautifully worked piece is only partially preserved. It was placed, apparently in this condition, in a foundation deposit box buried next to the entrance of the ante-cella to the temple. Besides this fragment the deposit contained only ashes and pieces of bricks.
K.K.

90
Statue of the goddess with the flowing vase

Site: Mari (Tell Hariri), Zimri-Lim Palace, room 64 and
  courtyard 106
Date: Early Old Syrian period, ca. 1800–1750 B.C.
Material: White stone
Height: 1.42 cm; *width of base:* 0.48 cm
Museum No.: Aleppo 1659
Literature: A. Parrot *Syria* 18 (1937) 78 / *MAM* II, 3 (1959) 5,
  Plates IV–VI, frontispiece // Strommenger and Hirmer
  Mesopotamien 88 Figs. 162, 163 // W. Orthmann
  Propyläen Kunstgeschichte 14, 292, Fig. 160b // Y. al-
  Khalesi "The Court of the Palms" *Bibliotheca
  Mesopotamica* 8 (1978) 37 // A. Parrot *Syria* 56 (1979) 411
  // Tokyo Exhibition No. 72 // Spycket *La Statuaire* 224

This statue was reconstructed from many fragments.
The horned headdress indicates her status as a goddess. Her hair is parted in the middle and falls in two
heavy braids to her shoulders. She wears rich jewelry:
several earrings, a necklace of six rows of beads with
a counterweight down her back, and triple-ringed
bracelets. The front of her laced dress is decorated
with a fish design; the sleeves are scalloped. The eye-
sockets have remnants of gypsum, but the eye inlays
are lost. A channel leads through the figure to the
vase in her hand, from which water once flowed.

   It has not been determined where this statue originally stood. The body was found in room 64 of the
Zimri-Lim Palace, the head in courtyard 106. On the
south wall of the courtyard, near the entrance to the
room, a large mural includes twin images of the goddess with the flowing vase. She stands facing the ruler
who, accompanied by a suppliant goddess, is worship-
ping Ishtar. The scene probably represents the investiture ceremony of King Zimri-Lim, which could have
taken place in adjacent rooms. Both the statue and the
wall painting can be dated to the palace's terminal
occupation period.
K.K.

91
Administrative text

Site: Mari (Tell Hariri), Zimri-Lim Palace, room 5
Date: Early Old Syrian period, reign of Zimri-Lim, ca.
  1775–1761 B.C.
Material: Clay
Height: 20.7 cm; *width:* 11.1 cm; *depth:* 4.5 cm
Museum No.: Aleppo 3140 (M. 1706) ·

90, left

Literature: M. Birot *ARM* 9 (1960) (= *Textes Cunéiformes du
  Louvre,* 30) 24–29, 335, No. 27

The precise purpose of this long list of names and
titles of "people from Mari" is not entirely clear. The
undamaged part of the tablet contains the names of
100 males, 52 females, 2 children, and 10 girls. Various titles and occupations are included. For example,

in the case of males, there are skilled artisans: washers, valets, singers, leather workers, cowhands, tailors, scribes, and gardeners; listed as household personnel are field workers, shepherds, cooks, stablemen, and servants. Also mentioned are millers and brewers. Female occupations include housekeepers, water carriers, and weavers. The text is dated to the 24th Abu (= the fourth month) of the year that "Zimri-Lim came to the aid of the ruler of Babylon for the second time." The "ruler of Babylon" was certainly Hammurabi, but we cannot fix the date exactly.
W.R.

92
Administrative text

Site: Mari (Tell Hariri), Zimri-Lim Palace, room 5
Date: Early Old Syrian period, reign of Zimri-Lim, ca. 1775–1761 B.C.
Material: Clay
Height: 15.3 cm; *width:* 9 cm; *depth:* 3.7 cm
Museum No.: Aleppo 3140 (M. 1713)
Literature: M. Birot *ARM* 9 (1960) (= *Textes Cunéiformes du Louvre,* 30) 111–116, No. 168

This is an account of the daily delivery of food for the royal household in the month of *Eburum* (the twelfth month). It lists milled grain, soaked grain, sourdough bread, *shipku*-barley, peas, *alappanu*-beer, and oil. On the last day of the month there are special deliveries for the king's sacrifices to the gods. Although the text is undated, it may belong to the reign of Zimri-Lim like the previous text from room 5.
W.R.

93
Foundation tablet

Site: Mari (Tell Hariri), *Sakhuru,* depot 5
Date: Beginning of the Third Dynasty of Ur, ca. 2100 B.C.
Material: Bronze
Height and width: 11.9 cm; *depth:* 0.4 cm
Museum No.: Aleppo 6821 (M. 1785)
Literature: A. Parrot *Syria* 21 (1940) Plate II4 / *Mari* 98 // G. Dossin *Syria* 21 (1940) 159 // M. Civil *RA* 56 (1962) 213

During the 1938 season of exploration at Tell Hariri the walls of a temple cella with large entrance pillars were excavated not far from the ziggurat. Nailed to the four corners of the walls were inscribed bronze plaques

which stated that "Niwar-Mer, *shakkanakku* (governor) of Mari, built this temple for Ninhursag." Immediately north of the cella was a connecting corridor. Under the opening of the western main portals of this corridor were buried a number of large clay bricks with carved square holes into which bronze plaques had been positioned. Here we show one of these plaques as an example of foundation deposits of the Ur III period.

The inscription on the plaque reads: "Apil-Kin, the mighty, governor of Mari, builder of the *Sakhuru,*" which was probably the name of the building in which these foundation deposits were found. From another text we know that the daughter of Apil-Kin married a son of Ur-Nammu, first king of the Ur III dynasty, and

92

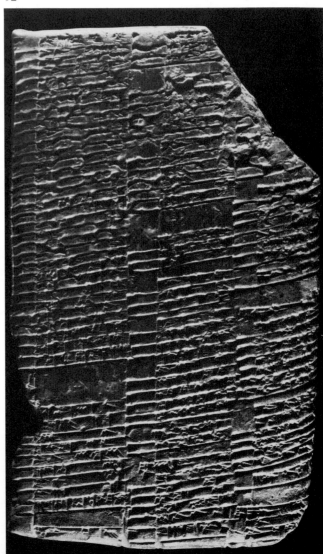

93

thus we can include this tablet and the building in the chronological framework of the Mesopotamian List of Kings.

K.K.

94
Foundation brick

Site: Mari (Tell Hariri), Shamash Temple
Date: Reign of King Yakhdun-Lim, ca. 1820–1800 B.C.
Material: Fired clay
Height: 41 cm; *width:* 40.5 cm; *depth:* 7 cm
Museum No.: Damascus S 2145
Literature: A. Parrot *Syria* 31 (1954) 161, Fig. 4 // G. Dossin *Syria* 32 (1955) 1–28 // J.-R. Kupper *IRSA* (1971) 245–249 (IVF 66)

This is one of the nine foundation bricks with a long inscription of King Yakhdun-Lim, son of another Mari king, Yaggid-Lim, found in the Shamash Temple. The bricks are inscribed in Old Babylonian style script with three columns on the obverse and one or two on the reverse. They were placed with the beginning of

the inscription facing down in the foundation walls.

The inscription starts by praising the sun god, Shamash, to whom the temple was dedicated. It continues by introducing King Yakhdun-Lim of Mari to whom the following deeds are ascribed: (1) a military campaign to the Mediterranean Sea; (2) a victorious battle with three kings from the middle Euphrates region, who were allies of the kingdom of Yamkhad/ Aleppo; (3) destruction of the city of Haman, the central fortress of the Hanaeans, a dominant tribe of pastoral nomads; (4) restoration work on the bank of the Euphrates; (5) construction of the temple dedicated to Shamash called *Egirzalaanki* ("the temple that is the glory of heaven and earth"). Then follow the various blessings and curses common to these inscriptions.

W.R.

95
Baking mold

Site: Mari (Tell Hariri), Zimri-Lim Palace, room 77
Date: Early Old Syrian period, ca. 1900–1750 B.C.
Material: Porous terracotta
Diameter: 22 cm; *depth:* 4.5 cm
Museum No.: Aleppo 1565 (M. 1033)
Literature: A. Parrot *Syria* 18 (1937) 75, Plate XII 1 / *MAM* II, 3 (1959) 34, Fig. 28, Plate XVII // Tokyo Exhibition No. 78

A group of fired but porous clay molds were found in the kitchen areas of the palace of King Zimri-Lim. Nearby in a large courtyard with two built-in ovens (one with a diameter of 3.75 m) storage vessels and basalt mortars were also retrieved (see Fig. 51). The molds from room 77 may have fallen from a collapsed upper story. None shows signs of direct contact with open fire. Most of the molds are rather shallow with incised designs in the bottom depicting both wild and domestic animals, mythological figures, and geometric patterns. The excavator assumed that the molds were used to prepare food for the royal table, and he believed they might have shaped cheeses or cakes. The porosity of the clay suggests that they would have been used for baking. The design of the mold in Cat. No. 95 shows two goats eating leaves off a tree.

K.K.

Figure 51
Workshop-courtyard in Zimri-Lim
Palace, Mari.

96
Baking mold

Site: Mari (Tell Hariri), Zimri-Lim Palace, room 77
Date: Early Old Syrian period, ca. 1900–1750 B.C.
Material: Porous terracotta
Height: 19 cm; *width:* 23.5 cm; *depth:* 8.2 cm
Museum No.: Aleppo 1561 (M. 1032)
Literature: A. Parrot *Syria* 18 (1937) 75, Plate XII 3 / *MAM*
II, 3 (1959) 35, Fig. 29, Plate XVIII // Tokyo Exhibition
No. 73

The design of this mold shows a bearded male in a
knee-length robe leading a stag by the horns and the

94, left

ca. 2100–1600 B.C.

231

neck. In front of them jumps a dog whose shape and head identify it as the *Saluki*, a hunting dog documented as early as the fifth millennium. A smaller stag appears in the left corner.

K.K.

97
Baking mold

Site: Mari (Tell Hariri), Zimri-Lim Palace, room 77
Date: Early Old Syrian period, ca 1900–1750 B.C.
Material: Porous terracotta
Height: 23.6 cm; *width:* 12.5 cm; *depth:* 6.8 cm
Museum No.: Aleppo 2169 (M. 1044)
Literature: A. Parrot *Syria* 18 (1937) 77, Fig. 13 / *MAM* II, 3 (1959) 37, Fig. 31, Plate XIX // Tokyo Exhibition No. 74

In the design of this mold a female figure sits on a bench with her hands supporting her breasts. She wears heavy necklaces and her hair is covered with a turbanlike scarf. Goddesses are often depicted naked and supporting their breasts, both on cylinder seals and terracotta figurines from the third to the second millennium B.C.

K.K.

98
Mold

Site: Mari (Tell Hariri), Zimri-Lim Palace, room 76
Date: Early Old Syrian period, ca. 1900–1750 B.C.
Material: Pink limestone
Height: 16 cm; *width:* 15.5 cm; *depth:* 6.5 cm
Museum No.: Aleppo 1571 (M. 1004)
Literature: A. Parrot *MAM* II, 3 (1959) 31, Fig. 27

A female figure is carved on the smoothly polished surface of a rather crudely cut piece of limestone. She wears rich jewelry around her neck, similar to that of Cat. No. 90, and large earrings; her thick hair reaches to her shoulders. The upper body is outlined with a thin groove. Since this is a fragment, we do not know why the body has been rendered separately from the head or even what function the piece served. Regardless of what was poured into the mold, the body would have to have been fashioned separately. This piece was found near the baking molds shown in Cat. Nos. 95–97 and may have had some connection with the kitchens.

K.K.

95, 96, 97, left

98

99
Fragment of a wall painting
See color plate p. 179

Site: Mari (Tell Hariri), Zimri-Lim Palace, courtyard 106
Date: Early Old Syrian period, ca. 1900–1750 B.C.
Material: Paint on gypsum plaster
Height: 47 cm; *width:* 52 cm
Museum No.: Aleppo 1666
Literature: A. Parrot *Syria* 18 (1937) 345 / *MAM* II, 2 (1958) 19, Fig. 18, Plate V 1 // Strommenger and Hirmer *Mesopotamien* 88 Fig. 164 bottom // A. Moortgat, *BaM* 3 (1964) 70 / *Die Kunst des Alten Mesopotamien* (1967) 76 // U. Seidl *Propyläen Kunstgeschichte* 14, 304, Fig. 188b

The thick plaster walls of courtyard 106 were decorated with wall paintings, some of which could be restored. This fragment shows part of a sacrificial procession from the south wall. A priest or servant leads a bull by a rope tied to its nose ring. He is wearing a woolen garment, decorated with a border of different material, over a knee-length robe (as we know from other figures). His soft hat is tied with two bands. The horns of the sacrificial animal have metal tips, and a moon crescent decorates its forehead. The representation of the bull's head is similar to that in statuary and glyptic art: we see the horns and forehead *en face*, while the rest of the head is in profile. This convention was common until the time of Hammurabi, and only later do we find representations entirely in profile. The figures are outlined in black; the colors are white, black, yellow, and reddish-brown. Blue and ochre are also seen on other fragments.

K.K.

100
Fragment of a wall painting
See color plate p. 178

Site: Mari (Tell Hariri), Zimri-Lim Palace, room 220
Date: Early Old Syrian period, ca. 1900–1750 B.C.
Material: Paint on gypsum plaster
Height: 12.5 cm; *width:* 9.6 cm
Museum No.: Damascus S (M. 4587)
Literature: A Parrot *Syria* 44 (1967) 4, Plate I 4 // Tokyo Exhibition No. 69

In 1966, during re-excavation of the two large rooms of the Zimri-Lim Palace, several additional pieces of fresco were found. This fragment of a bearded male was one of them. He is wearing a striped cap with a rolled-up brim. The excavator suggests that this represents a feather crown, but if we compare it with the contemporary feather crowns of winged creatures, it seems more likely to be the rounded cap of the worshiper. The fresco is painted in red, blue, and beige on a light brown background.

K.K.

101
Model of a house

Site: Supposedly from Salamiyya, near Hama
Date: Early Dynastic until Akkadian period, 2900–2290 B.C.
Material: Terracotta
Height: 42 cm; *length:* 54 cm; *depth:* 27 cm
Museum No.: Aleppo 1665
Literature: L. Wooley *Alalakh* (1955) 49, Plate IX // W. Khayata *APA* 5/6 (1974–1975) 171, Figs. 1–5

This large, completely preserved model has a partition with a round window-opening inside. From the outside the house appears to have two stories, but the inside does not have a dividing floor. Rows of birds, perhaps doves, appear under the molding on the outside walls.

A number of similar house models were found at the Early Dynastic Ishtar Temple at Ashur and in several Syrian contexts such as Emar of the fourteenth to thirteenth centuries. Textual and glyptic clues to the significance of such models suggest that they were votive objects. Dating is difficult since this type was found in both Early Dynastic and Akkadian contexts.

K.K.

102
Seal impression on a pot

Site: Ebla (Tell Mardikh), Sector B
Date: Old Syrian period, 1700–1650 B.C. (Mardikh IIIB)
Material: Fired clay
Height of impression: 7.5 cm
Museum No.: Aleppo 6331 (TM. 66. B. 207; TM. 65. B. 264)
Literature: P. Matthiae *MAIS* 1965 Plate 79: 3–4 / *MAIS* 1966 Plate 59: 1 / *Syria* 46 (1969) 1 / *Ebla* 143, Figs. 99–100 and 32 / *MonANE* 1/6 Plate XII

A cylinder seal was rolled on the shoulder of this vessel before it was fired. Since the seal was lightly rolled and the vessel made of rather coarse clay, the seal's qualities are only visible in part. However, several fragments permit us to reconstruct the design, as shown in Fig. 52.

A worshiper and a god stand under an Egyptian-inspired sun disk. Behind the god is an inscription and a goddess. The worshiper, who wears a robe with fringed edges, has long wavy hair and a beard. He faces the god, also dressed in a short robe, who wears a dagger at the waist and wields a club. He has a helmetlike headdress with several horns. It is not clear what he holds in his right hand, possibly, as suggested

101, right

OLD SYRIAN PERIOD

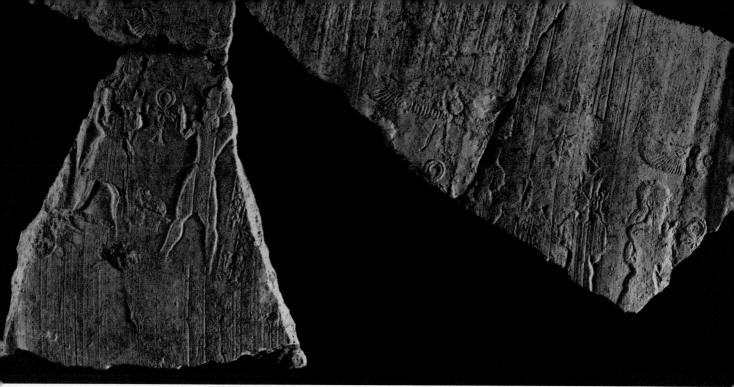

102

Figure 52
Seal impression on a pot (Cat. No. 102) from Tell Mardikh.

by the excavator, an axe and reins to the small bull on a platform below. An ankh fills the space between them. The excavator suggests that the god may be Adad. The goddess, possibly Anat, behind the inscription wears a long robe with a wide collar and a cylindrical horned headdress with a bird on top. A few details are visible: a heavy necklace of several strands of beads, earrings, and her hair gathered at the back of the neck. The object she carried in her right hand is broken off; it may have been a small ankh or a ring.
K.K.

103
Head-shaped cup
See color plate p. 178

Site: Ebla (Tell Mardikh), Sector B
Date: Old Syrian period, ca. 1650–1600 B.C. (Mardikh IIIB)
Material: Faience
Height: 7.3 cm; *diameter of rim:* 5.1 cm
Museum No.: Aleppo TM. 70. B. 930
Literature: P. Matthiae *Ebla* Fig. 101 / *Propyläen Kunstgeschichte* 14, 487, Fig. 423a

The face on this cup was made in a mold, while the

back of the head was sculpted. The strands of hair ending in curls are highlighted with black shadows. The hair on the back is indicated by a few black lines on a bluish background. Although the cup was not found in the temple, we may assume that it was meant as a votive offering. It is made of clay, first modeled, then fired, and in a later process glazed and fired again.

At the time of the earliest examples of writing, northern Syria was a center of faience production. At Tell Brak various faience objects were found, such as beads, rosettes, and animal figurines. Faience reached the height of its popularity in the second half of the second millennium, a period from which numerous vessels from Ashur, Babylon, and Ugarit are known (see Cat. Nos. 143–146).

K.K.

104
Stick pin
See color plate p. 180

Site: Ebla (Tell Mardikh), Hypogeum Q 78A, Tomb of the Princess
Date: Old Syrian period, 1825–1750 B.C.
Material: Gold
Length: 17.3 cm
Museum No.: Aleppo TM. 78. Q. 369
Literature: P. Matthiae *SEb* I (1979) 160, Fig. 74

In the center of a small courtyard in the Western Palace, limestone portals, blocked by heavy basalt slabs, guarded the entrance to the Tomb of the Princess, so called because on the lower step of the stairs were found the remains of a badly damaged skeleton of a girl, buried with nine pieces of impressive jewelry. Four of the pieces are shown here, in Cat. Nos. 104–107.

This gold pin was formed in one piece, the upper part was twisted, and an eight-pronged star was attached as the head.

K.K.

105
Bracelet
See color plate p. 180

Site: Ebla (Tell Mardikh), Hypogeum Q 78A, Tomb of the Princess
Date: Old Syrian period, 1825–1750 B.C.

Material: Gold
Diameter: 5.5–5.6 cm
Museum No.: Aleppo TM. 78. Q. 371
Literature: P. Matthiae *SEb* I (1979) 160, Fig. 74

This bracelet was one of the golden jewels found buried in the Tomb of the Princess. It was made by first attaching rows of tiny gold balls to a massive gold band with rounded ends. The band was then twisted and shaped into a bracelet.

K.K.

106
Ring-shaped ornament
See color plate p. 180

Site: Ebla (Tell Mardikh), Hypogeum Q 78A, Tomb of the Princess
Date: Old Syrian period, 1825–1750 B.C.
Material: Gold
Diameter: 2.9–3.1 cm
Museum No.: Aleppo TM. 78. Q. 366
Literature: P. Matthiae *SEb* I (1979) 160, Fig. 74 / *Archaeology* 33:2 (1980) 15

Only one such ring was found, and the excavator of the Tomb of the Princess suggests that it may have been a nose ring, although such rings have not been documented textually or pictorially. The ornament (perhaps an earring) is made of thick gold foil decorated with a granulated diamond pattern. Granulation, a technique already documented in Early Dynastic times, was accomplished by smelting gold in powdered charcoal so as to form tiny balls. The art consisted in melting the granules onto the ring without altering its shape. Similar granulated pieces of jewelry have been found at Byblos and Gaza.

K.K.

107
Necklace
See color plate p. 180

Site: Ebla (Tell Mardikh), Hypogeum Q 78A, Tomb of the Princess
Date: Old Syrian Period, 1825–1750 B.C.
Material: Gold, amethyst, lapis lazuli
Length: 10.2 cm; *width:* 2.5 cm
Museum No.: Aleppo TM. 78. Q. 367
Literature: P. Matthiae *SEb* I (1979) 160, Fig. 34 / *Akkadica* 17 (1980) 51, Fig. 16

This necklace, strung in modern times, consists of twenty-one pomegranate-shaped gold beads, an amethyst bead, and a rectangular center piece with an inset of lapis lazuli.
K.K.

108
Flask
See color plate p. 181

Site: Ebla (Tell Mardikh), Hypogeum Q 78A, Tomb of the Princess
Date: Old Syrian period, 1825–1750 B.C.
Material: Sardonyx
Height: 8.4 cm; *greatest diameter:* 6.5 cm
Museum No.: Aleppo TM. 78. Q. IA. 76
Literature: P. Matthiae *SEb* I (1979) 161, Fig. 62b / *Archaeology* 33:2 (1980) 8 // cf. P. Montet "Byblos et l'Egypte" *BAH* 11 (1929) Plate LXXI 608

Approximately seventy ceramic vessels, including imports from the Mediterranean coast and the region of Alalakh, were deposited in the Tomb of the Princess. Two stone vessels, one of sardonyx and a smaller one of opaque white stone, were also found here. They are fat-bellied flasks with long cylindrical necks, obviously modeled after metal bottles, known both from Byblos and from the Karum Kanesh (Kültepe) in Anatolia. The outer surface is smoothly polished, while the inside has horizontal traces of the drilling tools.
K.K.

109
Necklace
See color plate p. 1

Site: Ebla (Tell Mardikh), Hypogeum Q 78B2, Tomb of the Lord of the Goats
Date: Old Syrian period, ca. 1760–1700 B.C.
Material: Gold
Length: 4.4 cm; *width of longest part:* 3.8 cm
Museum No.: Aleppo TM. 79. Q. 250a–c
Literature: P. Matthiae *CRAI* (1980) 105, Fig. 8 / *SEb* IV (1981) 217–218, Figs. 59a–b / *I Tesori di Ebla* (Rome 1984) 123–124, Plate 78a

During the plundering of the Tomb of the Lord of the Goats, before the final destruction of the Ebla palace around 1650–1600 B.C., a number of pieces of jewelry placed with the deceased in the tomb were removed. Among them was this golden necklace in three parts,

each of which has a round pendant with attached star design. The necklace may have been dropped by the tomb robbers when they arrived at the adjacent Tomb of the Cistern through which they reached the burial chamber.

The three pieces were formed by fusing two layers of gold, the top layer consisting of four elaborately braided bands. A different manufacturing technique was used for the pendants: both the star and the circles are granulated. This type of necklace is documented on numerous clay figurines from the Old Syrian period, and the design and the structure of the decorations are typically Old Syrian, indicating that the necklace may date from the end of the eighteenth century B.C. The granulation technique can be compared to the splendid Babylonian medallions, especially from Dilbat and Larsa, which show similar rosettes decorated with stars. The original design and its careful execution permit comparison with the finest examples of jewelry from Byblos.
P.M.

110
Round lid

Site: Ebla (Tell Mardikh), Hypogeum Q 78C, Tomb of the Lord of the Goats
Date: Old Syrian period, ca. 1760–1700 B.C.
Material: Gold and lapis lazuli
Diameter: 2.9 cm; *thickness:* 0.1 cm
Museum No.: Aleppo TM. 79. Q. 200
Literature: P. Matthiae *I Tesori di Ebla* (Rome 1984) Plate 78e

This gold laminated disk with borders, whose patterns are faintly repeated on the back, may have been the cover or lid to a small case for precious objects, possibly attached to the top of a ceremonial standard. The decoration of the disk is executed with granulation and cloisonné. The center of the disk and two of the drops still have remains of their lapis lazuli inlays; the two other drops may have had paste inlays now lost. The lid is a typical product of the Old Syrian period, although it may be compared to a similar disk from Byblos, of a slightly earlier date, found in the treasure-filled vessel referred to as the Montet Jar (after P. Montet, who described its contents).
P.M.

110

---

others were found in the royal tombs at Byblos from the time of Sharuhen, and in the palace at Megiddo Level VIII.

P.M.

111
Necklace

See color plate p. 182

Site: Ebla (Tell Mardikh), Hypogeum Q 78C, Tomb of the Lord of the Goats
Date: Old Syrian period, ca. 1760–1700 B.C.
Material: Gold, rock crystal, grayish-green translucent stone
Length: 6.5 cm; *pendants:* 1.2 cm; *diameter:* 0.6 cm
Museum No.: Aleppo TM. 78. Q. 407
Literature: P. Matthiae *SEb* IV (1981) 219, Fig. 58 / *Antike Welt* 13 (1982) 11, illus. on cover / *I Tesori di Ebla* (Rome 1984) Plates 82d–e

This golden chain features two pendants made of different kinds of semi-precious stones ending in gold granulated caps attached to a small ring. It was found in the semi-circular Tomb of the Lord of the Goats. While the pendants lack a contemporary Near Eastern parallel, the gold chain with the interwoven links is well attested in Syro-Palestine. Two similar chains were also found in the same burial chamber, and

112
Ceremonial mace

Site: Ebla (Tell Mardikh), Hypogeum Q 78C, Tomb of the Lord of the Goats
Date: Old Syrian period, 1775–1750 B.C.
Material: Limestone, ivory, bronze, silver, and gold
Length of mace: 4.4 cm; *diameter:* 5.6 cm; *length of decorated segment:* 5 cm; *diameter:* 1.7 cm
Museum Nos.: Aleppo TM. 78. Q. 453; TM. 78. Q. 461
Literature: G. Scandone Matthiae *SEb* I (1979) 119–128, Figs. 36–40 // P. Matthiae *SEb* 1 (1979) 178–179 / *Akkadica* 17 (1980) 17, Fig. 19 / *SEb* 4 (1981) 221–223, Figs. 64a–h / *I Tesori di Ebla* (Rome 1984) 122, Plates 80b–e

The polished white limestone mace and the handle fragments of gold and precious materials may have been part of the same ceremonial object. They were found in pieces on the floor of the Tomb of the Lord of the Goats, the richest burial chamber of the royal palace at Ebla. This exquisitely made object is certainly of Egyptian origin. The ivory part of the handle is decorated with small oval silver and gold ornaments, but the really sensational feature is the carefully executed metallic section: applied to a silver base, gold monkeys with raised paws worship a row of gold hieroglyphs which form the personal name Hetepibre. This name belonged to an obscure pharaoh of the Thirteenth Dynasty, Hornedjheryotef, who reigned from 1775 to 1765 B.C.

It is astonishing to find an Egyptian pharaonic object from a dynasty of little importance in the tomb of an Eblaite lord. How did it get there? Was it part of the spoils of battle, or was it given to the nobleman by the Egyptian sovereign? We cannot answer these questions, but it is evident that the owner of the mace had had it for a long time. The hieroglyphs had fallen off and were reattached by an Eblaite artisan, who obviously know nothing of the Egyptian language, for he put the sign *htp* in the wrong place. This error is of historical importance, since it helps us date the tomb.

G.S.M.

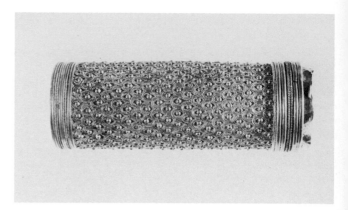

113
Handle for a standard

Site: Ebla (Tell Mardikh), Hypogeum Q 78C, Tomb of the
  Lord of the Goats
Date: Old Syrian period, 1760–1700 B.C.
Material: Gold
Length: 6.5 cm; *diameter:* 2.4 cm
Museum No.: Aleppo TM. 78. Q. 420
Literature: P. Matthiae *SEb* 1 (1979) 176, Fig. 78 / *I Tesori di
  Ebla* (Rome 1984) Plates 82f–g

This beautiful golden object, probably of Egyptian origin, was the cover of a cylindrical handle for a now-
lost scepter or ceremonial mace. It closely resembles
remnants of the ivory handle of a mace associated
with the Egyptian Pharaoh Hetepibre Hornedjheryotef
(Cat. No. 112), except for a slight difference in thickness. The design of minute scales, beautifully executed in a regular pattern, with granulation around
and inside the scales, is also similar to Egyptian handles of ceremonial maces from the Eleventh and
Twelfth Dynasties of the Middle Kingdom.
P.M.

114
Bowl with a lid

Site: Ebla (Tell Mardikh), Tomb of the Cistern
Date: Old Syrian period, 1750–1700 B.C.
Material: Alabaster
Height: 15.4 cm; *diameter:* 18 cm
Museum No.: Aleppo TM. 79. Q. 126; TM. 79. Q. 146
Literature: P. Matthiae *I Tesori di Ebla* (Rome 1984) Plate
  77b

112, left

This elegant bowl, restored from many fragments with a complete lid, was found in the Tomb of the Cistern, the latest of the royal second-millennium tombs at Ebla. Perhaps it originally came from the Tomb of the Lord of the Goats. It is possible that it was positioned close to the rock wall which was broken through to create a passage into the Tomb of the Cistern and that it thus arrived in the adjacent tomb. The material and the beautiful rendering indicate a possible Egyptian origin for the piece, from the last period of the Middle Kingdom or from the Second Intermediate Period. There are, however, no definite parallels from these periods, and similar bowls are depicted on wall paintings from the tombs of nobles of the Eighteenth Dynasty of the New Kingdom.

G.S.M.

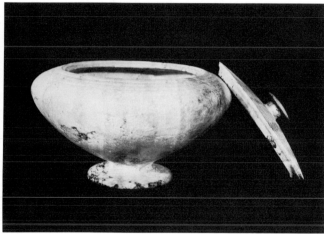

114

115
Goat-shaped protome
See color plate p. 181

Site: Ebla (Tell Mardikh), Hypogeum Q 78C, Tomb of the Lord of the Goats
Date: Old Syrian period, 1760–1700 B.C.
Material: Bronze, shell, lapis lazuli
Height: 6.7 cm; *length:* 13 cm; *width:* 3.2 cm
Museum No.: Aleppo TM. 78. Q. 447
Literature: P. Matthiae *SEb* I (1979) 172, Fig. 66 / *Akkadica* 17 (1980) 52, Fig. 17

From the Tomb of the Princess there is a connecting passage to another chamber which again is connected to a third. In all these rooms there were items belonging to the Lord of the Goats, including many ceramic vessels which, according to the excavator, are of a slightly later date than the ones found in the Tomb of the Princess. Farther away were bronze fittings for a ceremonial carriage, alabaster and silver vessels, gold jewelry, bronze weapons, gold ornaments for clothing, an Egyptian scepter, an ivory relief, and various furniture parts. Also retrieved here were two bronze decorative heads (protomes) of goats, which may have once ornamented the arms of a splendid throne. The excavator suggests that the Lord of the Goats may have been the high priest of Resheph, the god of war and plague, whose symbol was the goat.

K.K.

116
Cult basin

Site: Ebla (Tell Mardikh), Temple D
Date: Early Old Syrian period, ca. 1850 B.C. (Mardikh IIIA)
Material: Limestone
Length: 1.17 m; *height:* 0.64 m; *width:* 0.79 m
Museum No.: Aleppo 6474 (TM. 65. D. 226)
Literature: P. Matthiae *MAIS* (1965) 113, Plates XLII–LI / *Ebla* 142, Figs. 82–83 / *Propyläen Kunstgeschichte* 14,482 Fig. 412 / *MonANE* 1/6 Plates IX–X

This basin, with carved reliefs on three sides, may have been used in connection with a fertility ritual. The front upper register shows a scene from a ritual repast. On either side of a table are the seated king and queen, each holding a vessel in their right hand. Behind them stand servants with standards and vessels. The lower register shows a herd threatened by

lions; on the left side an archer defends the herd. In the front lower left corner there is an altar. The upper register of the left side of the basin shows a dragonlike monster with a scaly body and wings; his forelegs end in lion claws, while his hindlegs have bird talons. He has a snakelike tail and wears the divine horned crown on his lion head. A stream of water pours from his mouth. The monster's tail is grasped by a naked hero with side curls (a popular motif in Mesopotamia) who holds a fish in his right hand. The excavator suggests that the fish may be a symbol of the waters of the world. Behind him are two persons with slings. The center right side of the basin has a lion-headed naked hero holding two lions with their heads turned toward the observer.

This basin was found in the southwest corner of the cella of the large Temple D (see Fig. 48). Fragments of at least five additional relief basins were found at Ebla, all of them near or in temples.

K.K.

117

117
Fenestrated axe

Site: Ebla (Tell Mardikh), Hypogeum Q 78C, Tomb of the
   Lord of the Goats
Date: Old Syrian period, ca. 1760–1700 B.C.
Material: Bronze
Height: 9 cm; *width:* 8.3 cm; *depth:* 1.9 cm
Museum No.: Aleppo TM. 78. Q. 481
Literature: P. Matthiae *Akkadica* (1980) 53–62, Fig. 12 / *I
   Tesori di Ebla* (Rome 1984) Fig. 83b

Three axes were found in the Tomb of the Lord of the Goats: two so-called wide or fenestrated ("with windows") and one so-called long or duck-billed axe. The at least partial contemporaneity of the two types of axes is indicated by their joint presence in this tomb. Archaeologists had previously thought that the duck-billed type was derived from the fenestrated version.

This is the best preserved of the two fenestrated axes, a type unusual at Old Syrian Ebla but relatively common in contemporary Iran. These axes may have been Iranian imports, since four Iranian bronze bells were also found in the tomb. Fenestrated axes had some ritual value, illustrated by the splendid exemplars found at Byblos and by an Ebla fragment of a basalt statue of a king holding such an axe.

P.M.

116, left

118
Parts of a mold for a fenestrated axe
See color plate p. 183

Site: Ebla (Tell Mardikh), Tomb D 3712
Date: Old Syrian period, ca. 1850–1750 B.C.
Material: Andesite
Museum No.: Aleppo TM. 84. G. 30a–b

A funerary deposit of two parts of a mold for casting fenestrated axes was found next to the skeleton of an artisan during the excavation of a quarter of Ebla which had several metal workshops. This part of town, on the hillside of the acropolis, may have been the center for royal artisans. These molds, which were found one on top of the other, are in an excellent state of preservation. There are incised matching lines on both pieces to ensure flawless casting.

P.M.

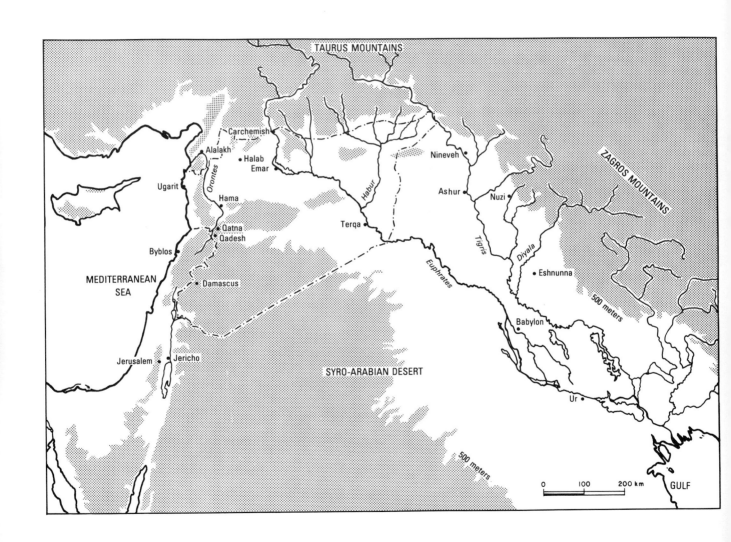

TAURUS MOUNTAINS

Carchemish
Alalakh
Halab
Emar
Ugarit
Hama
Qatna
Qadesh
Byblos

MEDITERRANEAN
SEA

Damascus

Jerusalem
Jericho

Orontes

Habur

Terqa

Euphrates

Nineveh

Ashur
Nuzi

Tigris

Diyala

Eshnunna

Babylon

Ur

ZAGROS MOUNTAINS

500 meters

SYRO-ARABIAN DESERT

500 meters

0   100   200 km

GULF

MIDDLE SYRIAN PERIOD
CA. 1600–1200 B.C.

EGYPTIAN AND HITTITE INFLUENCES IN SYRIA

KAY KOHLMEYER

IN THIS PERIOD IN NORTHERN SYRIA A NEW, NON-SEMITIC-SPEAKING group began to play an important historical role—the Hurrians. In Akkadian times it seems likely that these people had already established city-states on the Habur Plains of northeastern Syria. During the period of the Mari archives, rulers with Hurrian names appear in southeast Anatolia and northwest Syria. On the Habur Plains, and also in the west at Alalakh in the plain of Antioch, personal names recorded in cuneiform documents inform us of the presence of Hurrian immigrants. In the Middle Syrian period, Hurrian-speakers predominated within the population of Alalakh, as well as at Nuzi, near Kirkuk in northeastern Iraq.

Soon after the victory of the Hittite king Mursili I over Babylon—during a period of weakened state power in Anatolia and Mesopotamia—the kingdom of Mitanni came into existence. Within its great expanse, Mitanni included the Hurrian-speaking cities of northern Syria and Mesopotamia, from Nuzi to Alalakh. Washukanni, the capital city of this kingdom, remains one of the three great capital cities of the ancient Near East which have yet to be located, the other two being Agade and Shubat Enlil. The military superiority of Mitanni's ruling class was founded upon the use of light, horse-drawn war chariots. The so-called Indo-Aryan portion of the population is much contested in historical scholarship, and probably overestimated.

In north Syria, Mitanni came into conflict with the aggressive policies of the Egyptian New Kingdom. Just as the distant Mediterranean remained a goal for the Mesopotamian rulers, so the Euphrates appeared to the Egyptian pharaohs who strove to erect along its banks monuments to their own power. It was Thutmoses III (ca. 1490–1436 B.C.) who sought to systematically conquer western Syria; but a coalition of west Syrian rulers, led by the king of Qadesh (modern Tell Nebi Mend), stood in his path. At Megiddo in Palestine he attacked the coalition with its "hundred-thousands of men, the individuals of every foreign country, waiting in their chariots—330 princes, every one having his own army."[1] In subsequent campaigns he was able to move his forces farther north. In his thirty-third year he defeated the troops of Mitanni near Aleppo and forced the fleeing enemy to the Euphrates, which he crossed with ships obtained from the port of Byblos.

In spite of further campaigns, the Egyptians could not hold all of north Syria against the Mitanni empire. In the reign of Amenhotep II (ca. 1450–1425 B.C.) north Syria was divided into two spheres of influence: the northern sector extending south to Qatna (modern Mishrifé) under Mitannian rule and a southern portion under Egyptian control. Along the coast, however, Egyptian control extended still farther north, and included the city of Ugarit. This situation lasted until the middle of the fourteenth century B.C. The Mitanni-controlled region allowed individual cities their autonomy, apparently demanding only allegiance and tribute. The Egyptian-controlled sector, however, was directly under the aegis of Egyptian officials. This Egyptian influence in political and economic life is reflected in the culture of the Syrian port cities (see Cat. Nos. 132, 133, 137, 154, and 156).

In the north, meanwhile, a new power was emerging, the Hittites of Anatolia, with definite territorial aspirations directed toward the south and Syria. Their ambitions were no doubt prompted by an interest in controlling the trade from the Mediterranean to the east, the opportunities for booty, as well as the prestige which traditionally fell to those who controlled Syria. The great King Suppiluliuma, the actual founder of the Hittite empire, succeeded in defeating the troops of the Mitannian empire and installing his own sons as governors of Aleppo and Carchemish on the Euphrates. The Egyptians, of course, prevented the spread of his power farther to the south, but his grandson Muwatalli was able to loosen the borders between the two empires after a triumphant battle near Qadesh. The southern portion including Damascus remained Egyptian, but the northern fell to the Hittites. Ugarit had already come under Hittite influence in the reign of Suppiluliuma.

Although the arrangement of states in small political entities made them easy to conquer, they were difficult to govern. The economic and social organization of Syrian territory was considerably more complex than that of Anatolia and therefore required that the Hittite monarch extend considerable autonomy to the Syrian princes of his

[1]John A Wilson "The Barkal Stela" in J.B. Pritchard (ed.) *Ancient Near Eastern Texts* (2nd ed. Princeton 1955) 238.

realm, apart from the strategically important Carchemish on the Euphrates and the cult center at Aleppo. Vassal treaties bound the princes to the Hittite monarch, and through their oaths they were obliged to provide him with tribute and military support. The rulers of Carchemish were the king's governors, but they did not adjudicate especially difficult inner-Syrian matters; these were left for the Hittite monarch himself. One example of this is the divorce case of King Ammistamru II of Ugarit from the daughter of another vassal (see Cat. No. 161). This involved not only the threat of enmity between two Syrian subjects but also the important (for the Hittites) succession to the throne of Ugarit.

Suppululiuma's defeat of the Mitanni empire led to a collapse of power in northern Mesopotamia, and Assyria was able to free itself of Mitannian control and develop an independent foreign policy. Around 1300 B.C. the Assyrians conquered the Mitanni capital and then attempted to extend their power to the Euphrates. A conflict of interest with the Hittites, who saw their position in northern Syria now under threat, naturally resulted. A fragment from a letter written by the grandson of Suppiluliuma to the Assyrian king displays his hatred of the new north Syrian rival: "With the weapon you have won . . . Also mine . . . you are the victor and have become a great king. How do you then speak of brotherhood? . . . You and I, are we born of one mother?"

To protect his border, Suppiluliuma's son Mursili established a military support center at Ashtata on the banks of the Euphrates. The opposing forces are illustrated archaeologically in materials from Mari (Cat. Nos. 166, 167) and the more recent excavations at Dur-katlimmu (Tell Sheikh Hamad) on the Habur River. A decree of Hittite King Tudhaliya IV may be understood in the context of the imminent danger of war (Cat. No. 160). The same ruler initiated a trade blockade against the Assyrians which is reported in a state treaty with a west Syrian vassal: "A merchant (from you) shall not enter Assyria, a merchant from there you shall not permit in your country. He should not enter your land."

These difficulties continued as interior conflicts weakened central Hittite power in Anatolia and uprisings and economic downfall resulted. The last clay tablets from Ugarit report the ultimate catastrophe: severe famine within the Hittite empire and an invasion of foreign troops from "the Sea." According to the inscription of the Egyptian Pharaoh Rameses III, these "Sea People" turned Anatolia, Cyprus, northwest Syria, and Palestine into a wasteland. The cultural traditions of the region, however, were not torn from the Hittite realms but were maintained within the small Luwian successor states. This is the heritage which can be seen most clearly in the reliefs of 'Ain Dara (Cat No. 182).

UGARIT (RAS SHAMRA)

Location: 11 km north of Lattakiah, on the Mediterranean coast
Date: From the middle of the seventh millennium to the third century
   B.C.
Excavations: Since 1928 (Service des Antiquités de Beyrouth; Louvre, Paris; Directorate-General of Antiquities and Museums, Damascus and Centre de la Recherche Scientifique, Paris)
Publications:
Preliminary Reports: L. Albanese *Syria* 10 (1929) 16 // C.F.A. Schaeffer *Syria* 10 (1929) 285 / 12 (1931) 1 / 13 (1932) 1 / 14 (1933) 93 / 15 (1934) 105 / 16 (1935) 141 / 17 (1936) 105 / 18 (1937) 125 / 19 (1938) 193, 313 / 20 (1939) 277 / 28 (1951) 1 / 31 (1954) 14 / 47 (1970) 209 / 49 (972) 27 / *AAAS* 1 (1951) 5 / 2 (1952) 3 / 3 (1953) 117 / 4–5 (1954–1955) 149 / 7 (1957) 35 / 10 (1960) 133 / 11–12 (1961–1962) 187 / 13 (1963) 123 / 20 (1970) 7 / *AfO* 20 (1963) 206 / 21 (1966) 131 // H. de Contenson *Syria* 47 (1970) 1 / 49 (1972) 1 / 50 (1973) 13, 283 / 51 (1974) 1 / 54 (1977) 1 / *AAAS* 20 (1970) 13 / 22 (1972) 25 / 23 (1973) 121 / 25 (1975) 33 / 27–28 (1977–1978) 9 // J.–Cl. Margueron *Syria* 54 (1977) 151
Final Reports: C.F.A. Schaeffer *Ugaritica* I (1939) / *Ugaritica* II (1949) / *Ugaritica* III (1956) // C.F.A. Schaeffer et al. *Ugaritica* IV (1962) / *Ugaritica* V (1962) / *Ugaritica* VI (1969)
Publication of Tablets: A. Herdner *Corpus des textes en cunéiformes alphabetiques de Ras Shamra, Campagnes I à XI (1963) //* C. Virolleaud *Palais Royal d'Ugarit* II (1957) / V (1965) // J. Nougayrol III (1955) / IV (1956) / VI (1970)
Bibliography: M. Dietrich et al. *Ugarit-Bibliographie* I (1928–1950) *AOAT* 20 / 1 (1973) / II (1950–1959) *AOAT* 20/2 (1973) / III (1959–1966) *AOAT* 20/3 (1973) / IV *AOAT* 20/4 (1973)
General: G. Saadé *Ougarit, Métropole cananéene* (1979) // G. Young (ed.) *Ugarit in Retrospect: 50 Years of Ugarit and Ugaritic* (1981)

Ugarit was a blossoming coastal city, influenced by native as well as foreign merchants. The city's trade contacts across the Mediterranean had existed for centuries. Mari obtained its copper from Cyprus in the Old Syrian period, and this copper was certainly transferred to the coast and thence inland via the port city at Ugarit (see Fig. 53). Cretan ceramics, "Kamares ware," attest to the city's western relations. To the south, the city's coastal trade included exchange with Byblos, the famous "middleman" emporium with Egypt.

Perhaps under Egyptian influence important innovations in the recording of language—writing—were developed at Byblos and then Ugarit. A consonantal script with thirty signs, using a cuneiform-like

Figure 53
Ship from a wall painting in Thera.

writing system, appeared there. The order of the signs in Ugaritic is documented on a small tablet—the very same order of alphabetic signs as was later adopted by the Greek and Latin scripts (see the essay "Origins of the Alphabet").

Following the old traditions of Near Eastern city life, Ugarit was crossed by a few main streets, often leading to blind alleys or complex side-street arrangements. The streets were densely occupied by two-story dwellings, stores, and workshops constructed of stone and mortar. The multi-room houses usually centered on a courtyard. Family tombs were often situated under the house floors, covered with stones and archways. Entrance passages even included staircases. Richer houses had access to fountains, baths, and toilets, connected by various conduits. In its history the city has often been reconstructed with an arrangement of quarters, each assigned to specific craftsmen; for example, the southern quarter had its skilled goldsmiths and silversmiths, engravers and sculptors.

The port section of the city is the area today called Minet el-Beida. A walled tomb, accidentally uncovered by a farmer in 1928, attracted attention to this area and eventually led to the archaeological excavations at Ugarit. Here in the port area were situated the warehouses of merchants, coppersmiths, and manufacturers of the region's famous purple dye, "Phoenician blue." Foreign tradesmen from the Aegean, Egypt, Palestine, and other Syrian cities probably resided here.

When discussing the Hittite merchants, the texts from Ugarit focus on those from the city of Ura in Cilicia. Some of these merchants were agents of the Hittite king and often made large fortunes in Ugarit which they were able to transfer to their Hittite homeland. The Ugaritians considered them a plague: "The merchants, sons of Ura, are a heavy burden on the land of your servant," is the way they are described in a letter to the Hittite overlord Hattushili. In one of his edicts Hattushili orders the merchants to reside in Ugarit only during the summer and forbids them from appropriating houses in the city.

Poorer merchants and craftsmen served as simple soldiers in the military conscription; richer merchants joined more privileged groups of charioteers, occupied influential posts as advisors and administrators in the palace, and owned expensive plots of land. Treaties with other rulers provided royal merchants with immunity from prosecution and indemnification.

The palace of the fourteenth and thirteenth centuries B.C., which in its last occupational phase encompassed an area of approximately 6,500 square meters, was situated in the midst of a residential area. At various times additional courts and other sections were added to the building, originally one large dwelling area (Fig. 54A), then a court with surrounding rooms and a rectangular pillared hall (B). This kind of pillared gateway had been a characteristic of Syrian architecture from the time of the third-millennium palace at Ebla. The royal cemetery was situated under a room by the outer wall. Two additional courts, surrounded by regal rooms (C, D), were situated directly to the south. Many of the inscribed clay tablets are derived from this area. Two courts with pillared halls on the west (E) comprised the entrance to the palace and its southern quarter. In the chancellory (I) additional clay tablets were retrieved, some having been at the last moment in an oven for baking and preservation. Another court (L) featured a cultivated garden; a pillared hall formed the entrance to this court as well. Staircases found in many places are ample documentation that the palace was at least two stories tall.

The high mound in the northern area of the city—the acropolis—was dominated by two major temples, dedicated to the gods Dagan and Baal. Each consisted of a small, quadripartite hall and larger cella. In the interior and in the vicinity of the Baal Temple, stelae and fragments of stelae were retrieved, one with a depiction of the deity. This kind of tall stone monument, in the Bible called the "pillar of Baal" (2 Kings 3:2), was utilized in the Levant in place of the otherwise aniconic deity's statue. Excavations southwest of the Baal Temple uncovered two gold bowls (one is shown in Cat. No. 158), as well as a stele (Cat. No. 150). Stone anchors, perhaps votive offerings, were found in the vicinity of the temple and testify to the significance of sea trade for the city.

The city's fleet must have been extensive: 150 Ugaritic ships are mentioned in a Hittite letter. Trade goods were essentially the agricultural products of the hinterland: grain, olive oil, wine. Tin, lead, copper, and manufactured goods, such as textiles, were also traded, as well as works in bronze and other precious metals, decorative pieces and molds (Cat. Nos. 129–131), and objects like the sword with the inscription of Pharoah Merneptah (Cat. No. 149).
KAY KOHLMEYER

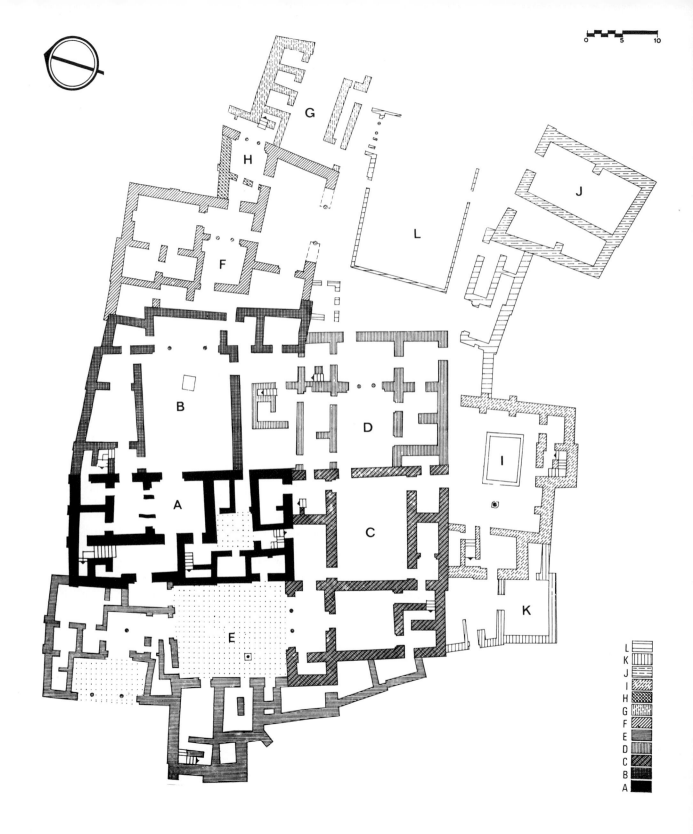

G

H

J

L

F

B

D

I

A

C

K

E

L	
K	
J	
I	
H	
G	
F	
E	
D	
C	
B	
A	

0   5   10

MIDDLE SYRIAN PERIOD

BACKGROUND TO THE BIBLE: UGARIT

DENNIS PARDEE

SINCE THE BEGINNING OF UGARITIC STUDIES IN 1929 THERE HAS BEEN a constant symbiosis between that domain and the domain of biblical studies. The Hebrew Bible has been an object of study in the Jewish and Christian communities for centuries, and this ancient scholarly tradition was drawn upon heavily in the decipherment and interpretation of the texts written in the Ugaritic language. In the decades since the pioneering work of 1929–1930 this debt has been repaid many times over, and the constant influx of new data from the ongoing excavations at Ugarit (modern Ras Shamra on the north Syrian coast) makes its contribution to the modern understanding of the Hebrew Bible and its world an ever-expanding one.

In order to avoid the extremes of a pan-Hebraistic approach to Ugarit or of a pan-Ugaritic approach to the Bible, both of which have at times marred Ugaritic-Hebrew studies, the parameters of comparison must be set out. On the negative side, first: the two cultures existed in different spheres, geographical, temporal, linguistic, and economic. That is, Ugarit was destroyed in ca. 1190 B.C. at the time of the invasions of the Sea Peoples, just when Hebrew culture as depicted in the Bible was beginning. Ugarit was on the coast of northern Syria, while the Hebrew kingdoms were centered in inland Palestine, from Galilee to the Negev. The people of Ugarit spoke and wrote in their own language, today termed Ugaritic, while the Israelites spoke and wrote Hebrew. Finally, though both cultures depended for basic foodstuffs and clothing on local sources, Ugarit had a more centralized economy with a greater emphasis on trade, especially by sea, than was the case in the inland Israelite kingdoms.

Just as pernicious as an approach which would attempt to explain Ugaritic or Hebrew culture entirely in contrast to the other would be one that ignored the similarities that do exist. The similarities of language are often cited as typical. Though a speaker of Ugaritic

Figure 54
Palace at Ugarit, with sequence of building phases.

probably could not have understood a speaker of Hebrew or vice versa, their languages were much closer to each other than they were to other Semitic languages—for example to Akkadian, the East Semitic language which served as *lingua franca* for the entire Near East from ca. 2000 to 500 B.C. Moreover, in such basic features of the language as phonology and syntax, Ugaritic had, as we know from the prose texts written in the final years before the destruction of Ugarit, evolved from the archaic language of poetry to a form of expression not distant from classical Hebrew. There was not a direct linear relationship between Ugaritic and Hebrew and—given the factors of geographical separation and religious differences—direct cultural ties leading to extensive linguistic borrowing probably would have been very limited even if Ugarit had survived into the Iron Age. Nevertheless, the archaic twenty-seven-letter consonantal inventory of the Ugaritic alphabet had already been reduced to twenty-five phonemes (*ḏ* and *ẓ* were frequently confused with other sounds; Hebrew has twenty-three consonantal phonemes). One syntactic feature so characteristic of Hebrew, the so-called *waw*-consecutive, was already attested sporadically in late Ugaritic. Also in the linguistically less weighty area of vocabulary there are many parallels between Ugaritic and Hebrew; though here it is a question of degree, for there are lexical parallels among all the Semitic languages.

It is in the area of literary devices and genres that some of the most intriguing differences and similarities lie. One of the most characteristic of Hebrew literary forms, the prose narrative (including myths, minor epics, novellas, stories, and "history" as understood at the time), is totally missing at Ugarit—not just in Ugaritic is it missing, but in the rest of the languages attested there—for all the Ugaritic myths and epics are in poetry. On the other hand, there are hundreds of economic and administrative texts from Ugarit, in both Ugaritic and Akkadian, while only a handful, very brief and difficult to interpret, have appeared in archaeological excavations in Palestine, and only allusions and remnants are present in the Bible itself.

An area in which something closer to parity exists is that of letters: though more letters have survived in Ugaritic than in Hebrew (about 100 vs. 50, including Hebrew letters found in excavations as well as fragments preserved in the Bible), the numbers are at least sufficient for comparison. And interesting as it is that there are many incidental likenesses and some comparable epistolographic formulae (e.g., Ugaritic *ṯtb rgm* ≃ Hebrew *hšb dbr*, "return word"), the most specifically epistolographic features of address, greetings, and closing are generally different in the two corpora. The Ugaritic formulary is closer to the Syro-Mesopotamian type of the preceding centuries, well known in the West from the Akkadian letters from Amarna, Alalakh, Mari, and Ugarit itself, while the Hebrew formulary is closer to that of the Aramaic letters of the fifth century B.C. on. Unfortunately we do not have comparative material to allow us to say what the evolution of West Semitic epistolary formulae was in the half-millennium which separated the latest Ugaritic letters from the earliest Hebrew ones.

The area of greatest literary similarity between the Ugaritic and Hebrew corpora is one, fortunately, in which the two cultures achieved what was arguably their greatest artistic contributions to human culture, certainly the greatest of which a record has been preserved. I refer to their poetry. Even here differences of genre exist: most Ugaritic poetry is mythological narrative, dealing with the exploits of the gods, especially of Baal, the Ugaritic god of rain and fertility, while the Hebrew poems are primarily lyrical, with only passing allusions to Canaanite mythology (e.g., Leviathan). Although Psalm 29, to cite an important example, shares many motifs with Ugaritic mythological poetry—indeed so "Canaanite" in this respect that many scholars consider it a Yahwized Baal-poem—it does not recount a mythological gest of Yahweh but is a hymn to his power. There are, therefore, many points of similarity in the biblical allusions to Canaanite mythological entities and motifs.

A far more important area of similarity, however, is that of poetic structure and rhetoric. Both poetries relied for their individual statements (micro-structure) and for their rhetorical progress (macro-structure) on various types of repetition, which range in the micro-structure from exact repetition of words or phrases to semantic repetition of similar concepts by means of different words. The major macro-structural segments were often marked off by repeated formulae or by the repetition of an entire segment with only those changes made which were necessary for the progression of the narrative. The building block of a poem in both languages was a two-element (bicolon) or three-element (tricolon) poetic line with parallelisms of sound, grammar, and meaning between the line segments. Examples of a bicolon:

ltbrk [krt] t'	Please pronounce a blessing on Noble Kirta,
ltmr n'mn [ǵlm] 'il	Please bless the goodly lad of El.
CTA 15 II 14–16[1]	

[1]The Ugaritic texts are cited according to the official edition by the Mission de Ras Shamra: André Herdner *Corpus des tablettes en cunéiformes alphabétiques découvertes à Ras Shamra-Ugarit de 1929 à 1939* (abbreviated *CTA*). Mission de Ras Shamra, Vol. IX (Paris: Librairie Nationale & Geuthner, 1963). Translations of Ugaritic and Hebrew texts are my own.

yhwh 'z l'mw ytn	May Yahweh give strength to his people,
yhwh ybrk 't-'mw	May Yahweh bless his people with well-
bšlwm	being.
Psalm 29:11	

The following are examples of one type of tricolon, known as a "staircase" because of the specific pattern of repetitive and grammatical parallelism:

ht 'bk b'lm	Behold, your enemy, O Baal,
ht 'ibk tmhs	Behold, your enemy shall you smite,
ht tsmt srtk	Behold, you shall strike down your adversary.
CTA 2 IV 8–9	
ky hnh 'ybyk yhwh	For behold, your enemies, O Yahweh,
ky hnh 'ybyk y'bdw	For behold, your enemies shall perish,
ytprdw kl p'ly 'wn	Shall be divided all doers of evil.
Psalm 92:10	

These patterns of repetition can occur within a line segment, between the segments of a poetic line (as in the examples just cited), or in near or distant patterns throughout a larger poem or unit of a poem. For an example of such extended repetition, the sevenfold occurrence of the word *ql*, "voice" but also "thunder," in Psalm 29 is often cited.

That there was a common Canaanite poetic heritage which the Hebrew poets shared, compared by some to the poetic traditions of the Homeric age, appears today assured by the many similar parallelistic devices employed by the Ugaritic and Hebrew poets. It remains an item of discussion, however, just how these devices came to be held in common and to what extent the details themselves or simply the principles underlying them were traditional in each culture. Once again, such questions will only be answered, if indeed ever they are, by the discovery of unimpeachably authentic remains from the half-millennium separating the Ugaritic texts from the Hebrew ones.

These mythological poems lead us to another area of comparison, that of religion. Here the contributions to modern knowledge have come primarily from the Ugaritic side. This is because the official Yahwistic monotheism of the culture in which the Hebrew Bible was produced brought about the suppression of Canaanite polytheism.

Remnants remain, of course, as in the long campaign against Baal worship recounted in both historical and prophetic books. A picture somewhat more varied than that given in the Hebrew Bible is also slowly emerging from archaeological excavations. For example, a sanctuary with an altar was unearthed at Tel Arad in the northern Negev, dating from a period when worship was supposed to have been centralized in Jerusalem. Even more revealing is what looks like the product of a scribe practicing epistolary greetings, written on a jar found at Kuntillet Ajrud in the northern Sinai. One reads "I bless you to Yahweh and to his 'Ashera.'" The precise meaning of the Hebrew phrase "his 'Ashera'" is disputed, but we do know that Ashera was the consort of El in the Ugaritic pantheon, and the corresponding word in the Hebrew inscription almost certainly refers to a female consort of Yahweh or to her cult symbol. Another example: from both mythological and practical ritual texts from Ugarit we know that an ancestor deity known as *'il'ib* ("god of the father") was extremely important at Ugarit. Though no trace of this deity is known from the Bible, a seal dating from about 600 B.C. with the inscription *l'bd'l'b* ("[Belonging] to 'Abd'il'ib") was published in 1864, long before the Ugaritic deity was known. Though the provenance of the seal is unknown, the find-date seems to preclude forgery, for the deity *'l'ib* was unknown before the discovery of Ugarit in 1929. This name, which means "Servant of 'Il'ib," is therefore a trace of evidence that the deity was still known and venerated somewhere in the Levant some six hundred years after the destruction of Ugarit.

These and many other such details indicate that under the veneer of official Yahwism there existed a popular religion, probably practiced both by "Canaanites" in Israel and by "reprobate" Israelites, which found its roots in the pre-Hebrew Canaanite religion, many details of which are now furnished by the Ugaritic texts. Moreover, Yahwism itself—whatever the origins of Yahwistic monotheism may have been—identified Yahweh with the old Semitic deity El and with the deity of the similar name Eloah and its plural Elohim (the latter is the Hebrew for "gods" and for "God"), while such literary productions as Psalm 29 or the phrophecies of Hosea show that the attribution of many of Baal's characteristics to Yahweh was part and parcel of official Yahwism. The study of the Ugaritic religious texts is of inestimable value in sorting out the constituent elements of Yahwism and in identifying the features of popular religion as they are revealed by archaeological discovery.

In the areas of economy and society there are again dark spots and light ones. From the literary perspective, for example, we have nothing from Ugarit approaching the legal sections of the Pentateuch, be it ethical (the Ten Commandments), ritual (the Ugaritic ritual texts tend to be descriptions of what had taken place or of what is to take place in a given ritual rather than prescriptions for all time, as some Hebrew ritual texts are presented), or social legislation. The building of the Israelite desert sanctuary is presented as a set of orders from Yahweh, rather than as permission from El followed by construction according to a traditional building-plan, as in the case of Baal's temple in a Ugaritic myth—here the comparison with the building of Solomon's temple (2 Samuel 7; 1 Kings 5–7) is more instructive, as one might expect from two urban contexts. Indeed, it is Israelite kingship which has been most illuminated by the Ugaritic administrative texts, at least as Samuel viewed it in his detailed condemnation of the royal institution in 1 Samuel 8, and as David and Solomon attempted to set it up. One may compare especially the detailed lists of officers in David's court (2 Samuel 8:15–18; 20:23–26) with the Ugaritic personnel lists (*CTA* 73–77) or the account of Solomon's attempt to set up a centralized provincial administration (1 Kings 4) with the Ugaritic administrative lists (*CTA* 80–147). It would appear that the Ugaritic monarchy was able to maintain a relatively strong hold on all aspects of the economy for the two centuries from which we have written records; whereas we know that the Israelite kingdom split in two after Solomon, and there are indications that loyalties to tribe and clan played a stronger balancing role against the crown in the Israelite kingdoms than may have been the case, at least judging from the primarily royal records, at Ugarit.

In matters of personal wealth and cultural sophistication we have reason to believe that at least at Ugarit itself the international trade for which that city was a center produced a standard of living beyond anything attained in Palestine. The well-built stone houses, each with a magnificent corbelled family tomb under one of the floors, the gold vessels and gold-plated statuary (of which surely only a fraction have survived to our day), the alabaster vessels, the finely decorated pottery—all surpass the discoveries at any one Palestinian site in quantity and usually in quality as well. One has the feeling that the wealth of Samaria at which Amos railed would not have measured up to the wealth of the Ugaritian royalty and nobility. We know from the many towns and cities of Palestine now excavated that the picture of concentration of wealth in Samaria painted by Amos, and in Jerusalem as described in the historical books, was probably basically correct; for most other towns were relatively small and poor in the biblical period. Unfortunately, there has been no extensive excavation in the Ugaritic hinterland, and we are thus unable to determine from archaeological data the relative wealth of metropolis and countryside. If the Ugaritic economy was more centralized than the Israelite one, however, we may surmise that the inhabitants of the towns of the Ugaritic territory would have led relatively simple lives as agriculturists and craftsmen.

As for literary sophistication, surely the myths of the great gods were known generally and were passed on from generation to generation by local poets. But we have no way of knowing whether traveling bards indoctrinated each town with the deeds of the ancestors of the Ugaritic royal line (as found in the Kirta epic) or whether each town was left to its own devices in such "political" matters. The relatively frequent shifting of the borders of Ugarit by its Hittite overlords leads one to believe that the loyal hinterland, its people steeped in Ugaritic royal epic, may have lain in a relatively restricted crescent around Ugarit itself. The same is true of Israel, of course, for most of the literary remains preserved in the Hebrew Bible either originated in the small state of Judah or else passed through a Judaean literary transmission.

In many respects, then, the comparability of Ugarit and the Bible resides in accidents of discovery: if the archives of Aleppo, Hama, Damascus, Byblos, Tyre, Sidon, Acco, or Ashdod had been found for the periods in question, they might have shown up more clearly the dissimilarities between the Ugaritic and Hebrew cultures. Giving thanks for what we have and for what it teaches us, however, we can say that Hebrew and the Hebrew Bible provided much to make Ugaritic and Ugaritic culture understandable to us. We also can acknowledge that the many details of Ugaritic society, revealed by the artifacts, by the texts in the various languages used there, but especially by the Ugaritic texts themselves, have thrown more light on Hebrew culture in general and on thousands of obscure details of the Hebrew Bible than has any other single source of comparison.

Recommended Reading

P. C. Craigie. *Ugarit and the Old Testament* (Grand Rapids: Eerdmans, 1983).

J. C. de Moor. "Ugarit." *The Interpreter's Dictionary of the Bible: Supplementary Volume* (Nashville: Abingdon, 1976).

L. R. Fisher and S. Rummel (eds.). *Ras Shamra Parallels*. Vols. I, II, III (Rome: Pontifical Biblical Institute, 1972, 1975, 1981).

J. C. L. Gibson. *Canaanite Myths and Legends* (2nd ed. Edinburgh: T. & T. Clark, 1978). Contains an English translation of all the major myths and epics.

G. D. Young (ed.). *Ugarit in Restrospect: 50 Years of Ugarit and Ugaritic* (Winona Lake, Ind.: Eisenbrauns, 1981).

EMAR (MESKENE)

Location: West bank of the Euphrates
Date: End of the fourteenth century to beginning of the twelfth century B.C. with additional settlement in the Roman through Islamic periods
Excavations: 1972–1974 (University of Strasbourg)
Publications: J.-Cl. Margueron *AAAS* 25 (1975) 73 / *Syria* 52 (1975) 53 / *Syria* 53 (1976) 193 / J.-Cl. Margueron (ed.) *Le moyen Euphrat* 235, 245, 265, 285 // D. Arnaud *Syria* 52 (1975) 87 // D. Deyer (ed.) *Meskéné-Emar: Dix ans de travaux, 1972–1982* (Paris 1982)

The most important port and river crossing was situated on the bend of the Euphrates—the city of Emar. This city was well known from Hittite and Mesopotamian sources even before its rediscovery. The great overland trade route from Aleppo and the Mediterranean ended here, where export ships were loaded with goods destined for Mesopotamia. The famous Old Babylonian itinerary text, which lists in detail the route from Larsa in southern Mesopotamia through northern Mesopotamia, the Habur Plains, the valley of the Balikh River, and onward to the west, has the city of Emar as its final objective.

The remains of the third-millennium city have yet to be uncovered, but the accidental discovery of fourteen clay tablets provided some evidence for the Middle Syrian period city. Apart from domestic structures, one official public building and three temples have been exposed. The library of one temple provided approximately 1,500 clay tablets and fragments. The two other temples, of the *langraum* ("long-room") type, have yielded tablets with the names of the deities to whom they were consecrated: the goddess Ishtar and the weather god Teshub or Adad. These documents will provide us with a useful index to the influence of the Hittites upon the cultures and politics of Emar.

Kay Kohlmeyer

END OF THE BRONZE AGE

JAMES D. MUHLY

WITHIN A SHORT PERIOD OF TIME, TRADITIONALLY DATED AROUND 1200 B.C., the great Late Bronze Age empires of the eastern Mediterranean came to an end and were never to be recreated in anything resembling what had been known during the fourteenth and thirteenth centuries. From Greece to the Levant there is evidence that the capitals of these empires were attacked and burned at about the same time. A century of archaeological work has uncovered the extensive debris of this destruction at such sites as Mycenae, Tiryns, Enkomi, Kition, Hazor, and Lachish. At Boghazköy (ancient Hattusha) the burning structural timbers fell into the streets between the acropolis buildings, creating a deposit of charcoal and ash over a meter deep.

These destructions at the end of the Late Bronze Age mark a crucial transition in the occupation of the sites in question. Some of them were never again inhabited; others were reoccupied only after a hiatus of some 300–400 years; a few were reoccupied almost immediately after being destroyed, but by a group of inhabitants who had a different, more impoverished material culture. The archaeological evidence for the existence of these destructions and for their date is relatively unambiguous; the historical interpretation of that evidence, however, has become the subject of great controversy.

Part of the reason for this controversy has been the confusion created by attempts to combine contemporary historical records, such as the royal inscriptions of the Egyptian pharaohs Ramses II (1279–1213 B.C.), Merneptah (1213–1203 B.C.), and Ramses III (1187–1156 B.C.), themselves highly tendentious texts, with later literary and folkloristic traditions relating to such "events" as the Dorian Invasion, the Phrygian Expansion into Anatolia, and the Exodus and Conquest of the Ancient Israelites.

While the Egyptian texts refer to massed invasions by land and by sea of various groups known collectively as the "Peoples of the Sea," it has been notoriously difficult to find any trace of such people in the archaeological record. Only the Philistines, who gave their name to what was thereafter to be known as Palestine (Greek *Palestinē*), subsequent to their settlement in the area as Egyptian garrison troops, can be identified in an archaeological context by their distinctive painted pottery. The other groups mentioned in the Egyptian texts, especially those who participated in the great raid on Egypt in the eighth year of the reign of Ramses III (1180 B.C.), remain enigmatic. Their identification has been the subject of endless speculation, much of it more amusing than convincing, ranging as far afield as Troy, Etruria, Sardinia, and Sicily.

What history does record is that following this wave of destructions, the empires of the Late Bronze Age were replaced by a series of small, independent states. The centuries from 1200 to 800 B.C. are often designated as representing a period of Petty Statism, which was brought to an end by the rise of imperial Assyria in the ninth century B.C. During the course of the eighth century, following a period of Assyrian weakness in the early years of that century, these small independent states came to an end as they were conquered one by one by Assyria and incorporated into the Assyrian system of provincial administration. Most of these conquests were carried out during the reigns of the Assyrian kings Tiglath-pileser III (744–727 B.C.) and Sargon II (721–705 B.C.).

The years 1200–800 saw the appearance of a number of states whose history is known more from textual than from archaeological evidence, from Assyrian royal inscriptions and from local texts written for the most part in native Semitic languages. In the north, in what is today southeastern Turkey and northern Syria, centered on the cities of Malatya, Carchemish, Aleppo, and Hama, there developed a series of Neo-Hittite or Syro-Hittite kingdoms, combining elements of Late Bronze Age Hittite and Luwian culture with local Aramaean and Assyrian elements. These kingdoms are to be identified with the Old Testament references to Hittites and with what the Assyrians knew as the land of Hatti. For purposes of producing monumental inscriptions on stone they continued to use the pictographic hieroglyphic script developed during the second millennium in order to write Luwian (one of the three Indo-European languages of Bronze Age Anatolia, the others being Hittite and Palaic). The extent to which the Luwian script actually represented a spoken language in the area remains unknown, but language does seem to provide the major element of continuity between these Iron

Age Hittite kingdoms and the Bronze Age Hittites of Central Anatolia. The Syrian site of 'Ain Dara, currently being excavated, represents one of our best examples of this type of Neo-Hittite site. Our most important historical evidence comes from Carchemish, excavated by the British during the early years of this century, where important historical texts are only now being translated, thanks to the great advances in our understanding of Hierglyphic Luwian made during the past ten years.

To the south, centered on the city of Damascus, there developed the Aramaean kingdom of Aram, often known as the kingdom of Aram-Damascus. References to Aramaeans, then known as Ahlamu, already appear in second-millennium texts from Kassite Babylonia, but at some point after 1200 they established a political unity governed from Damascus. As a language Aramaic soon came to dominate the entire Levant and eventually all of western Asia. Aramaic became the main spoken language of the Persian empire and was in use as far south as the island of Elephantine, at the first cataract on the Nile opposite modern Aswan. The kingdom of Aram-Damascus seems to have extended as far north as the site of Arslantash (ancient Hadatu), some 20 miles east of Carchemish. From Arslantash came a very important group of ivories, one of which was inscribed with the name of Haza'el, king of Damascus (ca. 843–796 B.C.) (See the essay "Syrian Ivory Carving.")

The coast of present-day Lebanon was inhabited by the Phoenicians. Like their Neo-Hittite neighbors to the north, the Phoenician cities never developed a unified political organization. Phoenician civilization was created through the achievements of a number of small cities or city-states, each functioning as an independent political entity. Occupying only a narrow strip of land along the coast, the Phoenician cities of Tyre, Sarepta, Sidon, Beirut, Byblos, and Arvad were forced to turn to trade and commerce in order to support themselves. Thus developed Phoenician commercial interests overland—with Aram-Damascus, the kingdoms of Israel and Judah, and Assyria—and overseas across the entire Mediterranean and even down the Atlantic coast of North Africa.

Most of the important Phoenician cities of the Early Iron Age had been major sites already in the Bronze Age and have remained major centers of habitation to the present day. Continuity of settlement was accompanied by continuity of place name. Cities such as Tyre, Sidon, and Beirut have had the same name since at least the second millennium B.C. It is precisely this continuity that has presented the most serious obstacle to the excavation of Phoenician sites. The remains of Iron and Bronze Age Sidon lie buried beneath the buildings of the modern city. As a result, the Phoenicians have for long been a people known only outside their homeland. Through the excavation of many Phoenician and Punic colonies throughout the Mediterranean world we have learned to identify a type of site (having a double harbor separated by a headland or point of land), a style of architecture (using ribs or pillars of well-dressed stone separated by sections of wall made of uncut field stones set in yellow clay), and a class of pottery (dominated by red burnished mushroom-lipped jugs and two-spouted lamps) which can be described as typically Phoenician.

This distinctive material culture has become known at many sites across the Mediterranean, as far west as Mogador, in present-day Morocco. But in no case was this material in an archaeological context that could be dated any earlier than the eighth century B.C. The most important of these Phoenician colonies, that of Carthage on the coast of modern Tunisia, was, according to tradition, established by a party sent out from Tyre in 814 B.C. Nothing from the limited excavation that has been carried out at the site (ancient Carthage being covered by the growing modern city of Tunis) can be dated any earlier than the late eighth century B.C. Other Phoenician colonies have foundation dates as early as ca. 1110 B.C., but nothing from any of these sites can be dated any earlier than the eighth century.

In the late 1960s it became possible to open excavations at the site of Sarepta, located midway between Sidon and Tyre, the one site in the Phoenician homeland not inhabited in modern times. With no remains later than Roman times to deal with, Sarepta offered the opportunity of uncovering a large part of the Iron Age and Late Bronze Age settlement. This work was in progress when excavation was interrupted by the Lebanese civil war and all the unfortunate events that have devastated Lebanon since the mid 1970s. Fortunately it had, by that time, been possible to excavate enough to show that the very material culture known from many sites outside Phoenicia was present also at Sarepta but again not in contexts that could be any earlier than the late ninth century.

Yet all the elements that have long been associated with the Phoenicians of the western Mediterranean, including the clay face masks, the small glass amulets, and the distinctive sign or symbol of the goddess Tanit, were present also at Sarepta. All this was clear evidence for a great homogeneity in material culture spread across the entire Mediterranean, but a homogeneity not known prior to the eighth century B.C. Yet the site of Sarepta was occupied as a Phoenician site centuries before ca. 800 B.C. Moreover there were inscriptions in the Phoenician language, especially those from Byblos, that could be dated as early as the twelfth century. There even was a Phoenician text from Sarepta that came from a thirteenth-century Late Bronze Age context. There also were the famous Old Testament references to Hiram, king of Tyre, a mid-tenth-century contemporary of Solomon, who supplied the latter with a fleet and with artisans skilled in working with metal and stone. The Assyrian king Tiglath-pileser I (1115–1077 B.C.) states that he marched to Mount Lebanon, cut down some of the famous cedars for beams to be shipped back to Assyria, and received tribute from Byblos, Sidon, and the island of Arvad. Clearly there was a recognized Phoenician culture, known from Phoenicia proper and from neighboring lands, that developed centuries before the great colonial expansion of the eighth century.

Tiglath-pileser I seems to refer to the area we know as Phoenicia as "the land Amurru," a term known already in the second millennium and meaning simply the "westland." For the Assyrians, Amurru was anything west of the Euphrates and the lands in question could be designated simply as those "beyond the river," a phrase in use at least from the time of the Assyrian king Tukulti-ninurta I (1244–1208 B.C.) down into Persian times. The area was also known as the land of Canaan, a name that, like Amurru, appears as early as the Mari letters of the eighteenth century B.C.

Modern translations of Late Bronze Age and Early Iron Age texts frequently use the toponym "Syria" to translate expressions such as "across the river" (Akkadian *Eber nari*). This is historically inaccurate and quite misleading. As a place name "Syria" does not appear before the seventh century B.C. The first use of the name seems to come in the works of the Greek lyric poet Kallinus of Ephesus, a usage that was continued by later Greek authors, especially the fifth-century historian Herodotus of Halicarnassus. The origins of the name are not at all clear, but the Greeks seem to have derived the name Syria from Assyria. Herodotus is the first author to distinguish between Syria and Assyria.

The Greeks certainly did not borrow the toponym Syria from Egypt. It is true that all modern translations of the Wenamun story, which dates to the mid-eleventh century B.C., make reference to Syria, Syrians, and to the eastern Mediterranean as the "great Syrian sea," but this is another example of the misleading terminology discussed above. In all these cases the Egyptian text uses the expression H;rw, to be vocalized as Huru. This name may originally have had some connection with the Hurrians, but by the time of the

Egyptian New Kingdom it had become strictly a geographical designation for what we know today as Syria and Lebanon.

According to one theory the name Canaan was derived from a word designating the purple-red dye for which the area has been famous throughout history. Tyrian purple, as the color was known to the Greeks and Romans, was made from the crushed shell of the sea snail *Murex trunculus*, and heaps of crushed *Murex* shells are a common feature at most Phoenician sites. An estimated 10,000 shells were required to produce 1 gram of pure purple dye. If the name Canaan does indeed derive from the color word *kinahhu*, then Canaan was the land of the purple dye and Canaanites those who produced it. The Greek names Phoenicia and Phoenician would then be but translations of the local terminology, derived from *phoinix*, the Greek designation for the same purple dye.

This would mean that Phoenicians were simply Canaanites in Greek disguise. This would in turn argue for a strong cultural continuity, not a historical break, from the Bronze Age into the Iron Age. Studies of the personal names attested in local Late Bronze Age and Early Iron Age texts from the area would tend to support such a conclusion. It must be borne in mind, however, that our knowledge of the Phoenician language is sorely defective. Although approximately 8,000 Phoenician texts are known today, they tend to be short and rather repetitious, preserving a total of less than 700 words, of which more than 300 appear only once.

In attempting to understand the cultural phenomenon that we have come to identify as Phoenician, the crucial question is the one of continuity from the Bronze Age into the Iron Age, from Canaanite to Phoenician. Are we dealing with the arrival of a new group of people or, as seems more likely on the basis of present evidence, with the gradual transformation of a local cultural tradition? This problem is central to any study of the archaeology and history of Syria in the Early Iron Age. If we recollect what is known about the other groups of people that make up the cultural configuration of Early Iron Age Syria—Neo-Hittites/Luwians, Aramaeans, and Phoenicians—we find that in every case we have a mix of Bronze Age and Iron Age elements and that it is very difficult to sort them out and to assess the relative importance of each. Of all the petty states of the Early Iron Age, those of the Aramaeans in Syria and of the ancient Israelites in Palestine seem to have the best claim to being *ab novo* creations of the Early Iron Age. That may be one of the main reasons why these two states became the dominant political forces in the Levant prior to the rise of imperial Assyria.

When we consider that the ribbed architecture so characteristic of all Phoenician sites first appears at Late Bronze Age Ras Shamra (ancient Ugarit), and that many of the artistic elements in Phoenician metalwork and ivory carving can be traced to objects in use in Ras Shamra at that period, we begin to realize the importance of Syria in this transition. Unfortunately the limited amount of work at Syrian sites occupied during this crucial transition period has resulted in a very defective presentation of the archaeological record and consequently in a considerable gap in our knowledge of Syrian archaeology for the period 1200–900 B.C. The same gap is to be found in Anatolia (modern Turkey), representing what is known as the Dark Age of Anatolian Archaeology. Such a gap obviously makes very difficult a study of the Bronze Age/Iron Age transition from any point of view.

The great cosmopolitan commercial center of Late Bronze Age Ugarit was destroyed at the end of the thirteenth century B.C. The excavator, C. F. A. Schaeffer-Forrer, found in the ruins of the ancient city, burned by a fire so intense that limestone ashlar building blocks had been melted into pure lime, a pottery kiln full of clay cuneiform tablets in the process of being baked. So sudden and so complete had been the destruction that the ancient scribes never had a chance to remove the tablets from the oven. Ugarit was, in fact, never again reoccupied, one of the factors that make it possible for the French excavators to expose such an extensive amount of the ancient settlement.

The exact nature of this destruction has been the subject of much discussion. The excavator refused to accept the existence of any foreign invader and insisted upon explaining the end of Ugarit in terms of an earthquake and attendant conflagration. Yet, at some distance inland, the site of Meskene (ancient Emar) on the Euphrates was also destroyed at the end of the Late Bronze Age. Dated legal contracts found in this destruction level suggest a date coinciding with the second year of the reign of the Kassite king Meli-Shipak, or 1185 B.C. Such a date is in keeping with the general idea that these destructions are to be placed in the early years of the reign of Ramses III. However they are to be explained, the destructions of Ugarit and Emar did bring to an end the Late Bronze Age in Syria as well as the Hittite domination that had existed there for at least 200 years before.

Ugarit and Emar were not reoccupied following these destructions, but such was not the case at Ras ibn Hani, located about 4.5 kilometers southwest of Ugarit and perhaps a summer palace for the queens of Ugarit during the fourteenth and thirteenth centuries B.C. Following a destruction which seems to have taken place just after that which brought Ugarit to an end, Ras ibn Hani was reoccupied for a period down to the middle of the tenth century B.C. The pottery from this reoccupation has yet to be studied in detail, but it does present obvious parallels with Mycenaean IIIC:1b pottery of the twelfth century B.C. as well as with contemporary local wares in Cyprus. A chronological sequence for the Iron Age in Syria has yet to be worked out in detail, but the excavators of Ras ibn Hani regard Iron I as dating from ca. 1200 to 700 B.C., with early Iron II lasting from 700 B.C. to the conquests of Alexander the Great in 330 B.C. On this basis the material from Ras ibn Hani would be Early Iron I.

The connections with Cyprus are of special interest in light of the important material recently excavated from tombs of the eleventh and tenth centuries at Palaepaphos-*Skales*, in southwestern Cyprus. Although the Phoenician colonization of Cyprus has recently been dated to the mid-ninth century, marked by the building of the great temple to the goddess Astarte at Kition, the material from Palaepaphos-*Skales* presents numerous examples of imported painted wares which have their best parallels in eleventh-century pottery from Tyre, Sarepta, and the Phoenician site of Tell Keisan in northern Palestine. The material from Palaepaphos-*Skales* emphasizes also the close connections between Phoenician and Philistine pottery in the eleventh century. Some of the best parallels for the finds from Cyprus come from the late Philistine ceramic repertoire from sites such as Megiddo, Level VIA. Clearly there was a great deal of cultural and commercial interchange between Syria, Palestine, and Cyprus in the centuries prior to the onset of Phoenician colonial expansion.

Although there is considerable scholarly disagreement on the subject, I would still argue that the expansion in question did not really get under way before the eighth century B.C. A century of archaeological exploration has not altered the fact that nothing from any of the Phoenician sites in the Far West can be dated earlier than the eighth century. The evidence from Phoenicia itself is even more conclusive. The German excavations at Kamid el-Loz, a site located roughly midway between Beirut and Damascus in the southern Biqa of Lebanon, produced a wealth of imported material from Mycenaean Greece, Cyprus, and Egypt during the period of Late Bronze Age occupation at what was then known as the site of Kumidi. At some point around 1200 B.C. Kumidi was destroyed, and following a short hiatus the site was reoccupied as a settlement, possibly Phoenician, that lasted into the ninth century B.C. From this "Phoenician" period at Kamid el-Loz comes a rich collection of carved ivories but not a single object imported from Greece, Cyprus, or Egypt. This same lack of imported material during the years 1200–900 B.C. is also true for the limited exposure undertaken at Tyre and Sarepta. The Old Testament describes a great age of international commerce during the days of Hiram, king of Tyre (969–936 B.C.), but this has yet to receive any support from contemporary archaeological evidence.

Of all the achievements of the Phoenicians, that of the development of the alphabet is certainly the most famous. The most remarkable story of the origin and expansion of alphabetic writing is recounted elsewhere (see "Origins of the Alphabet"), but two points are relevant here. The first is that the Late Bronze Age Phoenician inscription from Sarepta was written not in the standard cursive Phoenician alphabet but in the special cuneiform alphabet developed for writing Ugaritic. Recent excavations at the site of Hala Sultan Tekké, in southeastern Cyprus, just west of Kition, have produced a silver bowl with a short Phoenician inscription in an early-twelfth-century context. The inscription was again written using the cuneiform alphabet. The earliest Phoenician text from outside Phoenicia proper, written with the cursive Phoenician alphabet of twenty-two characters, seems to be the inscription on a bronze bowl from Teke Tomb J at Knossos (Crete), dating to ca. 1000 B.C. These facts should be kept in mind in evaluating any theory dating Phoenician cursive inscriptions from the western Mediterranean to the twelfth and eleventh centuries B.C.

The two Iron Age sites in Syria most closely associated with the Phoenicians are the coastal sites of Al Mina and Tell Sukas. In both cases the actual Phoenician presence has been obscured by the emphasis given to Greek colonists, the presence of Greek merchants in the Levant, and the Greek adaptation of the Phoenician alphabet. For the past fifty years it has been almost an axiom of classical scholarship that the Greek borrowing of the Phoenician alphabet took place at the site of Al Mina shortly after 800 B.C.

The reason for this insistence upon a Greek presence, upon Greek merchants and colonists at Al Mina and Tell Sukas (and now also at Ras el Basit, perhaps to be identified as the Greek Posideion) is the discovery of significant amounts of Greek pottery at all of these sites. The pottery was of a distinctive style most closely associated with Greek cities on the island of Euboea, and dated no earlier than the late ninth century B.C. Based upon the assumption that the local Phoenician inhabitants of the Syrian coast had no interest in Greek pottery, the mere existence of such pottery was seen as sufficient evidence to indicate the existence of an important, perhaps even a dominant Greek element at each site. Through Al Mina, as well as Tell Sukas and Ras el Basit, it was argued, Oriental ideas and customs entered the Greek world, producing what came to be known as the Orientalizing Period in Greek art.

The problem with all this is that there was little else, apart from the pottery, at Al Mina or Tell Sukas from which to identify the presence of resident Greeks. The layout of each site as well as the architecture of the buildings seemed to be thoroughly Oriental or Phoenician. Even the temples at Tell Sukas were Phoenician, not Greek, in basic design. Nor was there any evidence for the use of the Greek language, at least not before the sixth century B.C. (and even the sixth-century inscriptions were not found in a contemporary context). Even in the Classical period the graffiti from Al Mina, scratched on the bases of broken Athenian black-glazed drinking cups, were all in Phoenician, not Greek.

In addition to the imported Greek pottery there was also a large quantity of local Levantine or Phoenician ware. Al Mina, in particular, produced significant amounts of Cypriot pottery, again attesting to the close relationship between Cyprus and coastal Syria during the Iron Age. What was long thought to be one of the most characteristic Phoenician ceramic types, a single-handled neck-ridge juglet in Black-on-Red ware, has now been shown, on the basis of clay analysis, to have been made in Cyprus.

Examples of this juglet are known from Al Mina. They are also attested at the site of Tabbat al-Hammam, located just south of Arados. Investigated in the 1930s, in work available only in a preliminary report, Tabbat al-Hammam is of crucial importance as it provides what might well be the earliest artificial harbor installation in the eastern Mediterranean. The breakwater, or mole, built of ashlar blocks extending into the sea, seems to be a construction of the late ninth century B.C. As such it probably marks the beginning of Phoenician expansion into the Mediterranean, an expansion that took them first to Cyprus, then to the northern and southern coasts of the western Mediterranean, and eventually beyond the Straits of Gibraltar, one of the great commercial and colonial enterprises of the ancient world.

Recommended Reading

J. D. Hawkins. "The Neo-Hittite States in Syria and Anatolia." In *Cambridge Ancient History.* Vol. III, Part 1 (2nd ed. Cambridge: Cambridge University Press, 1981).

ORIGINS OF THE ALPHABET

FRANK MOORE CROSS

THE ALPHABET WAS INVENTED ONLY ONCE. ALL ALPHABETIC WRITing derives ultimately from an old Canaanite alphabet, and as we shall see, it was a revolutionary as well as unique gift to human civilization.

The ancient Near East spawned a number of writing systems. The earliest was the Sumerian, which appeared in Mesopotamia a century or two before 3000 B.C. coeval with the emergence of the Sumerian city-states. Shortly after, probably resulting from Sumerian stimulus, Egyptian heiroglyphic writing appeared—about 3000 B.C. Both systems originated in pictographs which represented words and then early developed into true word-syllabic writing, signs representing both words and syllables. Sumerian and Egyptian and other writing systems which followed—Proto-Elamite, ca. 3000; Proto-Indic, ca. 2200; Cretan, ca. 2000; Hittite, ca. 1500; Chinese, ca. 1300—were enormously complex and cumbersome. The Egyptian list of signs numbers more than 700, and though all of these were not in simultaneous use, it is a formidable task to learn even those commonly used in a single period. Sumerian writing, which simplified into cuneiform, has a sign list of nearly 600, of which about 300 were in ordinary use in a given era.

Given such complexity, only a scholar with years of training learned to read and write. Inevitably literacy remained the exclusive possession of a small, powerful, scribal elite. Ordinarily members of this elite were royal and priestly functionaries, attached to king and temple. In effect, writing was a monopoly of the court.

The introduction of the alphabet provided a new system of writing of breathtaking simplicity. The early alphabet used only twenty-seven or twenty-eight signs and was shortly simplified to twenty-two. The system was completely phonetic, with each sign representing a single consonantal phoneme. A person could learn to read and write in a matter of days or weeks.

The impact of the alphabet on the evolution of human civilization is difficult to exaggerate. Literacy spread like wildfire, and with it the democratization of higher culture. With the invention of the older writing systems, the ancient world slowly entered a transition from a wholly oral culture to one supplemented by writing. With the coming of the alphabet, societies still dominantly oral in the transmission of culture in a few centuries completed a revolutionary transformation to dominantly written means to preserve and transmit culture.

Alphabetic writing multiplied the sources of learning and literature and gave rise ultimately to new modes of viewing culture and new ways of thinking. Writing froze oral communication and made it visible, so to speak, to be examined and reexamined at leisure; alphabetic writing vastly facilitated such reflective scrutiny. A text could be deliberately studied and with such study arose new possibilities for critical and logical analysis. It is even possible to understand the innovations of ancient Greece—logical thought and skepticism—and of ancient Israel—the prophetic critique of state and society—as the fruits of alphabetic literacy.

How did the alphabet come into being? The modern era of the study of alphabetic origins began with the discovery of the Proto-Sinaitic inscriptions by Sir Flinders Petrie in 1905. Petrie, excavating at Serabit el Khadem in the Sinai Peninsula, found a dozen short texts inscribed in an unknown pictographic script. He dated them to about 1500 B.C., a date long disputed but now confirmed as almost certainly correct. Harvard expeditions in 1927, 1930, and 1935 greatly expanded the corpus of Proto-Sinaitic texts. The first tentative steps toward decipherment were taken by Sir Alan Gardiner in 1917. The distribution of the signs made evident that they were alphabetic, and Gardiner noted a recurrent series of signs: "oxgoad-house-eye-oxgoad-cross." (See Fig. 55.) Gardiner recognized that if the signs followed an acrophonic principle, their Canaanite value would be: *laba'lati*, "for the Lady." Ba'alat was a favorite epithet of the great Canaanite goddess Ashera, and since in Egypto-Canaanite syncretism Ba'lat was identified with Hathor, the Egyptian goddess whose temple dominated Serabit el-Khadem, the reading was highly suitable.

Gardiner propounded a theory that the old Canaanite alphabet, as we now call it, was acrophonically devised under the inspiration of Egyptian hieroglyphic writing. Acrophony is the principle of representing a sound by a picture or pictograph of an object whose name begins with the sound (phoneme): an apple for *a*, a ball for *b*, and so

Figure 55
Evolution of the early alphabet from Old Canaanite (Proto-Sinaitic) pictographs of ca. 1500 B.C. to the Linear Phoenician script of ca. 1000 B.C. Included is a column of early Greek alphabetic signs of a later date.

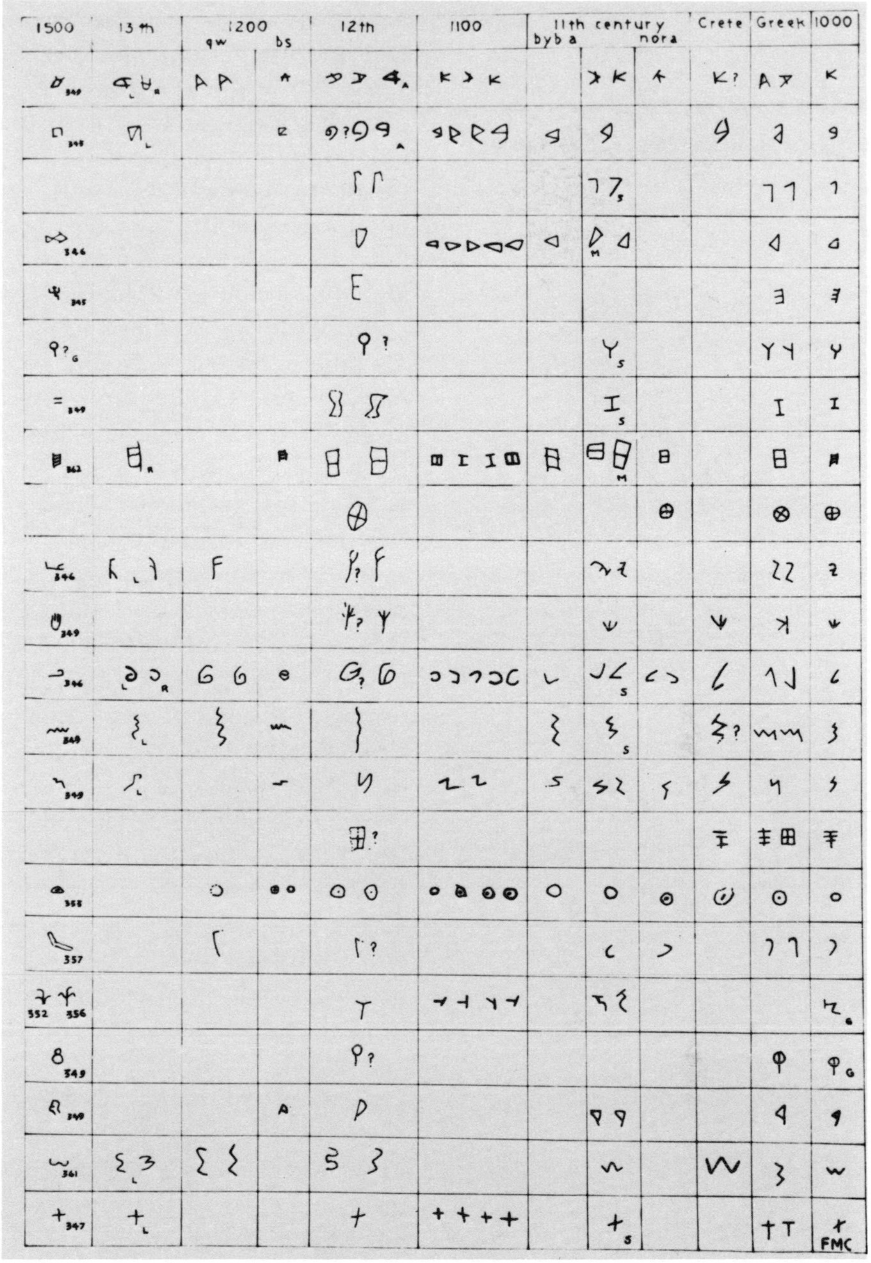

on. It was well known that the names of the letters in Phoenician and Hebrew were acrophonic: *'alef* or *'alp*, "ox"; *bêt*, "house"; *gimel* or *gaml*, "throwstick." However, a question remained: were the names primary, part of the invention of the alphabet, or secondary mnemonic devices? Gardiner's partial decipherment, and many attempts to extend it, were hotly debated, and nearly forty years passed before sufficient data were collected to settle the basic questions of how the alphabet was devised. Even today the early pictographic alphabet is not fully deciphered.

Over the years there has been a steady accumulation of early alphabetic inscriptions which now can be classified under two headings: (1) Old Canaanite inscriptions, transparently pictographic in origin, found in Syria-Palestine, belonging to the same genre as the pictographic script of Sinai; (2) Linear Phoenician inscriptions, easily read, an alphabetic script which is an ancestor of the Hebrew, Aramaic, and Greek scripts.

A word about terminology: arbitrarily we use the term Canaanite to refer to a people of a homogeneous culture who lived in Syria-Palestine before 1200 B.C. and spoke a related group of dialects. The name Canaan, known from biblical usage, stems from the Egyptian province of Canaan—Palestine west of the Jordan River—in the Late Bronze Age. After the series of destructive attacks which engulfed the Levant about 1200 B.C. (see the essay "End of the Bronze Age"), the remnant of the Canaanites, whose centers were now restricted to the Lebanese coast and northern Palestine, were called Phoenicians, their Greek name. Thus the Phoenicians' ancestors were Canaanites.

The Old Canaanite inscriptions in pictographic alphabetic signs date from ca. 1700 to 1200 B.C. The invention of the system took place probably in the eighteenth century—in the Hyksos age. Inscriptions in Early Linear Phoenician form a series beginning in the eleventh century. Actually the chronology of the Linear Phoenician series was settled only in the late 1940s and early 1950s. The precise relationship between the Old Canaanite alphabet and the Early Linear Phoenician script remained uncertain until 1953, when a group of inscribed arrowheads was found near Bethlehem at El-Khadr. These inscriptions from the end of the twelfth century proved to be missing links in the history of the alphabet. Five exist, three published in 1954, two published only in 1980 after being lost in the hands of private collectors for a quarter century. The El-Khadr arrowheads come from precisely the time when the Old Canaanite pictographs were evolving into the Early Linear Phoenician alphabet. Fortunately they contained virtually the same short inscription, one that could be

Figure 56
An inscribed bronze arrowhead
from El Khadr (ca. 1100 B.C.). Its
text reads ḥṣ ʿbdlb⟨ʿ⟩t, "the arrow
of ʿAbdlabiʾt."

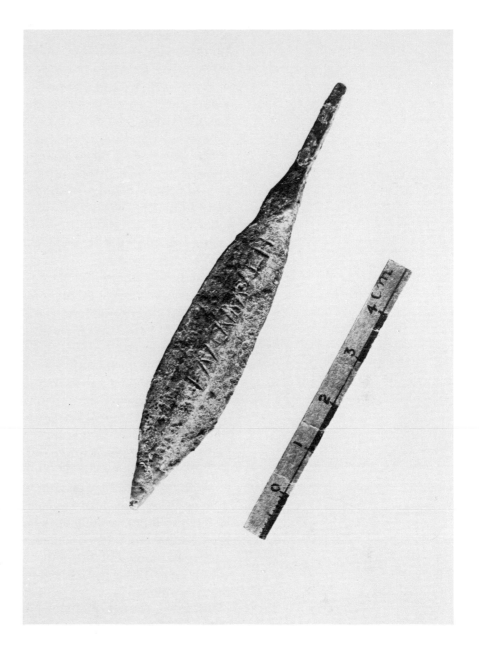

deciphered with certitude (see Fig. 56).

We now recognized clearly for the first time certain features of the two styles of alphabetic writing. The Old Canaanite alphabet was multidirectional: written horizontally right-to-left, left-to-right, and vertically. Boustrophedon (as the ox plows) writing was also used. In Linear Phoenician, the direction was fixed: right-to-left horizontal writing was standardized, and the stance of letters became fixed. In the El-Khadr arrowheads and the older Canaanite system, letters/pictographs faced away from the direction of writing. The Greek script was borrowed before the standardization of direction and stance. Early Greek was multidirectional and indeed standardized in horizontal left-to-right writing. Generally, therefore, Greek letters face in the opposite direction from Phoenician.

The discovery of the El-Khadr arrowheads led quickly to decipherment of the thirteenth-century ewer from Lachish in Palestine, and indeed to new readings of the Proto-Sinaitic texts. In 1977 and 1981 two additional twelfth-century inscriptions were published, one from Izbet Sartah in Israel which contained an abecedary of the same century further confirming our detailed description of the evolution of the early alphabet.

Meanwhile other important discoveries bearing on alphabetic origins were being made. Beginning in 1929 a series of magnificent epigraphic discoveries was made in Ugarit (modern Ras Shamra) on the coast of Syria. The main group of texts contains epic and mythological works inscribed in a cuneiform alphabet in an early Canaanite dialect of the fourteenth century B.C. It is now certain that this cuneiform alphabet was used throughout Syria-Palestine and that the Ugaritic alphabet can be called the Canaanite cuneiform alphabet. It is also certain that the system used in Ugaritic and a related one in Phoenicia and Palestine were developed under the inspiration of the Old Canaanite pictographic alphabet. Had there been any doubt, it was resolved by the discovery at Ugarit of abecedaries, first published in 1957. One group simply lists alphabetic signs following the precise order that survives in Hebrew, Aramaic, and Greek. Another abecedary, unfortunately broken, lists the signs of the Ugaritic alphabet in order and adds Babylonian signs, which permit us to reconstruct the names of the letters of the alphabet in the fourteenth century B.C. These names, beginning *'alp*, *bêt*, *gaml*, are ancestral to the later Phoenician and Greek names. These Ugaritic texts confirm other evidence that the names of the Old Canaanite signs and their order are at least as old as the fourteenth century B.C., and they add additional support to the view that the acrophonic principle, integral to the names of the signs, went back to the invention of the script.

The pictographic alphabet was devised under indirect influence of Egyptian hieroglyphic writing. Several of the pictographs are transparently derived from hieroglyphic models. Moreover, Egyptian writing has the peculiarity of giving notation only to the consonants in words and syllables, a peculiarity which survived in the Canaanite and Phoenician alphabets. In fact, Egyptian had what we call a pseudo-alphabet: signs representing a consonant and any vowel. However, they used such signs always in conjunction with biliteral and triliteral signs, so that Egyptian remained always a word-syllabic system; its pseudo-alphabet never functioned as an alphabet. The Canaanite system came into being when it was seen that one could write using a single consonant and any vowel (or no vowel). Such a system was ideally suited to West Semitic: each syllable in these languages begins with a consonant, and the vocalic structure is simple. Part of the invention was to devise pictographs representing consonantal phonemes on the acrophonic principle; part was to set the signs in a fixed order with fixed names, an order that survives to this day. The beauty of the invention is of course its simplicity—which required an extraordinary feat of abstraction.

To be sure, the Canaanite and Phoenician alphabets are incomplete in their notation of language, for no signs were devised to mark vowels. The Aramaeans upon borrowing the Phoenician alphabet developed a rudimentary system of denoting certain vowels, and these *matres lectionis* were used by Israelite scribes in the ninth century B.C. The first full system of signs for vowels was developed by the Greeks. The Phoenician system was most awkward for the writing of Greek: it contained many signs for consonants not used in that language and had no means to denote syllables beginning with a vowel. The alphabet was quickly modified, therefore, and signs, consonantal in Semitic, were co-opted for vowels in Greek—for example, the glottal stop, Phoenician *'alep*, became utilized to represent the vowel *a*.

The antiquity of the borrowing of the Greek alphabet has been the subject of much debate. Until very recently there was a consensus that the borrowing took place in the late ninth or the eighth century B.C. However, with our present knowledge of the evolution of the Old Canaanite and Linear Phoenician scripts, it has been recognized that the Greek script stems from an archetype of the eleventh century, at the time of transition from Old Canaanite to the Early Linear Phoenician. Evidently it was little used until the ninth century, in the interval being adapted to make a more efficient vehicle for recording the Greek tongue.

The Old South Arabic script was borrowed about 1300 B.C. and is ancestral to Ethiopic. The Aramaeans borrowed the Phoenician alphabet no later than the eleventh century. The Old Hebrew script diverged from Phoenician only in the tenth century in the time of David or Solomon. The Aramaic script has a remarkable history. It spread eastward, displacing older writing systems in Mesopotamia, Persia, and ultimately India. It is also the ancestor of the medieval Arabic script (by way of Nabataean) and of the medieval Hebrew script.

Recommended Reading

W. F. Albright. *The Proto-Sinaitic Inscriptions and Their Decipherment HTS* 22 (Cambridge, Mass.: Harvard University Press, 1966).

F. M. Cross. "Newly Found Inscriptions in the Old Canaanite and Early Phoenician Scripts." *Bulletin of the American Schools of Oriental Research* 238 (1980) 1–20.

B. S. J. Isserlin. "The Earliest Alphabetic Writing." In *Cambridge Ancient History.* Vol. III, Part 1 (3rd ed. Cambridge: Cambridge University Press, 1982).

J. Naveh. *Early History of the Alphabet* (Leiden: E. J. Brill, 1982).

119
Cylinder seal

Site: Ugarit (Ras Shamra), southern city
Date: Middle Syrian period, 1500–1400 B.C.
Material: Hematite
Height: 3 cm; *diameter:* 1.2 cm
Museum No.: Damascus S 2795 (RS. 23. 438)
Literature: C.F.A. Schaeffer *AfO* 20 (1963) 207, Fig. 23 left /
  AAAS 11/12 (1961/1962) Fig. 3 // cf. E. Porada *Corpus of
  Ancient Near Eastern Seals in North American Collections
  I: The Pierpont Morgan Library* (1948) Plate CXLIII No.
  945 E // B. Buchanan *Catalogue of Ancient Near Eastern
  Seals in the Ashmolean Museum I* (1966) Plate 35 No. 864

119

A bearded worshiper and a suppliant goddess face
each other with a star between them. The worshiper is
dressed in an open cloak with one leg exposed; the
goddess is wearing an ankle-length plain robe; they
both wear rounded caps. Behind them is a palm tree
with a guilloche dividing the scene into two registers.
The top register shows two couchant sphinxes with a
gazelle between them. Below the palm tree lie two
resting horned goats with birds on either side. A
guilloche forms the ground line. This beautiful seal
is carved in the Mittani style.
U.K.

120
Cylinder seal

Site: Ugarit (Ras Shamra)
Date: Late Old Syrian to Early Middle Syrian period,
  1700–1500 B.C.
Material: White stone, gold
Height: 2.2 cm; *diameter:* 0.85 cm
Museum No.: Aleppo 4603
Literature: Cf. B. Parker *Iraq* 11 (1949) Plate II 12 // D.
  Collon "The Seals from Tell Atchana/Alalakh" *AOAT* 27
  (1975) 90 No. 164

120

Cylinder seals were frequently mounted with caps of
precious metal, like this one which still retains its gold
caps. A suspension loop, by which the seal was worn
around the neck, was usually attached to the top cap.
The design of this seal, probably of Egyptian inspiration, shows lotus flowers in a double band.
U.K.

121

122

121
Cylinder seal

Site: Ugarit (Ras Shamra), surface "région egéene"
Date: Middle Syrian period, 1500–1300 B.C.
Material: Steatite
Height: 2.7 cm; *diameter;* 1.3 cm
Museum No.: Aleppo RS. 68. 30. 261

Under a winged sun disk on either side of a palm tree stands a naked hero with side curls. A worshiper wearing a long cloak and holding a sacrificial goat is presented to a seated god by a small suppliant figure. The god wears a horned crown and is seated on a tall throne, holding a club in his léft hand. This Mittani-style seal is less carefully executed than Cat. No. 119, but care was taken in depicting the typical Mittani palm tree.
U.K.

122
Cylinder seal

Site: Ugarit (Ras Shamra), "tranche nord G C 8. 4800"
Date: Middle Syrian period, 1500–1300 B.C.
Material: Steatite
Height: 2.3 cm; *diameter:* 1.1 cm
Museum No.: Aleppo RS. 68. 30. 259

In the design of this seal a god fights a sphinx, who is clawing at a goat. The god, dressed in a short robe and tall conical hat, attacks the sphinx with a spear and holds a club over his shoulder. There is a winged sun disk above the sphinx and a tree in front of the goat. Drill holes serve as filler motifs.
U.K.

123
Cylinder Seal

Site: Ugarit (Ras Shamra), Minat al-Beida harbor district
Date: Middle Syrian period, 1500–1300 B.C.
Material: Blue sintered quartz
Height: 2.1 cm; *diameter:* 1 cm
Museum No.: Aleppo 4731 (4128 M.B. 1932)
Literature: Cf. C. F. A. Schaeffer *Syria* 28 (1951) 9, Fig. 3 //
    A. Moortgat *Vorderasiatische Rollsiegel* (1940) Plate 65
    No. 550

The design of this seal is divided by incised lines into four side-by-side frames: a goat standing on his hind legs with a branch behind him, then three persons. The Egyptian influence is clear in the depiction of the figures, who all stand stiffly upright and wear Egyptian-inspired clothes and headdresses.
U.K.

123

125
Seal ring

Site: Ugarit (Ras Shamra), Tomb of Rap'anu
Date: Middle Syrian period, 1500–1300 B.C.
Material: Silver
Diameter of ring: 2.2 cm; *width of seal:* 2 cm
Museum No.: Aleppo RS. 68. 30. 288
Literature: Cf. C.F.A. Schaeffer *AAAS* 11–12 (1961–1962)
   Fig. 5 / *AfO* 20 (1963) 206, Fig. 20

The residential quarter of Ugarit was situated northeast of the Middle Syrian royal palace. The largest
house in this quarter, a two-storied structure with 34
rooms on the ground floor, belonged to an important
royal official, Rap'anu, according to the archives. Below the interior courtyard of this house there was a funerary chamber with small rooms attached, and from
here this silver seal ring was retrieved. Its design
shows a goat nibbling upon a palm tree. Seal rings
such as this first appear in Syria in the middle
of the second millennium B.C.
K.K.

124
Cylinder seal

Site: Ugarit (Ras Shamra)
Date: Middle Syrian period, 1500–1300 B.C.
Material: Steatite
Height: 1.3 cm; *diameter:* 1 cm
Museum No.: Aleppo 4785 (RS. 8088)
Literature: Cf. O.W. Muscarella (ed.) *Ladders to Heaven*
   (Toronto 1981) No. 217

Cylinder seals are almost always arranged horizontally. This seal is one of the very few engraved to present a vertical design, which shows a deity dressed in a
short robe, wearing a conical cap. He is standing on a
lion and holds a spear in each hand.
U.K.

126
Scale pans

Site: Ugarit (Ras Shamra)
Date: Middle Syrian period, 1500–1300 B.C.
Material: Bronze
Greatest diameters: 9.8 and 10 cm
Museum No.: Aleppo 4171; 4172
Literature: Cf. C.F.A. Schaeffer *Ugaritica* I (1939) 44, Fig. 33 / *Syria* 18 (1937) 148, Plate XXIV 2

127
Weights

Site: Ugarit (Ras Shamra)
Date: Middle Syrian period, 1500–1300 B.C.
Material: Hematite, lead, bronze
Length: 5.5, 2.5, 6.5 cm; *weight:* 91.5, 9.5, 6.5 g
Museum Nos.: Damascus S 5687 (RS. 56. 20. 61 B); S 5466 (RS. 21. 224); S 7146 (RS. 62. 25. 260)
Literature: Cf. C.F.A. Schaeffer *Syria* 18 (1937) 148, Fig. 13 / *Ugaritica I* (1939) 44, Fig. 34 / *AfO* 20 (1963) 209, Fig. 24

The scales (Cat. No. 126) and small weights were probably used by a merchant for weighing precious metals. Two of the weights, made of polished hematite, have bored holes on the bottom filled with lead; the larger weight has a bronze handle. The excavator reports that weights from both the Egyptian and the Mesopotamian systems of measure were found at Ugarit. Very likely they were used to weigh gold imported from Egypt. The relative value of gold was impressive but varied considerably across the Near East: in Egypt the exchange ratio was one part gold to two parts silver; in Ugarit the value was three to four parts silver to one part gold; while in Nuzi in northeastern Iraq the ratio was nine parts silver to one part gold.
K.K.

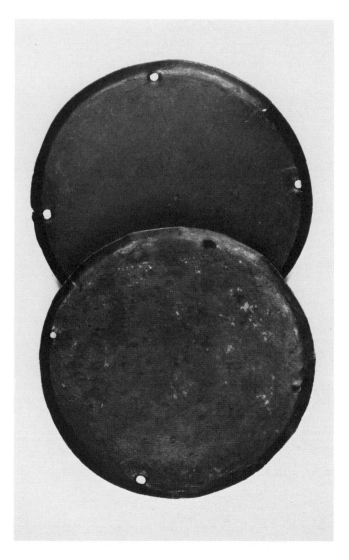

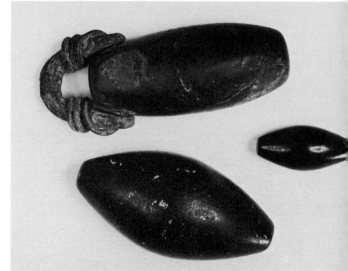

128, right

128
Weights in the shape of a bull and a lion

Site: Ugarit (Ras Shamra)
Date: Middle Syrian period, 1500–1300 B.C.
Material: Bronze, lead
Height of bull: 4.3 cm; *length:* 9 cm; *depth:* 4.5 cm; *weight:*
   465 g; *height of lion:* 3.1 cm; *length:* 7.6 cm; *depth:* 3 cm;
   weight: 180 g
Museum Nos.: Aleppo 4516, 4520
Literature: C.F.A. Schaeffer *Syria* 16 (1935) Plate XXXIII 5 /
   cf. *Ugaritica* I (1939) 44 / *AfO* 20 (1963) 209, Fig. 25

Many larger weights were modelled as resting animals, sometimes even as human heads. Here we show
a bull and a lion, both of them naturalistically rendered. Both weights have drilled holes on the bottom
filled with lead; on the bull weight the lead-filled hole
has been covered with a plate. If we assume the
Ugaritic basic weight of a shekel to be 9–9.3 grams,
the larger weight is 50 Ugaritic shekels, the smaller
one 20 shekels.
K.K.

129
Casting mold

Site: Ugarit (Ras Shamra)
Date: Middle Syrian period, 1500–1300 B.C.
Material: Steatite
Length: 15.7 cm; *width:* 4.3 cm; *depth:* 1.5 cm
Museum No.: Aleppo 4571 (RS. 55. 19. 224)
Literature: C.F.A. Schaeffer *Syria* 18 (1937) 152, Fig. 17 /
   Ugaritica I (1939) 44, Fig. 32

These two halves of a casting mold, once joined with
tacks or nails, were found in the house of a goldsmith.
The drill holes on top may have served to attach further parts. Marks on one side show how the parts
were put together. A richly decorated necklace or diadem may have been cast in this mold. The design includes birds of prey and sphinxes, with pomegranates
suspended below.
K.K.

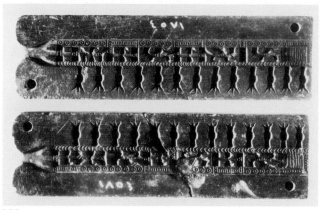

129

130
Pendant

See color plate p. 314

Site: Ugarit (Ras Shamra), Minat al-Beida harbor district,
   "dépôt d'enceinte" (dépôt 11)
Date: Middle Syrian period, 1500–1300 B.C.
Material: Gold
Height: 7.2 cm; *width:* 4 cm
Museum No.: Aleppo 4575
Literature: C.F.A. Schaeffer *Syria* 10 (1929) 289, Plate LIV 2
   // O. Negbi *Canaanite Gods in Metal* (Tel Aviv 1976) Fig.
   128 No. 1698 // cf. K.R. Maxwell-Hyslop *Western Asiatic
   Jewellery, ca. 3000–612 B.C.* (1971) 138

A number of Levantine gold pendants depict a naked
goddess *en face*, with hair set in the style of the Egyptian goddess Hathor. The goddess on this pendant
holds a flower standard in each hand; other pendants
show her holding snakes or goats. Sometimes she
stands on a lion or a crescent moon. We are not sure
which goddess she represents, since traits of Egyptian
as well as Mesopotamian styles can be seen here. On
an Egyptian New Kingdom stele she appears standing
on a lion as the goddess Qudshu, who may be comparable to Astarte as well as Anat. The best compari-
sons for the pendant are the depictions of naked goddesses made of terracotta from the late third and early
second millennia, which all may have had magic properties. Other pendants from Ugarit show the same
softly modelled outline of the body and the same details, which seem to be characteristic of Ugaritic workshops.
K.K.

131
Pendant

See color plate p. 314

Site: Ugarit (Ras Shamra)
Date: Middle Syrian period, 1500–1300 B.C.
Material: Gold
Height: 7 cm; *width:* 3.9 cm
Museum No.: Aleppo 4576
Literature: Cf. C.F.A. Schaeffer *Syria* 13 (1932) Plate IX /
   Syria 19 (1938) 322, Fig. 49 // O. Negbi *Canaanite Gods in
   Metal* (Tel Aviv 1976) Plate 52 bottom

On this pear-shaped pendant only the head, the
breasts, and the navel are modelled; the pubic hair
and a small tree are carelessly incised. Similar pendants where the body is reduced to individual features
are known from Tell Ajjul, Lachish, and Megiddo in
Palestine. A large number of such pendants were
found in Ugarit, often with the small incised tree, and
we can therefore rule out the theory that they were
imports from the south.
   A rectangular strip on top of this and the pendant in
Cat. No. 130 rolled into a loop to serve for suspension.
K.K.

132
Statuette of an enthroned god

Site: Ugarit (Ras Shamra), acropolis
Date: Middle Syrian period, 1500–1300 B.C.
Material: Bronze
Height without pegs: 12.4 cm
Museum No.: Aleppo 4529
Literature: O. Negbi *Canaanite Gods in Metal* (Tel Aviv
   1976) 46, Fig. 54 // C.F.A. Schaeffer *Syria* 17 (1936) 126,
   Plate XV 3 / *AfO* 21 (1966) 65, Fig. 12 // G. Roeder
   Mitteilungen aus der Ägyptischen Sammlung VI (Berlin
   1956) 38 (D. 18) Fig. 56

This small sculpture of a male enthroned deity belongs to a group of Syro-Palestinian bronze figurines.
In his left hand the unidentified deity once held a
scepter or a cup, while the right hand is raised in a
gesture of blessing. Three pegs, two under the feet
and one under the seat, served as attachments to a
throne and a footstool. The figure wears a reed crown
with ostrich feathers on both sides. This kind of headdress was often worn by Osiris, the Egyptian god of
death, but in Egyptian art it is also worn by the Syrian
gods Anat and Resheph. While the wide collar is a

132, right

ca. 1600–1200 B.C.

typical Egyptian ornament, the rendering here seems more abstract and simplified than in original Egyptian art. Over the long Syrian robe, decorated with ribbons, the deity wears a short pleated skirt or apron with horizontal stripes. The skirt is clearly inspired by the dress of the pharaohs of the New Kingdom; the middle piece, especially, looks like the uraeus (the stylized representation of the sacred asp) associated with Egyptian kings.

M.E.-K.

133
Statuette of a standing god

See color plate p. 315

Site: Ugarit (Ras Shamra), southern city
Date: Middle Syrian period, 1400–1300 B.C.
Material: Bronze, gold
Height: 12.2 cm; *width:* 4.3 cm; *depth:* 4.5 cm
Museum No.: Damascus S 3372 (RS. 23: 393)
Literature: C.F.A. Schaeffer *AAAS* 11–12 (1961–1962) 191, Fig. 6 / *AfO* 20 (1963) 206, Fig. 21 // D. Collon *Levant* 4 (1972) 113 // O. Negbi *Canaanite Gods in Metal* (Tel Aviv 1976) No. 1327 // Spycket *La Statuaire* 338

Four small bronzes originally wrapped in linen were found in a house in the southern part of the city of Ugarit: two statuettes of beardless deities, including this standing god; the enthroned god shown in Cat. No. 134; and a small figure of a bull, which may have been the top of a scepter. In the same house was a treasure of silver and electrum rings, earrings, pendants, and gold and silver bars, all of which suggests that the house may have belonged to a goldsmith.

This god raises his right arm and stretches his left forward. He wears a short skirt and a tall headdress ending in an elongated point, modelled after the "white crown" of Upper Egypt. Similar figurines hold a weapon in the right hand—dagger, club or spear. This type of striding armed deity is typically Levantine; sailors brought them to Greece—to Tiryns, Mycenae, Rhodes, and Thessaly.

The deity cannot be identified with certainty, but perhaps he is Baal or a weather god such as Resheph or Adad. The head and neck are covered with a thin layer of gold foil, while a similar statue in the Louvre shows traces of silver on the body. There are remnants of the linen wrapping on the back.

K.K.

134
Statuette of an enthroned god

See color plate p. 315

Site: Ugarit (Ras Shamra), southern city
Date: Middle Syrian period, 1400–1300 B.C.
Material: Bronze, gold
Height: 13.5 cm; *width:* 5 cm; *depth:* 9 cm
Museum No.: Damascus S 3573 (RS. 23. 394)
Literature: C.F.A. Schaeffer *AAAS* 11–12 (1961–1962) 191, Fig. 6 / *AfO* 20 (1963) 206, Fig. 21 / *AfO* 21 (1966) 65, Fig. 11 / *Syria* 43 (1966) Plate II // O. Negbi *Canaanite Gods in Metal* (Tel Aviv 1976) Fig. 129 No. 1442 // Saadé *Ougarit* 128, Fig. 35 // Spycket *La Statuaire* 341 // Tokyo Exhibition No. 113

This seated god, found together with Cat. No. 133, wears the same headdress and has the same gestures as Cat. No. 132, although it shows more local Syrian elements of style. Above the ears are drill holes that once held horns, the sign of divinity in the ancient Near East. He wears the Syrian wrap-around robe with rolled-up edge and sandals with wide double straps. The narrow oblong eye sockets were originally inlaid. The importance of this statuette, which conceivably represents the bearded god El, is evident from its gold-foil covering.

K.K.

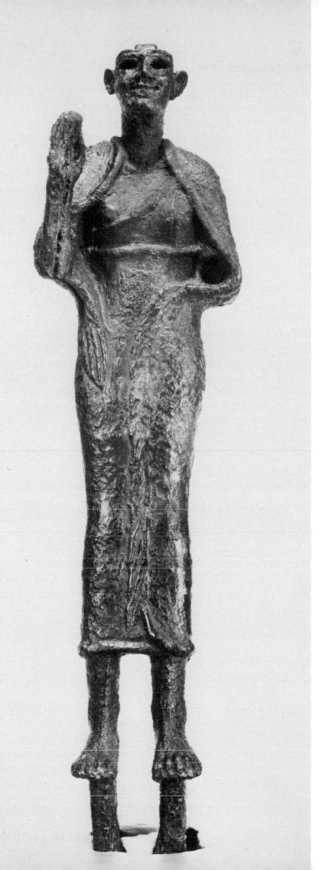

135
Statuette of a goddess (?)

Site: Ugarit (Ras Shamra), southern city
Date: Middle Syrian period, 1400–1300 B.C.
Material: Bronze
Height with modern base: 25.8 cm; *width:* 6 cm
Museum No.: Damascus S 3574 (RS. 23. 395)
Literature: C.F.A. Schaeffer *Syria* 43 (1966) 1, Fig. 2 Plate
    III // O. Negbi *Canaanite Gods in Metal* (Tel Aviv 1976)
    Fig. 129 No. 1630 // Tokyo Exhibition No. 116

This female statuette was found in a small workshop
near the house mentioned in Cat. Nos. 133 and 134.
Her left hand is covered by her fringed robe, and she
wears a belted dress under her robe. The statuette has
grooves on both sides, at the back of the neck and the
legs, and on the right arm. These grooves (often found
on Syrian bronzes from the second millennium) served
to attach a covering layer of finer material, such as
gold or silver. The left arm was cast separately, then
attached to the body, as was the headdress. Since
there seems no technical reason why the headdress
should not have been cast with the rest of the body, we
may assume that it was made of a different material.
Another Ugaritic statuette of a deity wears a steatite
headdress with electrum horns.
K.K.

136
Bronze statuette

Site: Ugarit (Ras Shamra)
Date: Middle Syrian period, 1500–1300 B.C.
Material: Bronze
Height: 13.7 cm; *width:* 3.7 cm; *depth:* 2.2 cm
Museum No.: Aleppo RS. 68. 30. 248
Literature: Cf. O. Negbi *Canaanite Gods in Metal* (Tel Aviv 1976) 42

Like the previous statuette, this one also has grooves for a layer of precious metal. Both arms, now lost, were cast separately. A peg on the head held the headdress. This figurine was placed on a base with two other figurines; the pegs under her feet are mold casting remnants. Another statuette from Ugarit,[1] also with attached arms and wearing a similar robe, was found within a level possibly dating from the nineteenth to the seventeenth century B.C. A precise date for the stylistic features of this statuette is therefore difficult to ascertain.
K.K.

[1]C.F.A. Schaeffer *Ugaritica* I (1939) Plate XXXI

137
Falcon-shaped ornament

Site: Ugarit (Ras Shamra)
Date: 1400–1300 B.C. (?)
Material: Bronze, inlaid with gold
Height excluding peg: 8.8 cm
Museum No.: Aleppo 4532
Literature: C.F.A. Schaeffer *Syria* 10 (1929) 288, Plate LII 1.3

The falcon was a divine symbol in Egypt, most often symbolizing the sun god Horus. On official occasions the pharaoh was accompanied by a falcon standard, and this piece may have had a similar purpose in Ugarit. It is impossible to determine whether this falcon is of Syrian or Egyptian origin.

The head has a drilled hole which once accommodated a sun disk. A raised cobra in front of the legs would protect the god by its poisonous fangs. The feathers, eyes, and breast are decorated with gold, inlaid in a process that involved hammering the precious

metal into the carved grooves. This technique was first documented at the end of the Middle Kingdom in Egypt; the earliest examples of definite date are two inlaid lids with representations of Queen Neferhotep from the Thirteenth Dynasty. This technique was used infrequently until the end of the Twenty-Second Dynasty.

M.E.-K.

138

138
Spindle bottle

Site: Ugarit (Ras Shamra)
Date Early Middle Syrian period, 1600–1350 B.C.
Material: Terracotta
Height: 32.3 cm; *greatest diameter:* 8.5 cm
Museum No.: Aleppo 4403 (RS. 8128)
Literature: Cf. C.F.A. Schaeffer *Ugaritica* II (1949) 138,
　　Figs. 51, 17

The spindle-shaped bottle was common along the
Levantine coast. It was often covered with a gray—or
as in this case red—slip of finely smoothed clay, then
fired. These vessels may have been used for storage,
for transportation of precious liquids, or for religious
ceremonies. This example has an inscribed mark on
the bottom identifying its workshop.

The shape may have originated in northwest Syria,
but similar bottles were also produced elsewhere. Especially common along the coast, they were also found
inland as well as in Palestine, Egypt, and Cyprus.
While this type of vessel was exported to Cyprus,
animal-shaped Cypriot vessels made their way to
Ugarit (see Cat No. 139).
K.K.

139
Bull-shaped jar
See color plate p. 314

Site: Ugarit (Ras Shamra), south acropolis, sector 20 E,
　　tomb 3464
Date: Early Middle Syrian period, 1600–1400 B.C.
Material: Terracotta
Height excluding restoration: 15.8 cm; *length:* 19.2 cm
Museum No.: Damascus S 6883 (RS. 61. 24. 435)
Literature: C.F.A. Schaeffer *AAAS* 13 (1963) Fig. 25 //
　　J.C. Courtois *Ugaritica* VII (1978) 290, Fig. 32

Found in a tomb in Ugarit, this import represents one
of the best types of Cypriot pottery, the so-called
Base-Ring II ware. Modelled in the shape of a bull, it
has a drilled hole through the snout serving as a spout.
The ears and horns are carefully rendered and the
eyes were originally inlaid. The surface of the vessel is
reddish brown, decorated with beige stripes.
K.K.

140
Cup shaped like the head of a lion

Site: Ugarit (Ras Shamra)
Date: Middle Syrian period, 1500–1300 B.C.
Material: Terracotta
Height: 16.2 cm
Museum No.: Damascus S 4217 (RS. 52. 16. 52)
Literature: Cf. C.F.A. Schaeffer *Ugaritica* VII (1978) 149 /
  Syria 19 (1938) Plate XIX

The bottom of this one-handled cup is in the form of a lion's head. The eyes are deeply carved, while the other features, such as the whiskers, are incised. A similar lion cup, found in 1962 with an Ugaritic inscription dedicating the vessel to "Resheph, the protector," dates from the thirteenth century B.C. The inspiration for these vessels can be found in the West: other animal-headed rhyta of Mycenaean style have been found in Ugarit and Minat-al-Beida. Such vessels were produced still earlier in Cyprus and Crete.[1]

K.K.

[1]P. Demarghe "Die Geburt der griechischer Kunst" in *Universum der Kunst* (1965) Fig. 219

141
Mycenaean rhyton

Site: Ugarit (Ras Shamra), residential area northeast of the
    palace, near tomb 4760
Date: Late Middle Syrian period, 1230–1200 B.C.
Material: Terracotta
Height excluding restoration: 36.5 cm; *reconstructed
    diameter at top:* 13.5 cm
Museum No.: Aleppo RS. 68. 30. 310
Literature: J. C. Courtois *Ugaritica* VII (1978) 310, Fig.
    37:12 // Cf. C.F.A. Schaeffer *Syria* 13 (1932) Plate IV /
    Syria 51 (1974) Plate II / *Ugaritica* II (1949) Fig. 91 // see
    also F. H. Stubbings *Mycenean Pottery from the Levant*
    (1951) // H.-G. Buchholz *AA* (1974) 400

From approximately 1390 B.C., at the beginning of the
reign of the Egyptian Pharaoh Amenhotep III, a type
of Mycenaean pottery distinguished by its painted designs (called Late Helladic IIIA/B) was imported into
the Levant in large quantities. Earlier, Mycenaean imports were scarce and restricted to the coastal area,
but at this time the trade expanded inland, from the
plain of Antioch to the Euphrates in the east, and as
far south as Palestine. A large number of such
Mycenaean imports were found in tombs at Ugarit.
   This vessel has a drilled hole at the tip and is decorated with six playing dolphins painted in reddish-
brown colors. Representations of sea life were common in the decorative repertoire of these seafarers.
K.K.

142
Mycenaean jug

Site: Ugarit (Ras Shamra)
Date: Late Middle Syrian period, 1300–1200 B.C.
Material: Terracotta
Height: 10.2 cm.; *greatest diameter:* 11.4 cm
Museum No.: Aleppo 4487
Literature: Cf. C.F.A. Schaeffer *Ugaritica* II (1949) Fig. 122
    // *AAAS* 13 (1963) Fig. 30

Jugs with two handles were often used for transporting
valuable liquids, such as rare oils or perfumes. Sometimes the spout is sealed; often there is a small drill
hole on top for easier pouring. This jug has a simple
decoration of reddish-brown bands with triangles on
top.
   It is often difficult to determine whether Mycenaean
pottery was imported or was produced in Ugarit by

142

Figure 57
Pilgrim flask from Minat al-Beida (cf. Cat. No. 143).

Mycenaean potters. Because of its fine clay, slip, and carefully painted decoration, this vessel is probably an import.
K.K.

143
Pilgrim flask
See color plate p. 316

Site: Ugarit (Ras Shamra)
Date: Late Middle Syrian period, 1300–1200 B.C.
Material: Faience
Height: 21.3 cm
Museum No.: Damascus S 6881 (RS. 61. 24. 433)

During the late Bronze Age, Mycenaean or Cypriot ceramic imports, usually with Aegean shapes and decorations, were quite common at coastal Levantine sites. This pilgrim flask is an unusual example of a native Levantine faience vessel decorated with spirals and dots of Aegean inspiration. A Mycenean flask found in a tomb at Minat al-Beida with a similar decoration may have inspired this one. The Mycenean example has seven spirals emerging from a central ring filled with a spiral (see Fig. 57). In our case, the spirals are reversed, starting at the outside and ending toward the circle on the middle of the flask.
K.K.

144
Imitation of a Mycenaean jug
See color plate p. 316

Site: Ugarit (Ras Shamra), tomb H 698
Date: Late Middle Syrian period, 1300–1200 B.C.
Material: Faience
Height: 8.3 cm; *greatest diameter:* 10.5 cm
Museum No.: Aleppo 6203 (RS. 66, 2H 698)
Literature: Cf. C.F.A. Schaeffer *Syria* 10 (1929) Plate III 4 //
    H.-G. Buchholz *AA* (1974) 458

Modelled after a Mycenaean jug with a handle, this vessel is simply decorated with circles, crosses, and dots: black on a light blue background. Poor firing of the jug resulted in a blistered glaze.
K.K.

145
Spoon-shaped bowl
See color plate p. 316

Site: Ugarit (Ras Shamra), "ville basse," tomb LVI
Date: Late Old Syrian to beginning of Middle Syrian period,
   1700–1680 B.C.
Material: Faience
Length: 15.6 cm; *diameter of bowl:* 8.1 cm
Museum No.: Aleppo 4557
Literature: C.F.A. Schaeffer *Syria* (1938) 241, Plate XXII 2

In the northeastern part of the city were a number of
large houses dating from the Old Syrian to the beginning of the Middle Syrian period. Below the houses
were approximately twenty graves, one of them containing some forty-four bodies accompanied by hundreds of pottery vessels. One of the grave goods was
this small faience vessel shaped like a spoon. The
handle ends in a turned-back head of a duck, very
similar to the cosmetic jar of Cat. No. 153. Their inspiration was probably Egyptian.
K.K.

146
Double-faced cup

Site: Ugarit (Ras Shamra)
Date: Middle Syrian period, 1300–1200 B.C.
Material: Faience
Height: 9.4 cm; *width:* 5.1 cm; *depth:* 6.4 cm
Literature: Cf. C.F.A. Schaeffer *Ugaritica* I (1939) Plate X,
   Fig. 94 // M. Falkner and B. Hrouda *RLA* III (1957–1971)
   297 // W. Culican *Levant* 3 (1971) 86 // P. Amiet *Die Kunst
   des alten Orient* (1977) Fig. 498

This cup, shaped as a double-faced female head, rests
on a tall hollow foot. Double-faced vessels are a special development of faience face vases. Their origin is
unclear, for they have been found in the east at Ashur,
in the west on Cyprus, and in the south in Palestine.
The theory that this type of vessel originated in northern Syria because of the style of the headdress finds
support in the early example of a face vessel from Tell
Mardikh (Cat. No. 103 on p. 00).
K.K.

146

147
Faience plate
See color place p. 317

Site: Ugarit (Ras Shamra), family grave
Date: Ca. 1300 B.C.
Material: Faience
Diameter: 13 cm
Museum No.: Damascus S 7179 (RS. 63. 26. 256)
Literature: C.F.A. Schaeffer *AfO* 21 (1966) 132, Fig. 15 //
   E. C. Straub *Die Nunschale: Eine Gefässgattung des
   Neuen Reiches: Münchner Ägyptologische Studien* 30
   (1974) 18, 65 // Tokyo Exhibition No. 135

This plate is decorated with Egyptian motifs: fish and
plants, including blue lotus buds. The aquamarine-
colored background represents water, the ocean or the

Nile. Such ceramic pieces with Egyptian decoration were frequently imported by Cyprus and coastal Levantine sites. The design probably represents the Egyptian deity Nun, creator of the ocean and life.
M.E.-K.

148
Sickle sword

Site: Ugarit (Ras Shamra), Chantier C
Date: Middle Syrian period, 1400–1300 B.C.
Material: Bronze
Length: 57.7 cm
Museum No.: Aleppo 4180
Literature: C.F.A. Schaeffer *Syria* 17 (1936) 145, Plate XVIII 2 // R. Maxwell-Hyslop *Iraq* 8 (1946) 41 (Type 34) // S. Schosske et al. (eds.) *Lexikon der Ägyptologie* III (1980) 819 // cf. *Staatliche Sammlung Ägyptischer Kunst* (Munich 1972) 52, Plate 24 (AS 5887)

This curved sickle sword was found at a level dating to the first half of the fourteenth century B.C. Although cast in one piece, the handle was fashioned from strips of organic material, perhaps bone, which are now lost. Handled sickle swords have a long history in the ancient Near East. The Early Dynastic statue of Eannatum from Lagash (2600 B.C.) shows a similar weapon in the king's right hand. This kind of sword is also found in the hands of other kings, heros, and deities on cylinder seals and terracotta plaques from the late third millenium B.C. On a wall painting from Mari the goddess Ishtar holds a sickle sword (Fig. 42). In later periods, the shape of the sickle sword continued to evolve: the handle was shortened, the blade was lengthened and straightened. Such ancient Near Eastern weapons have also been found in Egypt from New Kingdom and later times.
K.K.

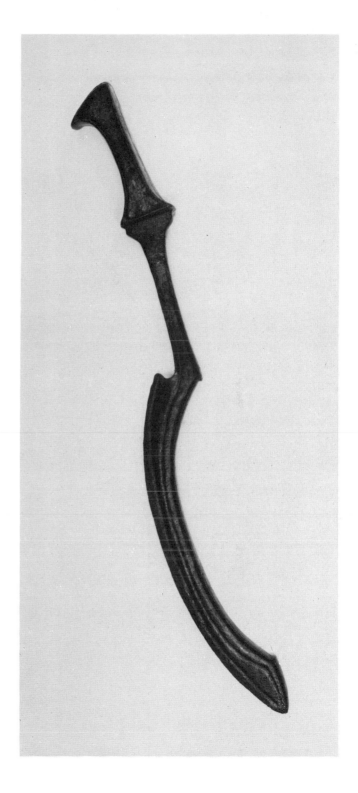

149
Sword inscribed with name of Merneptah

Site: Ugarit (Ras Shamra), residential quarter, east of palace
Date: Late Middle Syrian period, reign of Merneptah,
   1213–1204 B.C.
Material: Bronze
Length: 74.4 cm; *greatest width:* 5 cm
Museum No.: Damascus S 3591 (RS. 17. 90)
Literature: C.F.A. Schaeffer *Ugaritica* III (1956) 169, Figs.
   123, 124, Plate VIII / *AAAS* 3 (1953) 140, Fig. 15 // For the
   historical context see M. Liverani *Storia di Ugarit nell'età
   degli archivi politici: Studi Semitici* 6 (1962) 132 and H.
   Klengel *Geschichte Syriens* II 415 n. 114

We find yet another proof of the intensive trade between Ugarit and Egypt in this sword blade with an inscribed cartouche of Merneptah, pharaoh of the Nineteenth Dynasty. The handle, made of perishable
material, is now lost. The blade was found in the corner of a private courtyard with a dagger, a spear point,
and other weapons. The house may have belonged to a
dealer or manufacturer of weapons for the Egyptian
pharaohs.
K.K.

150
Stele depicting a treaty

Site: Ugarit (Ras Shamra), acropolis, near the Baal Temple
Date: Middle Syrian period, 1400–1300 B.C.
Material: Limestone
Height: 21.8 cm; *width:* 13.6 cm; *depth:* 6.9 cm
Museum No.: Aleppo 4418
Literature: C.F.A. Schaeffer *Syria* 17 (1936) Plate XIV /
   Ugaritica III (1956) 92, Plate VI // A. Parrot "Die
   Phönizier" *Universum der Kunst* (1977) Fig. 72 // G. Saadé
   Ougarit 104, Fig. 15 // P. Matthiae *Ars Syria* 69, Plate 22

Stelae, or stone commemorative monuments, either
inscribed or uninscribed, were used in secular or religious contexts from at least the third millennium B.C.
in the ancient Near East. An early example of this
commemorative art form is known from Ugarit of the
Old Syrian period, but this kind of monument is better
documented during the Middle Syrian period. The example here illustrates a typical theme: alliance, or
treaty making, between royal powers in superior ver-
sus dependent or equal partner roles, or alliances
("covenants") between gods and kings. Treaty and
covenant making in the ancient Near East is, of

150, right

course, as old as cities and states. Literary documentation for such treaties, alliances, and contracts extends from such matters as "trivial" land sales to subjects as "sublime" as divine protection. Most ancient Near Eastern commemorative stelae confirm the relations between royalty as treaty documents. Such diplomatic relationships are the archetypes for those described, for instance, in the patriarchal narratives of the Old Testament. A well-known example is the treaty between Jacob and Laban (Genesis 31).

In this stele two male figures stand facing each other under lotus buds. Both are wearing wrap-around garments with fringes that enclose one arm. The person to the left is almost a mirror image of the person on the right, and thus his left hand rather than his right remains free. This kind of depiction, rare in Syria, is common in contemporary Hittite reliefs. On the table between the two figures are documents, perhaps contracts.

One very significant difference between the two male figures must be noted, however. The left figure is bare-headed, while the right figure wears a conical cap. Bare-headed figures on other stelae from Ugarit seem to represent the king. often before the deity. Iconographically, however, the person on the right is clearly not a divine figure. It is possible, therefore, that this stele simply represents a treaty or covenant between two earthly powers—the king of Ugarit and a neighboring prince.

H.W.

151
Stele depicting the god El (?)

Site: Ugarit (Ras Shamra), residential area at acropolis
Date: Late Middle Syrian period, 1300–1200 B.C.
Material: Serpentine
Height: 45.5 cm; *width:* 29.5 cm; *depth:* 22.5 cm
Museum No.: Aleppo 4622
Literature: C.F.A. Schaeffer *Syria* 18 (1937) 128, Plate 17 // P. Matthiae *Ars Syra* (1962) 68, Plate 23 // K. Galling (ed.) *Biblisches Realexikon* (1977) 100 // A. Parrot "Die Phönizier," *Universum der Kunst* (1977) Fig. 7 // Tokyo Exhibition No. 122

Near the Dagan and Baal temples at Ugarit were private houses belonging to various artisans. One of these was a sculptor, and here we have one of his unfinished works: a worship-scene stele probably intended for a temple. Under the winged sun disk stands a worshiper facing a seated bearded god, perhaps El, head of the Ugaritic pantheon. He wears a horned crown (cf. Cat. No. 133) and a long wrap-around robe with fringes. The throne has armrests and a footstool, both richly decorated. The god's arms are in profile while the upper body is seen frontally; his left hand is raised in a greeting, while in his right he holds a flower. The worshiper is dressed in a tall cap and a long robe. He holds a staff, which ends in an animal head, and a jug from which he is about to pour a libation for the deity. His headdress with the uraeus (representation of the sacred asp) indicates his royal status. A similar headdress was found in the tomb of King Yapishemu-abi in Byblos.

K.K.

151, right

transporting vessel for oil or wine. Wall paintings show such flasks as Syrian trade goods. Fragments of these vessels have been retrieved from both funerary and domestic contexts at Ras Shamra. Wine and oil from the Near East was equally valued in Greece, where similar flasks have been found in Mycenae and Athens.

K.K.

153
Cosmetic pot with duck-shaped handle

Site: Ugarit (Ras Shamra)
Date: Middle Syrian period, 1400–1300 B.C.
Material: Ivory
Height: 6.5 cm; *length:* 12.5 cm; *width:* 5.2 cm
Museum No.: Aleppo 4535
Literature: Tokyo Exhibition No. 120 // cf. C.F.A. Schaeffer
   Syria 13 (1932) Plate VIII 2 / *Ugaritica* III (1939) 31,
   Fig. 23

For reasons of preservation we cannot show some of the most beautifully worked pieces of Ugaritic art: the ivory reliefs, the most important of which come from the palace, including a register with animal contests, hunting scenes, and depictions of the royal couple. Ivory existed in Syria. We know from a report from Pharaoh Thutmosis III that he went hunting for elephants at Apamea on the Orontes River, where the herd was said to include 120 animals.

Typical examples from the ivory workshops along the coast are small cosmetic pots. This one is elongated and ends in a handle in the form of a turned-back duck's head. The missing lid of the pot was originally attached in the same manner as is the duck's head. The stylized feathers at the back of the neck are beautifully rendered. A similar example with a small bird decorating the lid was found in a tomb at Sidon.[1] Examples are also known from Egypt.[2]

K.K.

[1]A. Parrot "Die Phönizier" *Universum der Kunst* (1977) Fig. 90
[2]A. Hermann *ZÄS* 68 (1932) 86, Plate IX

152
Two-handled flask with stand

Site: Ugarit (Ras Shamra), residential quarter
Date: Middle Syrian period, 1400–1300 B.C.
Material: Alabaster
Height of flask: 45.5 cm; *diameter without handles:* 28 cm
Museum No.: Aleppo 6198, 6199 (RS. 66. 29. 129)
Literature: Cf. C.F.A. Schaeffer *Syria* 54 (1977) Plate IX 3 //
   on Canaanite-trade pottery vessels see V. Grace in S.
   Weinberg (ed.) *The Aegean and the Near East* (1956) 80
   and R. Amiran *Ancient Pottery of the Holy Land* (1970)
   140

This type of luxury item, an alabaster flask, appears not only in its native Syria, but also in Palestine and Egypt, mostly brought to the latter countries as a

153

154

155

MIDDLE SYRIAN PERIOD

154
Figure of a female drummer

Site: Ugarit (Ras Shamra), tomb 3464
Date: Middle Syrian period, 1300–1200 B.C.
Material: Ivory
Height: 5.4 cm
Museum No.: Damascus S 3602 (RS. 24. 400)
Literature: C.F.A. Schaeffer *AAAS* 13 (1963) 132, Figs. 12,
   13 // cf. L. Manniche *Ancient Egyptian Musical
   Instruments* (Münchner Ägyptologische Studien 34)
   Berlin 1975)

The kneeling figure holds a drum or tambourine. The
delicate shape of the body and the hair hanging down
the back suggest the representation of a female. The
function of the piece is unclear. It reminds us of the
Egyptian figurines of servants which were to accompany their owner in the afterlife. Such figurines of musicians have been found, but none with a similar round
drum. This instrument only arrived in Egypt from the
Near East during the Eighteenth Dynasty, when the
figures of servants had already gone out of style. The
Egyptians regarded this type of drum as suitable for
female musicians; however, in the Egyptian representations the players are dancing rather than sitting, so
it is difficult to perceive Egyptian influence in this
small ivory figurine. Perhaps the excavator, C.F.A.
Schaeffer, was right when he suggested that this might
be a depiction of the Syrian goddess Anat, described
in a text found at Ugarit as a tambourine player.
M.E.-K.

155
Lotion container

Site: Ugarit (Ras Shamra), child's tomb northeast of Dagan
   Temple
Date: Ca. 1350 B.C.
Material of figure: limestone; *base:* calcite; *loin-cloth:* ivory
Height: 16.5 cm
Museum No.: Damascus S 3575 (RS. 22. 362)
Literature: C.F.A. Schaeffer *AAAS* 10 (1960) 135, Fig. 5 //
   P. Amiet *Die Kunst des Alten Orients* (Fribourg 1977) 447,
   Fig. 502 // cf. J. Vandier-d'Abbadie (Musée du Louvre,
   Dept. des Antiquités égyptiennes) *Catalogue des objets de
   toilette égyptiens* (Paris 1972) No. 393 // J. Vercoutter et al.
   *L'image du noir dans l'art occidental I: Des pharaons à la
   chute de l'empire romain* (Fribourg 1976) Fig. 1

The small male figurine, standing on a stool of calcite,
carries a heavy vessel on his left shoulder, a container

for fragrant lotion. His hair is gathered on top of his
head and his short skirt suggests that he is a Nubian
boy or possibly a young dwarf. The body proportions
point to the latter interpretation. There are very similar lotion containers in the Louvre and the British
Museum.

This piece is certainly Egyptian. Similar ones have
been found in Egypt from the Eighteenth Dynasty, a
period when there was intensive trade between Syria
and the land of the Nile. Our example was buried with
a child, together with other imports, such as Mycenaean ceramics, a necklace of faience, carnelian,
ivory, and gold beads, as well as a small ivory case
and a glass bottle. Such funerary gifts show the international relations of Ugarit (which was under the sov-
ereignty of Egypt at the time), and also the wealth of
the family who buried the child near the Dagan
Temple.
M.E.-K.

156
Fragments of a vessel

Site: Ugarit (Ras Shamra), palace
Date: Ca. 1300 B.C.
Height: 17.5 cm
Museum No.: Damascus S 4160 (RS. 15. 239)
Literature: C.F.A. Schaeffer *Ugaritica* III (Paris 1956) 164,
   Fig. 118 // Ch. Desroches-Noblecourt *Ugaritica* III (Paris
   1956) 179, Plate 126 // W. S. Smith *Interconnections in the
   Ancient Near East* (New Haven 1965) 29, Fig. 43

Under a decorated canopy stands a female with a flask
in her right hand facing a seated male. This scene
may easily be completed from Egyptian parallels: the
wife pours a drink for her comfortably seated husband. Between them is a table with a bull-shaped
rhyton. To the casual observer this tableau may seem
entirely Egyptian; even the headdress of the female—
stylized flowers on top of the hair—is well known from
depictions of Egyptian royal and noble ladies from the
Eighteenth Dynasty. However, a few details betray
this jar as a Syrian imitation, rather than an imported
Egyptian vessel. The commissioner of the jar was
probably "Niqmadu, the lord of the land of Ugarit,"
as the hieroglyphic inscription reads, in whose palace
the fragments were found.

An early theory was that the woman depicted was
an Egyptian princess, perhaps a daughter or grand-
daughter of Akhenaton, who had married Niqmadu.

156

157
Axe with iron blade
See color plate p. 317

Site: Ugarit (Ras Shamra), northwest part of city
Date: Middle Syrian period, 1400–1300 B.C.
Material: Copper, gold, iron
Length: 19.7 cm
Museum No.: Aleppo 4520
Literature: C.F.A. Schaeffer *Ugaritica* I (1939) 107, Figs.
    100–103, Plate XXII // R. Dussaud *Syria* 21 (1940) 97 //
    Strommenger and Hirmer *Mesopotamien* 94, Plate XXXIV
    // Tokyo Exhibition No. 119

This axe with a decorated head was a symbolic or
ceremonial object. Other such symbolic axes are
known: one from the Middle Elamite period found at
Tchoga-Zanbil in Iran is decorated with lion and boar
heads. A bronze axe found in an Ugaritic smithy was
decorated with a lion head. In our example, the iron
blade is held between two lion heads, while the back
of the axe head is shaped like the forepart of a boar.
Stylized incised motifs have been inlaid with gold in a
technique similar to that of the falcon in Cat. No. 137.
The axe was found near other votive offerings, among
them two statuettes, in a small shrine in the northwestern corner of the palace quarter.
K.K.

158
Gold bowl
See color plates pp. 318–319

Site: Ugarit (Ras Shamra), southwest of Baal Temple
Date: Middle Syrian period, 1400–1300 B.C.
Material: Gold
Height: 5 cm; *diameter:* 17–17.5 cm; *weight:* 179 g
Museum No.: Aleppo 4572
Literature: C.F.A. Schaeffer *Ugaritica* II (1949) 1, Plates
    II–V, VII // Strommenger and Hirmer *Mesopotamien* 94,
    Figs. 176–178, XXXIII–XXXIV // Tokyo Exhibition No. 114

This bowl is the most famous example of Ugaritic
goldsmith work. From a Ugaritic document we know
that gold bowls as well as pendants and rings belonged
to Queen Akhat-milku. It is possible that tribute to the
Hittite king and overlord also consisted of gold items.
The bowl was found together with a gold plate in a
trench southwest of the Baal Temple. Both items were
probably used in religious ceremonies.
    The outside of the bowl is decorated with three

Dynastic marriages were well known in the New Kingdom, but while the pharaohs accepted foreign
princesses into their own harems, they absolutely for-
bade Egyptian princesses to marry out of the country.
When one Babylonian king asked to marry an Egyptian, the father of Akhenaton, Amenhotep III, answered: "for ages we have not given a royal daughter
from Egypt to anybody." If the important king of
Babylon was refused an Egyptian princess, it is very
unlikely that this right would be granted to a mere
Syrian prince.
    Probably the wife of Niqmadu was Syrian. She
wears Egyptian-looking clothes, but her dress is decorated with ribbons in the Syrian style. The most likely
explanation is that Niqmadu ordered this vessel depicting himself and his Syrian wife to be made in the
Egyptian style.
M.E.-K.

MIDDLE SYRIAN PERIOD

159

concentric friezes, while a rosette decorates the bottom center. The first frieze has five gazelles standing next to stylized plants. It is clear that the artist did not come to terms with the space in this small band, for there was no room for the sixth gazelle, which should have been there to create symmetry. The middle frieze has two bulls with lowered heads facing each other on one half of the band—two lions on the other; the animals are separated by palm trees and there is a row of pomegranates above. The outer register shows two magical creatures: a sphinx and a winged lion with horns standing next to a luscious palm tree. An animal contest follows: lions attack deer; a lion attacks a griffin; there is a hunting scene in which two male figures fight an upright lion with dagger and spear; a stag appears below. Branches are added as a decorative element throughout the scene. The outlines and details are engraved or hammered out. The outer register is surrounded by guilloches.

The details borrowed from Egyptian art and the incorporation of Aegean as well as Near Eastern artistic elements are typical for the style which developed in the Ugaritic workshops, where this fine bowl was made.
K.K.

159
Royal land sale document

Site: Ugarit (Ras Shamra)
Date: Late Middle Syrian period, ca. 1300 B.C.
Material: Fired clay
Height: 7 cm; *width:* 5.9 cm; *depth:* 2.5 cm
Museum No.: Damascus S 4335 (RS. 16. 260)
Literature: C.F.A. Schaeffer *Syria* 31 (1954) Plate V /
    Ugaritica III (1956) 66, Figs. 92–99 // J. Nougayrol *Le
    palais royal d'Ugarit* III (1955) 98, Plate LXXXIV

This document is a deed regarding a piece of property. Against all rules, King Niqmepa signs over a piece of land and a house to his servant, Amanihu, for a payment of 150 shekels in gold (1.3–1.4 kg). The text, in Akkadian, reads: "As of today, Niqmepa, son of Niqmadu, king of Ugarit, has taken a piece of land and given it to his servant, Amanihu. (For his part) Amanihu has given 150 (shekels) gold to the king, his lord, in payment. Nobody can claim this (piece of property) from Amanihu later. Seal of Niqmepa, son of Niqmadu, king of Ugarit."

To seal official documents in the fourteenth and thirteenth centuries, the Ugaritic kings used two much older cylinder seals, an original and an almost identical copy. The impression on this tablet is of the original better-executed seal. The design has a typical presentation scene from the Ur III or Isin-Larsa period, when the *shakkanakkus* ruled at Mari. A worshiper and a suppliant goddess face a seated deity; there is a sun disk in a crescent above the scene. The seal inscription reads: "Yaqarum, son of Niqmadu, king of Ugarit." The name Yaqarum later became a form of title in Ugarit. The names mentioned on the cylinder seal may be identical with the names of certain divine kings of Ugarit, who are mentioned in a king list. It is possible that the original owner of the seal became one of the founders of the Ugaritic royal family.

Only by adding the final sentence in the document (in this case: seal of Niqmepa) did the seal become related to the present ruler. Seal rings, as well as cylinder seals, were used by Ugaritic kings and queens. We often find the oval impressions of such seal rings with a cylinder seal impression on the same tablet.
K.K./W.R.

160

Purchase of release from military service

Site: Ugarit (Ras Shamra), palace,.southern archive
Date: Late Middle Syrian period, ca. 1250 B.C.
Material: Clay
Height: 8.3 cm; *length:* 11.4 cm; *depth:* 3.3 cm
Museum No.: Damascus S 3565 (RS. 53. 17. 59)
Literature: C.F.A. Schaeffer *Ugaritica* III (1956) 24, Fig. 32
   // J. Nougayrol *Le palais royal d'Ugarit* IV (1956) 150,
   Plate IV

In this decree the Hittite King Tudhaliya IV declares
to Ini-Teshub, king of Carchemish, his governor in
Syria, that King Ammistamru II of Ugarit is released
from the army during the war with Shalmaneser I of
Assyria, and thereby free from indictment. The Ugarit
king has bought his freedom for 50 minas of gold
(ca. 25 kg). The seal inscription in Luwian hieroglyphs
reads: "Seal of Ini-Teshub, King of Carchemish."
   Translation of the slightly damaged tablet:
   (To) Ini-Teshub, king of Carchemish (son of

Shakhurunuwa), king of Carchemish: (my son, Tudhaliya), great king, king of Hatti, has set free Ammistamru, king of Ugarit (together with his soldiers and chariots). (Until the battle with) Ashur ends (the king of Ug)arit as well as his soldiers and chariots (need not) participate. (In the future) no (process) can be brought against the king of Ugarit. Even if the battle with Ashur (is over) (as soon as) the "Sun" has conquered the king of Ashur (and as soon as) they have made peace with each other, process cannot be brought against him (and his soldiers) and his chariots, and even later (process cannot be) brought (against him). The king of Ugarit has delivered 50 minas in gold on ten caravans from Bit-Duppashi to the "Sun."

A seal has been rolled across the tablet with the following design, framed by guilloche borders: next to an upright goat a weather god stands on two mountain deities and faces a king who is standing on a fantastic animal; both god and king wear a horned crown and hold a club over one shoulder. Behind the king a figure standing on a bull fights a lion with his spear; there is a small sphinx above. Since this tablet is sealed by Ini-Teshub, it must be the copy of the decree which was sent to the king of Ugarit for his records.
W.R./K.K.

161
Royal divorce decree

Site: Ugarit (Ras Shamra), palace, southern archive
Date: Late Middle Syrian period, ca. 1250 B.C.
Material: Clay
Height: 14.2 cm; *width:* 8.8 cm; *depth:* 6.2 cm; *seal diameter:* 5.2 cm
Museum No.: Damascus S 3566 (RS. 53. 17. 159)
Literature: C.F.A. Schaeffer *Ugaritica* III (1956) 19, Figs. 24–26 // J. Nougayrol *Le palais royal d'Ugarit* IV (1956) 126, Plate XXII // Tokyo Exhibition No. 133

This is a decree of the Hittite King Tudhaliya IV regarding the divorce of King Ammistamru II of Ugarit from the daughter of Benteshina, king of Amurru, the return of the dowry, and the royal succession in Ugarit. The cuneiform seal inscription reads: "Seal of Tudhaliya, the great king, king of Hatti, the hero, son of Hattushili, the great king, the hero, and of Puduhepa, great queen of Hatti, grandson of Mursili,

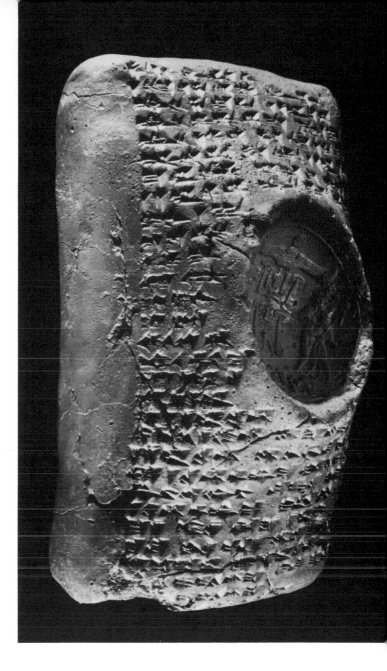

the great king, the hero." A translation of the decree reads:

> From my Sun, Tudhaliya, the great king, king of Hatti: Ammistamru, king of Ugarit married the daughter of Benteshina, king of Amurru. However, she had nothing but mischief in mind for Ammistamru. Therefore, Ammistamru, king of Ugarit, has divorced her. Forever! Now the daughter of Benteshina should take everything she brought into the house of Ammistamru and leave his house. Whatever Ammistamru has lost or sold may be claimed by the people of Amurru, and Ammistamru must reimburse them. Regarding Utrisharruma: he is the crown prince of Ugarit. If Utrisharruma says: "I want to join my mother," he should leave his royal robe on a stool and go away, and Ammistamru, king of Ugarit will choose another son as crown prince. If, after the death of Ammistamru, Utrisharruma takes his mother back and reinstates her as queen (mother), then Utrisharruma shall leave his royal robe on a stool and leave to go wherever he wants, and then my Sun will instate another son of Ammistamru as king.
>
> Hereafter the daughter of Benteshina cannot have any claims on her sons or daughters, or her sons-in-law; they belong to Ammistamru, king of Ugarit. In case she does claim them, this tablet should be shown to her.

The seal of the great Hittite king is deeply impressed on the obverse of the tablet (see Fig. 58). In Luwian hieroglyphs the inscription reads: "My Sun (represented by a winged sun disk) Tudhaliya, Labarna (a royal title similar to the Roman Caesar), the great king." Then follows his name in Hurrian, and repeated below, between two ankhs, his Hittite name and titles. In the design of the seal the king stands to the right dressed in a short robe embracing a similarly dressed deity. The king holds a spear while the god (called "weather god" in the inscription) holds a club. Facing them stands a female deity in a long robe. In one hand she holds a standard of sun signs indicating that she is the sun goddess Arima, the highest-ranking goddess in the Hittite pantheon.

W.R./K.K.

Figure 58
Seal impression on clay tablet (Cat. No. 161) from Ugarit.

162
Incantation against snake bites

Site: Ugarit (Ras Shamra), acropolis, priest's house
Date: Late Middle Syrian period, 1300–1200 B.C.
Material: Fired clay
Height: 24.5 cm; *width:* 16 cm; *depth:* 3.7 cm
Museum No.: Damascus S 6587 (RS. 61. 24. 244)
Literature: C. Virolleaud *Ugaritica* V (1968) 564–574 // cf. *GLECS* 9 (1961) 41, 50 / 10 (1964) 64–66 / *CRAI* XI (Leiden 1962) 105–113 // M. Astour *JNES* 27 (1968) 13–28 // A. Caquot *Syria* 46 (1969) 241–265 // E. Lipinski *UF* 6 (1974) 169–174 // M. Dietrich et al. *UF* 7 (1975) 121–125 // T.H. Gaster *JANES* 7 (1975) 33–51 // D. Pardee *JANES* 10 (1978) 83–108 // M. Tsevat *UF* 11 (1979) 759–778 // P. Xella *I testi rituali di Ugarit I* (1981) 224–240

This complete tablet, written in the alphabetic Ugaritic cuneiform, contains an incantation against snake bites. The text is not completely understood. Translation of the beginning follows:

> The mother of the stallion, the mare, daughter of the source, daughter of the stone, daughter of heaven, daughter of the underworld invokes (the sun

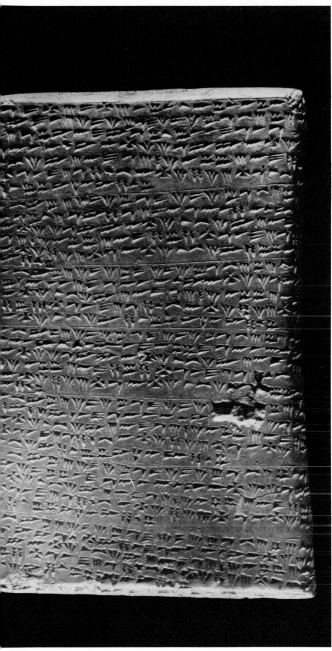

goddess) Shapash, her mother: Shapash, mother, bring my word to El at the source of the two rivers, at the place where the two depths flow together! (This is) the incantation against the snake bite, the poison of the scaly snake: destroy it and remove the poison. But see he lifts up the snake, feeds the scaly snake, places a chair and sits down.

The strophic lines are repeated twelve times with the invocation of other gods: Baal from the Saphon mountain, Dagan from Tuttul, the goddesses Anat and Astarte, the moon god Yarich from Laragat, the god of epidemic diseases, Rashap from Babtu, the goddess Astarte from Mari, Zizu-wa-Kamishu from Hurriyat, Milku from Ashtarat, the artisan god Kothar-wa-khasis from Crete, the deities Shakar-wa-Shalim from heaven.

Only the thirteenth god named, Horon from Masud, manages through magical rituals involving tamarisk and date clusters to dilute the poison and thereby make it harmless. The incantation ends with a dialogue between the mare and Horon which makes it clear that the snakes now have lost their power:

Recite the incantation around the houses, around the locked houses, around the bronze locks. Open up the house for the incantation, open up the house so that I, Horon, can enter. Open up the palace so that I can enter. As dowry, give me snakes; give me lizards as my wedding gift, snake babies as my present. Now I'll give you snakes as your dowry, baby snakes as your present.

W.R.

162

163

Terracotta relief of a goddess on a throne

Site: Emar (Meskene)
Date: Late Middle Syrian period, 1300–1200 B.C.
Material: Terracotta
Height: 12.9 cm; *width:* 8 cm; *depth:* 1.7 cm
Museum No.: Aleppo (Msk. 74. 382)
Literature: J.C. Margueron *Syria* 52 (1975) 71, Plate VIII 2

This terracotta plaque, made from a mold, shows a female deity seated on a low-backed throne, her feet resting on a footstool. She is wearing a horned crown and dressed in an ankle-length robe with banded borders. She holds a scepter in her right hand and possi-

163

bly a flower (or a vessel) in her left hand. Over her right shoulder is the faint outline of a bird.

Such votive plaques were mass produced in Mesopotamia by the time of the Third Dynasty of Ur, and they reached their height of popularity in the Old Babylonian period. They may have served as votive gifts to the temple, but more likely they were used in private votive shrines.

U.K.

164
Clay tablet of a king from Carchemish

Site: Emar (Meskene), Chantier A, "batiment officiel"
Date: Late Middle Syrian period, 1250 B.C.
Material: Terracotta
Height: 7.3 cm; *length:* 10.6 cm; *depth:* 2.7 cm
Museum No.: Aleppo (Msk. 73. 58)
Literature: D. Arnaud *AAAS* 25 (1975) 90

In this tablet the king of Carchemish communicates the improvement of one of his brother Heshmi-Teshub's decrees. The royal seal has been rolled horizontally across the tablet. The seal design is framed by guilloches, a common decorative motif in second-millennium Syrian seals. A god wearing a tall rounded hat with one horn holds a club over his left shoulder; in his right hand he holds a ceremonial axe. He wears a long robe over a short skirt, and a long pigtail hangs down his back. The inscription in front of him identifies him as the god Sharumma, the son of the weather god Teshub and Hebat, who was the protecting deity for the Hittite king Tudhaliya IV. The seal inscription is rather long: "Seal of Ini-Teshub, king of Carchemish, servant of Kubaba, son of Shakhurunuwa, grandson of Sharri-kushuk, great grandson of Suppiluliuma, the great king, king of Hatti, the hero." The title, servant of Kubaba, probably indicates that the king also served as high priest for the city deity of Carchemish. He furthermore relies on his descent from the famous Hittite king who came into power in Hattusha during a difficult political period and who proceeded to resurrect centralized power in Anatolia, to conquer northern Syria, to defeat the Hurrian Mittanni empire, and finally to put two of his sons on the throne: one in Aleppo, the other in Carchemish. Impressions of a very similar seal are known from the correspondence of Ini-Teshub, which was found at Ugarit.

K.K.

MIDDLE SYRIAN PERIOD

164

165
Liver model

Site: Emar (Meskene)
Date: Late Middle Syrian period, 1320–1200 B.C.
Material: Smoked terracotta
Height: 11 cm; *width:* 10.8 cm; *depth:* 4.1 cm
Museum No.: Aleppo (Msk. 7430)
Literature: D. Arnaud *AEPHE* V/83 (1974–1975) 144 / 88
(1979–1980) 214

Studying the shape of the livers of sacrificed animals

to predict future events was performed both in Syria and Mesopotamia. The priest would study the liver carefully, then draw his conclusions. Sometimes models of livers were shaped in clay and advice was written down for future reference and study. This liver model, which was found at Emar in the area of the Assad Sea, shows characteristic traits. At the top right is the pyramidal protrusion which the oracle priest called "the finger"; under that runs the gall bladder from left to right, also called "gall" by the Babylonians. The division between the left and right

165

They were probably made as teaching aids for beginning divination priests as they began to officiate at sacrifices. The models do not seem to be records of recently observed livers, because textual explanations on the models quote each other and some appear to be expansions of others. It also is likely that the thirty-two models were copied by one hand from still older material. In theory the art of liver divination was an attempt to be scientific and empirical, and at some period political events that occurred after a given liver was observed actually had been remembered and recorded for future reference.

The Mari livers are concerned with political predictions and also include references to previous rulers of Mesopotamia such as Sargon and Naram-Sin. They are thus the earliest of what have been called historical omens; in fact, some scholars have argued that liver divination represented an important way in which the ancients thought about their history.

D.C.S.

liver lobes was called "the palace gate." On the left side rises the papillary protrusion which probably was called "the bladder" by the Babylonians; below is a lightly carved line stretching toward the gall bladder. An indentation called "the path" is followed by another indentation parallel to the gall bladder, called "the reinforcement."

The text next to the gall bladder says: "when the left side of the gall bladder looks like a goat's tail, the enemy will take the booty away with them." Next to the path at the extreme left the inscription reads: "when the boundaries of the foundation of the 'standort' are wide, their god will abandon these people."

W.R.

THE OLDEST DIRECT WITNESSES TO THE PRACTICE OF liver divination are thirty-two clay models found in room 108 of the royal palace at Mari. The dates of the livers seem to be contemporary with the archival texts from the period of the early governors of Mari, around 1900–1820 B.C., and the language in which they are written is apparently a local form of early Old Babylonian.

166
Necklace
See color plate p. 318

Site: Mari (Tell Hariri), tomb 125
Date: Late Middle Syrian period, 1300–1200 B.C.
Material: Gold, lapis lazuli, agate, carnelian, blue artificial stone
Length of gold ornaments: 1.4 cm; *diameter of beads:* 1.4 cm
Museum No.: Aleppo 3897
Literature: A. Parrot *Syria* 18 (1937) 83, Plate XV 2 // K.R. Maxwell-Hyslop *Western Asiatic Jewellery, ca. 3000–612 B.C.* (1971) 34, 178 // cf. A. Parrot *Mari* 146 // J.L. Huot et al. *Iraq* 42 (1980) 121

After the destruction of Mari by Hammurabi, it was almost completely abandoned. A few thin-walled rooms in the northern part of the palace ruins indicate that some inhabitants may have continued to live here. But from Middle Syrian times we have some evidence of settlement: a complex of buildings which, according to the excavator, may have been the residence for the commander of a garrison and a cemetery for the soldiers and their families. Most of the graves were in the two large courtyards of the palace north of the ziggurat. Besides pottery the graves contained alabaster vessels, masks made of sintered quartz, faience

167

bowls, and jewelry made of precious metal and semi-precious stones. The most valuable find was no doubt this necklace. Quadrupled thinly rolled gold spirals are interspersed with flat beads of colored stones.
K.K.

167
Ring

Site: Mari (Tell Hariri)
Date: Late Middle Syrian period, 1300–1200 B.C.
Material: Shell, bitumen
Diameter: 2.5 cm
Museum No.: Aleppo 6548 (M. 4404)
Literature: Cf. *De Sumer à Babylone* (Collections du Musée du Louvre 1979) 65, Figs. 229–230

Very likely this ring was from a Middle Syrian grave. It is carved from shell and its fine execution is reminiscent of precious-metalwork. Three indentations with remnants of bitumen perhaps once held inlays of precious stones, although inlays of bitumen alone in light-colored materials such as limestone, alabaster, or shell were popular in the ancient Near East because of the color contrast.
K.K.

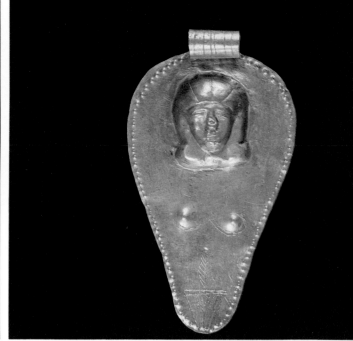

Cat. No. 130

Cat. No. 131

Cat. No. 139

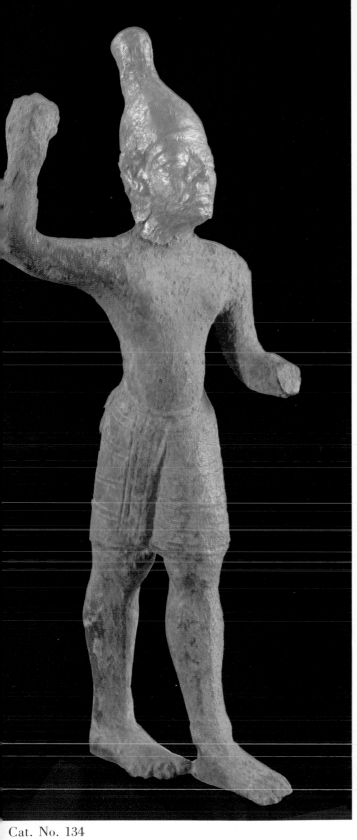

Cat. No. 134

Cat. No. 133

Cat. No. 143

Cat. No. 144

Cat. No. 145

Cat. No. 147

Cat. No. 157

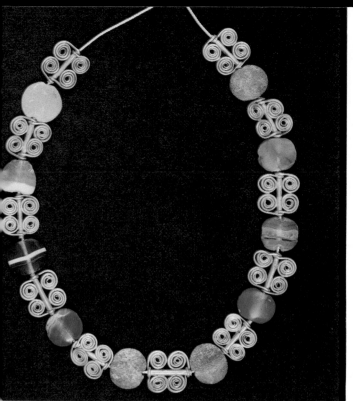

Cat. No. 166

Cat. No. 158

Cat. No. 158

Cat. No. 168

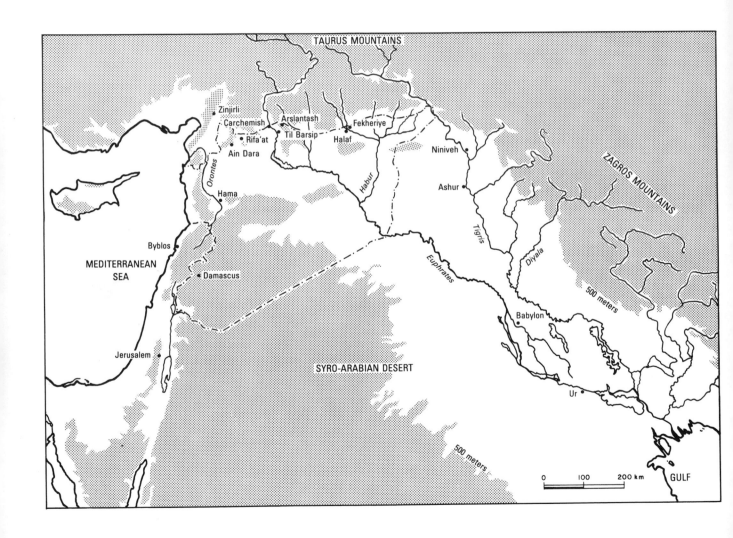

TAURUS MOUNTAINS

Zinjirli
Carchemish
Arslantash
Til Barsip
Fekheriye
Rifa'at
Halaf
Ain Dara
Niniveh
Orontes
Habur
Ashur
ZAGROS MOUNTAINS
Hama
Tigris
Byblos
Diyala
MEDITERRANEAN
SEA
Euphrates
500 meters
Damascus
Babylon
Jerusalem
SYRO-ARABIAN DESERT
Ur
500 meters
0   100   200 km   GULF

NEW SYRIAN PERIOD
CA. 1200–330 B.C.

ASSYRIAN DOMINATION, ARAMAEAN PERSISTENCE

EVA STROMMENGER

THE POLITICAL DESTINY OF SYRIA IN THE FIRST MILLENNIUM B.C. was increasingly determined by neighboring powers. Assyria, which had already infiltrated into the west, must be mentioned in the first place. The important trade routes through northern Mesopotamia, northern Syria, and Asia Minor had to be secured. We have already noted the "Assyrian" (Shamshi-Adad's) need for a control point on the Euphrates at Mari. In the first millennium, the Assyrian kings Assurnasirpal II and Shalmaneser III also concerned themselves with a secure land route to the Euphrates. Their military campaigns were directed toward the Mediterranean, but they did not deprive the princes of small states west of the Euphrates of their independence; swearing loyalty and paying tribute were considered sufficient. Through such tribute and booty the Assyrians obtained raw materials, luxury items, and labor.

Cities with splendid buildings were constructed in the areas controlled by the Assyrians as symbols of their power. One example is Hadatu (Arslantash), another was Kar Shalmaneser (ca. 856 B.C.), the old Til Barsip (Tell Ahmar), capital city of Bit Adini. Around 808 B.C. the independence of Guzana (Tell Halaf), capital of Bit Bahiani, was ended. The official architecture there followed the Assyrian style. The palace of Kar Shalmaneser was embellished with rich wall paintings (Cat. Nos. 168, 169) differing but little from those of the Assyrian heartland. In Hadatu, on the other hand, native sculptors were at work (Cat. No. 170). Valuable furniture, decorated with ivory carvings produced in workshops around Damascus, was brought as booty or "gifts" to Hadatu.

The military campaigns of the Assyrians usually lasted only a few months. Shortly after their withdrawal, the manifestations of loyalty were forgotten and payment of tribute was required again. Very often coalitions against the threat from the East were formed. When in 853

B.C. Shalmaneser III tried to take Damascus, twelve princes opposed him, among them Ahab of Israel and Gindibu the Arab. Victory eluding them, the Assyrians were forced to withdraw. In the middle of the eighth century the Assyrians effected a merger with Urartu, a powerful state to the northeast of Assyria which had extended its power to Arpad (modern Tell Rifa'at near Aleppo) and to Carchemish and now blocked the route to the raw materials of Asia Minor.

From the time of Tiglath-pileser III (744–727 B.C.), the Assyrians openly sought conquest with their campaigns to the West. This policy forced them into conflict with Egypt, often allied with the Phoenician and Palestinian states. Against such a coalition, King Sennacherib pushed toward Jerusalem in 701 B.C. These events gained a certain notoriety in antiquity among contemporary observers who were not free from malicious gloating. Three different sources document the story. In the Bible (2 Kings 19: 35) we read "That very night the angel of God went out and killed a hundred fourscore and five thousand in the Assyrian camp; they were all found to be dead bodies in the morning." Sennacherib's campaign reporter describes King Hezekiah as a caged bird, shut up in Jerusalem, as well as the rich booty, but is silent as to the abandonment of the campaign and the reasons for it. Herodotus, who knew of the campaign by hearsay, reports that mice ate the Assyrians' leather and the important parts of the weapons, rendering them useless. Historians today suspect that an epidemic, perhaps borne by rats, broke out among the Assyrian army.

The Assyrian kings Esarhaddon (681–669 B.C.) and Assurbanipal (669–627 B.C.) were able to extend their conquests as far as Egypt. The Egyptian pharaoh Psammetichus, however, was able to drive out the foreign rulers in 655 B.C. In 621 B.C., the Scyths invaded Syria and challenged the Nile region. In response, the Egyptians campaigned as far as the Euphrates.

Against this background of great international struggles we can attempt to define the native rulers, but only with the greatest difficulty. Some are known by name from the Assyrian field reports. For a very few rulers there are primary documents; but for most, their residences remain unexplored. In the area of Aleppo, with its center at Arpad (Tell Rifa'at), ruled Bit Agusi ("House of Agusi"). Toward the east, the land on both banks of the Euphrates belonged to Bit Adini, with its capital at Til Barsip (Tell Ahmar). On the Habur Plains there was Bit Bahiani with its capital at Guzana (Tell Halaf). In the northern Orontes Valley lay Hattina (Kinalua, perhaps modern 'Ain Dara), south of there lay Hamath (modern Hama), and finally, farther south, the state of Damascus.

Figure 59
Scribes writing in alphabetic script
and cuneiform, from a wall
painting at Tell Ahmar.

The most important population group were the Aramaeans, who spoke a West Semitic language and wrote with alphabetic Phoenician script. Easier by far to learn than cuneiform, the Phoenician script undoubtedly facilitated the spread of their language. Even the Assyrians used Aramaean scribes. In the war campaigns these scribes, writing with brushes on papyrus or parchment, stood next to their cuneiform-writing counterparts, who noted the booty on clay or wax tablets (Fig. 59).

The Aramaeans first appear in the campaign reports of Tiglath-pileser I (1113–1075 B.C.) as opponents worth watching. They were then a component of the pastoral nomadic tribes moving into the cultivated areas of sedentary inner Syria and northern and southern Mesopotamia from the Syrian steppes. Eventually they gained political influence in these regions. The names of their states, for instance Bit Agusi, point back to their old tribal forms of organization.

Part of inner Syria was heavily influenced around the beginning of the first millennium B.C. by a population speaking an Indo-European language—Luwian. The stone documents of these people, written in a kind of hieroglyphs, have been found not only in northern Syria but as far to the south as Hama. The relief from 'Ain Dara (Cat. No. 182) is a fine example of the Hittite precursors still evident in the art of these people.

Lastly, another language-defined group should be mentioned, the Arabs. They first appear in Assyrian reports of the ninth century B.C., where they are portrayed as Bedouin of the steppe lands (see Fig. 60). The Arab adaptation to this region was probably facilitated by the use of camels, replacing their earlier dependence upon nomadism based on sheep- and goat-herding. The Arabs, however, were not only pastoralists but also merchants leading caravans of camels through territories and along routes previously avoided. They also appear in Assyrian campaign reports as dangerous enemies. One of their leaders, Gindibu, has already been discussed. Women sometimes are mentioned along with their leaders.

The alliance of the Medes, a people of the Iranian plateau, and the Babylonians eventually led to the conquest of Nineveh, capital of the Neo-Assyrian empire. With the fall of the empire, the western territories fell to the Babylonians, whose crown prince Nebuchadnezzar II succeeded in defeating the pharaoh Necho in 605 B.C. near Carchemish and pushing the Egyptians back into Palestine. Syria thus became Babylonian and shortly thereafter a province of the enormous Achaemenid empire. When Alexander of Macedonia began his conquest of the Near East in 333 B.C., a new cultural epoch began, an epoch influenced culturally and politically by the West.

NEW SYRIAN PERIOD

Figure 60
Bedouin, from a wall painting in
the palace of Assurbanipal at
Nineveh.

THE ARAMAEANS

DANIEL C. SNELL

THE ARAMAEANS WERE A PEOPLE WHO SWEPT INTO SYRIA IN THE last part of the second millennium B.C., perhaps from the Syro-Arabian desert. Probably they at first were nomadic flock-herders who filtered into the marginal land around settlements, but later they moved from this niche into towns and cities, flooding into what is now Iraq, Lebanon, and Jordan, and began to exert a political influence. The scope of this ethnic movement was unparalleled in the ancient Near East until the arrival of the Arabs more than a millennium and a half later.

It is not clear when this movement began. The peoples called Ahlamu in cuneiform inscriptions in the second millennium appear not to have been Aramaeans; they may have been members of a specific nomadic tribe. But by the time of Tiglath-pileser I of Assyria (1116–1076 B.C.), it seems certain that the several descriptions of raids he conducted against the peoples he called Ahlamu Aramaya refer to marauding groups who spoke dialects of Aramaic.

We do not know whether the Hittite ethnic element was already established in northern Syria when the Aramaeans arrived, but the Aramaeans adopted many of the artistic modes of Hittite culture. The spread of the language the Aramaeans spoke shows that they assimilated many of the peoples whom they encountered. Aramaeans seem to have had a special ability to form new cultural syntheses in the spheres of art and statecraft.

Political system

The power and wealth of Aramaic-speakers derived not just from their numbers but also from their involvement in long-distance trade, especially the camel-borne trade across the Syrian desert. Perhaps because of the scope of their movements, the Aramaeans never

NEW SYRIAN PERIOD

managed to form a unified empire that dominated the whole region, but the small states that they came to control played significant roles on the international stage. The rise of these states must be seen as a response to Assyrian weakness, which may be partly attributable to the penetration of Aramaeans into Assyria itself around 1076. The Assyrian neglect of the West continued until the Neo-Assyrian kingdoms two hundred years later. In the power vacuum left by the Assyrians the Aramaeans formed many little states and several large ones.

We know relatively little about the internal administration of these Aramaean states. Several of them appear to have been ruled jointly with a single monarch called the king of at least two places. Such unions may have been only personal and temporary, lasting as long as the life of the ruler.

The most important of the states which the Assyrians encountered in the middle of the eighth century B.C. as they regained control of the region were Arpad in the north, centered on a city north of modern Aleppo; Hamath, ruled from the site of modern Hama; and Damascus, focused on the oasis that still bears the name. Although the Assyrians regarded these states as coherent and unified opponents, there are many indications that they were in fact composed of coalitions of smaller entities. We even have treaties between Arpad and what must have been a much smaller component state, Katikka. We see the extent of one such coalition in references in the Old Testament in I Kings 20:1 to the fact that the king of Damascus took the field with thirty-two other kings who were presumably his partners in the coalition that was the state. But these kings were subservient to the king of Damascus and could, as in I Kings 20:24, actually be replaced by him if he disliked their performance.

This extremely complex political world may have been the result of the independent tribal origins of the Aramaeans. These coalition states could change composition quickly, and one little king could withdraw from the protection of a great neighbor and go to the service of another. The Assyrians, with their more monolithic view of statecraft, were eventually effective in decimating the little kingdoms and destabilizing the bigger ones. Many of the Aramaean rulers seem to have been adept at making the best of the fact of Assyrian penetration, and some became Assyrian tributaries when they believed that served their interests. The Assyrians in turn used speakers of Aramaic extensively in the administration of their western conquests.

The Assyrian kings after an initial setback at the battle of Qarqar in 853 B.C. saw it as their primary task to secure the western flank of their empire by smashing the coalitions of Aramaic states which were ever ready to detect weakness in the Assyrians and to organize anti-Assyrian coalitions. This process was a long one with many reverses. But eventually under Tiglath-pileser III (744–727 B.C.) most of the states were forced into roles as parts of Assyrian provinces or as tribute-paying vassals. This subjugation continued under the inheritors of Assyrian imperialism, the Neo-Babylonians and the Persians.

Language

Rulers of Aramaean political units at first appear to have adopted the Phoenician alphabet and language to write their inscriptions, but soon they saw that their own language could be recorded in the same alphabet. From the tenth century B.C. we begin to get a variety of inscriptions on stone which record the dynastic adventures of several of the small north Syrian states.

The language the Aramaeans spoke was a West Semitic one, related to the Ugaritic language which had thrived on the Syrian coast before the arrival of the Aramaeans, and it was related to Phoenician and other West Semitic languages attested later. Like the other Semitic languages, Aramaic was built on roots consisting predominantly of three consonants. Unlike the Phoenician language, which was used in the coastal cities, it did not form its definite article by placing an element before the word to be made definite but rather after the word. Phoenician would express "king" as *malk*, "the king" as *hammalk*, but Aramaic would say *malkā'*.

An interesting sidelight to the history of the Aramaic language is that two of the inscriptions from the eighth century B.C. concerning two kings both called Panamuwa of Ya'udi (or Yu'addiya) are in a different dialect. The dialect does not appear to use the definite article and has some endings for grammatical cases, unlike the language of the other texts. The second Panamuwa's son also left inscriptions in a more standard dialect. This change is evidence of a switch from writing a local spoken dialect to a standard written language, even though the local dialect probably continued to be spoken. The prestige of standard Aramaic dictated that self-respecting princes use it in their inscriptions.

Aramaic soon became the *lingua franca* of the Assyrian empire because of the numbers of speakers of the language and perhaps also because of the Aramaeans' wide involvement in trade. In addition, a dialect of Aramaic was adopted as the chancellory language of the Persian empire. We are not certain where this dialect, which we call Imperial Aramaic, originated, but it is obvious that it was easily understood by educated people from Iran all the way to the Mediterranean, and even to some extent in Egypt after that country fell to the Persians (cf. II Kings 18:26 = Isaiah 36:11, where the Judaean negotiators beg an Assyrian general to speak Aramaic instead of the language the common people will understand).

The Aramaic language eventually came to replace most of the languages of greater Syria, and it continues to be spoken to this day in enclaves in several regions of the country. Its wide use as a spoken language is perhaps also reflected in the fact that two sections of the Bible are written in Aramaic: Daniel 2:4b–7:28 and Ezra 4:8–6:18, 7:12–26. There is also a term in Aramaic in Genesis 31:47, where Laban, Jacob's Aramaean cousin, calls the rock pile which the two of them had just set up *yegar shāhadūthā'*, which means "hill of witness" in Aramaic. In Jeremiah 10:11 the sentence in Aramaic is apparently addressed to exiles in Babylonia who spoke Aramaic. The biblical writers may have used Aramaic in these books to depict authentically the people described.

Legacy

The states the Aramaeans had formed were swallowed up in the empires of others, but the Aramaeans continued to be important cultural middlemen, conveying to the West the traditions of Mesopotamia and eventually also bringing to the East the knowledge of Greek philosophy and science in the later Aramaic dialects of Syriac. We could wish that archaeologists had recovered more of the physical remains of the earliest periods of Aramaean history, but in light of the recent exciting discovery of a very early bilingual Aramaic and Akkadian inscription from Tell Fekheriye on the Habur Plains we can look forward to the recovery in Syria of more monuments to the ingenuity and skill of this ancient people.

Recommended Reading

Ali Abou-Assaf, P. Bordreuil, and A. Millard. *La Statue de Tell Fekherye et son inscription assyro-araméene* (Paris: Editions Recherche sur les Civilisations, 1982).

R. Bowman. "Aramaeans, Aramaic and the Bible." *JNES* 7 (1948) 65–90.

J. C. L. Gibson. *Textbook of Syrian Semitic Inscriptions* II: *Aramaic Inscriptions* (Oxford: Clarendon, 1975).

F. Rosenthal. "Aramaic Studies during the Past Thirty Years." *JNES* 37/2 (1978) 81–91.

D. Snell. "Why Is There Aramaic in the Bible?" *Journal for the Study of the Old Testament* 18 (1980) 32–51.

TIL BARSIP/KAR SHALMANESER (TELL AHMAR)

Location: Northern Mesopotamia, on the left bank of the Euphrates, 20
   km south of Carchemish
Date: Late fifth millennium through fourth century B.C.
Excavation: 1929–1931 (Musée du Louvre)
Publications: F. Thureau-Dangin and M. Dunand *Til Barsib* (Paris 1936)

The crescent-shaped area of the ruins of Tell Ahmar ("red mound") have a diameter of about 1200 meters. At the highest elevation are the remains of an eighth-century-B.C. palace. Earlier levels under this building go back as far as the fifth millennium B.C. The remainder of the site is still largely unexplored, although in the eastern portion traces of lion gates appeared on the surface, and in many places stone reliefs and inscriptions have been found, including two large stelae of Assyrian King Esarhaddon (680–669 B.C.).

The large lion which guards the eastern gate has an inscription of the Assyrian field commander Shamshi-ilu (mid-eighth century B.C.). The name of the city at that time is also given: "Kar Shalmaneser" ("Shalmaneser city")

The Assyrian palace is only partially preserved here, so we have presented as well the plan of a similar structure at Arslantash. The residence of Kar Shalmaneser is famous, however, for its beautiful wall paintings. These are not restricted to ornamental friezes but also contain rich figurative compositions with historical scenes from the middle of the eighth century. Two pieces are displayed in *Ebla to Damascus:* Cat. Nos. 168 and 169. In the reign of the Assyrian king Assurbanipal (668–627 B.C.) the palace was renovated and a new style of wall painting was introduced. The palace of Kar Shalmaneser is therefore our most important source for the study of Assyrian painting. In both phases of wall painting the artists' work is in composition and execution pure Assyrian with no traces of local influence.

EVA STROMMENGER

HADATU (ARSLANTASH)

Location: Northern Mesopotamia, 30 km east of the Euphrates, 6 km
   south of the Turkish border
Date: Ninth–eighth and fourth centuries B.C.
Excavation: 1928 (Musée du Louvre)
Publications: F. Thureau-Dangin *Arslan-Tash* // G. Turner *Iraq* 30
(1968) 62

In the middle of the fertile Plain of Saruj lies a large oval mound, roughly 700 by 550 meters in size. The site's Turkish name, Arslantash, means "lionstone"; monumental lion statues of basalt lie undisturbed on the surface. Stone bas reliefs were also reported in the 1920s by local inhabitants. Many of these pieces ended up in the Istanbul Museum, since Syria was then part of the Ottoman Empire.

The excavations of 1928 provided some useful information concerning the history of the site and some of its structures. Most of the site remains unexplored, but we do know of the palace dating to the ninth–eighth century B.C., a large house, a cultic building, the city wall, and a Hellenistic temple.

The city wall was built of sun-dried mud bricks set upon a stone foundation. Three gates in the wall were guarded by lions, their socles decorated with reliefs depicting Assyrian soldiers and native tribute bearers. The lions and reliefs, stylistically dated to the reign of the Assyrian king Tiglath-pileser III (744–727 B.C.), are examples of Assyrian provincial style rather than imperial style. From the Akkadian inscription in cuneiform characters on the lions, we learn that they were set on the "gate of Hadatu," a city amalgamated into the Assyrian empire in the reign of Shalmaneser III and then made the seat of the provincial governor.

The palace features the typical Neo-Assyrian plan (Fig. 61). On one of three sides of an enclosed court lay a room in which the reigning king could receive a large number of visitors. On the back

Figure 61
Plan of the palace at Arslantash.

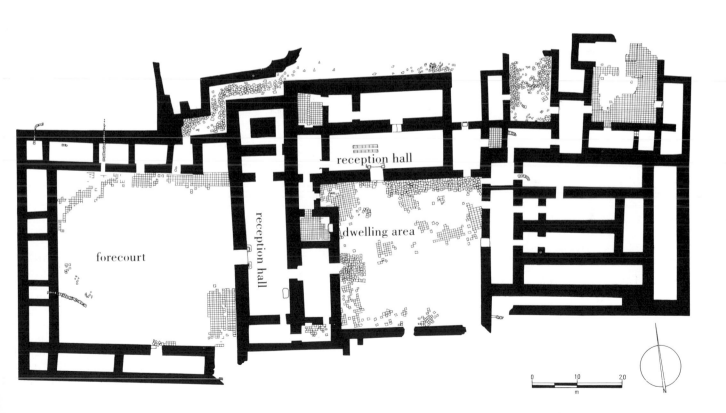

reception hall

reception hall

dwelling area

forecourt

side of this official presentation room, with side rooms and a staircase, was an inner court with the residential quarters of the family, which also served as a small reception room for private purposes. On the east was a large magazine-like complex. In a few rooms the excavator found the remains of wall paintings: horizontal friezes about 80 centimeters wide with rows of ornamental circles and squares, all set about 2 meters above the floor. East of the palace were found parts of a large house containing the remains of beds and other furnishings artfully decorated with ivory carvings (Cat. Nos. 171–177).

The Assyrian temple is only partially investigated. Its entrance was protected by two large bull statues, with inscriptions mentioning the lord of the building to be King Tiglath-pileser III and the temple's owner to be the goddess Ishtar. The decoration of this building included six divine statues with offering chests, among them Cat. No. 170.

Eva Strommenger

GUZANA (TELL HALAF)

Location: Northern Mesopotamia, the western extension of the Habur Plains, at the source of the Habur River, near Ras el-'Ain
Date: Sixth millennium B.C. and ninth–sixth centuries B.C.
Excavations: 1899, 1911–1913, 1927, 1929 (Baron Max von Oppenheim)
Publications: M. Frhr. v. Oppenheim *Der Tell Halaf* (Leipzig 1931) / *Tell Halaf: A New Culture in Oldest Mesopotamia* (London 1933) // H. Schmidt *Tell Halaf* I *Die Prähistorischen Funde* (Berlin 1943) // R. Naumann et al. *Tell Halaf* II *Die Bauwerke* (Berlin 1950) // A. Moortgat *Tell Halaf* III *Die Bildwerke* (Berlin 1955) // B. Hrouda *Tell Halaf* IV *Die Kleinfunde aus historischer Zeit* (Berlin 1962) // W. Orthmann *Untersuchungen zur späthethitischen Kunst* (Bonn 1971) 119–128, 178–182, 464, 465, 484, Plates 8–13 // H. Genge *Nordsyrisch-südanatolische Reliefs* (Copenhagen 1979) I, 125-141; II, *passim*

Tell Halaf is one of the most interesting archaeological sites in the Near East because of the material it yielded and the fate of that material. The site lies on the spring-filled headwaters of the Habur River, where the river crosses from Turkey to Syria. It was discovered in 1899 by Baron Max von Oppenheim, who, while attached to the German diplomatic mission in Cairo, was sent to survey the best route for the proposed Berlin-to-Baghdad railroad. While in the area he heard that villagers at Tell Halaf had discovered some strange carved stones when digging a grave, and he went to investigate. After three days of excavations von Oppenheim realized that he had found the facade of an elaborately sculptured temple. He filled in the area and "reserved" the site from the Turkish government for ten years.

Upon leaving the diplomatic service in 1911 von Oppenheim returned to Tell Halaf to excavate until interrupted by World War I in 1914. During those few years he exposed most of the citadel, much of the course of the fortification walls, and some buildings in the outer town. The famous sculpture which he retrieved there was stored in the excavation house, which fell into ruin when it was used as a fort during World War I. In 1927 von Oppenheim returned to the site, re-excavated the sculpture from the house, left part of it in Aleppo, and took the lion's share to Berlin. There he set it up, in a railroad barn, as the Tell Halaf Museum. During an air raid in 1943 the building caught fire and the heat shattered most of the sculpture and destroyed many of the records and photographs of the expedition. In spite of this disaster, determined German scholars have been able to publish the results of the excavation in a monumental series of four volumes, so that the lost material is still an essential part of the study of the ancient Near East. Some of von Oppenheim's share of the sculpture ended up in London, Paris, New York, and Baltimore, as well as Berlin.

The history of the site goes back to ca. 5000–4500 B.C., when it was occupied by the people of Tell Halaf culture, so named after the painted pottery which was first found here. This is an extremely fine, thin-walled ware, made by hand or on a slow wheel and decorated with a luminous glaze-like paint. Open bowls or jars are covered with rich polychrome designs, usually consisting of geometric patterns but occasionally including animals or human figures. Steatopygus figurines, stone amulets, and beads were also in use in the period, as well as circular buildings. Pottery from this early village culture, which had its center in

northern Iraq, has been found in a very wide area from Lake Van to northern Iraq, from the southern Turkish coast to Kurdistan.

The site of Tell Halaf was apparently abandoned for three and a half millennia after this early period. Then, around the beginning of the first millennium B.C. Tell Halaf became the seat of one of the easternmost of the Aramaic states which had spread over northern Syria. The town was known in Assyrian records as Guzana, capital of a region called Bit Bahiani. It paid tribute to Assyria off and on after 894 B.C. and became an Assyrian province in the eighth century. While some remains of the Assyrian occupation were found (a temple and a large house in the outer town, graves and tablets) the most impressive and important remains at the site date from the two phases of the Aramaic period (see Fig. 62). The name of the king of this last phase is known from building inscriptions. He was Kapara, son of Hadianu. As the king is not attested in Assyrian records, there is much debate as to how he and his monuments should be dated. Opinions on the matter vary from a date at the end of the second millennium B.C. to one in the early eighth century B.C. The official publications of the site argue for a date in the ninth century, but until more is known of the culture and art of the twelfth through the tenth centuries B.C. the possibility that some of the Aramaic material reaches back into these ages cannot be excluded.

The site consists of an outer town of about 70 hectares surrounded on three sides by a rectangular fortification (see Fig. 63). The curve of the river formed the fourth

Figure 62
The Temple-Palace at Tell Halaf.

side, and here on a steep 21-meter rise lay the citadel. This was fortified on the land side also by a rectangle, an unusual shape for Aramaic town defenses. On the river side, projecting out on a spur in the eastern corner of the citadel, is a small palace. This is set on the edge of the fortifications, which at this point are very thick and strongly built. The palace was isolated from the rest of the citadel by a thick wall at the back. It was entered only through a long, narrow, sloping passage which led from the river bank up through the heavy fortification wall.

The palace in its latest form consisted of three clusters of rooms separated by a long corridor. There was a suite with bedroom, bathroom, and two parlors, a separate bathing complex, and a harem which could only be reached by a bridge. Remains of a staircase suggest the building had at least two stories. The administrative part of the palace—two large courts sur-

rounded by small rooms—lay behind this small living unit farther inside the citadel. Two gates connected the courts to other areas.

The palace seems to have been a private, semi-fortified residence. Since no reception rooms were found there, it is thought that the king must have held court in the Temple-Palace, so named because it is believed to have served both functions. This extraordinary building, with its elaborately sculptured facade, lay behind the palace on the opposite side of the citadel, facing the river. The king coming from his palace would have had a good view of the remarkable structure, whereas visitors arriving from the town through the main gate to the citadel would first encounter the back of the building, which was imposingly constructed like a fortress with heavy corner bastions and three intermediate towers. Lining the lower courses of the 61-meter-long wall were sculptured orthostats, large vertical slabs,

NEW SYRIAN PERIOD

made of alternating black volcanic stone (basalt) and limestone painted red. A gate along the right side of the building led into the temple precinct. It was guarded by two stone creatures almost 2 meters high with human heads, wings, and the bodies of scorpions. One frowned, the other smiled.

Once in front of the building the visitor, passing a royal mausoleum, went up a broad flight of steps to a wide paved terrace. Here he was met by a rather startling statue of a bird of prey, with bulging inlaid eyes, set high on a column. Nearby was a bright altar made of green, yellow, and white glazed brick formed into rosettes and scaled patterns interspersed with lozenges and guilloches. Beyond lay an extraordinary sight. In the entrance way to the temple, 9 meters wide, were three giant caryatid figures,

Figure 63
Plan of Guzana (Tell Halaf).

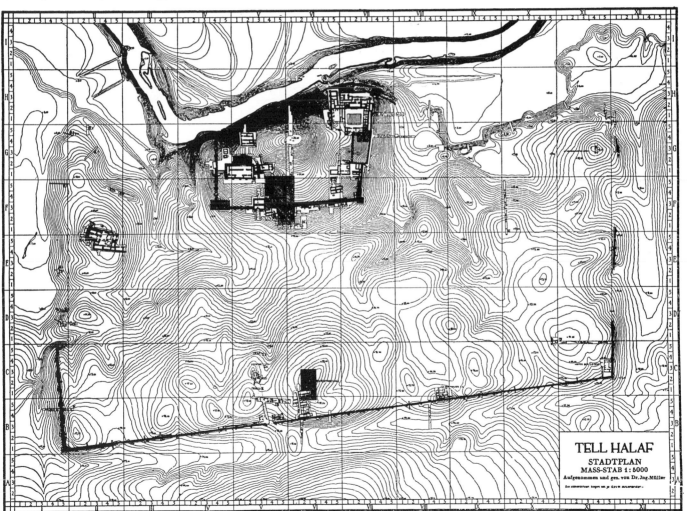

TELL HALAF
STADTPLAN
MASS-STAB 1 : 5000
Aufgenommen und gez. von Dr. Ing. Müller

each 3 meters high. In the center a male figure stood on a platform which was supported by a bull, 1.5 meters in height; on the right a woman stood over a lioness and on the left a male figure over a lion. Guarding the doors were female sphinxes with low foreheads and forboding faces. Beyond the doorway the front facade of the temple was decorated by sculptured orthostats depicting lions, gods, hunting scenes, and male sphinxes. All these figures were carved of black volcanic stone which would have emphasized the staring quality of the large inlaid eyes.

Passing between caryatids the visitor entered a wide, shallow room and faced another doorway, this time guarded by griffins with the same imposing large beak as the lone bird in front of the temple. The door led to another wide, shallow room where pillars on stone bases supported the roof. This was the main room, the hearth room, of this type of building (called *bit hilani*), which was characteristic of the city states of north Syria of the time. Here the excavators found *in situ* a rectangular cart made of bronze and iron on which the hearth could be moved about.

Although the plan of the building and the generous use of sculptural decoration can be matched in other Aramaic city states, nothing quite like the facade of the Temple-Palace has yet been found. King Kapara, who had the building made, boasts that he had done what his father and grandfather had not; but he did this in large part by re-using sculpture from buildings which once stood on the site. We know these existed from traces of an earlier Temple-Palace and from the fact that some of the haphazardly arranged small orthostats are still labeled "Temple of the Weather God"—inscriptions which Kapara's sculptors forgot to erase before carving his own inscription: "Palace of Kapara." The portico of the building was made by Kapara, but how much of the other sculpture is Kapara's and how much is re-used is still debated.

There is general agreement, however, that the haunting grave sculpture from the site predates Kapara. There seems to have been a cult of the dead at the site. One royal mausoleum has already been mentioned. Another in the same location had been covered by Kapara's time. Just outside the main entrance to the citadel from the town of Kapara's day two more large vaulted complexes thought to have been tombs were found. Nearby was a building with elaborate drainage facilities relating to ritual performances. Outside the citadel wall of pre-Kapara times were two impressive grave installations. Giant statues of seated women placed in small enclosures covered the shafts of cremation graves. The largest of these statues—which in its geometric simplicity was one of the most impressive monuments of ancient Near Eastern art—was destroyed in the Berlin air raid in 1943. The other, of a slightly more naturalistic style, can still be seen in Aleppo.

Just inside the outer town wall was still another installation which appears to have been used for the cult of the dead. Here was found a long, narrow building, entered from the short end, with a small side chamber; in plan it resembles the houses of the site. At the far end of the main room opposite the entrance was a platform which held an over-life-size statue of a couple seated on a bench. Slightly in front of these figures was a statue of a man standing on a basalt base, dangling a long sword from his left hand and carrying a boomerang over his right shoulder. Elsewhere in the room were smaller, much cruder statues of a similar type. An altar with an arrangement for liquid offerings stood in front of the figures, and beads were found on the floor. The funerary statues have more parallels in the second millennium than the first, but whether this is a matter of date or the outlandish quality of all of the sculpture from the site is not clear.

The primitive quality of the sculpture at Tell Halaf can be matched at some northwestern Syrian sites of the period such as Zinjirli and Karatepe, but the style, many of the compositions, and much of the subject matter is unique to Tell Halaf. This is particularly true of the 179 small orthostats, 1–1.2 meters high, which decorated the back of the Temple-Palace (see Fig. 64 and Cat. Nos. 178–181). Figures depicted on these stone slabs are characterized by very large noses and eyes. The men are bearded, wear their hair in a pigtail, and sometimes wear a sort of stocking cap. The sculptural quality of the figures is minimal: this is really drawing on stone. The background is cut away and the details are rendered by grooves. The drawing varies enormously: some figures are extremely awkward, whereas others, which probably copy small imported works of art, are more accomplished—for example, prancing horses, rampant goats, a camel. The orthostats with few exceptions were designed as separate units. Again, when copying well-known motifs—a lion hunt from a chariot, animal battles—the artists met with some success. When left

Figure 64
Small decorated orthostats in situ *at the rear of the Temple-Palace, Tell Halaf.*

on their own they produced awkward, even comical, compositions. When there was no room left for the prey in a chariot hunt scene, the wild bull was placed up in the air. One lion being hunted was so large that the archer who stalks him had to be put on its back. Such compositions read almost like hieroglyphs; others, such as a lion sprawled out eating his prey, are entirely new.

The art of Tell Halaf is so different from contemporary art in Syria that many believe the artists had an entirely different iconographical heritage. There is only one god represented on the orthostats, in contrast to a wealth of extraordinary mixed creatures—scorpion-bird-men, a merman, and a variety of winged animals and winged humans. One of the latter has six wings and is often cited as an example of Isaiah's seraph. There are many human figures: men in combat, archers, boomerang throwers, sling shooters, and cavalry men; men in hand-to-hand combat or wrestling; men fishing and picking dates. The orthostats are a heterogeneous lot, and several attempts have been made to subdivide them into groups. It is doubtful, however, that a completely logical arrangement can ever be found for these pieces. Here as elsewhere in north Syria in the early first millennium B.C. there seems to have been an enthusiasm for making sculpture *en masse* for its own sake. The artists drew on what they had seen, heard, or imagined—with much courage but without a systematic iconographical program.

JEANNY VORYS CANBY

IVORY CARVING

IRENE J. WINTER

TWO ASPECTS OF IVORY ARE CONSISTENTLY REFERRED TO IN THE ancient texts: its value as a commodity and its beauty as a material. The dowry of Queen Akhat-milku of Ugarit (Ras Shamra) in the second millennium B.C. included beds, footstools, and a chair inlaid with ivory; in the first millennium, Assyrian kings listed with evident pleasure the ivory and inlaid furniture they received as booty and tribute from the princes of Syria during their western campaigns. Divine images were manufactured of ivory, as was the statue of Shaushga (Ishtar) referred to by Tushratta of Mitanni, a kingdom of northwestern Syria during the second millennium, in one of the Amarna letters to Egyptian Pharaoh Amenhotep III. And on occasion the material is referred to metaphorically, as when the beauty of a goddess, probably Astarte, was likened to "an ivory panel . . . perfect and full of charm" in one of the poetic texts from Ras Shamra. The esteem in which ivory was held in antiquity was second only to that of precious metals, and it is in this light that the archaeological remains of ivory found in Syria and those attributed to Syrian workmanship found at other sites must be viewed. In fact, we know of one case in which a silver statue from Alalakh was melted down to provide silver ornaments for the grave of a ruler, but 30 shekels of its weight, a relatively large sum, was set aside for the setting of an ivory ornament.

The exact source of the ivory has been the subject of much scholarly debate. Surely ivory from the tusks of the African elephant could have been available via Egypt to the Mediterranean littoral and then inland to many Syrian sites; and ivory of the Indian elephant, which was imported quite early into Mesopotamia, could have been redistributed from there. But at least from the late second millennium through the early first millennium B.C. there were herds of elephant in Syria itself, in the marshy regions surrounding Aleppo and the

Habur River. Egyptian kings of the Eighteenth Dynasty, Thutmosis I and III (sixteenth–fifteenth century B.C.), make reference to hunting elephants in Syria, as do Assyrian kings from Tiglath-pileser I to Shalmaneser III (eleventh–ninth century B.C.). It is striking, however, that no references to elephants or to ivory sources in Syria have been found among the prolific texts dealing with trade and production of the early part of the second millennium, the Middle Bronze Age. It has been suggested therefore that perhaps the later elephant populations represent stocked rather than indigenous herds.

In any event, for the Late Bronze and Early Iron periods not only finished goods but also tusks have been uncovered in excavations: two from Alalakh of the Late Bronze Age and several fragments from 'al-Mina in the Early Iron Age; while tusks are reported as part of Shalmaneser III's booty from both Carchemish on the Euphrates and Patina in the Amuq valley. The presence of such tusks confirms stylistic and other arguments for Syrian ivory production, since the raw materials were at hand in both periods.

The question of how early fine ivory carving was being executed in Syria is a difficult one to answer because of the incompleteness of the archaeological record. Simple bone carvings and inlay fragments occur quite early. But even more important, a number of *wood* carvings have been excavated at Tell Mardikh (ancient Ebla) dating to the end of the Early Bronze Age, late third millennium B.C., which include complex scenes of fighting animals and human figures close in both subject matter and style to the later ivories. As the working of wood and ivory is very similar, employing identical tool kits and techniques, one may conclude that the technology for carving ivory was certainly present. However, whether fine woodworking was the precursor of ivory carving, or whether the two were done simultaneously while ivory remains were simply not preserved, is unclear.

In later periods, right through the early twentieth century as preserved in ethnographic accounts, there were whole villages in Syria that specialized in the carving of both wood and ivory—the more expensive, often religious, items being executed in ivory. But for the Early Bronze Age one might suggest that this was not the case. In general, ivory carvings have been found in very elite contexts— palaces and temples—reflecting their value. Since the wood carvings from Ebla were all found in the Royal Palace, one would expect that if ivory were being worked, some of the wood would have been inlaid or accompanied by pieces of ivory in this very context. It is therefore more probable that ivory was not yet being used as a medium for palace furnishings.

The earliest excavated examples of ivory date to the Middle Bronze Age, ca. 1800–1700 B.C. One, an ivory plaque some 5.5 centimeters in length and carved in relief, comes from a tomb in the lower city of Ebla. An open-work frieze was found in another Middle Bronze Age tomb at Byblos, and several inlay fragments were discovered in the Level VII temple at Alalakh. The subject matter of these pieces—a princely banquet-laden table and attendants on the plaque, and floral elements such as papyrus blossoms and palm fronds for the rest—all have counterparts among the ivories of the Late Bronze and Early Iron periods, as do the techniques of relief carving, open-work, and inlay. This would suggest strong continuity throughout.

It is only in the Late Bronze Age that we have the first evidence of substantial collections of ivory, accompanying the references to elephants hunted in Syria. These collections may reflect stockpiling of a valuable commodity or else the conspicuous display of what were surely desirable luxury goods.

The ivories discovered at Ras Shamra (ancient Ugarit) constitute the most important collection of the period. Finds include a large bifacial bed panel comprised of joined plaques of ivory (Fig. 65); inlay fragments that would have been part of a (now lost) wooden table some 3 meters in diameter; the head of a male, probably a divine

Figure 65
Ivory bed panel from Ugarit (Ras Shamra), fourteenth–thirteenth century B.C.

Exterior panel

Interior panel

figure, carved in the round; various small cosmetic items (e.g., Cat. No. 153); and the tip of a complete tusk carved with ornamental figures and designs. These pieces were all found together in the palace. It has been suggested that they were assembled in a workshop, but in fact little evidence supports this—no tools, no fragments that were clearly waste flakes as opposed to breakage, no indication of room function within palace quarters.

The style of these ivories reflects the diverse contacts of Late Bronze Age Syria. Principal influences are Egyptian motifs and details (see, e.g., Cat. No. 154). To a lesser degree we also see elements of Hittite iconography and symbolism and Mycenaean themes, with the Aegean predilection for movement and curvilinear forms. The large bed panel from Ras Shamra in particular (Fig. 65) shows evidence of many of these influences. Note, for example, on the exterior side, the Egyptian military helmet of the king (second plaque from left) and the courtier's dress (far right); while on the interior side, the central suckling goddess wears the Hittite royal symbol between the horns of her headdress. Yet the overall style is clearly Syrian—for example, the person of the nude goddess (exterior, far left, as compared with the gold pendant, Cat. No. 130), as well as various details, such as the weapons carried by two warriors (exterior, third plaque from right, compared with an actual bronze blade, Cat. No. 148).

The Ras Shamra assemblage in general suggests a multiplicity of models and sources, in the end all modified by and assimilated into Syrian taste. This would certainly reflect the historical situation of the International Age of the Late Bronze period, in which Ugarit maintained a wide network of foreign relations but was itself an important center of wealth, culture, and production.

The Ras Shamra ivories have been dated within the fourteenth to thirteenth centuries B.C. Roughly contemporary is a more restricted group of ivories excavated at Tell Fekheriye in the Habur region of northeast Syria. These latter ivories are quite homogeneous in style and type: they were all cut out in silhouette with little modelling; details were added by incised lines alone; and tenons protrude at top and bottom to facilitate mounting, presumably into wooden furniture, although the wood has not been preserved. Here themes of griffin-genii, winged sun disks, and "sacred trees" are more at home in the Hurrian or Hittite repertoire known also from cylinder seals. This is entirely in keeping with the location of Tell Fekheriye, as it would have fallen within the domain of the Hurrian kingdom of Mitanni which, at about 1400 B.C., became subject to the Hittites. Hence, the major ivory collections of the period reflect the differing ethnicities and foreign relations of the coastal and inland regions of the Late Bronze Age.

Those ivories first identified as Syrian of the Iron Age were in fact excavated at Nimrud (Kalhu), ancient capital of the Assyrians near Mosul. Great quantities of ivories from many varying traditions were hoarded in palaces and public buildings. Pieces were attributed to Syria on the basis of stylistic parallels with fixed monuments—stone reliefs and sculpture—known from north Syrian sites of the first millennium B.C. (cf. Fig. 66 with Cat. No. 180, a relief from Tell Halaf). These ivories evince a strong continuity with works of the Syrian Late Bronze period in themes, techniques of carving, and types of objects (cf., e.g., the chair panel from Nimrud, Fig. 67, with the Ras Shamra bed, Fig. 65), while at the same time they have also incorporated various elements of the Aegean and Hittite styles of the same period. There is a marked diminution of Egyptian elements evident in the ivories of this period, although Egyptian influence did remain strong along the Phoenician coast, which was also producing ivories in the Iron Age. In brief, Syrian-style ivories may be characterized by a greater sense of action, by squatter, more powerful

Figure 66
Syrian-style ivory pyxis from
Nimrud, ninth century B.C.

Figure 67
Ivory bed or chair panel from
Nimrud, eighth–seventh century
B.C.

proportions, and by more highly charged compositions, compared with the more quiescent, elegant, and slender figures harmoniously disposed in space of the contemporary Phoenician style.

Beyond the major divisions into Syrian and Phoenician groups, there is now sufficient evidence to suggest that several centers in northern Syria were producing fine ivory work from the ninth to the late eighth century B.C. This would include the kingdoms of Carchemish, Sam'al, Hama, and possibly also Patina, Arpad (Tell Rifa'at), and Guzana (Tell Halaf). A further South Syrian style may also be identified, with a probable center at Aram (Damascus).

A number of ivories from Arslantash included in the present exhibition are of Phoenician style (e.g., Cat. Nos. 173 and 174); however, a number of others would fall into this latter, South Syrian group (see Cat. Nos. 171, 172, 174, 177). They were accompanied by an inscribed ivory label, reading: ". . . To our lord, Haza'el," the name of a known ruler of Aram ca. 845–805 B.C. In addition, stylistically they fall into the southern group, incorporating recognizable but often mistaken Egyptianizing elements and compositions characteristic of the Phoenician school, with squatter proportions and greater intensity of movement, more characteristic of the North Syrian school. The frame for an ivory bed was actually among the excavated materials from Arslantash. The decorated plaques exhibited here (Cat. Nos. 171–177) are all tenoned for insertion into furniture and would have presumably belonged to just such a bed or chair. Since Arslantash is itself located in northern Syria, it has been suggested that the ivories were carried there as booty by Assyrian representatives sometime between the late ninth century and the ultimate annexation of the kingdom of Aram by Assyria in 732 B.C. It is all the more striking, therefore, that Assyrian inscriptions record the taking of the king of Aram's own ivory bed and throne as part of the captured booty in at least two campaigns.

The distribution of Syrian-style ivories in the Iron Age, from Hasanlu in northwest Iran, across Anatolia, to sites in mainland Greece, follows a path quite distinct from the more southerly distribution of Phoenician-style ivories, and it has been suggested that this reflects not only differing spheres of influence but also competitive and exclusive access to routes and markets. Hasanlu provides the best chronological peg for the ninth century *floruit* of the Syrian-style ivories, as it was destroyed ca. 805 B.C. The ivories found there include plaques and pyxides (cannister-like vessels) of pure North Syrian style, often identical with pieces also found at Nimrud (e.g., Fig. 66). Whether the ivories were acquired directly from their places of origin or were redistributed by the Assyrians cannot be determined, but these Syrian ivories in turn gave rise to a local style at Hasanlu that imitated the fine, imported pieces in cruder works showing similar themes. Thus, these North Syrian ivories had an impact, not only on the luxury markets of their time, but also on the artistic traditions of their neighbors.

The latest examples of Syrian ivories in the first millennium B.C. do not seem to go beyond the later part of the eighth century. This may be due in part to the depletion of the Syrian elephant herds, which provided ready sources of raw material. However, this terminus would also coincide with the annexation of virtually all of the north Syrian states by the Assyrian empire, as a result of which there were large-scale interruptions in urban production. It is more than likely that the depleted economies of the north Syrian states led to the cessation of local industries and the migration of craftsmen to other more prosperous centers. This phenomenon may well account for the Syrian influence observable in many seventh- and even sixth-century Greek ivories.

In the course of his Syrian campaigns Shalmaneser III of Assyria (858–824 B.C.) took much ivory booty and received ivory in tribute: ebony furniture set with ivory from Carchemish; ivory furniture overlaid with silver and gold from Bit Adini (from its capital, Til Barsip, on the Euphrates); and inlaid ivory furniture from Damascus. These references attest to the variety and geographical diversity of Syrian ivory production in the first millennium B.C. It is not at all impossible that the later Islamic and modern tradition of inlaid ivory and mother-of-pearl furniture from Damascus is the heir to a very ancient tradition. In any event, the Assyrian references also provide eloquent tribute from the past to the value of fine ivory work. They help to animate our understanding of the joy of the goddess Athirat, in the poem of Baal preserved among the tablets of Ras Shamra, at her gifts of a chair, footstool, and table fit "for a god." And they help us to reconstruct in our mind's eye the separate preserved plaques into complex, masterfully crafted pieces of furniture, while remembering the quality of carving and richness of detail of individual pieces.

Recommended Reading

Richard D. Barnett. *A Catalogue of the Nimrud Ivories in the British Museum* (2nd ed. London: British Museum, 1975) / "Ancient Ivories of the Middle East." *Qedem* (Jerusalem) 14 (1982).

Helene J. Kantor. "Syro-Palestinian Ivories." *JNES* 15 (1956) 153–174.

Max Mallowan and Georgina Herrmann. *Ivories from Nimrud (1949–1963) III: Furniture from SW7 Fort Shalmaneser* (Aberdeen: British School of Archaeology in Iraq, 1974).

Irene J. Winter. "Phoenician and North Syrian Ivory Carving in Historical Context: Questions of Style and Distribution." *Iraq* 38 (1976) 1–22.

'AIN DARA

Location: 40 km northwest of Aleppo, on the right bank of the Afrin River
Date: Tenth century B.C. to sixteenth century A.D.
Excavations: 1964, annually since 1976 (Directorate-General of Antiquities, Syria)
Publications: F. Seirafi *AAAS* 10 (1960) 87 (in Arabic) // F. Seirafi and A. Kirichian *AAAS* 15 (1965) 3 // A. Abu Assaf *AfO* 26 (1978/79) 147

'Ain Dara is a famous resort frequented by the city population of Aleppo; its rich oasis surrounded by trees provides shaded picnic spots. As an archaeological site

Figure 68
Topographic plan of 'Ain Dara.

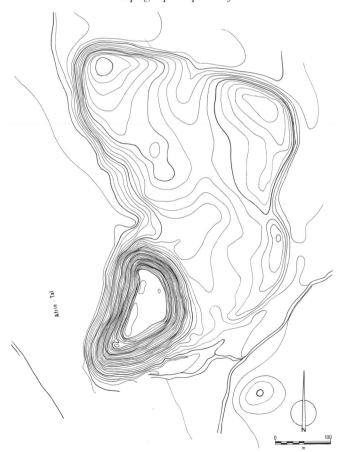

'Ain Dara only became important in 1954 when a shepherd found a basalt lion head in the den of a fox. He reported the find to the Directorate-General of Antiquities in Aleppo, and a small prospecting expedition was dispatched to the site. It was immediately noticed that the shepherd had stumbled upon a well-preserved, powerful gate figure, fallen on its side.

The ruins of 'Ain Dara lie on the right bank of the Afrin River and can be reached via Aleppo or by way of the famous Byzantine ruins at Qal'at Siman. The extensive, almost quadrilateral plan of the site comprises a residential city with a center on the southwest (Fig. 68). The entire city was once surrounded by a stone wall equipped with towers at its gates. The high center, or acropolis, consists of settlement ruins which fall off steeply on all sides. Excavations have been concentrated on the acropolis, especially the southern sector with the gate at which the lion was once situated.

Six settlements, dating from the ninth century B.C. through the sixteenth century A.D., have been identified in the excavations of the Directorate-General of Antiquities. These may be summarized as follows:

Level I lies directly under the surface. Small finds date it to the fifteenth–sixteenth century A.D. Erosional processes have carried off the remains of this occupation to such an extent that only a few very small stubs of walls remain. 'Ain Dara apparently was a settlement of little significance at this time.

Level 2 came to an end through a catastrophic fire of undetermined origin. Settlement apparently extended across the entire area of the acropolis, but the lower city remained unoccupied. The population was therefore quite limited. The Hellenistic period wall was rebuilt or restored in only a few places, and apparently still served to protect the population of the acropolis.

Houses and farmsteads were simple and densely packed. In one case a large farmstead could be defined as a living room and a divided stable. Walls of sun-dried brick were erected on stone foundations. Flat roofs were made of a layer of beams with reed matting, sealed with mud plaster. Strong wooden pillars set in the middle of the room supported the roof. Such flat roofs were annually resealed with mud plaster applied evenly over the roof with stone rollers. Examples of such have been found at 'Ain Dara.

The household inventory of one farmstead destroyed by fire has been preserved: three large clay containers filled with lentils, wheat, and chickpeas; a large hand mill and basalt mortar; a wooden threshing sledge, its underside set with chipped stone; clay utensils of all kinds including plates, basins, and cooking pots; iron plowshares, sickles, axes, arrows, and horse bits and stirrups. These implements belonged to a single house-

hold. Common equipment such as oil and wine presses was also present. Bread ovens, which were situated in public locations and occasionally inside houses, apparently were often used communally. Coins were found in small quantities. Some are especially valuable, since they date this level to the ninth to the thirteenth centuries A.D.

Level 3 belongs to the period of the Umayyad and Abassid kingdoms, on the basis of evidence provided by the small finds retrieved in excavation. The material illustrates the typically agrarian life of the population. The occupants of the succeeding level 2 renovated or rebuilt the houses of level 3; there are no dwellings between levels 2 and 3. Uninterrupted occupation from the sixth to the fifteenth or sixteenth century seems indicated. Prior to that, however, from the first to the sixth century, during the Roman period, 'Ain Dara was uninhabited. Under level 3 lies more than a meter of debris which separates it from level 4.

Level 4 represents the Hellenistic and Seleucid periods (ca. 330–64 B.C.). Settlement extended over the entire surface of the acropolis and was surrounded by a protective wall more than 2 meters high, armed with bastions and towers. The gate of the fortress has yet to be located within the still-limited area of excavation. Public buildings of this period have also not been exposed. A few wall remains provide occasional glimpses of typical houses. In one case a house floor was prepared from a cementlike material. The presence of roof tiles indicates that at least some of these houses were tiled rather than mud-plastered.

The well-protected nature of the

settlement suggests the existence of an administrative center, as in the case of the present-day town of Afrin. The few silver and bronze coins can be attributed to the reigns of Seleucid monarchs. The ceramics are either typically Hellenistic or are local wares for daily use such as plates, basins, bowls, and cooking pots.

Level 5 extends from the seventh to the fourth century B.C. This settlement has only been reached in one 100-square-meter area. The same building techniques used in earlier levels appear here, but stone is now used for sculpture, along with the entire basalt lions from the older level 6. In an apparently important building, a large lion was found in the corner of each of four rooms. In front of the 1.5-meter-wide entrance of the building there was a walkway of limestone slabs. The wooden door, which opened outward, was fastened to a vertical post which turned in a stone door socket.

Level 6 contains the remains of a still incompletely exposed tenth- to ninth-century temple situated in the northwestern portion of the acropolis. This building is a characteristic *bit hilani* structure featuring an entrance hall with one to three columns at its front end, an adjacent main room with a space for a hearth, and an arrangement of smaller rooms arranged around it. Often the front walls of such structures are decorated with small orthostats with animal sculptures in relief, while the columns stand on figuratively decorated pedestals. Characteristically these rooms are not arbitrarily enlarged by adjoining other rooms to them. Archaeological research in northern Mesopotamia and north Syria has shown that almost all palaces of the early Iron Age (1200–700 B.C.) belong to this *bit hilani* type. Differences between them are restricted to minor details such as size, staircases, and the number of rooms.

The 'Ain Dara temple is still not completely exposed; hence we cannot categorize it further. Its most striking feature relative to other contemporary north Syrian temples is its outer walls. In contrast to the so-called Temple-Palace of Tell Halaf (Fig. 62), the palaces of Zinjirli (Sam'al), Tell Tayinat, and Sakçe Gözü, the outer wall at 'Ain Dara is decorated with animal sculptures: lions and sphinxes. Unfortunately all of these were partially damaged by fire. On the two facades which meet in the south corner of the temple the lions stand opposite the sphinxes and look to the right and left respectively.

From the entrance hall, a corridor 3.6 meters wide and 2.6 meters deep, decorated with lions, leads to the main room. It has two steplike thresholds made of stone slabs in which are three large footprints pointing toward the interior of the temple. The first step contains two footprints next to each other; the second has only the left foot. Footprints are known in other cultural contexts. "Their very general sense is the immortality of a certain person or god at a certain place. . . . they are often considered as signs of ownership and often immortalize the place of appearance or the departure of a mythical being" (*AAAS* 21 [1971] 33). In the cult room toward which the footprints point, reliefs with mountain-god representations were found in 1963 (Cat. No. 182).

During the 1980 excavations a relief with the representation of the

Figure 69
Bas relief panel from 'Ain Dara.

warlike goddess Ishtar was found in a room adjacent to the cult room's corridor (Fig. 69). Earlier, this relief had probably stood in the south corner of this room. We may assume that here in the courtyard there remain more orthostats depicting a divine procession, one that the Ishtar relief might have led. Although the presence of mountain gods in the cult room and Ishtar nearby provide some clues as to whom the temple was consecrated, this cannot be answered at this time.

During the Iron Age, 'Ain Dara, in the fertile Afrin plain, was part of the realm of the petty princes established following the wave of the Sea Peoples across north Syria and southern Anatolia. The comparison of 'Ain Dara's architecture with other buildings in the area makes its chronological position clear. We can observe a complete correspondence in public buildings with regard to plans, outer walls, and entrances with orthostats and animal sculptures. The ancient name of the city still eludes us. M. Dunand and F. Seirafi assumed that 'Ain Dara is the ancient Kinalua, often mentioned in the Neo-Assyrian annals. Further excavation is certain to shed light on this as well as other questions.
Ali Abu Assaf

168
Detail of a wall painting—Assyrian officer
See color plate p. 319

Site: Til Barsip/Kar Shalmaneser (Tell Ahmar)
Date: Ca. 750 B.C.
Material: Paint on plaster
Height: 35 cm; *width:* 30 cm
Museum No.: Aleppo 231
Literature: F. Thureau-Dangin and M. Dunand *Til-Barsib*
(Paris 1936) // A. Parrot *Assur* (Munich 1961) Fig. 113

The large rooms in the palace of the governor of Kar
Shalmaneser had friezes painted on the walls showing
victorious military campaigns and the conquest of the
enemy. Such pictorial renderings in a governmental
building, where many people came, served as political
propaganda, and the Assyrians were masters of such
propaganda.

Only a few pieces of the paintings could be saved,
but whatever was recognizable at the time of the excavation was carefully copied. This is the head of an
armed officer of the royal guard who stood behind the
king (see Fig. 70). He is dressed in a short-sleeved
shirt covered with a shawl of patterned fringed material. His hair is held by a headband, and he wears an
earring.
E.S.

169
Detail of a wall painting—Assyrian court officials
See color plate p. 319

Site: Til Barsip/Kar Shalmanesser (Tell Ahmar)
Date: Ca. 750 B.C.
Material: Paint on plaster
Height: 40 cm; *width:* 3.8 cm
Museum No.: Aleppo 230
Literature: F. Thureau-Dangin and M. Dunand *Til-Barsib*
(Paris 1931) // A. Parrot *Assur* (Munich 1961) Figs. 113,
114

The two Assyrian officials are from the same frieze as
the officer in Cat. No. 168. They are attendants of the
seated king, who is receiving captives of war bearing
gifts and a prostrate enemy prince (see Fig. 70). The
two officials wear the same kind of clothes as the officer; the colors are black, blue, and various shades of
red, painted on a tan plaster background. The outlines
of the figures were first drawn in red or black, then
filled in with paint.
E.S.

Figure 70
The Assyrian king at the presentation of prisoners,
from a wall painting at Tell Ahmar.

170
Statue of a god

Site: Hadatu (Arslantash), Ishtar Temple
Date: Reign of Assyrian King Tiglath-pileser III,
   744–727 B.C.
Material: Basalt
Height of statue: 1.73 cm; *base:* 34 cm
Museum No.: Aleppo 51
Literature: Thureau-Dangin *Arslan-Tash* 10, 66 Plate I //
   E. Strommenger *Die neuassyrische Rundskulptur* (Berlin
   1970) 21, Fig. 10

From the ancient Near East only a few statues of deities are preserved. Since the depictions of gods in the
large temples were richly decorated with gold and jewels, it is rare to find such works in their original splendor. This statue from the Ishtar Temple of the provincial Assyrian town of Hadatu is one of six similar
statues once housed there. He holds a box in his
hands which probably was meant to receive votive
gifts. His short-sleeved robe, with a fringed shawl
wrapped around it, and his hair and beard show the
Assyrian fashion of the eighth century B.C. The bull-
horns on his headdress indicate his divine status, but
since he wears only two horns, he must have had an
inferior position in the pantheon. Rows of such lower
deities were often placed at the entrance to Neo-Assyrian temples. This statue was carved out of a square
block of basalt, and the body features are hardly recognizable under the garment. These statues from
Arslantash were locally produced in the provincial
style, although the models for them were Assyrian
from the upper Tigris.
E.S.

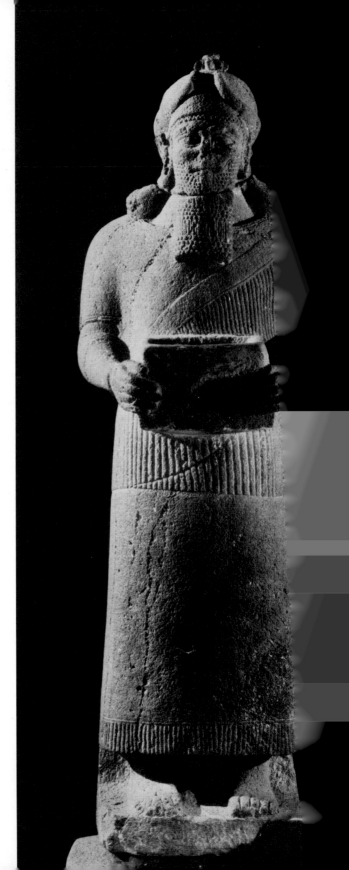

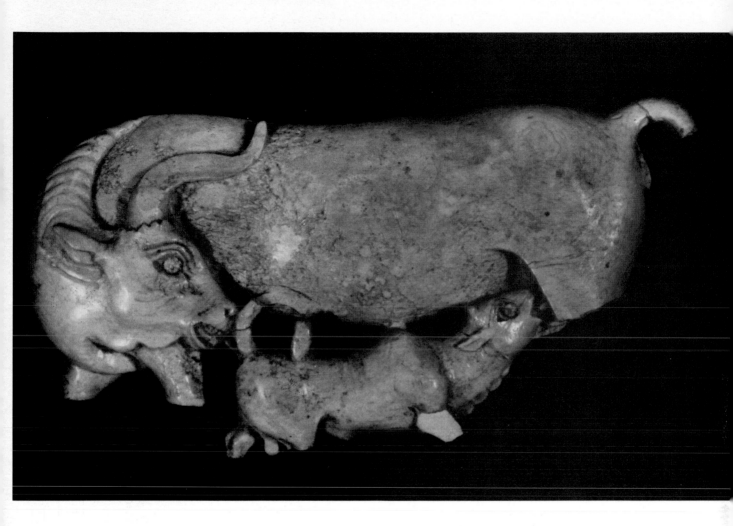

171
Ivory carving of cow with calf

Site: Hadatu (Arslantash)
Date: 850–800 B.C.
Material: Ivory
Height: 5.8 cm; *width:* 11.4 cm; *depth:* 1.5 cm
Museum No.: Aleppo 349 (9817)
Literature: Thureau-Dangin *Arslan-Tash* 121, Plate XXXIX
   71// cf. Thimme *Phönizische Elfenbeine* xxi, Figs. 23–28

This ivory carving was used on decorated furniture,
which was popular all over the ancient Near East.
Workshops have been found in Syria, Palestine, and
Phoenicia. King Solomon, for instance, ordered "a
large chair decorated with ivory and precious stones,"
and other rulers also had such furniture in their palaces. Among the tribute offerings from the Damascus
prince Benhadad III to the Assyrian king Adad-Nirari
III (805–782 B.C.) were "a bed of ivory and a sofa decorated and inlaid with ivory." The ivories from Arslantash may have been part of such involuntary gifts. A
small uncarved plaque of ivory has an inscription in
Aramaic stating that it belonged to certain Haza'el,
which was the name of the above-mentioned
Benhadad's father and predecessor. We therefore can
assume that the furniture belonged to Haza'el of Da-

172

mascus (ca. 844–806 B.C.), although we must acknowledge that there were other princes with the same name. One thing is certain: the ivories found at Arslantash were not locally produced but originated from southern workshops.

In the areas east of the Mediterranean there were numerous ivory workshops, all producing very similar carvings, and one may assume that the raw material was available in this area. We do have evidence that there were elephants in the Euphrates and Habur regions at the time. The furniture was made of wood, then covered with the carved ivories; sometimes the ivory plaques were solid, but more often they were carved in an open-work style. Indentations on the back of the ivories served as points of attachment. Sometimes the ivory reliefs were enhanced by gilding or by inlays of semi-precious stones, but only faint traces of such inlays remain.

The motif here—a cow licking her newborn calf— was well known in Mesopotamia from the beginning of the second millennium B.C. The Ugaritic literature tells us of a similar motif: "Like the heart of a cow longs for her calf, like the heart of a sheep longs for her lamb, so does the heart of Anat long for Baal." E.S.

172
Ivory carving of grazing deer

Site: Hadatu (Arslantash)
Date: 850–800 B.C.
Material: Ivory
Height: 5.9 cm; *width:* 10 cm; *depth:* 0.5 cm
Museum No.: Aleppo 310
Literature: Thureau-Dangin *Arslan-Tash* 118, Plate XXXVI
   61 // cf. Thimme *Phönizische Elfenbeine* xxii, Figs. 17–22

Like the previous example, these grazing deer were
part of a frieze assembled from individual small
plaques which were used to decorate furniture. This
piece was one of many similar mass-produced pieces,
and the quality of the carving is excellent. The types
of filling motifs in these plaques differed from workshop to workshop or from artisan to artisan. Sometimes the backs have incised inscriptions in Aramaic
indicating where the piece should be positioned on the
furniture, and often the artist would leave his mark.
E.S.

173

174

173
Ivory carving of a woman in a window

Site: Hadatu (Arslantash)
Date: 850–800 B.C.
Material: Ivory
Height: 8 cm; *width:* 9.1 cm; *depth:* 0.9 cm
Museum No.: Aleppo 314 (9808)
Literature: Thureau-Dangin *Arslan-Tash* 113, Plate XXXIV
   47 // Thimme *Phönizische Elfenbeine* xxiii, Figs. 12–16

A three-stepped recessed frame surrounds a rectangle, closed below by a balustrade with a smooth horizontal beam resting on four beautifully executed columns. Inside the frame appears a female head with an
Egyptian coiffure, a rectangular diadem, and earrings
of typical ninth-century Assyrian design. This beautiful bejeweled woman looking out of her window is
probably the demoness Kililu, the first of Ishtar's eighteen attendants. Two holes on the sides and the rough
back of the carving served to attach the plaque to its
background. An incised double circle is either the
mark of the workshop or the artist.
E.S.

ca. 1200–330 B.C.

174
Ivory carving of a sphinx

Site: Hadatu (Arslantash)
Date: 850–800 B.C.
Material: Ivory
Height: 7.9 cm; *width:* 5.9 cm; *depth:* 0.9 cm
Museum No.: Aleppo 361 (9833)
Literature: Thureau-Dangin *Arslan-Tash* 105, Plate XXXI 33

This sphinx has a human head with an Egyptian
coiffure; it wears a wide collar and a shield. Only
traces remain of the plants that originally filled the
background. On the back are two incised signs.
E.S.

175
Ivory carving of two sphinxes

Site: Hadatu (Arslantash)
Date: 850–800 B.C.
Material: Ivory
Height: 8.7 cm; *width:* 19.9 cm
Museum No.: Aleppo 304 (9813)
Literature: Thureau-Dangin *Arslan-Tash* 102, Plate XXVII
  22

Two sphinxes with ram's heads face one another with
the double crown of Egypt between them. Many of the
carved ivories, especially the so-called Phoenician
group to which these belong, are heavily influenced by
Egyptian art. They are, however, never exact copies of
the Egyptian models, for they have incorporated Near
Eastern traditions of style. In this case, wings were
added to the ram-headed sphinxes. This symmetrical
pair belongs to a continuous frieze in which the individual animals were separated by stylized plants. Unlike Cat. No. 171, this carving is open; that is, the figures are inside an open frame.
E.S.

175

176
Ivory carving of the birth of the sun god

Site: Hadatu (Arslantash)
Date: 850–800 B.C.
Material: Ivory, with remains of gold
Height: 9 cm; *width:* 8.3 cm; *depth:* ca. 0.9 cm
Museum No.: Aleppo 309 (9768)
Literature: Thureau-Dangin *Arslan-Tash* 93, Plate XIX 21 //
  Thimme *Phönizische Elfenbeine* xxi, Fig. 11

Two winged protecting deities with lilies in their hands
stand on either side of a lotus plant, while the small
sun god sits on the bud of the lotus flower. According
to Egyptian myth the sun god was born every morning
in an opening lotus blossom. The theme is thus entirely Egyptian. The composition, execution, and
many details, such as the double crown and the long
bull's tails of the two protecting gods, are also based

on Egyptian models, while the fringed robe is ancient Near Eastern.

Indentations in the four corners served to attach the plaque. On the back are three incised signs which cannot be read.

E.S.

177
Ivory carving of two men binding papyri

Site: Hadatu (Arslantash)
Date: 850–800 B.C.
Material: Ivory
Height: 10.4 cm; *width exclusive of restoration:* 9 cm; *depth:* 1.1 cm
Museum No.: Aleppo 305 (9785)
Literature: Thureau-Dangin *Arslan-Tash* 100, Plate XXXVI 21

NEW SYRIAN PERIOD

Also inspired by an Egyptian model, this relief represents the symbolic union between Upper and Lower Egypt by the tying together of a lily and a papyrus stalk. Two males dressed in Near Eastern clothes, but wearing the Egyptian double crown, face each other over a bunch of papyri, from which they both hold a stalk. The sun god, wearing a disk on his head and holding a scepterlike object, squats on top of the papyri.

E.S.

178
Small orthostat decorated with archer

Site: Guzana (Tell Halaf), west wall of the Temple-Palace
Date: 900–850 B.C.
Material: Basalt
Height: 57 cm; *width:* 37.5 cm; *depth:* 19 cm
Museum No.: Aleppo 196
Literature: A. Moortgat *Tell Halaf* III *Die Bildwerke* (Berlin 1955) 39, Plate 12b

A bearded male in a short skirt bends a large bow to shoot an arrow. Together with 178 similar small orthostats, this relief decorated the outer wall of the Temple-Palace of Guzana (see Fig. 64, which shows the orthostats *in situ*). Many of the reliefs have a short cuneiform inscription reading "Prince Kapara from Bit Bahiani." In this case we read only the name, Kapara, on the chest and upper arm. In other inscriptions he proclaims himself a great builder and renovator of the city. He removed the reliefs from an older building, erased the original inscription, and replaced it with his own. During the reign of Kapara the reliefs were positioned in a schematic pattern: gray basalt interspersed with reddish-colored limestone without regard for any meaningful pictorial sequence.

E.S.

179
Small orthostat decorated with rock thrower

Site: Guzana (Tell Halaf), south wall of the Temple-Palace
Date: 900–850 B.C.
Material: Basalt
Height: 63 cm; *width:* 32 cm; *depth:* 19 cm
Museum No.: Aleppo 188
Literature: A. Moortgat *Tell Halaf* III *Die Bildwerke* (Berlin
    1955) 44, Plate 20a

A bearded male wearing a headband and a wrap-
around skirt holds a stone in his right hand and some
sort of throwing stick in his left. Since the relief was
found out of order, we do not know what the sequence
was. Most often the reliefs have only one figure each:
with a sling, spear, or on horseback, for example. A
hunting scene from a chariot is a rare example of a
complicated design.

    Most of the reliefs have only the basic outlines
carved in the stone with hardly any modeling. Individual traits are rendered by incised lines. The heads are
disproportionately large, and the feet are executed in
a peculiar way. It seems as if the sculptor merely filled
the available space on his slab of stone with his composition.
E.S.

180
Small orthostat with lion

Site: Guzana (Tell Halaf), south wall of the Temple-Palace
Date: 900–850 B.C.
Material: Basalt
Height: 51 cm; *width:* 38 cm; *depth:* 19.5 cm
Museum No.: Aleppo 195
Literature: A. Moortgat *Tell Halaf* III *Die Bildwerke* (Berlin
    1955) 64, Plate 44b

This upright lion, which fills the slab diagonally, is a
typical example of animal depictions from Tell Halaf,
where we also find reliefs of stags, bulls, and os-
triches. The cuneiform inscription in the left upper
corner reads "Temple of the Weather God."
E.S.

181
Small orthostat

Site: Guzana (Tell Halaf), south wall of the Temple-Palace
Date: 900–850 B.C.
Material: Basalt
Height: 64 cm; *width:* 38.5 cm; *depth:* 20 cm
Literature: A. Moortgat *Tell Halaf* III *Die Bildwerke* (Berlin 1955) 89, Plate 92a

This winged bull belongs to a large group of fantastic animals which were particularly popular in the ancient Near East from the second millennium onward. It is possible that this piece originally formed part of a composition of two winged bulls facing each other over a plant or a palm tree, since a number of reliefs with a palm tree were found and this motif often was used as the central point in a heraldic design. The word "palace" can still be read in the upper left corner of the relief.
E.S.

182
Foundation relief with mountain god and bull-men

Site: 'Ain Dara
Date: 1000–900 B.C.
Material: Basalt
Height: 58 cm; *length:* 102 cm; *depth:* ca. 30 cm
Museum No.: Aleppo 6248
Literature: F. Seirafi and A. Kirichian *AAS* 15 (1965) 12, Plate Xa // W. Orthmann *Untersuchungen zur späthethitischen Kunst* (Bonn 1971) 56, 476, Plate 3

The foundation reliefs from the inside of the temple in 'Ain Dara are quite different from the ones from Tell Halaf: they are more modeled, clearly of a higher artistic and technical quality, and derive from a completely different school of artistic representation, one influenced by Hittite art.

The mountain god in the center of the relief shows strong Hittite stylistic traits, especially in the way the face is rendered. His robe with a scale design is of Anatolian origin, and he has Anatolian shoes with turned-up toes, while he wears the Mesopotamian horned crown. He is flanked by two bearded bull-men, who stand with their arms raised. In similar depictions of bull-men they usually hold a winged sun disk. In

'Ain Dara no remnants of such a winged sun disk were found, and one wonders whether the gods and bull-men here were supposed to "carry" the building.

This relief belongs to a series which included depictions of fantastic animals with either lion's or bird's heads replacing the bull-men.

E.S.

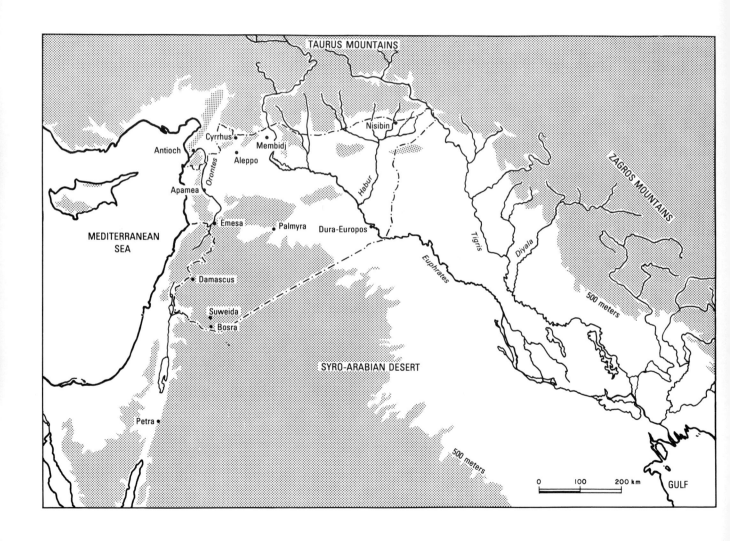

TAURUS MOUNTAINS

ZAGROS MOUNTAINS

Nisibin

Cyrrhus
Antioch
Membidj
Aleppo

Apamea
Orontes

Habur

Emesa
Palmyra
Dura-Europos

MEDITERRANEAN
SEA

Tigris

Diyala

Euphrates

Damascus

500 meters

Suweida
Bosra

SYRO-ARABIAN DESERT

Petra

500 meters

0   100   200 km

GULF

HELLENISTIC AND ROMAN PERIODS CA. 330 B.C.– A.D. 400

FROM ALEXANDER TO ROMAN RULE

EVA STROMMENGER

IN 334 B.C. ALEXANDER THE GREAT CONQUERED THE ACHAEMENID empire, which was then united with Macedonia under his rule. After the Battle of Issus in 333 B.C. he occupied Syria and then, in 331, Mesopotamia. After Alexander's death his empire was divided among his army commanders, who reigned as governors and slightly later as independent kings. One of these military commanders was Antigonus Monophthalmus (the one-eyed); Syria-Palestine and northern Mesopotamia fell within his realm. As the victor in the Battle of Ipsus in 301 B.C. in Asia Minor, Seleucus, the ruler of Babylon, gained control of these regions as well. Through defeats inflicted by the Romans in Asia Minor, and the Parthians to the east, the Seleucid empire was confined to the approximate area of the modern state of Syria. The region was conquered in 83 B.C. by Tigranes, king of Armenia. In 64 B.C. the Roman proconsul Pompey dethroned Tigranes and displaced the last Seleucid monarch. The province of "Syria" was annexed; it stretched from Issus to Damascus and toward the east from the Taurus Mountains to the mouth of the Habur River. Northern Mesopotamia then fell under the rule of the Parthians for two centuries.

In A.D. 165, under the emperor Marcus Aurelius, northwestern Mesopotamia became Roman territory up to a north-south line between the Balikh and the Habur rivers. In A.D. 194 the emperor Septimus Severus made all of the "land between the rivers, under the name 'Mesopotamia,'" a Roman province. The fortified border (the Roman *limes*) against the Syrian desert ran from Jebel Sais east to Palmyra, then west of Rusafa north to the Euphrates. There the *limes* turned southeast along the river toward the Habur and its northern source. At the Jebel Sinjar the *limes* turned eastward, following the southern edge of the mountain toward the Tigris. In the corner between the *limes* and the Euphrates lay the Roman vassal state of

Palmyra. Later, in 363, the border was pushed back to the Habur Plains, where it stayed until the Arab conquest of A.D. 634.

Only a short millennium encompasses the extent of classical antiquity and its Byzantine successors—the sequence of Macedonian Greeks, Romans, and Byzantine Christian rulers. Hellenization began with Alexander the Great and led to some fundamental changes in cultural life, noticeable particularly in the buildings and visual arts where works now appeared to follow Greek rules of form. The power center represented by the Iranian plateau, always pushing toward the Euphrates and beyond, first in the reigns of the Arsacid Parthians, then under the Sassanians, also left its traces upon the northern Mesopotamian and east Syrian landscape.

DURA-EUROPOS ON THE EUPHRATES

SUSAN MATHESON

AROUND 300 B.C. A MILITARY COLONY CALLED EUROPOS WAS FOUND-
ed by Nikanor, a general in the army of Seleucus I and governor of the
territory of Syria. The new settlement was situated on a plateau on
the west bank of the Euphrates River, bordered north and south by
ravines (see Fig. 71). It was an easily defensible position, vulnerable
only on its western side where it faced the desert, and its natural
defenses were reinforced early on by a massive wall with guard
towers encircling the city. A high area on the eastern side of the city
was also walled in to create a citadel. Farmland stretched along the
Euphrates' bank to the north and south of the town, irrigated by water
from the river.

The settlers in the new colony were Macedonian soldiers, veterans
of the wars of Alexander the Great and, after his death, the wars
among his successors who fought for control of his empire. Each
veteran was given land, which he could use and pass on to his heirs,
but to which was tied compulsory military service in the Seleucid
army for as long as the land remained in the veteran's family. These
Macedonians comprised the ruling class at Hellenistic Europos,
bringing their cultural institutions to the indigenous Aramaean population. The official language and the legal system were both Greek, as
indicated by a law governing the inheritance of property inscribed on
a papyrus document found in the city.

Although little survives of early Europos, certain Hellenistic features can be identified by analogy to other better-preserved Greek
cities in the Seleucid kingdom. The most obvious is the plan of the
city, a grid plan around a central agora (marketplace). Commercial
buildings defined the north side of the agora, while temples dedicated to the Greek gods bordered it to the south. Cults of Artemis,
Apollo, and Zeus had been established by the second century B.C.

HELLENISTIC AND ROMAN PERIODS

Figure 71
Aerial view of Dura-Europos.

From the scanty remains of the Seleucid Artemis temple, it appears to have been Greek in form, with an open rectangular courtyard inside a Doric colonnade, a monumental gate, and an altar in the center of the precinct. Pottery associated with this level of the temple suggests a date in the earliest phase of the city's history. Also at this time palaces were built on the citadel and on a second piece of high ground, called the Redoubt. Little else is known about the architecture of Hellenistic Europos.

Europos remained a Seleucid military colony until around 113 B.C., when it was integrated into the expanding Parthian empire. Parthian control of its territories was relatively loose, and cities like Europos retained a substantial degree of autonomy. This leniency, coupled with a certain Parthian philhellenism—manifested, for example, in their adoption of Greek as their official language—permitted the continuation of the Seleucid forms of civic administration and law at Europos, with the descendants of the original Macedonian settlers, who called themselves *Europaoi*, still serving as the local ruling class and aristocracy. Worship of the official gods of the Seleucid dynasty also continued.

In fact, these elements of Greek culture were merely a veneer on the surface of an increasingly orientalized city. During the two and a half centuries of Parthian control, the economic climate, the religious environment, the visual appearance, and even the name of the city changed to reflect a new balance in the population. The Greek name for the city, Europos, while still in use in official documents, was largely replaced in graffiti and other casual inscriptions by the name Dura, an Aramaic word meaning "fortress," which obviously reflected local perception of the city's role. The old Macedonian aristocracy, intermarried with the local Aramaean inhabitants, was superseded as the dominant cultural force by the far larger native population. The agriculturally based military colony became a busy and prosperous market town, an important stop on the caravan route connecting the Persian Gulf and Seleucia on the Tigris with Palmyra, Antioch, and the Mediterranean Sea.

The first signs of change occurred in the agora: houses and shops multiplied in number and were crowded together along small winding streets that completely broke up the regularity and openness of the Hellenistic marketplace. The beginning of this progressive filling in of the agora can be dated by associated pottery finds to the end of the second century B.C. The result was a covered oriental bazaar, or suq, probably quite similar in appearance to those seen in the Middle East today. Some relatively elaborate houses were built around the agora and near the residence of the Parthian governor on the Redoubt. A landslide destroyed much of the citadel in the first century B.C., and it is apparent that whatever government functions were served by the citadel palace were transferred to the Redoubt palace.

A considerable amount of newly acquired wealth was devoted to the building and renovation of temples. Nowhere is the rise to cultural prominence of the local population so evident as it is in the dedications, the architectural style, and the painting and sculpture of these temples.

The religious life of Dura was complex, dominated by three great goddesses. Artemis, whose temple had been among the earliest built, was clearly the original great goddess, and she apparently continued to be worshipped in her Greek form throughout the city's history. Perhaps because she retained her Greek identity, two other goddesses, Atargatis and Azzanathkona, who were more oriental in character, were brought to Dura and given temples in the first century A.D. Atargatis, purely Syrian, who was the chief goddess of the city of Hierapolis, appears to have been equal in importance to Artemis; names and genealogies of women from prominent Dura families appear in dedicatory inscriptions in the temples of both goddesses. The relation of the Dura Atargatis cult to that at Hierapolis is evident in the cult relief from the Atargatis temple (Fig. 72), which reflects in its essentials the three cult images from the shrine at Hierapolis as they are understood from literary evidence (Lucian *De Dea Syria* 31–33) and representations on coins.

Atargatis' temple was begun in A.D. 31, immediately adjacent to the Artemis Temple. Both were oriental in plan, the Artemis Temple having been rebuilt after it was destroyed by fire around the middle of

Figure 72
Cult relief of Atargatis and Hadad,
from Dura-Europos.

the first century B.C. A walled temple complex *(temenos)* with a single or primary entrance enclosed an open courtyard with the main sanctuary *(naos)* at its rear, opposite the entrance. Small shrines or chapels lined the interior of the temenos wall, dedicated by individual donors over the life of the temple, sometimes to gods other than the sanctuary's major deity. Varying in shape according to the demands of its location, this basic plan characterized the eight new temples built at Dura in the Parthian period, among them the temple of Dura's third great goddess, Azzanathkona.

The goddess Azzanathkona is known only at Dura, and the meaning of the name is uncertain. Dedicatory inscriptions in her temple date from as early as A.D. 31, and later inscriptions show that she was identified with Artemis. The cult relief from her temple, however, showing her seated on a throne between two lions with her hand raised in an oriental gesture of blessing, clearly indicates that she is one of the Syrian mother goddesses. The worship of a Greek goddess from the Seleucid era, a Syrian goddess from one of the great Near Eastern cult centers, and a purely local version of the great goddess is characteristic of the variety of religious experience at Dura.

Evidence for close cultural contact between Dura and Palmyra is found in the dedications of three temples at Dura to gods specifically associated with Palmyra. A temple in the desert outside the main gate was built by two Palmyrene residents for Bel and Yarhibol, according to a Palmyrene inscription of 33 B.C; while a second temple, near the agora and dating from before the first century A.D, is identified as the Temple of the Gaddé, or Fortunes, from a pair of reliefs dedicated by a Palmyrene named Hairan in A.D 159. The third Palmyrene temple, and the most important, is the temple of Bel, in the northwest corner of the city. The walls of this temple were filled with paintings from the Parthian and subsequent Roman periods showing scenes of devotees sacrificing with incense to the Palmyrene triad of divinities: Bel, Yarhibol, and Aglibol. Significant as evidence for the religious history of Dura, these paintings and similar examples from other temples also provide a glimpse of the appearance and dress of Dura's inhabitants.

Armed gods played an important role at Dura, and these may once again reflect the influence of nearby Palmyra and the settlements around it. Gods wearing a Hellenistic or Roman cuirass, sometimes with Parthian trousers, appear frequently in painting and sculpture dedicated by Palmyrenes in Dura's temples; these images presumably follow Palmyrene traditions. Representations of Arsu, Yarhibol, and Aphlad are in this group. In contrast to these cuirassed deities are the gods in indigenous dress and armament, wearing a tunic and mantle and carrying a spear, a small round shield, often a bow and arrow and sword. Some of these gods can be identified, including Arsu, Asheru, and Sa'ad, while others are anonymous; most appear to be Arab gods, local armed protectors of the nomads, worshipped in rustic shrines in the Palmyrene settlements. They are often appropriately mounted on horseback or camel. Their popularity at Dura was probably encouraged by the need for protection of the caravan trade that supported the city's prosperity.

At no time in Dura's history could it be considered a major artistic center. With the exception of architecture, little of the Greco-Roman style which characterized so much of the art of Antioch reached Palmyra, let alone Dura, and the mediocre quality of much of its art prevents meaningful comparison with the impressive sculptures from other Parthian cities. Art at Dura was almost solely in the service of religion, and the strictly frontal style that characterizes Dura's painting and sculpture, a style totally lacking in concern for movement or anatomical accuracy, was particularly suitable for religious iconography. The influence of Palmyrene art on that of Dura is strong, as can be seen not only in the close relation of their sculptural styles but also in the use of Palmyrene limestone and in the presence of Palmyrene artists' signatures on scuplture found in Dura's temples.

Dura remained under Parthian control until the second century A.D. The city's position on the disputed border between the Parthian and Roman empires made it the object of attempted military take-overs and a pawn in diplomatic negotiations; it was taken briefly by the emperor Trajan and his forces ca. A.D. 113 but returned to the Parthians by his successor, Hadrian. Dura was finally captured in 165 by a Roman force commanded by Lucius Verus, and it remained under Roman control until it fell to the Sassanian king Shapur I after a siege in A.D. 256, ending the history of settlement at the site.

The Romans installed a garrison at Dura, strengthened under Septimius Severus around A.D. 211, which appropriated the northern third of the city for its camp. Civilian inhabitants were displaced and forced into increasingly crowded residential areas south of the old agora, while new baths, administrative buildings, and temples were built by the Romans in the northern sector. The old Seleucid forms of local government, which had survived throughout the Parthian period, were replaced by Roman law, and Dura became a military outpost and finally a colony on the eastern border of the Roman Empire.

Certain aspects of Parthian Dura remained, however. Worship of the official Roman pantheon was required for the soldiers, but the civilian population continued to worship the Seleucid, Palmyrene, and other Syrian gods as they had under Parthian rule. New, if small, communities of Christians and Jews grew up in Dura in the late second century A.D. Each of these two congregations adapted a private house as a place of worship, decorating the new synagogue (now reconstructed in the National Museum, Damascus) and the Christian baptistery with remarkable wall paintings of biblical subjects. Members of a Palmyrene contingent in the Roman garrison erected a shrine to the Persian god Mithras, which they decorated with paintings of scenes from the god's life. The use of figured wall paintings in these unusual contexts at Dura appears to have been stimulated by the local artistic tradition seen in the Parthian temples of Bel and Zeus Theos and probably reflects a particular unorthodoxy among the members of these religious communities.

The large majority of the artifacts discovered at Dura during the excavations carried out by Yale University and the French Académie des Inscriptions et Belles Lettres in the 1920s and 1930s date from the Roman occupation. This is particularly true of the small finds, including rarely preserved items like textiles, leather shoes, and baskets, as well as the more common pottery, glass, and coins. These finds, along with papyrus documents dealing with both civic and military matters, give an unusually detailed picture of life in an eastern Roman province, a picture which indicates that indigenous Syrian cultural traditions remained strong.

Recommended Reading

C. Hopkins. *The Discovery of Dura-Europos* (New Haven: Yale University Press, 1979).

S. Matheson. *Dura-Europos* (New Haven: Yale University Art Gallery, 1982).

A. Perkins. *The Art of Dura-Europos* (Oxford: Oxford University Press, 1973).

M.I. Rostovtzeff. *Dura-Europos and Its Art* (Oxford: Oxford University Press, 1938).

ROME IN SYRIA

F. E. PETERS

IN ITS MATURITY THE ROMAN EMPIRE WAS COMPOSED OF A SERIES OF administrative units called provinces, which stretched from Britain and Morocco on the west to what was called Mesopotamia (much of modern Iraq) on the east. The empire was in fact a conglomerate, centrally and often loosely controlled by the emperor and his bureaucracy in Rome, locally administered by a Roman provincial governor, and protected by Roman legions stationed within the provinces. The prevailing policy was pacification and prosperity; its chief instruments were the Roman army, Roman law, and urbanization.

None of the provinces was a charter member of the Roman state; each had to be acquired in one fashion or another, and Syria was added to this complex political organism called the Roman Empire before its maturity, and indeed before there was an empire at all. The dynamically expanding Italian city-state of Rome was drawn into the Near East by the collapse of the old regimes descended from Alexander the Great and his Greco-Macedonian generals in the fourth century B.C.—Ptolemy in Egypt and Seleucus and his successors in the area that stretched from the Mediterranean to the Pamirs. By the first pre-Christian century these latter dynasts were no longer capable of sustaining themselves against their own populations, predatory warlords, the rising Parthians to the east, or even against the pirates who were infesting the eastern Mediterranean and disrupting the commerce upon which all of them, and Rome besides, had grown rich.

The Romans had little tolerance for pirates on their sea-lanes or for a power vacuum in the Near East, and after years of absent but nonetheless real intervention in the eastern Mediterranean, the Roman senate in 67 B.C. vested one of its premier generals with a limited military mandate, an *imperium*, to clear out the pirates in the coves around southern Turkey. The *imperator* Pompey accomplished his mission and then in 66 B.C. was given a more extended command covering most of western Anatolia, where new successes drew him deeper into the disintegrating affairs of the Seleucids. By the time Pompey returned to Rome it had become—neither willingly nor quite unwillingly—the successor state to the Seleucid kingdom and its assorted clients in Syria and Palestine and of course the inheritor of its enemies, debts, and problems as well.

Thus Syria became a Roman province, and not the least of them; indeed, it was one of the brightest jewels in the chaplet of provinces that ringed the Roman Mediterranean. For the Seleucids Syria was a conquest squandered, a rich land they had made richer and then could not hold through their own ineffectiveness. It would be many centuries before Rome would suffer such political debility, and so for them Syria became what it was in the process of becoming before the end of the Seleucid regime, a prosperous land resplendent with that finest of eastern Hellenic products—the city.

The Romans promoted urbanization, and in Syria their cities extended and adorned the Seleucid foundations. Alexander the Great had a reputation as a city-builder in antiquity, but it was actually his Seleucid successors who did the building, planted the colonies, and installed in their Syrian heartland the municipal institutions that sum up in concrete and practical form the ideals of Hellenism. The Romans were Hellenes in the same sense: they affirmed municipal autonomy and self-government and they fostered the political and cultural institutions that made the process possible—a curia of local citizens, municipal magistrates, the rule of law. The governor of a Roman province cared for provincial security, collected the imperial taxes, and administered Roman justice; the cities ruled themselves and their immediate agricultural hinterlands.

From the first to the third Christian centuries, notably in the second, the Romans built and enlarged in Syrian land through outright imperial endowment, but just as often through local landowners who continued to share the Greco-Roman ideal of private investment in the public good, particularly in the form of civic and municipal amenities. Syria was, and remains even today, a land of temples, theaters, and baths: from the great sanctuaries of Baal at Palmyra and of Jupiter at Baalbek and Damascus, to the magnificent 17,000-seat theater at Bostra and such jewel-like creations as the nymphaeum and odeon at Qanawat, the exquisite temples at Atil, Sanamayn, and Dumayr, and the intimate, almost miniature, playhouse at Palmyra.

Some complexes rose directly from imperial intent, like that built at what had been Shuhba, a village which had the fortune to be the birthplace of the Emperor Philip (A.D. 243–249) and so predictably became Philippopolis. The Romans quickly redid the place—"the Romans" invariably meaning the Roman army, which in Syria spent far more of its time and energies on the construction of public works than in military campaigning. They followed the customary rectangular city plan with main and cross streets at right angles, a temple to the deified imperial family, an elaborate hall of justice, splendid baths supplied by a new aqueduct, and, as a sure reflection of the agricultural wealth that surrounded the place, sumptuous villas decorated in the high and sure style of Roman mosaicists.

Many of the Romans' urban showplaces are buried under modern cities: Roman Damascus, Beirut, and Aleppo are only barely discernible under their contemporary descendants, while Emesa and Epiphania have all but disappeared under the cities today called Homs and Hama. We can scarcely recognize Antioch, one of the Mediterranean's great Greco-Roman metropolises, through the ravages that wars, earthquakes, and malaria have wrought upon that city, but others are still fresh and astonishing through their ruins: Cyrrhus and Apamaea in northern Syria, Palmyra out on the great Syrian steppe, and Bostra, the present-day Busra-eski Sham, in the south.

And also in the south, on the plains and slopes around the Jebel Druze, we have the physical clues to the sources of the wealth that made Syria one of the most dazzling provinces of the Roman Empire at its height. Scattered around the countryside, standing solitary amidst rich fields of grain or near the centers of modest villages, are the remains of country villas whose construction and decor still bespeak the very best that the Romans ever did with chisel and stone. These were the houses of rich landowners, men who profited from what one ancient source called a land "overflowing with grain, wine and oil." The Romans husbanded and cultivated the natural resources of a rich soil and adequate rainfall and even extended it beyond nature's own limits. Through careful water management and a combination of natural and artificial irrigation they pushed the limits of the arable land eastward onto the steppe, even to places where it does not extend today.

The high-quality Syrian grain was consumed by the growing urban population of the province and by the legions and auxiliaries stationed there; Syrian wine and olive oil were exported in bulk around the empire; and for the luxury trade Syrian fruits, ointments, and unguents were available. Textiles were woven and dyed in Syria, chiefly at Tyre, which had a near monopoly on the process, and likewise exported. Roman imperial taxes were primarily on land and its produce, so some part of the province's agricultural wealth was skimmed off in taxes and kind for the empire's needs and pleasures. But the base remained sound and stable for centuries, and there was enough profit to circulate through the cities and towns and support—in a rich and attractive style—the Romans and the Romanized landowners and artisans who lived there. As the elegant ruins testify, Syrian life was unmistakably the good life in the second century A.D. One legion went into open revolt when threatened with a change of post from Syria to Germany.

The Seleucids were the original Hellenizers and colonizers in Syria; the Romans built deeper and broader and higher. The Seleucids were a regional power; the Romans an international one. Just as Romans of whatever nationality came to live, trade, or serve in Syria, so Syrians began to move out and back along that same international network of commerce and administration and make their own colonies in other provinces of the empire. Syrians traded in France, served in the army in Tunisia and along the Danube, and brought their food, their customs, and their local cults—one of them Christianity—with them. Syrians even ruled in Rome itself: in the third century a powerful priestly family of Emesa clothed itself in imperial purple and a Syrian Arab presided as emperor over Rome's celebration of the millennium of its own foundation.

These men and women had to some extent become Romans, by status as Roman citizens and by culture as members of the ecumenical world of shared Greco-Roman values and ideals. That world had two official languages in the East: Greek, the *lingua franca* of the trade in goods and ideas, and Latin, the language of Roman administration and the military. Behind them, so muted that we cannot catch it at first, was a third language and culture which neither disappeared nor was assimilated by the more public, official, and prestigious Hellenism—the Syriac. This local Syro-Aramaic culture did not find the full range of its literary voice until Christianity gave it tongue in the fourth century, but it was there all the time. In the countryside surely, but even in the large cities there was a significant number of the population who continued to speak their native Semitic Aramaic.

Some Syrians—the peasant population in the hinterland, for instance—were completely untouched by the high Greco-Roman culture of the cities; but there was also a local Syrian intelligentsia who knew and adopted Roman ways without losing their own. We can see them, for example, in the local artists who decorated the lintels and jambs of Roman temples in Syria with luxuriant designs of vines and grapes whose rich but controlled profusion owes nothing to Hellas or Rome. We can observe them in the funerary portraits of Palmyra, where proud and assured Syrian faces still stare back at us from beneath their eastern finery. They stand calmly in their priestly robes in the temple frescoes from Dura-Europos. Their extraordinary religious practices tumble forth from Lucian's literary sketch of the lives of Syrian fakirs in the second century or Eunapius' fourth-century collection of the biographies of Syrian philosophers, magicians, and theurgists, some of whom would have been completely at home in Athens, while others dwelled an infinite distance from the cool slopes of Hellenic Olympus or the stately processions of Rome. The early Christians railed against those Syrian pagans, but all of them—ascetics, magicians, and priests—eventually found their place in Syrian Christianity as well.

For us, as for the Romans, Syria represented the best that the provincial system could produce in the high empire. There was peace behind secure natural frontiers and under the protection of the Roman army. The cities of Syria with their flourishing trades and crafts were rich in material goods, and the process of syncretistic assimilation to the ideals of Hellenism produced a local culture that, like the local art, was easy and assured with the already "classical" past and redolent of the norms and motifs of an eastern present and a still distant Islamic future. Under the Romans Syrian culture, whether in letters, religion, or the plastic arts, was provincial in the best sense: it spoke in the *koine* of the empire but in accents that were unmistakably and attractively Syrian.

Recommended Reading

F. Heichelheim. "Roman Syria" in T. Frank (ed.). *An Economic Survey of Ancient Rome* IV (Baltimore: Johns Hopkins University Press, 1938).

Philip Hitti. *History of Syria, Including Lebanon and Palestine* (New York: Macmillan, 1951).

Horst Klengel. *The Art of Ancient Syria* (South Brunswick and New York: Barnes, 1972).

M. I. Rostovtzeff. *Social and Economic History of the Roman Empire*. 2 vols. (2nd ed. Oxford: Oxford University Press, 1957).

PALMYRA: THE CARAVAN CITY

ADNAN BOUNNI

PALMYRA

Location: Oasis 150 km east of Homs, 170 km southwest of Raqqa, at the Jebel Bishri

Date: Fourth century B.C. to third century A.D. (textual references as early as nineteenth century B.C.)

Excavations: Field research from 1751 (see text for history of excavations)

Publications:

General: J. Dawkins and R. Wood *The Ruins of Palmyra* (London 1753) // B. Mortiz "Zur antiken Topographie der Palmyrene" *Abhandlungen der Konigl. preuss. Akademie der Wissenschaften zu Berlin* (1889) // W. Wright *An Account of Palmyra and Zenobia* (New York 1895) // H. Ingholt *Studier over palmyrensk skulptur* (Copenhagen 1928) / *Two Unpublished Tombs from the Southwest Necropolis of Palmyra, Syria* (Beirut 1974) // Th. Wiegand *Palmyra* (Berlin 1932) // R. Pfister *Textiles de Palmyre découverts par le Service des antiquités* (Paris 1934) / *Nouveaux textiles de Palmyre* (Paris 1937) // Daniel Schlumberger (with H. Ingholt et al.) *La Palmyrène du nord-ouest* (Paris 1951) // J. Starcky *Palmyra* (Paris 1952) / *Palmyra: bilan et perspectives* (Colloque de Strasbourg 18–20 Oct. 1973, Université des sciences humaines de Strasbourg, Centre de recherche sur le Proche Orient et la Grece antique, 3 (Strasbourg 1976) // K. Michalowski et al. *Palmyra: Fouilles polonaises* I–VII (Warsaw 1960–1977) / *Palmyra* (New York 1970) // A. Bounni *al-Fann at-Tadmuri* (Damascus 1963) / *Le sanctuaire de Nabu* (Damascus 1982) // P. Collart and J. Vicari *Le sanctuaire de Baalshamin à Palmyre* I–VI (Neuchatel 1969–1975) // H. Seyrig, R. Amy, and E. Will *Le temple de Bel à Palmyra* (Paris 1975) // M. A. R. Colledge *The Art of Palmyra* (London 1976) // H. J. W. Drijvers *The Religion of Palmyra* (Leiden 1976) // H. Stern *Les mosaiques des maisons d'Achille et de Cassiopée à Palmyre* (Paris 1977) // I. Browning *Palmyra* (London 1979) // J. Teixidor *The Pantheon of Palmyra* (Leiden 1979)

Inscriptions: C. J. M. Vogüée *Syria centrale. Inscriptions semitiques* (Paris 1868–1877) // J.-B. Chabot *Choix d'inscriptions de Palmyre* (Paris 1922) // J. Cantineau *Inventaire des inscriptions de Palmyre* I–IX (Beirut 1930–1936) / *Grammaire de palmyrenien épigraphique* (Paris 1935) // F. Rosenthal *Die Sprache der palmyrenischen Inschriften und ihre Stellung innerhalb des aramaischen* (Leipzig 1936) // J. Starcky *Inventaire des inscriptions de Palmyre* X (Damascus 1949) // J. Teixidor *Inventaire des inscriptions de Palmyre* XI (Beirut 1965) // J. K. Stark *Personal Names in Palmyrene Inscriptions* (Oxford 1971) // A. Bounni and J. Teixidor *Inventaire des inscriptions de Palmyre* XII (Damascus 1975)

The oasis at Palmyra, sustained by a sulfurous spring rising out of a limestone ravine, was a regularly visited rest stop and caravan station for the traffic between Syria and Mesopotamia. The etymology of its ancient name, Tadmor, is unknown. By Greco-Roman times the oasis was called Palmyra, perhaps because of the extensive palm groves there.

Under the name Tadmor, Palmyra is known from inscriptions of the second millennium B.C. through the Assryian archives of merchants stationed at Kültepe (ancient Kanesh) on the Anatolian plateau. Slightly later the name recurs on the clay tablets from Mari, and in the fourteenth and thirteenth centuries B.C. it appears on a clay document from Emar (Meskene). The annals of Tiglath-pileser I mention the town about 1100 B.C.

Remains of older settlements, including the ancient Tadmor, perhaps lie under the 200-by-200-meter enclosure of the Temple of Bel (Fig. 73). The buildings of the Hellenistic city, which flourished here from the fourth century B.C.,

Figure 73
The Temple of Bel at Palmyra.

are seriously damaged, mainly because of new constructions of the first century A.D. Most of the visible structures, which extend over more than 12 square kilometers, date from the first three Christian centuries.

Syria became a Roman province in 63 B.C. Palmyra, however, maintained its independence as an Arabian principality and enjoyed—according to Pliny the Elder[1]—a privileged position between the two large contending empires, Rome and Parthia. Both, it seems, were interested in protecting Palmyra. In 41 B.C. Marcus Antonius undertook a futile push toward the city. The Palmyrenes had, as Appian reports, gained a key trade and political position.[2] They procured exotic goods from India, Arabia, and Persia, then traded them to the Romans. When, precisely, Palmyra was amalgamated into the Roman state is a contested issue. Perhaps this occurred under Tiberius (A.D. 14–37), at which point the Roman Empire would have consolidated its control over Syria's trade routes and the ports of Syria, Egypt, and Anatolia.

In the second half of the first century A.D. Palmyra was occupied by a Roman garrison. The city's own famous archers, cavalry, and camel riders from the time of Trajan (A.D. 98–117) participated in the defense of the Empire's borders on the Danube, in England, and in Africa. In A.D. 106 after the fall of Petra, on the trade route from south Arabia to Syria, Palmyra became the most important trading center in the Orient. Its great prosperity was expressed in the restoration of old monumental buildings and the construction of temples. Under Hadrian (A.D. 117–138)

Palmyra achieved the status of a free city as Hadriana Palmyra and in the name of its "Council of Advisors and People" defined its own taxes and proclaimed its own decisions. Caracalla raised the city to the rank of a Roman colony in A.D. 212.

The founding of the Sassanian empire in A.D. 228 resulted in the loss of Palmyra's control over trade routes. The Palmyrenes then sought new economic opportunities under the leadership of a well-known Arabic family. Odainat, the head of this family, held the title of governor within the small province. In 262 and 267 he led two campaigns against the Sassanians, reaching as far as Ctesiphon, the Sassanian capital east of Baghdad. Odainat—the hope simultaneously of Palmyra and Rome—was murdered along with his older son under mysterious circumstances. Since his other son was too young to succeed him, his wife, Zenobia, took the post of regent. Highly intelligent, knowledgeable, and ambitious, Zenobia knew full well the political terrain of the Orient and the weaknesses of Rome. With the empire threatened from within and without, she did not hesitate to proclaim her independence of Rome. She soon conquered all of Syria, and her armies marched toward Egypt and Anatolia. The emperor Aurelian, forced to react quickly, defeated the Palmyrene army at Antioch and Emesa (Homs). Zenobia retreated to Palmyra, where Aurelian laid siege to her heavy defenses. Zenobia attempted to flee to the Sassanians but was caught and imprisoned in 272. In this critical situation the Palmyrenes rose up and massacred the occupying Roman garrison.

Aurelian's retaliation was devastating.

Palmyra's economic prosperity made it an important city in the ancient world. An oligarchical class of merchants and caravaneers amassed considerable riches by exacting high tolls from caravans. The luxurious life style of the Palmyrene aristocracy was displayed in its fondness for temples, palaces, collonaded streets, and statues which conferred a kind of immortality on the rich citizens they depicted (Fig. 74). Entertainment was provided by the theater, thermal baths, and banquets. Wealth was also expended on funerary monuments, such as tombs (Fig. 75) and ornamental sculpture of high quality (see Cat. Nos. 185–195).

Michael Rostovtzeff, the excavator of Dura, quite correctly identified it as "the city of carvans." The most "noble" of the Palmyrenes, free and prosperous, were the merchants, in particular the owners or leaders of caravans, which constituted the hub of the economic life of Palmyra. Indeed, Palmyrene social order, religious beliefs, and the worldview of its citizens were all products of the city's caravan economy.

By the seventeenth century, European travellers to the Orient were drawn to Palmyra. The Neapolitan Pietro della Valle (1616–1625), the Frenchman Jean-Baptiste Tavernier (1638), English merchants from Aleppo (1678, 1691), the Frenchmen Girod and Sautet (1705), and the Swede Cornelius Loos (1710) all visited the city. They returned to Europe with copies of inscriptions, drawings of ruins, and incredible travel stories.

The visit of two Englishmen—R. Wood and H. Dawkins—in 1751 had far-reaching effects. Their work, *The Ruins of Palmyra*, appeared in English and French in 1753 and signalled the beginning of Palmyra's systematic exploration. One year later, the Frenchman J. J. Barthelémy and the Englishman J. Swinton deciphered the Palmyrene alphabet. An ever-larger number of researchers then followed: L. F. Cassas, C. F. Volney, Ch. M. de Voguëé, R. Ker Porter. In 1861 W. H. Waddington copied a number of inscriptions. In 1870 the German A. D. Mordtmann edited several new texts, and E. Sachau, who visited the city in 1879, dedicated many articles to it.

In 1881 a Russian, S. A. Lazarew, discovered the tax laws of the city. Ten years later a Russian exploration group transported this important document to Russia, where today it is in the Hermitage Museum. The wall paintings of the chamber tomb of the "Three Brothers" were investigated then as well. In 1899 M. Sobernheim discovered a chamber tomb in the "Valley of the Tombs" and took the first photographs of Palmyra. Research on the entire city was begun in 1902 and reconstituted in 1917, under the direction of Th. Wiegand. A few isolated problems were researched,[3] while A. Musil—in 1908, 1912, and 1915—undertook explorations of the more distant reaches of the city.

In 1914 a project of the Académie des Inscriptions et Belles Lettres under the direction of A. Jaussen and R. Savignac copied all hitherto-known texts. These were subsequently published by J. B. Chabot. In 1924 and 1928 H. Ingholt initiated excavations in the western necropolis area. In 1929 A. Gabriel completed the first precise topographic plan of the city. New epigraphic research was undertaken by J. Cantineau which has continued through the work of J. Starcky in 1949, J. Teixidor in 1965, A. Bounni and J. Teixidor in 1975.

The large Temple of Bel (Fig. 73) was cleared in 1929–1930 by Henri Seyrig, who was then Director of the Antiquities Service of Syria and Lebanon. Together with the Director of the National Museum in Damascus, Prince Ja'far al-Hassani, Seyrig during 1934–1940 was the most important proponent of archaeological research at Palmyra. R. Amy, E. Will, M. Ecochard, R. Duru, and others undertook the excavations and reconstruction of the Temple of Bel, the chamber tomb

of Yarhai (Fig. 76), now exhibited in the National Museum, Damascus, the agora, the Villa Cassiopeia, and the Valley of the Tombs (Fig. 75). D. Schlumberger investigated the environs of Palmyra, and J. Starcky published the first comprehensive summary of Palmyrene research results.

After Syria achieved independence in 1946 national research at Palmyra escalated considerably. Selim Abdul-Hak excavated there in 1952 with Obeid Taha and Nazmi Kheir in the southeast necropolis. Beginning in 1957 Adnan Bounni, director of excavations for the Directorate-General of Antiquities, initiated what has become some twenty years of research at Palmyra. Nassib Saliby, Obeid Taha, and Khaled Assad have been his principal collaborators.

This most recent period of research has focused upon the Valley of the Tombs, the main street, the Temple of Nabu, the agora, the Nyphae A and B, and the Street of Baal-shamin. Important restoration work has been undertaken in the temples of Bel, Baal-shamin, and Nabu, the main street, the Tetrapylon, the Tomb Temple, and the north and west necropolises. These restorations were the work of several architects: W. Hariri, N. Khier, A. Moufti, R. Douhman, Y. Jabali, A.Ostrasz, and J. Seigne. All of the technical work was executed by the master mason Saleh Taha.

In the past few years Khaled Assad, Director of Antiquities and Museums for Palmyra, has worked with Ali Taha and Ahmed Taha on excavation and restoration, especially in the northern fortress, the main street, and the Temple of Arsu. Foreign archaeological mis-

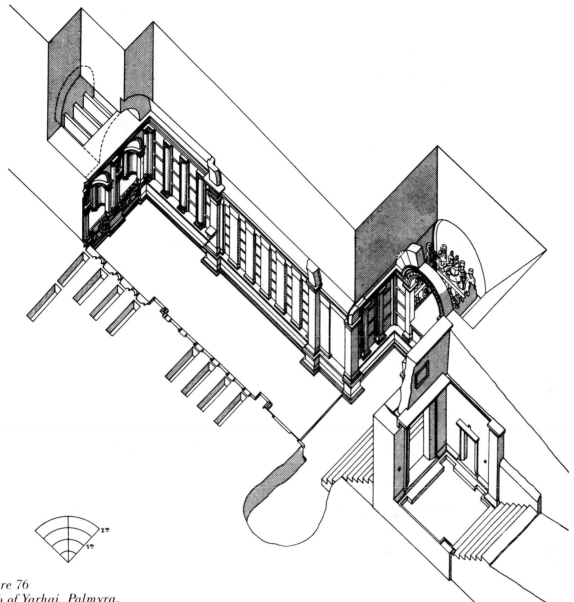

Figure 76
Tomb of Yarhai, Palmyra.

sions have been authorized by the
Syrian government to participate in
the excavations of several monuments: P. Collart and his Swiss colleagues worked on the Temple of
Baal-shamin in 1954–1956; since
1959 K. Michalowski has led his
Polish colleagues, followed by A.

Sadurska and M. Gawlikowski, in
the area of Diocletian's camp.
Comte du Mesnil du Buisson led
the 1966–1967 excavations in the
court of the Bel Temple and excavated the Temple of Bel-hamon and
of Manut on the peak of Jebel al-
Muntar.

ROMAN ART IN SYRIA

KLAUS PARLASCA

IN THE CENTURIES BEFORE AND AFTER THE BIRTH OF CHRIST THE Syrian realm comprised many political entities, petty principalities, and city-states of various size and significance. From the first century A.D. a strong centralizing process became evident, while local activity was still accommodated in the cultural sphere. Hieropolis (modern Membidj) became the central point for the veneration of the Syrian goddess, while further west, at Emesa, the Roman presence also generated considerable influence. The impressive military and trade center of Dura-Europos on the Euphrates enjoyed special status of another sort as the locus for many of the changes in the Syrian border. In addition to Dura-Europos, the exhibition *Ebla to Damascus* provides two other foci for Roman art in Syria: Palmyra and the southwestern Hauran region, which both display local self-reliance as well as supra-regional qualities in their artistic landscapes.

Palmyra presents to the modern observer an incomparable panorama. The city's ruins feature public buildings, temples, and tombs in equal measure. With the annexation of the Nabataean empire and its capital at Petra under the emperor Trajan in A.D. 107, Palmyra experienced an enormous economic upswing. The city flourished for more than a hundred years and then came to an abrupt end through the dynastic ambitions of its rulers, especially the famous Queen Zenobia, which brought about the destruction of the city of Aurelian in A.D. 276. The geographically strategic situation of Palmyra, however, protected it from complete annihilation. During the Byzantine period a certain afterbloom persisted, as several churches demonstrate, some even built in the city area proper.

In the realm of art, an important position is occupied by Palmyra's rich tomb sculpture, exemplified by Cat. Nos. 185–195. All of these sculptures come from subterranean tombs uncovered since the 1850s in either illicit robberies or systematic offical excavations. A number of projects sponsored by the Directorate General of Antiquities since World War II have revealed especially important monuments. These include a group of religious reliefs (Cat. Nos. 183, 184) as well as individual attempts at portrait sculpture (Cat. Nos. 196, 197). Since the second half of the first century, tomb sculpture has been a highly desirable commodity on the art market. As a result, the plunder of the cemeteries in late antiquity and in modern times has taken its toll. All the more important, therefore, is the testimony of the excavated pieces from the houses of wealthy citizens, including the richly figured cornice fragments shown in Cat. Nos. 198–203.

Within Palmyrene funerary art, the dominant relief portraits served as sealing stones of *loculi*, or burial slots, which in the tomb chambers were set in several rows against one another. This space-saving system was employed both in subterranean burial complexes *(hypogea)* and in funerary houses or tower tombs. In addition, there are reliefs on sarcophagi which provide thematic treatments of the customary funeral banquet. As a rule, the male deceased are depicted with seated deceased females (Cat. Nos. 189–191). Scenes clearly representing a death cult, such as a relief in Damascus with the deceased laid out on a bier, are quite uncommon.

The numerous funerary relief portraits supposedly represent the individuals named in their inscriptions. However, the number of actually individualized characteristics represented is very small, and the sculptured busts and reliefs seem limited to repetitions of general types. The male bust in Cat. No. 195 is one of the few exceptions; here the hair style and facial features are expressively rendered.

There were numerous other types of portraits besides stone funerary reliefs in Palmyra. The columns set along the streets (Fig. 74), in the temples, and in the agora featured shrines and bronze statues of which only a few remain. Other statues were manufactured of local limestone or imported marble. The artistic quality of the undoubtedly costly marble statues is surprisingly mediocre, giving the otherwise interesting Cat.No. 185 only limited artistic significance.

One of the special features of Palmyrene art is its presentation of the particular mixed culture of East and West. In the medium of sculpture this is particularly visible in the depiction of clothing fashions. For the most part men wear the Greek mantle of the eastern Roman Empire, while women are dressed in Oriental garb.

The relief busts of the deceased from Membidj (Cat. No. 204) and at Belkis (Seleucia in the Euphrates) have numerous parallels with Palmyrene sculpture, including contrasting Roman and Oriental dress for men and women. Here the relief portrait is also used as the cover for a sarcophagus, as at Palmyra. However, it is relatively easy to distinguish these reliefs from those of Palmyra, first of all by their inscriptions. At Palmyra, apart from a few bilingual inscriptions, the indigenous Aramaic language is used, whereas at Membidj and Belkis the inscriptions are exclusively Greek.

A second source of difference is the stone used. In Palmyra it is limestone, whereas basalt is prevalent in Membidj and Belkis. In relatively treeless Hauran, with its volcanic domes and lava fields, both the architecture and sculpture made extensive use of black basalt (see Cat. Nos. 207–209). The quality of these works is not outstanding, but the local workshops were nevertheless able to produce expressive sculpture.

In the sphere of stone sculpture, votive works were predominant, with depictions of either deities or dedicants. Their individual styles illustrate the different streams of Syrian art, classical elements mixing with Oriental motifs to form a kind of folk art. Votive sculpture is usually small in scale. Among the statuettes an Aphrodite with Eros seated on her shoulder is a popular type (Cat. No. 218). The relative frequency of this group suggests representation of a local Syrian cult.

High-quality glazed ceramics represent most of the imported materials found in Syria. This is true of the singular Hellenistic jug of the *lagynos* type (Cat. No. 224). It probably is derived from workshops in Asia Minor, like the goblet (Cat. No. 225) and the *skyphos* (Cat. No. 226). Although sherd finds document the spread of glazed ceramics from Asia Minor as far south as Petra, South Arabia, and Egypt, the distribution of vessels in private Damascus collections is probably a function of the art market.

183, right

183
Votive relief with Heracles and other gods

Site: Palmyra, Bel Temple
Date: 100–1 B.C.
Material: Yellowish limestone
Height: 22.5 cm; *width:* 35 cm
Museum No.: Damascus 4242/10050
Literature: H. Seyrig *Syria* 24 (1945) 62, 79, No. 1 Plate 1 =
   Antiquités syriennes 4 (Paris 1953) 1, 18, Plate 1 // M.
   Morehart *Berytus* 12 (1956–1957) 59, No. 10 Fig. 10 // R.
   du Mesnil du Buisson *Les tessères et les monnaies de
   Palmyra* (Paris 1962) 209, Fig. 140 // M. Gawlikowski
   Etudes et travaux (1) (Warsaw 1966) 149, Fig. 3 // H. Seyrig
   Syria 47 (1970) 107, Fig. 28 // E. Lukasiak *Studia
   palmyrenskie* 5 (Warsaw 1974) 17, Fig. 9 // M.A.R.
   Colledge *The Art of Palmyra* (London 1976) 45, Fig. 36 //
   H.J.W. Drijvers *The Religion of Palmyra* (Leiden 1976) 12,
   25, Plate 14 // J. Teixidor *The Pantheon of Palmyra* (Leiden
   1979) 113, 136, Plate 31:2

This unfinished relief was reused in antiquity and
found built into the wall of a well under the Bel Temple
in Palmyra. It depicts four standing deities. Heracles
is at the left, easily recognized by his attributes, a lion
skin and a club; perhaps he represents Nergal, the
equivalent of Heracles in ancient Near Eastern mythology. Next to him stands an unidentified female deity
with a halo around her head. Several suggestions as to
her identity have been put forward: Venus, Belti,
Astarte, Herta, Nanai. She is followed by two male
deities with curly hair, halos, and palm branches in
their right hands. The god to the left with a large crescent moon resting on top of his head is Aglibol, the
one to the right probably Yarhibol, the sun god. Originally the relief may have continued to the right, where
one would expect Bel, the ancient Baal, the main deity
of Palmyra, and possibly, as in other reliefs, "the
founder" (see Cat. No. 184).

On aesthetic grounds this relief belongs to the
provincial Palmyrene style in its most archaic
Hellenistic phase. The upper bodies and heads of all
four figures are presented strictly *en face*. The finely
modeled faces with their expressive large eyes and
carefully stylized coiffures and beards sharply contrast with the sketchy carving of the clothes.
K.P.

184
Votive relief with Allat and Shamash

Site: Khirbat Wadi Suana, Diabal al-Bal'as
Date: Ca. A.D. 150
Material: White limestone
Height: 28 cm; *width:* 34 cm
Museum No.: Damascus 2605/5216
Literature: D. Schlumberger *La Palmyrene du nord-ouest*
   (Paris 1951) 70, 117, Plate 31:1 // Abdul-Hak Catalogue
   (1951) 31, No. 6 Plate 12:1 // J. Wais *Studia palmyrenskie* 4
   (Warsaw 1970) 50, Fig. 45 // M.A.R. Colledge *The Art of
   Palmyra* (London 1976) 49, Fig. 39 // H.J.W. Drijvers *The
   Religion of Palmyra* (Leiden 1976) 20,33, Plate 56:1 /
   Hommages à M. Vermaseren 1 (Leiden 1978) 333 No. c,
   Plate 65 // H. Seyrig *Syria* 48 (1971) 349

This relief was found in a small rural shrine 58 kilometers northwest of Palmyra. The goddess Allat,
equivalent to Athena, stands to the left. Her clothes
and attributes are similar to those of the Greek model,
especially the shield, helmet, and spear. A Medusa-
head forms the center piece of her aegis, the goatskin
which covers her upper body. In the middle of the triad
we recognize the sun god Shamash holding a burning
torch in his left hand, while the right is raised in a
blessing gesture. He is dressed in a long-sleeved tunic
and a robe which covers his back and is fastened with
a brooch on the right shoulder, like the Greek
chlamys. He wears a diadem and has a halo around
his head. To the right of Shamash stands "the founder" dressed in a long-sleeved chiton and a robe, the
edge of which he holds in his left hand. He makes a
votive incense offering on a small altar on a stand with
his right hand. His fashionable hair style and his
beard date the relief to the reign of Hadrian (A.D.
76–138), or to the beginning of the reign of his successor, Antonius Pius. From a number of similar desert shrine reliefs we know that the goddess Allat was
especially popular among the Arabic population.
Shamash, as well as Yarhibol and Malakbel, the third
sun god in the Palmyrene pantheon, were also worshiped in the surrounding areas from Emesa (Homs) in
the west to Hatra in the northeast.
K.P.

184, right

185
Tomb relief of a seated girl

Site: Palmyra
Date: A.D. 1–100
Material: White limestone
Height: 41 cm; *width:* 36 cm
Museum No.: Damascus 24
Literature: M.A.R. Colledge *The Art of Palmyra* (London 1976) 244, No. 3c

Judging from its proportions, this relief probably served as the seal of a tomb, like many other portrait reliefs. A small girl, dressed in a beltless long-sleeved chiton, sits on an upholstered stool. She wears two thick necklaces and long earrings ending in beads. Her hair is combed back and covered by a flat turban. She holds a dove in front of her chest with her left hand, a gesture used exclusively in depictions of deceased children. Behind her is a piece of suspended cloth, also indicating death. Her posture is somewhat stiff, in spite of the right hand under her cheek. Large staring eyes give her round face a stern look. Typologically this sculpture is unique: apparently it belongs to a relatively early group of tomb reliefs that show the deceased in full figure, usually standing rather than sitting.

K.P.

186
Tomb relief of a standing woman

Site: Palmyra, Tomb of Ta'ai
Date: A.D. 100–120
Material: White limestone
Height: 62 cm; *width:* 25 cm
Museum No.: Damascus 18798
Literature: S. Abdul-Hak *AAAS* 2 (1952) 243, No. 34; 249, Plates 11:2, 265, Plate 4:2

This beautiful representation of a young noblewoman, with its carefully rendered details, idealizes Palmyrene women's fashions. The woman is dressed in a chiton decorated with ribbons on the front and on the sleeves, interspersed with carefully stitched pleats; her outer robe is belted and fastened on the left shoulder. Her hair is covered with a large shawl reaching the ground; the edge of the shawl she holds with her right hand, while her left arm is partly covered by it.

185, left

ca. 330 B.C.–A.D. 400

189

Funerary sculpture of a couple

Site: Palmyra
Date: A.D. 100–150
Material: White limestone
Height: 55 cm; *width:* 94 cm
Museum No.: Damascus 19
Literature: H. Ingholt *Studier over palmyrensk Skulptur*
(Copenhagen 1928) 94, No. PS 62 / *Berytus* 2 (1935) 68,
Plate 28:1 // Abdul-Hak *Catalogue* (1951) 30 No. 4 Plate
10:2 // Zouhdi *Catalogue* (1976) 124 // H. J. W. Drijvers
The Religion of Palmyra (Leiden 1976) 22, 37 Plate 76

188, left

Originally this group was a high relief with a semi-
circular background, positioned over a door inside a
subterranean tomb. The reclining figure, who represents the deceased, rests his left elbow on a pillow. He
wears typical Parthian clothes—long pants with wide
decorative borders, a short shirt, a chlamyslike robe,
and wide protective leggings below the knees, fastened with some sort of garters. This outfit was developed by Parthian horsemen in Iran. The wreath with a
miniature portrait of a priest indicates the deceased's
occupation.

In typical fashion, his wife sits in an armchair to the

192

192
Funerary relief of Nebula

Site: Palmyra, Tomb of Ta'ai
Date: A.D. 125–150
Material: White limestone
Height: 50 cm; *width:* 42 cm
Museum No.: Damascus 18797
Literature: S. Abdul-Hak *AAAS* 2 (1952) 240, No. 29, Plate
  4:2, 265 Plate 4:2 // Gawlikowski *Recueil* 11 No. 16

According to the Palmyrene inscription, this is a portrait of Nebula, son of Ma'nu, son of Ta'ai. The deceased wears a chiton and a robe draped over the left
shoulder—Greek garments also widely worn in the
Eastern provinces of the Roman Empire. The hair
style, with long strands hanging down the back, is Oriental, as is the beard and the long moustache. In his
left hand he holds a *schedula*, a strip of paper used for
writing legal documents, which may indicate his occupation as a businessman or a scribe. His only jewel
is a ring with a stone which he wears on the little finger of the left hand. The cloth hung behind him indicates that he is the deceased. Unlike many other such
portraits, therefore, this relief was made after his
death. The style and the fashion of the beard together
with the less rigid rendering of the eyes indicate a date
in the second quarter of the second century A.D.
K.P.

193
Funerary relief of Aliyat

Site: Palmyra, southeastern necropolis, Hypogeum 2
Date: A.D. 125–150
Material: White limestone
Height: 59 cm; *width:* 49 cm
Museum No.: Damascus 7444
*Literature: Deuxième exposition des découvertes
  archéologiques des années 1954–1955 . . . au Musée
  National de Damas* (Damascus n.d.) 38, No. 10

In this relief the woman, who turns slightly to the
right, is wearing a long-sleeved chiton made of relatively heavy material and a shawl which she holds with
her left hand; with her right hand she grasps its edge.
A cloth, indicating death, is hung behind her. Her jewelry consists of a thick twisted necklace with a round
pendant, a thin chain, wide braided bracelets, and two
rings on her right hand. The lack of a turban, head-

193, right

This fragment was no doubt part of a wall relief decorating a tomb. It had a richly profiled frame on the top
and sides. The deceased was the main figure, as is indicated by the remnants of the Palmyrene inscription.
Next to him stood the figure of a small girl dressed in
a chiton with a wide tasseled shawl over her shoulders. Her rich jewelry is striking: a necklace with pendants of two moon crescents and a sun disk, earrings,
and two elaborately braided bracelets. Her hair is
gathered close to the head, and she has a small braid,
which indicates that she is quite young. The rich jewelry tells us that she is the daughter of the house, not
a servant.
K.P.

HELLENISTIC AND ROMAN PERIODS

band, and headdress is unusual.[1] The slightly waved hair is parted in the middle. This simple hair style is reminiscent of coiffures from the Hadrian period. The Palmyrene inscription in the upper right corner names the deceased: Aliyat, daughter of Taimarsu, son of Mogim.

K.P.

[1]The few comparison pieces were published by H. Ingholt *Berytus* 3 (1936) 114, and in "Parthian Sculptures from Hatra" *Memoirs of the Connecticut Academy of Arts and Sciences* 12 (1954) 11.

194
Funerary relief of Aqmat

Site: Palmyra, western necropolis, Tomb of Shalamallat
Date: A.D. 150–200
Material: White limestone
Height: 60.5 cm; *width:* 50 cm
Museum No.: Palmyra B 1758/6582
Literature: A. Bounni and N. Saliby *AAAS* 7 (1957) 47
   No. 12, Plate 3:2 in Arabic // A. Bounni *AAAS* 11–12
   (1961–1962) 156, No. 14 // Gawlikowski *Recueil* 20, No. 37

This portrait shows the idealized features of a woman dressed in a chiton with a shawl covering her head. She wears a turban under which a headband or diadem covers the hair. At the temples long strands of hair are combed back and tucked into the turban. Besides the headband her only jewelry is a small double ring on the little finger of her left hand, in which she holds a spool and a spindle. Her right hand pulls the shawl forward on the left shoulder, creating an assymmetrical effect. According to the Palmyrene inscription, this is the deceased Aqmat, daughter of Hairan, son of Bonnur, and the mother of Nebozabad, son of Barikai.

K.P.

195
Funerary relief of a male

Site: Palmyra
Date: A.D. 225–250
Material: White limestone
Height: 48 cm; *width:* 39 cm
Museum No.: Damascus 8769

Behind the male figure, dressed in a Greek robe, hangs the cloth which indicates that this is a funerary

194, left

195

work. On a pillar to the right lies a wreath of honor. The top of a small palm branch can be seen in his left hand. The unique facial features of the portrait with short-cropped hair can be dated rather accurately.[1] The deeply drilled pupils probably had inlays of colored glass which, together with partial painting, strengthened the animated expression of the sculpture.

K.P.

[1]Cf. a portrait at Stanford University, No. 17205, in *From Icon to Image*, catalogue of an exhibit, November 1962– January 1964, Plate 3a, which probably was made by the same artist and which may be a portrait of a relative.

196
Female head

Site: Palmyra, garden of the Bel Temple
Date: A.D. 1–50
Material: Limestone
Height: 13 cm; *width:* 9.5 cm
Museum No.: Palmyra B 2252/8089
Literature: Tokyo Exhibition No. 188

This fragment is probably from a free-standing statue. The forehead is framed by a series of curls, while the hair at the temples is combed sideways toward the top of the head. The hair behind the wide ribbon is only schematically rendered. The face is dominated by large eyes, whose fully visible irises impress the ob-

server with their intense gaze. The coiffure shows no specific signs of Roman fashion, but the old-fashioned rendering of the eyes indicates that this is one of the earliest Palmyrene sculptures.
K.P.

197
Female head

Site: Palmyra
Date: Ca. A.D. 130
Material: Marble (large crystals)
Height: 35 cm; *width:* 24 cm
Museum No.: Damascus 43
Literature: Zouhdi *Catalogue* (1976) 121, No. 1

196

197

198

A few marble statues from Palmyra have been preserved which are stylistically similar to this head. Since marble does not exist in Syria, these statues were probably made elsewhere and then transported to Palmyra. In spite of their higher monetary value, artistically they are rather mediocre. The rendering of this head is nondescript. The hair is parted in the middle, combed back over the ears, and a braided wreath

across the top is partially covered by a scarf. The coiffure and the clothing are of a style neither royal nor local. Rather, she reminds us of the older statue of Faustina, wife of the emperor Antonius Pius. In the statue of Faustina the hair part is simply and schematically rendered and the ears are left free. The same was true for the statue of Sabina, wife of Hadrian, whose hair style differs slightly by being divided in the

middle by a wreath. We therefore would date this head to the reign of Hadrian (A.D. 76–138), and the rendering of the eyes suggest a date toward the end of the reign.
K.P.

198–203
Six plaster heads

Site: Palmyra, 200–203 from the construction site of the Hotel Meridien
Date: Ca. A.D. 200
Material: Plaster
Dimensions: (198) *height:* 14 cm; *width* 27.5 cm; (199) *height:* 15.5 cm; *width:* 13 cm; (200) *height:* 15 cm; *width:* 15 cm; (201) *height:* 18 cm; *width:* 12.5 cm; (202) *height:* 22 cm; *width:* 13 cm; (203) *height:* 20 cm; *width:* 15 cm
Museum Nos.: (198) Damascus 5963/13753; (199) 5948/13730; the rest have provisional site Nos. 10, 7, 21, and 23
Literature: Cf. M.A.R. Colledge *Art of Palmyra* (London 1976) 104, Fig. 136 (with mistaken interpretation) // Tokyo Exhibition No. 187

The heads shown here were originally part of plaster moldings placed about two thirds up the wall in the sumptuously decorated rooms of a private house at Palmyra. Cat. Nos. 198 and 199 were originally positioned on the top part of a horizontal relief molding. The plain part of the molding was plastered on the walls, and the heads were pressed into it while it was still wet. Several details were executed afterward—for example, the hair of Cat. No. 198—just before the plaster dried completely. There are similar decorations in Pompeian wall paintings.[1]

Iconographically, we can only partly determine the motifs. Cat. Nos. 202 and 203 are clearly theater masks, characterized by their wide-open mouths and eyes. Perhaps No. 202 is supposed to be the Trojan King Priam because of his peaked cap. The head of a youth with a similar cap (No. 201) may be a representation of Paris. The young girl wearing a scarf (No. 200) is obviously from the realm of comedies. The series from the Hotel Meridien site is of much better quality than others from Palmyra and elsewhere in the Roman Empire.[2]
K.P.

[1]A. Allroggen-Bedel *Maskendarstellungen in der römisch-kampanischen Wandmalerei* (Munich 1974).

[2]Cf. M. Blanchard-Lemée *Maisons à mosaiques du quartier central de Djemila (Cuicul)* (Paris 1975) 193, Figs. 91–92.

199

200

201

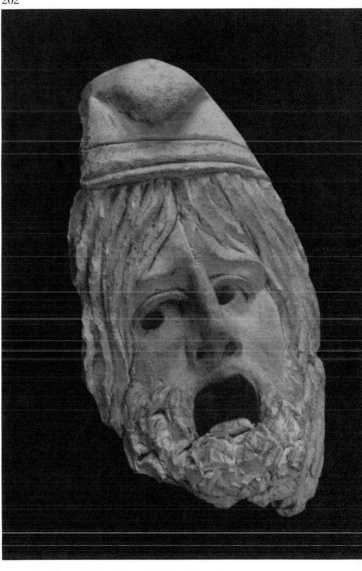

202

407

203

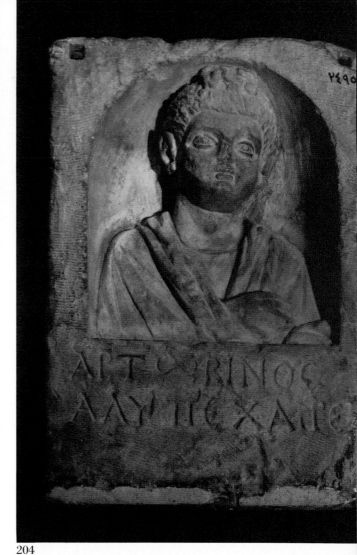

204

204
Tombstone carved in relief

Site: Membidj
Date: A.D. 150–200
Material: Yellow limestone
Height: 61 cm; *width:* 41.5 cm
Museum No.: Damascus 3495/7386

This tombstone has a carved portrait of a young boy framed in a semi-circular niche above an inscription. His clothes and the inscription identify him as male;

the short-cropped hair with a few longer locks on top indicate youth. The inscription gives his name as Artobinos, and an exclamation follows which can be translated as: "may you be free of grief" or "may nobody cause you grief." The figure's slight turn to the left loosens the composition. The frame of the portrait was probably meant to suggest a small shrine. The holes in the two top corners had inserted hooks, from which garlands could be hung.
K.P.

205
Votive relief dedicated to Aphlad

Site: Dura-Europos, Temple of Adonis
Date: Ca. A.D. 54
Material: White limestone
Height: 51 cm; *width:* 31 cm
Museum No.: Damascus 2124/4488
Literature: C. Hopkins in *The Excavations at Dura-Europos: Preliminary Report of the Fifth Season 1931–1932* (New Haven 1934) 106, Plate 13 / *Berytus* 3 (1936) 6, Plate 3:1 // H. Seyrig *Berytus* 3 (1936) 138 // M. Rostovtzeff *Caravan Cities* (Oxford 1932) 186, 218, Plate 32:1 / *Yale Classical Studies* 5 (1935) 226, 233, Figs. 36, 38 // O. Eissfeldt *Tempel und Kulte syrischer Städte in hellenistisch-römischer Zeit: Der Alte Orient* 40 (Leipzig 1941) 139, Plate 14:3 // J. Starcky *Syria* 26 (1949) 56, 81, Fig. 5 // H. Th. Bossert *Altsyrien* (Tübingen 1951) 39, Fig. 566 // Abdul-Hak *Catalogue* (1951) 10, No. 5, Plate 4:1 // E. H. Kantorowicz *Proceedings of the American Philosophical Society* 105 (1961) 377, Fig. 24 = *Selected Studies* (New York 1965) 12, Plate 5:24 // M.A.R. Colledge *The Parthians* (London 1967) 160, Fig. 67 / *Parthian Art* (London 1977) 99, Plate 33 // D. Schlumberger *Der hellenisierte Orient* (Baden-Baden 1969) 106, Fig. 17 // H. Klengel *Syria antiqua* (Leipzig 1971) 111, Fig. p. 72 // A. Perkins *The Art of Dura-Europos* (Oxford 1973) 19, 77, Plate 31 // H.J.W. Drijvers *The Religion of Palmyra* (Leiden 1976) 18, 31, Plate 47:2 // R. A. Stucky *Syria* 53 (1976) 134 // Zouhdi *Catalogue* (1976) 132 // S. B. Downey *The Stone and Plaster Sculpture. Excavations at Dura-Europos: Final Report* III 1,2 (Los Angeles 1977) 7, No. 1 Plate 1 // C. Hopkins *The Discovery of Dura-Europos* (New Haven 1979) 87, Plate 88 // J. Teixidor *The Pantheon of Palmyra* (Leiden 1979) 65, 102, 136, Plate 33 // P. Linant de Bellefons "Aphlad" *Lexicon Iconographicum Mythologiae Classicae* 1 (Zürich 1981) 879, Plate 699. For inscription see also L. Robert *Hellenica* 13 (1965) 120, 124 n. 4 // J. T. Milik *Dedicaces faites par des dieux* (Paris 1972) 136 // E. Lipinski *Orientalia* 45 (1976) 69

On the right a bearded god stands on a pedestal resting on two winged griffins. He wears a cuirass with buckled leather straps, decorated with stars and with two rows of fringes above the knees. He has on heavy stockings and high boots with cross-lacings. In his right hand he holds an object, perhaps a stylus, and in his left, a scepter. The polos on his head is decorated with bejeweled bands. To the left stands a bare-footed priest wearing the pointed cap often seen on northern Syrian priests; unlike Palmyrene priests depicted (see Cat. No. 189) his hair is visible here. He holds a typical implement for sacrifice in his left hand, a votive

wine vessel, while with his right hand he reaches across to place a ball of incense on the flaming altar.

The long Greek inscription gives further details: "This foundation of the sanctuary of Aphlad, called god of the village of Anath on the Euphrates, Adadiabos, the son of Zabdibolos, son of Silloi erected as his offering on behalf of the safety of himself, his children, and all his house." Below there is a graffita carelessly scratched by a later visitor. Aphlad was the local version of Baal at Anath; the word "foundation" refers to both the place and the relief. The date A.D. 54 is derived from a dated inscription found at the same location.

K.P.

206
Wall painting with victory goddess
See color plate p. 426

Site: Dura-Europos, Parthian Bath
Date: A.D. 166–200
Material: Paint on plaster
Height: 1.28 cm; *width:* 0.85 cm
Museum No.: Damascus 1969/4955
Literature: F.E. Brown *The Excavations at Dura-Europos. Preliminary Report of the Sixth Season 1932–1933* (New Haven 1936) 51,63, Plate 41:1 // R. du Mesnil du Buisson *Les peintures de la synagogue de Doura-Europos* (Rome 1939) 32 n. 1, Fig. 27 // Abdul-Hak *Catalogue* (1951) 12 No. 10, Plate 3:1 top // D. Schlumberger *Der hellenisierte Orient* (Baden-Baden 1969) 71, Plate p. 74 // A. Perkins *The Art of Dura-Europos* (Oxford 1973) 25,34, Fig. 28 // Zouhdi *Catalogue* (1976) 132 // Tokyo Exhibition No. 217 // C. Hopkins *The Discovery of Dura-Europos* (New Haven 1979) 125, Figs. pp. 126 and 127

This representation of a winged goddess of victory was found on top of a pillar in a small bath, apparently built shortly after the Roman conquest in A.D. 165. The goddess is standing on a globe, holding a wreath decorated with ribbons in her right hand, a palm branch in her left, both characteristic symbols of victory. Her hair is piled high on her head in a chignon. The different colors of her garment indicate that the painter was not certain what his courageous model should wear: the goddess appears to be dressed in a belted short chiton of a pink color with a flounce at the hips, but the change to green betrays the painter's mistaken notion that the material around the legs

should be a different garment. The one exposed leg appearing from the chiton is often found in Roman art.
K.P.

207
Statue of Athena-Allat

Site: Suaida
Date: Ca. A.D. 50–100
Material: Black basalt
Height: 1.59 m
Museum No.: Damascus 4219/5216
Literature: Abdul-Hak *Catalogue* (1951) 57, No. 3 Plates 24 middle 25 // A. Abel *Bulletin de la Société Royale d'Archéologie de Bruxelles* 49 (1956–1957) 5 // H. Klengel *Syria antiqua* (Leipzig 1971) Fig. p. 102 // Zouhdi *Catalogue* (1976) 115 No. 2 Fig. 48 // Tokyo Exhibition No. 176 // H.J.W. Drijvers *Phoenix 26* (1980) 84, Fig 28 // see also the modern 5-pound note of the Syrian National Bank

The goddess wears sandals and a chiton over which a pleated blouse reaches her hips. Her chest is covered with an aegis—a goatskin decorated with a Medusa head. The rendering of the sleeves and helmet betrays a lack of familiarity with Greek garments; it looks like armor with the sleeves of the chiton underneath, and the helmet has an almost baroque outline with the separately worked crest. On her left arm the goddess wears a round shield with a Medusa head (a well-known element to ward off evil). In her raised right hand she once held a spear. The position of her feet, and the garment swirling back reminds us of the many other statues of victory from the same workshops.

The native population presumably saw this statue as the goddess Allat, the equivalent of Athena. The base has a Greek votive inscription: "For the health of our ruler," not mentioning the emperor by name. The rendering of the eyes indicates a date around the turn of the first century A.D.
K.P.

208
Tombstone with relief of a woman

Site: Harah (Hauran)
Date: A.D. 100–200
Material: Black basalt
Height: 1.06 cm; *width:* 42 cm
Museum No.: Damascus 1350/2978
Literature: Abdul-Hak *Catalogue* (1951) 60 No. 9, Plates 23:2 left, 29:2 b // Zouhdi *Catalogue* (1976) 112, Fig. 44

205, left

207

ca. 330 B.C.–A.D. 400

This irregularly shaped tombstone shows a female figure standing on a square pedestal. She is dressed in a long chiton with a large tasseled shawl covering her head; on her feet she wears simple sandals. Her hair has thick wavy strands. Her only jewelry is a bead necklace. The inscription names the deceased: Bersis, daughter of Narcellos, who died at fifteen years of age. In spite of the rather crude rendering of details, the figure shows a well-balanced distribution of body weight and proportion, emphasized by the graceful draping of the garments.

K.P.

209
Head of a goddess

Site: Oasis near Damascus
Date: A.D. 100–200
Material: Black basalt
Height: 30 cm
Museum No.: Damascus 1944/4199
Literature: Abdul-Hak *Catalogue* (1951) 74 No. 2, Plate
    38:21a

This head, broken off a statue, shows a thick mass of corkscrew curls, which evokes (but only accidentally) the coiffure of the Egyptian goddess Isis. The hair is crowned by a wreath of leaves with an emblem in the center, and part of a necklace is preserved. The idealized facial features seem almost lifeless, although a certain mastery of sculpting technique is apparent. This head is an example of provincial alienation from the usual idealized Roman type of sculpture.

K.P.

210
Bronze shield portrait of a goddess

Site: Banyas (Hauran)
Date: A.D. 150–200
Material: Bronze
Diameter: 38.8 cm; *height of bust:* 34 cm
Museum No.: Damascus 16967
Literature: Zoudhi *Catalogue* (1976) 90 No. 1, Fig. 30 //
    H. Klengel *Syria antiqua* (Leipzig 1971) 111, Fig. p. 98

This shield portrait, *clipeata imago*, consists of two parts: the hollow portrait which still has remains of lead filling and the shield which forms the frame. The

208

209, right

HELLENISTIC AND ROMAN PERIODS

back has six pegs for hanging on a wall, or perhaps it was set in the center of a gable, like a series of images of gods and similar portraits.[1] Since this portrait is not life-size, it may have been a votive object. This and an example of a male portrait from the time of Trajan (the beginning of the second century A.D.) in Ankara are the only bronze examples of this size.[2] Our figure, dressed in a chiton with buttoned sleeves, probably represents an unidentified goddess. The hair style and the diadem give no definite clues, but she might be Aphrodite. The rendering of the eyes date her to the second half of the second century A.D.
K.P.

[1]Cf. P. Hommel *Studien zu den römischen Figurengiebeln der Kaiserzeit* (Berlin 1954) 110.
[2]R. Winkes *Clipeata Imago: Studien zu einer römischen Bildnisform* (Bonn 1969) 73, 132.

211
Gold brooch
See color plate p. 427

Site: Origin unknown (museum purchase)
Date: A.D. 1–200
Material: Gold
Height with pendant: 11.8 cm; *greatest diameter:* 5.5 cm
Museum No.: Damascus 4318/10127

This richly ornamented brooch, with a horizontal needle on the back, was used to fasten loosely draped garments on the shoulder. Attached at the bottom of the piece are three braided chains ending in heart-shaped pendants.
K.P.

212
Gold earring
See color plate p. 427

Site: Origin unknown (museum purchase)
Date: A.D. 200–300
Material: Gold
Height: 6 cm; *width:* 2.4 cm
Museum No.: Damascus 1554/7225
Literature: Cf. H. Hoffman and V. von Claer *Antiker Gold- und Silberschmuck . . . Hamburg* (Mainz 1968) 139 No. 90 // T. Hackens *Catalogue of the Classical Collection. Classical Jewellery* (Providence 1976) 116, No. 52

210, left

This piece of jewelry consists of a circular, partially twisted ring with an oval buckle on top decorated with three spirals. From the bottom of the earring hang six tiny gold balls with chains. This kind of earring is found throughout Syria with slight variations.
K.P.

213
Pair of gold earrings
See color plate p. 427

Site: Dair al-Hadjar (Hauran)
Date: A.D. 1–100
Material: Gold with garnets
Height: 4.7 cm; *width:* 6.1 cm
Museum No.: Damascus 2545/5119
Literature: B. Zouhdi *AAAS* 21 (1971) 101 No. 34, Plate 18 (cf. 100 No. 29, Plate 17) // J. El-Chehadeh *Untersuchungen zum antiken Schmuck in Syrien* (Diss. Berlin 1972) 6, 8, No. 4 with illus. // cf. K. Schmitt-Korte *Die Nabatäer—Spuren einer arabischen Kultur der Antike* (Exhibition Catalogue Hannover and Frankfurt/Main 1976–1977) 64, Fig. 39 a–d = *Die Nabatäer—Erträge einer Ausstellung* (Bonn 1981) Plate 88 // T. Hackens *Catalogue of the Classical Collection. Classical Jewellery* (Providence 1976) 113 Nos. 50–53

These elaborate semi-circular earrings are made of thin gold foil richly ornamented with granulation. On one side is a small bird with inlaid garnet eyes. This type of jewelry has been associated with the regime of the Nabataeans, which ended in A.D. 106.
K.P.

214
Bronze lamp

Site: Hauran
Date: Ca. 100 B.C.–A.D. 100
Material: Bronze
Height: 9.5 cm; *length:* 18.2 cm
Museum No.: Damascus 20252

Oil lamps were an important household object in the classical world. Their many variations were often shaped with much imagination. This example of a lamp with two wicks is apparently unique. The two

214

long snouts appear from the body of a prancing horse. The rectangular filling hole on the back was probably closed with a separate lid shaped like a rider. Only the reins and part of the hinge are preserved. The tail of the horse is shaped into a circular handle. A typologically related lamp, shaped like a bull, in the Brooklyn Museum shows definite Iranian stylistic elements.[1]

K.P.

[1]Brooklyn Museum L.50.17; cf. Ch. K. Wilkinson in *The Guennol Collection* I (New York 1975) 9, with three illustrations.

215
Miniature bronze vessel

Site: Lebanon (?) (museum purchase)
Date: A.D. 1–100
Material: Bronze
Height: 7.5 cm; *greatest diameter:* 5.5 cm
Museum No.: Damascus 6027/13855
Literature: Tokyo Exhibition No. 210

This small vessel has three feet, two loops for hanging, and a lid shaped like a lion mask. The bottom is
lost. On the inside are two pipes which may have held
glass tubes. It was probably used as an ink well. The
sides show in relief a frieze of female dancers who
hold hands; one of them plays the lyre. Similar motifs
are often found on decorated wells. To use the motif
on a small vessel containing fluids is both beautiful
and original.
K.P.

216
Vessel shaped as a Nubian head
See color plate p. 428

Site: Hauran
Date: A.D. 1–100
Material: Bronze inlaid with silver
Height: 19.1 cm; *width:* 10.6 cm
Museum No.: Damascus 14854
Literature: Zoudhi *Catalogue* (1976) 114, Fig. 45 // cf. K.
   Majewski *Archeoloqia* 14 (1936) 95–126, Fig. 37

This vessel probably served as a container for incense
or spices. It has a small lid on top of the head. The
ethnic type depicted—a Nubian youth with corkscrew
curls—mirrors the exotic origin of the contents. This
small, carefully worked piece of art was decorated
with different inlays, but only the black corroded
silver pupil of the right eye remains. The thin necklace with its crescent-moon pendant was probably of
silver, while the emblem of the wreath presumably
was made of colored stone. The remains of ferric ox-
ide on the handle indicate that a chain was attached
here. The vessel was undoubtedly an import, most
likely from Alexandria.
K.P.

215

217
Vessel shaped as a Nubian boy

Site: Zawiya, in southern Syria
Date: A.D. 1–100
Material: Bronze
Height: 18.2 cm; *lower width:* 7.2 cm
Museum No.: Damascus 4081/8927
Literature: Zoudhi *Catalogue* (1976) 114

This container is closely related to Cat. No. 216 in
both design and use. This type of sculptured vessel

was very popular during the Hellenistic period, and representations of exotic types enjoyed great popularity until the Imperial period. The Nubian boy is wearing an apron and sits on a rock. Two similar ink wells or perfume flasks, also in the shape of seated Nubian boys, are located in the Bibliothèque Nationale, Paris.[1]

K.P.

[1]See G.H. Beardsley *The Negro in Greek and Roman Civilization* (Baltimore 1929) 124, Nos. 257, 262, 263.

218
Statuette of Aphrodite with Eros

Site: Origin unknown (museum purchase)
Date: Ca. A.D. 100–200
Material: Marble
Height: 24 cm
Museum No.: Damascus 6028/13856
Literature: D.K. Hill *Journal of the Walters Art Gallery* (Baltimore) 31–32 (1968–1969) 9, Fig. 5

This statue, which was reassembled from fragments, shows a goddess dressed in a chiton with a shawl over her shoulders. In her raised right hand she holds a "hand garland," in the lowered left, an apple. The hair is parted in the middle and does not show any kind of ornament. A small winged Eros can be seen on her left shoulder. There are numerous examples of this motif, all made of marble, documenting the popularity of depictions of mythological themes. Since these statues are found very frequently in Syria,[1] it is highly unlikely that they represent an imitation of the Roman Venus Genetrix by the famous sculptor Arkhesilaos in Rome dating to the time of Caesar.

K.P.

[1]For futher examples in Damascus see Abdul-Hak *Catalogue* (1951) 353 Nos. 1, 4, 9; Plate 53:2 // D. K. Hill *Journal of the Walters Art Gallery* 31–32 (1968–1969) 9, Fig. 4.

217, left

219
Statuette of Isis from Byblos

Site: Origin unknown (museum purchase)
Date: A.D. 50–100
Material: Bronze
Height including base: 29.6 cm; *width of base:* 12.6 cm
Museum No.: Damascus 7620
Literature: Deuxième exposition des découvertes archéologiques des années 1954–1955 . . . au Musée Nationale de Damas (Damascus) 39, No. 1 // Zoudhi *Catalogue* (1976) 89, Fig. 26

A naked goddess stands on a semi-circular, three-footed pedestal with a step in the middle. In her right hand she holds a small unidentified object (in similar statues it is often a small globe or an apple), and in her left she holds a mirror with a lid. She wears her thick hair in a heavy chignon, and a large headdress consisting of several parts rests on her comparatively small head. The headdress is put together from a diadem with serrated edges and an Isis crown, consisting of a double feather with cow horns, two slanted grain sheaves, and a sun disk. These details, however, are only vaguely indicated in this example. Other depictions of this goddess are widespread along the Syrian coast.[1] She is Isis of Byblos, a variation of Astarte, who again corresponds to the Greek Aphrodite.
K.P.

[1]For the crown see A. de Ridder "Les Bronzes" *Collection de Clercq* III (Paris 1904) Plate 17, No. 97; Plates 21–23, Nos. 106, 107, 109, 110, 114.

220
Two women with tambourines

Site: Salamiya at Hama (1931)
Date: A.D. 1–100
Material: Red-brown clay with remains of pink paint on light green background
Height: 13.2 cm; *width:* 7.5 cm; *depth:* 4.1 cm
Museum No.: Damascus 1614/3528
Literature: M. Rostovtzeff *Yale Classical Studies* 5 (1935) 183, Fig. 17 // H. Ingholt *Berytus* 3 (1936) 86 n. 32 // Abdul-Hak *Catalogue* (1951) 92 // Zouhdi *Catalogue* (1976) 97, Fig. 36 // M.A.R. Colledge *Parthian Art* (London 1977) 101, illus. 40b // Tokyo Exhibition No. 190

The two tambourine players sit in a tentlike frame which—as parallels show—apparently was an orna-

218, right

ment for a camel. The two women wear the same garments and hair style. The hair is parted in the middle
and decorated with a diadem; single strands of hair
reach the shoulders. Their dresses are cut very low.
Musicians were probably connected to the cult of the
temples, and the tambourine was a popular instrument
in the Near East. A similar pair, riding a camel, is in
the Ny Carlsberg Glyptotek, Copenhagen.[1]
K.P.

[1]Museum No. 2809; H. Ingholt "Parthian Sculptures from
Hatra" *Memoirs of the Connecticut Academy of Arts and
Sciences* 12 (1954) 10, Plate 2.1.

221
Two standing musicians

Site: North Syria
Date: A.D. 1–100
Material: Clay with remnants of pinkish paint
Height: 16.4 cm; *width:* 9.4 cm; *depth:* 3.7 cm
Museum No.: Damascus 3248/7003
Literature: Abdul-Hak *Catalogue* (1951) 92

The woman on the right plays a double flute, while the
one on the left beats a drum. They both wear long garments reaching the floor and belted at the hips. Their
hair, simply parted in the middle, is decorated with a
diadem. It is not clear whether this is supposed to be
a religious scene like Cat. No. 220. The almost identical motif and the similarly low cut garments indicate
that the two pairs came from the same workshop.
Other pairs of female musicians are known elsewhere
in the Near East.[1]
K.P.

[1]See, e.g., M. Rostovtzeff *Yale Classical Studies* 5 (1935)
183, Fig. 22.

219, left

220

221

222
Votive statuette of a bull

Site: Bludan, near Damascus
Date: A.D. 1–100
Material: Bronze
Height: 14 cm; *length:* 21.8 cm; *width:* 7.4 cm
Museum No.: Damascus 13151
Literature: B. Zouhdi *AAAS* 11–12 (1961–1962) 89. 2 plates

ca. 330 B.C.–A.D. 400ca. 330 B.C.–A.D. 400

222

before p. 97 / *Catalogue* (1976) 88 No. 2 // M.P. Speidel
Mithras-Orion. Greek Hero and Roman Army God (Leiden
1980) preface, 39, Plate 1

The naturalistic figure of a young bull leaning forward
in a tensed pose is a votive offering to Orion from a
Roman soldier. The Greek inscription on the base
reads: "The veteran Thamanaios dedicàted (it) piously
to the god Orion." Here we have an example of a military cult figure. Orion was originally a human Greek
hero, but later he was seen as the astrological con-
stellation of Taurus.

K.P.

223

Lamp cover in the form of a child's head

Site: Homs (museum purchase)
Date: A.D. 100–200(?)
Material: Terracotta
Height: 16 cm; *width and depth:* 11 cm
Museum No.: Damascus 18787
Literature: B. Zouhdi *AAAS* 10 (1969) 77. Fig. 10 // J.W.
    Hayes *Ancient Lamps in the Royal Ontario Museum* I
    (Toronto 1980) 143 No. 565

This lamp cover shaped like a child's head could be

hung from the loop on top. A large opening on the back served to hold a small oil lamp, which would illuminate the drilled eyes. Smoke and hot air could escape through holes on the top. Similar lamp covers existed in other shapes, but this local design seems to be unique.

K.P.

224
Lagynos (jug)
See color plate p. 429

Site: Masyaf (museum purchase)
Date: A.D. 100–200
Material: Terracotta with multi-colored glaze
Height: 11.2 cm; *diameter:* 7.9 cm
Museum No.: Damascus 6017/13842

This type of jug (called *lagynos* in Greek) has a nearly hemispherical lower part, a flat wide shoulder, and a comparatively long neck—a shape which was prevalent in Hellenistic pottery. This example was probably made in Asia Minor, where such lead-glazed ceramics enjoyed wide popularity during the later Hellenistic period. The decoration for the glaze was stenciled, and the foot, neck, and handle were added to the main body of the vessel. There is a leaf pattern on the lower part, then a continuous row of spirals, while the shoulder of the jug is decorated with a meander border. This jug seems to be unique.

K.P.

225
Goblet
See color plate p. 429

Site: Aleppo (?) (museum purchase)
Date: 100 B.C.–A.D. 100
Material: Clay
Height: 12.8 cm; *diameter:* 15.6 cm
Museum No.: Damascus 5753/13160
Literature: Tokyo Exhibition No. 193

This drinking cup without handles was shaped in a hemispherical mold, while the foot and the rim were made on a potter's wheel. The rim and interior are ochre-colored, while the outside has green lead glaze. The goblet was probably made in a workshop in Asia Minor.

K.P.

226
Skyphos (two-handled cup)
See color plate p. 429

Site: Origin unknown (museum purchase)
Date: 100 B.C.–A.D. 100
Material: Clay
Height: 7.6 cm; *width with handles:* 15.9 cm
Museum No.: Damascus 5754/13131
Literature: Abdul-Hak *Catalogue* (1951) 97 No. 2 // A. Hochuli-Gysel *Kleinasiatische glasierte Reliefkeramik (50 B.C.–50 A.D.) und ihre oberitalischen Nachahmungen* (Bern 1977) 176, Plate 58

This two-handled cup, called in Greek a *skyphos*, is one of the best examples of this genre from Asia Minor. This type of glazed ceramics was widely popular in antiquity, and examples have been found as far away as Petra, Yemen, and Egypt. The production process was similar to that of Cat. No. 225, but the details, such as the relief decoration on the sides, indicate that it was made in a workshop in Ismir, on the west coast of Turkey.

K.P.

227
Vessel in the form of a camel

Site: Homs (museum purchase)
Date: 100–1 B.C.
Material: Terracotta
Museum No.: Damascus 3614/8357
Literature: Tokyo Exhibition No. 195 // cf. J.H. Iliffe *Quarterly of the Department of Antiquities in Palestine* 11 (1945) 17 No. 88 Plate 6

Animal-shaped vessels from the ancient Near East are documented very early. The Greeks adopted this type of pottery and continued to produce similar vessels, so that the genre became part of classical culture as well. This example shows a resting camel, with the filling hole and the handle shaped on top of the saddle, while the mouth of the camel serves as the spout. A relatively close parallel is known from Jordan.

K.P.

227, right

Cat. No. 206

Cat. No. 211

Cat. No. 212

Cat. No. 213

Cat. No. 224

Cat. No. 216

Cat. No. 225

Cat. No. 226

Cat. No. 230

Cat. No. 231

Cat. No. 232

Cat. No. 249

Cat. No. 250

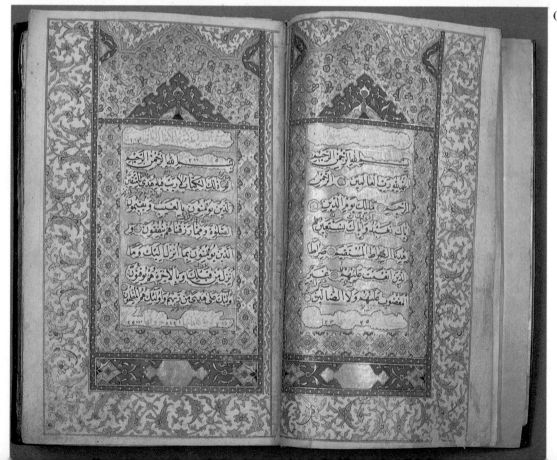

Cat. No. 257

Cat. No. 258

Cat. No. 259, top   Cat. No. 260, bottom

Cat. No. 265

434

Cat. No. 269

Cat. No. 270

Cat. No. 273

Cat. No. 276

Cat. No. 277

Cat. No. 278

BYZANTINE PERIOD
CA. A.D. 400–600

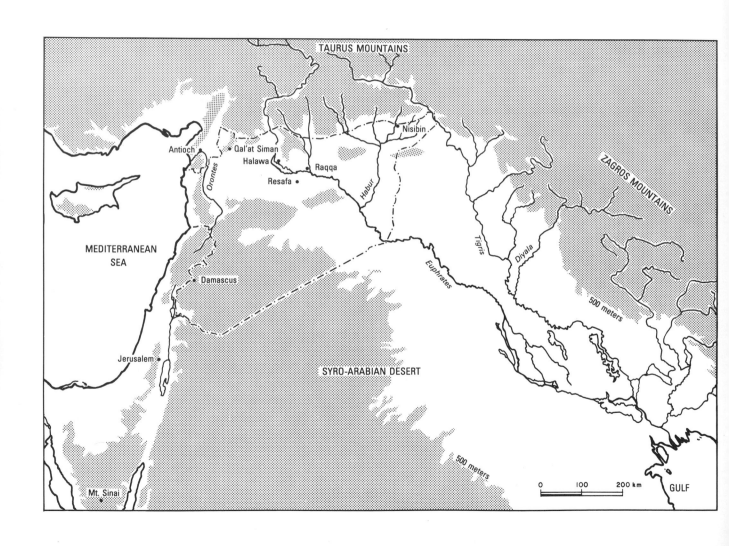

TAURUS MOUNTAINS

Antioch
Qal'at Siman
Halawa
Resafa
Raqqa
Nisibin
Orontes
Habur
Tigris
Diyala
Euphrates
ZAGROS MOUNTAINS
500 meters

MEDITERRANEAN
SEA

Damascus

Jerusalem

SYRO-ARABIAN DESERT

500 meters

Mt. Sinai

0   100   200 km

GULF

A CULTURAL LANDSCAPE IN THE BYZANTINE PERIOD

CHRISTINE STRUBE

A REGION THAT NEVER FAILS TO LEAVE A LASTING IMPRESSION UPON visitors to Syria is the northern limestone mountains with their extensive ruins. This is the part of Syria which has, since the publications of the Marquis de Voguée in 1865–1877, been considered to present the essence of early Byzantine architecture. Outside of Syria, in the Mediterranean area only a very few buildings of the fourth to seventh centuries remain with their original walls unchanged by later additions or alterations. The importance of Syria, then, is the fact that the northern massif has about 150 churches and hundreds of houses of this period, many well enough preserved to allow detailed reconstruction.

The limestone massif, called Belus in antiquity, consists of series of ranges between 400 and 800 meters in elevation, stretching west of the current Aleppo-to-Hama road, often interrupted by large and small plains. On these peaks are approximately 750 ruined sites, an extraordinarily high density, even though most were villages rather than cities. The history of these sites begins with the first century, when Syria was a Roman province, but their golden epoch was under Byzantine rule, from the fourth to the seventh centuries. During this period a relatively minor component of the population spoke Greek and constituted a kind of upper class, while most people spoke Syriac, a northwest Semitic language descended from Aramaic. These villages were under the administrative authority of the capitals slightly to the north, such as Antioch, and Apamea to the south, not far from modern Hama. Little remains today of Antioch, while ancient Apamea has recently been investigated by Belgian archaeologists under the direction of J. Ch. Balty.

The dead cities include not only churches from the fourth to seventh centuries but also simple houses, public meeting places, marketplaces and bazaars, baths and tombs from the first to seventh centuries. The contrast between the spare mountainous landscape of today and the rich ruins is so great that it is difficult to avoid asking where these cities came from and how they attained their high level of social and economic life. We must assume, for starters, that deforestation of the mountains led to the subsequent devastation of the slopes. The Russian architect G. Tchalenko initiated the fundamental research on such questions which interrelate geographic, historical, and archaeological data.

In antiquity cereal agriculture was really only possible on the plains. Wealth in the mountainous regions was derived from the cultivation of olive trees, a monoculture supplemented on the fringes of the terrain by grape and fig cultivation. The protracted and difficult opening of the mountain territories was initiated from the outside, of course. Rich landowners of the plains built seasonal villas on the slopes, planted olive trees, and then waited the requisite ten to twelve years before the trees began to bear fruit. The cultivation of olive trees began in the first century, when Syria was still a Roman province.

Economic prosperity in the region was dependent upon the unhindered export of olive oil and the import of goods for daily use. The end of the trade and thus of the olive groves was brought about by political events: the Persian war (603–630), the blockage of the Mediterranean, and the ultimate disruption of the old trade routes. The settlements of the region were not destroyed by the Arabs but abandoned by their inhabitants, for there was no alternative to the olive monoculture. Most of the settlements of the first to seventh centuries remained unoccupied—their churches, houses, and tombs preserved—up to their rediscovery in 1935.

The processing of limestone played a major role in the development of Belus from the start. The extensive use of this raw material— for cisterns, and presses for oil and wine, for example—explains the considerable skill that the local workshops displayed. Inhabitants of these mountain settlements busied themselves with olive cultivation only part of the year; the remainder found them working in quarries and at masonry. Professional teams were probably also imported for the more important buildings in the region.

The best-known architectural monument of these limestone mountains, and surely one of the most important early Christian structures of the Mediterranean world, is the pilgrimage center of Qal'at Siman (Figs. 77 and 78). The church was built around the pillar upon which Saint Simeon lived for many years in strict asceticism. The powerful design of this building harks back to the work commissioned by Emperor Zenon in Byzantium (476–491).

Figure 77
Qal'at Siman.

Figure 78
The remains of the last pillar of Saint Simeon Stylites, Qal'at Siman.

ca. A.D. 400–600

445

Figure 79
The basilica in Qalbloze.

Figure 80
The church in Qasr ibn Wardan.

The stylites

The cult of the Syrian stylites (Greek = "of a pillar") is named after the monk Simeon whose choice of an ascetic life initially met with considerable resistance within monastic and church circles. The respect accorded to Simeon, even in his lifetime, however, can be understood as the transference of the honor previously accorded to martyrs. Through his holy life the ascetic became a martyr.

Simeon came into the world the son of a Cilician farmer in 386. At the age of sixteen he entered the cloister of Teleda, which he left ten years later, going to Telanisos, now Deir Siman, where he lived in a small community for three years. Then, in the throes of his asceticism, he had a pillar constructed on which he lived. This pillar was soon replaced by taller ones; the last was 17–20 meters high. Simeon spent a total of forty-two years on them. When the saint died in 459, the last pillar became a holy relic, the cross-shaped memorial monument at the center of the shrine at Qal'at Siman (see Fig. 78).

Contemporary reports provide information for the life of the saint and the degree of admiration and attention excited by his difficult asceticism, which certainly surpassed all other forms in his lifetime. His fame was so widespread that—as a result of the worldwide trade relations of Antioch—pilgrims from Gaul, England, Spain, and Italy came to Qal'at Siman. The saint was not only held in great honor among Christians but also among Arabs and Persians. Fifteen years before his death, reports Bishop Theodoret of Cyrrhus, pictures of Simeon hung in the workshops of Rome.

To what extent can we reconstruct the saint's pillar, of which only the bottom now remains? The standing surface of the 17–20-meter-high limestone pillar was about 2 meters wide; this is clear from the later pillars and portrayals of the stylites. To keep the crowds back, and to prevent the splitting of chips for souvenirs and relics, a structure was erected around the base of the pillar. After a few hours of sleep the saint spent the greater part of the day standing on the pillar. Once a week a servant or student brought him food with the help of a ladder (see Cat. No. 240). He was protected from the elements by his sheepskin monk's clothing. A small conduit within the pillar probably facilitated the saint's hygienic requirements. Stylite asceticism, however, also elicited resistance and reproach because of its glorification of the individual, its attracting attention at all costs, although Simeon's own modesty and humility did silence his critics. While his own life was far removed from the ordinary, Simeon Stylites was aware of the daily life and religious questions of his time;

he was consulted about church conflicts, was an effective missionary, interpreted the law in conflicting situations, and addressed pilgrims.

The pilgrimage shrine of Qal'at Siman

After the death of Saint Simeon in 459 a cross-shaped structure of limestone was erected around his pillar. At the central part of the cross an octagon opened in wide and high arches onto three arms of the cross. Only the east arm of the cross contained an actual church where the liturgy was recited; the other arms served as assembly halls for pilgrims. It cannot yet be determined whether the octagon was covered or was an open court surrounding the pillar. In G. Tchalenko's reconstruction (Fig. 81) a hypothetical wooden cupola has been drawn in. Further investigation, perhaps around the slab floor of the octagon, may provide clues to this question.

On the southeast side of the memorial building there is a cloister with a church, and in front of the northern arm of the cross there is a common tomb for the monks. Across from this building complex, about 150 meters away, a second group of buildings was constructed. It includes a large baptistery, a basilica on the south, and two long buildings providing accommodations for pilgrims. To help understand the opposition of the two buildings and the close connection between the baptistery and the pilgrim shelter, one must realize that the visitors to the shrine were not baptized. Since the unbaptized were not allowed to enter the shrine, they could stay overnight in the nearby shelter prior to their baptism.

Pilgrims climbed from Deir Siman—a site that owed its existence to them—over the Via Sacra to the shrine. They passed three structures, the first formed like a triumphal arch. Small sales booths on the left and right sold clothing, oil, and souvenirs. A second gate led to the area in front of the baptisterium, a third provided access to the narrow area, where the eye fell upon the splendidly decorated entry hall of the memorial building. The center of the entire complex is the pillar of Simeon. The cross-shaped structures focus attention upon it, while the cloister, where the organization of pilgrimages and care of the shrine took place, is clearly subordinate to the memorial building.

Other expressions of Syrian Christian art

Another example of a mid-fifth-century limestone building, which typically features block construction without the use of mortar, is the Qalbloze basilica (Fig. 79). Built in 450, it is the earliest example of the type in which wide-spanned arcades on pillars replace the interior pillar positions.

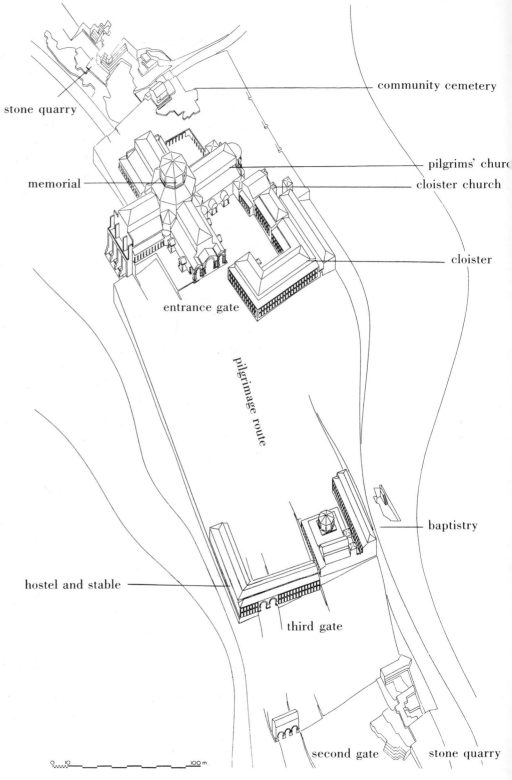

Figure 81
Reconstruction of the plan of
Qal'at Siman.

stone quarry

community cemetery

pilgrims' church

memorial

cloister church

cloister

entrance gate

pilgrimage route

baptistry

hostel and stable

third gate

second gate

stone quarry

0 10   100 m.

BYZANTINE PERIOD

Testifying to the architectural diversity found in Syria at this time—a result of the range of materials and influences present—is the fortress complex near Qasr ibn Wardan in the desert steppe (Fig. 80). This includes a basilica, a representative palace-like building, and a barracks, erected in 564. In its construction basalt, limestone, and baked brick were used together, giving the exterior of the building a carefully planned colorful appearance.

Wall painting is the great unknown art of the fourth to seventh centuries. One finds in Apamea traces of painting and in one case, the Bel Temple at Palmyra, the remains of a church fresco, but even that is in bad condition. While it is possible that new discoveries will fill this lacuna, it seems certain that the majority of the paintings are already lost. The frescoes shown here from the Mar Yaqub cloister near Qara (Cat. Nos. 230 and 231) are not only a valuable remnant of the still poorly known paintings of the centuries after the Arab conquest; they comprise, moreover, a document for the life of the Christian congregation under Arab rule.

The floor mosaics of the dated church at Halawa (A.D. 471), a site which lies in Osrhoene on the Euphrates, represent a major genre of Syrian Christian art (Cat. No. 232, on p. 431). Floor mosaics were laid in the interior of both sacred and secular structures. Common themes in both cases are garden landscapes, Nile and hunting scenes, and activities of daily life. As in other churches of the fifth and sixth centuries, the mosaics of Halawa with animal symbols and paradisiacal landscapes point to the resurrection of eternal life.

RUSAFA–SERGIOPOLIS: PILGRIM SHRINE AND CAPITAL

THILO ULBERT

On the Euphrates there is a church which is dedicated to Sergios, a famous saint. The earlier inhabitants out of honor and loyalty called the place Sergiopolis and surrounded it with a modest fortress that would deter a sudden attack by the Saracens. . . .Later, however, the shrine became quite wealthy through the donation of valuables. In consideration of this the Emperor Justinian took it upon himself to protect the site. He surrounded the place with an extraordinarily strong wall and provided an abundance of water for the inhabitants with the construction of reservoirs. He added houses, walls, and other buildings that usually decorate a city. Also, he put a garrison there for the defense of the city wall in case of emergency.[1]

IN THIS SHORT DESCRIPTION, PROCOPIUS OF CAESAREA, HISTORIAN for Emperor Justinian I (527–565) characterizes the origins and the history of a city in north Syria on the Euphrates which reached its apogee in the sixth century A.D. The foundations of Rusafa may go back as far as the Assyrian period, however, for it is conceivable that the city can be identified with the Resef mentioned in the Bible (Isaiah 37: 12). Archaeological evidence for this early settlement is, however, still lacking.

We are on firmer historical ground in late antiquity when Rusafa was a strategic boundary between Rome and the Parthians. Native cavalry were then situated within a modest garrison. Through the martyrdom of Sergios, an officer of the eastern Roman army, the site became quite famous in the early fourth century. The tomb of Sergios in front of the city wall eventually became a pilgrimage shrine, and churches and shelters were built for the pilgrims. Rusafa, now called Sergiopolis, became the site of a metropolitan bishopric. (See Fig. 82.)

Christian Rusafa ceased to flourish with the Arab conquest of the seventh century. The city experienced a last moment of fame as a capital under the Umayyad caliph Hisham (724–743). The Middle Ages apparently saw the coexistence of Islam and Christianity at Rusafa. Recent archaeological work has shown that the main cathedral functioned into the thirteenth century. The large court of the cathedral, once the meeting place of pilgrims, became the site of the main mosque shortly after the conquest. The desert city's life ended in the thirteenth century, probably as a result of the Mongol invasions.

[1]Procopius, *De aedificiis* II 9, 3–8. (Translation O. Veh.)

Figure 82
Aerial view of Rusafa from the northwest.

Johannes Kollwitz directed the archaeological research at Rusafa from 1952 until his death in 1968. Two of the early Christian basilicas were explored under his direction. The complete investigation of the city wall (Fig. 83) was undertaken by Walter Karnapp. After an interruption of eight years, the German Archaeological Institute has resumed work at Rusafa under the direction of Thilo Ulbert.

The current research program at Rusafa is twofold: first, complete topographic documentation for all visible monuments inside and outside the city wall: second, the investigation of any large buildings in the city which have not yet been explored. The first part of the program aims to obtain information from surface surveys of areas

Figure 83
The city gate in Rusafa.

already documented with aerial photography, through the systematic retrieval of surface finds and through small excavations of irrigation works, cemeteries, and areas outside the city wall, including the hardly visible but very significant remains of early Islamic mud-brick architecture. With this work we hope to complete a picture of an important city of late antiquity with the minimal expenditure of time and money.

Documentation for the city wall—the feature which gives the site its singular appearance—was concluded in the earlier stages of research. This fortification system is almost completely preserved, its rectangular form enclosing an area of almost 21 hectares (the sides average 500 by 400 meters). The wall includes fifty watch towers, four main gates, bulwarks, and stairways. These, like the equally imposing cisterns in the southwest corner of the city, date to the time of Emperor Justinian.

Procopius does not mention any sacred buildings that were built by Justinian (who was responsible for the erection of the remarkable Hagia Sophia in Constantinople). Revenue derived from pilgrims apparently allowed the church to finance the construction of its own basilica. Among the three sixth-century churches still in ruins, the

Figure 84
The basilica in Rusafa.

so-called central building which was investigated by Kollwitz is architecturally the most interesting, together with Basilica B, a large pillared building less well preserved.

Within the framework of the new research program, we have worked since 1976 on the documentation for Basilica A, the most comprehensive of the ruins inside the city (Fig. 84). Surprisingly, it can be demonstrated that this church was maintained to the end of the city's life. Much can be learned about the city as a whole from Basilica A's additions, its destruction by earthquake, and its restorations. One inscription found *in situ* must be counted as one of the most important discoveries here: it informs us that a Bishop Abraham of Sergiopolis dedicated the church in 559 to the Holy Cross. Here we have the first fixed dating of the large building at Rusafa which soon after became and remained a cathedral until the last days of the city.

A first-floor mosaic has also been recovered from the city. Although this mosaic has been extensively damaged by earthquakes, its life-size depictions of animals are among the finest of the early Byzantine period. Both the style and the materials used—imported marble from Greece and Asia Minor—illustrate Rusafa's wide-ranging connections with the outside world.

The coexistence of Christendom and Islam at Rusafa during the early Middle Ages, attested by the large mosque in the north court of the basilica, has already been mentioned. Other early Islamic building plans have been recovered as well. One investigated by Katarina Otto-Dohrn, a colleague of Kollwitz's, has been identified as a palace of the Umayyad ruler Hisham.

In archaelogical studies of late antiquity, Byzantium, and the early Islamic period, Rusafa-Sergiopolis has become a fixed point for discussions of defensive city-building techniques, church architecture, sculpture, and pilgrim life within Syria and adjacent lands. Although many questions remain—such as the date of the site's earliest settlement, the location of the original tomb of Sergios, the existence of church buildings prior to the sixth century—past and current research activities are filling many gaps in our understanding of urban life in late antiquity.

Recommended Reading

W. Karnapp. *Die Stadtmauer von Rusafa in Syrien* (Berlin 1976).

J. Kollwitz. *AA* (1954) 119 / *AA* (1957) 141 / *AA* (1963) 328.

T. Ulbert. *AA* (1977) 563 / *JbAC* Suppl. 8 (1980) 559.

SYRIA BETWEEN BYZANTIUM AND ISLAM

BENJAMIN R. FOSTER

WHEN THE AILING AND DEFEATED BYZANTINE EMPEROR HERACLIUS in 636 looked his last upon Syria, a former Roman province wrested from his control by the Muslim conquerors, he exclaimed, "Farewell, O Syria, and what an excellent country this is for the enemy!" The Muslim conquest of Syria was momentous for the history of this region. Syria was an early center of Judaism and of Christianity in its various and often contentious eastern branches. In addition, for many centuries it had been a center of Hellenistic culture in its distinctive Near Eastern version and also part of the western and eastern Roman Empire. Prior to the Muslim conquest, many Arabs, some of them Christians, had already taken up residence in Syria, and one of their local kingdoms, known as Ghassan, had been recognized by the Byzantine emperors as a client state in the vain hope of safeguarding the imperial frontiers to the south and east.

At first the Muslim conquerors, ruling from Mecca, made few changes in the government and religious organization of the conquered lands, for they were content to collect taxes and to preside over conquests further afield. Yet with the establishment in 651 of the Umayyad caliphate in Damascus, capital of an increasingly secularized empire stretching from Spain to Central Asia, the Near Eastern world was drastically different from what it had been merely a century earlier. The eastern Roman, or Byzantine, Empire, ancient and proud as it was, faced a challenge not only on the field of battle (for the Muslims never ceased their efforts to conquer the rest of Byzantium), but also in the realm of faith and self-identity. Here was a new, revealed, aggressive, scriptural religion spread by a brilliant succession of military successes, a religion so sure of itself that, according to Muslim historians, an early caliph is said to have written to all the great kings of his age (including Heraclius), urging their immediate submission to Islam.

One may consider first the military and political confrontation of the two powers. The frontier between Byzantium and Islam ran roughly where that of Syria and Turkey runs today. The mountain passes separated march districts controlled by the two opposing sides. Each spring, for centuries after the conquest of Syria, thousands of Muslims massed into armies and raiding parties to cross the frontier and assault Byzantine fortresses in the hope of booty, prisoners, and expansion of Islam. These campaigns became the subject of a rich epic tradition in both Greek and Arabic. The poems give us a picture of a sometimes bloody, sometimes chivalrous, sometimes cruel, sometimes picaresque adventurism long before the Crusades. Each side earned the grudging respect of the other, and showed courage, determination, and adaptability as the conflict went on.

The climax of all Arab assaults on Byzantium was reached in 717, when the Arabs marched against the capital, Constantinople, by land and sent a large fleet to attack the city from the sea. The combination of "Greek fire" (liquid fire that was directed at the enemy through bronze tubes), a singularly harsh winter, the death of the caliph in Damascus, and the mighty land walls of Constantinople left the expedition a debacle. News of it reached as far as England, and the siege grew to a splendidly embroidered legend in medieval Muslim and Christian historiography.

With the collapse of the Umayyad caliphate in 750 and the transfer of the "state" to Baghdad under the Abbasids, Syria continued to be the staging ground for the great struggle between Christianity and Islam. Some idea of the expenditure of treasure alone in this effort can be gleaned from a budget copied from the caliph's archives of the early ninth century. This informs us that the revenues of the Syrian frontier provinces were about 70,000 dinars, of which 40,000 were used for maintenance costs of fortifications, 30,000 for troop salaries, and a deficit of 120,000 was incurred to meet additional expenses and to pay the costs of the raiding expeditions. On the other side, the Byzantine payroll for one military district for 810 is reputed to have been 13,000 talents of gold.

The ninth-century Abbasid caliph Harun al-Rashid, better known to us as the insatiable tale-hearer of the Arabian Nights, led in his turn a campaign against Byzantium, taking a number of forts and sending a raiding party to Cyprus. As an Arab poet expressed it:

Harun has thundered perils frightening,
His sword flashing ruin like bolts of lightning.
His banners now with victory fly,
They pass us waving like clouds in the sky![1]

The continuing conflict between Byzantium and Islam was carried on as well in the world of ideas. Christian theologians crossed pens

1. Abu al-'Atahiyah, quoted by al-Mas'udi in his account of a single combat between a Greek and an Arab during Harun's siege of Heraclea: *Muruj al-Dhahab* (Beirut 1965) 1:371.

with imaginary Saracens, and Muslim savants composed elegant and often heated responses. The debate was lively and long, and not without humor and even indecency. At first the Christians enjoyed a distinct advantage. Orthodox Christianity had been battling for many years to arrive at a definitive understanding of the nature of Christ; as veterans of this effort, all branches of the faith, including the Nestorians and Syrian Christians, were adept at polemics and partisan exegesis. So the Orthodox church turned to do battle with Islam as it had with the Jacobites, Nestorians, Monophysites, Manichaeans, and numerous other "heresies," and as before the dispute was mainly a Christological one. A polemical debate is of course impossible without some common ground to debate from, so the initial Christian polemical efforts were little more than ridicule of what Christians took to be the errors and confusions of Islam. As with so many other areas, Muslims mastered the necessary techniques in an incredibly short time, and so by the beginning of the ninth century they were well prepared to face all comers. They labored under the disadvantage of arguing both from the Bible and the Koran, whereas the Christian apologists as a group knew little of the Koran. No doubt an important impetus to the development and systematization of Muslim theology was the polemical onslaught that Muslim thinkers had to face, especially in Syria.

The lot of Christians living in Syria under the caliphate was a mixed one, like that of any subject people. In general, religious freedom was tolerated, with isolated instances of persecution, though expansion of the faith and prosyletizing were forbidden. Lives of Christian saints, as one would expect, paint a gloomy picture. Removed from the speculation and discursive thought of the theologians, popular religion was prey to superstition, vague fears and real suffering, marvels and forebodings. The symbolism of the apocalypse and the shadowy figure of the Antichrist could only too easily be given substance in the Arab conquests and the prophet of Islam. Muslims too suffered persecution at Christian hands for their faith, and an Arab poet once remarked that "the prison of a Christian is a Muslim grave."[2]

Beyond the confrontation on Syrian soil of two great faiths, championed by the two great political powers of the eastern Mediterranean, lay some respect and admiration on both sides. After the initial Byzantine contempt for the warrior of the desert comes astonishment and envy at the spectacular achievements of Islam. As a Byzantine emperor or patriarch is said to have written to Harun al-Rashid: "You possess in abundance the very finest goods and things that seem to us very precious and difficult to produce . . . let us not be fighting as

2. Marwan ibn Abi Hafsah, quoted by Tabari, *Tarikh al-Uman wal-Mulūk* (ed. de Goeje et al. Leiden 1879–1901) 3:707. For five laudatory couplets on the occasion of Harun's destruction of a Byzantine fortress at Safsaf, the grateful caliph gave this same poet 5000 dinars, his own mantle, ten Greek slave girls, and a steed from his own stables (Tabari *Tarikh* 3:742). A triumphal Byzantine poem of this type concentrates rather on the power of God; cf. S. Lampros *Historika Meletemata* (Athens 1884) 129–132.

though we were godless and had no lives to lose, emulating out of hatred the warfare of demons against mankind. . . ."[3] Perhaps the most lasting result of all this conflict was the rending asunder of the eastern and western Mediterranean worlds into cultural, religious, and political divisions still apparent in our own time. One is compelled to offer some positive results of this conflict and confrontation as well.

In the first instance, the challenge and response of two great faiths helped each to define itself, both within and in the face of attack. The continuing development of medieval Christian and Muslim theology owes much to the necessity of confronting a respected and feared opponent. The Arab conquerors, to some extent urban in background, mingled with the indigenous, already mixed population of greater Syria; but they maintained, even in the new urban environment there, proud memories of their tribal lineage in Arabia. The Muslim builders of the great desert palaces of Syria and Jordan and the magnificent mosques of Damascus and Jerusalem had before them monuments of long-lived Syrian architectural traditions. Mosaic, tile work, engraving, glass blowing, manuscript illumination, weaving, carpentry, and metal working were all native Syrian arts in antiquity and all were destined to flourish under Muslim rule to such an extent that one forms from them, first and foremost, one's notions of "Islamic art."

Syria was always a mixed and productive cultural environment, especially in the Hellenistic and early Islamic periods, for here the great rival empires of the late classical and early Middle Ages first acted out their destinies. The spiritual, incorporeal qualities of Byzantine art and the grace and symmetry of the art of Islam were in no small measure influenced by their early greater Syrian environment, where each developed together and separately. What the Muslims came to learn of both Christianity and Judaism, not to mention classical civilization, may initially at least be traced to the multilingual culture of Syria. Here a local form of Aramaic, known as Syriac, a language belonging to the same family as Arabic, was widely used in Christian communities for religious, historical, and philosophical discourse. This language, lying between Greek and Arabic, as it were, helped the communication between them, both in direct translation and in the transmission of ideas. The classical legacy, expanded and refined by the Muslims, was in due course to be returned to Europe in the Renaissance, even though Byzantium itself fell to the Muslim Turks in the fifteenth century and the caliphates of Damascus and Baghdad were by then only memories.

3. Cedrenus *Compendium Historiarum* ed. Niebuhr (Bonn 1838) 2:34–35 // Leo Grammaticus *Chronographia* ed. Bekker (Bonn 1842) 203–204 // Georgios Monachus *Chronicon Syntomon* ed. De Boor (Leipzig 1904) 2:773. The authenticity of this letter is open to doubt.

In the trapezoidal panels, framed by borders of stylized branches, a cross and a vine leaf are recognizable. The upper part of the cross has been chiselled off, perhaps when the capital was removed from a Christian building and reused during the Islamic period.

E.S.

229
Capital with monogram

Site: Origin unknown, imported from Asia Minor
Date: A.D. 550–600
Material: Marble
Height: 35 cm; *top surface:* 45 × 45 cm
Museum No.: Damascus 5143
Literature: Cf. Wulff *Bildwerke* I 57 No. 168

This capital, slightly larger than Cat. No. 228, may have belonged to the front of an altar. It is decorated with horizontal zigzag bands which are framed above and below with staffs and heart-shaped leaves. On two sides there is a cross-shaped monogram in a round medallion. The capital was later made into a goblet: the interior was hollowed out and provided with a side spout.

E.S.

228
Capital with cross and vine leaf

Site: Raqqa, imported from Asia Minor
Date: A.D. 550–700
Material: Marble
Height: 26 cm; *Top surface:* 29.5 × 29.5 cm
Museum No.: Damascus A. 1869
Literature: Zouhdi *Catalogue* (1976) 255

Although architectural sculpture of high quality was produced in Syria from native stone during the early Christian period (see Figs. 77,78) capitals were occasionally imported. They were particularly valued if the stone was rare—for instance, marble—even when the quality of the carving was rather poor, as is the case with this sculpture.

This and the following capital were imported from Asia Minor, hence not from the center of Byzantium but from the provinces. Considering the small size of these capitals, we suggest that they may have belonged to a ciborium, a canopied structure above an altar.

ca. A.D. 400–600

230

Fragment of wall painting with three saints

See color plate p. 430

Site: Monastery church Mar Yaqub near Qara, 89 km north
  of Damascus
Date: A.D. 1100–1200
Material: Paint on plaster
Height: 79 cm; *width:* 103 cm
Museum: Damascus
Literature: Cf. J. Nasrallah *Bulletin d'études orientales* 10
  (1943–44) 5 / *AAAS* 2 (1952) 149 / *AAAS* 6 (1956) 63 / *AAAS*
  8–9 (1958–1959) 59 / *AAAS* 11–12 (1961–1962) 45 // J. Leroy
  AAAS 25 (1975) 95

In 1975, in the apse of a small monastery church near
Qara, the remains of frescoes were found under more
recent wall plaster. Two segments of these frescoes are
shown here. Today Qara in the Qalamun Mountains is
a small market town of 7,000 inhabitants; in antiquity
the main road from Damascus to the cities of north
Syria passed through here. Qara was christianized
quite early, and according to legend the apostle
Thomas preached in Qalamun. Many churches in the
region are dedicated to him. The place was apparently
quite significant during the Byzantine period. At the
time of the Synod of Chalcedon (451) it was the seat of
a bishopric, and Qara remained entirely Christian until the conquest of Baibar (1266), when the population
was either butchered or deported. However, a few
Christians later returned, Qara was rebuilt, and today
approximately 500 Christians (Catholic and Greek
Orthodox) live here. The monastery, dedicated to
Saint Jacob, is situated a few kilometers northwest of
Qara. It was abandoned in 1908, but the church—
which contained the frescoes—remains in good condition.

One fragment shows three persons with halos,
dressed in shirtlike garments. The head of the left figure—with short hair, a stubby beard, and energetic
features—is still partially preserved. What he holds in
his right hand raised to his chest is not discernible:
perhaps it is a scroll. He is possibly Saint Andreas.
The figure in the middle holds a scroll in his left hand
while his right hand is raised in a gesture of blessing.
The Greek inscription on his left is difficult to read; at
the very bottom we can recognize three letters which
may have belonged to an older fresco. This figure may
represent Saint John, the Evangelist, the youngest of
the apostles. Little of the third figure remains. His

right hand is raised in a gesture of prayer.[1] Between
him and the middle figure are the remains of a Syriac
and a Greek inscription. Syriac (a late Aramaic language), spoken by the people of Qalamun, was used in
the liturgy here until the eighteenth century. Neo-
Aramaic is still spoken in three nearby villages to this
day.

The beauty and proportions of this fresco suggest a
date in the twelfth century.

J.N.

[1]Cf. J. Leroy *AAAS* 25 (1975) 102.

231

Fragment of wall painting with Saint Michael

See color plate p. 430

Site: Monastery church Mar Yaqub near Qara
Date: 1100–1200
Material: Paint on plaster
Height: 62 cm; *width:* 92 cm
Museum: Damascus

This fragment shows an angel, probably Saint
Michael, with a halo and spread wings. His hair is
held by a band with a gem in the middle. The left
hand, raised to his chest, holds a spear, the point of
which is lost. The raised right hand has the palm
turned outward.[1]

J.N.

[1]Cf. an icon from Constantinople from the tenth century
in A. Grabar *La peinture byzantine* (Geneva 1953) 186.

232

Floor mosaic from a church

See color plate p. 431

Site: Halawa, on the left bank of the Euphrates
Date: A.D. 471
Material: Assorted stones
Dimensions: (left to right, height × length): 1.61 × 1.31 m;
  1.65 × 1.35 m; 1.54 × 1.39 m; 1.70 × 1.30 m
Museum: Damascus
Literature: J. Balty *Mosaiques antiques de Syrie* (Brussels
  1977) 126 No. 58 // A. Abou Assaf *AAAS* 22 (1972) 136
  Plate 141:2 (inscription) // cf. R. van den Broek *The Myth
  of the Phönix* (Leiden 1972) // P. Canivet *Byzantion* 49
  (1979) 57

Syrian archaeologists discovered a few square

meters of a mosaic floor from the center aisle and the apse of a church in the small town of Halawa in 1971. Two inscriptions with the same content, in Greek and Syriac, mention the date 471 and the name of Bishop Nonnos, who is well known from synod records. He succeeded Bishop Ibas in 457 and died in 471, the year mentioned in the inscription, which thereby provides one basis for dating Near Eastern mosaics.

The mosaic of the apse is almost completely preserved. Representations of animals, trees, and plants are symmetrically arranged. In the center is the main figure (not illustrated): the mythological bird Phoenix with a halo standing on a small hill. The Phoenix is the pinnacle of a triangle, the base of which is formed by the second important element of this composition: two sheep facing each other on opposite sides of a pomegranate tree (illustrated). This scene is frequently found in churches from this period. A duck and a goose, weeds, flowers, and shrubs fill the background. Above are two cypresses with double crowns, an apple and a pear tree and next to the Phoenix a bull and a unicorn (not illustrated); there is a small tree above the Phoenix. The entire mosaic is framed by a red border studded with jewels and semi-precious stones. The outer frieze, only partially preserved, is decorated with plant and Nile River motifs, such as fish, ducks, and birds. Such motifs are common in Near Eastern churches from the fifth and sixth centuries.

The Halawa mosaic is almost contemporary with the floor mosaic of the portico of Apamea (A.D. 469), which shows that there existed an essentially decorative Syrian style characterized by the absence of depth and shading. The animals and the plants are quite stylized and stand isolated from the monochrome background. We have here an imaginary composition, with symbolic instead of narrative elements. It is not by accident that the Phoenix occupies a key position at the pinnacle of the triangle. In antiquity the Phoenix was the symbol of immortality; Christianity adopted the figure and reinterpreted its symbolism to represent belief in eternal life. The sheep on either side of the pomegranate tree symbolize the souls, the tree itself, eternity—a symbolism already witnessed in pre-Christian tombs. The two animals in the upper frieze may be interpreted symbolically as well: in a Roman text from the beginning of the first century the bull and unicorn are described as symbols of the crucified Christ.

J.B.

233
Horseshoe-shaped table top

Site: Hama
Date: A.D. 350–400
Material: Marble
Width: 108 cm; *length:* 107.5 cm; *depth with modern frame:* 7.5 cm
Museum No.: Damascus 4952
Literature: G. Roux *Tables chrétiennes en marbre découvertes à Salamine: Salamine de Chypre* IV (Paris 1973) 134, Fig. 66 // M. Bonfioli *Una mensa a sigma a Roma: Atti della Pontificia Accademia romana di archeologia, Rendic.* 50 (Rome 1977–1978) 114 // cf. G. Tchalenko *Eglises de village de la Syrie du nord* (1979) Figs. 117,118

This table top was found in Hama in a well, and it is therefore not known whether it came from a church, a tomb, or a private house. Its back cannot be examined because the individual fragments were set in plaster during restoration of the piece. The flat table surface is framed by an elegant border frieze of animals following each other or in contests: lions, bears, antelopes, stags, and deer. In the left corner is a portrait of a beardless male wearing a diadem, and in the right corner a portrait of a female wearing a crown and a pearl necklace. On the outside the frieze is bordered by an astragal showing a string of beads. Similar table tops—either horseshoe-shaped or round—were widespread in the eastern Mediterranean. We do not know where they were made, perhaps in Constantinople or Antioch? None of them is earlier than the fourth century, and a few date from the fifth and sixth centuries.

Our piece belongs to the more elaborately decorated table tops, with the astragal as an ornament on the outer rim. Other examples show scenes from the Old and New Testaments or representations of ancient mythology—never, however, mixing pagan and Christian scenes. Hunting scenes and depictions of animals are frequent, but as they are common to both sacred and profane symbolism, they do not answer our question as to the original use of the table tops. The shape is found in representations of the Last Supper, where Christ and the apostles are often assembled around a horseshoe-shaped table. This fact raises the question of whether we are perhaps dealing with an altar plate, but no evidence for this theory has been found, and more often it seems clear that these pieces were used as table tops holding sacred objects. A north Syrian church had a horseshoe-shaped table standing on a raised platform near the altar, which probably held

the Bible and the cross while mass was being read. Besides such use in the early churches, the table may have been used in cults for the dead and may have held the funerary meal.

C.S.

234
Basalt cross

Site: Hauran
Date: A.D. 500–700
Material: Basalt
Height: 90.5 cm; *width:* 65 cm; *depth:* 25 cm
Museum No.: Damascus 152
Literature: R. M. Mouterde *Les découvertes intéressant l'archéologie chrétienne, récemment effectuées en Syrie: Congresso archeologia* (Ravenna 1932) 465, Fig. 8 // *Dictionnaire d'archéologie chrétienne et de liturgie* XV: 2. col. 1717 No. 10965

Very few figurative reliefs from early Syrian Byzantine art are preserved. This piece is one of only six known stone reliefs with representations of the stylites, a cult that developed around the Syrian Saint Simeon. In the more recent works about stylites, it is not mentioned because it was thought to be lost shortly after its publication as a drawing by Mouterde (1932: see *Literature* above). At first sight, the composition looks like two overlapping standing pillars divided by two suspended horizontal persons forming a cross. The two pillars have a basis and a simply profiled capital but are not of equal importance, as indicated by their different size. The lower pillar is crowned with a wreath, and on either side of its capital are two circular medallions, perhaps meant to indicate the sun and the moon (their design is completely worn off). The two figures carrying the wreath are probably meant to represent angels, although they have neither halos nor wings.

This representation may be interpreted on the basis of the iconography of Simeon the Elder and the Younger. Two angels carrying a wreath are depicted on a pilgrim memento from Qal'at Siman (Cat. No. 240) as well as on numerous other depictions of stylites. The small upper pillar has a parallel on a relief in Paris, but it is not known whether it is to be understood as a symbol of victory over death or whether it represents two stylites, teacher and student. It is unfortunate that the representations on the sides of the larger pillar are

233, left

234

lost, since they might have indicated which stylite is meant. In depictions of Simeon the Younger, his mother, Saint Martha, and his student often appear on either side of the pillar.

In the composition as a whole there is a close connection between the depiction of the stylites and the symbolism of the cross. The abstract rendering, depicting only the pillars and not the stylites themselves, has close parallels in north Syria, and this is one of the best examples of the Syrian fondness for abstract symbolism. Another example is found in two Syrian depictions of the crucifixion, where Christ himself forms the cross.

C.S.

235

235
Clay pilgrim flask

Site: Homs (museum purchase)
Date: A.D. 400–600
Material: Terracotta
Height: 6.3 cm; *depth:* 2.2 cm
Museum No.: Damascus 1769/3895
Literature: Cf. the close parallels in Berlin and Paris: Wulff
    Bildwerke I Nos. 1350, 1387 // E. Coche de la Ferté
    L'antiquité Chrétienne au Musée du Louvre (1958) No. 64

Such flasks, made of glass, clay, or metal, held sacred
oil or water. They were available as souvenirs at
shrines or other places of pilgrimage. They resemble
—whether round or oval—shepherds' flasks, and they
had either handles or holes for attaching a carrying
strap. They were decorated with representations of
saints or depictions of New Testament miracles.
   On the front of this flask is a bearded apostle standing under an arcade; he has an incense vessel in his
right hand and with his left he holds an open book to
his chest. On the back the same apostle (perhaps
Paul) is depicted with two followers in a sailboat.
C.S.

236
Clay pilgrim flask

Site: Zabadani near Damascus
Date: A.D. 400–500
Material: Terracotta
Height: 10 cm; *depth:* 2 cm
Museum No.: Damascus 10279
Literature: Cf. L. Y. Rahmani *Israel Exploration Journal* 10
    (1966) 71, Plate 8A

This round pilgrim flask is meant to hold sacred oil.
Both sides have the same representation—the Annunciation of the Virgin Mary—and the same Greek inscription—XERE KAI XARI TO MENHO KYRIOC META
COY, "Be greeted, most gracious one, the Lord is with
you." Mary is shown in a high-backed chair, wearing a
halo; in her raised right hand she holds a spinning
wheel while her left moves the thread. On the right an
angel approaches her, a hand raised in greeting; between them is the star of Bethlehem.
   Iconographic representation of the Annunciation is
only rarely documented—for example, on a monument
in Ravenna—and it is therefore especially important
that there is a flask corresponding exactly to ours in

the Department of Antiquities in Jerusalem. Both
flasks were made at the same shrine, and since they
were both found in the Syrian-Palestinian area, we
may assume that they were produced there.
C.S.

237
Clay lamp

Site: Hauran
Date: A.D. 600–800
Material: Terracotta
Height: 9 cm; *length:* 15.5 cm
Museum No.: Damascus 12802
Literature: Cf. Zouhdi *AAAS* 24 (1974) Plate 175:57 // E. Day
    Berytus 7 (1942) 64, Plate XII

This lamp has a design of stylized branches. A cross
with a medallion forms part of the wide handle.
Lamps with striated patterns were common in the
sixth century, but the highly arched shape of this lamp
indicates a later date, the seventh–eighth centuries.
C.S.

238
Mold for a lamp

Site: Damascus (museum purchase)
Date: A.D. 400–600
Material: Limestone
Height: 5 cm; *length:* 14.5 cm; *width:* 11.5 cm; *length of
    lamp:* 12 cm
Museum No.: Damascus 6746/15628
Literature: Cf. Zouhdi *AAAS* 24 (1974) Plates 173:49,51

The top part of an oil lamp was shaped in this negative
mold. The finished lamp had a circular body with a
flat handle, a rounded spout with concave sides, and a
hole for the wick in front, common in Byzantine
lamps. This lamp contains a number of decorative
motifs which usually appear only individually. There is
a shell design in front of the burning hole, a stylized
leaf design on the handle, while the top has vines with
birds pecking at grapes. The outer rim is decorated
with a string of pearls. Vines with animals was a popular motif for both Roman and Byzantine lamps, but
only seldom is the rendering as vivid and differenti-
ated as in this example. Similarly shaped lamps from
the fifth and sixth centuries have been excavated in
Syria, and the design of birds and vines is not un-

236, 237, right

ca. A.D. 400–600

238

design elements, such as birds and plants, are arranged symmetrically around this central tree. The carefully worked small globes distributed over the field indicate that the stamp was made in the second half of the seventh or perhaps the beginning of the eighth century. The composition of the scene has parallels in Syrian mosaics (see Cat. No. 232) and in miniature art from the fifth and sixth centuries. If this stamp was made for Christians, the scene could be interpreted as a heavenly one. But the date of origin requires caution, since the iconographic elements and the structure of the design have Islamic parallels. Therefore, we cannot be sure whether this bread stamp was commissioned by Christians.
C.S.

known in this period; however, none of the numerous excavated lamps correspond exactly in form and decoration to this mold.
C.S.

239
Bread stamp

Site: North Syria (museum purchase)
Date: A.D. 650–750
Material: Terracotta
Diameter: 6.5 cm; *depth:* 4.5 cm
Museum No.: Damascus 4044
Literature: G. Galavaris *Bread and Liturgy. The Symbolism of Early Christian and Byzantine Bread Stamps* (Madison 1970)

From about the fourth century Christians used different stamps for regular bread and for bread for the communion. It is, however, often impossible to distinguish clearly between the two types of bread stamps. Crosses and animal symbols such as fish and stags appear on both kinds, and without an inscription it is not clear whether the stamps were meant for communion or not.

In our example the main scene depicts two gazelles standing on either side of the tree of life; all the other

240, 241
Pilgrim mementos

Site: Qal'at Siman
Date: A.D. 400–600
Material: Terracotta
Diameter: 2.8–3 cm; 2.4 cm
Museum Nos.: Damascus 3613/4047
Literature: G. Tchalenko *Villages antiques de la Syrie du nord* III (Paris 1958) 43, Figs. 25,26,28 // P. Castellana and R. Fernandez *Les saints stylites syriens* (1975) 175, Fig. 28 // V. Elbern *Jdl* 80 (1965) 287, Fig. 6

The concept of a "blessing" was projected onto objects which pilgrims obtained at shrines and could bring home as salutary souvenirs or holy mementos. The memento with a stylite representation is significant since it was found in the pilgrimage shrine of Qal'at Siman and therefore depicts Simeon the Elder rather than his successor, Simeon the Younger. Saint Simeon is depicted standing on his pillar. We recognize the high base of the pillar and the balustrade which surrounds the platform on top. The saint wears the Syrian monk's garb with a pointed hood, there is a cross above his head, and two angels are offering him wreaths. At the foot of the pillar there is an incense-burning stand on one side and a ladder extends to the platform of the pillar. The angels with the wreaths symbolize the triumph of the martyrs or saints, while the incense stand signifies that offerings and prayers were given at the pillar. The depiction of a servant or student next to the ladder is well known from other representations of stylites.

239

240

241

469

242

The second memento (Cat. No. 241) shows the three
holy kings approaching Mary, who sits on a throne
with the child in her lap. The three bearded kings
wear short tunics and have their hands concealed in
their garments. The star of Bethlehem shines above.
The three kings wear globular headdresses similar to
those of the Persian Sassanian kings.
C.S.

242
Candelabrum

Site: Damascus (museum purchase)
Date: A.D. 400–600
Material: Bronze
Height: 10.5 cm; *length:* 28.5 cm
Museum No.: Damascus 6474/15247
Literature: K. Weitzmann *Age of Spirituality* (Princeton
   1979) Nos. 557, 559 // Wulff *Bildwerke* I No. 1008

Originally the central globe had four arms, of which
two remain; they are shaped like branches and end in
animal (perhaps dolphin) heads. One arm is mounted
upside down. On top of the globe is a lotus blossom
ending in a ring for hanging the lamp, while the bottom of the globe is decorated with a simple cross.
   Two other candelabra, one in the Metropolitan
Museum in New York and the other in the Hermitage

Museum in Leningrad, resemble this piece. The candelabrum in New York has six branches extending from a central globe ending in circular flat plates with chains suspended. The Leningrad example has a mid-section shaped like a three-aisled church; the branch-shaped arms end in dolphin heads with wide rings that held glass lamps. The light construction of our example, which is very similar to the one in Leningrad, indicates that the glass lamp holders were suspended directly from the four arms.
C.S.

243
Votive cross

Site: Aleppo (museum purchase)
Date: A.D. 500–1000
Material: Bronze
Length: 37.2 cm; *preserved width:* 17 cm
Museum No.: Aleppo 5180
Literature: Cf. F. Seirafi *AAAS* 10 (1960) Fig. 19 // Wulff
　　Bildwerke I Nos. 944, 945

Unfortunately the lower part of this cross, which would have indicated whether it was carried, mounted, or possibly suspended, is not preserved. However, the size of the cross excludes the possibility of its being part of a candelabrum or lamp. The arms are irregularly decorated with a design of circles within circles, and there are circular plates at the corners. The simple ornamentation and lack of any inscription make it impossible to accurately date the object. It may be from the sixth century or considerably later.
C.S.

244
Bronze lamp

Site: Aleppo (museum purchase)
Date: A.D. 400–600
Material: Bronze
Height: 14 cm; *length:* 24.5 cm
Museum No.: Aleppo 6147
Literature: Cf. the bronze lamps with stands from Syria in
　　Ross *Catalogue of the Byzantine and Early Medieval*
　　Antiquities in the Dumbarton Oaks Collection (Washington
　　1962) Nos. 34, 39, also 37

The bronze lamps shown here (Cat. Nos. 244–247) were all purchased from art dealers. Some of them have parallels only in museums outside Syria, while

243

244

ca. A.D. 400–600

others have at least the shape in common with excavated Syrian lamps. In the case of Cat. No. 246 we may assume that it came from one of the best Syrian workshops.

A square indentation on the bottom of the lamp in No. 244 indicates that it was mounted on a stand. The lamp is unusually long, with quite a large opening. The lid, decorated with a dolphin, was cast separately and fastened with a hinge. The handle is ornamented with a Latin cross surrounded by a heart-shaped frame. Similar lamps, some with stands, have been found in Syria.

C.S.

245
Peacock-shaped lamp

Site: Damascus (museum purchase)
Date: A.D. 500–600
Material: Bronze
Height: 10 cm; *length:* 14 cm, *with chain,* 36 cm
Museum No.: Damascus 6485/13220
Literature: Cf. B. Zouhdi *AAAS* 24 (1974) 161 // M. C. Ross
    Archaeology 13 (1960) 134 / *Catalogue* I No. 41 // Wulff
    Bildwerke I No. 768

This lamp is shaped like a peacock; the hole for the wick is in the tail, and the top feathers form the lid of

246

the filling hole. The lid was cast separately and is attached with a hinge. All the details—the wing feathers, the comb on top of the head, the eyes, and the beak—are carefully incised.

Approximately a dozen such lamps are known. Most of them stood on a table or a stand, but a few, like this one, had optional chains for hanging.

The peacock as a symbol of paradise has a long history in ancient Near Eastern art, and it survived in reliefs, mosaics, and the miniature art of the Byzantine period.

C.S.

246
Foot-shaped lamp

Site: Homs (museum purchase)
Date: A.D. 500–600
Material: Bronze
Height: 12.5 cm; *length:* 16 cm; *height with chain:* 35 cm
Museum No.: Damascus 6178
Literature: Cf. K. Weitzmann *Age of Spirituality* (Princeton 1979) No. 317

Foot-shaped lamps were popular in the Hellenistic-Roman and Byzantine periods. The lamps were usually shaped like a right foot with a sandal; they had

chains for hanging or carrying. The toes form the opening for the wick in this case, while the spout for pouring the oil is in the ankle. The lid is an elaborate double-tiered round structure with two parts which are individually hinged and which can be opened separately. The lid probably represents the dome of a church.

In the Metropolitan Museum, New York, there is a foot-shaped lamp so similar to our piece that it is possible they were made in the same workshop.
C.S.

247
Incense lamp

Site: Homs (museum purchase)
Date: A.D. 500–600
Material: Bronze
Height: 16 cm; *upper diameter:* 12.5–14 cm
Museum No.: Damascus 6152/14708
Literature: Cf. K. Weitzmann *Age of Spirituality* (Princeton 1979) Nos. 531, 544

This goblet-shaped vessel, suspended on three chains, may have been a hanging lamp, but its size suggests that it was used as an incense vessel, swung by hand. The shape of the vessel has parallels in the famous Syrian silver goblets and also in numerous glass goblets found in Syrian excavations. As these date from the sixth century, we suggest a similar date for this lamp.
C.S.

ISLAMIC PERIOD
CA. 600–1600

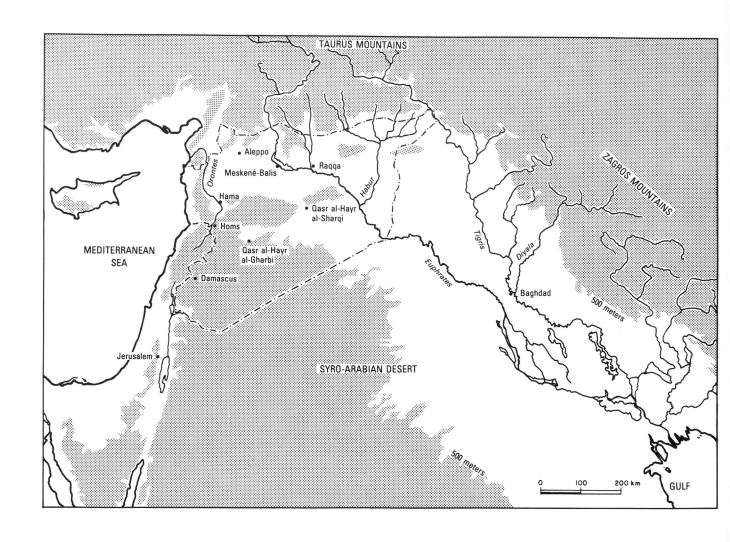

TAURUS MOUNTAINS

ZAGROS MOUNTAINS

MEDITERRANEAN
SEA

• Aleppo

Meskené-Balis
• Raqqa

Hama
• Qasr al-Hayr
al-Sharqi

• Homs

Qasr al-Hayr
al-Gharbi

• Damascus

Orontes

Habur

Tigris

Diyala

Euphrates

• Baghdad

500 meters

Jerusalem

SYRO-ARABIAN DESERT

500 meters

0   100   200 km

GULF

ISLAMIC DAMASCUS AND ALEPPO

JERE L. BACHARACH

DAMASCUS AND ALEPPO ARE ISLAMIC CITIES: THEIR POPULATION IS overwhelmingly Muslim, the social and religious organizations are predominantly Islamic, and almost all the remaining historical monuments are associated with Islam (see Fig. 85). But the transformation of these two great cities into centers of Islamic learning and culture was a slow and complex process reaching its pinnacle approximately five centuries after the original conquests.

During the decade following the death of the Prophet Muhammad (632) Muslim armies continued the policies he had established of bringing more and more territory under Muslim political and military control. The caliphs, successors of Muhammad to leadership of the community, directed these first military activities from western Arabia, particularly from the city of Medina. The armies, primarily composed of Arab cavalry, demonstrated brilliant military qualities as they defeated much larger forces of Persian Sassanians in Iraq and Iran and Byzantines in Greater Syria and then Egypt. These military forays involved minimal disruption of the activities and livelihood of the local populations, so that when Damascus and Aleppo permanently surrendered to Muslim conquerors at the end of 636 the most significant change was that taxes had to be paid to a new master. Local Christian communities probably enjoyed greater freedom than they had under the enforced orthodoxy of Byzantine rule.

Not only did the Muslim conquerors not force the populace to convert; it is even doubtful that they encouraged it. In addition, in order to separate this numerically small and newly converted military elite from the bulk of the population, Muslims established for themselves a series of garrison enclaves as their military and political centers. Initially Syria was governed from a small center on the Golan Heights called al-Jabiya and not from Damascus.

In 639 Mu'awiya (d. 680) was appointed, by the caliph, governor of

Figure 85
Aleppo in the eighteenth century.

the territories of Syria. By 656 he was engaged in a power struggle
with 'Ali, the fourth caliph who was also the Prophet's first cousin and
son-in-law. The results of this first civil war were momentous, creating a permanent split in the Muslim community. One group, the
minority, who believed that 'Ali and his family should have been the
immediate successors of Muhammad, were to be known as the
Shi'ites. The majority of the community, the Sunni, accepted the
historical development as it took place and were willing to recognize
Mu'awiya as the next caliph and 'Ali as the fourth.

Symbolic of Mu'awiya's victory in 661 following the death of 'Ali was the establishment of Damascus as the political and military capital of the Islamic world. Thus Damascus became the center of an empire which was to stretch from southern France and the Iberian Peninsula to the Indus River in India and the region of Transoxiana in the modern U.S.S.R. The dynasty was called the Umayyad after Mu'awiya's grandfather, Umayya, and lasted until 750, with the most important period for the history of Damascus being the end of the seventh and first decades of the eighth century.

The Umayyad caliph Abd al-Malik (685–705) instituted major changes which would stress the Islamic and Arab identity of the ruling elite. His requirement that all government documents be written in Arabic acted as a stimulus for religious conversion by some of the urban elite and bureaucracy as Arabic and Islam became totally intertwined: for Muslims, God had revealed his Truth in Arabic to the Prophet Muhammad. Abd al-Malik also introduced new coins which featured Arabic inscriptions rather than representations of rulers or religious figures with Greek or medieval Persian inscriptions, as was customary on Byzantine and Persian coins. Finally, to commemorate the triumph of Islam over all previous religions, Abd al-Malik had built in Jerusalem, at the site of the Second Jewish Temple, the magnificent structure known as the Dome of the Rock. Jerusalem, with this unique building, was to become the third holiest Muslim city after Mecca and Medina.

Abd al-Malik's son al-Walid (705–715) established a major building policy whose most spectacular creation was the Umayyad Mosque in Damascus. Using the site of a Roman *temenos* (sanctuary) which had become the locale of the Church of Saint John, al-Walid called upon the best craftsmen from Constantinople and within his empire to construct and decorate his new mosque. The basic style included a large open courtyard and a covered area on the side closest to Mecca (the *qibla* direction). The walls were covered with elaborate mosaics (Fig. 86). Art historians debate whether the mosaic scenes of unwalled cities represent towns conquered by Muslims or symbolic renditions of Koranic visions of paradise. Whatever the original significance of these images, they have been lost as Muslims soon established for themselves a visual vocabulary for their religious and public buildings which stressed geometric design, floral and vine patterns, and calligraphy. This tradition rejected the use of human, animal, or "realistic" presentations. Even the use of mosaics as a decorative technique fell into disfavor and was rarely used after the Umayyad era.

cultural life were accomplished by Nur al-Din (1146–1174), leader of the Zangid dynasty, by various members of the Ayyubid dynasty (1171–1250), and by numerous sultans and governors associated with Mamluk rule (1250–1517).

Nur al-Din undertook a *jihad* or holy war against the enemies of Sunni Islam, which included both Crusaders and Shi'ite Muslims. He took control of Aleppo from his father and began a major construction program which included rebuilding the city walls, restoring the Umayyad Mosque, creating a hospital (*maristan*), establishing a house of justice (*Dar al-'Adl*), endowing residences (*khanaqah*s) for *sufi*s (mystics), building new schools (*madrasa*s), and turning the citadel into the seat of government. Many of these activities represented new developments for the Syrian communities. Madrasas as centers of Sunni learning had been created in the Muslim East and were now carried to the Syrian Sunni community through the patronage of Nur al-Din. Eventually he would build six madrasas in Aleppo and numerous others in Damascus and elsewhere. The spread of sufi orders represented another religious development which had important social and economic implications, because the Sunni population could organize themselves along sufi lines as well as by quarters.

In 1154 Nur al-Din took Damascus and made it one of his administrative centers. His incorporation of this ancient city into his territories had been a result of Crusader pressures against the former Muslim rulers of the city, in particular, the military campaigns associated with the Second Crusade. Nur al-Din's program in Damascus paralleled that of Aleppo, and the physical character of the city rapidly changed as madrasas, khanaqahs, a Dar al-'Adl, a maristan, a rebuilt city wall, and a restored citadel emerged. Nur al-Din was eventually buried in Damascus, as was the founder of the Ayyubid dynasty, Salah al-Din (1171–1194).

The Ayyubid period marked the high point for Damascus and Aleppo as centers of Muslim religious, cultural, and intellectual activities. The building program begun by Nur al-Din continued with the addition by the Ayyubid rulers of new madrasas, khanaqahs, and other buildings. The Ayyubids rebuilt the citadels of both Aleppo and Damascus, making the former one of the most formidable and impressive medieval fortifications in the Middle East. Although numerous rulers after Nur al-Din stressed their Sunni Islamic identity and thus created a critical link between themselves and the majority of the population, the fact that the palace and primary governmental offices were placed in the citadel emphasized the distance between the rulers and ruled. This gap was accentuated by ethnic differences:

Nur al-Din was of Turkish background, the Ayyubids Kurdish, and the Mamluk rulers of a non-Islamic, slave origin, people who were imported primarily from Central Asia, converted, freed, and then established themselves as military and political rulers of the region.

The Mamluks had seized power in 1250 in Egypt. But it was the Mongol invasion of Syria in 1260 after these Central Asian non-Muslim warriors had sacked Baghdad which brought to an end the Ayyubid dynasty and the establishment of Mamluk power. After defeating the Mongols, the Mamluks seized Damascus and Aleppo and for the next 250 years ruled these cities from Cairo. Aleppo suffered the most, as it was a frontier post which exchanged hands between Mamluks and Mongols and then became a jumping-off point for Mamluk campaigns into Asia Minor. Damascus, which had been partially sacked by Mongols in 1260 and restored under initial Mamluk rule, quickly found itself subordinate to developments in Cairo. During the fourteenth century many buildings, including mosques, madrasas, and water fountains, were built under Mamluk patronage, but the population as a whole suffered extortions by these non-Arab Muslims.

The Mamluk attempts to monopolize economic activities for their own benefit and their constant internecine warfare also had a negative impact on the welfare of the local Syrian and Egyptian populations. The power of the gangs of young men increased as they were used by different Mamluk factions or were able to seize opportunities when Mamluk rule was lax. The political and—for about a century—economic conditions changed for the better when all of Syria and Egypt fell under the control of the Ottoman sultans after the military campaigns of Sultan Selim I in 1516 and 1517. Aleppo and Damascus were now part of an empire centered in Istanbul.

The process by which these two important cities were transformed from Byzantine Christian cities into centers of a rich and varied Muslim life is not recorded in the historical sources. However, the architectural record as well as the accounts of the activities of numerous rulers allows the reconstruction of many of the changes. The first Muslim dynasty, the Umayyads, established a visible Muslim presence by building the first mosques. Although political power shifted from Syria to Iraq, conversion continued, and when Aleppo and Damascus became the focus of major political developments in the late eleventh and twelfth centuries, their populations had become overwhelmingly Muslim. The rule of Zangids, Ayyubids, and Mamluks changed the physical character of the cities by the addition of numerous buildings which emphasized the Islamic identification of both the rulers and the population. The religious practices also shifted as intellectual activities were centered in madrasas and many individuals joined sufi organizations. Even the relationship between the rulers and ruled changed as the rulers set themselves up in citadels which dominated the urban setting. Following the Ottoman conquest in the early sixteenth century, Aleppo and Damascus became two among numerous provincial cities, and their cultural, artistic, and political lives declined.

Recommended Reading

N. Elissèff. "Dimashk." *Encyclopaedia of Islam.* 2nd ed. Vol. II.

Oleg Grabar. *The Formation of Islamic Art* (New Haven: Yale University Press, 1973).

R. Stephen Humphreys. "Damascus." *Dictionary of the Middle Ages.* Vol. IV (1984) / *From Saladin to the Mongols* (Albany: SUNY Press, 1977).

Ira M. Lapidus. "Aleppo." *Dictionary of the Middle Ages.* Vol. I (1982) / *Muslim Cities in the Later Middle Ages* (Cambridge, Mass.: Harvard University Press, 1967).

J. Sauvaget. "Halab." *Encyclopaedia of Islam.* 2nd ed. Vol. III.

QASR AL-HAYR AL-GHARBI

Location: On the Raqqa–Damascus desert route, near Jebel Rawaq, some 60 km southwest of Palmyra

Dates: First century A.D., construction of the Harbaqa dam and creation of an artificial oasis and establishment of the communications route along the Roman road to Palmyra; 559, foundation of a monastery by the Ghassanid prince al-Harith ibn Jabala; 724–727, reactivation of the oasis by the Umayyad caliph Hisham and foundation of a palace city; 1187 to beginning of the fourteenth century, installation of a mail station in the ruins of the palace

Exploration: 1930, air and topographic survey of oasis (A. Poidebard); 1936–1938, excavation of Umayyad structures (D. Schlumberger); 1939–1950, reconstruction of the gate wings of the palace in the National Museum, Damascus (M. Ecochard)

Publications: A. Poidebard *La Trace de Rome dans le desert de Syrie* (1934) 187 // D. Schlumberger *Syria* 20 (1939) 195, 324 / *Syria* 25 (1946) 86 // S. Abd al-Haqq *AAAS* 1/1 (1951) 129 (Arabic part 5) // K. A. C. Creswell *Early Muslim Architecture* 1–2 (2nd ed. Oxford 1969) 506

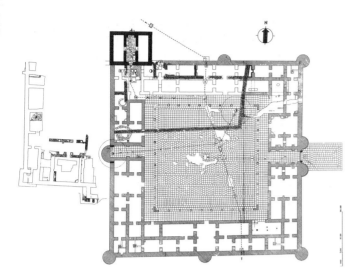

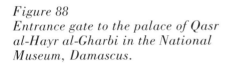

Figure 87
Palace of Qasr al-Hayr al-Gharbi.

Figure 88
Entrance gate to the palace of Qasr
al-Hayr al-Gharbi in the National
Museum, Damascus.

Qasr al-Hayr al-Gharbi includes more than 19 kilometers of ruins which stretch along the valley of the Jebel Rawaq. In the first century A.D. Palmyrene builders constructed the 600-meter-long Harbaqa dam, which made possible the first agricultural use of the district. A canal 18 kilometers long passes north from the valley, eventually opening into an open-water reservoir. In a circle about 3 kilometers wide several buildings are situated, two of them epigraphically dated: the ruined tower of a Christian cloister built in 559 by the Ghassanid prince al-Harith ibn Jabala, and a caravanserai commissioned in 727 by the Umayyad caliph Hisham. Until the excavations of

1936–1938, which proved the site to be an early Islamic palace complex, these two buildings were considered Roman-period ruins.

The nucleus of the site is the palace of the caliph Hisham (724–743), which includes the tower of the Ghassanid cloister. This square building, 70 meters on a side, with its nobly decorated facade, overlooks the river valley in a commanding fashion (Figs. 86–89). Grouped around an arcaded court were six self-enclosed dwelling areas with their own staircases to what was the second story. Four of these two-story buildings apparently served as residences for the ruling family and court, while the east facade wing with two main en-

Figure 89, 90
Detail from the entrance gate of the
palace at Qasr al-Hayr al-Gharbi.

trances and adjacent rooms was reserved for the caliph himself.

The decorative features of the
palace are especially noteworthy:
wall paintings utilizing both court
styles and historical genres (Cat.
Nos. 255, 256), wood reliefs with
plant decorations (Cat. No. 254), and
rich stucco reliefs on the exterior
and court facades (Cat. Nos. 251–
253). In the extension of figural
stucco relief an over-life-size figure
sometimes occupies the central
position. The decorative themes
are obviously related to the structure's main functions: in one case,
the presence of royal power is indicated, in another, natural and animal representations and hunting
scenes occupy a strikingly wide expanse. The decorations, in other
words, reflect the dual use of the
structure, as royal residence and
caliph's pleasure palace.

This double function is also apparent in other structures at the
oasis. A small bath about 30 meters
north of the residence also features

decorative wall painting and stucco
relief. The rooms of the bath were
themselves decorated with marble
slabs with relief adornment (Cat.
No. 257).

An unwalled garden area of more
than a kilometer's length some 3
kilometers from the palace was
watered by a canal flowing from
the Harbaqa dam. The garden was
divided into small four-sided beds,
overrun with small canals, and
probably included animal enclosures as well. A water reservoir situated 1,800 meters away regulated
the flow of water into the garden. A
mill and a caravanserai were also
provided with water from this reservoir. The existence of the mill
testifies to the agricultural use to
which at least some land parcels
were put.

The caravanserai is the second
largest structure within the palace
complex. Two wings extend from
the facade, which provides general
access to the public court. The
south wing is a mosque, identified

by its prayer niche. The north wing served as a watering area. Particularly important is the inscription on the portal of the caravanserai (now preserved in the National Museum, Damascus); it provides the date of the foundation for the entire Ummayad palace area:

In the name of God. There is no God but Him alone and none next to Him. The completion of this work falls upon the servant of God, Hisham, the ruler of the faithful. God may make his obligation a reward: Constructed by the hands of Thabit, son of Abu Thabit in the month of Rajab of the year 109.

The entire complex then can be attributed to the Umayyad caliph Hisham, who chose not to reside in the capital at Damascus but in the Syrian desert. This same caliph also commissioned the construction of the pilgrimage city at Rusafa and the structures at Qasr al-Hayr al-Sharqi, some 90 kilometers east of Palmyra (see Fig. 90). All of the desert residences of Hisham lying in the region of Palmyra made use of pre-Islamic building plans and decorative elements. The four-sided palace building with round bastions is actually derived from the plans of Roman military installations. The decorative features of these structures even reused ancient pieces, such as portions of the palace and caravanserai portals. The reversion to older building traditions at Qasr al-Hayr al-Gharbi is all the more impressive in consideration of the multiple construction specialties of the complex's craftsmen, who came from all parts of the Umayyad realm. In spite of its diverse origins and a dependence upon more ancient local models, architectural work of considerable individuality was constructed.

Village farming communities are conspicuously absent from this region; hence an interest in agricultural production could not have been the reason for the revivification of the oasis. The construction of an estate for the exclusive use of the buildings' owners explains these desert developments. Hunting and other courtly pleasures, however, were not the only functions served by this complex. The decoration provides the signs of a royal presence practically situated at the junction of trade routes and the pastoral movements of Arab tribes.

MICHAEL MEINECKE

QASR AL-HAYR AL-SHARQI

OLEG GRABAR

FOR MOST TRAVELERS TO SYRIA, TOURISTS OR SCHOLARS ALIKE, Palmyra, the fabled "caravan city" half-way between the Damascus–Aleppo axis to the west and the Euphrates to the east, has been the easternmost outpost of their visits. The narrow asphalted road from Homs or the less clearly defined track from Damascus ended in the spectacular ruins of Zenobia's city. The Jezireh ("the island," or the land between the Tigris and Euphrates) was another world connecting the highlands of Anatolia with the flat alluvial plains of lower Iraq, and Rusafa was its outpost into what was called the Syrian desert. More accurately it is identified in Arabic sources as the *badiya*, a steppe-like zone, dusty and forbidding most of the time, but covered with flowers and grasses and adaptable to agriculture if watered by strong rains or irrigation. Just about half-way between Palmyra and Rusafa or the Euphrates lie the spectacular ruins known as Qasr al-Hayr al-Sharqi (the eastern Qasr al-Hayr): two large enclosures with walls remaining in part over 12 meters high (Fig. 91) and traces of occupations and constructions extending over several square kilometers. From the point of view of traditional scholarly interpretations of Syrian archaeology and also of the more casual visitor, these ruins appear as an anomaly, an oddity, fitting neither with the settled cultures associated with the Roman Empire nor with a nomadic world usually devoid of monumental architecture.

Yet two clues exist for an understanding of these ruins. One derives from historical geography and from the existence, attested by Roman, Byzantine, and early Arab sources, of a string of settlements linking Palmyra with Rusafa. To some the ruins were part of a complex defensive system known as the *limes*, the frontier protecting the Roman Empire to the west; to others they were part of a north-south trade route connecting the Euphrates with Damascus or Homs; to others yet, they were both. The prevalent hypothesis, however, was

Figure 91
*Qasr al-Hayr al-Sharqi, after
excavation.*

that the site was a Roman military outpost, and thus it was labelled in the *Guide Bleu* and on most archaeological maps. The presence in the ruins of a Palmyrene inscription further strengthened the argument for a date in the second or third century.

The second clue had been found and then lost by a French traveler, the consul Rousseau, who passed by in 1808. It was an inscription reused in a mosque located in one of the enclosures, commemorating the building of a city *(madina)* in A.D. 728–729 by order of the caliph Hisham, the most powerful ruler of the first Islamic dynasty, the Umayyads, who ruled over most of Spain and had reached India and the frontiers of China. Thus an alternate explanation of Qasr al-Hayr was that it was one of a number of Umayyad settlements at the edges of the desert and the frontiers of cultivation throughout Syria, Jordan, and Palestine. The great French scholar Jean Sauvaget had even tentatively suggested that Qasr al-Hayr was a settlement of Hisham's known as al-Zaiturra. Other data like the presence of a mosque and a tower, interpreted (incorrectly, as it turned out) to be a minaret, further suggested that much of Qasr al-Hayr was early Islamic, but the Roman explanation tended to prevail.

Between 1964 and 1972 seven seasons of excavations were carried out at Qasr al-Hayr under the auspices of the Kelsey Museum of

Archaeology at the University of Michigan and the Department of Fine Arts at Harvard University. The results of these excavations can be summarized easily enough. Even though utilizing older spoils which may have been brought from as far away as Palmyra, Qasr al-Hayr al-Sharqi was an Umayyad foundation probably completed at the time of Hisham, but it did not consist of a princely pleasure palace in the midst of gardens and agricultural enterprises like Qasr al-Hayr al-Gharbi to the west. It was instead an aristocratic settlement comprising five distinct elements: a large enclosure with six nearly identical residences, a mosque, a formal administrative building, and oil presses; an imposing caravanserai with a beautifully preserved facade; a bath; a huge outer enclosure protected by a complex system of sluices, serving probably for animal husbandry rather than agriculture; and an irrigated area with a few simpler houses.

Two historico-cultural phenomena explain Qasr al-Hayr. One is the transformation, as a result of the creation of the Muslim world, of a frontier area into a zone of commercial and social communications and exchanges. The extensive economic and military development of the Eupharates Valley and the importance taken by Iraq within the budding Muslim world gave a radically new and different function to the steppe of north-central Syria; it became a key place in the movement of people from southern Iraq to Aleppo and from Damascus to the Euphrates Valley. The second phenomenon is the immense wealth amassed by the ruling Umayyad dynasty, a wealth which allowed them to invest into mercantile economy with unheard-of lavishness. Archaeological surveys and investigations uncovered underground canalizations of nearly 30 kilometers and a technology of building which had to have been imported at great expense from many parts of Arabia and the Fertile Crescent. A number of political events, perhaps matrimonial alliances of early Muslim princes with major nomadic tribes, may explain why this spot received such munificence.

Two additional aspects of what is known of Qasr al-Hayr deserve some elaboration. One pertains to its history, the other to what may be called its anthropology. A general assumption of early Islamic history and culture in Syria has been that with the fall of the Umayyad dynasty in 750 the whole country entered into a period of decline until the great revival of the eleventh century. With the exception of the Euphrates Valley itself, whose development was continued under the early Abbasids since it was their military and commercial life-line to the Mediterranean and Anatolia, the rule was consistently applied until the twentieth century to the semi-arid zone of the so-called

Syrian desert. The excavation of Qasr al-Hayr suggests that the assumption of decline and disappearance must be modified, or at least modulated, with respect to much of that area.

To begin with, a decline in use did not take place after the fall of the Umayyad dynasty (as happened in so many other places) but at some time in the ninth century or even the tenth, when the power of the Abbasids declined as well. Qasr al-Hayr al-Sharqi fulfilled an economic function independent of political vagaries. For example, when a large section of the wall of the caravanserai fell after an earthquake, it was so well repaired that only a very careful analysis of the masonry revealed its restoration. Little seems to have happened at Qasr al-Hayr in the eleventh century, and the site may indeed have been abandoned. But in the twelfth the ruins of the early settlement were reused for a small urban center—whatever is implied by the medieval Arabic word *bulayd*. This was something more than a village, for its houses were arranged next to each other along crooked streets and it had an extended system of water distribution, yet it lacked the large common spaces of a true medieval city or a material culture of ceramics that was not entirely imported from elsewhere.

Although the argument can be made that it was the settlement known to medieval geographies as al-Urd, its name is not really important, for it was but one of a probably large number of settlements reflecting the expansion of active life in Syria during Zangid and Ayyubid times, an expansion the early Mamluks sought but failed to hold together. Why Qasr al-Hayr was abandoned is not altogether clear, although the general decline of the Euphrates Valley after the Mongol invasions was no doubt a major consideration. It was a slow abandonment: canalizations were no longer repaired, cisterns no longer relined, houses no longer rebuilt; people left with their treasures and belongings, leaving behind only broken fragments of mundane implements. From the middle of the fourteenth century onward, only occasional and temporary settlements are attested. The few visitors either left their mark by scribbling their presence on a wall, like one Mansur b. Abbas who was there in 1393–1394 on his way to Baghdad, or recollected their memories of a brief sojourn, like the French consul Rousseau in 1808.

This history of Qasr al-Hayr al-Sharqi over nearly a millennium is interesting not only as the explanation of a spectacular ruin over time. It is equally fascinating for what I have called its anthropological implications, its ways of pointing at issues of life, behavior, and relations which extend much beyond a specific moment of history and yet which govern the peculiarities of any one archaeologically defined period.

Three such issues stand out. The first one, almost dictated by the ecology and geography of the area, is the relationship between nomadic and settled life. The technology of the Umayyad Qasr al-Hayr was that of the settled world brought artificially into an inhospitable area by imperial fiat. It made visible and present both the forms (fancy doorways flanked by towers, stucco decoration, large courtyard dwellings, colonnades and porticoes surrounding paved open areas) and the ways of life (bathing, manufacturing, trading) of Syrian or Mesopotamian cities to a setting which was primarily that of the great nomadic tribes. These two worlds, however different, needed each other as consumers of each other's products and as partners in the movement of goods and people. The equilibrium which developed in Umayyad and early Abbasid times was in fact controlled by the settled world, as its monumental creations spread out in the badiya with hardly any defensive or protective apparatus. But as time went on, with variations which can only be guessed, nomadic values began to predominate and eventually took over until the social and technological—probably irreversible—changes of the second half of the twentieth century.

Qasr al-Hayr is a prime example of settlements found in Central Asia, in the Arabian world, and on the edges of the Sahara in which two sets of values coexist more or less successfully and permanently but whose components are very difficult to retrieve from archaeological evidence alone. One example of the problem may suffice. The ceramics from Qasr al-Hayr were entirely imported and therefore fancier types occurred in higher percentages than in ordinary settled sites. One explanation may well be that nomadic implements in leather, textile, or other perishable but easily transportable materials predominated over glass or ceramics.

The second issue is that of the importance of the initial investment in creating a place like Qasr al-Hayr. This was not a slowly growing settlement which acquired at some point a major external impetus. It was at its most developed and most grandiose at the very beginning. What this initial development did was more than create a setting for a specific time: investing in a water system in order to develop the infrastructure of life in the badiya acted to modify the ecological structure of the area and to make all subsequent settlements possible. The question is whether the resilience of life after such an investment is measurable, whether it is possible to develop a formula which would imply the degree of consciousness of future growth which its creators had in mind.

Finally, Qasr al-Hayr offers an excellent example of the spread of a material culture to an area quite remote from the sources of manufacture—in this case Iraq, Egypt, and western Syria. It illustrates the exact nature of a universal Muslim culture which, in many ways like Roman imperial culture, was able through means which are still insufficiently elucidated to make available even to distant places examples of the most elegant objects known in capitals. There were luster ceramics and glass objects at Qasr al-Hayr, not as many perhaps as at Hama, Samarra, or Raqqa, but enough to make one aware of a complex culture transcending a specific place. No real explanation can be provided for the discovery at Qasr al-Hayr of a gold coin from Morocco (incorrectly identified in the published volumes), but its presence is yet another demonstration of the fact that Qasr al-Hayr al-Sharqi is not simply an interesting curiosity in the rich archaeological history of medieval Syria, but a small segment within a much wider spectrum of time and space.

Recommended Reading

Oleg Grabar, Renata Holod, James Knudstad and William Trousdale. *City in the Desert* (Cambridge, Mass.: Harvard University Press, 1978), 2 vols.

RAQQA/RAFIQA

Location: On left bank of the Euphrates, west of its juncture with the Balikh River

Dates: Alongside the early historic settlement of Tell Bica, Alexander the Great founded a new city with the name Nicephorium, which remained until the Islamic conquest of 639. In the further development of the city two stages can be discerned of flourishing city life: 722–836: foundation of a new city, Rafiqa, west of Raqqa, and a seasonal summer residence of the caliph and capital city of the Abbasid kingdom; 1159–1259; under the leadership of the Zangids and the Ayyubids, through the destruction of the Mongols

Exploration: 1907–1908, first topographic investigation and building survey (F. Sarre and E. Herzfeld); 1924, exposure of kilns (E. de Lorey); 1933, soundings at the city wall (D. Schlumberger); 1944–1945, partial excavation of Palace A ca. 380 m north of the city wall (N. Dunand and R. Duru); 1950–1954, excavation of Palaces B, C, and D ca. 1200 m northeast of city wall through the Syrian Antiquities Department (N. Saliby); 1968–1969, additional excavation of Palace A with southern additions (K. Tuweir); from 1976, excavation and restoration of Qasr al Banat (Castle of the Maidens), the city wall, and the plans of Heraqla, some 8 km west of the city (K. Tuweir)

Publications: F. Sarre and E. Herzfeld *Archäologische Reise im Euphrat-und Tigris-Gebiet* 2 (1920) 349 // K. A. C. Creswell *Early Muslim Architecture* 2 (1940) 39, 165 // J. Sauvaget *Ars Islamica* 13/14 (1948) 31 // S. Abdul-Hak *AAAS* 1:1 (1951) 111 // N. Saliby *AAAS* 4:5 (1954) 205 (Arabic part 25) // M.A. al-'Usch *AAAS* 7 (1957) (Arabic part 51) // K. Tuweir *Das Altertum* 25:2 (1979) 93

The modern city of Raqqa, on the left bank of the Euphrates, not far from the mouth of the Balikh River, stands on truly historical ground. In the Greco-Roman and Byzantine periods (third century B.C. through seventh century A.D.) the city bore a variety of names: Nicephorium, Calinicum, and Leontopolis. Archaeological remains of these periods are limited to architectural elements (pillars, arches) later re-used in Islamic buildings. In A.D. 639–640 the city came under the rule of the Arabs, who named it Raqqa, meaning "flat, even land." Medieval sources report that the famous Umayyad caliph of Damascus, Hisham ibn Abd al-Malik, owned two palaces here.

Raqqa underwent a complete renovation under the caliph al-Mansur (722). West of it he built the city Rafiqa in horseshoe shape after the model of the famous round city of Baghdad. What Baghdad was like in those days can only be determined from contemporary reports, for the walls of the city of this period remain to be recovered. At Raqqa, however, impressive remains stand from the golden period of Rafiqa. More than half of the city wall is preserved; only the southern portion along the river bank has completely disappeared.

When the caliph of Baghdad from 769 to 803, Harun al-Rashid, made Rafiqa his residence, the city expanded in the east and the north far beyond the circular wall. The ninth and tenth centuries are called the city's golden age. Rafiqa later suffered under the conflicts of the different Islamic dynasties, but in 1166 the later sultan of Damascus, Nur al-Din Zangi, renewed the hall facade of the Great Mosque. In 1182 Rafiqa came under the control of the Ayyubid ruler Salah al-Din (Saladin). During the period of his rule the famous glazed ceramics known as "Raqqa ware" were produced.

After the invasion of the Mongols and the fall of Baghdad in 1258, Rafiqa lost its significance and was finally abandoned. The Arab historian Abu al-Fida reported in 1321 that the city was a ruin with no inhabitants. So it remained until the nineteenth century, when Arab nomads and Circassian immigrants founded a small hamlet with the old name Raqqa, in the southwest corner of the earlier Rafiqa, inside and beyond the city wall. The inhabitants began to carry off the old stone structures to erect new homes. They also sought out old vessels of the famous Raqqa ware for sale on the European antiquities market. In this fashion bricks from the city wall and from the Great Mosque came to be distributed over a wide area.

The population of Raqqa grew quickly after 1960 with the immigration of former nomads, farmers from outlying villages, and those from other areas of Syria. Today

Raqqa has a population of approximately 200,000 inhabitants. Almost the entire old city area is inhabited, while much of the population is settled in a wide area outside of the old city walls. These new settlements among the ruins of the old present a great many difficulties for archaeological research.

Rafiqa was not limited to the walled city. On aerial photographs one can see extensive tracts of ruins to the north and east of the "city." Here are large structures, still mostly uninvestigated. Initial small excavations were undertaken in 1906, during the period of Ottoman rule, by the Istanbul Museum under Makridi Bey, but this research was never published. A very precise description of the site in 1907–1908 has been provided by Ernst Herzfeld.[1] In 1944 the French architect Duru investigated a portion of the palace from the period of Harun al-Rashid, north of the city wall (Palace A). His results also remain unpublished. Two noteworthy palaces from the ninth century were investigated by Nassib Saliby at the commission of the Directorate-General of Antiquities.[2] Saliby also later exposed other parts of Palace A and two additional structures.

In 1977 the Directorate-General of Antiquities began a long-term project to investigate and restore the remaining ruins of old Rafiqa. Immediate results included the observations that the walls of the Great Mosque, as well as the city wall, were not built of mud brick, as previously assumed,[3] but rather of layers of baked brick. The wall has since been restored with baked brick.

Another large structure in the old city has also been excavated and restored. The residents of today's Raqqa call this building Qasr al-Banat (Castle of the Maidens). Herzfeld accorded the vestiges of its beautifully decorated brick wall special attention.[4] He assigned it a date in the twelfth century. The function of this building remains enigmatic, although the writer has continued the excavations there for several years.

A rectangular stone plastered court with a central fountain forms the heart of this building. On each side are large, open-vaulted halls (iwan), with separate side rooms. The complex to the north is perhaps a reception room for guests. Qasr al-Banat is an exceptional example of brick architecture with walls decorated with niches and "stalactites," arches with ornamental relief, windows with richly decorated stucco and colored glass.

The contrast presented by the center axis of the iwan and the assymetrical order of the adjacent rooms is striking. This suggests the secular rather than the sacred character of the structure. The principle of the four-crossed iwan is a sign of mosques, Koranic schools, and hospitals of the eleventh–thirteenth centuries in much of Iran, Iraq, and Syria. Only one palace structure with this kind of plan is documented, the Lashkari Bazaar of Afghanistan, where stucco work similar to that of Qasr al-Banat also appears.

The ruins of Heraqla, some 8 kilometers west of Raqqa, have also been investigated. The city which once lay directly on the Euphrates, is now some 3 kilometers away. In 1879, E. Sachau visited this site and came to consider it a Roman castellum.[5] Ernst

[1]F. Sarre and E. Herzfeld *Archäologische Reise im Euphrat- und Tigris-Gebiet* II (Berlin 1920) 349.
[2]N. Saliby *AAAS* 4–5 (1954–1955) 205 / *AAAS* 6 (1956) (Arabic 26).
[3]K.A.C. Creswell *Early Muslim Architecture* (1958) 158.
[4]Sarre and Herzfeld 158.
[5]E. Sachau *Reise in Syrien und Mesopotamien* (Leipzig 1883) 244.

Herzfeld, however, recognized Heraqla's connection with the Abbasid caliph of Baghdad, Harun al-Rashid.[6] Medieval historians (e.g., Tabari, Yaqut, and Masudi) report that Harun al-Rashid triumphed over the city called Heraklion (modern Turkish Eregil in Konya province) in a battle with the Byzantine emperor Nikophorus. The medieval historians embellished the event with the following story: Harun al-Rashid saw among the prisoners of Heraklion a beautiful young woman, whom he took for himself. He then built a castle between Raqqa and Balis (Meskene), which he called Heraqla in honor of the girl's home town. We will see, however, that the plan of Heraqla is more a symbol of victory than a pleasure palace.

The city has a terrace with rectangular towers and uneven sides of 100, 102, 104, and 106 meters. It is constructed of large house stones using lime mortar and large lime-stone blocks. The wall is casemate-like with earth-filled spaces to increase stability. In the middle of each side of the terrace there is a large rectangular hall (iwan) which opens to the outside. Two outer steps lead to the outside and the terrace. The terrace stands in the midst of the towered wall, 500 meters in diameter, built of gypsum. It has four gates, each a different shape: the north gate is round, the east is octagonal, the west is hexagonal, and the south gate is square.

The post-Byzantine date of the structure is assured by the reuse of a house block with an inscribed cross. The Arabic name of a stone-cutter is preserved on a block from the south gate. The type of terrace, the plan of the city, its long-lasting building materials, all suggest a victory monument—perhaps the victory of Harun al-Rashid over the Byzantine emperor.
KASSEM TUWEIR

[6] Sarre and Herzfeld 162.

SCIENCE IN MEDIEVAL SYRIA

DAVID A. KING

FROM THE NINTH CENTURY TO THE FIFTEENTH, MUSLIM SCIENTISTS excelled in every branch of scientific knowledge. Syria in particular witnessed the activity of several scholars prominent in the field of astronomy. In this brief overview (which excludes the biological and medical sciences), we shall present an account of the works of some of the major figures in this scientific tradition in Syria.

The works of Habash and al-Battani from the ninth and early tenth centuries will serve as an introduction to Islamic astronomy in general and astronomy in Muslim Syria in particular. In the tenth century a Damascene mathematician wrote the first account of decimal fractions, and his work will be used to demonstrate some Muslim innovations in arithmetic. In the early thirteenth century a major work on mechanical technology was compiled in north Syria; this treatise by al-Jazari reflects the sophisticated level of automata available in the central lands of Islam. In the fourteenth century, Syria was again the scene of a vigorous astronomical tradition represented by the works of Ibn al-Sarraj, Ibn al-Shatir, and al-Khalili. An account of the works of these three scholars will serve to illustrate the culmination of three different aspects of Islamic astronomy. The reader will notice that several of these works survive only in unique manuscripts and should also bear in mind that most of these works have been investigated only during the present century and in some cases only in the past few years.

The observations of al-Ma'mun

In Baghdad in the early ninth century the Abbasid Caliph al-Ma'mun commissioned a group of astronomers to make two sets of observations in order to determine the terrestrial distance corresponding to one degree of latitude. One of these observation programs was conducted in the desert between Raqqa and Palmyra in Syria. According to the reports, a solar meridian altitude measurement was made and then the group moved along the meridian until the solar midday altitude differed by one degree: the distance between the observation posts then provided the required result.

Al-Ma'mun also commissioned a group of astronomers to make a series of observations in Damascus, after a similar series had been conducted in Baghdad. Special instruments were constructed for solar and lunar observations made from Dayr Murran, a monastery on Qasiyun Mountain overlooking Damascus. The instruments included a meridian quadrant of a radius of about 5 meters for observing celestial altitudes and 5-meter-long iron gnomon for observing shadow lengths. Based on these observations a new set of tables was compiled, this being the ultimate purpose of all medieval observational programs. The observatory was demolished in the ninth century and never rebuilt.

Habash al-Hasib: The leading astronomer of the ninth century

Habash worked mainly in Baghdad, but although he was employed by the Abbasid Caliph al-Ma'mun, he does not appear to have participated in the team observations commissioned by the caliph. He was familiar with both the Greek and the Persian-Indian traditions which so profoundly influenced early Islamic astronomy. He prepared two *zij*es, or astronomical handbooks with tables, one in each tradition; unfortunately both are lost. The *zij* of Ptolemy, compiled in Alexandria about A.D. 150 and better known as the *Almagest*, was the main vehicle for the transmission of classical mathematical astronomy to the Islamic commonwealth.

One other *zij* by Habash does survive, however, and because of this one we include him in this survey of astronomy in Syria. Habash came to Damascus and made observations there, and then compiled the *Damascus Zij*. This survives in a unique manuscript in Istanbul with an anonymous recension available in another manuscript in Berlin. The *Damascus Zij* is a work of remarkable sophistication. It contains material on chronology, trigonometric functions, spherical astronomy, and planetary astronomy. In his eclipse theory, Habash used an iterative process of successive approximations which is usually associated with Kepler (ca. 1600). Also, he presented a highly sophisticated and mathematically accurate solution to the problem of finding the *qibla*, or local direction of Mecca from any locality, which Muslims must face during their prayers and other ritual acts. He further devised a highly ingenious set of auxiliary trigonometric tables for solving problems of spherical astronomy, that is, the mathematics of the apparent daily rotation of the heavens. Habash also wrote treatises on astronomical instruments.

Al-Battani and the arabicization of Greek astronomy

Muhammad ibn Jabir al-Battani is one of the most celebrated of Muslim astronomers. His *Zij*—a work of major importance—survives in a unique Arabic manuscript preserved in the Escorial and in a Latin translation by Plato of Tivoli, who flourished in Barcelona in the first half of the twelfth century. The work is a sober survey of Ptolemaic astronomy, incorporating the results of the author's own observations made in Raqqa between 877 and 918 and including also eclipse observations made in Antioch in 901.

The *Zij* of al-Battani symbolizes the victory of the Ptolemaic tradition over the Indian-Persian tradition in Islamic astronomy. In his trigonometry, for example, the sine to base 60 succeeds Ptolemy's cumbersome chord function and the Indian sines to base 150 used by earlier Muslim astronomers. In his planetary theory there is no trace of Indian models. He presents chapters on the prediction of the visibility of the lunar crescent and on the determination of the qibla: in both cases, his treatment is much more practical than that of Habash. Al-Battani's *Zij* was highly regarded not only in the Muslim world; it was also very influential in Europe, being quoted by no less than Peurbach, Copernicus, Tycho Brahe, Kepler, and Galileo.

Al-Uqlidisi: Inventor of decimal fractions

In the middle of the tenth century Abu 'l-Hasan al-Uqlidisi compiled a treatise on arithmetic in Damascus. This survives in a unique manuscript preserved in Istanbul. Called after Uqlidis, or Euclid, he may have earned his name for his mathematical abilities or because he earned his livelihood preparing copies of Euclid's *Elements*. We have no biographical details of consequence, save that he had travelled widely and inspected numerous works on arithmetic.

Much of the material in al-Uqlidisi's treatise is standard: a presentation of Hindu numerals, the place-value concept, arithmetical operations including square roots. But there are several innovations. First he discusses arithmetical operations (addition, subtraction, multiplication, and division) for numbers in the decimal and the sexagesimal (base 60) systems. It was the latter (derived from Babylonian and Greek usage) which was standard among the astronomers. Secondly, this is the earliest known text containing a treatment of decimal fractions. He advocates the use of a decimal marker, a stroke above the units, and gives several examples of calculations with decimal fractions.

Al-Uqlidisi's work was apparently not widely known in the Islamic East. The next treatment of decimal fractions occurs in the arithmetic of al-Kashi (Samarqand, ca. 1425), and it was Simon Stevin (Netherlands, ca. 1600) who was responsible for their adoption in Europe.

Al-Jazari on mechanical devices

Al-Jazari worked for the ruler of the Artuqid dynasty centered on Diyarbekr (in what is now southeastern Turkey) in the late twelfth and early thirteenth centuries. He was an engineer and compiled an encyclopaedic work on mechanical devices to serve or to delight the affluent. He makes no mention of mechanical devices for military purposes, on which several other treatises were available.

His book contains descriptions and diagrams for intricate water-clocks, blood-letting devices, mechanical flutes, mechanisms for raising water for irrigation purposes, and "toys for grown-ups." The latter included machines in which mechanized serving girls proffer glasses and fill them with wine. There is also a description of a monumental decorated door with the earliest account of green-sand casting, a technique not recorded in Europe until the sixteenth century.

While no automata survive from the Islamic Middle Ages, the historical sources mention several individual examples, and there is every reason to suppose that such devices were quite popular. Most of the dozen or so surviving manuscripts of al-Jazari's work were copied in Mamluk Egypt and Syria between the thirteenth and sixteenth centuries. His treatise, the most comprehensive of Islamic works on the subject, was apparently unknown in the medieval West.

Developments in astronomy in the thirteenth century

Damascus seems to have been an active center of astronomy in the twelfth and early thirteenth centuries. The biographical dictionaries of that period list several recent and contemporary scholars concerned with the sciences, mainly in Damascus, although they were involved more in teaching than in writing treatises. A revival of astronomy in Cairo around 1250 was influential in Syria.

The thirteenth-century Syrian astronomer al-'Urdi compiled a treatise on theoretical astronomy which was a forerunner to later developments at the Maragha Observatory in northwest Iran. Al-'Urdi left Damascus for Maragha before writing this treatise, but, as we shall see below, the writings of the Maragha school were to influence Syrian astronomy in the fourteenth century.

Abu 'l-Fida', Ayyubid prince of Hama about 1300, is known to have compiled a *zij*, now lost. Several astronomers patronized by him produced works on theoretical astronomy and instruments. But activity at his court was apparently without influence on later astronomy either in Syria or elsewhere.

Syrian astronomy from the fourteenth century onward was mainly practiced by *muwaqqit*s, that is, astronomers associated with the major mosques and madrasas whose particular concern was astronomical timekeeping and the regulation of the times of prayer. In Islam the times of the five daily prayers are defined astronomically. The Islamic day begins at sunset with the *maghrib* prayer. The *'isha'* prayer begins a nightfall, and the *fajr* prayer begins at daybreak. The *zuhr* prayer begins at midday and the afternoon *'asr* prayer at a time defined by shadow lengths.

In the early centuries of Islam it was the muezzins who regulated the times of prayers even in major mosques, using the techniques of folk astronomy such as observing shadow lengths by day and the risings of the lunar mansions by night. The institution of the muwaqqit seems to have been started in Egypt in the thirteenth century. As we shall see, the major school of astronomers in Damascus in the fourteenth century were muwaqqits associated with the Umayyad Mosque, and various other astronomers served there in the same capacity until the nineteenth century.

Ibn al-Sarraj and the culmination of Islamic instrumentation

Ibn al-Sarraj worked in Aleppo around 1325. We have little biographical information about him and he does not appear to have been associated with any religious institutions. So, unlike all the other Syrian astronomers we shall mention, he was not a muwaqqit. He turned his attention to devising a series of astrolabes and other instruments that could be used to solve all of the problems of spherical astronomy and timekeeping for any latitude.

The apparent rotation of the heavens about the observer may be conveniently represented by a celestial globe resting in a circular frame as the horizon and able to rotate about an axis aligned with the celestial pole. Ancient and medieval globes bear markings for prominent fixed stars and the ecliptic, which is the apparent path of the sun against the background of the stars. The astrolabe is a two-dimensional representation of this kind of celestial globe, achieved by means of a mathematical projection called stereographic, first devised by Hipparchus about 150 B.C. The stars and the ecliptic are represented on a grid which rotates over one of a series of plates for different latitudes, bearing markings representing the local horizon, meridian, and altitudes above the horizon. To use the instrument one simply takes an altitude measurement of a particular celestial body and places the marker for that body over the corresponding altitude circle on the plate below: the astrolabe then displays the instantaneous configuration of the heavens relative to the local horizon, and the grid can be moved to simulate and measure the passage of time.

Muslim astronomers inherited the astrolabe from the Greeks and made considerable advances in its theory and construction. One of the most interesting developments is the universal astrolabe which serves all latitudes with a single plate. It was devised by the eleventh-century Andalusian astronomer al-Shakkaz.

Ibn al-Sarraj actually devised two kinds of universal astrolabes. The first is simply a reinvention of the instrument of al-Shakkaz, which was not known in the Muslim East. When Ibn al-Sarraj realized that he had been preceded, he made a more sophisticated variety; a unique example of his handiwork survives in the Benaki Museum in Athens. A treatise on its use has also survived, written by the fifteenth-century Cairo muwaqqit al-Wafa'i, who owned the very instrument now in Athens.

Ibn al-Sarraj's astrolabe, which is universal from five different aspects (Fig. 92), is the most sophisticated astrolabe from the Near East and Europe in the entire medieval and Renaissance period. His other instruments include calculating devices of great sophistication. A treatise on all the instruments known to him, written in his own hand, was discovered in Dublin in 1982 and awaits study.

Ibn al-Shatir and the culmination of Islamic theoretical astronomy

Ibn al-Shatir was the head of a team of muwaqqits at the Umayyad Mosque in Damascus in the mid-fourteenth century. In spite of his interest in timekeeping, his major contribution was in the development of planetary models which did not have the problems inherent in those of Ptolemy.

Ibn al-Shatir compiled a treatise on theoretical astronomy in which he presented the reasoning behind his new planetary models. Building on the earlier writings of the astronomers at the Maragha Observatory (including al-'Urdi), he devised a new lunar model which represented with a substantial measure of success the longitude of

Figure 92
The universal astrolabe of Ibn al-Sarraj, which can be used to solve problems of spherical astronomy for all terrestrial latitudes in five different ways.

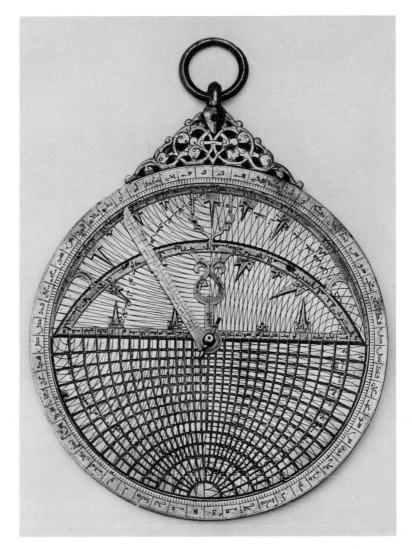

the moon and its distance from the earth, plus a series of planetary models with secondary epicycles replacing the ingenious but problematic Ptolemaic equant. These models are mathematically equivalent to those elaborated by Copernicus some 150 years after the time of Ibn al-Shatir. This discovery, made in the 1950s, aroused considerable interest in Islamic planetary theory which has not subsided. A direct influence of Ibn al-Shatir's models on Copernicus has yet to be established, but it remains a distinct possibility.

Ibn al-Shatir also compiled a *zij* appropriately called *Al-Zij al-*

Jadid (The New Astronomical Tables), which contains solar, lunar, and planetary tables based on his new models. It remained popular in Syria for several centuries, both in its original form and in several different recensions by later astronomers.

Ibn al-Shatir's contributions to instrument design were also considerable. For example, he made a large astrolabic clock described by a contemporary historian who saw it in the astronomer's home. He constructed a large (2 × 1 m) sundial for the Umayyad Mosque in Damascus (Fig. 93). Sundials had been in widespread use in the Near East in the Greco-Roman period, and Muslim astronomers made considerable advances in sundial theory and construction. The surviving fragments of Ibn al-Shatir's sundial are now on display in the National Archaeological Museum in Damascus, and an exact replica, made by the nineteenth-century muwaqqit al-Tantawi, is still *in situ* on the minaret. The instrument displays time in both seasonal and equinoctial hours, as well as time relative to the afternoon prayer and the prayers at nightfall and daybreak. It is without doubt the most splendid sundial known from the Middle Ages.

Figure 93
A reconstruction of the magnificent sundial constructed by Ibn al-Shatir for the main minaret of the Umayyad Mosque in Damascus.

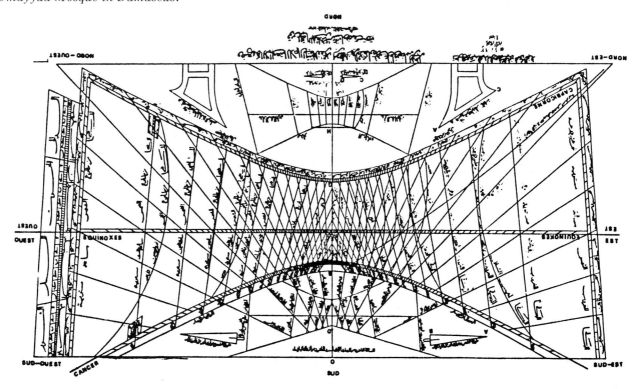

Al-Khalili and the culmination of Islamic astronomical timekeeping

The major figure in the field of timekeeping at Damascus was a contemporary of Ibn al-Shatir named al-Khalili. As far as we know, no corpus of tables for timekeeping was compiled for the latitude of Damascus before the mid-fourteenth century. Al-Khalili computed an extensive set of tables for the new parameters (local latitude and obliquity of the ecliptic) derived from the observations of Ibn al-Shatir. His tables for timekeeping by the sun and regulating the times of the five prayers were used in Damascus until the nineteenth century. They exist in numerous manuscript copies and were first investigated about ten years ago. The main tables display the time since sunrise and the time remaining until midday for each degree of observed solar altitude and of solar longitude (corresponding roughly to each day of the year). The others display various functions relating to the times of prayer, again with values computed for each degree of solar longitude: the functions tabulated include the duration of morning and evening twilight, the altitude of the sun at the beginning and end of the afternoon prayer, and the time when the sun is in the direction of Mecca.

Syrian astronomers prepared prayer tables for the latitudes of Tripoli and Aleppo after the model of the Damascus corpus, and the achievements of these astronomers in astronomical timekeeping inspired further activity in Cairo. In the fourteenth century a corpus of tables for timekeeping for the latitude of Tunis was prepared along the lines of the Damascus tables, and Syrian astronomers, perhaps those associated with the Umayyad Mosque in the fourteenth century, seem to have prepared the first set of prayer tables for Istanbul. All of the impressive achievements of Ottoman astronomers in timekeeping owe their inspiration to the earlier Egyptian and Syrian tradition.

Al-Khalili also turned his attention to universal solutions and compiled a set of auxiliary tables for solving problems of spherical astronomy for all latitudes, based on three trigonometric functions. These auxiliary tables contain over 13,000 entries, and successive applications of the various functions tabulated lead to the solution of any problem in spherical astronomy for any latitude. Earlier Muslim astronomers from the ninth century onward, the most notable of whom was Habash, had compiled isolated sets of simpler and less sophisticated auxiliary functions, but al-Khalili arrived at the final solution. His auxiliary tables were used by later Syrian, Egyptian, and Turkish astronomers.

Al-Khalili's greatest computational achievement, however, was in the compilation of a table displaying the qibla, or local direction of Mecca, for each degree of latitude and longitude, based on an accurate mathematical formula. Earlier astronomers from the ninth century onward who had compiled qibla tables had contented themselves with much simpler approximate formulae. Again al-Khalili arrived at a final solution to one of the most important problems confronting the Muslim astronomers.

Science in Syria under the Ottomans

Not all creative scientific activity in Syria came to an end with the destruction of Damascus by the Mongols in 1402. About 1425 Shihab al-Din al-Halabi produced some new tables for timekeeping for Damascus. About seventy-five years later, al-Salihi produced a Syrian recension of the *Zij* of Ulugh Beg of Samarqand. And about 1650 al-Qazwini produced a recension of the *Zij* of Ibn al-Shatir. Each of these individuals was a muwaqqit at the Umayyad Mosque in Damascus. We should also mention Ibn al-Ha'im, who worked as a teacher at a madrasa in Jerusalem in the early fourteenth century: he wrote mostly on the algebra of the complicated Islamic laws of inheritance, and mathematics in Syria after his time was concerned mainly with the same subject.

The Ottoman Turks found themselves heirs to the Egyptian and Syrian traditions, as well as to the works of the Samarqand astronomers, some of whom had close ties to Istanbul. The most famous Muslim astronomer of the sixteenth century, Taqi 'l-Din ibn Ma'ruf, who directed the Istanbul Observatory, was a Syrian who had lived both in Egypt and in Palestine and was familiar with the rich heritage of Mamluk astronomy. In the eighteenth century the Ottomans came into contact with European astronomy, and the "*zijes*" of the French astronomers Lalande and Cassini were translated into Turkish and their tables adapted to the longitude of Istanbul. Other versions were later prepared in Arabic for Damascus and Cairo.

Astronomy continued to be studied in Damascus and Aleppo, as well as Cairo, after Istanbul had become the center of astronomical activity in the Islamic world. Different and virtually independent schools likewise continued to flourish in the Maghreb and in Safavid Iran. The preparation of annual ephemerides and the copying of tables for timekeeping for the use of the muwaqqits continued apace. The compilation of treatises on different kinds of instruments such as quadrants and sundials also continued until the nineteenth century, but there was nothing new in these after the fifteenth century. The great scientists of such caliber as Habash, al-Battani, and Ibn al-Shatir had been virtually forgotten. Only in this century have their works been brought back to life by historians of science using the few surviving manuscripts and instruments.

Recommended Reading

Articles "al-Battani," "Habash al-Hasib," "al-Khalili," "Ibn al-Shatir," "al-Jazari," "al-Khalili," "al-Uqlidisi," in *Dictionary of Scientific Biography.* 16 vols. (New York: Scribner's, 1970–1980).

D. R. Hill. *The Book of Knowledge of Ingenious Mechanical Devices* (Dordrecht, 1974).

E. S. Kennedy and I. Ghanem (eds.). *The Life and Work of Ibn al-Shatir: An Arab Astronomer of the Fourteenth Century* (Aleppo, 1976).

D. A. King, "The Astronomy of the Mamluks." *Isis* 74 (1983) 531–555 / "Astronomical Timekeeping in Fourteenth-Century Syria." *Proceedings of the First International Symposium on the History of the Arabic Science, Aleppo, 1976* Vol. II (Aleppo, 1978).

A. S. Saidan. *Arithmetic of al-Uqlidisi* (Dordrecht, 1978).

248
Marble fragment with ink inscription

Site: Qasr al-Hayr al-Gharbi, palace
Date: Before 743
Material: Marble, fragmented on three sides; broken close
  to right edge
Height: 7.8 cm; *width:* 6.4 cm; *depth:* 1.5 cm
Museum No.: Damascus A. 17978
Literature: Dja'far al-Hasani in D. Schlumberger *Syria* 20
  (1939) 372, Fig. 29 // A. Grohmann *Arabische Paläographie*
  1 (1967) 115

Early Islamic inscriptions were written in ink on stone
plates, as well as on papyrus, wood, bone, parchment,
and other materials. Under the first caliph, Abu Bakr
(632–634), when the gathering of the holy book of
Islam, the Koran, was begun, the legacy of the prophet Muhammad included fragments of individual
chapters of the Koran written on pieces of stone.

This marble plate found at Qasr al-Hayr al-Gharbi is
the oldest of such inscriptions preserved. It contains
five lines of a letter from the caliph Hisham (who died
in 743) to his nephew and successor al-Walid Abi
l-Abbas: "In the name of god . . . / from Hish(am . . .
to) / (a)l-Walid A(bi l-Abbas) / . . . son of Yusuf. . . ."
The text is written with a quill in black ink; the writing
style, also know from papyri inscriptions, is a slanted
variant of the so-called *Kufi*-ductus, the earliest form
of Arabic script which is characterized by angular
lines. Since the back of the marble plate retains a few
introductory attempts at the same letter, this may be a
draft which Hisham composed during his stay at the
palace of Qasr al-Hayr al-Gharbi, built by him in 727
(see also Cat. Nos. 251–258).
M.M.

249
Page of the Koran
See color plate p. 432

Site: Damascus, Umayyad Mosque
Date: Before 911
Material: Parchment, torn at the edges
Height: 22 cm; *length:* 30.5 cm
Museum No.: Damascus A. 338
Literature: *Catalogue* (1969) 223, Fig. 127 // *Guide* (1980)
  209, Fig. 83 // cf. A. J. Arberry *The Koran Illuminated*
  (1967) 8, Plates 19–20.

Since the collection of Muhammad's prophetic revela-

248

tions were to be spread in the original Arabic version
only, and since the religious teaching was confined to
the Arabic language as well, the Koran became the
connecting link between all Muslims, regardless of
native language. Commensurate with the vast cultural
and historical significance of the Koran, the examples
of early Islamic inscriptions are particularly richly embellished. This piece of parchment, containing the last
two pages of a handwritten Koran, is one of the oldest
dated examples. The reverse has six lines of dedication in the *Kufi*-ductus:

This segment of the Koran is commissioned and

there are / these thirty segments for the / Friday Mosque in Damascus / 'Abd al-Mun'im Ibn Ahmad, by which he wishes the reward / of god, and the continuation of his prosperity / in Dhu l-Qa'da in the year 298 (= 1–30 July 911).

Other pages of this Koran are kept in the Chester Beatty Library in Dublin (MS 1421). The illuminated page which originally was opposite the last line of the Koran combines geometric and plant motifs. The center, bordered by rectangular woven ornaments in gold with red and blue, is inspired by an earlier tradition of pre-Islamic floor mosaics and book illuminations, while the medallion on the left side is influenced by Mesopotamian decorative art.

M.M.

250
Koran manuscript
See color plate p. 432

Site: Damascus (?) (museum purchase)
Date: 1689
Material: Written in black ink on paper, diacritical marks in red, illumination in gold, light and dark blue, red, pink, and light green; leather binding stamped with two gold tones
Height of page: 21.3 cm; *width:* 12.7 cm; *cover width:* 14 cm
Museum No.: Damascus A. 6676

This Koran, bound in leather, has supplementary instructions for prayer and is a characteristic example of later editions. A colophon (in a different handwriting) gives us the date and the name of the illuminator of the manuscript:

He who had the honor of illuminating this Koran / the artist in need of God's grace, Musa, a student of the dervish Muhammad 'Arif; (it was finished) during the night of the 29th / Ramadan the holy month, in the year 1100 after the Hegira of the Prophet (= 16 July 1689), to him the highest blessing and perfect / salutation.

In the twelfth century a rounded script, rather than the earlier *Kufi*, was introduced in Syria. The larger-sized letters were favorable for the tall, rectangular-shaped books which replaced the square format of those written in the *Kufi*-ductus (Cat. No. 249). To facilitate reading, the text of the Koran was written with a complete set of diacritical marks which indicated the exact pronunciation.

The two richly illuminated first pages contain in eight lines the first two chapters, or suras, of the 114 into which the Koran is divided. The first line gives the title of the sura and the contents, then come the seven lines of text:
(Right: Sura 1, the Beginning):

In the name of Allah, the beneficent, the merciful
Praise be to Allah, the Lord of the worlds
The beneficent, the merciful
Master of the day of requital
Thee do we serve and thee do we beseech for help
Guide us on the right path
The path of those upon whom thou hast bestowed favors
Not those upon whom wrath is brought down, nor those who go astray

(Left: Sura 2, the Cow):

In the name of Allah, the beneficient, the merciful
I, Allah, am the best knower
This book, there is no doubt in it, is a guide to those who keep their duty
Who believe in the unseen and keep up prayer and spend out of what we have given them
And who believe in that which has been revealed to thee and that which was revealed before thee, and of the Hereafter they are sure
These are on the right course from their lord and these it is who are successful

The last ninth line includes additions by the copyist regarding the length of the individual suras. The first two pages, which are connected in content, are also illuminated together and framed by borders of finely executed golden leaves with details in red and blue. These pages have individual geometric borders surrounding the text, with a wide elaborate plant design on top. The black, sometimes golden text written in the *Thuluth*-ductus is set in white clouds on a gold background.

M.M.

251
Fragment of a female figure

Site: Qasr al-Hayr al-Gharbi, palace
Date: Ca. 727
Material: Stucco
Height: 40.7 cm, assembled from many pieces
Museum: Damascus
Literature: D. Schlumberger *Syria* 20 (1939) 349, Fig. 21

During the excavations of the Qasr al-Hayr al-Gharbi palace, an unusually large number (ca. 50,000) of decorative stucco fragments were recovered. Although the outer walls were only a few meters high at the time of excavation, it was possible to reconstruct the portal of the palace, which once stood more than 14 meters, in the courtyard of the Damascus Museum—partly from the ornamental sequence of the many fragments (see Fig. 88). On the semi-circular towers flanking the portal, which were inspired by the Roman style of nearby Palmyra, it was possible to reconstruct the stucco decorations almost completely. They were set above a 5-meter-tall stone foundation divided into two friezes, decorated with geometric ornamental designs. The upper frieze consists of an architectural arrangement of portraits with a gallery of niches above.

The elaborately sculpted modeled pieces are especially noteworthy. This bust of a naked woman with long braids, a crownlike headdress, and earrings gives a good impression of the decorations (see Fig. 89). The builder of the palace, the Umayyad caliph Hisham, occupies a central place in the cycle of portraits decorating the portal, so perhaps the accompanying figures represent members of his family.

In spite of the stylized features of the face and the clumsily rendered body, the dependence on and inspiration from ancient portraits is apparent (cf. Cat. Nos. 186, 187, 194). This portrait of a woman with a bird in her left hand reminds us of portraits of the Roman goddess Atargatis, who usually is depicted holding a dove.
M.M.

251, left

252
Plaster relief of a nut tree

Site: Qasr al-Hayr al-Gharbi, palace
Date: Ca. 727
Material: Plaster
Height: 106 cm
Museum: Damascus
Literature: London Catalogue (1976) 298, No. 469

During the reconstruction of the facade, a plaster cast of this relief was placed in the first niched panel on the right portal tower (see Fig. 90). The naturalistic representation of the branched tree with nutlike fruits and a vine climbing up its trunk has close parallels in early Islamic building decoration—for example, in the glass mosaics in the Umayyad Mosque in Damascus (see Fig. 86), which was completed in 714. In both cases, the inspiration from ancient models is clearly visible (see Cat. No. 232). The material, however, points in another direction; although several stucco and plaster sculptures were found in nearby Palmyra (see Cat. Nos. 198-203) which may have served as models, there is no evidence for a local continuing tradition of such sculpture before the eighth century. The use of stucco reliefs also has Mesopotamian connections, since Mesopotamian art was a source of inspiration for the art of the beginning of the Islamic period. Since the ruling Sassanians used stucco extensively as a decorative material, we suspect that Mesopotamian artisans were brought here to produce this early Islamic decoration.
M.M.

253
Plaster relief of a male figure

Site: Qasr al-Hayr al-Gharbi, palace
Date: Ca. 727
Material: Plaster, assembled from many fragments
Height: 54 cm
Museum No.: Damascus A. 4794 + 2665
Literature: Cf. D. Schlumberger *Syria* 20 (1939) 330

The existence of an upper story of the palace was indicated by the existence of the many stucco fragments. Apparently the square inner courtyard was surrounded by a double arcade which led to living rooms and side rooms. The portraits from the facade of the upper story, partially reconstructed in the Damascus Museum, demonstrate the elaborate artistic plan of

the noble builder. This isolated relief of a male figure
clearly shows the ancient heritage; the lightly turned
head with curly hair and a beard is clearly inspired by
Roman portraits, as seen in large numbers on the
tomb reliefs from Palmyra (Cat. Nos. 191–192). The
garment he wears gracefully draped over his shoulder
and left arm also looks like a Roman toga.
M.M.

254
Wood carving

Site: Qasr al-Hayr al-Gharbi, palace
Date: Ca. 727
Material: Carved with traces of gilt and blue paint
Height: 9.7 cm; *width:* 39.5 cm
Museum No.: Damascus A. 16582
Literature: D. Schlumberger *Syria* 20 (1939) 324 // *London
    Catalogue* (1976) 280 No. 429 // cf. E. Pauty *Les bois
    sculptés jusqu'à l'époque ayyoubide* (1931) 6 No. 2293,
    8946 Plate III

The major decorations of the palace were in the eastern part of the building. Adjoining the main portals
elaborately ornamented with stucco were rooms with
wall paintings simulating marble. Above these rooms,
accessible by two wooden stairways in the northeastern and southeastern corners of the inner courtyard, were the public rooms and the hall for audiences
given by the nobleman who built the palace. The few
fragments of wooden decorations came from these upper rooms. They may have formed part of a panel, and
in spite of their fragmented state, they give a fairly
good impression of the elaborate architectural decoration.
    The climbing vines on this relief, clearly inspired by
ancient models (see also the marble relief in Cat. No.
274) were originally gilded, while their contrasting
background was painted blue.
M.M.

253, *right*
252, *left*   254, *below*

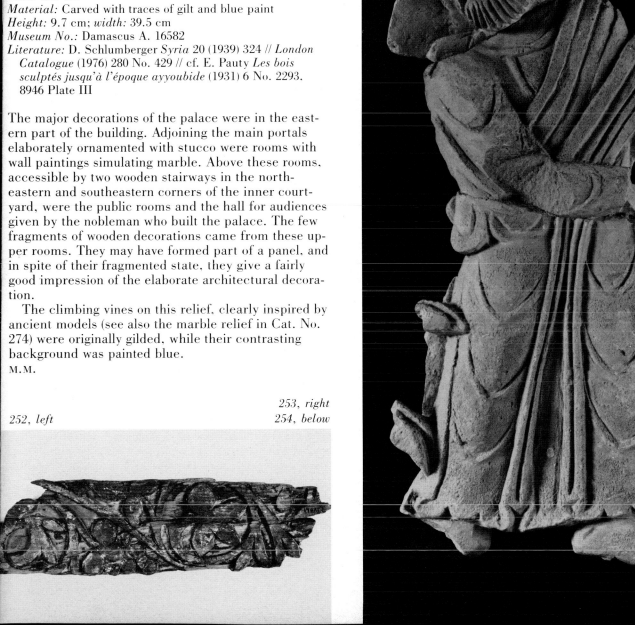

255
Marble relief

Site: Qasr al-Hayr al-Gharbi, bath
Date: Ca. 727
Material: Marble
Height: 45.7 cm; *width:* 22.8 cm
Museum No.: Damascus A. 17988
Literature: Cf. *London Catalogue* (1976) 298 No. 468 (A. 17989)

The bath, situated about 30 meters north of the palace, belonged to the estate of the caliph and was richly decorated. The inner walls had frescoes simulating marble, paintings of climbing vines, as well as marble reliefs. The similarity between the bath decorations and the stucco reliefs from the neighboring palace lead us to believe that the two structures were built at the same time.

From the original, apparently splendid wall decorations, only a few fragments remain, including this marble relief. Together with a matching relief, also in the Damascus Museum (A. 17989), it formed part of a door frame. The relief is elaborately decorated with symmetrical branches reaching up and around a fat-bellied richly ornamented goblet. The design is reminiscent of the mosaic decoration in the Umayyad Mosque in Damascus (Fig. 86), which has motifs showing both local inspiration and Sassanian influence.
M.M.

256
Stucco relief

Site: Raqqa/Rafiqa, Palace B
Date: Ca. 835
Material: Stucco, assembled from many fragments
Height: 132 cm; *width:* 60 cm
Museum: Damascus
Literature: S. Abdul-Hak *AAAS* 1/1 (1951) 117, Fig. 7 (left) // cf. D. T. Rice *Ars Islamica* 1 (1934) 61, 65 Fig. 10

From 1950 to 1952 the so-called Palace B, approximately 1 kilometer northeast of the walled city of Raqqa, was excavated. According to painted Kufi inscriptions (now in the Damascus Museum) this mudbrick palace dates from the reign of the Abbasid caliph al-Mu'tasim (833–842). Judging from the monumental size of the palace (168 × 74 meters) and the

255

rich building decoration, this must have been the residence of a member of the ruling family.

As with the Umayyad Palace of Qasr al-Hayr al-Gharbi (see Cat. Nos. 251–253), the primary decorative means here was stucco reliefs, but they were limited to friezes meant to accentuate parts of the building. The entrance from the public rooms to the private quarters was richly decorated, and this fragment formed part of a door frame here. Four- and six-petalled rosette medallions alternate, filled with vines and leaves in an unbroken pattern; the spaces between the medallions are decorated with small shoots of vines.

The stylistic distance from the comparatively naturalistic stuccos of the Umayyad period is evident and is emphasized by the complete lack of figurative representations. However, compared with the slated carving style developed shortly before in Raqqa (see Cat. No. 261), the shapes of the plants, although stylized, are still essentially naturalistic. Apparently these two completely different styles developed concurrently.

The dark shaded effect executed by deep carving is characteristic for the somewhat earlier, closely connected stucco decorations in Hira (near Kufa in Iraq), where, however, the dependence on Sassanian models is more pronounced.
M.M.

257
Fragment of a fresco with female head
See color plate p. 433

Site: Qasr al-Hayr al-Gharbi, palace
Date: Ca. 727
Material: Paint on plaster, assembled from many fragments
Height: 39 cm; *width* 41 cm
Museum: Damascus
Literature: London Catalogue (1976) 316 No. 497c // cf. D.
    Schlumberger *Syria* 20 (1939) 325

The public rooms, the audience hall, and the throne room of the caliph were situated above the portals to the eastern part of the palace. Two monumental floor frescoes were found in the enclosed stairways leading to the upper story. The representations are partly borrowed from classical iconography, partly inspired by Eastern—that is, Sassanian—models, such as the royal hunt. Originally the rooms on the upper floor were furnished with similar wall paintings.

256

Only a few fragments of the frescoes are preserved. This fragment of a female head, shown in three-quarter profile, presumably belonged to a court scene. The face of the apparently noble lady has idealized, stylized features; she wears an elegant turban, knotted under the chin, and valuable dangling earrings.
M.M.

258
Fragment of a fresco with prisoners (?)
See color plate p. 433

Site: Qasr al-Hayr al-Gharbi, palace
Date: Ca. 727
Material: Paint on plaster assembled from many fragments
Museum: Damascus
Literature: Catalogue (1969) 164 // *Guide* (1980) 152 // cf. D. Schlumberger *Syria* 20 (1939) 325

Apart from scenes of courtly life in the palace of the caliph, the wall paintings of the upper floor apparently also had representations of historical events, which is evident in a group of male faces squeezed together, whose caricaturelike features indicate a subordinate social position. They may represent a group of prisoners from an Umayyad conquest.

For combinations of courtly and historical scenes, the bath frescoes from Qusair 'Amra (60 km east of Amman in Jordan) offer clear parallels; there, conquered lords from neighboring states are depicted next to bathing scenes and allegorical representations of ancient origin. A few of the figures in the bath have Greek inscriptions, which are helpful for identification. Our frescoes also had inscriptions, but only a few carefully drawn Greek letters are preserved.

Here again we have a connection with the local pre-Islamic art of wall painting. It may be assumed that experts from Mesopotamia were called in to collaborate with native Syrian artists on these frescoes, as was the case in Cat. Nos. 251–253.
M.M.

259
Painted wood plaque
See color plate p. 433

Site: Raqqa/Rafiqa, Palace B
Date: ca. 835
Material: Wood, painted blue, red, and ochre, with black outlines

Length: 52.2 cm; *width:* 11.1 cm
Museum No.: Damascus A. 16063
Literature: N. Saliby *AAAS* 4–5 (1954–1955) 210 // cf. S. Abdul-Hak *AAAS* 1 (1951) 114

This wooden fragment from the public rooms of Palace B seems not to have been originally much larger. The central frieze is bordered by wide framing stripes with a zigzag pattern on the narrow sides. The design shows a climbing floral motif where goblet-shaped flowers are interspersed with clusters of four connected leaves.

The rendering here is less abstract than in Cat. No. 260 and therefore looks more like the stucco decorations of the palace. These fragments of wooden panels prove that several styles of decoration were used simultaneously.
M.M.

260
Painted wood plaque
See color plate p. 433

Site: Raqqa/Rafiqa, Palace B
Date: Ca. 835
Material: Wood with traces of red, ochre, and black paint, fragmented
Length: 13 cm; *width:* 35 cm
Museum No.: Damascus A. 16064
Literature: N. Saliby *AAAS* 4/5 (1954–1955) 210 // cf. S. Abdul-Hak *AAAS* 1 (1951) 114

The large public rooms south of the main audience hall in Palace B (see Cat. No. 262) were the only rooms richly decorated with wooden panels and reliefs. This fragment of an originally square wooden panel may have formed part of a coffered ceiling. In the center of the fragment we can distinguish a four-pointed star filled with plant motifs, from which a goblet-shaped ornamental flower grows. The symmetrically designed floral pattern is in the Raqqa style.
M.M.

261
Marble capital

Site: Raqqa/Rafiqa
Date: Ca. 800
Material: Marble bas-relief, one corner damaged, another broken off

261

262

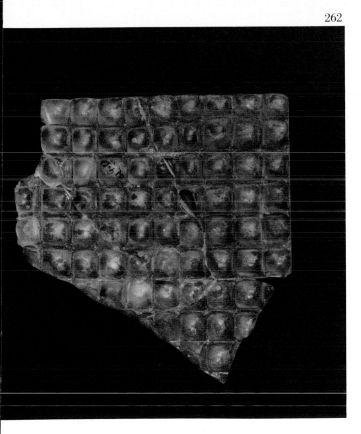

Height: 25 cm: *length/width:* 29–30 cm
Museum No.: Damascus A. 9687
Literature: Cf. E. Herzfeld in Sarre and Herzfeld
   Archäologische Reise im Euphrat- and Tigris-Gebiet II
   (Berlin 1920) 352, Fig. 322 / IV (1920) Plate CXL 2–4 //
   M. S. Dimand *Ars Islamica* 4 (1937) 323, Fig 45

A new style of decoration was characteristic for the
Abbasid period. Instead of the earlier modelled sculpting or naturalistic carving, this was more abstract,
the design created by slanted incised or engraved
lines. Although the style usually is connected to Samarra, the capital of the Abbasids situated 130 kilometers north of Baghdad, we have some early examples of the style from Raqqa, from the time of Caliph
al-Mansur (772), who instituted a major rebuilding of
the city and in the process moved the architectural
center from Baghdad to Raqqa, which enjoyed a short
glorious period as the residence of the caliphat.

It is possible that this capital was part of one of the
new buildings commissioned by Harun al-Rashid, who
made Raqqa the capital city during his twelve-year
reign (796–808). This marble capital shows the final
stage of development of the ancient acanthus design.
M.M.

262
Plate of glass

Site: Raqqa/ Rafiqa, Palace B
Date: Ca. 835
Material: glass plate, assembled from seven fragments
Height 11.2 cm; *length:* 11.8 cm (accompanying plaster bed,
   height: 6 cm, *width:* 10.8 cm)
Museum No.: Damascus A. 16036
Literature: Catalogue (1969) 175, Fig. 79 // *Guide* (1980) 161,
   Fig. 32 // cf. S. Abdul-Hak *AAAS* 1:1 (1951) 115, Fig. 4 //
   N. Saliby *AAAS* 4–5 (1954–1955) 210, 72 (Fig. 8 in Arabic
   part)

Many fragments of glass floor tiles were found in one
of the public rooms in the southern wing of Palace B,
which could be reached from the central inner courtyard. The entire floor of the room (ca. 12 × 7.5 m)
had been covered with the shiny small green glass
tiles (11.6 × 12.4 cm), giving a luxurious look to the
room fully equaling the earlier frescoed floor (Cat. No.
257) or floor mosaics (Cat. No. 232) of larger buildings.
M.M.

Egypt. Numerous glass sherds, including fragments of similar goblets made of blue glass, which were found during the excavation of Palace B in 1952, attest to the existence of a glass workshop in Raqqa. The tiled glass floor (No. 262), also from Palace B, gives further evidence of local glass production.
M.M.

263
Glass cup

Site: Raqqa/Rafiqa (museum purchase)
Date: Ca. 850
Material: Honey-colored glass with incised design, numerous mistakes
Height: 8.2 cm; *diameter:* 8.5 cm
Museum No.: Damascus A. 11403
Literature: Catalogue (1969) 269, Fig. 159 // M. A. al-'Ush *Archaeology* 24 (1972) 202, 3 illus, // *London Catalogue* (1976) 137 No. 120 // *Guide* (1980) 253, Fig. 121

This almost cylindrical cup has four decorative horizontal friezes; the decoration was presumably incised with a diamond. The center frieze on the cup is framed with borders of simple geometric designs, divided into ten panels by vertical bands. The panels are decorated with various surprisingly naturalistic leaf designs; two alternating abstracts motifs form the upper frieze.

The free-form naturalistic rendering of the main frieze makes this small cup a masterpiece of early Islamic glass art. It was probably produced in Raqqa, but glasses with similar designs are known from Nishapur in Iran, Samarra in Iraq, and Cairo in

264
Ceramic vessel

Site: Raqqa/Rafiqa, Palace A, imported from Hira (Iraq)
Date: Before 775
Material: Ceramic with molded decoration, assembled from fragments
Height: 7.5 cm; *diameter:* 12.2 cm
Museum No.: Damascus A. 17261
Literature: M. A. al-'Usch *AAAS* 10 (1960) Arabic part 140, Plate 1 Fig. 9; Plate 2 Fig. 8; Plate 15 Fig. 22 // A. Grohmann *Arabische Paläographie* I (1971) 73, 86, Fig. 54, Plate 14:2 // *London Catalogue* (1976) 213 No. 250, illus. // cf. D. T. Rice *Ars Islamica* 1 (1934) 66, Fig. 18 (middle)

This fragment of a fat-bellied vase or bowl is distinguished by its thin-walled sides, which remind us of glass vessels (see No. 263). It is only sparsely decorated. The foot has a stamped decoration of eight palm trees forming a medallion with a braided ring around it; otherwise the only design is an inscribed frieze in the *Kufi*-ductus or script style. The inscription gives the bowl special significance since it mentions the commissioner, the place of production, and the name of the artist: "work of the Christian Ibrahim, [made] in al-Hira [for] the Emir Sulaiman [so]n of the ruler of the true believers."

Thus this bowl was commissioned by the son of a ruling caliph, a certain prince Sulaiman, who perhaps was the son of the Umayyad caliph Abd al-Malik (685–705). Considering the find spot, however, an identification with the son of the Abbasid caliph al-Mansur (754–775) of the same name seems more likely, as he founded the new city Rafiqa near Raqqa in 772. It is plausible that al-Mansur in the course of his extensive building activities erected a palace for his son, possibly in the area of the north wall, where this bowl was found. If this is so, the vessel dates from between 772 and 775 (death of al-Mansur).

The bowl was not produced in Raqqa, however, but, according to the inscription, in Hira (near Kufa at the lower Euphrates in Iraq) 650 kilometers southeast of Raqqa, in the workshop of a Christian master potter, Ibrahim (Abraham). Sherds of similar ceramics with Kufi inscriptions have been found in Hira, where there is evidence for a large Christian population in the eighth century. The production technique using molds (see Cat. No. 268) made it possible to produce a large number of identical vessels, and there may have been a considerable import trade from Hira.

This bowl is a beautiful example of early Islamic ceramics; its technical perfection can be compared to that of the Roman *terra sigilata* ware which was imported to both Syria and Mesopotamia.

M.M.

265
Ceramic bowl
See color plate p. 434

Site: Qal'at Jabar
Date: 1200–1250
Material: Ceramic with glossy paint and glaze, small pieces restored in plaster
Diameter: 41 cm; *height* 14.3 cm
Museum: Aleppo

Literature: A. R. Zaqzouq *Antiquités de l'Euphrate* 42. // cf. J. Sauvaget *Poteries syro-mésopotamiennes* (Paris 1932) 25 No. 150, Plate 45 // V. Poulsen in Riis and Poulsen *Hama* 4:2 (Copenhagen 1957) 198, Figs. 667, 669 // A. Bahgat *La céramique égyptienne de l'époque musulmane* (1922) Plate 54

There are a few examples of figurative, glazed ceramics from Raqqa, and in most cases only two colors of underglaze are used, here golden brown on a background of light beige, corresponding to a similar two-colored plate (Cat. No. 270) in black on turquoise. The representations, usually individual figures or animals, occupy the center of the bowls and may have been inspired by contemporary Egyptian and Iranian painted, glazed pottery. This large, well-preserved bowl belongs to this rare group. It was excavated by the Syrian Department of Antiquities inside the fortress of Qal'at Jabar, 60 kilometers west of Raqqa.

The painted sun with female features surrounded by two circles of rays is extraordinary. Motifs from the realm of astrology are not otherwise found in the figurative repertoire of Raqqa ceramics, but they have iconographic parallels in the later unglazed pottery from Damascus as well as in Egyptian and Iranian pottery. The arabesque decoration and the abstract border frieze which looks like writing (see Cat. No. 271) indicate that this bowl came from the workshops of Raqqa.
M.M.

266
Turquoise ceramic bowl
See color plate p. 435

Site: Raqqa (museum purchase)
Date: 1150–1200
Material: Incised ceramic with turquoise glaze
Diameter: 14.8 cm; *height:* 5.3 cm
Museum No.: Damascus A. 1388
Literature: Catalogue (1969) 170 // *Guide* (1980) 157 // cf. V. Poulsen in Riis and Poulsen *Hama* 4:2 (Copenhagen 1957) 148, Fig. 458

The production process of Islamic ceramics changed in the twelfth century as it became influenced by Chinese porcelain. For example, the addition of sand created a better glaze which fused with the body of the vessel during firing. This resulted in a growing production of glazed ceramics with more colors and more finely designed ornamental and figurative decorations.

This small bowl from Raqqa belongs to the early phase of this development. The incised floral ornamentation, which completely fills the vessel, is closer to the earlier tradition with its formal structure and stylized detail (see Cat. Nos. 259, 261) than the modern arabesque forms (see Cat. Nos. 271, 272). The turquoise-colored glaze, which looks darker in the ornamental engravings, is especially characteristic of the glazed ceramic from Raqqa.

When the Raqqa workshops began producing glazed vessels is not known, but we may assume that it occurred in conjunction with the second blossoming of the city under Nur al-Din Mahmud ibn Zangi in 1159. M.M.

267

267

267
Pilgrim flask

Site: North Syria, Raqqa (?) (museum purchase)
Date: 1200–1300
Material: Decorated ceramic, neck and one handle restored
Height: 25.5 cm; *thickness:* 15 cm
Museum No.: Damascus A. 2065
Literature: Catalogue (1969) 241 // *Guide* (1980) 226 // cf. J. Sauvaget *Poteries syro-mésopotamiennes* (Paris 1932) 25 No. 147 Plate 27 // V. Poulsen in Riis and Poulsen *Hama* 4:2 (Copenhagen 1957) 248, Fig. 885 // E. Baer *Sphinxes and Harpies* (1965) 17, Fig. 34

The large drum-shaped pilgrim flasks are a characteristic form of Syrian unglazed ceramics. They were brought on trips as water flasks, hung by the handles or straps, and as a result of the porosity of the clay the water stayed cool. The production of the vessels was simple, since the same mold was used for both sides. This flask, found in the region of Antioch, is distinguished by an unusual design: a striding harpy, a mythical creature with the body of a bird and a female head, is being attacked by a bird. This hybrid creature, as well as sphinxes, were especially popular motifs in the twelfth and thirteenth centuries.

Vessels of this kind were probably produced in several places, but at this time we have evidence of extensive ceramic production only in Raqqa and Damascus. Inside the walled city of Raqqa, potters' kilns were found in 1924; additional ceramic workshops were discovered containing sherds of unglazed pottery in 1950. The workshops of Raqqa continued their production until the Mongol invasion in 1259, at which time the production was moved to Damascus. The vessels, excavated in the potters' quarter of the northern suburb al-Salihiya—among them technical and iconographically similar flasks—date mainly to the late thirteenth century. M.M.

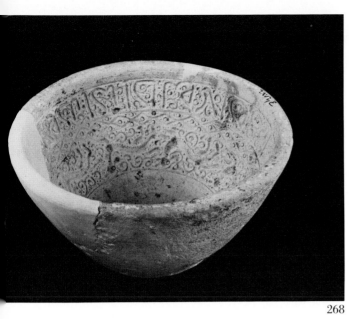

268

268
Mold for decorated bowl

Site: North Syria, Raqqa (?) (museum purchase)
Date: 1200–1300
Material: Ceramic with negative relief, one piece along the
   rim broken off in antiquity
Diameter: 17 cm; *height:* 8.7 cm
Museum No.: Damascus A. 6876
Literature: M. A. al-ʿUsch *AAAS* 10 (1960) Arabic part 169,
   Plate 15 Fig. 25 // see F. Sarre in Sarre and Herzfeld
   Archäologische Reise im Euphrat- und Tigris-Gebiet III
   (1911) Plate LXV 1.6 / IV (1920) 15 // *Düsseldorf Catalogue*
   (1973) 120, Nos. 155 f.

Hollow molds with a negative relief were used to form
unglazed ceramic bowls by the early Islamic period
(see Cat. No. 264). The wet clay was pressed into the
mold to receive the imprint before being fired. Other
vessels were shaped in two semi-globular molds, then
joined; finally neck, foot, and handles were attached.
This technique made it possible to produce a large
number of identical vessels with minimum trouble and
expense.

   Two of the bowls made in this mold are preserved in
the Damascus Museum (A.7370, 13974). When the
bowls were made, a piece of the mold was already
missing, but the empty spaces in the relief decoration
were retouched with simple carving. The mold and

vessels therefore also have an identical, fragmented
inscription: "Lasting(?) power, prosperity in abundance and . . . flourishing to the owners." It is interesting that the mold was used after it was damaged.
Similar bowls with animal friezes and wishes of prosperity are also known from Turkey, through Mesopotamia, to Iran. One of the production centers for
these vessels was presumably Raqqa, where unglazed
pottery (Cat. No. 267) as well as glazed ceramics (Cat.
Nos. 265–266) have been found.
M.M.

269
Ceramic bowl
See color plate p. 436

Site: Raqqa (museum purchase)
Date: 1200–1250
Material: Ceramic with black drawing under transparent
   turquoise glaze; some faults
Diameter: 27 cm; *height:* 7 cm
Museum No.: Damascus A. 13423
Literature: M. A. al-ʿUsch *al-Madjalla* 5/56 (1961) 110, Fig.
   1 // *Catalogue* (1969) 169, Fig. 68 // *Guide* (1980) 156, Fig.
   19 // cf. E. J. Grube *Kunst des Orients* 4 (1963) 56, Fig. 14
   // E. Atil *Art of the Arab World* (1975) 77 No. 31, illus. // U.
   Porter *Medieval Syrian Pottery* (1981) 13, Plate V

At the beginning of the thirteenth century, turquoise
glazed ceramics were developed further at Raqqa by
adding black underglaze, a technique employed also in
contemporary Iran. This bowl is of especially high
quality and almost unique in a design very different
from the usual animal and plant decorations. In the
shallow bottom is a striding camel, loosely silhouetted
and set off against the background of plants.

   In the Freer Gallery of Art in Washington there is
an almost identical bowl (No. 47.8), with the same dimensions and a heron in the center. The two bowls
may be attributed to the same workshop, even the
same master. The silhouette borders, which in this
genre define the background clearly, are unusual in
contemporary Persian ceramics but appeared in Egyptian vessels in the late twelfth century.
M.M.

270
Ceramic bowl
See color plate p. 436

Site: Raqqa (museum purchase)
Date: 1200–1250
Material: Ceramic with turquoise and blue painting under colorless, glossy glaze, assembled from many pieces
Diameter: 27 cm; *height:* 12.5 cm
Museum No.: Damascus A. 13076
Literature: M. A. al-'Usch *al-Madjalla* 5/56 (1961) 112, Fig. 3 // *Catalogue* (1969) 170, Fig. 72 // *London Catalogue* (1976) 230, No. 302 // *Guide* (1980) 157, Fig. 23 // cf. E. J. Grube *Kunst des Orients* 4 (1963) 65, Fig. 22 // E. Atil *Art of the Arab World* (1975) 81, No. 34

The connection with Egypt which can be observed in the turquoise and black bowl (Cat. No. 269) is continued through the introduction of another ceramic technique: in a second firing a metallic decorative glaze is burned on. This complicated process of production had a long tradition reaching back to early Islamic ceramics of the ninth century in Mesopotamia. One reason for the popularity of the shiny metallic ceramics may have been that possession of vessels made of precious metals was not permitted for religious reasons and thus metallic ceramics were a substitute; the cheaper price may also have played a role.

Most such vessels from Raqqa have abstract designs, unlike their inspirational models from Egypt and Iran which usually have figurative designs. The decoration is the characteristic golden brown on a white background. The metallic sheen covers either the white background or the golden brown design. The main accent is on the plant motif in the center and the wide border. The abstract motifs are of secondary importance; writing plays only a subordinate role and is here—as often in ceramics from the eighth century—only a pseudo-inscription without meaning, framing the central motif. Such careless use of Arabic script is often found in this type of ceramics from Raqqa.

This bowl is an especially excellent example because of two additional colors of glaze in the decoration: the main frieze has alternating turquoise and cobalt blue underglaze.
M.M.

271
Wood carving

Site: Qal'at Jabar or Raqqa (?)
Date: 1000–1050
Material: Wood plaque with negative relief
Height: 36.3 cm; *width:* 23 cm
Museum No.: Damascus A. 3647
Literature: R. Ettinghausen in G. C. Miles (ed.) *Archeologia Orientalia in Memoriam Ernst Herzfeld* (1952) 76 // *Catalogue* (1969) 217, Fig. 125 (A. 3645) // *London Catalogue* (1976) 281, No. 432 (A. 3645) // *Guide* (1980) 204 // cf. K. A. C. Creswell *Muslim Architecture of Egypt* 1 (1952) 84, 129, Plates 33, 39 // E. Pauty *Les bois sculptés jusqu'à l'époque ayyoubide* (1931) 30, 51, Plates XXIII, LX

The relief belongs to a group of eight wood panels which have been in the Damascus Museum since 1933 and 1941 (A. 1480, 1482–1484; 3645–3648). Since they were found in the area of Raqqa, they have been connected with the flourishing Abbasid period (ninth–tenth centuries). The central design of abstract vines also speaks for this date.

The smaller vines that fill the central goblet, however, point to a later date, as do the separated leaves which form the basic element for the arabesques characteristic of Islamic decoration. Because this variation in ornamentation only spread in the eleventh century, we may date the relief to this time.

A further point is given by the number of equally large, vertical ornamental details of parallel pieces, which create a frieze. Presumably the panels belonged to a wooden door similar to those from the early Christian period in Syria.
M.M.

272
Bronze candlestick

Site: Meskene/Balis
Date: Ca. 1250
Material: Cast in bronze
Height: 21 cm; *width:* 26.5 cm
Museum: Aleppo
Literature: Aleppo catalogue (1974) 4 // cf. R. Hariri in A. U. Pope (ed.) *A Survey of Persian Art* III (1939) 2492 VI (1939) Plate 1313 B

This bronze object which apparently served as a candle holder was found in the excavation of the Institut

271, right

272

Français d'Études Arabes de Damas in Meskene, the medieval city Balis (on the Euphrates 65 kilometers west of Raqqa). A comparable piece in the Cleveland Museum of Art, certainly produced in the same workshop, tells us about the function and date of this piece.

The object was probably originally used as a folding table, with the lion heads serving as the base for a round table top. In our example, however, traces show that one of the lion heads was broken off early, and because it could no longer fulfil its original purpose, the candle holder in the center was added (a part which naturally is missing from the item in Cleveland) and the object was transformed into a candlestick.

The damage to one of the lion heads and the subsequent repair and transformation of the object probably took place in the workshop shortly after the piece was made. This may explain why the final decoration which distinguishes the Cleveland piece was left undone.

The Cleveland object is beautifully decorated with inlays of silver thread, a technique characteristic of metal workshops in the area of the Tigris and Euphrates. In the middle of the thirteenth century traveling artisans, mostly from Mosul, also worked for Ayyubid customers in Syria. In any case, these objects were only in use for a short time, since the Mongols sacked both the town of Balis and the nearby metropolis of Raqqa in 1259. This historical event is the reason for the excellent state of preservation of this piece and gives us a narrow framework for its date.
M.M.

273
Gold bracelet
See color plate p. 437

Site: Euphrates area (museum purchase)
Date: 1000–1100
Material: Gold foil
Diameter: 11–13 cm; *thickness:* 1.8–2.5 cm; *diameter of ornament:* 4.4 cm
Museum No.: Damascus A. 2799
Literature: Catalogue (1969) 209, Fig. 116 // *London Catalogue* (1976) 202, No. 242 // *Guide* (1980) 197, Fig. 72 // cf. E. Atil *Art of the Arab World* (1975) 41, No. 14

This large bracelet, perfectly preserved except for the five missing inset jewels, was found in Raqqa, as was a similar piece now in the Freer Gallery of Art in Washington (No. 48.25). Such splendid bracelets of

gold or silver were worn in pairs on the wrists or on the upper arms over the sleeves of elegant garments.

The material of this bracelet is embossed gold foil shaped into a tube. The seam on the inside is covered with a running decorative stripe with a scale pattern, which also divides the slanted inscription of blessings, written in the angular *Kufi*-ductus, into ten parts: "Lasting power / permanent happiness / eternal success / true, pious blessing / complete grace, prosperity / lasting, eternal power / . . ./ perseverance, kindness / constant happiness / to the owner."

There is a hinge between the third and fourth parts of the inscription. The elaborate clasp, which is held together with a gold peg, is richly decorated with filigree crowns originally alternating with inset jewels. The inside of the clasp is decorated with tiny filigree work. The crowns give us an indication of the date of origin. Similar filigreed jewelry is known from Egypt and elsewhere in Syria, and there are Egyptian inscribed woodcarvings in the same style, all dating from the eleventh and twelfth centuries.
M.M.

274
Marble relief

Site: Damascus, Umayyad Mosque
Date: 714–715
Material: Marble
Height: 162 cm; *width:* 45 cm
Museum No.: Damascus A. 11
Literature: K. A. C. Creswell *Early Muslim Architecture* (1932) 120, Plate 47a, I/II (1969) 177, Plate 62A.a.c. // cf. M. van Berchem *Mémoires présentés à l'Institut Égyptien* 3 (1897) 429, 507, Plate 10, Fig. 7

The main mosque of Damascus, commissioned from 707 to 714–715 by Caliph al-Walid, was richly decorated, inspired by late ancient Near Eastern art, with marble reliefs and glass mosaics. While large parts of the mosaics on the upper wall have been preserved, the original marble panels which covered the lower wall have almost all been lost. This relief, however—the only one of eight similar pieces which survived the fire of 1893—gives some indication of the original marble decoration.

Each of four inscribed slabs, which sat in the transept columns leading to the main prayer niche, were flanked by a pair of marble reliefs. Two of the inscrip-

tions which are in the Damascus Museum (Nos. A.5, A.7) refer among other things to the new marble panels on the transept columns commissioned in 1082–1083 by the Iranian Seljuk sultan Malikshah and his son Tutusch, governor of Syria. This, however, is an older piece; the inscribed plates are considerably smaller (120 × 57 cm) and must have been set in additional marble frames to match these reliefs. Old photos show that new reliefs were added with a pattern similar to the older ones, identical in composition but of simpler ornamentation.

This narrow rectangular relief has a diamond-shaped motif with a central medallion. The middle panel and the four corner panels are framed with strings of beads and filled with vines. Although this ornamentation is in agreement with ancient models, the combination of geometric and plant motifs as well as the completely filled panel is characteristic of Islamic decorative art. The relief also matches the rest of the original decoration of the Umayyad mosque and can thus be dated to the Islamic art of the original building in 714–715.

M.M.

275
Wooden screen

Site: Damascus, Duqaq Mausoleum
Date: 1104
Material: Carved poplar with small bone inlays
Height: 213.5 cm; *width:* 246 cm
Museum No.: Damascus A. 97a
Literature: J. Bourgoin *Précis de l'art arabe* (1892) Plate III 25 // Dj. A. al-Hasani *Musée National Syrien* (1931) 16, Plate 16 // *RCEA* No. 2891 // E. Herzfeld *Ars Islamica* 10 (1943) 62, Fig. 76, 81 // J. Sauvaget *Syria* 24, 3–4 (1944–1945) 220 // *Catalogue* (1969) 219, Fig. 123 // *Guide* (1980) 206, Fig. 81 // cf. E. Pauty *Les bois sculptés jusqu'à l'époque ayyoubide* (1931) 65, 67, Plates LXXV f. LXXX ff.

This masterpiece of medieval wood carving can be dated from an adjoining piece in the Damascus Museum (A.97b) which has a fragmented inscription in the *Kufi*-ductus on a background of vines: "This screen was commissioned [. . . Abu Dja'] for Muhammad Ibn al-Hasan Ibn Ali, the sincere friend of the ruler of the faithful, God has taken from him [this work] in the month of the year 497 [= 1103–1104]."

The named donor can be identified as Zain al-Daula Muhammad al-Khwarizmi, the vizier of the Syrian

274, left

275, right

Seljuk ruler Duqaq (1095–1104), who had this piece made the year the ruler died. The wooden screen has been erroneously connected with the Musalla al-Idain Mosque in the southern suburb of Damascus, which was built a century later (1211). J. Bourgoin gave us a clue as to the true location, when he described (in 1892) the screen as an enclosure "of the cenotaph of a tomb," which can refer only to the mausoleum of Duqaq (built in 1104). This tomb, commissioned by Duqaq's mother, Safwat al-Mulk, was part of a large building complex in the western part of the city which formed part of the so-called Peacock Cloister (Chanqah Tawusiya) founded by Duqaq. In 1110–1111 the tomb of Safwat al-Mulk was erected here also.

The two lower parts of the once 2.8-meter-tall screen are worked as posts, with relief carving on the front only. The lowest part has double decorative pillars, while the second part has a more elaborately worked row of single pillars. The top piece has decorative panels where geometric designs alternate with arabesques. The back has ornamental friezes framing the panels, while a Koran inscription in *Kufi*-ductus forms the frame of the front panels. First the formula: "in the name of Allah," then Sura 5, verses 55–56:

> Only Allah is your friend and his messenger and those who believe, those who keep up prayer and pay the poor-rate, and they bow down.
> And whoever takes Allah and his messenger and those who believe for friend—surely the party of Allah, they shall triumph.

M.M.

276
Ceramic bowl
See color plate p. 438

Site: Damascus (museum purchase)
Date: 1250–1300
Material: Ceramic with black drawing under turquoise glaze, assembled from pieces, restored with plaster in places
Diameter: 37.5 cm; *height:* 10.7 cm
Museum No.: Damascus A. 3827
Literature: M. A. al-'Usch *al-Ma'rifa* 1:5 (1962) 102, Fig. 6 // *Catalogue* (1969) 248, Fig. 139 // *Guide* (1980) 232, Fig. 102 // cf. G. Contenau *Syria* 5 (1924) 205

Technically, this large bowl corresponds to the early-thirteenth-century black and turquoise bowl from

Raqqa (Cat. 269), but the decoration is very different. The large center is decorated with a motif of cross-shaped vines which gracefully branch out toward the border frieze, while the diagonal lines end in medallions. The sketchy individual leaves are more freely painted than the dominating stylized arabesques in Raqqa ceramics (Cat. Nos. 265, 270). The generous composition with empty space between the vines contradicts the general tendency to completely fill all spaces. This indicates a later date of origin, as does the inscribed frieze subdivided into four medallions with blessing formulas: "Lasting power, growing happiness / safe life, constant / destiny, great prosperity / growing happiness to the owner." The type of script used here with the elongated lettering is elegantly effective.

The vessel was probably produced after the Mongol destruction of Raqqa in the early Mamluk period, when Damascus became a center for ceramic production.

M.M.

277
Ceramic bowl
See color plate p. 438

Site: Northern Italy, (museum purchase)
Date: 1475–1500
Material: Incised ceramic, brown and green painting under colorless glaze; assembled from many pieces
Diameter: 10.2 cm; *height:* 5 cm
Museum No.: Damascus A. 1464
Literature: *Catalogue* (1969) 246 // *Guide* (1980) 230 // cf. B. Rackham *Catalogue of Italian Maiolica* (1972) 423

The ceramic production in Damascus was temporarily interrupted by the occupation of Timur (1401) but experienced a renewed upswing in the fifteenth century by the immigration of Iranian artisans. The technical and formal repertoire, however, remained limited. Most of the ceramics produced were glazed with blue over white and had almost no figurative representations. During this period of Syrian pottery tradition, the import of European ceramics grew, especially from Spain and Italy.

This small bowl, found in the Christian quarter near the east gate of Damascus, corresponds technically to the incised local ware. The Renaissance profile of a young man, the zigzag border, and the colors identify

this piece as an import from northern Italy. Similar bowls have been found in Egypt and Cyprus, indicating artistic exchange between the Orient and the Occident, furthered by trade. This bowl may have belonged to the household of one of the many Italian traders of wool and spices who resided in Damascus.
V.M.B.

278
Ceramic vase
See color plate p. 439

Site: Damascus (museum purchase)
Date: 1250–1300
Material: Ceramic, painted blue, black, and red with colorless glaze
Height: 22.9 cm
Museum No.: Damascus A. 7016
Literature: M. A. al-'Usch *al-Ma'rifa* 2:3 (1963) 108, Fig. 3 // *Catalogue* (1969) 247, Plate XV // *Guide* (1980) 231, Plate 4, Fig. 101 // cf. E. Kühnel *Islamische Kleinkunst* (1963) 128

This vase represents a type of multicolored painted ceramic usually connected with the workshops of Rusafa, an early Christian city 45 kilometers southeast of Raqqa. Sherds of a similar type, however, have been found at Raqqa. This vase is distinguished by figurative representations: the body shows two elegantly drawn striding bluish black peacocks with spread tails. The effective color contrast between the dark painting and the white background is further enhanced by red and blue accents. The neck of the vase is decorated with six climbing blue and red birds framed by gentle arabesques.

The shape of the vessel and the decoration are quite different from Raqqa ware, where figurative presentations were inspired by Iranian flat and heavy individual figures. The stylized birds of the vase have parallels in early Islamic turquoise and black ceramics from Damascus. The free variations of vine compositions correspond to the animated stylized birds here. The technical dependence on the Raqqa workshop repertoire indicates a date shortly after the founding of the Damascus workshops.
M.M.

279
Apothecary jar
See color plate p. 440

Site: Damascus
Date: 1300–1350
Material: Ceramic, painted and glazed, restored
Height: 26.5 cm
Museum No.: Aleppo 5999
Literature: Cf. U. Scerrato *Arte islamica a Napoli* (1967) 48, No. 68 Fig. 49

Apothecary jars, also called *albarelli*, with graceful narrowing bodies which facilitated their removal from shelves, are the best-known products from the ceramic workshops of Damascus. Such vessels served as containers for export of exotic fruits and spices and were therefore widespread in Europe. Fourteenth- and fifteenth-century inventories from Italy, France, and Spain attest to the widespread use and high value of the Damascus jars. After Timur's conquest of Damascus (1401), the Spanish ceramic center in Valencia took over the production of such jars, inspired by the Damascus model.

The albarelli were often richly decorated with gold on cobalt blue glaze, but more often had blue and black colors under transparent glaze; the decoration was usually spirals or vertical ornamental bands. This jar belongs to the simple examples with parallel stripes of vines which are comparable, in proportion and decor, to a dated (1317–1318) albarello in the Museo di Capodimonte in Naples.
M.M.

280
Helmet

Site: Aleppo (museum purchase)
Date: 1400–1500
Material: Iron with brass mountings
Height: 25 cm
Museum No.: Damascus A. 1555
Literature: Cf. H. Stöcklein *Ars Islamica* 1 (1934) 213, Fig. 13 // D. Barrett *Islamic Metalwork in the British Museum* (1949) XVII, XXIII, Plate 30 // L. A. Mayer *Mamluk Costumes* (1952) 41, Plate VII

Shortly after 1400 the production of Mamluk bronze works in Syria came to an end. The artistic tradition ended with the conquest of Timur and the deportation of Damascus artists to Turkestan in 1401. Although

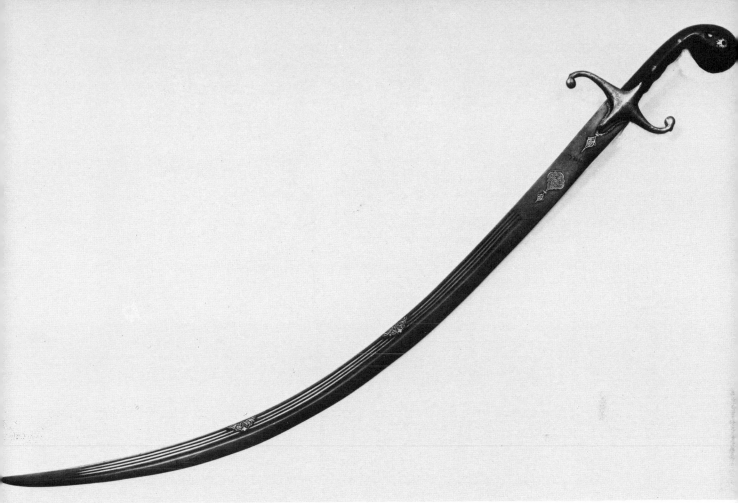

281

the bronze workshops were limited to producing less demanding vessels with simple incised decorations, the contemporary weapon workshops produced armor decorated with gold and jewels. The extensive weapon collections in the Topkapi Museum in Istanbul brought there after the Ottoman conquest of Syria and Egypt (1516–1517) attest to this production.

The Mamluk helmet in Aleppo is a comparatively simple example whose conical shape is characteristic for the fifteenth century. The nose plate—which has a drop-formed end which presumably indicated rank—and the eye shield are preserved. The helmet was originally provided with an additional neck protection and neck flaps.

M.M.

281
Saber

Site: Iran (museum purchase)
Date: 1600–1700(?)
Material: Steel blade with gold inlay and engraved inscription, horn handle, silver guard
Length: 98 cm
Museum No.: Damascus A. 16737
Literature: Cf. L. A. Mayer *Islamic Armourers and Their Works* (1962) 26, Plates IV Va // C. Pauseri *Gladius* 4 (1965) 5

A genre of sabres of hard steel is connected with Damascus; their blades show a characteristic design still used today in woven damasks. Swords of this kind were highly desired in Europe after Napoleon's Egyptian expedition, which renewed European interest in the Orient. These weapons were mainly produced in Iran and exported in large numbers to Europe.

This completely preserved sabre is inscribed on the right side of the blade under the handle with a religious formula—"Oh! fulfiller of all Wishes"—two engraved cartouches, and a signature—"Work of Asad Allah." The left side has a partially deciphered religious formula of gold script in a medallion frame: "Oh lord of all kingdoms, save us from destruction! . . ."

Asad Allah is known from other signatures, some of them including the place of origin "from Isfahan," and is considered one of the finest weapon smiths producing the highest quality swords. Although we do not know his exact dates, he belonged to the group of artists who were employed by the court of Shah Abbas I (1588–1629) in Isfahan, Iran. Swords with the name Asad Allah, according to the historical inscriptions, were distributed from the early seventeenth to the early nineteenth century, and his signature was considered a mark of outstanding quality.
M.M.

BIBLIOGRAPHIC ABBREVIATIONS

As in *Land des Baal* (Mainz 1982), the following works are cited in abbreviated form in bibliographical sources in the essays, site descriptions, and catalogue entries in *Ebla to Damascus*. As is also the case in *Land des Baal*, only the initial pages of journal articles are cited, not the concluding pages.

AA	*Archäologischer Anzeiger im Jahrbuch des Deutschen Archäologishen Instituts* (Berlin)
ÄA	*Ägyptologische Abhandlungen* (Wiesbaden)
AAAS	*Annales Archéologiques Arabes Syriennes* (Damascus)
AASOR	*Annual of the American Schools of Oriental Research* (New Haven, Conn.)
Abdul-Hak *Catalogue* (1951)	A. and S. Abdul-Hak *Catalogue Illustré du Département des Antiquités Gréco-Romaines au Musée de Damas* (1951)
AEPHE	*Annuaire École Pratique des Hautes Études* (Paris)
AfO	*Archiv für Orientforschung.* Internationale Zeitschrift für Wissenschaft vom Vorderen Orient (Berlin/Graz)
AJA	*American Journal of Archaeology.* Journal of the American Institute of Archaeology (Princeton, N.J.)
Akkadica	*Akkadica.* Periodique bimestrial de la Fondation Assyriologique Georges Dossin (Brussels)
Aleppo Catalogue	*Liste de Vitrines de l'Exposition des Découvertes de la Campagne Internationale de Sauvegardes des Antiquités de la Vallée de l'Euphrate au Musée d'Alep* Nov. 16, 1974
Das Altertum	*Das Altertum.* Sektion für Altertumskunde bei der Deutschen Akademie der Wissenschaften zu Berlin (Berlin)
Antiquités de l'Euphrate	*Antiquités de l'Euphrate. Exposition de la Campagne International de Sauvegarde des Antiquites de l'Euphrate* (Aleppo 1974)
AOAT	*Alter Orient und Altes Testament.* Veröffentlichungen zur Kultur und Geschichte des Alten Orients und des Alten Testaments (Neukirchen/Vluyn)
APA	*Acta Praehistorica et Archaeologica* (Berlin)
Archaeology	*Archaeology.* An Official Publication of the Archaeological Institute of America (New York)
Archeologia	*Archeologia Warszawa.* Rocznik Instytutu Historii Kultury Materialnej Polskiej Akademii Nauk (Warsaw/Wroclaw)
ARM	*Archives Royales de Mari* (Paris 1950—)
Ars Islamica	*Ars Islamica.* University of Michigan and Freer Gallery of Art (Ann Arbor 1934–1951)
Ars Orientalis	*Ars Orientalis.* University of Michigan and Freer Gallery of Art (Ann Arbor 1954—)
BAH	*Bibliothèque Archéologique et Historique.* Institut Français d'Archéologie de Beyrouth (Paris)

BaM	*Baghdader Mitteilungen.* Deutsches Archäologisches Institut. Abteilung Baghdad (Berlin)		B. Zouhdi *A Concise Guide to the National Museum of Damascus* (Damascus 1980)
Berytus	*Berytus.* Archaeological Studies (Copenhagen)	*Iraq*	*Iraq.* Subsidized by the British Academy, British School of Archaeology in Iraq (London)
BiblArch	*Biblical Archaeologist.* A Publication of the American Schools of Oriental Research (Durham, N.C.)	*IRSA*	E. Sollberger and J.-R. Kupper *Inscriptions royales sumeriennes et akkadiennes* in *Littératures anciennes du Proche-Orient* 3 (1971)
BJ	*Bonner Jahrbücher des Rheinischen Landesmuseums in Bonn und des Vereins von Altertumsfreunden im Rheinlande* (Cologne/Graz/Kevelaer)	*JANES*	*Journal of the Ancient Near Eastern Society of Columbia University* (New York)
BJV	*Berliner Jahrbuch für Vor- und Frühgeschichte.* Museum für Vor- und Frühgeschichte (Berlin)	*JbAC*	*Jahrbuch für Antike und Christentum.* F. J. Dölger-Institut an der Universität Bonn (Münster)
Braun-Holzinger *Beterstatuetten*	E. A. Braun-Holzinger *Frühdynastische Beterstatuetten* in *Abhandlungen der Deutschen Orient-Gesellschaft* 19 (Berlin 1977)	*JdI*	*Jahrbuch des Deutschen Archäologishen Instituts* (mit Beiblatt) (und) Archäologischer Anzeiger (Berlin)
Byzantion	*Byzantion.* Revue Internationale des Études Byzantines (Brussels)	*JNES*	*Journal of Near Eastern Studies.* Continuing the American Journal of Semitic Languages and Literatures (Chicago)
Catalogue (1969)	M. A. al-'Usch, A. Djoundi, and B. Zouhdi *Catalogue du Musée National de Damas* (Damascus 1969)	Klengel *GS* II	H. Klengel *Geschichte Syriens im 2.Jahrtausend v.u.Z.* Part II: *Mittel- und Südsyrien.* Deutsche Akademie der Wissenschaften zu Berlin, Institut für Orient-Forschung, Veröffentlichung No. 70 (Berlin 1969)
Cauvin *Les premiers villages*	J. Cauvin *Les premiers villages de Syrie-Palestine du IXème aux VIIème millénaire avant JC* (Lyon 1978)	*Levant*	*Levant.* Journal of the British School of Archaeology in Jerusalem (London)
CRAI	*Compte Rendu de la Recontre Assyriologique Internationale*	*London Catalogue* (1976)	*The Arts of Islam, Hayward Gallery, 8 April–4 July 1976* (London 1976)
CRAIBL	*Comptes Rendus de l'Academie des Inscriptions et Belles Lettres* (Paris)	*MAIS* 1964	A. Davico et al. *Missione archaeologica italiana in Siria.* Rapporto prelim. della campagna 1964. Università di Roma, Centro di Studi Semitici, Serie Archaeologica 8 (Rome 1965)
Düsseldorf Catalogue (1973)	*Islamische Keramik, Hetjens-Museum, Düsseldorf* (Düsseldorf 1973)		
Gawlikowski *Recueil*	M. Gawlikowski *Recueil d'inscriptions palmyréniennes provenant de fouilles syriennes et polonaises récentes à Palmyre* in *Mémoires présentés par divers savants à l'Académie des Inscriptions et Belles Lettres* 16 (Paris 1974)	*MAIS* 1965	G. Castellino et al. . . . campagna 1965 (Tell Mardikh) . . . Serie Archaeologica 10 (Rome 1967)
GLECS	*Comptes Rendus des Séances: Groupe Linguistique d'Études Chamito-Sémitiques* (Paris)	*MAIS* 1966	A. Davico et al. . . . . campagna 1966 (Tell Mardikh) . . . Serie Archaeologica 13 (Rome 1967)
Guide (1980)	M. A. al-'Usch, A. Djoundi, and		

MAM I–IV   A. Parrot *Mission archéologique de Mari* I. Serie archéologique: I. *Le temple d'Ishtar* (1956); II. *Le palais*, 1. *Architecture* (1958); 2. *Peintures murales* (1958); 3. *Documents et monuments* (1959); III. *Les temples d'Ishtarat et de Ninni-zaza* (1967); IV. *Le trésor d'Ur* (1968)

Margueron (ed.) *Le Moyen Euphrate*   J.-Cl. Margueron (ed.) *Le Moyen Euphrate, Zones de contact et d'échanges* in *Travaux de Centre de Recherche sur le Proche-Orient et la Grèce Antiques* 5 (Strasbourg 1980)

MARI   *Mari Annales de Recherches Interdisciplinaires* (Paris)

Matthiae *Ars Syra*   P. Matthiae *Ars Syra. Contributi alla storia dell'arte figurativa siriana nelle età del medio e tardo bronzo.* Università di Roma, Centro di Studi Semitici, Serie Archeologica 4 (Rome 1962)

Matthiae *Ebla*   P. Matthiae *Ebla. Un impero ritrovato* (Turin 1977)

Matthiae *MonANE* 1/6   P. Matthiae *Ebla in the Period of the Amorite Dynasties and the Dynasty of Akkade.* Sources and Monographs, Monographs on the Ancient Near East 1/6 (1969)

MDOG   *Mitteilungen der Deutschen Orient-Gesellschaft zu Berlin* (Berlin)

Mellaart *Çatal Hüyük*   J. Mellaart *Çatal Hüyük. Stadt aus der Steinzeit* (Bergisch-Gladbach 1967)

OLZ   *Orientalistische Literaturzeitung.* Monatsschrift für die Wissenschaft vom ganzen Orient und seinen Beziehungen zu den angrenzenden Kulturkreisen. Deutsche Akademie der Wissenschaften zu Berlin (Berlin)

Palais Royal d'Ugarit   *Le palais royal d'Ugarit.* Mission de Ras Shamra (Paris)

Parrot *Mari*   A. Parrot *Mari. Capitale fabuleuse* (Paris 1974)

Pettinato *Catalogo*   G. Pettinato *Catalogo dei testi cuneiformi di Tell Mardikh-Ebla:* *Materiali epigrafici di Ebla* 1. Istituto Universario Orientale di Napoli, Seminario di Studi Asiatici, Series Maior I (Naples 1979)

Phoenix   *Phoenix.* Vooraziatisch-Egyptisch Genootschap Ex Oriente Lux (Leiden)

Propyläen-Kunstge-schichte   W. Orthmann (ed.) *Der alte Orient: Propyläen-Kunstgeschichte* Band 14 (Berlin 1975)

RA   *Revue d'Assyriologie et d'Archéologie Orientale* (Paris)

RCEA   E. Combe, J. Sauvaget, and G. Wiet (eds.) *Répertoire chronologique d'épigraphie arabe* 1–16 (Cairo 1931–1964)

Riis and Poulsen *Hama*   P. J. Riis and V. Poulsen *Hama. Fouilles et recherches 1931–1938* Vol. 4:2: *Les verreries et poteries médiévales.* Nationalmuseets Skrifter, Større Beretninger 3 (Copenhagen 1957)

RLA   *Reallexikon der Assyriologie und Vorderasiatischen Archäologie* (Berlin/Leipzig; Berlin/New York)

RM   *Mitteilungen des Deutschen Archäologischen Instituts.* Römische Abteilung (Heidelberg)

Saadé *Ougarit*   G. Saadé *Ougarit. Metropole cananéenne* (Beirut 1979)

Saeculum   *Saeculum.* Jahrbuch für Universalgeschichte (Freiburg/Munich)

SEb   *Studi Eblaiti.* Missione Archaeologia Italiana in Siria (Rome)

SMS   *Syro-Mesopotamian Studies* (Malibu, Calif.)

Spycket *La statuaire*   A. Spycket *La statuaire du Proche-Orient Ancien* in *Handbuch der Orientalistik*, Seventh Division, Vol. I, Second Sec. (Leiden/Cologne 1981)

Strommenger *Habuba Kabira*   E. Strommenger *Habuba Kabira. Eine Stadt vor 5000 Jahren* (Mainz 1980)

Strommenger and Hirmer *Mesopotamien*   E. Strommenger and M. Hirmer *Fünf Jahrtausende Mesopotamien* (Munich 1962)

Studi Semitici	*Studi Semitici.* Università di Roma, Centro di Studi Semitici (Rome)
Sumer	*Sumer.* A Journal of Archaeology in Iraq. The Republic of Iraq, Directorate-General of Antiquities (Baghdad)
Syria	*Syria.* Revue d'Art Oriental et d'Archéologie. Institut Français d'Archéologie de Beyrouth (Paris)
Thimme *Phönizische Elfenbeine*	J. Thimme *Phönizische Elfenbeine. Möbelverzierungen des 9. Jahrhunderts v. Chrs. Bildhefte des Badischen Landesmuseums Karlsruhe* (Karlsruhe 1973)
Thureau-Dangin *Arslan-Tash*	E. Thureau-Dangin *Arslan-Tash* (Paris 1931)
Tokyo Exhibition	N. Egami, J. Sugiyama, and T. Sugimura *The Exhibition of Treasures of Syrian Antiquity* (Tokyo 1977)
UAVA	*Untersuchungen zur Assyriologie und Vorderasiatischen Archäologie.* Ergänzungsbände zur Zeitschrift für Assyriologie und Vorderasiatische Archäologie (N.S. Berlin)
Ugaritica	C. F. A. Schaeffer *Ugaritica: Mission de Ras Shamra* III. *BAH* 31 (Paris 1939)
Ugartica II	C. F. A. Schaeffer *Ugaritica* II: *Mission de Ras Shamra* V. *BAH* 47 (Paris 1949)
Ugaritica III	C. F. A. Schaeffer *Ugaritica* III: *Mission de Ras Shamra* VIII. *BAH* 64 (Paris 1956)
Ugaritica IV	C. F. A. Schaeffer *Ugaritica* IV: *Mission de Ras Shamra* XV. *BAH* 74 (Paris 1962)
Ugaritica V	E. Laroche et al. *Ugaritica* V: *Mission de Ras Shamra* XVI. *BAH* 80 (Paris 1968)
Ugaritica VI	C. F. A. Schaeffer (ed.) *Ugaritica* VI: *Mission de Ras Shamra* XVII. *BAH* 81 (Paris 1969)
Ugaritica VII	C. F. A. Schaeffer (ed.) *Ugaritica* VII: *Mission de Ras Shamra* XVIII. *BAH* 99 (Paris 1978)
Ugarit-Forschungen	*Ugarit-Forschungen.* Internationales Jahrbuch für die Altertumskunde Syrien-Palästinas (Neukirschen-Vluyn)
Wulff *Bildwerke* I	O. Wulff *Altchristliche und mittelalterliche byzantinische und italienische Bildwerke* Part I (2nd ed. 1909)
Wulff *Bildwerke* II	O. Wulff *Altchristliche und mittelalterliche byzantinische und italienische Bildwerke* Part II (2nd ed. 1911)
ZA	*Zeitschrift für Assyriologie und Vorderasiatische Archäologie* (Leipzig/Berlin)
ZÄS	*Zeitschrift für Ägyptische Sprache und Altertumskunde* (Leipzig/Berlin)
ZDPV	*Zeitschrift des Deutschen Palästina-Vereins.* Zugleich Organ des Deutschen Evangelischen Insituts für Altertumswissenschaft des Heiligen Landes. Deutscher Verein zur Ergorschung Palästinas (Leipzig/Stuttgart/Wiesbaden)
Zouhdi *Catalogue* (1976)	B. Zouhdi, Département des Antiquités Syriennes aux Époques Grecque, Romaine et Byzantine *Catalogue de Musée National de Damas* (Damascus 1976)

LIST OF ILLUSTRATIONS AND THEIR SOURCES

Forschungen 7 (1975) No. 139. *Page 97*

Fig. 22. Seal impression of King Abban of Yamkhad belonging to the Aleppo Group, drawn by Dominique Collon in "The Seal Impressions of Tell Atchana/ Alalakh" *AOAT* 27 (1975) No. 3. *Page 97*

Fig. 23. Seal impression of cylinder with Aegean elements in the Erlenmeyer Collection, after Dominique Collon in "The Aleppo Workshop" *Ugarit-Forschungen* 13 (1981) No. 7. *Page 99*

Fig. 24. Seal impression of King Niqmepa of Yamkhad, drawn by Dominique Collon in "The Aleppo Workshop" *Ugarit-Forschungen* 13 (1981) No. 6. *Page 99*

Fig. 25. Early Mitannian cylinder of sintered quartz from Alalakh, after Dominique Collon in "The Alalakh Cylinder Seals" *BAR* int. ser. 132 (1982) No. 91. *Page 99*

Fig. 26. Syro-Mitannian cylinder of hematite from Ugarit, after C. F. A. Shaeffer *Corpus I des cylindres-sceaux de Ras Shamra-Ugarit et d'Enkomi-Alasia* (Paris 1983) 44, R.S. 20.043. *Page 99*

Figs. 27–31. Reconstructed seal impressions from Habuba Kabira South of Cat. Nos. 22–27, drawn by Dessa Rittig. *Pages 106–109*

Fig. 32. Amulet impressions from Tell Brak of Cat. Nos. 36–39, drawn by Heide Fleck. *Page 116*

Fig. 33. Plan of the Temples of Ishtarat and Ninni-zaza at Mari, after A. Parrot *MAM* III (1967)

Plate II, drawn by Alfred Hofstetter. *Page 131*

Fig. 34. Palace temple at Mari, after A. Parrot *Mari* Fig. 44, drawn by Alfred Hofstetter. *Page 133*

Fig. 35. Topographic plan of Tell Mardikh, after P. Matthiae *Akkadica* 17 (1980) Fig. 2, drawn by Alfred Hofstetter. *Page 135*

Fig. 36. Axiometric plan of Royal Palace G at Tell Mardikh, after P. Matthiae *Ebla, un impero ritrovato* (1977) Fig. 12, drawn by Alfred Hofstetter. *Page 136*

Figs. 37, 38. Cuneiform tablets *in situ*, archives room, Palace G, Ebla, photos by Maurizio Necci. *Pages 142, 143*

Fig. 39. Inlay figure from Mari, after A. Parrot *Sumer/Assur* suppl. 1969 (1970) Fig. 29, drawn by Alfred Hofstetter. *Page 155*

Fig. 40. Reconstruction of relief plaque, Cat. No. 70, after J. Boese "Altmesopotamische Weihplatten" *UAVA* 6 (1971) Plates XXVI, XXVII, drawn by Alfred Hofstetter. *Page 165*

Fig. 41. Plan of Zimri-Lim Palace at Mari, after A. Parrot *MAM* II, 1 (1958), drawn by Alfred Hofstetter. *Page 196*

Fig. 42. Detail of mural, Zimri-Lim Palace, Mari, after J. Lauffray *MAM* II, 2 (1958) Plate XI. *Page 197*

Fig. 43. Plan of Building Level II at Tell Leilan, from H. Weiss *BiblArch* 48 (1985) 9. *Page 208*

Fig. 44. Isometric plan of Building Level II at Tell Leilan, from H. Weiss *BiblArch* 48 (1985) 17. *Page 209*

Fig. 45. Spiral columns, Building Level II, Tell Leilan, photo Harvey Weiss. *Page 212*

Fig. 46. City gate A, Tell Mardikh, after P. Matthiae *SEb* III 5–8 (1980), drawn by Alfred Hofstetter. *Page 214*

Fig. 47. Temple D, Tell Mardikh, after P. Matthiae *Ebla, un impero ritrovato* (1977) Fig. 30, drawn by Alfred Hofstetter. *Page 215*

Fig. 48. Ritual basin *in situ*, Temple D. Tell Mardikh, photo by Maurizio Necci. *Page 215*

Fig. 49. Seal impression on clay envelope, Terqa, ca. 1720 B.C., photo Joint Expedition to Terqa. *Page 221*

Fig. 50. Hoard of beads found in Ninkarrak Temple, Terqa, photo Joint Expedition to Terqa. *Page 221*

Fig. 51. Workshop-courtyard in Zimri-Lim Palace, Mari, after A. Parrot *MAM* II 1 (1958), Plate L 1, drawn by Alfred Hofstetter. *Page 231*

Fig. 52. Seal impression on a pot from Tell Mardikh, after P. Matthiae *Syria* 46 (1969) Fig. 1, drawn by Gerhard Andrées. *Page 236*

Fig. 53. Ship from a wall painting in Thera, from S. Marinatos in D. Gray "Seewesen" F. Matz and H.-G. Buchholz (eds.) *Archaeologica Homerica* I G (1974) Fig. 26. *Page 250*

Fig. 54. Palace at Ugarit, after C.F.A. Schaeffer *Ugaritica* IV (1962) Fig. 21. *Page 252*

Fig. 55. Evolution of the early alphabet from Old Canaanite

Fig. 89, 90. Detail from entrance gate, photos by K. Anger. *Page 486*

Fig. 91. Qasr al-Hayr al-Sharqi, photo by Oleg Grabar. *Page 489*

Fig. 92. Universal astrolabe of Ibn al-Sarraj, Benaki Museum, Athens, No. 13178. *Page 503*

Fig. 93. Reconstruction of sundial of Ibn al-Shatir for Umayyad Mosque, Damascus, courtesy Alain Brieux, Paris. *Page 504*

Maps of Syria preceding each chapter, by Sharon Shmiedel and Harvey Weiss.

Photo credits for Cat. Nos.: all of the objects were photographed by Ingrid Strüben except for the following: Cat. Nos. 5, 7, 36–39, 68, 74, 75, 125, 167, 240, and 241 by Jürgen Liepe; Cat. No. 78 by Eric Long, Smithsonian Photographic Services; Cat. Nos. 77, 83, 84, 109–114, 117, 118, and cover by Dr. Maurizio Necci / Lorenzo de Masi Fotografo.

CHRONOLOGICAL OVERVIEW:
10,000 B.C.–A.D. 1900

A.D.

1900 Treaty of Lausanne creates French Mandate, 1923; Syrian independence from France, 1946

1500 Ottoman dynasty controls Syria, 1517–1917

1300 Mamluk dynasty

1200 Mongol invasion, 1258; Mamluk dynasty in Egypt and Syria, 1250–1517

1100 Crusaders conquer Jerusalem; Ayyubid dynasty, 1171–1250

1000 Seljuk dynasty, 1078–1113

900 Hamdanid princes rule north Syria

800 Abassid dynasty, 750–1258, with capital at Baghdad; Rafiqa and Heraqla constructions by Harun al-Rashid

700 Umayyad Mosque built in Damascus; Qasr al-Hayr al Gharbi and al-Sharqi built by caliph Hisham, 724–743

600 Hejira, beginning of Islamic era, 622; death of Muhammad, 632; Umayyad dynasty, 651–750, capital Damascus

500 Sassanian king seizes Antioch, 540; traditional date for birth of Muhammad, 570

400 Death of Saint Simeon, 459, and foundation of pilgrimage shrine at Qal'at Siman

300 Namarah inscription in classical Arabic, 328; Constantine the Great moves capital to Byzantium

200 Fall of Dura-Europos, 256; Zenobia rules Palmyra, 268; Aurelian seizes Palmyra, 272

100 Romans take Dura-Europos, 164

100 Syria becomes province of Rome, 64

B.C.

200 Antioch founded, 250

300 Alexander the Great enters Syria; Dura-Europos founded

500 Syria annexed into the Persian empire, 550

600 Collapse of Neo-Assyrian empire, 612

700 Assyrians conquer Damascus

800 Til Barsip; Hama, Damascus powerful kingdoms

900 Guzana capital of Bit Bahiani; Tell Fekheriye statue with bilingual inscription

541

1000	Aramaean movements into Syria
1100	Neo-Hittite kingdoms of north Syria
1200	Invasion of Sea Peoples, destruction of coastal cities from Cilicia to Egypt
1300	Alphabetic writing of Ugaritic; Battle of Qadesh on the Orontes between Egypt and Hittites, 1285
1400	Ugarit, palace and archives, until destruction by Sea Peoples
1500	Mitanni kingdom controls northern Mesopotamia
1600	Kingdom of Yamkhad; Hittite raid across Syria to Babylon, 1595; Old Babylonian period ends
1700	Death of Shamshi-Adad, 1781; destruction of Mari by Hammurabi, 1750
1800	Zimri-Lim rules Mari; Hammurabi rules Babylon
1900	Amorite dynasties rule major cities: Qatna, Halab, Ebla, Mari, Shubat Enlil, Babylon
2000	*Shakkanakku* period at Mari
2100	Amorite movements across Syria and Mesopotamia; Third Dynasty of Ur, 2111–2003
2200	End of Akkadian dynasty; Gutian disruptions
2300	Destruction of Ebla; Naram-Sin palace at Tell Brak
2400	Ebla Palace G and archives, literary and other texts in Eblaite
2500	Foundation of walled cities on Habur Plains: Mozan, Leilan, Hamoukar
2600	Presargonic palaces at Mari; Royal Cemetery at Ur
2700	Earliest evidence for cuneiform writing of Akkadian
2800	Cuneiform writing of Sumerian
2900	Early Dynastic period in southern Mesopotamia; Ninevite V period in northern Mesopotamia
3000	Eye Temples at Tell Brak; end of Sumerian colony period
3500	Foundation of Mesopotamian colonies along Euphrates: Habuba Kabira/Qannas, Jebel Aruda
4500	Ubbayid period in southern Mesopotamia
5000	Halaf period in northern Mesopotamia and Syria; first villages in southern Mesopotamia
6000	Ramad
7000	Bouqras
8000	Beginning of Neolithic agricultural villages: Mureybit, Abu Hureyra
9000	End of Pleistocene, beginning of Holocene
10000	End of Palaeolithic hunting and gathering

Ebla to Damascus was published by the Smithsonian Institution Traveling Exhibition Service under the direction of Andrea Price Stevens, Publications Officer

Edited by Diana Menkes
Art direction by Polly Sexton Design
Book production by Barbara Leckie

Typeset in Bodoni by Carver Photocomposition, Arlington, Virginia
Color separations by Verlag Philipp von Zabern, Mainz, West Germany

Printed on Warren's Lustro Offset Enamel dull by Eastern Press, New Haven, Connecticut

The three publications which accompanied the European versions of the exhibition *Ebla to Damascus* are the following:

Land des Baal: Syrien—Forum der Völker und Kulturen, edited by Eva Strommenger and Kay Kohlmeyer (Mainz am Rhein: Verlag Philipp von Zabern, 1982).

Au pays de Baal et d'Astarté: 10,000 ans d'art en Syrie, edited by Pierre Amiet (Paris: Association Française d'Action Artistique, 1983).

Da Ebla a Damasco, edited by Paolo Matthiae, Stefania Mazzoni Archi, and Gabriella Scandone Matthiae (Rome: Editrice Electa, 1985).